NTC's Dictionary of QUOTATIONS

NTC's Dictionary of QUOTATIONS

Robin Hyman

Printed on recyclable paper

National Textbook Company
a division of *NTC Publishing Group* • Lincolnwood, Illinois USA

This edition first published in 1994 by National Textbook Company,
a division of NTC Publishing Group, 4255 West Touhy Avenue,
Lincolnwood (Chicago), Illinois 60646-1975 U.S.A.

Published in the United Kingdom by Bell & Hyman Limited.

Manufactured in the United States of America.
ISBN 0-8442-5753-2 (hardbound edition)
ISBN 0-8442-5754-0 (softbound edition)

4 5 6 7 8 9 ML 9 8 7 6 5 4 3 2 1

Introduction

This dictionary of famous quotations has been designed as a useful and comprehensive reference work and also as a book that I hope will give pleasure to readers who use it as an anthology. The selection of entries, as well as the arrangement in a single rather than double column, is intended to encourage the browser and to entice anyone looking up specific quotations. The number of quotations selected from an author is not, of course, any indication of the author's popularity or literary merit. Some authors, like Pope and Wilde, wrote in an epigrammatic form that lends itself well to quotation; by comparison few novelists, apart from Dickens, have this particular quality. The criterion in selection is what is likely to be familiar to the general reader whose mother tongue is English. A few quotations are also included from French, German, Greek, Italian, Latin, and Spanish sources that seem likely to be known to many readers and in all such cases a translation is given. In addition to quotations, more than 1,000 proverbs are included. Often one does not know whether a familiar phrase is proverbial or whether it has a specific literary origin. Because of this it seemed helpful to include the best-known proverbs.

It is often extremely difficult to assess the degree of familiarity of quotations and this is particularly true when considering what to include from contemporary writing and speech. Which of the following, for example, are likely to be remembered in, say, 2050?

"*One small step for man, one giant leap for mankind.*" Neil Armstrong, the first man on the moon.

"*In a hierarchy every employee tends to rise to his level of incompetence,*" Laurence J. Peter and Raymond Hull, The Peter Principle.

"*Three passions, simple but overwhelmingly strong, have governed my life: the longing for love, the search for knowledge, and unbearable pity for the suffering of mankind.*" The Autobiography of Bertrand Russell, Vol. I, Prologue.

Many quotations from the twentieth century are included in this book but, as the test for selection is that a quotation is likely to remain well-known for several years, I have excluded most current television and radio sayings, advertising slogans, and political phrases. I hope in a future edition to have the opportunity to consider whether the three quotations above and many others from literature and speech of recent years show signs of standing the test of time.

The quotations in the book have been arranged alphabetically by author and, wherever possible, line references have been given in poems, and act and scene references in plays. The name of the speaker has been given in all quotations from plays, and this enables one to discover without reference to the original text that, for example, it was Marcellus, and not Hamlet or Horatio as one might have supposed, who said, "Something is rotten in the state of Denmark."

A comprehensive index with more than 25,000 entries has been provided at the end of the dictionary and this index contains the key words in each quotation. It gives not only the page reference, but the number of the quotation on the page. From this index it is easy to quickly trace a half-remembered quotation by looking up one of the key words and, also, should one refer to individual words in the index like *man* or *beauty*, find quotations on these subjects. References in most cases are to the Oxford Editions of Standard Authors, but line references obviously vary from edition to edition with authors, like Shakespeare, who wrote partly in prose and partly in poetry.

Many friends gave encouragement and helpful advice during the five years of preparation of this book. Thanks are due in particular to the Rev. S. R. Cutt for his assistance in the selection of quotations from the Bible; Mrs. E. M. Hatt who undertook the immense task of compiling the index; and Miss Barbara Hall and Miss Pamela Jones for their careful checking of the proofs. Librarians in England and the United States have answered numerous enquiries with great courtesy, and the staff of the British Museum has been especially helpful. The verification of contemporary references has in many cases been made easier by the ready cooperation of the writers and speakers themselves.

ROBIN HYMAN

TO MY MOTHER AND FATHER
WHO TAUGHT ME TO ENJOY READING

ACTON, John Emerich Edward Dalberg, 1st Baron, 1834–1902

1 Power tends to corrupt, and absolute power corrupts absolutely. Great men are almost always bad men . . . There is no worse heresy than that the office sanctifies the holder of it. *Historical Essays and Studies, Appendix, Letter to Bishop Mandell Creighton*

ADAMS, John Quincy, 1767–1848

2 Think of your forefathers! Think of your posterity! *Speech, Plymouth, Massachusetts, 22 Dec. 1802*

ADAMS, Sarah Flower, 1805–1848

3 Nearer, my God, to thee,
Nearer to thee!
E'en though it be a cross
That raiseth me. *Nearer, my God, to Thee*

ADDISON, Joseph, 1672–1719

4 'Tis not in mortals to command success,
But we'll do more, Sempronius; we'll deserve it. PORTIUS *Cato, Act 1, Scene 2*

5 The woman that deliberates is lost. MARCIA *Ib, Act 4, Scene 1*

6 Thus I live in the world rather as a Spectator of mankind, than as one of the species, by which means I have made myself a speculative statesman, soldier, merchant, and artisan, without ever meddling with any practical part of life. *The Spectator, No. 1, 1 March 1711*

7 Sunday clears away the rust of the whole week. *Ib, No. 112, 9 July 1711*

8 [*Sir Roger*] told them, with the air of a man who would not give his judgment rashly, that 'much might be said on both sides.' *Ib, No. 122, 20 July 1711*

9 The spacious firmament on high,
With all the blue ethereal sky,
And spangled heavens, a shining frame,
Their great Original proclaim. *Ib, No. 465, 23 Aug. 1712, Ode*

10 A woman seldom asks advice until she has bought her wedding clothes. *Ib, No. 475, 4 Sept. 1712*

11 We are always doing something for posterity, but I would fain see posterity do something for us. *Ib, No. 583, 20 Aug. 1714*

12 See in what peace a Christian can die. *Last words*

ADY, Thomas, c. 1655

13 Matthew, Mark, Luke, and John,
The bed be blest that I lie on.
Four angels to my bed,
Four angels round my head,
One to watch, and one to pray,
And two to bear my soul away. *A Candle in the Dark*

AKINS, Zoe, 1886–1958

1 The Greeks Had a Word For It. *Title of play, 1930*

ALCUIN, 735–804

2 *Vox populi, vox dei.* The voice of the people is the voice of God.
Letter to Charlemagne

ALDRICH, Henry, 1647–1710

3 If all be true that I do think,
There are five reasons we should drink:
Good wine—a friend—or being dry—
Or lest we should be by and by—
Or any other reason why. *Reasons for Drinking*

ALEXANDER, Cecil Frances, 1818–1895

4 All things bright and beautiful,
All creatures great and small,
All things wise and wonderful,
The Lord God made them all. *All Things Bright and Beautiful*

5 The rich man in his castle,
The poor man at his gate,
God made them, high or lowly,
And order'd their estate. *Ib*

6 Once in royal David's city
Stood a lowly cattle shed,
Where a Mother laid her Baby
In a manger for His bed:
Mary was that Mother mild,
Jesus Christ her little child. *Once in Royal David's City*

7 There is a green hill far away,
Without a city wall,
Where the dear Lord was crucified,
Who died to save us all. *There is a Green Hill*

ALLAINVAL, Abbé Léonor d', 1700–1753

8 *L'embarras des richesses.* A superfluity of good things. *Title of play, 1726*

ALLINGHAM, William, 1824–1889

9 Up the airy mountain
Down the rushy glen,
We daren't go a-hunting,
For fear of little men. *The Fairies*

AMBROSE, St., 340?–397?

10 *Si fueris Romae, Romano vivito more;*
Si fueris alibi, vivito sicut ibi.
When in Rome, live as the Romans do; when elsewhere, live as they live elsewhere *Advice to St. Augustine, quoted by Jeremy Taylor*

ANDERSEN, Hans Christian, 1805–1875

11 The Ugly Duckling. *Title of story*

ANONYMOUS

Advertisements

1 Daddy, what did YOU do in the Great War? *Recruiting Poster, 1914–18 War*

2 Drinka pinta milka day. *Milk Marketing Board*

3 Friday night is Amami night.

4 Guinness is good for you.

5 Is your journey really necessary? *Railway Poster, 1939–45 War*

6 That schoolgirl complexion. *Palmolive Soap*

7 Stop me and buy one. *Wall's Ice Cream*

8 They come as a boon and a blessing to men,
The Pickwick, The Owl, and the Waverley pen.

9 Top People take *The Times*.

10 Worth a guinea a box. *Beecham's Pills*

11 You want the best seats; we have them. *Keith Prowse & Co. Ltd.*

Ballads

12 In Scarlet town, where I was born,
There was a fair maid dwellin',
Made every youth cry *Well-a-way*!
Her name was Barbara Allen. *Barbara Allen's Cruelty, Stanza 1*

13 The King sits in Dunfermline town
Drinking the blude red wine. *Sir Patrick Spens, 1*

14 To Noroway, to Noroway,
To Noroway o'er the faem;
The King's daughter o' Noroway,
'Tis thou must bring her hame. *Ib, 13*

15 There were three ravens sat on a tree,
They were as black as they might be.
The one of them said to his make,
'Where shall we our breakfast take?' *The Three Ravens, 1*

16 As I was walking all alane
I heard twa corbies making a mane:
The tane unto the tither did say,
'Whar shall we gang and dine the day?' *The Twa Corbies*

Epitaphs

17 Here lie I and my four daughters,
Killed by drinking Cheltenham waters.
Had we but stuck to Epsom salts,
We wouldn't have been in these here vaults. *Cheltenham Waters*

18 Here lies a man who was killed by lightning;
He died when his prospects seemed to be brightening.
He might have cut a flash in this world of trouble,
But the flash cut him, and he lies in the stubble. *At Great Torrington, Devon*

1 Here lies a poor woman who was always tired,
She lived in a house where help wasn't hired:
Her last words on earth were: 'Dear friends, I am going
To where there's no cooking, or washing, or sewing,
For everything there is exact to my wishes,
For where they don't eat there's no washing of dishes.
I'll be where loud anthems will always be ringing,
But having no voice I'll be quit of the singing.
Don't mourn for me now, don't mourn for me never,
I am going to do nothing for ever and ever.' *On a Tired Housewife*

2 Here lies my wife,
Here lies she;
Hallelujah!
Hallelujee! *At Leeds*

3 Here lies the body of Richard Hind,
Who was neither ingenious, sober, nor kind. *On Richard Hind*

4 Here lies the body of Mary Ann Lowder,
She burst while drinking a seidlitz powder.
Called from the world to her heavenly rest,
She should have waited till it effervesced. *On Mary Ann Lowder*

5 Here lies Will Smith—and, what's something rarish,
He was born, bred, and hanged, all in the same parish. *On Will Smith*

6 Mary Ann has gone to rest,
Safe at last on Abraham's breast,
Which may be nuts for Mary Ann,
But is certainly rough on Abraham. *Mary Ann*

7 Stranger! Approach this spot with gravity!
John Brown is filling his last cavity. *A Dentist*

8 This is the grave of Mike O'Day
Who died maintaining his right of way.
His right was clear, his will was strong,
But he's just as dead as if he'd been wrong. *20th century*

Limericks

9 There was a faith-healer of Deal,
Who said, 'Although pain isn't real,
If I sit on a pin
And it punctures my skin,
I dislike what I fancy I feel.'

10 There was a young lady of Riga,
Who went for a ride on a tiger;
They returned from the ride
With the lady inside,
And a smile on the face of the tiger.

11 There was a young man of Boulogne
Who sang a most topical song.
It wasn't the words
That frightened the birds,
But the horrible *double entendre*.

1 There was a young man of Japan
Whose limericks never would scan;
When they said it was so,
He replied, 'Yes, I know,
But I always try to get as many words into the last line as ever I possibly can.'

2 There was a young woman called Starkie,
Who had an affair with a darky.
The result of her sins
Was quadruplets, not twins—
One black, and one white, and two khaki.

3 There was an old man from Darjeeling,
Who boarded a bus bound for Ealing,
He saw on the door:
'Please don't spit on the floor',
So he stood up and spat on the ceiling.

4 There's a wonderful family called Stein,
There's Gert and there's Epp and there's Ein;
Gert's poems are bunk,
Epp's statues are junk,
And no one can understand Ein.

For other limericks, see Arnold Bennett (28:9), A. H. R. Buller (63:1), A. H. Euwer (109:1), M. E. Hare (128:11), R. A. Knox (155:14), Edward Lear (158:12 and 13), D. L. Merritt (170:6), and W. C. Monkhouse (183:1).

Play

5 Everyman, I will go with thee and be thy guide,
In thy most need to go by thy side. KNOWLEDGE *Everyman (15th century morality play)*

Poems and Sayings

6 A beast, but a just beast. *Of Dr. Temple, Headmaster of Rugby*

7 From ghoulies and ghosties and long-leggety beasties
And things that go bump in the night,
Good Lord, deliver us! *Scottish prayer*

8 He that fights and runs away
May live to fight another day. *Musarum Deliciae (17th century)*

9 'How different, how very different, from the home life of our own dear Queen!' *Irvin S. Cobb, A Laugh a Day. Remark of Victorian lady after a performance of Antony and Cleopatra*

10 I always eat peas with honey
I've done it all my life,
They do taste kind of funny,
But it keeps them on the knife. *Peas*

11 I know two things about the horse,
And one of them is rather coarse. *The Horse (20th century)*

1 If all the world were paper,
And all the sea were ink,
And all the trees were bread and cheese,
What should we do for drink? *If All the World were Paper (17th century)*

2 King Charles the First walked and talked
Half an hour after his head was cut off. *Peter Puzzlewell, A Choice Collection of Riddles, Charades, and Rebuses (18th century)*

3 Lizzie Borden took an axe
And gave her mother forty whacks;
When she saw what she had done,
She gave her father forty-one. *On an American Trial of the 1890's*

4 Miss Buss and Miss Beale
Cupid's darts do not feel.
How different from us,
Miss Beale and Miss Buss. *On Two Victorian Headmistresses*

5 Please to remember
The Fifth of November,
Gunpowder treason and plot. *Guy Fawkes Day*

6 The rabbit has a charming face;
Its private life is a disgrace. *The Rabbit (20th century)*

7 Sumer is icumen in
Lhude sing cucu!
Groweth sed and bloweth med
And springth the wude nu. *Sumer is Icumen In (13th century)*

Songs

8 Absence makes the heart grow fonder. *Davison, Poetical Rhapsody, 1602*

9 The animals went in one by one,
There's one more river to cross. *One More River*

10 As I sat on a sunny bank,
On Christmas Day in the morning,
I spied three ships come sailing by. *Carol, As I sat on a Sunny Bank*

11 Begone, dull care! I prithee begone from me!
Begone, dull care, you and I shall never agree. *Begone Dull Care*

12 The bells of hell go ting-a-ling-a-ling
For you but not for me. *Song of 1914–18 War*

13 The Campbells are comin', oho, oho. *The Campbells are Comin'*

14 Come, landlord, fill the flowing bowl,
Until it doth run over . . .
For to-night we'll merry, merry be,
To-morrow we'll be sober. *Come, Landlord, Fill the Flowing Bowl*

15 Come lasses and lads, get leave of your dads,
And away to the Maypole hie,
For every he has got him a she,
And the fiddler's standing by. *Come Lasses and Lads*

1 Early one morning, just as the sun was rising,
I heard a maid singing in the valley below:
'Oh, don't deceive me; Oh, never leave me!
How could you use a poor maiden so?' *Early One Morning*

2 Frankie and Johnny were lovers, lordee, and how they could love,
Swore to be true to each other, true as the stars above;
He was her man, but he done her wrong. *Frankie and Johnny*

3 God rest you merry, gentlemen,
Let nothing you dismay. *God Rest You Merry*

4 Greensleeves was all my joy,
  Greensleeves was my delight,
Greensleeves was my heart of gold,
  And who but Lady Greensleeves. *Greensleeves*

5 Ha, ha, ha, you and me,
Little brown jug, don't I love thee! *The Little Brown Jug*

6 Here's a health unto his Majesty, . . .
Confusion to his enemies, . . .
And he that will not drink his health,
I wish him neither wit nor wealth,
Nor yet a rope to hang himself. *Here's a Health unto his Majesty*

7 Here we come gathering nuts in May
    Nuts in May,
On a cold and frosty morning. *Children's Song*

8 The holly and the ivy,
When they are both full grown,
Of all the trees that are in the wood,
The holly bears the crown.
The rising of the sun
And the running of the deer,
The playing of the merry organ,
Sweet singing in the choir. *Carol, The Holly and the Ivy*

9 I feel no pain, dear mother, now
But oh, I am so dry!
O take me to a brewery
And leave me there to die. *Shanty*

10 In Dublin's fair city, where the girls are so pretty,
I first set my eyes on sweet Molly Malone,
As she wheeled her wheelbarrow, through streets broad and narrow,
Crying, Cockles and mussels! alive, alive, O! *Cockles and Mussels*

11 She was a fishmonger, but sure 'twas no wonder,
For so were her father and mother before. *Ib*

12 In good King Charles's golden days,
When loyalty no harm meant,
A zealous High Churchman was I,
And so I got preferment. *The Vicar of Bray*

13 And this is law, that I'll maintain,
Unto my dying day, Sir,
That whatsoever King shall reign,
I'll be the Vicar of Bray, Sir. *Ib*

1 It is good to be merry and wise,
It is good to be honest and true,
It is best to be off with the old love,
Before you are on with the new. *Songs of England and Scotland, 1835*

2 My Bonnie is over the ocean,
My Bonnie is over the sea,
My Bonnie is over the ocean,
Oh, bring back my Bonnie to me. *My Bonnie*

3 Now I am a bachelor, I live by myself and I work at the weaving trade,
And the only only thing that I ever did wrong
Was to woo a fair young maid. *Weaver's Song*

4 She sighed, she cried, she damned near died: she said 'What shall I do?'
So I took her into bed and covered up her head
Just to save her from the foggy, foggy dew. *Ib*

5 Oh, I went down South for to see my Sal,
Sing 'Polly-wolly-doodle' all the day! *Polly-Wolly-Doodle*

6 Oh, 'tis my delight on a shining night, in the season of the year.
The Lincolnshire Poacher

7 Old soldiers never die;
They only fade away. *War Song, 1914–18*

8 O, No, John! No, John! No, John! No! *O, No, John*

9 O, Shenandoah, I long to hear you
Away, you rolling river. *Shenandoah*

10 O ye'll tak' the high road, and I'll tak' the low road,
And I'll be in Scotland afore ye,
But me and my true love will never meet again,
On the bonnie, bonnie banks o' Loch Lomon'.
The Bonnie Banks o' Loch Lomon'

11 She was poor but she was honest
Victim of a rich man's game.
First he loved her, then he left her,
And she lost her maiden name. *She was Poor but she was Honest*

12 See her on the bridge at midnight,
Saying 'Farewell, blighted love.'
Then a scream, a splash and goodness,
What is she a-doin' of? *Ib*

13 It's the same the whole world over,
It's the poor wot gets the blame,
It's the rich wot gets the gravy.
Ain't it all a bleedin' shame? *Ib*

14 Some talk of Alexander, and some of Hercules,
Of Hector and Lysander, and such great names as these;
But of all the world's brave heroes there's none that can compare
With a tow, row, row, row, row, row for the British Grenadier.
The British Grenadiers

15 The sons of the prophet were brave men and bold,
And quite unaccustomed to fear,
But the bravest by far in the ranks of the Shah
Was Abdul the Bulbul Amir. *Abdul the Bulbul Amir*

1 Swing low sweet chariot,
Comin' for to carry me home,
I looked over Jordan an' what did I see?
A band of Angels coming after me,
Comin' for to carry me home. *Swing Low, Sweet Chariot*

2 There is a lady sweet and kind,
Was never face so pleased my mind;
I did but see her passing by,
And yet I love her till I die. *Passing By*

3 There is a tavern in the town,
And there my dear love sits him down,
And drinks his wine 'mid laughter free,
And never, never thinks of me. *There is a Tavern in the Town*

4 Fare thee well, for I must leave thee,
Do not let this parting grieve thee,
And remember that the best of friends must part. *Ib*

5 Tom Pearse, Tom Pearse, lend me your grey mare,
All along, down along, out along Lee.
For I want for to go to Widdicombe Fair,
Wi' Bill Brewer, Jan Stewer, Peter Gurney, Peter Davey, Dan'l Whiddon,
Harry Hawk, Old Uncle Tom Cobbleigh and all. *Widdicombe Fair*

6 We're here because we're here because we're here because we're here. *Army Song, 1914–18*

7 What shall we do with the drunken sailor
Early in the morning?
Hoo-ray and up she rises
Early in the morning. *What shall we do with the Drunken Sailor?*

French

8 *Liberté! Égalité! Fraternité!* Liberty! Equality! Fraternity! *French Revolution*

9 *Revenons à nos moutons.* Let us return to our sheep (i.e. to the subject). *Maistre Pierre Pathelin*

Greek

10 Nothing in excess. *In the temple at Delphi*

Latin

11 *Ad majorem Dei gloriam.* To the greater glory of God. *Motto of the Society of Jesus*

12 *Et in Arcadia ego.* I too am in Arcadia. *Inscription on tomb*

13 *Gaudeamus igitur,*
Iuvenes dum sumus.
Let us be happy while we are young. *Students' song (13th century)*

14 *Tempora mutantur, et nos mutamur in illis.* Times change, and we change with them. *Quoted in Harrison, Description of Britain, 1577*

ARABIAN NIGHTS

1 Who will change old lamps for new ones? . . . new lamps for old ones? *The History of Aladdin*

2 Open Sesame! *The History of Ali Baba*

ARCHIMEDES, 287–212 B.C.

3 Give me a firm place to stand, and I will move the earth. *On the Lever*

4 I have found it! [Eureka!] *On making a discovery*

ARISTOTLE, 384–322 B.C.

5 Man is by nature a political animal. *Politics, Book 1*

6 Inferiors revolt in order that they may be equal, and equals that they may be superior. Such is the state of mind which creates revolutions. *Ib, Book 5*

7 Plato is dear to me, but dearer still is truth. *Attributed*

ARNOLD, George, 1834–1865

8 The living need charity more than the dead. *The Jolly Old Pedagogue*

ARNOLD, Matthew, 1822–1888

9 The sea is calm to-night,
The tide is full, the moon lies fair
Upon the Straits. *Dover Beach*

10 Is it so small a thing
To have enjoy'd the sun,
To have lived light in the spring,
To have loved, to have thought, to have done? *Empedocles on Etna*

11 Come, dear children, let us away;
Down and away below. *The Forsaken Merman*

12 Children dear, was it yesterday
(Call yet once) that she went away? *Ib*

13 She left lonely for ever
The kings of the sea. *Ib*

14 Who saw life steadily, and saw it whole:
The mellow glory of the Attic stage. *Sonnets, To a Friend*

15 Wandering between two worlds, one dead,
The other powerless to be born. *The Grande Chartreuse*

16 Strew on her roses, roses,
And never a spray of yew.
In quiet she reposes:
Ah! would that I did too. *Requiescat*

17 To-night it doth inherit
The vasty Hall of Death. *Ib*

18 Go, for they call you, Shepherd, from the hill. *The Scholar Gipsy, 1*

19 All the live murmur of a summer's day. *Ib, 20*

20 Tired of knocking at Preferment's door. *Ib, 35*

21 Before this strange disease of modern life,
With its sick hurry, its divided aims. *Ib, 203*

1 Still nursing the unconquerable hope,
Still clutching the inviolable shade. *The Scholar Gipsy, 211*

2 Others abide our question. Thou art free.
We ask and ask: Thou smilest and art still,
Out-topping knowledge. *Shakespeare*

3 Truth sits upon the lips of dying men. *Sohrab and Rustum*

4 And that sweet City with her dreaming spires
She needs not June for beauty's heightening. *[Of Oxford] Thyrsis, 19*

5 The pursuit of perfection, then, is the pursuit of sweetness and light. *Culture and Anarchy*

6 Thus we have got three distinct terms, Barbarians, Philistines, Populace, to denote roughly the three great classes into which our society is divided. *Ib*

7 Home of lost causes, and forsaken beliefs, and unpopular names, and impossible loyalties! *[Of Oxford] Essays in Criticism, First Series, Preface*

8 I am bound by my own definition of criticism: a disinterested endeavour to learn and propagate the best that is known and thought in the world. *Ib, Functions of Criticism at the Present Time*

9 In poetry, no less than in life, he is 'a beautiful and ineffectual angel, beating in the void his luminous wings in vain.' *[Of Shelley] Ib, Second Series*

10 Culture is the passion for sweetness and light, and (what is more) the passion for making them prevail. *Literature and Dogma, Preface*

11 Culture, the acquainting ourselves with the best that has been known and said in the world, and thus with the history of the human spirit. *Ib*

ARNOLD, Thomas, 1795–1842

12 What we must look for here is, first, religious and moral principles; secondly, gentlemanly conduct; thirdly, intellectual ability. *Address to his Scholars at Rugby*

13 My object will be, if possible, to form Christian men, for Christian boys I can scarcely hope to make. *Letter on appointment as Headmaster of Rugby, 1828*

ASAF, George (George H. Powell), 1880–1951

14 What's the use of worrying?
It never was worth while,
So, pack up your troubles in your old kit-bag,
And smile, smile, smile.
Pack up your Troubles in your old Kit-Bag (1915)

ASQUITH, Herbert Henry, 1st Earl of Oxford and Asquith, 1852–1928

15 Wait and see. *Various Speeches, 1910*

AUDEN, Wystan Hugh, 1907—1973

16 To save your world you asked this man to die:
Would this man, could he see you now, ask why? *Epitaph for an Unknown Soldier*

1 When statesmen gravely say—'We must be realistic—'
The chances are they're weak and therefore pacifistic:
But when they speak of Principles—look out—perhaps
Their generals are already poring over maps. *Footnotes*

2 Lay your sleeping head, my love,
Human on my faithless arm. *Lay your Sleeping Head*

3 To the man-in-the-street, who, I'm sorry to say
Is a keen observer of life,
The word Intellectual suggests straight away
A man who's untrue to his wife. *Note on Intellectuals*

4 Our researchers into Public Opinion are content
That he held the proper opinions for the time of year;
When there was peace, he was for peace; when there was war, he went.
The Unknown Citizen

AUGUSTINE, St., 354–430

5 Give me chastity and continence, but not yet. *Confessions, 8*

AUSTEN, Jane, 1775–1817

6 The yeomanry are precisely the order of people with whom I feel I can have nothing to do. A degree or two lower, and . . . I might hope to be useful to their families in some way or other. EMMA *Emma, Ch. 4*

7 One half of the world cannot understand the pleasures of the other. EMMA *Ib, Ch. 9*

8 Nobody is healthy in London, nobody can be. MR WOODHOUSE *Ib, Ch. 12*

9 Human nature is so well disposed towards those who are in interesting situations, that a young person, who either marries or dies, is sure of being kindly spoken of. *Ib, Ch. 22*

10 Business, you know, may bring money, but friendship hardly ever does. JOHN KNIGHTLEY *Ib, Ch. 34*

11 It will, I believe, be everywhere found, that as the clergy are, or are not what they ought to be, so are the rest of the nation. EDMUND *Mansfield Park, Ch. 9*

12 To sit in the shade on a fine day, and look upon verdure is the most perfect refreshment. FANNY *Ib, Ch. 9*

13 Let other pens dwell on guilt and misery. *Ib, Ch. 48*

14 But are they all horrid, are you sure they are all horrid? CATHERINE MORLAND *Northanger Abbey, Ch. 6*

15 A woman, especially if she have the misfortune of knowing anything, should conceal it as well as she can. *Ib, Ch. 14*

16 One does not love a place the less for having suffered in it, unless it has all been suffering, nothing but suffering. *Persuasion, Ch. 20*

17 It is a truth universally acknowledged, that a single man in possession of a good fortune must be in want of a wife. *Pride and Prejudice, Ch. 1*

18 Happiness in marriage is entirely a matter of chance. *Ib, Ch. 6*

19 How can you contrive to write so even? MISS BINGLEY *Ib, Ch. 10*

1 It is happy for you that you possess the talent of flattering with delicacy. May I ask whether these pleasing attentions proceed from the impulse of the moment, or are the result of previous study? MR BENNET
Pride and Prejudice, Ch. 14

2 Nobody is on my side, nobody takes part with me: I am cruelly used, nobody feels for my poor nerves. MRS BENNET *Ib, Ch. 48*

3 'I am afraid' replied Elinor, 'that the pleasantness of an employment does not always evince its propriety.' *Sense and Sensibility, Ch. 13*

4 What dreadful hot weather we have! It keeps me in a continual state of inelegance. *Letter, 18 Sept. 1796*

AUSTIN, Alfred, 1835–1913

5 An earl by right, by courtesy a man. *The Season*

6 Across the wires the electric message came:
'He is no better, he is much the same.' *On the Illness of the Prince of Wales, Attributed*

BACON, Francis, 1st Baron Verulam, 1561–1626

7 My Essayes . . . come home, to Mens Businesse, and Bosomes.
Essays. Dedication

8 What is truth? said jesting Pilate, and would not stay for an answer.
Essay 1. Of Truth

9 Men fear death, as children fear to go in the dark; and as that natural fear in children is increased with tales, so is the other. *2. Of Death*

10 It is as natural to die as to be born; and to a little infant, perhaps, the one is as painful as the other. *Ib*

11 All colours will agree in the dark. *3. Of Unity in Religion*

12 Revenge is a kind of wild justice; which the more man's nature runs to, the more ought law to weed it out. *4. Of Revenge*

13 Prosperity is the blessing of the Old Testament; adversity is the blessing of the New. *5. Of Adversity*

14 Prosperity is not without many fears and distastes; and adversity is not without comforts and hopes. *Ib*

15 Prosperity doth best discover vice; but adversity doth best discover virtue.
Ib

16 He that talketh what he knoweth, will also talk what he knoweth not.
6. Of Simulation and Dissimulation

17 The joys of parents are secret, and so are their griefs and fears.
7. Of Parents and Children

18 Children sweeten labours, but they make misfortunes more bitter. *Ib*

19 He that hath wife and children hath given hostages to fortune; for they are impediments to great enterprises, either of virtue or mischief.
8. Of Marriage and Single Life

20 Wives are young men's mistresses; companions for middle age; and old men's nurses. *Ib*

21 He was reputed one of the wise men, that made answer to the question, when a man should marry? A young man not yet, an elder man not at all.
Ib

1 Nuptial love maketh mankind; friendly love perfecteth it; but wanton love corrupteth and embaseth it. *Essay 10. Of Love*

2 Men in great places are thrice servants: servants of the sovereign or state; servants of fame; and servants of business. *11. Of Great Place*

3 There is in human nature generally more of the fool than of the wise. *12. Of Boldness*

4 If the hill will not come to Mahomet, Mahomet will go to the hill. *Ib*

5 In charity there is no excess. *13. Of Goodness, and Goodness of Nature*

6 If a man be gracious and courteous to strangers, it shews he is a citizen of the world. *Ib*

7 New nobility is but the act of power; but ancient nobility is the act of time. *14. Of Nobility*

8 So when any of the four pillars of government are mainly shaken or weakened (which are religion, justice, counsel, and treasure), men had need to pray for fair weather. *15. Of Seditions and Troubles*

9 Money is like muck, not good except it be spread. *Ib*

10 The remedy is worse than the disease. *Ib*

11 A little philosophy inclineth man's mind to atheism; but depth in philosophy bringeth men's minds about to religion. *16. Of Atheism*

12 It were better to have no opinion of God at all, than such an opinion as is unworthy of him. *17. Of Superstition*

13 Travel, in the younger sort, is a part of education; in the elder, a part of experience. *18. Of Travel*

14 It is a miserable state of mind to have few things to desire and many things to fear. *19. Of Empire*

15 Nothing destroyeth authority so much as the unequal and untimely interchange of power pressed too far, and relaxed too much. *Ib*

16 There be that can pack the cards, and yet cannot play well. *22. Of Cunning*

17 Be so true to thyself, as thou be not false to others. *23. Of Wisdom for a Man's Self*

18 He that will not apply new remedies must expect new evils: for time is the greatest innovator. *24. Of Innovations*

19 To choose time is to save time. *25. Of Dispatch*

20 The French are wiser than they seem, and the Spaniards seem wiser than they are. *26. Of Seeming Wise*

21 Whosoever is delighted in solitude is either a wild beast or a god. *27. Of Friendship*

22 Riches are for spending. *28. Of Expense*

23 Age will not be defied. *30. Of Regiment of Health*

24 Suspicions amongst thoughts are like bats amongst birds, they ever fly by twilight. *31. Of Suspicion*

25 Of great riches there is no real use, except it be in the distribution. *34. Of Riches*

26 Nature is often hidden, sometimes overcome, seldom extinguished. *38. Of Nature in Men*

1 A man that is young in years may be old in hours, if he have lost no time. *Essay 42. Of Youth and Age*

2 Virtue is like a rich stone, best plain set. *43. Of Beauty*

3 Houses are built to live in, and not to look on. *45. Of Building*

4 God Almighty first planted a garden. And indeed it is the purest of human pleasures. *46. Of Gardens*

5 Studies serve for delight, for ornament, and for ability. *50. Of Studies*

6 To spend too much time in studies is sloth. *Ib*

7 Some books are to be tasted, others to be swallowed, and some few to be chewed and digested. *Ib*

8 Reading maketh a full man; conference a ready man; and writing an exact man. *Ib*

9 Histories make men wise; poets witty; the mathematics subtile; natural philosophy deep; moral grave; logic and rhetoric able to contend. *Ib*

10 Fame is like a river, that beareth up things light and swoln, and drowns things weighty and solid. *53. Of Praise*

11 The place of justice is an hallowed place. *56. Of Judicature*

12 If a man will begin with certainties, he shall end in doubts, but if he will be content to begin with doubts, he shall end in certainties. *The Advancement of Learning, 1, 5, 8*

13 Hope is a good breakfast, but it is a bad supper. *Apophthegms, 36*

14 I have taken all knowledge to be my province. *Letter to Lord Burleigh, 1592*

15 God's first creature, which was light. *The New Atlantis*

16 There are four classes of Idols which beset men's minds. To these for distinction's sake I have assigned names—calling the first class, Idols of the Tribe; the second, Idols of the Cave; the third, Idols of the Market-place; the fourth, Idols of the Theatre. *Novum Organum*

17 Nature, to be commanded, must be obeyed. *Ib*

BAGEHOT, Walter, 1826–1877

18 *The Times* has made many ministries. *The English Constitution, Ch. 1*

19 Women—one half the human race at least—care fifty times more for a marriage than a ministry. *Ib, Ch. 2*

20 Of all nations in the World, the English are perhaps the least a nation of pure philosophers. *Ib*

21 Poverty is an anomaly to rich people. It is very difficult to make out why people who want dinner do not ring the bell. *Literary Studies, 2*

BAIRNSFATHER, Charles Bruce, 1888–1959

22 Well, if you knows of a better 'ole, go to it. *Fragments from France, 1*

BALFOUR, Arthur James, 1848–1930

23 The energies of our system will decay, the glory of the sun will be dimmed, and the earth, tideless and inert, will no longer tolerate the race which has

for a moment disturbed its solitude. Man will go down into the pit, and all his thoughts will perish. *The Foundations of Belief, Part 1, Ch. 1*

1 It is unfortunate, considering that enthusiasm moves the world, that so few enthusiasts can be trusted to speak the truth. *Letter to Mrs Drew, 1918*

BALL, John, ?–1381

2 When Adam delved and Eve span,
Who was then the gentleman? *Text for sermon on Peasants' Revolt*

BARHAM, Richard Harris, 1788–1845

3 A servant's too often an impudent elf;
—If it's business of consequence, *do it yourself*! *The Ingoldsby Legends, The Ingoldsby Penance, Moral*

4 The Jackdaw sat on the Cardinal's chair!
Bishop and abbot, and prior were there. *Ib, The Jackdaw of Rheims*

5 Never, I ween,
Was a prouder seen,
Read of in books, or dreamt of in dreams,
Than the Cardinal Lord Archbishop of Rheims! *Ib*

6 He long lived the pride of that country side,
And at last in the odour of sanctity died. *Ib*

7 He smiled and said, 'Sir, does your mother know that you are out?' *Ib, Misadventures at Margate*

BARING-GOULD, Sabine, 1834–1924

8 Now the day is over,
Night is drawing nigh,
Shadows of the evening
Steal across the sky. *Now the Day is over*

9 Onward, Christian soldiers
Marching as to war,
With the Cross of Jesus
Going on before. *Onward, Christian Soldiers*

BARNUM, Phineas Taylor, 1810–1891

10 There's a sucker born every minute. *Attributed*

BARRIE, Sir James Matthew, 1860–1937

11 When the first baby laughed for the first time, the laugh broke into a thousand pieces and they all went skipping about, and that was the beginning of fairies. PETER PAN *Peter Pan, Act 1*

12 Every time a child says 'I don't believe in fairies' there is a little fairy somewhere that falls down dead. PETER PAN *Ib*

13 To die will be an awfully big adventure. PETER PAN *Ib, Act 3*

14 Do you believe in fairies? Say quick that you believe. If you believe, clap your hands! PETER PAN *Ib, Act 4*

15 One's religion is whatever he is most interested in, and yours is Success. KATE *The Twelve-Pound Look*

1 You've forgotten the grandest moral attribute of a Scotsman, Maggie, that he'll do nothing which might damage his career. JOHN SHAND
What Every Woman Knows, Act 2

BARRINGTON, George, 1755–1810?

2 True patriots we; for be it understood,
We left our country for our country's good. *Prologue for opening of Playhouse, Sydney, 16 Jan. 1796 by company of convicts*

BATEMAN, Edgar, 19th century

3 Wiv a ladder and some glasses,
You could see to 'Ackney Marshes,
If it wasn't for the 'ouses in between. *If it wasn't for the 'Ouses in between*

BATES, Katherine Lee, 1859–1929

4 America! America!
God shed His grace on thee
And crown thy good with brotherhood
From sea to shining sea! *America the Beautiful*

BAYLY, Thomas Haynes, 1797–1839

5 Absence makes the heart grow fonder,
Isle of Beauty, Fare thee well! *Isle of Beauty*

BEATTY, David, 1st Earl Beatty, 1871–1936

6 There's something wrong with our bloody ships to-day.
Remark during Battle of Jutland, 1916

BEAUMONT, Francis, 1584–1616

7 What things we have seen,
Done at the Mermaid! heard words that have been
So nimble, and so full of subtle flame,
As if that everyone from whence they came
Had meant to put his whole wit in a jest,
And had resolved to live a fool the rest
Of his dull life. *Letter to Ben Jonson*

8 Mortality, behold and fear!
What a change of flesh is here. *On the Tombs in Westminster Abbey*

BEAUMONT, Francis, 1584–1616, and FLETCHER, John, 1579–1625

9 But what is past my help is past my care. *The Double Marriage, Act 1, Scene 1*

10 There is no other purgatory but a woman. ELDER LOVELESS
The Scornful Lady, Act 3, Scene 1

BECKETT, Samuel, 1906—

11 Nothing happens, nobody comes, nobody goes, it's awful! ESTRAGON
Waiting for Godot, Act 1

1 VLADIMIR: That passed the time.
ESTRAGON: It would have passed in any case.
VLADIMIR: Yes, but not so rapidly. *Waiting for Godot, Act* 1

2 Habit is a great deadener. VLADIMIR *Ib, Act 3*

BECKFORD, William, 1759–1844

3 I am not over-fond of resisting temptation. *Vathek*

BECON, Thomas, 1512–1567

4 For when the wine is in, the wit is out. *Catechism, 375*

BEE, Bernard Elliott, 1823–1861

5 There is Jackson standing like a stone wall. *First Battle of Bull Run, 1861*

BEECHING, Henry Charles, 1859–1919

6 First come I; my name is Jowett.
There's no knowledge but I know it.
I am Master of this College:
What I don't know isn't knowledge. *The Masque of Balliol*

BEERBOHM, Sir Max, 1872–1956

7 Most women are not so young as they are painted. *A Defence of Cosmetics*

8 Zuleika, on a desert island, would have spent most of her time in looking for a man's footprint. *Zuleika Dobson, Ch. 2*

9 She was one of the people who say, 'I don't know anything about music really, but I know what I like.' *Ib, Ch. 9*

BEERS, Ethel Lynn, 1827–1879

10 All quiet along the Potomac to-night,
No sound save the rush of the river,
While soft falls the dew on the face of the dead—
The picket's off duty forever. *All Quiet Along the Potomac*

BEHN, Aphra, 1640–1689

11 Love ceases to be a pleasure, when it ceases to be a secret. *La Montre, or The Lover's Watch, Four o'clock*

12 Variety is the soul of pleasure. WILLMORE *The Rover, Part 2, Act 1*

13 Fine clothes, rich furniture, jewels and plate are more inviting than beauty unadorn'd. PETRONELLA *Ib, 4, 2*

BELLOC, Hilaire, 1870–1953

14 Child! do not throw this book about;
Refrain from the unholy pleasure
Of cutting all the pictures out!
Preserve it as your chiefest treasure. *The Bad Child's Book of Beasts, Dedication*

1 When people call this beast to mind,
They marvel more and more
At such a little tail behind,
So large a trunk before. *The Bad Child's Book of Beasts, The Elephant*

2 The Chief Defect of Henry King
Was chewing little bits of String. *Cautionary Tales, Henry King*

3 Physicians of the Utmost Fame
Were called at once; but when they came
They answered, as they took their Fees,
'There is no Cure for this Disease.' *Ib*

4 'Oh, my Friends, be warned by me,
That Breakfast, Dinner, Lunch and Tea
Are all the Human Frame requires. . . .'
With that the Wretched Child expires. *Ib*

5 When I am dead, I hope it may be said:
'His sins were scarlet, but his books were read.' *Epigrams, On His Books*

6 Lord Finchley tried to mend the Electric Light
Himself. It struck him dead: And serve him right!
It is the business of the wealthy man
To give employment to the artisan. *Ib, Lord Finchley*

7 The accursèd power which stands on Privilege
(And goes with Women, and Champagne and Bridge)
Broke—and Democracy resumed her reign:
(Which goes with Bridge, and Women and Champagne).
Ib, On a General Election

8 The Devil, having nothing else to do,
Went off to tempt My Lady Poltagrue.
My Lady, tempted by a private whim,
To his extreme annoyance, tempted him.
Ib, On Lady Poltagrue, A Public Peril

9 I said to Heart, 'How goes it?' Heart replied:
'Right as a Ribstone Pippin!' But it lied. *The False Heart*

10 I'm tired of Love: I'm still more tired of Rhyme.
But Money gives me pleasure all the time. *Fatigue*

11 Birds in their little nests agree
With Chinamen, but not with me. *On Food*

12 Remote and ineffectual Don
That dared attack my Chesterton. *Lines to a Don*

13 The Microbe is so very small
You cannot make him out at all.
More Beasts for Worse Children, The Microbe

14 Lord Hippo suffered fearful loss
By putting money on a horse
Which he believed, if it were pressed,
Would run far faster than the rest. *More Peers, Lord Hippo*

1 Lord Lucky, by a curious fluke,
Became a most important duke.
From living in a vile Hotel
A long way east of Camberwell
He rose in less than half an hour
To riches, dignity and power. *More Peers, Lord Lucky*

2 When I am living in the Midlands
That are sodden and unkind,
I light my lamp in the evening:
My work is left behind;
And the great hills of the South Country
Come back into my mind. *The South Country*

3 If I ever become a rich man,
Or if ever I grow to be old,
I will build a house with deep thatch
To shelter me from the cold,
And there shall the Sussex songs be sung
And the story of Sussex told. *Ib*

4 I will hold my house in the high wood
Within a walk of the sea,
And the men that were boys when I was a boy
Shall sit and drink with me. *Ib*

5 Do you remember an Inn,
Miranda? *Tarantella*

BENNETT, Enoch Arnold, 1867–1931

6 'Ye can call it influenza if ye like,' said Mrs. Machin. 'There was no influenza in my young days. We called a cold a cold.' *The Card, Ch. 8*

7 'And yet,' demanded Councillor Barlow . . . 'what great cause is he identified with?'
'He is identified,' said the speaker, 'with the great cause of cheering us all up.' *Ib, Ch. 12*

8 Being a husband is a whole-time job. That is why so many husbands fail. They cannot give their entire attention to it. CULVER *The Title, Act I*

9 There was a young man of Montrose,
Who had pockets in none of his clothes,
When asked by his lass
Where he carried his brass,
He said, 'Darling, I pay through the nose.' *Limerick*

BENSON, Arthur Christopher, 1862–1925

10 Land of Hope and Glory, Mother of the Free,
How shall we extol thee, who are born of thee?
Wider still and wider shall thy bounds be set;
God who made thee mighty, make thee mightier yet.
Land of Hope and Glory (Music by Sir Edward Elgar)

BENTHAM, Jeremy, 1748–1832

1 The greatest happiness of the greatest number is the foundation of morals and legislation. *The Commonplace Book*

BENTLEY, Edmund Clerihew, 1875–1956

2 The Art of Biography
Is different from Geography.
Geography is about Maps,
But Biography is about Chaps.
Biography for Beginners, Introductory Remarks

3 Sir Christopher Wren
Said, 'I am going to dine with some men.
If anybody calls
Say I am designing St. Paul's.' *Ib, Sir Christopher Wren*

4 What I like about Clive
Is that he is no longer alive.
There is a great deal to be said
For being dead. *Ib, Clive*

5 Sir Humphry Davy
Detested gravy.
He lived in the odium
Of having discovered Sodium. *Ib, Sir Humphry Davy*

6 George the Third
Ought never to have occurred.
One can only wonder
At so grotesque a blunder. *More Biography, George the Third*

7 When their lordships asked Bacon
How many bribes he had taken
He had at least the grace
To get very red in the face. *Baseless Biography, Bacon*

BENTLEY, Nicolas Clerihew, 1907—

8 Cecil B. de Mille,
Rather against his will,
Was persuaded to leave Moses
Out of 'The Wars of the Roses'. *Clerihew*

BERLIN, Irving, 1888—

9 Come on and hear, come on and hear, Alexander's Ragtime Band.
Alexander's Ragtime Band

BERNARD, William Bayle, 1807–1875

10 A Storm in a Teacup. *Title of Farce*

BETJEMAN, Sir John, 1906—

11 The Church's Restoration
In eighteen-eighty-three
Has left for contemplation
Not what there used to be. *Hymn*

12 Miss J. Hunter Dunn, Miss J. Hunter Dunn,
Furnish'd and burnish'd by Aldershot sun. *A Subaltern's Love Song*

THE BIBLE

(Quotations are from the Authorised Version, 1611, unless otherwise stated)

Old Testament

Genesis

1 In the beginning God created the heaven and the earth.
And the earth was without form, and void. *1, 1–2*

2 And God said, Let there be light: and there was light. *1, 3*

3 So God created man in his own image, in the image of God created he him; male and female created he them. *1, 27*

4 Be fruitful, and multiply, and replenish the earth. *1, 28*

5 And God saw everything that he had made, and, behold, it was very good. *1, 31*

6 And the Lord God took the man, and put him into the garden of Eden to dress it and to keep it. *2, 15*

7 And the Lord God said, It is not good that the man should be alone; I will make him an help meet for him. *2, 18*

8 And the rib, which the Lord God had taken from man, made he a woman. *2, 22*

9 This is now bone of my bones, and flesh of my flesh. *2, 23*

10 And they were both naked, the man and his wife, and were not ashamed. *2, 25*

11 Ye shall be as gods, knowing good and evil. *3, 5*

12 And they sewed fig leaves together, and made themselves aprons. *3, 7*

13 In the sweat of thy face shalt thou eat bread. *3, 19*

14 For dust thou art, and unto dust shalt thou return. *3, 19*

15 The mother of all living. *3, 20*

16 Am I my brother's keeper? *4, 9*

17 And the Lord set a mark upon Cain. *4, 15*

18 And all the days of Methuselah were nine hundred sixty and nine years. *5, 27*

19 There were giants in the earth in those days. *6, 4*

20 There went in two and two unto Noah into the ark, the male and the female. *7, 9*

21 And the ark rested in the seventh month, on the seventeenth day of the month, upon the mountains of Ararat. *8, 4*

22 And the dove came in to him in the evening; and, lo, in her mouth was an olive leaf pluckt off. *8, 11*

23 While the earth remaineth, seedtime and harvest, and cold and heat, and summer and winter, and day and night shall not cease. *8, 22*

24 Whoso sheddeth man's blood, by man shall his blood be shed. *9, 6*

25 I do set my bow in the cloud. *9, 13*

26 Even as Nimrod the mighty hunter before the Lord. *10, 9*

27 Therefore is the name of it called Babel; because the Lord did there confound the language of all the earth. *11, 9*

1 His hand will be against every man, and every man's hand against him. *Genesis, 16, 12*

2 Shall not the Judge of all the earth do right? *18, 25*

3 If I find in Sodom fifty righteous within the city, then I will spare all the place for their sakes. *18, 26*

4 But his wife looked back from behind him, and she became a pillar of salt. *19, 26*

5 In thy seed shall all the nations of the earth be blessed. *22, 18*

6 He sold his birthright unto Jacob. *25, 33*

7 Esau my brother is a hairy man, and I am a smooth man. *27, 11*

8 The voice is Jacob's voice, but the hands are the hands of Esau. *27, 22*

9 A ladder set up on the earth, and the top of it reached to heaven. *28, 12*

10 He made him a coat of many colours. *37, 3*

11 Behold, this dreamer cometh. *37, 19*

12 Jacob saw that there was corn in Egypt. *42, 1*

13 Ye shall eat the fat of the land. *45, 18*

14 Unstable as water, thou shalt not excel. *49, 4*

Exodus

15 Now there arose up a new king over Egypt, which knew not Joseph. *1, 8*

16 I have been a stranger in a strange land. *2, 22*

17 Behold, the bush burned with fire, and the bush was not consumed. *3, 2*

18 A land flowing with milk and honey. *3, 8*

19 I AM THAT I AM. *3, 14*

20 Ye shall no more give the people straw to make brick. *5, 7*

21 Let my people go, that they may serve me. *8, 1*

22 This is the finger of God. *8, 19*

23 Darkness which may be felt. *10, 21*

24 But the Lord hardened Pharaoh's heart, and he would not let them go. *10, 27*

25 The Lord smote all the firstborn in the land of Egypt. *12, 29*

26 And the children of Israel went into the midst of the sea upon the dry ground. *14, 22*

27 Would to God we had died by the hand of the Lord in the land of Egypt, when we sat by the flesh pots, and when we did eat bread to the full. *16, 3*

28 And when the children of Israel saw it, they said one to another, It is manna: for they wist not what it was. And Moses said unto them, This is the bread which the Lord hath given you to eat. *16, 15*

29 I am the Lord thy God, which have brought thee out of the land of Egypt, out of the house of bondage. *20, 2*

30 Thou shalt have no other gods before me. *20, 3*

31 Thou shalt not make unto thee any graven image. *20, 4*

1 For I the Lord thy God am a jealous God, visiting the iniquity of the fathers upon the children unto the third and fourth generation of them that hate me. *Exodus, 20, 5*

2 Thou shalt not take the name of the Lord thy God in vain. *20, 7*

3 Remember the sabbath day, to keep it holy.
Six days shalt thou labour, and do all thy work:
But the seventh day is the sabbath of the Lord thy God. *20, 8–10*

4 Honour thy father and thy mother: that thy days may be long upon the land which the Lord thy God giveth thee. *20, 12*

5 Thou shalt not kill. *20, 13*

6 Thou shalt not commit adultery. *20, 14*

7 Thou shalt not steal. *20, 15*

8 Thou shalt not bear false witness against thy neighbour. *20, 16*

9 Thou shalt not covet thy neighbour's house, thou shalt not covet thy neighbour's wife, nor his manservant, nor his maidservant, nor his ox, nor his ass, nor any thing that is thy neighbour's. *20, 17*

10 Thou shalt give life for life,
Eye for eye, tooth for tooth, hand for hand, foot for foot. *21, 23–24*

11 Thou shalt not suffer a witch to live. *22, 18*

12 Thou art a stiffnecked people. *33, 3*

Leviticus

13 Let him go for a scapegoat into the wilderness. *16, 10*

14 Ye shall be holy; for I the Lord your God am holy. *19, 2*

15 And thou shalt not glean thy vineyard, neither shalt thou gather every grape of thy vineyard; thou shalt leave them for the poor and stranger. *19, 10*

16 Thou shalt love thy neighbour as thyself. *19, 18*

17 Thou shalt rise up before the hoary head, and honour the face of the old man. *19, 32*

Numbers

18 The Lord bless thee, and keep thee: The Lord make his face shine upon thee, and be gracious unto thee: The Lord lift up his countenance upon thee, and give thee peace. *6, 24–26*

19 We will go by the king's high way. *20, 17*

20 Let me die the death of the righteous, and let my last end be like his! *23, 10*

Deuteronomy

21 Hear, O Israel: The Lord our God is one Lord. *6, 4*

22 And thou shalt love the Lord thy God with all thine heart, and with all thy soul, and with all thy might. *6, 5*

23 Man doth not live by bread only, but by every word that proceedeth out of the mouth of the Lord doth man live. *8, 3*

24 As a man chasteneth his son, so the Lord thy God chasteneth thee. *8, 5*

1 And now, Israel, what doth the Lord thy God require of thee, but to fear the Lord thy God, to walk in all his ways, and to love him and to serve the Lord thy God with all thy heart and with all thy soul. *Deuteronomy, 10, 12*

2 Love ye therefore the stranger: for ye were strangers in the land of Egypt. *10, 19*

3 For the poor shall never cease out of the land. *15, 11*

4 Thou shalt not muzzle the ox when he treadeth out the corn. *25, 4*

5 I have set before you life and death, blessing and cursing: therefore choose life, that both thou and thy seed may live. *30, 19*

6 He kept him as the apple of his eye. *32, 10*

7 Jeshurun waxed fat, and kicked. *32, 15*

8 As thy days, so shall thy strength be. *33, 25*

9 The eternal God is thy refuge, and underneath are the everlasting arms. *33, 27*

Joshua

10 Be strong and of a good courage. *1, 6*

11 Hewers of wood and drawers of water. *9, 21*

12 Sun, stand thou still upon Gibeon; and thou, Moon, in the valley of Ajalon. *10, 12*

Judges

13 I arose a mother in Israel. *5, 7*

14 The stars in their courses fought against Sisera. *5, 20*

15 She brought forth butter in a lordly dish. *5, 25*

16 Have they not divided the prey; to every man a damsel or two? *5, 30*

17 Faint, yet pursuing. *8, 4*

18 Say now Shibboleth. *12, 6*

19 Out of the eater came forth meat, and out of the strong came forth sweetness. *14, 14*

20 He smote them hip and thigh. *15, 8*

21 If I be shaven, then my strength will go from me. *16, 17*

22 He bowed himself with all his might; and the house fell upon the lords, and upon all the people that were therein. *16, 30*

23 From Dan even to Beer-sheba. *20, 1*

24 Every man did that which was right in his own eyes. *21, 25*

Ruth

25 Whither thou goest, I will go; and where thou lodgest, I will lodge: thy people shall be my people, and thy God my God. *1, 16*

26 The Lord do so to me, and more also, if ought but death part thee and me. *1, 17*

27 And she went, and came, and gleaned in the field after the reapers. *2, 3*

1 Samuel

28 Speak, Lord; for thy servant heareth. *3, 9*

29 It is the Lord: let him do what seemeth him good. *3, 18*

1 Quit yourselves like men. *I Samuel, 4, 9*

2 Is Saul also among the prophets? *10, 11*

3 The Lord hath sought him a man after his own heart. *13, 14*

4 Agag came unto him delicately. *15, 32*

5 Man looketh on the outward appearance, but the Lord looketh on the heart. *16, 7*

6 David took an harp, and played with his hand. *16, 23*

7 Saul hath slain his thousands, and David his ten thousands. *18, 7*

8 David therefore departed thence, and escaped to the cave Adullam. *22, 1*

2 Samuel

9 How are the mighty fallen! *1, 19*

10 Tell it not in Gath, publish it not in the streets of Askelon; lest the daughters of the Philistines rejoice, lest the daughters of the uncircumcised triumph. *1, 20*

11 Saul and Jonathan were lovely and pleasant in their lives, and in their death they were not divided: they were swifter than eagles, they were stronger than lions. *1, 23*

12 Thy love to me was wonderful, passing the love of women. *1, 26*

13 Abner with the hinder end of the spear smote him under the fifth rib. *2, 23*

14 Would God I had died for thee, O Absalom, my son, my son! *18, 33*

15 The sweet psalmist of Israel. *23, 1*

1 Kings

16 Divide the living child in two. *3, 25*

17 There came of all people to hear the wisdom of Solomon. *4, 34*

18 The barrel of meal shall not waste, neither shall the cruse of oil fail. *17, 14*

19 How long halt ye between two opinions? *18, 21*

20 There ariseth a little cloud out of the sea, like a man's hand. *18, 44*

21 A still small voice. *19, 12*

22 Elijah passed by him, and cast his mantle upon him. *19, 19*

2 Kings

23 Go up, thou bald head. *2, 23*

24 There is death in the pot. *4, 40*

25 The driving is like the driving of Jehu the son of Nimshi; for he driveth furiously. *9, 20*

Esther

26 Let it be written among the laws of the Persians and the Medes, that it be not altered. *1, 19*

27 The king loved Esther above all the women. *2, 17*

Job

1 Naked came I out of my mother's womb, and naked shall I return thither: the Lord gave, and the Lord hath taken away; blessed be the name of the Lord. *1, 21*

2 Shall mortal man be more just than God? shall a man be more pure than his maker? *4, 17*

3 Man is born unto trouble, as the sparks fly upward. *5, 7*

4 Though he slay me, yet will I trust in him. *13, 15*

5 Man that is born of a woman is of few days, and full of trouble. *14, 1*

6 Miserable comforters are ye all. *16, 2*

7 I am escaped with the skin of my teeth. *19, 20*

8 I know that my redeemer liveth. *19, 25*

9 The price of wisdom is above rubies. *28, 18*

10 I was eyes to the blind, and feet was I to the lame. *29, 15*

11 Great men are not always wise. *32, 9*

12 Who is this that darkeneth counsel by words without knowledge? *38, 2*

13 Hath the rain a father? *38, 28*

14 Canst thou draw out leviathan with an hook? *41, 1*

15 I have heard of thee by the hearing of the ear: but now mine eye seeth thee. *42, 5*

Psalms

16 Why do the heathen rage, and the people imagine a vain thing? *2, 1*

17 Out of the mouth of babes and sucklings hast thou ordained strength. *8, 2*

18 What is man, that thou art mindful of him? *8, 4*

19 Thou hast made him a little lower than the angels. *8, 5*

20 The fool hath said in his heart, There is no God. *14, 1*

21 Keep me as the apple of the eye, hide me under the shadow of thy wings. *17, 8*

22 The heavens declare the glory of God; and the firmament sheweth his handywork. *19, 1*

23 Day unto day uttereth speech, and night unto night sheweth knowledge. *19, 2*

24 More to be desired are they than gold, yea, than much fine gold: sweeter also than honey and the honeycomb. *19, 10*

25 Let the words of my mouth, and the meditation of my heart, be acceptable in thy sight, O Lord, my strength, and my redeemer. *19, 14*

26 Some trust in chariots, and some in horses: but we will remember the name of the Lord our God. *20, 7*

27 The Lord is my shepherd; I shall not want. *23, 1*

28 He maketh me to lie down in green pastures: he leadeth me beside the still waters. *23, 2*

29 Yea, though I walk through the valley of the shadow of death, I will fear no evil: for thou art with me; thy rod and thy staff they comfort me. *23, 4*

1 The earth is the Lord's, and the fulness thereof; the world, and they that dwell therein. *Psalms, 24, 1*

2 Weeping may endure for a night, but joy cometh in the morning. *30, 5*

3 Into thy hands I commend my spirit. *31, 6, Book of Common Prayer version*

4 Praise the Lord with harp: sing unto him with the psaltery and an instrument of ten strings. *33, 2*

5 Sing unto him a new song; play skilfully with a loud noise. *33, 3*

6 O taste and see that the Lord is good. *34, 8*

7 The Lord is nigh unto them that are of a broken heart. *34, 18*

8 But the meek shall inherit the earth. *37, 11*

9 I have been young, and now am old; yet have I not seen the righteous forsaken, nor his seed begging bread. *37, 25*

10 I myself have seen the ungodly in great power: and flourishing like a green bay-tree. *37, 36, Book of Common Prayer version*

11 Lord, make me to know mine end, and the measure of my days. *39, 4*

12 Blessed is he that considereth the poor. *41, 1*

13 God is our refuge and strength, a very present help in trouble. *46, 1*

14 Purge me with hyssop, and I shall be clean: wash me, and I shall be whiter than snow. *51, 7*

15 The sacrifices of God are a broken spirit: a broken and a contrite heart, O God, thou wilt not despise. *51, 17*

16 Oh that I had wings like a dove! *55, 6*

17 They are like the deaf adder that stoppeth her ear. *58, 4*

18 They grin like a dog, and run about through the city. *59, 6, Book of Common Prayer version*

19 Make a joyful noise unto God. *66, 1*

20 They go from strength to strength. *84, 7*

21 I had rather be a doorkeeper in the house of my God, than to dwell in the tents of wickedness. *84, 10*

22 For a thousand years in thy sight are but as yesterday when it is past, and as a watch in the night. *90, 4*

23 The days of our years are threescore years and ten; and if by reason of strength they be fourscore years, yet is their strength labour and sorrow; for it is soon cut off, and we fly away. *90, 10*

24 So teach us to number our days, that we may apply our hearts unto wisdom. *90, 12*

25 He shall cover thee with his feathers, and under his wings shalt thou trust. *91, 4*

26 Thou shalt not be afraid for the terror by night; nor for the arrow that flieth by day. *91, 5*

27 Nor for the pestilence that walketh in darkness; nor for the destruction that wasteth at noonday. *91, 6*

28 Like as a father pitieth his children, so the Lord pitieth them that fear him. *103, 13*

1 As for man, his days are as grass: as a flower of the field, so he flourisheth. *Psalms, 103, 15*

2 Wine that maketh glad the heart of man. *104, 15*

3 The iron entered into his soul. *105, 18, Book of Common Prayer version*

4 They that go down to the sea in ships, that do business in great waters. *107, 23*

5 They reel to and fro, and stagger like a drunken man, and are at their wits' end. *107, 27*

6 The fear of the Lord is the beginning of wisdom. *111, 10*

7 The mountains skipped like rams, and the little hills like lambs. *114, 4*

8 They have mouths, but they speak not: eyes have they, but they see not. *115, 5*

9 They have ears, but they hear not: noses have they, but they smell not. *115, 6*

10 I said in my haste, All men are liars. *116, 11*

11 Precious in the sight of the Lord is the death of his saints. *116, 15*

12 It is better to trust in the Lord than to put confidence in man. *118, 8*

13 The stone which the builders refused is become the head stone of the corner. *118, 22*

14 I am for peace: but when I speak, they are for war. *120, 7*

15 I will lift up mine eyes unto the hills, from whence cometh my help. *121, 1*

16 The sun shall not smite thee by day, nor the moon by night. *121, 6*

17 The Lord shall preserve thy going out and thy coming in from this time forth, and even for evermore. *121, 8*

18 They that sow in tears shall reap in joy. *126, 5*

19 Except the Lord build the house, they labour in vain that build it. *127, 1*

20 It is vain for you to rise up early, to sit up late, to eat the bread of sorrows: for so he giveth his beloved sleep. *127, 2*

21 Behold, how good and how pleasant it is for brethren to dwell together in unity! *133, 1*

22 By the rivers of Babylon, there we sat down, yea, we wept, when we remembered Zion. *137, 1*

23 We hanged our harps upon the willows in the midst thereof. *137, 2*

24 Sing us one of the songs of Zion. *137, 3*

25 How shall we sing the Lord's song in a strange land? *137, 4*

26 If I forget thee, O Jerusalem, let my right hand forget her cunning. *137, 5*

27 If I do not remember thee, let my tongue cleave to the roof of my mouth. *137, 6*

28 I am fearfully and wonderfully made. *139, 14*

29 Set a watch, O Lord, before my mouth; keep the door of my lips. *141, 3*

30 The eyes of all wait upon thee; and thou givest them their meat in due season. *145, 15*

31 Put not your trust in princes. *146, 3*

Proverbs

1 The fear of the Lord is the beginning of knowledge. *1, 7*

2 Whom the Lord loveth he correcteth. *3, 12*

3 Her ways are ways of pleasantness, and all her paths are peace. *3, 17*

4 Go to the ant, thou sluggard; consider her ways, and be wise. *6, 6*

5 For wisdom is better than rubies. *8, 11*

6 Wisdom hath builded her house, she hath hewn out her seven pillars. *9, 1*

7 Stolen waters are sweet, and bread eaten in secret is pleasant. *9, 17*

8 A wise son maketh a glad father: but a foolish son is the heaviness of his mother. *10, 1*

9 The memory of the just is blessed. *10, 7*

10 In the multitude of counsellers there is safety. *11, 14*

11 As a jewel of gold in a swine's snout, so is a fair woman which is without discretion. *11, 22*

12 A virtuous woman is a crown to her husband: but she that maketh ashamed is as rottenness in his bones. *12, 4*

13 Hope deferred maketh the heart sick. *13, 12*

14 He that spareth his rod hateth his son: but he that loveth him chasteneth him betimes. *13, 24*

15 Righteousness exalteth a nation. *14, 34*

16 A soft answer turneth away wrath. *15, 1*

17 A merry heart maketh a cheerful countenance. *15, 13*

18 Better is a dinner of herbs where love is, than a stalled ox and hatred there-with. *15, 17*

19 Pride goeth before destruction, and an haughty spirit before a fall. *16, 18*

20 Even a fool, when he holdeth his peace, is counted wise. *17, 28*

21 Wealth maketh many friends. *19, 4*

22 Wine is a mocker, strong drink is raging: and whosoever is deceived thereby is not wise. *20, 1*

23 Even a child is known by his doings. *20, 11*

24 It is naught, it is naught, saith the buyer; but when he is gone his way, then he boasteth. *20, 14*

25 The glory of young men is their strength. *20, 29*

26 A good name is rather to be chosen than great riches. *22, 1*

27 Train up a child in the way he should go: and when he is old, he will not depart from it. *22, 6*

28 If thine enemy be hungry, give him bread to eat; and if he be thirsty, give him water to drink:
For thou shalt heap coals of fire upon his head, and the Lord shall reward thee. *25, 21–22*

29 As cold waters to a thirsty soul, so is good news from a far country. *25, 25*

30 A whip for the horse, a bridle for the ass, and a rod for the fool's back. *26, 3*

31 As a dog returneth to his vomit, so a fool returneth to his folly. *26, 11*

1 Whoso diggeth a pit shall fall therein. *Proverbs, 26, 27*

2 Open rebuke is better than secret love. *27, 5*

3 Faithful are the wounds of a friend. *27, 6*

4 He that maketh haste to be rich shall not be innocent. *28, 20*

5 Where there is no vision, the people perish. *29, 18*

6 Give me neither poverty nor riches; feed me with food convenient for me. *30, 8*

7 There be three things which are too wonderful for me, yea, four which I know not: The way of an eagle in the air; the way of a serpent upon a rock; the way of a ship in the midst of the sea; and the way of a man with a maid. *30, 18–19*

8 Who can find a virtuous woman? for her price is far above rubies. *31, 10*

Ecclesiastes

9 Vanity of vanities, saith the Preacher, vanity of vanities; all is vanity. *1, 2*

10 What profit hath a man of all his labour which he taketh under the sun? *1, 3*

11 One generation passeth away, and another generation cometh: but the earth abideth for ever. *1, 4*

12 There is no new thing under the sun. *1, 9*

13 For in much wisdom is much grief: and he that increaseth knowledge increaseth sorrow. *1, 18*

14 To every thing there is a season, and a time to every purpose under the heaven. *3, 1*

15 A threefold cord is not quickly broken. *4, 12*

16 God is in heaven, and thou upon earth: therefore let thy words be few. *5, 2*

17 The sleep of a labouring man is sweet. *5, 12*

18 A good name is better than precious ointment; and the day of death than the day of one's birth. *7, 1*

19 For as the crackling of thorns under a pot, so is the laughter of the fool. *7, 6*

20 Say not thou, What is the cause that the former days were better than these? for thou dost not inquire wisely concerning this. *7, 10*

21 Be not righteous over much. *7, 16*

22 Whatsoever thy hand findeth to do, do it with thy might. *9, 10*

23 The race is not to the swift, nor the battle to the strong, neither yet bread to the wise, nor yet riches to men of understanding, nor yet favour to men of skill; but time and chance happeneth to them all. *9, 11*

24 Cast thy bread upon the waters: for thou shalt find it after many days. *11, 1*

25 Rejoice, O young man, in thy youth. *11, 9*

26 Remember now thy Creator in the days of thy youth, while the evil days come not, nor the years draw nigh, when thou shalt say, I have no pleasure in them. *12, 1*

27 Man goeth to his long home. *12, 5*

28 Of making many books there is no end; and much study is a weariness of the flesh. *12, 12*

1 Let us hear the conclusion of the whole matter: Fear God, and keep his commandments: for this is the whole duty of man. *Ecclesiastes, 12, 13*

The Song of Solomon

2 Let him kiss me with the kisses of his mouth: for thy love is better than wine. *1, 2*

3 I am black, but comely, O ye daughters of Jerusalem. *1, 5*

4 I am the rose of Sharon, and the lily of the valleys. *2, 1*

5 His banner over me was love. *2, 4*

6 Stay me with flagons, comfort me with apples: for I am sick of love. *2, 5*

7 Rise up, my love, my fair one, and come away. *2, 10*

8 For, lo, the winter is past, the rain is over and gone. *2, 11*

9 The flowers appear on the earth; the time of the singing of birds is come, and the voice of the turtle is heard in our land. *2, 12*

10 Our vines have tender grapes. *2, 15*

11 Until the day break, and the shadows flee away. *2, 17*

12 I sleep, but my heart waketh. *5, 2*

13 Terrible as an army with banners. *6, 4*

14 Love is strong as death; jealousy is cruel as the grave. *8, 6*

15 Many waters cannot quench love. *8, 7*

Isaiah

16 The ox knoweth his owner, and the ass his master's crib. *1, 3*

17 Though your sins be as scarlet, they shall be as white as snow. *1, 18*

18 They shall beat their swords into plowshares, and their spears into pruning-hooks: nation shall not lift up sword against nation, neither shall they learn war any more. *2, 4*

19 What mean ye that ye beat my people to pieces, and grind the faces of the poor? *3, 15*

20 Woe unto them that call evil good, and good evil. *5, 20*

21 A virgin shall conceive, and bear a son, and shall call his name Immanuel. *7, 14*

22 The people that walked in darkness have seen a great light. *9, 2*

23 For unto us a child is born, unto us a son is given: and the government shall be upon his shoulder: and his name shall be called Wonderful, Counseller, The mighty God, The everlasting Father, The Prince of Peace. *9, 6*

24 The wolf also shall dwell with the lamb, and the leopard shall lie down with the kid; and the calf and the young lion and the fatling together; and a little child shall lead them. *11, 6*

25 How art thou fallen from heaven, O Lucifer, son of the morning! *14, 12*

26 Watchman, what of the night? *21, 11*

27 Let us eat and drink; for to-morrow we shall die. *22, 13*

28 Set thine house in order: for thou shalt die. *38, 1*

29 All flesh is grass. *40, 6*

1 Behold, the nations are as a drop of a bucket. *Isaiah, 40, 15*

2 A bruised reed shall he not break, and the smoking flax shall he not quench. *42, 3*

3 There is no peace, saith the Lord, unto the wicked. *48, 22*

4 How beautiful upon the mountains are the feet of him that bringeth good tidings. *52, 7*

5 He is despised and rejected of men; a man of sorrows, and acquainted with grief. *53, 3*

6 All we like sheep have gone astray. *53, 6*

7 He is brought as a lamb to the slaughter. *53, 7*

8 Seek ye the Lord while he may be found, call ye upon him while he is near. *55, 6*

9 For my thoughts are not your thoughts, neither are your ways my ways, saith the Lord. *55, 8*

10 Is it such a fast that I have chosen? a day for a man to afflict his soul? *58, 5*

11 To give unto them beauty for ashes, the oil of joy for mourning, the garment of praise for the spirit of heaviness. *61, 3*

Jeremiah

12 They have healed also the hurt of the daughter of my people slightly, saying, Peace, peace; when there is no peace. *6, 14*

13 Is there no balm in Gilead; is there no physician there? *8, 22*

14 Can the Ethiopian change his skin, or the leopard his spots? *13, 23*

15 As the clay is in the potter's hand, so are ye in mine hand, O house of Israel. *18, 6*

16 The fathers have eaten a sour grape, and the children's teeth are set on edge. *31, 29*

Lamentations

17 Is it nothing to you, all ye that pass by? behold, and see if there be any sorrow like unto my sorrow. *1, 12*

18 Remembering mine affliction and my misery; the wormwood and the gall. *3, 19*

19 His compassions fail not. They are new every morning. *3, 22–23*

20 It is good for a man that he bear the yoke in his youth. *3, 27*

Ezekiel

21 They four had one likeness, as if a wheel had been in the midst of a wheel. *10, 10*

22 The king of Babylon stood at the parting of the way. *21, 21*

23 O ye dry bones, hear the word of the Lord. *37, 4*

24 Son of man, set thy face against Gog, the land of Magog. *38, 2*

Daniel

25 And he commanded the most mighty men that were in his army to bind Shadrach, Meshach, and Abed-nego, and to cast them into the burning fiery furnace. *3, 20*

1 MENE, MENE, TEKEL, UPHARSIN. *Daniel, 5, 25*

2 Thou art weighed in the balances, and art found wanting. *5, 27*

3 Thy kingdom is divided, and given to the Medes and Persians. *5, 28*

4 The law of the Medes and Persians, which altereth not. *6, 12*

5 They brought Daniel, and cast him into the den of lions. *6, 16*

6 The Ancient of days. *7, 13*

7 O Daniel, a man greatly beloved. *10, 11*

Hosea

8 I desired mercy, and not sacrifice; and the knowledge of God more than burnt offerings. *6, 6*

9 They have sown the wind, and they shall reap the whirlwind. *8, 7*

10 I drew them with cords of a man, with bands of love. *11, 4*

Joel

11 Rend your heart, and not your garments. *2, 13*

12 The years that the locust hath eaten. *2, 25*

13 Your old men shall dream dreams, your young men shall see visions. *2, 28*

14 Multitudes in the valley of decision. *3, 14*

Amos

15 Can two walk together, except they be agreed? *3, 3*

16 Prepare to meet thy God. *4, 12*

17 Woe to them that are at ease in Zion. *6, 1*

Jonah

18 So they cast lots, and the lot fell upon Jonah. *1, 7*

19 Jonah was in the belly of the fish three days and three nights. *1, 17*

20 And God said to Jonah, Doest thou well to be angry for the gourd? *4, 9*

21 And should not I spare Nineveh, that great city, wherein are more than sixscore thousand persons that cannot discern between their right hand and their left hand; and also much cattle? *4, 11*

Micah

22 They shall sit every man under his vine and under his fig tree. *4, 4*

23 O my people, what have I done unto thee? and wherein have I wearied thee? *6, 3*

24 What doth the Lord require of thee, but to do justly, and to love mercy, and to walk humbly with thy God? *6, 8*

Habakkuk

25 Thou art of purer eyes than to behold evil. *1, 13*

26 Write the vision, and make it plain upon tables, that he may run that readeth it. *2, 2*

Haggai

1 The glory of this latter house shall be greater than of the former. *2, 9*

Zechariah

2 Is not this a brand plucked out of the fire? *3, 2*

3 Who hath despised the day of small things? *4, 10*

4 What are these wounds in thine hands? Then he shall answer, Those with which I was wounded in the house of my friends. *13, 6*

Malachi

5 Have we not all one father? hath not one God created us? *2, 10*

6 The Lord, whom ye seek, shall suddenly come to his temple. *3, 1*

7 Unto you that fear my name shall the Sun of righteousness arise with healing in his wings. *4, 2*

The New Testament

St. Matthew

8 Where is he that is born King of the Jews? for we have seen his star in the east, and are come to worship him. *2, 2*

9 Rachel weeping for her children, and would not be comforted, because they are not. *2, 18*

10 Repent ye: for the kingdom of heaven is at hand. *3, 2*

11 The voice of one crying in the wilderness. *3, 3*

12 O generation of vipers, who hath warned you to flee from the wrath to come? *3, 7*

13 Man shall not live by bread alone, but by every word that proceedeth out of the mouth of God. *4, 4*

14 Follow me, and I will make you fishers of men. *4, 19*

15 Blessed are the meek: for they shall inherit the earth. *5, 5*

16 Blessed are the pure in heart: for they shall see God. *5, 8*

17 Ye are the salt of the earth: but if the salt have lost his savour, wherewith shall it be salted? *5, 13*

18 An eye for an eye, and a tooth for a tooth. *5, 38*

19 Resist not evil: but whosoever shall smite thee on thy right cheek, turn to him the other also. *5, 39*

20 Love your enemies. *5, 44*

21 He maketh his sun to rise on the evil and on the good, and sendeth rain on the just and on the unjust. *5, 45*

22 Let not thy left hand know what thy right hand doeth. *6, 3*

23 Use not vain repetitions. *6, 7*

24 After this manner therefore pray ye: Our Father which art in heaven, Hallowed be thy name. Thy kingdom come. Thy will be done in earth, as it is in heaven. Give us this day our daily bread. And forgive us our debts, as we forgive our debtors. And lead us not into temptation, but deliver us from evil: For thine is the kingdom, and the power, and the glory, for ever. Amen. *6, 9–13*

1 No man can serve two masters. *St. Matthew, 6, 24*

2 Ye cannot serve God and mammon. *Ib*

3 Consider the lilies of the field, how they grow; they toil not, neither do they spin. *6, 28*

4 Sufficient unto the day is the evil thereof. *6, 34*

5 Judge not, that ye be not judged. *7, 1*

6 Neither cast ye your pearls before swine. *7, 6*

7 Therefore all things whatsoever ye would that men should do to you, do ye even so to them: for this is the law and the prophets. *7, 12*

8 Enter ye in at the strait gate. *7, 13*

9 Beware of false prophets, which come to you in sheep's clothing, but inwardly they are ravening wolves. *7, 15*

10 A man under authority. *8, 9*

11 What went ye out into the wilderness to see? A reed shaken with the wind? *11, 7*

12 He that is not with me is against me. *12, 30*

13 One pearl of great price. *13, 46*

14 A prophet is not without honour, save in his own country. *13, 57*

15 If the blind lead the blind, both shall fall into the ditch. *15, 14*

16 Thou art Peter, and upon this rock I will build my church; and the gates of hell shall not prevail against it. *16, 18*

17 The keys of the kingdom of heaven. *16, 19*

18 Get thee behind me, Satan. *16, 23*

19 Except ye be converted, and become as little children, ye shall not enter into the kingdom of heaven. *18, 3*

20 But whoso shall offend one of these little ones which believe in me, it were better for him that a millstone were hanged about his neck, and that he were drowned in the depth of the sea. *18, 6*

21 If thine eye offend thee, pluck it out. *18, 9*

22 Until seventy times seven. *18, 22*

23 It is easier for a camel to go through the eye of a needle, than for a rich man to enter into the kingdom of God. *19, 24*

24 For many are called, but few are chosen. *22, 14*

25 Render therefore unto Caesar the things which are Caesar's; and unto God the things that are God's. *22, 21*

26 Ye blind guides, which strain at a gnat, and swallow a camel. *23, 24*

27 Wars and rumours of wars. *24, 6*

28 For unto every one that hath shall be given, and he shall have abundance: but from him that hath not shall be taken away even that which he hath. *25, 29*

29 As a shepherd divideth his sheep from the goats. *25, 32*

30 Inasmuch as ye have done it unto one of the least of these my brethren, ye have done it unto me. *25, 40*

1 Ye have the poor always with you. *St. Matthew, 26, 11*

2 Watch and pray, that ye enter not into temptation: the spirit indeed is willing, but the flesh is weak. *26, 41*

3 He took water, and washed his hands before the multitude, saying, I am innocent of the blood of this just person. *27, 24*

4 I am with you alway, even unto the end of the world. *28, 20*

St. Mark

5 They that are whole have no need of the physician, but they that are sick. *2, 17*

6 The sabbath was made for man, and not man for the sabbath. *2, 27*

7 If a house be divided against itself, that house cannot stand. *3, 25*

8 He that hath ears to hear, let him hear. *4, 9*

9 My name is Legion: for we are many. *5, 9*

10 For what shall it profit a man, if he shall gain the whole world, and lose his own soul? *8, 36*

11 I believe: help thou mine unbelief. *9, 24*

12 What therefore God hath joined together, let not man put asunder. *10, 9*

13 Suffer the little children to come unto me, and forbid them not: for of such is the kingdom of God. *10, 14*

14 Is it not written, My house shall be called of all nations the house of prayer? but ye have made it a den of thieves. *11, 17*

15 And there came a certain poor widow, and she threw in two mites, which make a farthing. *12, 42*

16 Take ye heed, watch and pray. *13, 33*

17 Before the cock crow twice, thou shalt deny me thrice. *14, 30*

18 Crucify him. *15, 13*

St. Luke

19 There was no room for them in the inn. *2, 7*

20 And there were in the same country shepherds abiding in the field, keeping watch over their flock by night. *2, 8*

21 Ye shall find the babe wrapped in swaddling clothes, lying in a manger. *2, 12*

22 Glory to God in the highest, and on earth peace, good will toward men. *2, 14*

23 Be content with your wages. *3, 14*

24 Physician, heal thyself. *4, 23*

25 No man putteth new wine into old bottles. *5, 37*

26 No man, having put his hand to the plough, and looking back, is fit for the kingdom of God. *9, 62*

27 The labourer is worthy of his hire. *10, 7*

28 Fell among thieves. *10, 30*

29 He passed by on the other side. *10, 31*

30 Friend, go up higher. *14, 10*

1 The poor, and the maimed, and the halt, and the blind. *St. Luke, 14, 21*

2 Joy shall be in heaven over one sinner that repenteth, more than over ninety and nine just persons, which need no repentance. *15, 7*

3 And he would fain have filled his belly with the husks that the swine did eat. *15, 16*

4 Bring hither the fatted calf, and kill it. *15, 23*

5 I cannot dig; to beg I am ashamed. *16, 3*

6 The children of this world are in their generation wiser than the children of light. *16, 8*

7 Make to yourselves friends of the mammon of unrighteousness. *16, 9*

8 The crumbs which fell from the rich man's table. *16, 21*

9 Between us and you there is a great gulf fixed. *16, 26*

10 Remember Lot's wife. *17, 32*

11 I thank thee, that I am not as other men are. *18, 11*

12 Out of thine own mouth will I judge thee. *19, 22*

13 Father, forgive them; for they know not what they do. *23, 34*

St. John

14 In the beginning was the Word, and the Word was with God, and the Word was God. *1, 1*

15 The true Light, which lighteth every man that cometh into the world. *1, 9*

16 He came unto his own, and his own received him not. *1, 11*

17 The Word was made flesh, and dwelt among us. *1, 14*

18 Can there any good thing come out of Nazareth? *1, 46*

19 Ye must be born again. *3, 7*

20 The wind bloweth where it listeth. *3, 8*

21 For God so loved the world, that he gave his only begotten Son, that whosoever believeth in him should not perish, but have everlasting life. *3, 16*

22 Men loved darkness rather than light, because their deeds were evil. *3, 19*

23 Judge not according to the appearance, but judge righteous judgment. *7, 24*

24 He that is without sin among you, let him first cast a stone at her. *8, 7*

25 I am the light of the world. *8, 12*

26 The night cometh, when no man can work. *9, 4*

27 The good shepherd giveth his life for the sheep. *10, 11*

28 Jesus wept. *11, 35*

29 A new commandment I give unto you, That ye love one another. *13, 34*

30 In my Father's house are many mansions. *14, 2*

31 Greater love hath no man than this, that a man lay down his life for his friends. *15, 13*

32 Whither goest thou? *16, 5*

33 Pilate saith unto him, What is truth? *18, 38*

34 What I have written I have written. *19, 22*

35 Blessed are they that have not seen, and yet have believed. *20, 29*

Acts of the Apostles

1 Silver and gold have I none; but such as I have give I thee. *3, 6*

2 Thy money perish with thee, because thou hast thought that the gift of God may be purchased with money. *8, 20*

3 He went on his way rejoicing. *8, 39*

4 It is hard for thee to kick against the pricks. *9, 5*

5 God is no respecter of persons. *10, 34*

6 In him we live, and move, and have our being. *17, 28*

7 Great is Diana of the Ephesians. *19, 34*

8 It is more blessed to give than to receive. *20, 35*

9 A citizen of no mean city. *21, 39*

10 Brought up in this city at the feet of Gamaliel. *22, 3*

11 I appeal unto Caesar. *25, 11*

12 Hast thou appealed unto Caesar? unto Caesar shalt thou go. *25, 12*

13 I was not disobedient unto the heavenly vision. *26, 19*

14 Almost thou persuadest me to be a Christian. *26, 28*

Romans

15 The just shall live by faith. *1, 17*

16 These, having not the law, are a law unto themselves. *2, 14*

17 Death hath no more dominion over him. *6, 9*

18 The wages of sin is death. *6, 23*

19 For the good that I would I do not: but the evil which I would not, that I do. *7, 19*

20 And we know that all things work together for good to them that love God. *8, 28*

21 If God be for us, who can be against us? *8, 31*

22 So we, being many, are one body in Christ, and every one members one of another. *12, 5*

23 Let love be without dissimulation. Abhor that which is evil; cleave to that which is good. *12, 9*

24 Rejoice with them that do rejoice, and weep with them that weep. *12, 15*

25 Be not wise in your own conceits. *12, 16*

26 Vengeance is mine; I will repay, saith the Lord. *12, 19*

27 Be not overcome of evil, but overcome evil with good. *12, 21*

28 The powers that be are ordained of God. *13, 1*

29 Love worketh no ill to his neighbour: therefore love is the fulfilling of the law. *13, 10*

30 None of us liveth to himself, and no man dieth to himself. *14, 7*

31 We then that are strong ought to bear the infirmities of the weak. *15, 1*

1 Corinthians

32 I have planted, Apollos watered; but God gave the increase. *3, 6*

33 Absent in body, but present in spirit. *5, 3*

1 Know ye not that a little leaven leaveneth the whole lump? *I Corinthians, 5, 6*

2 All things are lawful unto me, but all things are not expedient. *6, 12*

3 It is better to marry than to burn. *7, 9*

4 All things to all men. *9, 22*

5 If a woman have long hair, it is a glory to her. *11, 15*

6 When I became a man, I put away childish things. *13, 11*

7 Now we see through a glass, darkly; but then face to face. *13, 12*

8 And now abideth faith, hope, charity, these three; but the greatest of these is charity. *13, 13*

9 Let your women keep silence in the churches. *14, 34*

10 Let all things be done decently and in order. *14, 40*

11 One born out of due time. *15, 8*

12 By the grace of God I am what I am. *15, 10*

13 O death, where is thy sting? O grave, where is thy victory? *15, 55*

2 Corinthians

14 The letter killeth, but the spirit giveth life. *3, 6*

15 We walk by faith, not by sight. *5, 7*

16 God loveth a cheerful giver. *9, 7*

17 For ye suffer fools gladly, seeing ye yourselves are wise. *11, 19*

18 A thorn in the flesh. *12, 7*

19 My grace is sufficient for thee: for my strength is made perfect in weakness. *12, 9*

Galatians

20 The right hands of fellowship. *2, 9*

21 Ye are fallen from grace. *5, 4*

22 Bear ye one another's burdens. *6, 2*

23 Be not deceived; God is not mocked: for whatsoever a man soweth, that shall he also reap. *6, 7*

Ephesians

24 Be ye angry, and sin not: let not the sun go down upon your wrath. *4, 26*

25 For this cause shall a man leave his father and mother, and shall be joined unto his wife, and they two shall be one flesh. *5, 31*

26 Put on the whole armour of God. *6, 11*

27 For we wrestle not against flesh and blood, but against principalities, against powers, against the rulers of the darkness of this world, against spiritual wickedness in high places. *6, 12*

Philippians

28 Work out your own salvation with fear and trembling. *2, 12*

29 Whose God is their belly, and whose glory is in their shame. *2, 19*

30 Our conversation is in heaven. *3, 20*

31 The peace of God, which passeth all understanding. *4, 7*

1 Whatsoever things are true, whatsoever things are honest, whatsoever things are just, whatsoever things are pure, whatsoever things are lovely, whatsoever things are of good report; if there be any virtue, and if there be any praise, think on these things. *Philippians, 4, 8*

2 I have learned, in whatsoever state I am, therewith to be content. *4, 11*

Colossians

3 Touch not; taste not; handle not. *2, 21*

4 Set your affection on things above, not on things on the earth. *3, 2*

1 Thessalonians

5 Remembering without ceasing your work of faith, and labour of love. *1, 3*

6 Pray without ceasing. *5, 17*

7 Prove all things: hold fast that which is good. *5, 21*

2 Thessalonians

8 If any would not work, neither should he eat. *3, 10*

1 Timothy

9 Not greedy of filthy lucre. *3, 3*

10 Refuse profane and old wives' fables. *4, 7*

11 Let no man despise thy youth. *4, 12*

12 Drink no longer water, but use a little wine for thy stomach's sake and thine often infirmities. *5, 23*

13 For we brought nothing into this world, and it is certain we can carry nothing out. *6, 7*

14 The love of money is the root of all evil. *6, 10*

15 Fight the good fight of faith. *6, 12*

2 Timothy

16 All scripture is given by inspiration of God. *3, 16*

17 I have fought a good fight, I have finished my course, I have kept the faith. *4, 7*

Titus

18 Unto the pure all things are pure. *1, 15*

Hebrews

19 It is appointed unto men once to die, but after this the judgment. *9, 27*

20 It is a fearful thing to fall into the hands of the living God. *10, 31*

21 Faith is the substance of things hoped for, the evidence of things not seen. *11, 1*

22 Whom the Lord loveth he chasteneth. *12, 6*

23 Let brotherly love continue. *13, 1*

24 Jesus Christ the same yesterday, and today, and for ever. *13, 8*

James

25 Faith without works is dead. *2, 20*

1 The tongue can no man tame; it is an unruly evil. *James, 3, 8*

2 Resist the devil, and he will flee from you. *4, 7*

3 Ye have heard of the patience of Job. *5, 11*

1 Peter

4 All flesh is as grass. *1, 24*

5 Honour all men. Love the brotherhood. Fear God. Honour the king. *2, 17*

6 Giving honour unto the wife, as unto the weaker vessel. *3, 7*

7 Charity shall cover the multitude of sins. *4, 8*

8 Be sober, be vigilant; because your adversary the devil, as a roaring lion, walketh about, seeking whom he may devour. *5, 8*

2 Peter

9 The dog is turned to his own vomit again; and the sow that was washed to her wallowing in the mire. *2, 22*

10 One day is with the Lord as a thousand years, and a thousand years as one day. *3, 8*

1 John

11 Shutteth up his bowels of compassion. *3, 17*

12 God is love. *4, 8*

13 There is no fear in love; but perfect love casteth out fear. *4, 18*

2 John

14 The elder unto the elect lady. *1, 1*

Revelation

15 I am Alpha and Omega, the beginning and the ending. *1, 8*

16 Be thou faithful unto death, and I will give thee a crown of life. *2, 10*

17 He shall rule them with a rod of iron. *2, 27*

18 I will not blot out his name out of the book of life. *3, 5*

19 Because thou art lukewarm, and neither cold nor hot, I will spue thee out of my mouth. *3, 16*

20 Behold, I stand at the door, and knock. *3, 20*

21 He went forth conquering, and to conquer. *6, 2*

22 Behold a pale horse: and his name that sat on him was Death, and Hell followed with him. *6, 8*

23 And when he had opened the seventh seal, there was silence in heaven about the space of half an hour. *8, 1*

24 The bottomless pit. *9, 1*

25 They had tails like unto scorpions, and there were stings in their tails. *9, 10*

26 Let him that hath understanding count the number of the beast: for it is the number of a man; and his number is Six hundred threescore and six. *13, 18*

27 A place called in the Hebrew tongue Armageddon. *16, 16*

1 And I saw a new heaven and a new earth: for the first heaven and the first earth were passed away; and there was no more sea. *Revelation, 21, 1*

2 The holy city, new Jerusalem, coming down from God out of heaven, prepared as a bride adorned for her husband. *21, 2*

3 And God shall wipe away all tears from their eyes; and there shall be no more death, neither sorrow, nor crying, neither shall there be any more pain: for the former things are passed away. *21, 4*

4 If any man shall add unto these things, God shall add unto him the plagues that are written in this book. *22, 18*

Apocrypha

1 Esdras

5 The first wrote, Wine is the strongest.
The second wrote, The king is strongest.
The third wrote, Women are strongest: but above all things Truth beareth away the victory. *3, 10*

6 Great is Truth, and mighty above all things. *4, 41*

2 Esdras

7 I shall light a candle of understanding in thine heart, which shall not be put out. *14, 25*

Tobit

8 If thou hast abundance, give alms accordingly: if thou have but a little, be not afraid to give according to that little. *4, 8*

9 So they went forth both, and the young man's dog with them. *5, 16*

Wisdom of Solomon

10 Let us crown ourselves with rosebuds, before they be withered. *2, 8*

11 Through envy of the devil came death into the world. *2, 24*

12 The souls of the righteous are in the hand of God, and there shall no torment touch them. *3, 1*

13 The corruptible body presseth down the soul. *9, 15*

14 O Lord, thou lover of souls. *11, 26*

Ecclesiasticus

15 My son, if thou come to serve the Lord, prepare thy soul for temptation. *2, 1*

16 A faithful friend is the medicine of life. *6, 16*

17 Miss not the discourse of the elders. *8, 9*

18 Open not thine heart to every man. *8, 19*

19 Give not thy soul unto a woman. *9, 2*

20 Forsake not an old friend. *9, 10*

21 Judge none blessed before his death. *11, 28*

22 He that toucheth pitch shall be defiled therewith. *13, 1*

23 Be not made a beggar by banqueting upon borrowing. *18, 33*

1 All wickedness is but little to the wickedness of a woman. *Ecclesiasticus, 25, 19*

2 Let thy speech be short, comprehending much in few words. *32, 8*

3 Honour a physician with the honour due unto him. *38, 1*

4 How can he get wisdom . . . whose talk is of bullocks? *38, 25*

5 Let us now praise famous men, and our fathers that begat us. *44, 1*

6 Rich men furnished with ability, living peaceably in their habitations. *44, 6*

7 And some there be, which have no memorial. *44, 9*

8 Their bodies are buried in peace; but their name liveth for evermore. *44, 14*

1 Maccabees

9 Consider ye throughout all ages, that none that put their trust in him shall be overcome. *2, 61*

2 Maccabees

10 When he was at the last gasp. *7, 9*

11 It was an holy and good thought. *12, 45*

The Book of Common Prayer

12 We have erred, and strayed from thy ways like lost sheep. *Morning Prayer, General Confession*

13 We have left undone those things which we ought to have done; And we have done those things which we ought not to have done. *Ib, Ib*

14 As it was in the beginning, is now, and ever shall be: world without end. *Ib, Gloria*

15 The noble army of Martyrs. *Ib, Te Deum*

16 Give peace in our time, O Lord. *Ib, Versicles*

17 Whose service is perfect freedom. *Ib, Second Collect, for Peace*

18 In Quires and Places where they sing. *Ib, Rubric after Third Collect*

19 When two or three are gathered together in thy Name thou wilt grant their requests. *Ib, Prayer of St. Chrysostom*

20 Lighten our darkness. *Evening Prayer, Third Collect, for Aid against all Perils*

21 Defend us from all perils and dangers of this night. *Ib, Ib*

22 Have mercy upon us miserable sinners. *Litany*

23 Envy, hatred, and malice, and all uncharitableness. *Ib*

24 All the deceits of the world, the flesh, and the devil. *Ib*

25 In the hour of death, and in the day of judgement. *Ib*

26 Preserve to our use the kindly fruits of the earth. *Ib*

27 All sorts and conditions of men. *Prayer for all Conditions of men*

28 All who profess and call themselves Christians. *Ib*

29 Those who are any ways afflicted, or distressed, in mind, body, or estate. *Ib*

30 Patience under their sufferings, and a happy issue out of all their afflictions. *Ib*

1 Our creation, preservation, and all the blessings of this life. *A General Thanksgiving*

2 Read, mark, learn, and inwardly digest. *Collect, 2nd Sunday in Advent*

3 All our doings without charity are nothing worth. *Ib, Quinquagesima Sunday*

4 Jews, Turks, Infidels, and Hereticks. *Ib, Third Collect for Good Friday*

5 A right judgement in all things. *Ib, Whit-Sunday*

6 The author and giver of all good things. *Ib, 7th Sunday after Trinity*

7 Whom truly to know is everlasting life. *Ib, St. Philip and St. James's Day*

8 Constantly speak the truth, boldly rebuke vice, and patiently suffer for the truth's sake. *Ib, St. John Baptist's Day*

9 An open and notorious evil liver. *Holy Communion, Introductory Rubric*

10 Grant that the old Adam in this Child may be so buried, that the new man may be raised up in him. *Publick Baptism of Infants, Blessing*

11 Renounce the devil and all his works. *Ib*

12 The pomps and vanity of this wicked world. *Catechism*

13 To order myself lowly and reverently to all my betters. *Ib*

14 To keep my hands from picking and stealing. *Ib*

15 To do my duty in that state of life, unto which it shall please God to call me. *Ib*

16 An outward and visible sign of an inward and spiritual grace. *Ib*

17 Being now come to the years of discretion. *Order of Confirmation*

18 If any of you know cause, or just impediment. *Solemnization of Matrimony*

19 Brute beasts that have no understanding. *Ib*

20 Let him now speak, or else hereafter for ever hold his peace. *Ib*

21 Wilt thou have this Woman to thy wedded wife? *Ib*

22 To have and to hold from this day forward, for better for worse, for richer for poorer, in sickness and in health, to love and to cherish, till death us do part. *Ib*

23 To love, cherish, and to obey. *Ib*

24 With this Ring I thee wed, with my body I thee worship, and with all my worldly goods I thee endow. *Ib*

25 Those whom God hath joined together let no man put asunder. *Ib*

26 I pronounce that they be Man and Wife together. *Ib*

27 The Office ensuing is not to be used for any that die unbaptized, or excommunicate, or have laid violent hands upon themselves. *Burial of the Dead, Introductory Rubric*

28 Man that is born of a woman hath but a short time to live, and is full of misery. *Ib*

29 In the midst of life we are in death. *Ib*

30 We therefore commit his body to the ground; earth to earth, ashes to ashes, dust to dust. *Ib*

BICKERSTAFFE, Isaac, 1735?–1812?

1 There was a jolly miller once
Lived on the river Dee;
He worked and sang from morn till night;
No lark more blithe than he. *Love in a Village, Act 1, Scene 5*

2 I care for nobody, not I,
If no one cares for me. *Ib*

3 But if I'm content with a little
Enough is as good as a feast. *Ib, Act 3, Scene 1*

BICKERSTETH, Edward Henry, 1825–1906

4 Peace, perfect peace, in this dark world of sin?
The blood of Jesus whispers peace within. *Songs in the House of Pilgrimage*

BINYON, Laurence Robert, 1869–1943

5 They shall grow not old, as we that are left grow old:
Age shall not weary them, nor the years condemn.
At the going down of the sun and in the morning
We will remember them. *For the Fallen (1914–18)*

BIRRELL, Augustine, 1850–1933

6 That great dust-heap called 'history'. *Obiter Dicta, 1st series, Carlyle*

BISMARCK, Otto von, 1815–1898

7 *Nach Canossa gehen wir nicht*. We will not go to Canossa. *Speech Reichstag, 14 May 1872*

8 *Blut und Eisen*. Blood and Iron. *Speech, Prussian Chamber, 28 Jan. 1886*

BLACKSTONE, Sir William, 1723–1780

9 The king never dies. *Commentaries on the Laws of England, Book 1, 7*

10 That the king can do no wrong, is a necessary and fundamental principle of the English constitution. *Ib, Book 3, 17*

11 It is better that ten guilty persons escape than one innocent suffer. *Ib, Book 4, 27*

BLAIR, Eric, see ORWELL, George

BLAKE, William, 1757–1827

12 To see a World in a grain of sand,
And a Heaven in a wild flower,
Hold Infinity in the palm of your hand,
And Eternity in an hour. *Auguries of Innocence, 1*

13 A robin redbreast in a cage
Puts all Heaven in a rage. *Ib, 5*

14 A truth that's told with bad intent
Beats all the lies you can invent. *Ib, 53*

15 Man was made for joy and woe;
And when this we rightly know,
Thro' the world we safely go. *Ib, 56*

1 God appears, and God is Light,
To those poor souls who dwell in Night;
But does a Human Form display
To those who dwell in realms of Day. *Auguries of Innocence, 129*

2 Does the Eagle know what is in the pit
Or wilt thou go ask the Mole?
Can Wisdom be put in a silver rod,
Or Love in a golden bowl? *The Book of Thel, Thel's Motto*

3 Mutual Forgiveness of each vice,
Such are the Gates of Paradise. *The Gates of Paradise, Prologue*

4 He who bends himself a Joy
Doth the wingèd life destroy;
But he who kisses the Joy as it flies
Lives in Eternity's sunrise.
Gnomic Verses, XVII, Several Questions Answered

5 For a Tear is an Intellectual thing;
And a Sigh is the sword of an angel king;
And the bitter groan of a Martyr's woe
Is an arrow from the Almighty's bow. *Jerusalem, f. 52*

6 He who would do good to another must do it in Minute Particulars.
General Good is the plea of the scoundrel, hypocrite, and flatterer.
Ib, f. 55

7 I care not whether a man is Good or Evil; all that I care
Is whether he is a Wise Man or a Fool. Go! put off Holiness,
And put on Intellect. *Ib, f. 91*

8 And did those feet in ancient time
Walk upon England's mountains green?
And was the holy Lamb of God
On England's pleasant pastures seen?

Bring me my bow of burning gold!
Bring me my arrows of desire!
Bring me my spear! O clouds, unfold!
Bring me my chariot of fire!

I will not cease from mental fight,
Nor shall my sword sleep in my hand,
Till we have built Jerusalem
In England's green and pleasant land. *Milton, Preface*

9 Mock on, mock on, Voltaire, Rousseau;
Mock on, mock on; 'tis all in vain!
You throw the sand against the wind,
And the wind blows it back again. *Mock on, mock on, Voltaire, Rousseau*

10 Never seek to tell thy love,
Love that never told can be;
For the gentle wind does move
Silently, invisibly. *Never seek to tell thy Love*

11 Soon as she was gone from me,
A traveller came by,
Silently, invisibly:
He took her with a sigh. *Ib*

1 A petty sneaking knave I knew—
O! Mr. Cromek, how do ye do? *On Cromek*

2 Love seeketh not itself to please,
Nor for itself hath any care,
But for another gives its ease,
And builds a Heaven in Hell's despair.
Songs of Experience, The Clod and the Pebble

3 My mother groan'd, my father wept,
Into the dangerous world I leapt;
Helpless, naked, piping loud,
Like a fiend hid in a cloud. *Ib, Infant Sorrow*

4 But if at the Church they would give us some ale,
And a pleasant fire our souls to regale,
We'd sing and we'd pray all the livelong day,
Nor ever once wish from the Church to stray. *Ib, The Little Vagabond*

5 Tiger! Tiger! burning bright
In the forests of the night,
What immortal hand or eye
Could frame thy fearful symmetry? *Ib, The Tiger*

6 When the stars threw down their spears,
And water'd heaven with their tears,
Did he smile his work to see?
Did he who made the Lamb make thee? *Ib*

7 Piping down the valleys wild,
Piping songs of pleasant glee,
On a cloud I saw a child. *Songs of Innocence, Introduction*

8 'Pipe a song about a Lamb!'
So I piped with merry cheer. *Ib*

9 Little Lamb, who made thee?
Dost thou know who made thee? *Ib, The Lamb*

10 My mother bore me in the southern wild,
And I am black, but O! my soul is white. *Ib, The Little Black Boy*

11 When the voices of children are heard on the green,
And laughing is heard on the hill. *Ib, Nurse's Song*

12 Can I see another's woe,
And not be in sorrow too? *Ib, On Another's Sorrow*

13 Whether on Ida's shady brow,
Or in the chambers of the East,
The chambers of the sun, that now
From ancient melody have ceas'd. *To the Muses*

14 How have you left the ancient love
That bards of old enjoy'd in you!
The languid strings do scarcely move!
The sound is forc'd, the notes are few! *Ib*

15 Without Contraries is no progression. Attraction and Repulsion, Reason and Energy, Love and Hate, are necessary to Human existence.
The Marriage of Heaven and Hell, The Argument

16 Energy is Eternal Delight. *Ib, The Voice of the Devil*

1 The road of excess leads to the palace of wisdom. *The Marriage of Heaven and Hell, Proverbs of Hell*

2 He who desires but acts not, breeds pestilence. *Ib*

3 A fool sees not the same tree that a wise man sees. *Ib*

4 Damn braces. Bless relaxes. *Ib*

5 Exuberance is Beauty. *Ib*

6 Where man is not, nature is barren. *Ib*

7 If the doors of perception were cleansed everything would appear to man as it is, infinite. *Ib, A Memorable Fancy*

BORROW, George Henry, 1803–1881

8 There's night and day, brother, both sweet things; sun, moon, and stars, brother, all sweet things; there's likewise a wind on the heath. Life is very sweet, brother; who would wish to die? *Lavengro, Ch. 25*

BOSQUET, Marshal Pierre, 1810–1861

9 *C'est magnifique, mais ce n'est pas la guerre.* It is magnificent, but it is not war. *Watching the Charge of the Light Brigade, Balaclava, 1854*

BOSSIDY, John Collins, 1860–1928

10 And this is good old Boston,
The Home of the bean and the cod,
Where the Lowells talk to the Cabots,
And the Cabots talk only to God. *On the Aristocracy of Harvard*

BOULTON, Sir Harold Edwin, 1859–1935

11 When Adam and Eve were dispossessed
Of the garden hard by Heaven,
They planted another one down in the West,
'Twas Devon, glorious Devon! *Glorious Devon*

12 Speed, bonny boat, like a bird on the wing;
'Onward!' the sailors cry;
Carry the lad that's born to be king
Over the sea to Skye. *Skye Boat Song*

BOURDILLON, Francis William, 1852–1921

13 The night has a thousand eyes,
And the day but one;
Yet the light of the bright world dies
With the dying sun. *Light*

BOWEN, Charles, 1st Baron, 1835–1894

14 The rain it raineth on the just
And also on the unjust fella:
But chiefly on the just, because
The unjust steals the just's umbrella. *Sichel, Sands of Time*

BOWEN, Edward Ernest, 1836–1901

15 Forty years on, growing older and older,
Shorter in wind, as in memory long.
Feeble of foot, and rheumatic of shoulder,
What will it help you that once you were strong? *Forty Years On, Harrow School Song*

BRADFORD, John, 1510?–1555

1 There, but for the grace of God, goes John Bradford. *Remark on seeing some criminals led to execution*

BRATHWAITE, Richard, 1588?–1673

2 To Banbury came I, O profane one!
Where I saw a Puritane-one
Hanging of his cat on Monday,
For killing of a mouse on Sunday. *Barnabee's Journal, I*

BRIDGES, Robert, 1844–1930

3 Awake, my heart, to be loved, awake, awake!
The darkness silvers away, the morn doth break,
It leaps in the sky: unrisen lustres slake
The o'ertaken moon. Awake, O heart, awake! *Awake, My Heart, to be Loved*

4 I heard a linnet courting
His lady in the spring. *I heard a Linnet courting*

5 I never shall love the snow again
Since Maurice died. *I never shall love the Snow again*

6 Perfect little body, without fault or stain on thee,
With promise of strength and manhood full and fair! *On a Dead Child*

7 When Death to either shall come,—
I pray it be first to me. *When Death to either shall come*

BRIGHT, John, 1811–1889

8 The Angel of Death has been abroad throughout the land; you may almost hear the beating of his wings. *Speech, House of Commons, 23 Feb. 1855*

9 England is the mother of parliaments. *Speech, Birmingham, 18 Jan. 1865*

10 The right honourable gentleman . . . has retired into what may be called his political Cave of Adullam. *Speech, House of Commons, 13 March 1866*

11 Force is not a remedy. *Speech, Birmingham, 16 Nov. 1880*

BRONTË, Emily, 1818–1848

12 No coward soul is mine,
No trembler in the world's storm-troubled sphere:
I see Heaven's glories shine,
And faith shines equal, arming me from fear. *Last Lines*

13 Vain are the thousand creeds
That move men's hearts: unutterably vain;
Worthless as wither'd weeds. *Ib*

14 Riches I hold in light esteem,
And Love I laugh to scorn;
And lust of fame was but a dream
That vanish'd with the morn. *The Old Stoic*

15 O! dreadful is the check—intense the agony—
When the ear begins to hear, and the eye begins to see;
When the pulse begins to throb—the brain to think again—
The soul to feel the flesh, and the flesh to feel the chain. *The Prisoner*

BROOKE, Rupert, 1887–1915

1 Blow out, you bugles, over the rich Dead. *The Dead*

2 Just now the lilac is in bloom
All before my little room. *The Old Vicarage, Grantchester*

3 For England's the one land, I know,
Where men with Splendid Hearts may go. *Ib*

4 Stands the Church clock at ten to three?
And is there honey still for tea? *Ib*

5 If I should die, think only this of me:
That there's some corner of a foreign field
That is forever England. *The Soldier*

6 A dust whom England bore, shaped, made aware,
Gave, once, her flowers to love, her ways to roam,
A body of England's, breathing English air,
Washed by the rivers, blest by suns of home. *Ib*

7 And laughter, learnt of friends; and gentleness,
In hearts at peace, under an English heaven. *Ib*

BROOKS, Phillips, 1835–1893

8 O little town of Bethlehem,
How still we see thee lie;
Above thy deep and dreamless sleep
The silent stars go by. *O Little Town of Bethlehem*

BROWN, Thomas, 1663–1704

9 I do not love thee, Doctor Fell,
The reason why I cannot tell;
But this alone I know full well,
I do not love thee, Doctor Fell. *Translation of Martial, Epigrams, 1, 32*

BROWN, Thomas Edward, 1830–1897

10 A garden is a lovesome thing, God wot! *My Garden*

BROWNE, Charles Farrar, see WARD, Artemus

BROWNE, Sir Thomas, 1605–1682

11 He who discommendeth others obliquely commendeth himself.
Christian Morals

12 I dare, without usurpation, assume the honourable style of Christian.
Religio Medici, Part 1, 1

13 All things are artificial, for nature is the art of God. *Ib, 16*

14 I am of a constitution so general that it consorts and sympathiseth with all things. I have no antipathy, or rather idiosyncrasy, in diet, humour, air, any-thing. *Ib, Part 2, 1*

15 It is the common wonder of all men, how among so many million of faces, there should be none alike. *Ib, 2*

16 No man can justly censure or condemn another, because indeed no man truly knows another. *Ib, 4*

1 I could be content that we might procreate like trees, without conjunction, or that there were any way to perpetuate the world without this trivial and vulgar way of coition. *Religio Medici, Part 2, 9*

2 Lord, deliver me from myself. *Ib, 10*

3 Man is a noble animal, splendid in ashes, and pompous in the grave. *Urn Burial, Ch. 5*

BROWNE, Sir William, 1692–1774

4 The King to Oxford sent a troop of horse,
For Tories own no argument but force:
With equal skill to Cambridge books he sent,
For Whigs admit no force but argument. *Reply to Trapp's Epigram* *(see 318:1)*

BROWNING, Elizabeth Barrett, 1806–1861

5 Let no one till his death
Be called unhappy. Measure not the work
Until the day's out and the labour done. *Aurora Leigh, Book 5*

6 Since when was genius found respectable? *Ib, Book 6*

7 Do you hear the children weeping, O my brothers,
Ere the sorrow comes with years? *The Cry of the Children*

8 I tell you hopeless grief is passionless. *Grief*

9 What was he doing, the great god Pan,
Down in the reeds by the river? *A Musical Instrument*

BROWNING, Robert, 1812–1889

10 Love, we are in God's hand.
How strange now, looks the life he makes us lead!
So free we seem, so fettered fast we are! *Andrea del Sarto*

11 Ah, but a man's reach should exceed his grasp,
Or what's a heaven for? *Ib*

12 One who never turned his back but marched breast forward,
Never doubted clouds would break,
Never dreamed, though right were worsted, wrong would triumph,
Held we fall to rise, are baffled to fight better,
Sleep to wake. *Asolando, Epilogue*

13 Just when we are safest, there's a sunset-touch,
A fancy from a flower-bell, some one's death,
A chorus-ending from Euripides,—
And that's enough for fifty hopes and fears
As old and new at once as Nature's self,
To rap and knock and enter in our soul. *Bishop Blougram's Apology*

14 No, when the fight begins within himself,
A man's worth something. *Ib*

15 Oh, the little more, and how much it is!
And the little less, and what worlds away! *By The Fire-side, 39*

16 We loved, sir—used to meet:
How sad and bad and mad it was—
But then, how it was sweet! *Confessions*

1 Oh, to be in England
Now that April's there,
And whoever wakes in England
Sees, some morning, unaware,
That the lowest boughs and the brushwood sheaf
Round the elm-tree bole are in tiny leaf,
While the chaffinch sings on the orchard bough
In England—now! *Home-Thoughts, from Abroad*

2 And after April, when May follows,
And the whitethroat builds, and all the swallows! *Ib*

3 That's the wise thrush; he sings each song twice over,
Lest you should think he never could recapture
The first fine careless rapture! *Ib*

4 Nobly, nobly Cape Saint Vincent to the North-west died away;
Sunset ran, one glorious blood-red, reeking into Cadiz Bay.
Home-Thoughts, from the Sea

5 Whoso turns as I, this evening, turn to God to praise and pray,
While Jove's planet rises yonder, silent over Africa. *Ib*

6 I sprang to the stirrup, and Joris, and he;
I galloped, Dirck galloped, we galloped all three.
How they brought the Good News from Ghent to Aix

7 Escape me?
Never—
Beloved!
While I am I, and you are you. *Life in a Love*

8 Just for a handful of silver he left us,
Just for a riband to stick in his coat. *The Lost Leader*

9 Never glad confident morning again! *Ib*

10 Ah, did you once see Shelley plain,
And did he stop and speak to you?
And did you speak to him again,
How strange it seems, and new! *Memorabilia*

11 Never the time and the place
And the loved one all together! *Never the Time and the Place*

12 Dante, who loved well because he hated,
Hated wickedness that hinders loving. *One Word More, 5*

13 Where my heart lies, let my brain lie also! *Ib, 14*

14 God be thanked, the meanest of his creatures
Boasts two soul-sides, one to face the world with,
One to show a woman when he loves her. *Ib, 17*

15 It was roses, roses all the way. *The Patriot*

16 Hamelin Town's in Brunswick,
By famous Hanover city;
The river Weser, deep and wide,
Washes its wall on the southern side.
The Pied Piper of Hamelin, 1

17 Rats!
They fought the dogs and killed the cats,
And bit the babies in the cradles. *Ib, 2*

1 With shrieking and squeaking
In fifty different sharps and flats. *The Pied Piper of Hamelin, 2*

2 If I can rid your town of rats
Will you give me a thousand guilders?'
'One? fifty thousand!'—was the exclamation
Of the astonished Mayor and Corporation. *Ib, 6*

3 And the muttering grew to a grumbling;
And the grumbling grew to a mighty rumbling;
And out of the houses the rats came tumbling. *Ib, 7*

4 So, munch on, crunch on, take your nuncheon,
Breakfast, supper, dinner, luncheon! *Ib*

5 'You threaten us, fellow? Do your worst,
Blow your pipe there till you burst!' *Ib, 9*

6 All the little boys and girls,
With rosy cheeks and flaxen curls,
And sparkling eyes, and teeth like pearls,
Tripping and skipping, ran merrily after
The wonderful music with shouting and laughter. *Ib, 12*

7 The year's at the spring,
And day's at the morn;
Morning's at seven;
The hill-side's dew-pearled;
The lark's on the wing;
The snail's on the thorn;
God's in His heaven—
All's right with the world. *Pippa Passes, 1, Morning*

8 All service ranks the same with God—
With God, whose puppets, best and worst,
Are we: there is no last nor first. *Ib, 4, Night*

9 Grow old along with me.
The best is yet to be,
The last of life, for which the first was made:
Our times are in His hand
Who saith 'A whole I planned,
Youth shows but half; trust God: see all nor be afraid!' *Rabbi Ben Ezra*

10 Let age approve of youth, and death complete the same! *Ib*

11 What of soul was left, I wonder, when the kissing had to stop?
A Toccata of Galuppi's, 14

BUCHANAN, Robert Williams, 1841–1901

12 The Fleshly School of Poetry. *Title of article in the Contemporary Review, Oct. 1871*

13 She just wore
Enough for modesty—no more. *White Rose and Red, Part 1, 5*

BUFFON, Georges Louis Leclerc, Comte de, 1707–1788

14 *Le style est l'homme même.* Style is the man himself. *Discours sur le style*

BULLER, Arthur Henry Reginald, 1874–1944

1 There was a young lady named Bright,
Whose speed was far faster than light;
She set out one day
In a relative way,
And returned home the previous night. *Limerick*

BULWER-LYTTON, Edward, 1803–1873

2 Here Stanley meets,—how Stanley scorns, the glance!
The brilliant chief, irregularly great,
Frank, haughty, rash,—the Rupert of Debate. *The New Timon, 1, 6*

3 Beneath the rule of men entirely great,
The pen is mightier than the sword. *Richelieu, 2, 2*

BUNN, Alfred, 1796?–1860

4 I dreamt that I dwelt in marble halls,
With vassals and serfs at my side. ARLINE *The Bohemian Girl, Act 2*

BUNYAN, John, 1628–1688

5 Some said, John, print it; others said, Not so;
Some said, It might do good; others said, No.
Pilgrim's Progress, Author's Apology

6 As I walked through the wilderness of this world. *Ib, Part 1*

7 The name of the slough was Despond. *Ib*

8 The gentleman's name that met him was Mr. Worldly Wiseman. *Ib*

9 It beareth the name of Vanity Fair, because the town where 'tis kept is lighter than vanity. *Ib*

10 Mr. Facing-both-ways. *Ib*

11 A castle called Doubting Castle, the owner whereof was Giant Despair. *Ib*

12 So I awoke, and behold it was a dream. *Ib*

13 He who would valiant be
'Gainst all disaster,
Let him in constancy
Follow the Master.
There's no discouragement
Shall make him once relent
His first avowed intent
To be a pilgrim. *Ib, Part 2, English Hymnal Version*

14 I'll fear not what men say,
I'll labour night and day
To be a pilgrim. *Ib*

15 He that is down needs fear no fall;
He that is low, no pride. *Ib, Shepherd Boy's Song*

16 So he passed over, and all the trumpets sounded for him on the other side.
Ib

BURGESS, Gelett, 1866–1951

1 I never saw a Purple Cow,
I never hope to see one;
But I can tell you, anyhow,
I'd rather see than be one. *The Purple Cow*

2 Ah, yes, I wrote the 'Purple Cow'—
I'm sorry, now, I wrote it!
But I can tell you anyhow,
I'll kill you if you quote it. *Reply*

BURGON, John William, 1813–1888

3 Match me such marvel save in Eastern clime,
A rose-red city half as old as time. *Petra, 132*

BURKE, Edmund, 1729–1797

4 The concessions of the weak are the concessions of fear.
Speech on Conciliation with America, 22 March 1775

5 The use of force alone is but *temporary*. It may subdue for a moment; but it does not remove the necessity of subduing again: and a nation is not governed, which is perpetually to be conquered. *Ib*

6 I do not know the method of drawing up an indictment against an whole people. *Ib*

7 All government, indeed every human benefit and enjoyment, every virtue, and every prudent act, is founded on compromise and barter. *Ib*

8 The people are the masters. *Speech on the Economical Reform, 11 Feb. 1780*

9 He was not merely a chip of the old block, but the old block itself.
Of Pitt's first speech, 26 Feb. 1781

10 There is, however, a limit at which forbearance ceases to be a virtue.
Observations on 'The Present State of the Nation', 1769

11 But the age of chivalry is gone. That of sophisters, economists, and calculators, has succeeded; and the glory of Europe is extinguished for ever.
Reflections on the Revolution in France

12 Man is by his constitution a religious animal. *Ib*

13 Superstition is the religion of feeble minds. *Ib*

14 Good order is the foundation of all good things. *Ib*

15 Example is the school of mankind, and they will learn at no other.
Letters on a Regicide Peace, 1, 1796

16 And having looked to government for bread, on the very first scarcity they will turn and bite the hand that fed them.
Thoughts and Details on Scarcity

17 If any ask me what a free government is, I answer, that, for any practical purpose, it is what the people think so.
Letter to the Sheriffs of Bristol, 1777

18 Liberty, too, must be limited in order to be possessed. *Ib*

19 Among a people generally corrupt, liberty cannot long exist. *Ib*

20 The greater the power, the more dangerous the abuse.
Speech, House of Commons, 7 Feb. 1771

1 I am convinced that we have a degree of delight, and that no small one, in the real misfortunes and pains of others.
On the Sublime and Beautiful, 1, 14

2 Power gradually extirpates from the mind every humane and gentle virtue.
A Vindication of Natural Society

BURNET, Bishop Gilbert, 1643–1715

3 There was a sure way to see it lost, and that was to die in the last ditch.
History of his own Times, 1

BURNEY, Fanny (Mme D'Arblay), 1752–1840

4 Dancing? Oh, dreadful! How it was ever adopted in a civilised country I cannot find out; 'tis certainly a Barbarian exercise, and of savage origin.
MR MEADOWS *Cecilia, Bk. 3*

5 'True, very true ma'am,' said he, yawning, 'one really lives nowhere; one does but vegetate and wish it all at an end.' MR MEADOWS *Ib, Bk. 4*

6 Indeed, the freedom with which Dr. Johnson condemns whatever he disapproves is astonishing. *Diary, 23 Aug. 1778*

BURNS, John, 1858–1943

7 Every drop of the Thames is liquid history.
Attributed by Sir Frederick Whyte

BURNS, Robert, 1759–1796

8 Ae fond kiss, and then we sever! *Ae Fond Kiss, 1*

9 But to see her was to love her,
Love but her, and love for ever. *Ib, 11*

10 Had we never lov'd sae kindly,
Had we never lov'd sae blindly,
Never met—or never parted,
We had ne'er been broken-hearted. *Ib, 13*

11 Flow gently, sweet Afton, among thy green braes,
Flow gently, I'll sing thee a song in thy praise. *Afton Water, 1*

12 Should auld acquaintance be forgot,
And never brought to min'? *Auld Lang Syne, 1*

13 We'll tak a cup o' kindness yet,
For auld lang syne. *Ib, 7*

14 Freedom and Whisky gang thegither! *The Author's Earnest Cry and Prayer, 185*

15 Gin a body meet a body
Coming through the rye;
Gin a body kiss a body,
Need a body cry? *Coming through the Rye, 5*

16 I wasna fou, but just had plenty. *Death and Doctor Hornbrook, 14*

17 On ev'ry hand it will allow'd be,
He's just—nae better than he should be.
A Dedication to Gavin Hamilton, 25

18 A man's a man for a' that. *For a' that and a' that, 12*

1 Green grow the rashes O,
  Green grow the rashes O;
The sweetest hours that e'er I spend,
  Are spent amang the lasses O! *Green Grow the Rashes, 1*

2 The wisest man the warl' saw,
  He dearly lov'd the lasses O. *Ib, 19*

3 The golden hours on angel wings
  Flew o'er me and my dearie;
For dear to me as light and life
  Was my sweet Highland Mary. *Highland Mary, 13*

4 There's some are fou o' love divine,
  There's some are fou o' brandy. *The Holy Fair, 239*

5 John Anderson my jo, John,
  When we were first acquent,
Your locks were like the raven,
  Your bonnie brow was brent. *John Anderson My Jo, 1*

6 True it is, she had one failing,
  Had a woman ever less? *Lines, written under picture of Miss Burns*

7 Nature's law,
That man was made to mourn. *Man was Made to Mourn, 31*

8 Man's inhumanity to man
  Makes countless thousands mourn! *Ib, 55*

9 O Mary, at thy window be,
  It is the wish'd, the trysted hour! *Mary Morison, 1*

10 Wee, sleekit, cow'rin', tim'rous beastie,
O what a panic's in thy breastie! *To a Mouse, 1*

11 I'm truly sorry man's dominion
Has broken Nature's social union. *Ib, 7*

12 The best laid schemes o' mice an' men
    Gang aft a-gley,
An' lea'e us nought but grief an' pain
    For promis'd joy. *Ib, 39*

13 Still thou art blest compar'd wi' me!
The present only toucheth thee:
But oh! I backward cast my e'e
    On prospects drear!
An' forward tho' I canna see,
    I guess an' fear! *Ib, 43*

14 My heart's in the Highlands, my heart is not here;
My heart's in the Highlands a-chasing the deer;
Chasing the wild deer, and following the roe,
My heart's in the Highlands, wherever I go.
My Heart's in the Highlands, 1

15 My love is like a red red rose
  That's newly sprung in June:
My love is like the melodie
  That's sweetly play'd in tune. *A Red, Red Rose*

1 Scots, wha hae wi' Wallace bled,
Scots, wham Bruce has aften led,
Welcome to your gory bed,
Or to victorie. *Scots, Wha Hae, 1*

2 Liberty's in every blow!
Let us do or die! *Ib, 23*

3 Some hae meat, and canna eat,
And some wad eat that want it;
But we hae meat and we can eat,
And sae the Lord be thankit. *The Selkirk Grace*

4 But pleasures are like poppies spread—
You seize the flow'r, its bloom is shed;
Or like the snow falls in the river—
A moment white, then melts for ever. *Tam o' Shanter, 59*

5 Ye banks and braes o' bonnie Doon,
How can ye bloom sae fresh and fair?
How can ye chant, ye little birds,
And I sae weary fu' o' care? *Ye Banks and Braes, 1*

6 Thou minds me o' departed joys,
Departed never to return. *Ib, 7*

7 And my fause lover stole my rose,
But ah! he left the thorn wi' me. *Ib, 15*

BURTON, Robert, 1577–1640

8 All my joys to this are folly,
Naught so sweet as Melancholy. *Anatomy of Melancholy, Author's Abstract of Melancholy*

9 *Hinc quam sit calamus saevior ense patet.* From this it is clear how much more cruel the pen is than the sword. *Ib, Part 1*

10 England is a paradise for women, and hell for horses: Italy a paradise for horses, hell for women. *Ib, Part 3*

11 One religion is as true as another. *Ib*

12 Be not solitary, be not idle. *Ib, Last words*

BUSSY-RABUTIN, Comte de, 1618–1693

13 *L'absence est à l'amour ce qu'est au feu le vent; il éteint le petit, il allume le grand.* Absence is to love what wind is to fire; it extinguishes the small, it inflames the great. *Histoire Amoureuse des Gaules*

BUTLER, Samuel, 1612–1680

14 When civil fury first grew high,
And men fell out they knew not why. *Hudibras, 1, 1, 1*

15 For every why he had a wherefore. *Ib, 1, 1, 132*

16 Oaths are but words, and words but wind. *Ib, 2, 2, 107*

17 What makes all doctrines plain and clear?
About two hundred pounds a year.
And that which was prov'd true before
Prove false again? Two hundred more. *Ib, 3, 1, 1277*

1 He that complies against his will,
Is of his own opinion still. *Hudibras, 3, 3, 547*

2 The souls of women are so small,
That some believe they've none at all. *Miscellaneous Thoughts*

BUTLER, Samuel, 1835–1902

3 It has been said that the love of money is the root of all evil. The want of money is so quite as truly. *Erewhon, Ch. 20*

4 I keep my books at the British Museum and at Mudie's.
The Humour of Homer, Ramblings in Cheapside

5 Life is one long process of getting tired. *Note-books, Life, 7*

6 Life is the art of drawing sufficient conclusions from insufficient premises. *Ib, 9*

7 All progress is based upon a universal innate desire on the part of every organism to live beyond its income. *Ib, 16*

8 To live is like love, all reason is against it, and all healthy instinct for it.
Ib, Higgledy-Piggledy, Life and Love

9 Stowed away in a Montreal lumber room
The Discobolus standeth and turneth his face to the wall;
Dusty, cobweb-covered, maimed and set at naught,
Beauty crieth in an attic and no man regardeth.
O God! O Montreal! *A Psalm of Montreal*

10 The advantage of doing one's praising for oneself is that one can lay it on so thick and exactly in the right places. *The Way of All Flesh, Ch. 34*

11 A man's friendships are, like his will, invalidated by marriage—but they are also no less invalidated by the marriage of his friends. *Ib, Ch. 75*

12 'Tis better to have loved and lost than never to have lost at all. *Ib, Ch. 77*
(see also *84:18 and 312:13*)

13 Brigands demand your money or your life; women require both.
Attributed

BYROM, John, 1692–1763

14 Christians awake, salute the happy morn,
Whereon the Saviour of the world was born. *Hymn for Christmas Day*

15 God bless the King, I mean the Faith's Defender;
God bless—no harm in blessing—the Pretender;
But who Pretender is, or who is King,
God bless us all—that's quite another thing. *To an Officer in the Army*

BYRON, George Gordon, 6th Baron, 1788–1824

16 In short, he was a perfect cavaliero,
And to his very valet seem'd a hero. *Beppo, 33*

17 I like the weather, when it is not rainy,
That is, I like two months of every year. *Ib, 48*

18 Maidens, like moths, are ever caught by glare,
And Mammon wins his way where Seraphs might despair.
Childe Harold's Pilgrimage, Canto 1, 9

1 Adieu, adieu! my native shore
Fades o'er the waters blue. *Childe Harold's Pilgrimage, Canto 1, 13*

2 My native Land—Good Night! *Ib*

3 There was a sound of revelry by night,
And Belgium's capital had gather'd then
Her Beauty and her Chivalry, and bright
The lamps shone o'er fair women and brave men. *Ib, Canto 3, 21*

4 On with the dance! let joy be unconfined;
No sleep till morn, when Youth and Pleasure meet
To chase the glowing Hours with flying feet. *Ib, 3, 22*

5 I have not loved the world, nor the world me;
I have not flatter'd its rank breath, nor bow'd
To its idolatries a patient knee. *Ib, 3, 113*

6 I stood in Venice, on the Bridge of Sighs;
A palace and a prison on each hand. *Ib, Canto 4, 1*

7 Yet, Freedom! yet thy banner, torn, but flying,
Streams like the thunder-storm *against* the wind. *Ib, 4, 98*

8 While stands the Coliseum, Rome shall stand;
When falls the Coliseum, Rome shall fall;
And when Rome falls—the World. *Ib, 4, 145*

9 There is a pleasure in the pathless woods,
There is a rapture on the lonely shore,
There is society, where none intrudes,
By the deep Sea, and music in its roar:
I love not Man the less, but Nature more. *Ib, 4, 178*

10 What men call gallantry, and gods adultery,
Is much more common where the climate's sultry. *Don Juan, Canto 1, 63*

11 A little still she strove, and much repented,
And whispering 'I will ne'er consent'—consented. *Ib, 1, 117*

12 Sweet is revenge—especially to women. *Ib, 1, 124*

13 Pleasure's a sin, and sometimes sin's a pleasure. *Ib, 1, 133*

14 Man's love is of man's life a thing apart,
'Tis woman's whole existence. *Ib, 1, 194*

15 Man, being reasonable, must get drunk;
The best of life is but intoxication. *Ib, Canto 2, 179*

16 Alas! the love of women! it is known
To be a lovely and a fearful thing. *Ib, 2, 199*

17 In her first passion woman loves her lover,
In all the others all she loves is love. *Ib, Canto 3, 3*

18 'Tis melancholy, and a fearful sign
Of human frailty, folly, also crime,
That love and marriage rarely can combine. *Ib, 3, 5*

19 All tragedies are finish'd by a death,
All comedies are ended by a marriage. *Ib, 3, 9*

20 Dreading that climax of all human ills
The inflammation of his weekly bills. *Ib, 3, 35*

21 The isles of Greece, the isles of Greece!
Where burning Sappho loved and sung,

Where grew the arts of war and peace,
  Where Delos rose, and Phoebus sprung!
Eternal summer gilds them yet,
But all, except their sun, is set. *Don Juan, Canto 3, 86, 1*

1 The mountains look on Marathon—
  And Marathon looks on the sea;
And musing there an hour alone,
  I dream'd that Greece might still be free. *Ib, 3, 86, 3*

2 And if I laugh at any mortal thing,
  'Tis that I may not weep. *Ib, Canto 4, 4*

3 There is a tide in the affairs of women,
  Which, taken at the flood, leads—God knows where. *Ib, Canto 6, 2*

4 A lady of a 'certain age,' which means
Certainly aged. *Ib, 6, 69*

5 And, after all, what is a lie? 'Tis but
  The truth in masquerade. *Ib, Canto 11, 37*

6 'Tis strange the mind, that very fiery particle,
Should let itself be snuff'd out by an article. [*John Keats*] *Ib, 11, 60*

7 Now hatred is by far the longest pleasure;
Men love in haste, but they detest at leisure. *Ib, Canto 13, 6*

8 The English winter—ending in July,
  To recommence in August. *Ib, 13, 42*

9 Society is now one polish'd horde,
Form'd of two mighty tribes, the *Bores* and *Bored*. *Ib, 13, 95*

10 'Tis strange,—but true; for truth is always strange;
  Stranger than fiction: if it could be told,
How much would novels gain by the exchange! *Ib, Canto 14, 101*

11 I'll publish, right or wrong:
Fools are my theme, let satire be my song.
English Bards and Scotch Reviewers, 5

12 'Tis pleasant, sure, to see one's name in print;
A book's a book, although there's nothing in't. *Ib, 51*

13 A man must serve his time to every trade
Save censure—critics all are ready made. *Ib, 63*

14 As soon
Seek roses in December—ice in June;
Hope constancy in wind, or corn in chaff;
Believe a woman or an epitaph,
Or any other thing that's false, before
You trust in critics, who themselves are sore. *Ib, 75*

15 Better to err with Pope, than shine with Pye. *Ib, 102*

16 Fare thee well! and if for ever,
  Still for ever, fare thee well. *Fare Thee Well, 1*

17 Who kill'd John Keats?
  'I,' says the Quarterly,
So savage and Tartarly;
  ''Twas one of my feats.' *John Keats*

1 Maid of Athens, ere we part,
Give, oh give me back my heart! *Maid of Athens, ere we Part*

2 She walks in beauty, like the night
Of cloudless climes and starry skies;
And all that's best of dark and bright
Meet in her aspect and her eyes. *She Walks in Beauty*

3 So, we'll go no more a roving
So late into the night,
Though the heart be still as loving,
And the moon be still as bright. *So, we'll go no more a roving*

4 Though the night was made for loving,
And the day returns too soon,
Yet we'll go no more a roving
By the light of the moon. *Ib*

5 When we two parted
In silence and tears,
Half broken-hearted
To sever for years,
Pale grew thy cheek and cold,
Colder thy kiss;
Truly that hour foretold
Sorrow to this. *When we two parted*

6 If I should meet thee
After long years,
How should I greet thee?—
With silence and tears. *Ib*

7 I awoke one morning and found myself famous. *Entry in Memoranda after publication of Childe Harold*

BYRON, Henry James, 1834–1884

8 Life's too short for chess. *Our Boys, Act I*

CAESAR, Augustus, 63 B.C.–A.D. 14

9 *Quintili Vare, legiones redde.* Quintilius Varus, give me back my legions. *Suetonius, Divus Augustus, 23*

10 *Ad Kalendas Graecas soluturos.* To be paid at the Greek Kalends. *Ib, 87*

CAESAR, Julius, 102?–44 B.C.

11 *Gallia est omnis divisa in partes tres.* All Gaul is divided into three parts. *De Bello Gallico, I, I*

12 *Iacta alea est.* The die is cast. *On Crossing the Rubicon, 49* B.C.

13 *Veni, vidi, vici.* I came, I saw, I conquered. *After Victory at Zela, 47* B.C.

14 *Et tu, Brute.* You too, Brutus? *Last Words, attributed*

15 Caesar's wife must be above suspicion. *Plutarch, Life of Caesar*

CALVERLEY, Charles Stuart, 1831–1884

16 The auld wife sat at her ivied door
(Butter and eggs and a pound of cheese)
A thing she had frequently done before;
And her spectacles lay on her aproned knees. *Ballad*

1 The heart which grief hath cankered
Hath one unfailing remedy—the Tankard. *Beer*

2 For I've read in many a novel that, unless they've souls that grovel,
Folks *prefer* in fact a hovel to your dreary marble halls. *In the Gloaming*

3 How Eugene Aram, though a thief, a liar, and a murderer
Yet, being intellectual, was amongst the noblest of mankind. *Of Reading*

4 I have a liking old
For thee, though manifold
Stories, I know, are told,
Not to thy credit. *Ode to Tobacco*

CAMDEN, William, 1551–1623

5 Betwixt the stirrup and the ground
Mercy I asked, mercy I found. *Epitaph for a Man killed by falling from his Horse*

CAMPBELL, Roy, 1902–1957

6 You praise the firm restraint with which they write,
I'm with you there, of course:
They use the snaffle and the curb all right,
But where's the bloody horse? *On Some South African Novelists*

CAMPBELL, Thomas, 1777–1844

7 O leave this barren spot to me!
Spare, woodman, spare the beechen tree. *The Beech-Tree's Petition*

8 A chieftain to the Highlands bound
Cries 'Boatman, do not tarry!
And I'll give thee a silver pound
To row us o'er the ferry.' *Lord Ullin's Daughter*

9 'Tis distance lends enchantment to the view,
And robes the mountain in its azure hue. *Pleasures of Hope, 1, 7*

10 Ye mariners of England
That guard our native seas,
Whose flag has braved, a thousand years,
The battle and the breeze. *Ye Mariners of England*

11 Now Barabbas was a publisher. *Attributed*

CAMPION, Thomas, 1567–1620

12 Follow thy fair sun, unhappy shadow. *Follow thy Fair Sun*

13 There is a garden in her face,
Where roses and white lilies grow. *There is a Garden in her Face*

14 There cherries grow, which none may buy
Till 'Cherry Ripe' themselves do cry. *Ib*

CANNING, George, 1770–1827

15 I called the New World into existence to redress the balance of the Old.
Speech, 12 Dec. 1826

16 But of all plagues, good Heaven, thy wrath can send,
Save me, oh, save me, from the candid friend. *New Morality, 209*

17 Pitt is to Addington
As London is to Paddington. *The Oracle*

CAREY, Henry, 1693?–1743

1 God save our Gracious King,
Long live our noble King,
God save the King.
Send him victorious,
Happy and glorious. *God Save the King. Origin is disputed. See Dr. Percy A. Scholes, God Save the Queen, 1954*

2 Confound their politics
Frustrate their knavish tricks. *Ib*

3 Of all the girls that are so smart
There's none like pretty Sally;
She is the darling of my heart
And she lives in our alley. *Sally in our Alley*

CARLYLE, Thomas, 1795–1881

4 A witty statesman said, you might prove anything by figures. *Essay on Chartism*

5 Genius (which means transcendent capacity of taking trouble, first of all). *Frederick the Great, Bk. 4, Ch. 3*

6 A whiff of grapeshot. *History of the French Revolution, 1, 5, 3*

7 The seagreen Incorruptible. [*Robespierre*] *Ib, 2, 4, 4*

8 No great man lives in vain. The history of the world is but the biography of great men. *Heroes and Hero-Worship, 1, The Hero as Divinity*

9 The true University of these days is a collection of books. *Ib, 5, The Hero as Man of Letters*

10 History is the essence of innumerable biographies. *Essay on History*

11 No man who has once heartily and wholly laughed can be altogether irreclaimably bad. *Sartor Resartus, Bk. 1, Ch. 4*

CARNEGIE, Dale, 1888—

12 How to Win Friends and Influence People. *Title of Book*

CARNEY, Julia A. Fletcher, 1823–1908

13 Little drops of water, little grains of sand,
Make the mighty ocean and the pleasant land.
So the little minutes, humble though they be,
Make the mighty ages of eternity. *Little Things*

CARROLL, Lewis (Charles Lutwidge Dodgson), 1832–1898

14 'What is the use of a book,' thought Alice, 'without pictures or conversation?' *Alice's Adventures in Wonderland, Ch. 1*

15 She found a little bottle on it, ('which certainly was not here before,' said Alice,) and round its neck a paper label, with the words 'DRINK ME' beautifully printed on it in large letters. *Ib, Ch. 1*

16 'Curiouser and curiouser!' cried Alice. *Ib, Ch. 2*

17 How doth the little crocodile
Improve his shining tail,
And pour the waters of the Nile
On every golden scale!

How cheerfully he seems to grin,
  How neatly spread his claws,
And welcomes little fishes in
  With gently smiling jaws! ALICE *Alice's Adventures in Wonderland, Ch. 2*

1 'I'll be judge, I'll be jury,' said cunning old Fury: 'I'll try the whole cause, and condemn you to death.' *Ib, Ch. 3*

2 The Duchess! The Duchess! Oh my dear paws! Oh my fur and whiskers! THE WHITE RABBIT *Ib, Ch. 4*

3 'You are old, Father William,' the young man said,
  'And your hair has become very white;
And yet you incessantly stand on your head—
  Do you think at your age, it is right?'
'In my youth,' Father William replied to his son,
  'I feared it might injure the brain;
But, now that I'm perfectly sure I have none,
  Why, I do it again and again.' ALICE *Ib, Ch. 5*

4 'I have answered three questions, and that is enough,'
  Said his father; 'don't give yourself airs!
Do you think I can listen all day to such stuff?
  Be off or I'll kick you downstairs!' ALICE *Ib, Ch. 5*

5 'If everybody minded their own business,' the Duchess said in a hoarse growl, 'the world would go round a deal faster than it does.' *Ib, Ch. 6*

6 Speak roughly to your little boy,
  And beat him when he sneezes:
He only does it to annoy,
  Because he knows it teases. THE DUCHESS *Ib, Ch. 6*

7 I speak severely to my boy,
  I beat him when he sneezes;
For he can thoroughly enjoy
  The pepper when he pleases! THE DUCHESS *Ib, Ch. 6*

8 Twinkle, twinkle, little bat!
How I wonder what you're at! THE HATTER *Ib, Ch. 7*

9 Up above the world you fly,
Like a tea-tray in the sky. THE HATTER *Ib, Ch. 7*

10 'Take some more tea,' the March Hare said to Alice, very earnestly.
'I've had nothing yet,' Alice replied in an offended tone, 'so I can't take more.'
'You mean you can't take *less*,' said the Hatter: 'it's very easy to take *more* than nothing.' *Ib, Ch. 7*

11 The Queen was in a furious passion, and went stamping about, and shouting 'Off with his head!' or 'Off with her head!' about once in a minute. *Ib, Ch. 8*

12 Everything's got a moral, if only you can find it. THE DUCHESS *Ib, Ch. 9*

13 Take care of the sense, and the sounds will take care of themselves. THE DUCHESS *Ib, Ch. 9*

14 'Why did you call him Tortoise, if he wasn't one?' Alice asked.
'We called him Tortoise because he taught us,' said the Mock Turtle angrily: 'really you are very dull!' *Ib, Ch. 9*

15 'Reeling and Writhing, of course, to begin with,' the Mock Turtle replied; 'and then the different branches of Arithmetic—Ambition, Distraction, Uglification, and Derision.' *Ib, Ch. 9*

1 'That's the reason they're called lessons,' the Gryphon remarked: 'because they lessen from day to day.' *Alice's Adventures in Wonderland, Ch. 9*

2 'Will you walk a little faster?' said a whiting to a snail.
'There's a porpoise close behind us, and he's treading on my tail.'
THE MOCK TURTLE *Ib, Ch. 10*

3 Will you, won't you, will you, won't you, will you join the dance?
THE MOCK TURTLE *Ib, Ch. 10*

4 'Tis the voice of the Lobster; I heard him declare,
'You have baked me too brown, I must sugar my hair.' ALICE
Ib, Ch. 10

5 Soup of the evening, beautiful Soup! THE MOCK TURTLE *Ib, Ch. 10*

6 'The Queen of Hearts, she made some tarts,
All on a summer day:
The Knave of Hearts, he stole those tarts,
And took them quite away!' THE WHITE RABBIT (reading)
Ib, Ch. 11

7 They told me you had been to her,
And mentioned me to him:
She gave me a good character,
But said I could not swim. THE WHITE RABBIT (reading)
Ib, Ch. 12

8 'No, no!' said the Queen. 'Sentence first—verdict afterwards.'
'Stuff and nonsense!' said Alice loudly. *Ib, Ch. 12*

9 'Twas brillig, and the slithy toves
Did gyre and gimble in the wabe;
All mimsy were the borogoves,
And the mome raths outgrabe. ALICE (reading)
Through the Looking-Glass, Ch. 1

10 One, two! One, two! And through and through
The vorpal blade went snicker-snack!
He left it dead, and with its head
He went galumphing back. ALICE (reading) *Ib, Ch. 1*

11 'And hast thou slain the Jabberwock?
Come to my arms, my beamish boy!
O frabjous day! Callooh! Callay!'
He chortled in his joy. ALICE (reading) *Ib, Ch. 1*

12 Now, *here*, you see, it takes all the running *you* can do, to keep in the same place. If you want to get somewhere else, you must run at least twice as fast as that! THE QUEEN *Ib, Ch. 2*

13 'If you think we're wax-works,' he said, 'you ought to pay, you know.
Wax-works weren't made to be looked at for nothing. Nohow!'
TWEEDLEDUM *Ib, Ch. 4*

14 Tweedledum and Tweedledee
Agreed to have a battle;
For Tweedledum said Tweedledee
Had spoiled his nice new rattle. ALICE *Ib, Ch. 4*

15 'Contrariwise,' continued Tweedledee, 'if it was so, it might be; and if it were so, it would be: but as it isn't, it ain't. That's logic.' *Ib, Ch. 4*

16 The sun was shining on the sea,
Shining with all his might:
He did his very best to make

The billows smooth and bright—
And this was odd, because it was
The middle of the night. TWEEDLEDEE (reciting *The Walrus and The Carpenter*) *Through the Looking-Glass, Ch. 4*

1 'It's very rude of him,' she said,
'To come and spoil the fun!' TWEEDLEDEE *Ib, Ch. 4*

2 The Walrus and the Carpenter
Were walking close at hand;
They wept like anything to see
Such quantities of sand:
'If this were only cleared away,'
They said, 'it *would* be grand!' TWEEDLEDEE *Ib, Ch. 4*

3 'If seven maids with seven mops
Swept it for half a year,
Do you suppose,' the Walrus said,
'That they could get it clear?'
'I doubt it,' said the Carpenter,
And shed a bitter tear. TWEEDLEDEE *Ib, Ch. 4*

4 'The time has come,' the Walrus said,
'To talk of many things:
Of shoes—and ships—and sealing-wax—
Of cabbages—and kings—
And why the sea is boiling hot—
And whether pigs have wings.' TWEEDLEDEE *Ib, Ch. 4*

5 'I weep for you,' the Walrus said:
'I deeply sympathize.'
With sobs and tears he sorted out
Those of the largest size,
Holding his pocket-handkerchief
Before his streaming eyes. TWEEDLEDEE *Ib, Ch. 4*

6 'O Oysters,' said the Carpenter,
'You've had a pleasant run!
Shall we be trotting home again?'
But answer came there none—
And this was scarcely odd, because
They'd eaten every one. TWEEDLEDEE *Ib, Ch. 4*

7 The rule is, jam to-morrow and jam yesterday—but never jam to-day. THE QUEEN *Ib, Ch. 5*

8 Humpty Dumpty sat on a wall:
Humpty Dumpty had a great fall.
All the King's horses and all the King's men
Couldn't put Humpty Dumpty in his place again. ALICE *Ib, Ch. 6*

9 'They gave it me,' Humpty Dumpty continued thoughtfully, . . . 'for an un-birthday present.' *Ib, Ch. 6*

10 'When *I* use a word,' Humpty Dumpty said in rather a scornful tone, 'it means just what I choose it to mean—neither more nor less.' *Ib, Ch. 6*

11 In winter, when the fields are white,
I sing this song for your delight— HUMPTY DUMPTY *Ib, Ch. 6*

12 In spring, when woods are getting green,
I'll try and tell you what I mean. HUMPTY DUMPTY *Ib, Ch. 6*

1 I sent a message to the fish:
I told them 'This is what I wish.' HUMPTY DUMPTY *Through the Looking-Glass, Ch. 6*

2 The little fishes of the sea,
They sent an answer back to me.
The little fishes' answer was
'We cannot do it, Sir, because—'. HUMPTY DUMPTY *Ib, Ch. 6*

3 I said it very loud and clear;
I went and shouted in his ear. HUMPTY DUMPTY *Ib, Ch. 6*

4 He's an Anglo-Saxon Messenger—and those are Anglo-Saxon attitudes. THE KING *Ib, Ch. 7*

5 It's as large as life, and twice as natural! HAIGHA *Ib, Ch. 7*

6 The Lion looked at Alice wearily. 'Are you animal—or vegetable—or mineral?' he said, yawning at every other word. *Ib, Ch. 7*

7 I'll tell thee everything I can;
  There's little to relate.
I saw an aged aged man,
  A-sitting on a gate. THE KNIGHT *Ib, Ch. 8*

8 'Speak when you're spoken to!' the Red Queen sharply interrupted her. *Ib, Ch. 9*

9 No admittance till the week after next! CREATURE WITH A LONG BEAK *Ib, Ch. 9*

10 'You look a little shy; let me introduce you to that leg of mutton,' said the Red Queen. 'Alice—Mutton; Mutton—Alice.' *Ib, Ch. 9*

CARY, Phoebe, 1824–1871

11 And though hard be the task,
'Keep a stiff upper lip.' *Keep a Stiff Upper Lip*

CASTLING, Harry, 19th century

12 Let's all go down the Strand. *Title of Song*

CATO, Marcus Porcius, 234–149 B.C.

13 *Delenda est Carthago.* Carthage must be destroyed. *Plutarch, Life of Cato*

CATULLUS, Gaius Valerius, 87–54? B.C.

14 *Vivamus, mea Lesbia, atque amemus*
Rumoresque senum severiorum
Omnes unius aestimemus assis.
Let us live, my Lesbia, and love, and pay no heed to all the talk of censorious old men. *Carmina, 5*

15 *Da mi basia mille.*
Give me a thousand kisses. *Ib*

16 *Odi et amo. Quare id faciam, fortasse requiris.*
Nescio, sed fieri sentio et excrucior.
I hate and love. Why I do so, perhaps you ask.
I do not know, but I feel it and am in torment. *Ib, 85*

17 *Atque in perpetuum, frater, ave atque vale.*
And for ever, brother, hail and farewell! *Ib, 101*

CAVELL, Edith, 1865–1915

1 I realise that patriotism is not enough. I must have no hatred or bitterness towards anyone. *Last Words*

CERVANTES, Miguel de, 1547–1616

2 The knight of the sorrowful countenance. *Don Quixote, Part 1, Ch. 19*

3 Every man is as Heaven made him, and sometimes a great deal worse. *Ib, Part 2, Ch. 4*

4 There are only two families in the world, my old grandmother used to say, The *Haves* and the *Have-Nots*. *Ib, Ch. 20*

5 A private sin is not so prejudicial in the world as a public indecency. *Ib, Ch. 22*

6 Tell me what company thou keepest, and I'll tell thee what thou art. *Ib, Ch. 23*

CHAMBERLAIN, Joseph, 1836–1914

7 Provided that the City of London remains as at present, the Clearing-house of the World. *Speech, Guildhall, London, 19 Jan. 1904*

8 The day of small nations has long passed away. The day of Empires has come. *Speech, Birmingham, 12 May 1904*

CHAMBERLAIN, Neville, 1869–1940

9 In war, whichever side may call itself the victor, there are no winners, but all are losers. *Speech, Kettering, 3 July 1938*

10 I believe it is peace for our time . . . peace with honour. *Broadcast after Munich Agreement, 1 Oct. 1938*

11 Hitler has missed the bus. *Speech, House of Commons, 4 April 1940*

CHANDLER, John, 1806–1876

12 Conquering kings their titles take
From the foes they captive make:
Jesu, by a nobler deed
From the thousands He hath freed. *Conquering Kings their Titles Take*

CHARLES I of Great Britain, 1600–1649

13 Never make a defence or apology before you be accused. *Letter to Lord Wentworth, 3 Sept. 1636*

CHARLES II of Great Britain, 1630–1685

14 He had been, he said, a most unconscionable time dying; but he hoped that they would excuse it. *Macaulay, History of England, Vol. 1, Ch. 4*

15 Not a religion for gentlemen. [*Presbyterianism*] *Burnet, History of My Own Time, Vol. 1, Bk. 2, Ch. 2*

16 Let not poor Nelly starve. [*Said on his death-bed*] *Ib, Vol. 2, Bk. 3, Ch. 17*

17 Better than a play. *On House of Lords Debate on Divorce Bill, 1670*

CHARLES V, Holy Roman Emperor, 1500–1558

18 I speak Spanish to God, Italian to women, French to men, and German to my horse. *Attributed*

CHARLES, Hughie, see PARKER, Ross

CHAUCER, Geoffrey, 1340?–1400

1 When that Aprille with his shoures sote
The droghte of Marche hath perced to the rote. *The Canterbury Tales, Prologue, 1*

2 He was a verray parfit gentil knight. *Ib, 72*

3 He was as fresh as is the month of May. *Ib, 92 (Squire)*

4 And Frensh she spak ful faire and fetisly,
After the scole of Stratford atte Bowe,
For Frensh of Paris was to hir unknowe. *Ib, 124 (Prioress)*

5 He yaf nat of that text a pulled hen,
That seith, that hunters been nat holy men. *Ib, 177 (Monk)*

6 What sholde he studie, and make himselven wood,
Upon a book in cloistre alwey to poure,
Or swinken with his handes, and laboure,
As Austin bit? How shal the world be served?
Lat Austin have his swink to him reserved. *Ib, 184 (Monk)*

7 A Clerk ther was of Oxenford also,
That un-to logik hadde longe y-go. *Ib, 285*

8 As lene was his hors as is a rake. *Ib, 287 (Clerk)*

9 For him was lever have at his beddes heed
Twenty bokes, clad in blak or reed,
Of Aristotle and his philosophye,
Than robes riche, or fithele, or gay sautrye.
But all be that he was a philosophre,
Yet hadde he but litel gold in cofre. *Ib, 293 (Clerk)*

10 Souninge in moral vertu was his speche,
And gladly wolde he lerne, and gladly teche. *Ib, 307 (Clerk)*

11 No-wher so bisy a man as he ther nas,
And yet he semed bisier than he was. *Ib, 321 (Man of Law)*

12 It snewed in his hous of mete and drinke. *Ib, 345 (Franklin)*

13 His studie was but litel on the bible. *Ib, 438 (Doctor)*

14 For gold in phisik is a cordial,
Therfore he lovede gold in special. *Ib, 443 (Doctor)*

15 She was a worthy womman al hir lyve,
Housbondes at chirche-dore she hadde fyve,
Withouten other companye in youthe. *Ib, 459 (Wife of Bath)*

16 This noble ensample to his sheep he yaf,
That first he wroghte, and afterward he taughte. *Ib, 496 (Parson)*

17 If gold ruste, what shal iren do? *Ib, 500 (Parson)*

18 But Cristes lore, and his apostles twelve,
He taughte, and first he folwed it himselve. *Ib, 527 (Parson)*

19 His walet lay biforn him in his lappe,
Bret-ful of pardoun come from Rome al hoot. *Ib, 686 (Pardoner)*

20 The smyler with the knyf under the cloke. *Ib, The Knight's Tale, 1141*

21 This world nis but a thurghfare ful of wo,
And we ben pilgrimes, passinge to and fro;
Deeth is an ende of every worldly sore. *Ib, Ib, 1989*

22 So was hir joly whistle wel y-wet. *Ib, The Reve's Tale, 235*

1 Tragedie is to seyn a certeyn storie,
As olde bokes maken us memorie,
Of him that stood in greet prosperitee
And is y-fallen out of heigh degree
Into miserie, and endeth wrecchedly. *The Canterbury Tales, The Monk's Prologue, 85*

2 Mordre wol out, that see we day by day. *Ib, The Nun's Priest's Tale, 232*

3 My sone, keep wel thy tonge and keep thy freend. *Ib, The Maunciple's Tale, 319*

4 The lyf so short, the craft so long to lerne,
Th'assay so hard, so sharp the conquering. *The Parlement of Foules, 1*

5 For of fortunes sharp adversitee
The worst kinde of infortune is this,
A man to have ben in prosperitee,
And it remembren, whan it passed is. *Troilus and Criseyde, 3, 1625*

6 Go, litel book, go litel myn tragedie. *Ib, 5, 1786*

7 O moral Gower, this book I directe
To thee. *Ib, 5, 1856*

CHESTERFIELD, Philip Dormer Stanhope, 4th Earl of, 1694–1773

8 Be wiser than other people if you can, but do not tell them so. *Letter to his Son, 19 Nov. 1745*

9 Whatever is worth doing at all is worth doing well. *Ib, 10 March 1746*

10 An injury is much sooner forgotten than an insult. *Ib, 9 Oct: 1746*

11 Take the tone of the company you are in. *Ib, 9 Oct. 1747*

12 Advice is seldom welcome; and those who want it the most always like it the least. *Ib, 29 Jan. 1748*

13 In my mind, there is nothing so illiberal and so ill-bred, as audible laughter. *Ib, 9 Mar. 1748*

14 A man of sense only trifles with them [*women*], plays with them, humours and flatters them, as he does with a sprightly and forward child; but he neither consults them about, nor trusts them with, serious matters. *Ib, 5 Sept. 1748*

15 Idleness is only the refuge of weak minds. *Ib, 20 July 1749*

16 Women are much more like each other than men: they have, in truth, but two passions, vanity and love; these are their universal characteristics. *Ib, 19 Dec. 1749*

17 Every woman is infallibly to be gained by every sort of flattery, and every man by one sort or other. *Ib, 16 March 1752*

18 Unlike my subject will I frame my song,
It shall be witty and it shan't be long. *Epigram on 'Long' Sir Thomas Robinson*

19 Give Dayrolles a chair. *Last words*

CHESTERTON, Gilbert Keith, 1874–1936

20 The strangest whim has seized me . . . After all
I think I will not hang myself to-day. *A Ballade of Suicide*

1 When fishes flew and forests walked
And figs grew upon thorn,
Some moment when the moon was blood
Then surely I was born. *The Donkey*

2 The devil's walking parody
On all four-footed things. *Ib*

3 Fools! For I also had my hour;
One far fierce hour and sweet;
There was a shout about my ears,
And palms before my feet. *Ib*

4 White founts falling in the Courts of the sun,
And the Soldan of Byzantium is smiling as they run. *Lepanto*

5 Strong gongs groaning as the guns boom far,
Don John of Austria is going to the war. *Ib*

6 Before the Roman came to Rye or out to Severn strode,
The rolling English drunkard made the rolling English road.
The Rolling English Road

7 The night we went to Birmingham by way of Beachy Head. *Ib*

8 For there is good news yet to hear and fine things to be seen,
Before we go to Paradise by way of Kensal Green. *Ib*

9 Smile at us, pay us, pass us, but do not quite forget,
For we are the people of England, that never have spoken yet.
The Secret People

10 God made the wicked Grocer
For a mystery and a sign,
That men might shun the awful shops
And go to inns to dine. *The Song Against Grocers*

11 And Noah he often said to his wife when he sat down to dine,
'I don't care where the water goes if it doesn't get into the wine'.
Wine and Water

12 The human race, to which so many of my readers belong.
The Napoleon of Notting Hill, Bk. 1, Ch. 1, Opening Words

CHEVALIER, Albert, 1861–1923

13 'Wot cher!' all the neighbours cried,
'Who're yer goin' to meet Bill?
Have yer bought the street Bill?'
Laugh! I thought I should have died,
Knock'd 'em in the Old Kent Road. *Knock'd 'em in the Old Kent Road*

14 We've been together now for forty years,
An' it don't seem a day too much;
There ain't a lady livin' in the land
As I'd 'swop' for my dear old Dutch! *My Old Dutch*

CHEVALIER, Maurice, 1888–1972

15 I prefer old age to the alternative. *Remark, 1962*

CHURCHILL, Charles, 1731–1764

1 Be England what she will,
With all her faults, she is my country still. *The Farewell, 27*

2 The danger chiefly lies in acting well;
No crime's so great as daring to excel. *Epistle to William Hogarth*

3 He for subscribers baits his hook,
And takes your cash, but where's the book?
No matter where; wise fear, you know,
Forbids the robbing of a foe;
But what, to serve our private ends,
Forbids the cheating of our friends? [*Dr Johnson and his Dictionary*]
The Ghost, 3, 801

CHURCHILL, Lord Randolph Spencer, 1849–1894

4 The old gang. [*Members of the Conservative Government*]
Speech, House of Commons, 7 March 1878

5 An old man in a hurry. [*Gladstone*] *Speech, June 1886*

6 I never could make out what those damned dots meant. [*The decimal point*]
Quoted in Winston Churchill's Biography

CHURCHILL, Sir Winston Leonard Spencer, 1874–1965

7 It cannot in the opinion of His Majesty's Government be classified as slavery in the extreme acceptance of the word without some risk of terminological inexactitude. *Speech, House of Commons, 22 Feb. 1906*

8 The maxim of the British people is 'Business as usual'.
Speech, Guildhall, London, 9 Nov. 1914

9 The German dictator, instead of snatching the victuals from the table, has been content to have them served to him course by course.
Speech, House of Commons, 5 Oct. 1938

10 I cannot forecast to you the action of Russia. It is a riddle wrapped in a mystery inside an enigma. *Broadcast, 1 Oct. 1939*

11 I would say to the House, as I said to those who have joined the Government: 'I have nothing to offer but blood, toil, tears and sweat.'
Speech, House of Commons, 13 May 1940

12 Victory at all costs, victory in spite of all terror, victory however long and hard the road may be; for without victory there is no survival. *Ib*

13 We shall not flag or fail. We shall fight in France, we shall fight on the seas and oceans, we shall fight with growing confidence and growing strength in the air, we shall defend our island, whatever the cost may be, we shall fight on the beaches, we shall fight on the landing grounds, we shall fight in the fields and in the streets, we shall fight in the hills; we shall never surrender. *Speech, House of Commons, 4 June 1940*

14 Let us therefore brace ourselves to our duties, and so bear ourselves that, if the British Empire and its Commonwealth last for a thousand years, men will still say, 'This was their finest hour'. *Speech, House of Commons, 18 June 1940*

15 Never in the field of human conflict was so much owed by so many to so few. *Speech, House of Commons, 20 Aug. 1940*
on R.A.F. in Battle of Britain

1 *Nous attendons l'invasion promise de longue date. Les poissons aussi.*
We are waiting for the long-promised invasion. So are the fishes.
Broadcast to the French People, 21 Oct. 1940

2 Here is the answer which I will give to President Roosevelt. . . . Give us the tools, and we will finish the job. *Broadcast, 9 Feb. 1941*

3 What kind of a people do they [*the Japanese*] think we are?
Speech, U.S. Congress, 26 Dec. 1941

4 When I warned them [*the French Government*] that Britain would fight on alone whatever they did, their generals told their Prime Minister and his divided Cabinet: 'In three weeks England will have her neck wrung like a chicken.' Some chicken! Some neck! *Speech, Canadian Parliament, 30 Dec. 1941*

5 This is not the end. It is not even the beginning of the end. But it is, perhaps, the end of the beginning. *Speech, Mansion House, London, 10 Nov. 1942*

6 Let me, however, make this clear, in case there should be any mistake about it in any quarter. We mean to hold our own. I have not become the King's First Minister in order to preside over the liquidation of the British Empire.
Ib

7 The soft under-belly of the Axis. *Speech, House of Commons, 11 Nov. 1942*

8 The problems of victory are more agreeable than those of defeat, but they are no less difficult. *Ib*

9 There is no finer investment for any community than putting milk into babies. Healthy citizens are the greatest asset any country can have.
Broadcast: A Four Years' Plan, 21 March 1943

10 I view with profound misgivings the retreat of the American Army to our line of occupation in the central sector, thus bringing Soviet power into the heart of Western Europe and the descent of an iron curtain between us and everything to the eastward. *Cable to President Truman, 4 June 1945*
Quoted in The Second World War, Vol. 6, Triumph and Tragedy, 1954, p. 523

11 From Stettin in the Baltic to Trieste in the Adriatic, an iron curtain has descended across the Continent. *Speech, Westminster College, Fulton, U.S.A., 5 March 1946*

12 This is the sort of English up with which I will not put. *Attributed*
Marginal comment on document, quoted by Sir Ernest Gowers in Plain Words, 1948, p. 74

13 In War: Resolution. In Defeat: Defiance. In Victory: Magnanimity. In Peace: Goodwill. *The Second World War, Vol. 1, The Gathering Storm, 1948, Moral of the Work*

14 I have never accepted what many people have kindly said, namely that I inspired the nation. It was the nation and the race dwelling all round the globe that had the lion heart. I had the luck to be called upon to give the roar. *Speech on 80th birthday, Westminster Hall, 30 Nov. 1954*

CIBBER, Colley, 1671–1757

15 One had as good be out of the world, as out of the fashion.
Love's Last Shift, Act 2

16 Stolen sweets are best. *The Rival Fools, Act 1*

CICERO, Marcus Tullius, 106–43 B.C.

1 *Nihil tam absurde dici potest, quod non dicatur, ab alique philosophorum.* There is nothing so absurd but some philosopher has said it. *De Divinatione, 2, 58*

2 *Salus populi suprema est lex.* The good of the people is the chief law. *De Legibus, 3, 3, 8*

3 *Summum bonum.* The greatest good. *De Officiis, 1, 2*

4 *Cedant arma togae, concedant laurea laudi.* Let wars give way to peace, laurels to paeans. *Ib, 1, 22*

5 *Mens cuiusque is est quisque.* The mind of each man is the man himself. *De Republica, 6, 26*

6 *O tempora! O mores!* What times! What customs! *In Catilinam, 1, 1*

7 *Civis Romanus sum.* I am a Roman citizen. *In Verrem, 5, 57, 147*

8 *O fortunatam natam me consule Romam!* O happy Rome, born when I was consul. *Quoted in Juvenal, 10, 22*

CLAY, Henry, 1777–1852

9 I had rather be right than be President. *Speech, 1850*

CLEMENS, Samuel Langhorne, see TWAIN, Mark

CLEVELAND, Stephen Grover, 1837–1908

10 However plenty silver dollars may become, they will not be distributed as gifts among the people. *First Annual Message as President of U.S.A., 8 Dec. 1885*

CLIVE, Lord Robert, 1725–1774

11 By God, Mr. Chairman, at this moment I stand astonished at my own moderation! *Reply during Parliamentary Inquiry, 1773*

CLOUGH, Arthur Hugh, 1819–1861

12 A world where nothing is had for nothing. *The Bothie of Tober-na-Vuolich, 8, 5*

13 How pleasant it is to have money. *Dipsychus, Part 1, Scene 4*

14 And almost every one when age,
Disease, or sorrows strike him,
Inclines to think there is a God,
Or something very like Him. *Ib, Part 1, Scene 5*

15 Thou shalt have one God only; who
Would be at the expense of two? *The Latest Decalogue, 1*

16 Thou shalt not kill; but needst not strive
Officiously to keep alive. *Ib, 11*

17 Thou shalt not covet; but tradition
Approves all forms of competition. *Ib, 19*

18 'Tis better to have fought and lost,
Than never to have fought at all. *Peschiera*

1 Say not the struggle naught availeth,
The labour and the wounds are vain,
The enemy faints not, nor faileth,
And as things have been, things remain. *Say not the struggle naught availeth*

2 For while the tired waves, vainly breaking,
Seem here no painful inch to gain,
Far back through creeks and inlets making
Comes silent, flooding in, the main. *Ib*

3 And not by eastern windows only,
When daylight comes, comes in the light,
In front the sun climbs slow, how slowly,
But westward, look, the land is bright. *Ib*

COBBETT, William, 1762–1835

4 To be poor and independent is very nearly an impossibility. *Advice to Young Men*

5 But what is to be the fate of the great wen [*London*] of all? *Rural Rides*

COBORN, Charles, 1852–1945

6 Two lovely black eyes,
Oh, what a surprise!
Only for telling a man he was wrong,
Two lovely black eyes! *Two Lovely Black Eyes*

COKE, Sir Edward, 1552–1634

7 How long soever it hath continued, if it be against reason, it is of no force in law. *First Institute*

8 A man's house is his castle. *Third Institute*

9 Six hours in sleep, in law's grave study six,
Four spend in prayer, the rest on Nature fix. *Pandects*

COLERIDGE, Hartley, 1796–1849

10 She is not fair to outward view
As many maidens be;
Her loveliness I never knew
Until she smiled on me. *Song, She is not Fair*

COLERIDGE, Samuel Taylor, 1772–1834

11 It is an ancient Mariner,
And he stoppeth one of three.
'By thy long grey beard and glittering eye,
Now wherefore stopp'st thou me?' *The Rime of the Ancient Mariner, Pt. 1, 1*

12 He holds him with his glittering eye. *Ib, 1, 13*

13 The Sun came up upon the left,
Out of the sea came he!
And he shone bright, and on the right
Went down into the sea. *Ib, 1, 25*

1 The bride hath paced into the hall,
Red as a rose is she. *The Rime of the Ancient Mariner, Pt. 1, 33*

2 The ice was here, the ice was there,
The ice was all around:
It cracked and growled, and roared and howled,
Like noises in a swound! *Ib, 1, 59*

3 With my cross-bow
I shot the albatross. *Ib, 1, 81*

4 The fair breeze blew, the white foam flew,
The furrow followed free;
We were the first that ever burst
Into that silent sea. *Ib, Pt. 2, 103*

5 As idle as a painted ship
Upon a painted ocean. *Ib, 2, 117*

6 Water, water, every where,
And all the boards did shrink;
Water, water, every where,
Nor any drop to drink. *Ib, 2, 119*

7 I bit my arm, I sucked the blood,
And cried, A sail! a sail! *Ib, Pt. 3, 160*

8 Her lips were red, her looks were free,
Her locks were yellow as gold:
Her skin was as white as leprosy,
The Night-mare Life-in-Death was she,
Who thicks man's blood with cold. *Ib, 3, 190*

9 I fear thee, ancient Mariner!
I fear thy skinny hand! *Ib, Pt. 4, 224*

10 Alone, alone, all, all alone,
Alone on a wide wide sea!
And never a saint took pity on
My soul in agony. *Ib, 4, 232*

11 The many men, so beautiful!
And they all dead did lie:
And a thousand thousand slimy things
Lived on; and so did I. *Ib, 4, 236*

12 The moving Moon went up the sky,
And no where did abide:
Softly she was going up,
And a star or two beside. *Ib, 4, 263*

13 Oh sleep! it is a gentle thing,
Beloved from pole to pole! *Ib, Pt. 5, 292*

14 We were a ghastly crew. *Ib, 5, 340*

15 Quoth he, 'The man hath penance done,
And penance more will do.' *Ib, 5, 408*

16 Like one, that on a lonesome road
Doth walk in fear and dread,
And having once turned round walks on,
And turns no more his head;
Because he knows, a frightful fiend
Doth close behind him tread. *Ib, Pt. 6, 446*

1 No voice; but oh! the silence sank
Like music on my heart. *The Rime of the Ancient Mariner, Pt. 6, 498*

2 O Wedding-Guest! this soul hath been
Alone on a wide wide sea:
So lonely 'twas, that God himself
Scarce seemed there to be. *Ib, Pt. 7, 597*

3 He prayeth well, who loveth well
Both man and bird and beast. *Ib, 7, 612*

4 He prayeth best, who loveth best
All things both great and small;
For the dear God who loveth us,
He made and loveth all. *Ib, 7, 614*

5 A sadder and a wiser man,
He rose the morrow morn. *Ib, 7, 624*

6 A sight to dream of, not to tell! *Christabel, 1, 253*

7 And constancy lives in realms above;
And life is thorny; and youth is vain;
And to be wroth with one we love
Doth work like madness in the brain. *Ib, 2, 410*

8 I see, not feel, how beautiful they are! *Dejection: An Ode, 38*

9 I may not hope from outward forms to win
The passion and the life, whose fountains are within. *Ib, 45*

10 Swans sing before they die—'twere no bad thing
Should certain persons die before they sing.
Epigram on a Volunteer Singer

11 In Xanadu did Kubla Khan
A stately pleasure-dome decree:
Where Alph, the sacred river, ran
Through caverns measureless to man
Down to a sunless sea. *Kubla Khan, 1*

12 A savage place! as holy and enchanted
As e'er beneath a waning moon was haunted
By woman wailing for her demon-lover! *Ib, 14*

13 Through wood and dale the sacred river ran,
Then reached the caverns measureless to man. *Ib, 26*

14 And 'mid this tumult Kubla heard from far
Ancestral voices prophesying war! *Ib, 29*

15 It was a miracle of rare device,
A sunny pleasure-dome with caves of ice! *Ib, 35*

16 Weave a circle round him thrice,
And close your eyes with holy dread,
For he on honey-dew hath fed,
And drunk the milk of Paradise. *Ib, 51*

17 This Lime-tree Bower my Prison! *Title of Poem*

18 Tranquillity! thou better name
Than all the family of Fame! *Ode to Tranquillity*

19 That willing suspension of disbelief for the moment, which constitutes poetic faith. *Biographia Literaria, Ch. 14*

1 Our myriad-minded Shakespeare. *Biographia Literaria, Ch. 15*

2 Summer has set in with its usual severity.
Remark quoted in C. Lamb's letter to V. Novello, 9 May 1826

3 I wish our clever young poets would remember my homely definitions of prose and poetry; that is, prose = words in their best order;—poetry = the best words in the best order. *Table Talk, 12 July 1827*

4 No mind is thoroughly well organized that is deficient in a sense of humour. *Table Talk*

5 What comes from the heart, goes to the heart. *Ib*

COLLINGS, Jesse, 1831–1921

6 Three acres and a cow. *Slogan for Land Reform, 1885*

COLLINS, Mortimer, 1827–1876

7 A man is as old as he's feeling,
A woman as old as she looks. *The Unknown Quantity*

COLLINS, William, 1721–1759

8 To fair Fidele's grassy tomb
Soft maids, and village kinds shall bring
Each op'ning sweet, of earliest bloom,
And rifle all the breathing Spring. *Dirge in Cymbeline, 1*

9 Hamlets brown, and dim-discover'd spires. *Ode to Evening, 37*

10 How sleep the brave, who sink to rest,
By all their country's wishes blest! *Ode written in the Year 1746, 1*

11 By fairy hands their knell is rung,
By forms unseen their dirge is sung;
There Honour comes, a Pilgrim grey,
To bless the turf that wraps their clay,
And Freedom shall a-while repair,
To dwell a weeping hermit there! *Ib, 7*

12 When Music, heavenly maid, was young. *The Passions, An Ode for Music, 1*

13 With eyes up-rais'd, as one inspir'd,
Pale Melancholy sate retir'd. *Ib, 57*

14 O Music, sphere-descended Maid,
Friend of Pleasure, Wisdom's aid. *Ib, 95*

COLMAN, George, 1762–1836

15 Mum's the word. *The Battle of Hexham, Act 2, Scene 1*

16 When taken
To be well shaken. *Newcastle Apothecary*

COLTON, Charles Caleb, 1780?–1832

17 Men will wrangle for religion; write for it; fight for it; anything but—live for it. *Lacon, 1, No. 25*

18 When you have nothing to say, say nothing. *Ib, No. 183*

19 Imitation is the sincerest form of flattery. *Ib, No. 217*

20 Examinations are formidable even to the best prepared, for the greatest fool may ask more than the wisest man can answer. *Ib, No. 322*

1 The debt which cancels all others. *Lacon, 2, No. 66*

CONFUCIUS, 551-479 B.C.

2 Men's natures are alike; it is their habits that carry them far apart. *Analects*

3 Study the past, if you would divine the future. *Ib*

4 Learning without thought is labour lost; thought without learning is perilous. *Ib*

CONGREVE, William, 1670–1729

5 Music has charms to soothe a savage breast,
To soften rocks, or bend a knotted oak. ALMERIA
The Mourning Bride, Act 1

6 Heaven has no rage like love to hatred turned,
Nor hell a fury like a woman scorned. ZARA *Ib, Act 3*

7 They come together like the coroner's inquest, to sit upon the murdered reputations of the week. FAINALL *The Way of the World, Act 1, Scene 1*

8 'Tis for the honour of England, that all Europe should know that we have blockheads of all ages. FAINALL *Ib, Act 1, Scene 5*

9 A wit should no more be sincere, than a woman constant; one argues a decay of parts, as t'other of beauty. WITWOUD *Ib, Act 1, Scene 6*

10 Here she comes i' faith full sail, with her fan spread and streamers out, and a shoal of fools for tenders. MIRABELL *Ib, Act 2, Scene 5*

11 I am persecuted with letters—I hate letters—nobody knows how to write letters; and yet one has 'em, one does not know why.—They serve one to pin up one's hair. MRS MILLAMENT *Ib*

12 MRS MILLAMENT: I believe I gave you some pain.
MIRABELL: Does that please you?
MRS MILLAMENT: Infinitely; I love to give pain. *Ib*

13 Lord, what is a lover, that it can give? Why, one makes lovers as fast as one pleases, and they live as long as one pleases, and they die as soon as one pleases: and then if one pleases one makes more. MRS MILLAMENT *Ib*

14 Love's but the frailty of the mind,
When 'tis not with ambition join'd. SONG *Ib, Act 3, Scene 12*

15 O, nothing is more alluring than a levee from a couch in some confusion. LADY WISHFORT *Ib, Act 4, Scene 1*

16 I nauseate walking; 'tis a country diversion, I loathe the country and everything that relates to it. MRS MILLAMENT *Ib, Act 4, Scene 4*

17 Let us never visit together, nor go to a play together, but let us be very strange and wellbred: let us be as strange as if we had been married a great while; and as wellbred as if we were not married at all. MRS MILLAMENT *Ib, Act 4, Scene 5*

18 These articles subscribed, if I continue to endure you a little longer, I may by degrees dwindle into a wife. MRS MILLAMENT *Ib*

1 I hope you do not think me prone to any iteration of nuptials.
LADY WISHFORT *The Way of the World, Act 4, Scene 12*

2 O, she is the antidote to desire. WAITWELL *Ib, Act 4, Scene 14*

CONNELL, James, 1852–1929

3 Then raise the scarlet standard high!
Beneath its shade we'll live and die!
Though cowards flinch, and traitors jeer,
We'll keep the Red Flag flying here! *The Red Flag*

CONNOLLY, Cyril, 1903—1974

4 As repressed sadists are supposed to become policemen or butchers so those with irrational fear of life become publishers. *Enemies of Promise*

CONNOR, T. W., 19th century

5 She was one of the early birds,
And I was one of the worms. *She was a Dear Little Dickie-Bird*

CONRAD, Joseph, 1857–1924

6 You shall judge of a man by his foes as well as by his friends.
Lord Jim, Ch. 34

7 A work that aspires, however humbly, to the condition of art should carry its justification in every line. *The Nigger of the Narcissus, Preface*

8 The sea never changes and its works, for all the talk of men, are wrapped in mystery. *Typhoon, Ch. 2*

9 The belief in a supernatural source of evil is not necessary; men alone are quite capable of every wickedness. *Under Western Eyes, Part 2*

COOLIDGE, Calvin, 1872–1933

10 There is no right to strike against the public safety by anybody, anywhere, any time. *On the Boston police strike, 14 Sept. 1919*

11 He said he was against it. *When asked what a clergyman had said in a sermon on sin*

COOPER, James Fenimore, 1789–1851

12 The Last of the Mohicans. *Title of Novel*

CORBUSIER, Le, 1887—1965

13 *Une maison est une machine-à-habiter.* A house is a machine for living in.
Vers une architecture, 1923

CORNEILLE, Pierre, 1606–1684

14 *À vaincre sans péril, on triomphe sans gloire.* We triumph without glory when we conquer without danger. DON GOMÈS *Le Cid, Act 2, Scene 2*

15 *Faites votre devoir, et laissez faire aux dieux.* Do your duty and leave the rest to the Gods. LE VIEIL HORACE *Horace, Act 2, Scene 8*

CORNFORD, Frances Crofts, 1886–1960

16 O why do you walk through the fields in gloves.
Missing so much and so much?

O fat white woman whom nobody loves
Why do you walk through the fields in gloves
When the grass is as soft as the breast of doves
  And shivering-sweet to the touch? *To a Fat Lady Seen from a Train*

CORNUEL, Anne Bigot de, 1605–1694

1 *Il n'y a pas de héros pour son valet de chambre.* No man is a hero to his valet.
Lettres de Mlle. Aissé, 13 Aug. 1728

COUBERTIN, Baron Pierre de, 1863–1937

2 *L'important dans ces olympiades, c'est moins d'y gagner que d'y prendre part. . . . L'important dans la vie ce n'est point le triomphe mais le combat.* The most important thing in the Olympic Games is not winning but taking part. . . . The essential thing in life is not conquering but fighting well.
Speech at Banquet to Officials of Olympic Games, London, 24 July 1908

COUÉ, Émile, 1857–1926

3 *Tous les jours, à tous points de vue, je vais de mieux en mieux.* Every day, in every way, I am getting better and better. *Formula for his cures by auto-suggestion*

COUSIN, Victor, 1792–1867

4 *L'art pour l'art.* Art for art's sake. *Lecture at Sorbonne, 1818*

COWARD, Noel, 1899–1973

5 The Stately Homes of England
How beautiful they stand,
To prove the upper classes
Have still the upper hand. *Operette, Act 1, Scene 7, The Stately Homes of England*

6 And tho' if the Van Dycks have to go
And we pawn the Bechstein Grand,
We'll stand by the Stately Homes of England. *Ib*

7 A room with a view—and you
  And no one to worry us
No one to hurry us. *This Year of Grace, Act 1, A Room with a View*

8 At twelve noon the natives swoon
And no further work is done.
But mad dogs and Englishmen
Go out in the midday sun. *Words and Music, Mad Dogs and Englishmen*

9 Don't let's be Beastly to the Germans. *Title of song*

10 Don't put your Daughter on the Stage, Mrs. Worthington. *Title of song*

11 Poor Little Rich Girl. *Title of song*

COWLEY, Abraham, 1618–1667

12 God the first garden made, and the first city Cain. *The Garden*

13 This only grant me, that my means may lie
Too low for envy, for contempt too high. *Of Myself*

COWLEY, Hannah, 1743–1809

14 But what is woman?—only one of Nature's agreeable blunders.
DOILEY *Who's the Dupe? Act 2, Scene 2*

COWPER, William, 1731–1800

1 Hark! the Gaul is at her gates! *Boadicea*

2 Regions Caesar never knew
Thy posterity shall sway,
Where his eagles never flew,
None invincible as they. *Ib*

3 He found it inconvenient to be poor. *Charity, 189*

4 A moral, sensible, and well-bred man
Will not affront me, and no other can. *Conversation, 193*

5 Pernicious weed! whose scent the fair annoys,
Unfriendly to society's chief joys,
Thy worst effect is banishing for hours
The sex whose presence civilises ours. *Ib, 251*

6 John Gilpin was a citizen
Of credit and renown,
A train-band captain eke was he,
Of famous London town. *John Gilpin, 1*

7 Tomorrow is our wedding day
And we will then repair
Unto the Bell at Edmonton
All in a chaise and pair. *Ib, 2*

8 O'erjoyed was he to find
That, though on pleasure she was bent,
She had a frugal mind. *Ib, 8*

9 Away went Gilpin—who but he?
His fame soon spread around;
He carries weight! he rides a race,
'Tis for a thousand pound! *Ib, 29*

10 The dinner waits, and we are tired:
Said Gilpin, So am I! *Ib, 37*

11 Said John, 'It is my wedding-day,
And all the world would stare,
If wife should dine at Edmonton,
And I should dine at Ware.' *Ib, 49*

12 'Twas for your pleasure you came here,
You shall go back for mine. *Ib, 50*

13 Now let us sing, Long live the King,
And Gilpin long live he;
And when he next doth ride abroad,
May I be there to see! *Ib, 63*

14 What peaceful hours I once enjoyed!
How sweet their memory still!
But they have left an aching void,
The world can never fill. *Olney Hymns, 1*

15 God moves in a mysterious way,
His wonders to perform;
He plants His footsteps in the sea,
And rides upon the storm. *Ib, 35*

1 Toll for the brave,
The brave that are no more:
All sunk beneath the wave,
Fast by their native shore. *On the Loss of the Royal George*

2 How much a dunce that has been sent to roam
Excels a dunce that has been kept at home. *Progress of Error, 415*

3 Thou god of our idolatry, the press. *Ib, 461*

4 Absence of occupation is not rest,
A mind quite vacant is a mind distressed. *Retirement, 623*

5 I sing the Sofa. *The Task, 1, The Sofa, 1*

6 God made the country, and man made the town. *Ib, 1, 749*

7 England, with all thy faults, I love thee still,
My country. *Ib, 2, The Timepiece, 206*

8 Variety's the very spice of life
That gives it all its flavour. *Ib, 2, 606*

9 Detested sport,
That owes its pleasure to another's pain. *Ib, 3, The Garden, 326*

10 Now stir the fire, and close the shutters fast,
Let fall the curtains, wheel the sofa round,
And, while the bubbling and loud-hissing urn
Throws up a steamy column, and the cups,
That cheer but not inebriate, wait on each,
So let us welcome peaceful evening in. *Ib, 4, The Winter Evening, 36*

11 Nature is but a name for an effect
Whose cause is God. *Ib, 6, The Winter Walk at Noon, 223*

12 I would not enter on my list of friends
(Though graced with polished manners and fine sense,
Yet wanting sensibility) the man
Who needlessly sets foot upon a worm. *Ib, 6, 560*

13 The twentieth year is well-nigh past,
Since first our sky was overcast:
Ah, would that this might be the last
My Mary! *To Mary*

14 I am monarch of all I survey
My right there is none to dispute. *Verses supposed to be written by Alexander Selkirk*

15 O Solitude! Where are the charms
That sages have seen in thy face?
Better dwell in the midst of alarms
Than reign in this horrible place. *Ib*

CRABBE, George, 1754–1832

16 Habit with him was all the test of truth,
'It must be right: I've done it from my youth.' *The Borough, Letter 3, The Vicar, 138*

17 Books cannot always please, however good;
Minds are not ever craving for their food. *Ib, Letter 24, Schools, 402*

18 A master-passion is the love of news. *The Newspaper, 279*

1 Secrets with girls, like loaded guns with boys,
Are never valued till they make a noise. *Tales of the Hall, 11, The Maid's Story, 84*

CRASHAW, Richard, 1612?–1649

2 I would be married but I'd have no wife,
I would be married to a single life. *On Marriage*

3 Whoe'er she be,
That not impossible she
That shall command my heart and me. *Wishes to his Supposed Mistress*

CREIGHTON, Mandell, 1843–1901

4 No people do so much harm as those who go about doing good. *Life, 1904*

CROKER, John Wilson, 1780–1857

5 A game which a sharper once played with a dupe, entitled 'Heads I win, tails you lose.' *Croker Papers*

6 We now are, as we always have been, decidedly and conscientiously attached to what is called the Tory, and which might with more propriety be called the Conservative, party. *Quarterly Review, Jan, 1830*

CROMWELL, Oliver, 1599–1658

7 I beseech you, in the bowels of Christ, think it possible you may be mistaken. *Letter to the General Assembly of the Church of Scotland, 3 Aug. 1650*

8 What shall we do with this bauble? There, take it away. *Speech dismissing Parliament, 20 April 1653*

9 It is not fit that you should sit here any longer! . . . you shall now give place to better men. *Speech to the Rump Parliament, 22 Jan. 1654*

10 Mr. Lely, I desire you would use all your skill to paint my picture truly like me, and not flatter me at all; but remark all these roughnesses, pimples, warts, and everything as you see me, otherwise I will never pay a farthing for it. *Horace Walpole's Anecdotes of Painting, Ch. 12*

CUMBERLAND, Bishop Richard, 1631–1718

11 It is better to wear out than to rust out. *Quoted in G. Horne, The Duty of Contending for the Faith*

CUMMINGS, Edward Estlin, 1894–1962

12 a politician is an arse upon
which everyone has sat except a man. *a politician*

13 anyone lived in a pretty how town
(with up so floating many bells down)
spring summer autumn winter
he sang his didn't he danced his did. *anyone lived in a pretty how town*

14 Humanity i love you because
when you're hard up you pawn your
intelligence to buy a drink. *humanity i love you*

CUNNINGHAM, Allan, 1784–1842

1 A wet sheet and a flowing sea,
A wind that follows fast,
And fills the white and rustling sail,
And bends the gallant mast. *A Wet Sheet and a Flowing Sea*

2 It's hame and it's hame, hame fain wad I be,
O, hame, hame, hame to my ain countree! *It's Hame and It's Hame*

CURRAN, John Philpot, 1750–1817

3 The condition upon which God hath given liberty to man is eternal vigilance. *Speech on the Right of Election of Lord Mayor of Dublin, 10 July 1790*

DACRE, Harry, 19th century

4 Daisy, Daisy, give me your answer, do!
I'm half crazy, all for the love of you!
It won't be a stylish marriage,
I can't afford a carriage,
But you'll look sweet upon the seat
Of a bicycle made for two! *Daisy Bell*

DANA, Charles Anderson, 1819–1897

5 When a dog bites a man that is not news, but when a man bites a dog, that is news. *What is News? The New York Sun, 1882*

DANTE, Alighieri, 1265–1321

6 *Lasciate ogni speranza voi ch'entrate.* Abandon hope, all ye who enter here. *Divine Comedy, Inferno, 3, 9*

7 *Nessun maggior dolore,*
Che ricordarsi del tempo felice
Nella miseria.
There is no greater sorrow than to recall a time of happiness when in misery. *Ib, 5, 121*

8 *L'amor che muove il sole e l'altre stelle.* The love that moves the sun and the other stars. *Ib, Paradiso, 33, 145*

DANTON, Georges Jaques, 1759–1794

9 *De l'audace, encore de l'audace, et toujours de l'audace!* Boldness, and again boldness, and always boldness! *Speech, French Legislative Committee, 2 Sept. 1792*

DARWIN, Charles Robert, 1809–1882

10 Man with all his noble qualities . . . still bears in his bodily frame the indelible stamp of his lowly origin. *The Descent of Man, Last Words*

11 I have called this principle, by which each slight variation, if useful, is preserved, by the term of Natural Selection. *The Origin of Species, Ch. 3*

12 The expression often used by Mr. Herbert Spencer of the Survival of the Fittest is more accurate, and is sometimes equally convenient. *Ib, Ch. 3*

DAVENANT, Sir William, 1606–1668

13 I shall sleep like a top. CELANIA *The Rivals, Act 3*

1 Awake, awake! the morn will never rise,
Till she can dress her beauty at your eyes. *Song*

DAVIES, William Henry, 1871–1940

2 What is this life if, full of care,
We have no time to stand and stare? *Leisure*

3 Sweet Stay-at-Home, sweet Well-content. *Sweet Stay-at-Home*

DAVIS, Jefferson, 1808–1889

4 All we ask is to be let alone. *Attributed remark, Inaugural Address as President of Confederated States of America, 1861*

DAY LEWIS, Cecil, 1904–1972

5 Nothing so sharply reminds a man he is mortal
As leaving a place
In a winter morning's dark, the air on his face
Unkind as the touch of sweating metal. *Departure in the Dark*

6 Tempt me no more; for I
Have known the lightning's hour,
The poet's inward pride,
The certainty of power. *Tempt me no more*

DECATUR, Stephen, 1779–1820

7 Our country! In her intercourse with foreign nations, may she always be in the right; but our country, right or wrong. *Speech, Norfolk, Virginia April 1816*

DEFOE, Daniel, 1660?–1731

8 I takes my man Friday with me. *Robinson Crusoe, Pt. 1*

9 Wherever God erects a house of prayer,
The Devil always builds a chapel there;
And 'twill be found, upon examination,
The latter has the largest congregation. *The True-Born Englishman, Pt. 1, 1*

10 And of all plagues with which mankind are curst,
Ecclesiastic tyranny's the worst. *Ib, Pt. 2, 299*

DEKKER, Thomas, 1570?–1641?

11 Golden slumbers kiss your eyes,
Smiles awake you when you rise. *Patient Grissil, Act 4, Scene 2*

12 Brave shoemakers, all gentlemen of the gentle craft. *The Shoemaker's Holiday, Act 3, Scene 1*

DE LA MARE, Walter, 1873–1956

13 Look thy last on all things lovely,
Every hour. *Farewell*

14 'Is there anybody there?' said the Traveller,
Knocking on the moonlit door. *The Listeners*

15 'Tell them I came, and no one answered,
That I kept my word,' he said. *Ib*

1 Softly along the road of evening,
  In a twilight dim with rose,
Wrinkled with age, and drenched with dew,
  Old Nod, the shepherd, goes. *Nod*

2 Three jolly Farmers
Once bet a pound
Each dance the others would
Off the ground. *Off the Ground*

3 Slowly, silently, now the moon
Walks the night in her silver shoon. *Silver*

DENMAN, Thomas, 1st Baron, 1779–1854

4 Trial by jury itself, instead of being a security to persons who are accused, will be a delusion, a mockery, and a snare. *Judgment in O'Connell v. The Queen, 4 Sept. 1844*

DENNIS, John, 1657–1734

5 A man who could make so vile a pun would not scruple to pick a pocket. *The Gentleman's Magazine, 1781*

DE QUINCEY, Thomas, 1785–1859

6 Murder considered as one of the Fine Arts. *Title of Essay*

DESCARTES, René, 1596–1650

7 *Cogito, ergo sum.* I think, therefore I am. *Le Discours de la Méthode*

DICKENS, Charles, 1812–1870

8 'There are strings', said Mr. Tappertit, 'in the human heart that had better not be wibrated.' *Barnaby Rudge, Ch. 22*

9 This is a London particular . . . A fog, miss. *Bleak House, Ch. 3*

10 I expect a judgment. Shortly. MISS FLITE *Ib*

11 It is a melancholy truth that even great men have their poor relations. *Ib, Ch. 28*

12 'God bless us every one!' said Tiny Tim, the last of all. *A Christmas Carol, Stave 3*

13 'I am a lone lorn creetur',' were Mrs. Gummidge's words . . . 'and everythink goes contrairy with me.' *David Copperfield, Ch. 3*

14 Barkis is willin'. BARKIS *Ib, Ch. 5*

15 I have known him [*Mr. Micawber*] come home to supper with a flood of tears, and a declaration that nothing was now left but a jail; and go to bed making a calculation of the expense of putting bow-windows to the house, 'in case anything turned up,' which was his favourite expression. *Ib, Ch. 11*

16 Annual income twenty pounds, annual expenditure nineteen nineteen six, result happiness. Annual income twenty pounds, annual expenditure twenty pounds ought and six, result misery. MR MICAWBER *Ib, Ch. 12*

17 We are so very 'umble. URIAH HEEP *Ib, Ch. 17*

18 I only ask for information. ROSA DARTLE *Ib, Ch. 20*

19 'It was as true', said Mr. Barkis, 'as taxes is. And nothing's truer than them.' *Ib, Ch. 21*

1 Accidents will occur in the best-regulated families. MR MICAWBER
David Copperfield, Ch. 28

2 I'm Gormed—and I can't say no fairer than that. MR PEGGOTTY
Ib, Ch. 63

3 When found, make a note of. CAPTAIN CUTTLE *Dombey and Son, Ch. 15*

4 Whatever was required to be done, the Circumlocution Office was beforehand with all the public departments in the art of perceiving—HOW NOT TO DO IT. *Little Dorrit, Bk. 1, Ch. 10*

5 Let us be moral. Let us contemplate existence. MR PECKSNIFF
Martin Chuzzlewit, Ch. 10

6 Here's the rule for bargains: 'Do other men, for they would do you.' That's the true business precept. JONAS CHUZZLEWIT *Ib, Ch. 11*

7 He'd make a lovely corpse. MRS GAMP *Ib, Ch. 25*

8 Oh Sairey, Sairey, little do we know what lays afore us! MRS GAMP
Ib, Ch. 40

9 At Mr. Wackford Squeers' Academy, Dotheboys Hall . . . Youth are boarded, clothed, booked, furnished with pocket-money, provided with all necessaries, instructed in all languages living and dead . . . No extras, no vacations, and diet unparalleled. *Nicholas Nickleby, Ch. 3*

10 Every baby born into the world is a finer one than the last. *Ib, Ch. 36*

11 My life is one demd horrid grind! MR MANTALINI *Ib, Ch. 64*

12 Oliver Twist has asked for more. BUMBLE *Oliver Twist, Ch. 2*

13 Known by the *sobriquet* of 'The artful Dodger.' *Ib, Ch. 8*

14 I only know two sorts of boys. Mealy boys, and beef-faced boys.
MR GRIMWIG *Ib, Ch. 14*

15 'If the law supposes that,' said Mr. Bumble . . . , 'the law is a ass—a idiot.'
Ib, Ch. 51

16 The question about everything was, would it bring a blush to the cheek of a young person? *Our Mutual Friend, 1, 11*

17 Not presume to dictate, but broiled fowl and mushrooms—capital thing!
JINGLE *Pickwick Papers, Ch. 2*

18 Kent, sir—everybody knows Kent—apples, cherries, hops and women.
JINGLE *Ib*

19 I wants to make your flesh creep. JOE, THE FAT BOY *Ib, Ch. 8*

20 'It's always best on these occasions to do what the mob do.'
'But suppose there are two mobs?' suggested Mr. Snodgrass.
'Shout with the largest,' replied Mr. Pickwick. *Ib, Ch. 13*

21 Can I unmoved see thee dying
On a log,
Expiring frog! MRS LEO HUNTER *Ib, Ch. 15*

22 'Sir,' said Mr. Tupman, 'you're a fellow.' 'Sir,' said Mr. Pickwick, 'you're another!' *Ib*

23 Mr. Weller's knowledge of London was extensive and peculiar. *Ib, Ch. 20*

24 Take example by your father, my boy, and be very careful o' vidders all your life, specially if they've kept a public house, Sammy. MR WELLER
Ib

1 Poverty and oysters always seem to go together. SAM WELLER *Pickwick Papers, Ch. 22*

2 Wery glad to see you indeed and hope our acquaintance may be a long 'un, as the gen'l'm'n said to the fi' pun' note. SAM WELLER *Ib, Ch. 25*

3 Wen you're a married man, Samivel, you'll understand a good many things as you don't understand now; but vether it's worth goin' through so much, to learn so little, as the charity-boy said ven he got to the end of the alphabet, is a matter o' taste. MR WELLER *Ib, Ch. 27*

4 A double glass o' the inwariable. MR WELLER *Ib, Ch. 33*

5 Poetry's unnat'ral; no man ever talked poetry 'cept a beadle on boxin' day. MR WELLER *Ib*

6 It's my opinion, sir, that this meeting is drunk. STIGGINS *Ib*

7 Chops and Tomata sauce. Yours, Pickwick. *Ib, Ch. 34*

8 Put it down a we, my lord, put it down a we! MR WELLER *Ib*

9 Oh Sammy, Sammy vy worn't there a alleybi! MR WELLER *Ib*

10 Anythin' for a quiet life, as the man said wen he took the sitivation at the lighthouse. SAM WELLER *Ib, Ch. 43*

11 A smattering of everything, and a knowledge of nothing. *Sketches by Boz, Tales, Ch. 3, Sentiment, Minerva House*

12 It is a far, far, better thing that I do, than I have ever done; it is a far, far, better rest that I go to, than I have ever known. SIDNEY CARTON *A Tale of Two Cities, Ch. 15*

DICKINSON, Emily, 1830–1886

13 Success is counted sweetest
By those who ne'er succeed. *Poems, Part 1, Life*

14 How dreary to be somebody!
How public, like a frog
To tell your name the livelong day
To an admiring bog! *Ib*

15 Parting is all we know of heaven,
And all we need of hell. *Ib*

16 There's a certain slant of light,
On winter afternoons,
That oppresses, like the weight
Of Cathedral tunes. *Ib, Part 2, Nature*

17 Because I could not stop for Death,
He kindly stopped for me;
The carriage held but just ourselves
And Immortality. *Ib, Part 4, Time and Eternity*

18 If I shouldn't be alive
When the robins come,
Give the one in red cravat
A memorial crumb. *Ib*

DIOGENES, 412?–323? B.C.

19 Stand a little less between me and the sun. *Plutarch, Life of Alexander, 14*

DIONYSIUS of Halicarnassus, 40?–8 B.C.

1 History is philosophy teaching by examples. *Ars rhetorica, 11, 2*

DISRAELI, Benjamin, 1st Earl of Beaconsfield, 1804–1881

2 I will sit down now, but the time will come when you will hear me. *Maiden Speech, House of Commons, 7 Dec. 1837*

3 The right honourable gentleman [*Sir Robert Peel*] caught the Whigs bathing, and walked away with their clothes. *Speech, House of Commons, 28 Feb. 1845*

4 A Conservative government is an organised hypocrisy. *Ib, 17 Mar. 1845*

5 The question is this: Is man an ape or an angel? I, my lord, am on the side of the angels. *Speech, 25 Nov. 1864*

6 An author who speaks about his own books is almost as bad as a mother who talks about her own children. *Speech, Glasgow, 19 Nov. 1873*

7 Lord Salisbury and myself have brought you back peace—but a peace I hope with honour. *Speech, House of Commons, 16 July 1878*

8 A sophistical rhetorician [*Gladstone*] inebriated with the exuberance of his own verbosity. *Speech, 27 July, 1878*

9 Youth is a blunder; manhood a struggle; old age a regret. SIDONIA *Coningsby, Bk. 3, Ch. 1*

10 Every woman should marry—and no man. HUGO BOHUN *Lothair, Ch. 30*

11 To be conscious that you are ignorant is a great step to knowledge. *Sybil, Bk. 1, Ch. 5*

12 I was told that the Privileged and the People formed Two Nations. *Ib, Bk. 4, Ch. 8*

13 Variety is the mother of enjoyment. *Vivian Grey, Bk. 5, Ch. 4*

14 She is an excellent creature, but she never can remember which came first, the Greeks or the Romans. [*Of his wife*] *Attributed*

15 When I want to read a novel I write one. *Attributed*

DODGSON, Charles Lutwidge, see CARROLL, Lewis

DONNE, John, 1573–1631

16 And new Philosophy calls all in doubt,
The Element of fire is quite put out;
The Sun is lost, and th' earth, and no man's wit
Can well direct him where to look for it. *An Anatomy of the World, 205*

17 Come live with me, and be my love,
And we will some new pleasures prove
Of golden sands, and crystal brooks,
With silken lines, and silver hooks. *The Bait*

18 Reason is our Soul's left hand, Faith her right,
By these we reach divinity. *To the Countess of Bedford, 1*

19 Love built on beauty, soon as beauty, dies.
Elegies, No. 2, The Anagram, 27

1 No Spring, nor Summer beauty hath such grace,
As I have seen in one Autumnal face. *Elegies, No. 9, The Autumnal, 1*

2 Whoever loves, if he do not propose
The right true end of love, he's one that goes
To sea for nothing but to make him sick. *Ib, No. 18, Love's Progress, 1*

3 Licence my roving hands, and let them go,
Before, behind, between, above, below.
O my America! my new-found-land,
My Kingdom, safeliest when with one man man'd.
Ib, No. 19, Going To Bed, 25

4 Death be not proud, though some have called thee
Mighty and dreadful, for, thou art not so,
For, those, whom thou think'st, thou dost overthrow,
Die not, poor death. *Holy Sonnets, 10*

5 Go, and catch a falling star,
Get with child a mandrake root,
Tell me, where all past years are,
Or who cleft the Devil's foot. *Song, Go and Catch a Falling Star*

6 But I do nothing upon myself, and yet I am mine own Executioner. *Devotions, 12*

7 No man is an Island, entire of itself; every man is a piece of the Continent, a part of the main. *Ib, 17*

8 Any man's death diminishes me, because I am involved in Mankind; And therefore never send to know for whom the bell tolls; it tolls for thee. *Ib, 17*

DONNELLY, Ignatius, 1831–1901

9 The Democratic Party is like a mule—without pride of ancestry or hope of posterity. *Speech, Minnesota Legislature*

DOUGLAS, William, 1672–1748

10 And for bonnie Annie Laurie
I'll lay me down and dee. *Annie Laurie*

DOWSON, Ernest Christopher, 1867–1900

11 I have been faithful to thee, Cynara! in my fashion. *Non Sum Qualis Eram*

DOYLE, Sir Arthur Conan, 1859–1930

12 It has long been an axiom of mine that the little things are infinitely the most important. *The Adventures of Sherlock Holmes, A Case of Identity*

13 It is quite a three-pipe problem. *Ib, The Red-Headed League*

14 You know my methods, Watson. *The Memoirs of Sherlock Holmes, The Crooked Man*

15 'Excellent!' I [*Dr. Watson*] cried. 'Elementary,' said he [*Holmes*]. *Ib*

16 He [*Professor Moriarty*] is the Napoleon of crime. *Ib, The Final Problem*

1 'Is there any point to which you would wish to draw my attention?'
'To the curious incident of the dog in the night-time.'
'The dog did nothing in the night-time.'
'That was the curious incident,' remarked Sherlock Holmes.
The Memoirs of Sherlock Holmes, Silver Blaze

2 An experience of women which extends over many nations and three continents. *The Sign of Four*

3 When you have eliminated the impossible, whatever remains, however improbable, must be the truth. *Ib*

4 The Baker Street irregulars. *Ib*

5 London, that great cesspool into which all the loungers of the Empire are irresistibly drained. *A Study in Scarlet*

6 The vocabulary of 'Bradshaw' is nervous and terse, but limited. *Ib*

DRAKE, Sir Francis, 1540?–1596

7 I have singed the Spanish king's beard. *After destroying on 19 April 1587, a vast amount of shipping in the Harbour of Cadiz*

8 There is plenty of time to win this game, and to thrash the Spaniards too. *20 July 1588, while playing bowls, when the Armada was sighted*

DRAYTON, Michael, 1563–1631

9 Fair stood the wind for France
When we our sails advance. *Agincourt*

10 Ill news hath wings, and with the wind doth go,
Comfort's a cripple and comes ever slow. *The Barrons' Wars, 2*

11 Neat Marlowe, bathed in the Thespian springs,
Had in him those brave translunary things
That the first poets had. *Of Poets and Poesy*

12 Since there's no help, come let us kiss and part—
Nay, I have done, you get no more of me;
And I am glad, yea glad with all my heart
That thus so cleanly I myself can free. *Sonnets, 61, The Parting*

DRUMMOND, Thomas, 1797–1840

13 Property has its duties as well as its rights. *Letter to the Earl of Donoughmore, 22 May, 1838*

DRYDEN, John, 1631–1700

14 In pious times, e'r Priest-craft did begin,
Before Polygamy was made a Sin. *Absalom and Achitophel, Pt. 1, 1*

15 What e'r he did was done with so much ease,
In him alone, 'twas Natural to please. *Ib, 1, 27*

16 Of these the false Achitophel was first,
A Name to all succeeding Ages curst.
For close Designs and crooked Counsels fit,
Sagacious, Bold, and Turbulent of wit. *Ib, 1, 150*

17 A fiery Soul, which working out its way,
Fretted the Pigmy Body to decay:

And o'r informed the Tenement of Clay.
A daring Pilot in extremity;
Pleas'd with the Danger, when the Waves went high
He sought the Storms; but, for a Calm unfit,
Would Steer too nigh the Sands to boast his Wit.
Great Wits are sure to Madness near alli'd
And thin Partitions do their Bounds divide. *Absalom and Achitophel, 1, 156*

1 Bankrupt of Life, yet Prodigal of Ease. *Ib, 1, 168*

2 For Politicians neither love nor hate. *Ib, 1, 223*

3 But far more numerous was the Herd of such,
Who think too little, and who talk too much. *Ib, 1, 533*

4 A man so various, that he seem'd to be
Not one, but all Mankind's Epitome.
Stiff in Opinions, always in the wrong;
Was Everything by starts, and Nothing long:
But, in the course of one revolving Moon,
Was Chymist, Fidler, States-man, and Buffoon. *Ib, 1, 545*

5 So over Violent, or over Civil,
That every Man, with him, was God or Devil.
In squandring Wealth was his peculiar Art:
Nothing went unrewarded, but Desert. *Ib, 1, 557*

6 Did wisely from Expensive Sins refrain,
And never broke the Sabbath, but for Gain. *Ib, 1, 587*

7 During his Office, Treason was no Crime.
The Sons of Belial had a Glorious Time:
For Shimei, though not prodigal of pelf,
Yet lov'd his wicked Neighbour as himself. *Ib, 1, 597*

8 Nor is the Peoples Judgment always true:
The Most may err as grosly as the Few. *Ib, 1, 781*

9 Beware the Fury of a Patient Man. *Ib, 1, 1005*

10 The Midwife laid her hand on his Thick Skull,
With this Prophetick blessing—Be thou Dull. *Ib, Pt. 2, 476*

11 The lovely Thais by his side,
Sate like a blooming Eastern Bride. *Alexander's Feast, 9*

12 None but the Brave deserves the Fair. *Ib, 15*

13 Sound the Trumpets; beat the Drums. *Ib, 50*

14 Bacchus Blessings are a Treasure;
Drinking is the Soldiers Pleasure;
Rich the Treasure;
Sweet the Pleasure;
Sweet is Pleasure after Pain. *Ib, 56*

15 Let old Timotheus yield the Prize,
Or both divide the Crown:
He rais'd a Mortal to the Skies;
She drew an Angel down. *Ib, 167*

16 Errors, like Straws, upon the surface flow;
He who would search for Pearls must dive below. *All for Love, Prologue*

1 Men are but children of a larger growth. DOLABELLA *All for Love, Act 4, Scene 1*

2 Her Poverty was glad; her Heart content,
Nor knew she what the Spleen or Vapors meant.
The Cock and the Fox, 29

3 He [*Shakespeare*] was the man who of all modern, and perhaps ancient poets, had the largest and most comprehensive soul.
Essay of Dramatic Poesy

4 He was naturally learned; he needed not the spectacles of books to read nature; he looked inwards, and found her there. *Ib*

5 Here lies my wife: here let her lie!
Now she's at rest, and so am I. *Epitaph intended for Dryden's Wife*

6 For truth has such a face and such a meen
As to be lov'd needs only to be seen. *The Hind and the Panther, 1, 33*

7 Of all the Tyrannies on humane kind
The worst is that which Persecutes the mind.
Let us but weigh at what offence we strike,
'Tis but because we cannot think alike. *Ib, 1, 239*

8 And love's the noblest frailty of the mind. CORTEZ *The Indian Emperor, Act 2, Scene 2*

9 For all the happiness mankind can gain
Is not in pleasure, but in rest from pain. CORTEZ *Ib, Act 4, Scene 1*

10 All heiresses are beautiful. ALBANACT *King Arthur, Act 1, Scene 2*

11 Three Poets, in three distant Ages born,
Greece, Italy, and England did adorn.
The first in Loftiness of Thought surpass'd,
The next in Majesty, in both the last:
The Force of Nature could no farther go;
To make a third she join'd the former two. *Lines under Portrait of Milton*

12 Cousin Swift, you will never be a poet.
Quoted in Johnson's Lives of the Poets, Swift

13 All humane things are subject to decay,
And, when Fate summons, Monarchs must obey:
This Fleckno found, who, like Augustus, young
Was call'd to Empire and had govern'd long:
In Prose and Verse was own'd, without dispute
Through all the realms of Non-sense, absolute. *Mac Flecknoe, 1*

14 Shadwell alone my perfect image bears,
Mature in dullness from his tender years;
Shadwell alone of all my Sons is he
Who stands confirm'd in full stupidity.
The rest to some faint meaning make pretence,
But Shadwell never deviates into sense. *Ib, 15*

15 For I am young, a Novice in the Trade,
The Fool of Love, unpractis'd to persuade. *Palamon and Arcite, 3, 325*

16 Happy the Man, and happy he alone,
He who can call to-day his own:
He who, secure within, can say,
To-morrow do thy worst, for I have liv'd to-day.
Translation of Horace, 3, 65

1 Arms, and the man I sing, who, forced by fate,
And haughty Juno's unrelenting hate. *Translation of Virgil, Aeneid, I, 1*

DUFFIELD, George, 1818–1888

2 Stand up! Stand up for Jesus! *Hymn*

DUMAS, Alexandre, 1803–1870

3 *Tous pour un, un pour tous.* All for one, and one for all. *The Three Musketeers*

DUNBAR, William, 1460?–1520?

4 London, thou art the flower of Cities all! *In honour of the City of London*

5 *Timor mortis conturbat me.* *Lament for the Makaris*

DYER, Sir Edward, 1540–1607

6 My mind to me a kingdom is. *Title of poem*

DYER, John, 18th century

7 And he that will this health deny,
Down among the dead men let him lie! *Here's a Health to the King*

EDISON, Thomas Alva, 1847–1931

8 Genius is one per cent inspiration and ninety-nine per cent perspiration. *Newspaper interview*

EDWARD III of England, 1312–1377

9 Let the boy win his spurs. *Of the Black Prince at Crécy, 1345*

EDWARD VIII of Great Britain, 1894–1972

10 I have found it impossible to carry the heavy burden of responsibility and to discharge my duties as King as I would wish to do without the help and support of the woman I love. *Broadcast, 11 Dec. 1936*

EDWARDS, Oliver, 1711–1791

11 I have tried too in my time to be a philosopher; but, I don't know how, cheerfulness was always breaking in. *Boswell's Johnson, 17 April 1778*

EINSTEIN, Albert, 1879–1955

12 I never think of the future. It comes soon enough. *Interview, 1930*

ELIOT, George (Mary Ann Evans), 1819–1880

13 A prophetess? Yea, I say unto you, and more than a prophetess—a uncommon pretty young woman. *Adam Bede, Ch. 1.*

14 It's but little good you'll do a-watering the last year's crop. *Ib, Ch. 18*

15 The happiest women, like the happiest nations, have no history. *The Mill on the Floss, Bk. 6, Ch. 3*

16 Animals are such agreeable friends—they ask no questions, they pass no criticisms. *Scenes of Clerical Life, Mr. Gilfil's Love Story, Ch. 7*

ELIOT, Thomas Stearns, 1888–1965

1 Because I do not hope to turn again
Because I do not hope
Because I do not hope to turn. *Ash-Wednesday*

2 The readers of the Boston Evening Transcript
Sway in the wind like a field of ripe corn. *The Boston Evening Transcript*

3 Time present and time past
Are both perhaps present in time future,
And time future contained in time past. *Burnt Norton*

4 Human kind
Cannot bear very much reality. *Ib*

5 Here I am, an old man in a dry month,
Being read to by a boy, waiting for rain. *Gerontion*

6 Thoughts of a dry brain in a dry season. *Ib*

7 We are the hollow men
We are the stuffed men
Leaning together
Headpiece filled with straw. *The Hollow Men*

8 Between the idea
And the reality
Between the motion
And the act
Falls the Shadow. *Ib*

9 This is the way the world ends
Not with a bang but a whimper. *Ib*

10 Ash on an old man's sleeve
Is all the ash the burnt roses leave.
Dust in the air suspended
Marks the place where a story ended. *Little Gidding*

11 Let us go then, you and I,
When the evening is spread out against the sky
Like a patient etherised upon a table. *The Love Song of J. Alfred Prufrock*

12 In the room the women come and go
Talking of Michelangelo. *Ib*

13 The yellow fog that rubs its back upon the window panes. *Ib*

14 I have measured out my life with coffee spoons. *Ib*

15 I grow old . . . I grow old . . .
I shall wear the bottoms of my trousers rolled. *Ib*

16 Shall I part my hair behind? Do I dare to eat a peach?
I shall wear white flannel trousers, and walk upon the beach.
I have heard the mermaids singing, each to each. *Ib*

17 I do not think that they will sing to me. *Ib*

18 Macavity, Macavity, there's no one like Macavity.
Macavity: The Mystery Cat

19 The winter evening settles down
With smell of steaks in passageways. *Preludes, I*

1 And the wind shall say 'Here were decent godless people;
Their only monument the asphalt road
And a thousand lost golf balls.' *The Rock*

2 Birth, and copulation, and death.
That's all the facts when you come to brass tacks. *Sweeney Agonistes, Fragment of an Agon*

3 April is the cruellest month, breeding
Lilacs out of the dead land, mixing
Memory and desire, stirring
Dull roots with spring rain. *The Waste Land, The Burial of the Dead, 1*

4 I read, much of the night, and go south in the winter. *Ib, 18*

5 When lovely woman stoops to folly and
Paces about her room again, alone,
She smoothes her hair with automatic hand,
And puts a record on the gramophone. *Ib, The Fire Sermon, 253*

6 Webster was much possessed by death
And saw the skull beneath the skin. *Whispers of Immortality*

7 You've missed the point completely, Julia:
There were no tigers. That was the point. ALEX
The Cocktail Party, Act 1, Scene 1

8 You shouldn't interrupt my interruptions:
That's really worse than interrupting. JULIA *Ib, Act 3*

9 Yet we have gone on living,
Living and partly living. CHORUS *Murder in the Cathedral, Act 1*

10 The last temptation is the greatest treason:
To do the right deed for the wrong reason. THOMAS *Ib*

11 However certain our expectation
The moment foreseen may be unexpected
When it arrives. THOMAS *Ib, Act 2*

ELIZABETH I of England, 1533–1603

12 I will make you shorter by a head. *Chamberlin, Sayings of Queen Elizabeth*

13 I know I have the body of a weak and feeble woman, but I have the heart and stomach of a King, and of a King of England too. *Speech at Tilbury on the Approach of the Spanish Armada*

14 Though God hath raised me high, yet this I count the glory of my crown: that I have reigned with your loves. *The Golden Speech, 1601*

15 All my possessions for a moment of time. *Last words*

ELLERTON, John, 1826–1893

16 Now the labourer's task is o'er;
Now the battle day is past;
Now upon the farther shore
Lands the voyager at last. *Now the Labourer's Task*

17 The day thou gavest, Lord, is ended,
The darkness falls at thy behest. *The Day Thou Gavest*

ELLIOTT, Ebenezer, 1781–1849

18 What is a communist? One who has yearnings
For equal division of unequal earnings. *Epigram*

EMERSON, Ralph Waldo, 1803–1882

1 Art is a jealous mistress. *Conduct of Life, Wealth*

2 The louder he talked of his honour, the faster we counted our spoons. *Ib, Worship*

3 Nothing great was ever achieved without enthusiasm. *Essays, Circles*

4 A Friend may well be reckoned the masterpiece of Nature. *Ib, Friendship*

5 The only reward of virtue is virtue; the only way to have a friend is to be one. *Ib*

6 There is properly no history; only biography. *Ib, History*

7 All mankind love a lover. *Ib, Love*

8 The reward of a thing well done is to have done it. *Ib, New England Reformers*

9 Every man is wanted, and no man is wanted much. *Ib, Nominalist and Realist*

10 In skating over thin ice, our safety is in our speed. *Ib, Prudence*

11 Whoso would be a man must be a nonconformist. *Ib, Self-Reliance*

12 To be great is to be misunderstood. *Ib*

13 Nothing can bring you peace but yourself. *Ib*

14 Next to the originator of a good sentence is the first quoter of it. *Letters and Social Arms, Quotation and Originality*

15 By necessity, by proclivity, and by delight, we all quote. *Ib*

16 Every hero becomes a bore at last. *Representative Men, Uses of Great Men*

17 Never read any book that is not a year old. *Society and Solitude, Books*

18 Hitch your wagon to a star. *Ib, Civilization*

19 Poverty consists in feeling poor. *Ib, Domestic Life*

20 We boil at different degrees. *Ib, Eloquence*

21 America is a country of young men. *Ib, Old Age*

22 Can anybody remember when the times were not hard, and money not scarce? *Ib, Works and Days*

23 If a man write a better book, preach a better sermon, or make a better mouse-trap than his neighbour, though he build his house in the woods, the world will make a beaten path to his door. *Attributed*

EMPSON, William, 1906—

24 Seven Types of Ambiguity. *Title of book*

ESTIENNE, Henri, 1531–1598

25 *Si jeunesse savait; si vieillesse pouvait.* If only youth knew; if only age could. *Les Prémices*

EUCLID, c. 300 B.C.

26 *Quod erat demonstrandum.* Which was to be proved. *Translated from the Greek*

27 There is no royal road to geometry. *Said to Ptolemy I*

EUWER, Anthony Henderson, 1877—

1 As a beauty I'm not a great star,
There are others more handsome by far;
But my face—I don't mind it
Because I'm behind it;
It's the folks out in front that I jar. *Limerick*

EVELYN, John, 1620–1706

2 I saw Hamlet Prince of Denmark played, but now the old plays begin to disgust this refined age. *Diary, 26 Nov. 1661*

FARQUHAR, George, 1678–1707

3 There's no scandal like rags, nor any crime so shameful as poverty.
ARCHER *The Beaux Strategem, Act 1, Scene*

4 How a little love and good company improves a woman. MRS SULLEN
Ib, Act 4, Scene 1

5 Spare all I have, and take my life. SCRUB *Ib, Act 5, Scene 2*

FERDINAND I, Holy Roman Emperor, 1503–1568

6 *Fiat justitia, et pereat mundus.* Let justice be done, though the world perish.
Attributed

FIELDING, Henry, 1707–1754

7 When widows exclaim loudly against second marriage, I would always lay a wager that the man, if not the wedding-day, is absolutely fixed on.
Amelia, Bk. 6, Ch. 10

8 I am as sober as a Judge. *Don Quixote in England, 3, 14*

9 Oh! the roast beef of England,
And old England's roast beef. *The Grub Street Opera, 3, 3*

10 Public schools are the nurseries of all vice and immorality.
Joseph Andrews, Bk. 3, Ch. 5

11 Thwackum was for doing justice, and leaving mercy to heaven.
Tom Jones, Bk. 3, Ch. 10

FISHER, John Arbuthnot, 1st Baron, 1841–1920

12 Sack the lot! *Letter to The Times, 2 Sept. 1919*

FITZGERALD, Edward, 1809–1883

13 Awake! for Morning in the Bowl of Night
Has flung the Stone that puts the Stars to Flight:
And Lo! the Hunter of the East has caught
The Sultan's Turret in a Noose of Light. *Rubáiyát of Omar Khayyám*
(1st ed.) Verse 1

14 Come, fill the Cup, and in the Fire of Spring
The Winter Garment of Repentance fling:
The Bird of Time has but a little way
To fly—and Lo! the Bird is on the Wing. *Ib, 7*

15 Here with a Loaf of Bread beneath the Bough,
A Flask of Wine, a Book of Verse—and Thou
Beside me singing in the Wilderness—
And Wilderness is Paradise enow. *Ib, 11*

1 The Worldly Hope men set their Hearts upon
Turns Ashes—or it prospers; and anon,
Like snow upon the Desert's dusty Face
Lighting a little Hour or two—is gone. *Rubáiyát of Omar Khayyám, Verse 14*

2 Ah, my Belovéd, fill the Cup that clears
TO-DAY of past Regrets and future Fears:
To-morrow!—Why, To-morrow I may be
Myself with Yesterday's Sev'n Thousand Years. *Ib, 20*

3 Ah, make the most of what we yet may spend,
Before we too into the Dust descend;
Dust into Dust, and under Dust, to lie,
Sans Wine, sans Song, sans Singer, and—sans End! *Ib, 23*

4 One thing is certain, that Life flies;
One thing is certain, and the Rest is Lies;
The Flower that once has blown for ever dies. *Ib, 26*

5 I came like Water, and like Wind I go. *Ib, 28*

6 There was a Door to which I found no key:
There was a Veil past which I could not see. *Ib, 32*

7 Ah, fill the Cup:—what boots it to repeat
How Time is slipping underneath our Feet:
Unborn TO-MORROW, and dead YESTERDAY,
Why fret about them if TO-DAY be sweet! *Ib, 37*

8 Better be merry with the fruitful Grape
Than sadden after none, or bitter, Fruit. *Ib, 39*

9 You know, my Friends, how long since in my House
For a new Marriage I did make Carouse:
Divorced old barren Reason from my Bed,
And took the Daughter of the Vine to Spouse. *Ib, 40*

10 The Grape that can with Logic absolute
The Two-and-Seventy jarring Sects confute. *Ib, 43*

11 'Tis all a Chequer-board of Nights and Days
Where Destiny with Men for Pieces plays:
Hither and thither moves, and mates, and slays,
And one by one back in the Closet lays. *Ib, 49*

12 The Moving Finger writes; and, having writ,
Moves on: nor all thy Piety nor Wit
Shall lure it back to cancel half a Line,
Nor all thy Tears wash out a Word of it. *Ib, 51*

13 And that inverted Bowl we call The Sky,
Whereunder crawling coop't we live and die,
Lift not thy hands to *It* for help—for It
Rolls impotently on as Thou or I. *Ib, 52*

14 Who *is* the Potter, pray, and who the Pot? *Ib, 60*

15 Indeed the Idols I have loved so long
Have done my Credit in Men's Eye much wrong:
Have drown'd my Honour in a shallow Cup,
And sold my Reputation for a Song. *Ib, 69*

1 And when Thyself with shining Foot shall pass
Among the Guests Star-scattered on the Grass,
And in thy joyous Errand reach the Spot
Where I made one—turn down an empty Glass! *Rubáiyát of Omar Khayyám, Verse 75*

FLECKER, James Elroy, 1884–1915

2 For lust of knowing what should not be known,
We take the Golden Road to Samarkand. *Hassan, 5, 2*

3 I have seen old ships sail like swans asleep,
Beyond the village which men still call Tyre. *The Old Ships*

FLETCHER, John, see BEAUMONT, Francis

FLORIO, John, 1553?–1625

4 England is the paradise of women, the purgatory of men, and the hell of horses. *Second Fruits*

FOCH, Ferdinand, Marshal, 1851–1929

5 *Mon centre cède, ma droite recule, situation excellente. J'attaque.* My centre is giving way, my right is retreating. Situation excellent. I shall attack. *Message to Joffre, Sept. 1914*

FONTAINE, Jean de la, 1621–1695

6 *Elle alla crier famine*
Chez la fourmi sa voisine.
She went to cry famine at her neighbour's the ant's. *Fables, 1, 1, La Cigale et la Fourmi*

7 *Aide-toi, le ciel t'aidera.*
Help yourself and heaven will help you. *Ib, 6, 18, Le Chartier Embourbé*

FOOTE, Samuel, 1720–1777

8 He is not only dull in himself, but the cause of dullness in others. *Boswell's Life of Johnson*

FORD, Henry, 1863–1947

9 History is bunk. *In court, during libel action against Chicago Tribune, 1919*

FORD, John, 1586–1639?

10 He hath shook hands with time. BASSANES *The Broken Heart, Act 5, Scene 2*

11 'Tis Pity She's a Whore. *Title of Play*

FORD, Lena Guilbert, ?–1916?

12 Keep the home fires burning, while your hearts are yearning,
Though your lads are far away they dream of home;
There's a silver lining through the dark cloud shining,
Turn the dark cloud inside out, till the boys come home.
Keep the Home Fires Burning

FORGY, Howell Maurice, 1908—

13 Praise the Lord and pass the ammunition. *Said at Pearl Harbour, 7 Dec. 1941*

FORSTER, Edward Morgan, 1879–1970

1 It will be generally admitted that Beethoven's Fifth Symphony is the most sublime noise that has ever penetrated into the ear of man. *Howards End, Ch. 5*

2 Two Cheers for Democracy. *Title of Book*

FOSTER, Sir George Eulas, 1847–1931

3 In these somewhat troublesome days when the great Mother Empire stands splendidly isolated in Europe. *Speech, Canadian House of Commons, 16 Jan. 1896*

FOSTER, Stephen Collins, 1826–1864

4 Gwine to run all night!
Gwine to run all day!
I bet my money on de bob-tail nag,
Somebody bet on de bay. *Camptown Races*

5 I dream of Jeanie with the light brown hair.
Jeanie with the Light Brown Hair

6 Down in de cornfield
Hear dat mournful sound!
All de darkies am a weeping
Massa's in de cold, cold ground. *Massa's in de Cold, Cold Ground*

7 Weep no more, my lady,
Oh! weep no more to-day!
We will sing one song for the old Kentucky Home,
For the old Kentucky Home far away. *My Old Kentucky Home*

8 'Way down upon de Swanee Ribber. *Old Folks at Home*

9 All de world am sad and dreary,
Ev'ry-where I roam.
O darkies, how my heart grows weary,
Far from de old folks at home. *Ib*

10 Gone are the days when my heart was young and gay,
Gone are my friends from the cotton fields away,
Gone from the earth to a better land I know. *Poor old Joe*

11 I'm coming, I'm coming,
For my head is bending low,
I hear the gentle voices calling
'Poor old Joe.' *Ib*

12 Dere's no more hard work for poor old Ned,
He's gone whar de good niggers go. *Uncle Ned*

FRANKLIN, Benjamin, 1706–1790

13 Remember that time is money. *Advice to a Young Tradesman*

14 No nation was ever ruined by trade. *Essays, Thoughts on Commercial Subjects*

15 Be in general virtuous, and you will be happy. *Ib, On Early Marriages*

16 Here Skugg lies snug
As a bug in a rug. *Letter to Miss G. Shipley, 26 Sept. 1772*

1 We must indeed all hang together, or, most assuredly, we shall all hang separately. *Remark at signing of Declaration of Independence, 4 July 1776*

2 There never was a good war or a bad peace. *Letter to Josiah Quincy, 11 Sept. 1783*

3 Our Constitution is in actual operation; everything appears to promise that it will last; but in this world nothing is certain but death and taxes. *Letter to Jean-Baptiste Leroy, 13 Nov. 1789*

4 Man is a tool-making animal. *Boswell's Life of Johnson, 1778*

FREDERICK THE GREAT of Prussia, 1712–1786

5 You rogues, do you want to live for ever? *When the Guards hesitated at Kolin, 1757*

6 My people and I have come to an agreement which satisfies us both. They are to say what they please, and I am to do what I please. *Attributed*

FROHMAN, Charles, 1860–1915

7 Why fear death? It is the most beautiful adventure in life. *Last words before going down in the Lusitania*

FROST, Robert, 1875–1963

8 Earth's the right place for love:
I don't know where it's likely to go better. *Birches*

9 Most of the change we think we see in life
Is due to truths being in and out of favour. *The Black Cottage*

10 And nothing to look backward to with pride,
And nothing to look forward to with hope. *The Death of the Hired Man*

11 Home is the place where, when you have to go there,
They have to take you in. *Ib*

12 Some say the world will end in fire,
Some say in ice,
From what I've tasted of desire
I hold with those who favour fire. *Fire and Ice*

13 My apple trees will never get across
And eat the cones under his pines, I tell him.
He only says, 'Good fences make good neighbours.' *Mending Wall*

14 Something there is that doesn't love a wall,
That wants it down. *Ib*

15 Happiness makes up in Height for what it Lacks in Length. *Title of poem*

16 Like a piece of ice on a hot stove, a poem must ride on its own melting. A poem may be worked over once it is in being but may not be worried into being. *Preface, Collected Poems*

FRY, Christopher, 1907—

17 Why so shy, my pretty Thomasina?
Thomasin, O Thomasin,
Once you were so promising. 1ST GUARD, singing. *The Dark is Light Enough, Act 2*

1 I travel light; as light
That is, as a man can travel who will
Still carry his body around because
Of its sentimental value. THOMAS *The Lady's Not For Burning, Act 1*

2 What after all
Is a halo? It's only one more thing to keep clean. THOMAS *Ib*

3 What is official
Is incontestable. It undercuts
The problematical world and sells us life
At a discount. HUMPHREY *Ib*

4 Where in this small-talking world can I find
A longitude with no platitude? THOMAS *Ib, Act 3*

5 The best
Thing we can do is to make wherever we're lost in
Look as much like home as we can. NICHOLAS *Ib*

6 Try thinking of love, or something.
Amor vincit insomnia. PRIVATE PETER ABLE *A Sleep of Prisoners*

FULLER, Thomas, 1608–1661

7 There is a great difference between painting a face and not washing it. *Church History, Book 7*

8 A proverb is much matter decorated into few words. *The History of the Worthies of England, Ch. 2*

9 He knows little who will tell his wife all he knows. *The Holy State and the Profane State, The Good Husband*

10 Learning hath gained most by those books by which the printers have lost. *Ib, Of Books*

FYLEMAN, Rose, 1877–1957

11 There are fairies at the bottom of our garden. *Fairies*

GALBRAITH, John Kenneth, 1908—

12 The Affluent Society. *Title of book*

13 Wealth is not without its advantages and the case to the contrary, although it has often been made, has never proved widely persuasive. *The Affluent Society, Ch. 1*

GALILEO, 1564–1643

14 *Eppur si muove.* But it does move. *Attributed*

GARBO, Greta, 1905—

15 I want to be alone. *Attributed*

GARDNER, Augustus P., 1865–1918

16 Wake up, America. *Speech, 16 Oct. 1916*

GARRICK, David, 1717–1779

17 For physic and farces
His equal there scarce is;

His farces are physic,
His physic a farce is. *Epigram, Written soon after Dr Hill's farce called 'The Rout' was acted*

1 Come, cheer up, my lads, 'tis to glory we steer,
To add something more to this wonderful year;
To honour we call you, as free-men, not slaves,
For who are so free as the sons of the waves?
Heart of oak are our ships,
Jolly tars are our men.
We always are ready,
Steady, boys, steady;
We'll fight and we'll conquer again and again. *Heart of Oak*

2 Here lies Nolly Goldsmith, for shortness called Noll,
Who wrote like an angel, but talked like poor Poll. *Impromptu Epitaph on Goldsmith*

GAVARNI, Paul, 1801–1866

3 *Les enfants terribles.* The embarrassing young. *Title of series of prints*

GAY, John, 1685–1732

4 O ruddier than the cherry
O sweeter than the berry. *Acis and Galatea, 2*

5 Do you think your mother and I should have liv'd comfortably so long together, if ever we had been married? PEACHUM *The Beggar's Opera, Act 1, Scene 8*

6 MACHEATH: If with me you'd fondly stray
POLLY PEACHUM: Over the hills and far away. *Ib, Scene 13*

7 How happy could I be with either,
Were t'other dear charmer away! MACHEATH *Ib, Act 2, Scene 13*

8 She who has never loved has never lived. ASTARBE *The Captives, 2, 2*

9 Whence is thy learning? Hath thy toil
O'er books consumed the midnight oil? *Fables, Introduction*

10 Where yet was ever found a mother,
Who'd give her booby for another? *Ib, Part 1, No. 3*

11 Those who in quarrels interpose,
Must often wipe a bloody nose. *Ib, No. 34*

12 'Tis a gross error held in schools,
That fortune always favours fools. *Ib, Part 2, No. 12*

13 Life is a jest; and all things show it.
I thought so once; but now I know it. *My Own Epitaph*

GEORGE II of Great Britain, 1683–1760

14 Oh! he is mad, is he? Then I wish he would *bite* some other of my generals. *Of General Wolfe*

GEORGE V of Great Britain, 1865–1936

15 Wake up, England. *Title of reprinted speech*

16 How is the Empire? *Last Words*

GIBBON, Edward, 1737–1794

1 To the University of Oxford I acknowledge no obligation; and she will as willingly renounce me for a son, as I am willing to disclaim her for a mother. I spent fourteen months at Magdalen College; they proved the fourteen months the most idle and unprofitable of my whole life. *Autobiography*

2 Crowds without company, and dissipation without pleasure. [*London*] *Ib*

3 History, which is, indeed, little more than the register of the crimes, follies, and misfortunes of mankind. *Decline and Fall of the Roman Empire, Ch. 3*

4 All that is human must retrograde if it does not advance. *Ib, Ch. 71*

GIBBONS, Stella, 1902—

5 Something nasty in the woodshed. *Cold Comfort Farm*

GILBERT, Sir William Schwenk, 1836–1911

6 In enterprise of martial kind,
When there was any fighting,
He led his regiment from behind—
He found it less exciting. DUKE OF PLAZA-TORO *The Gondoliers, Act 1*

7 That celebrated,
Cultivated,
Underrated,
Nobleman,
The Duke of Plaza-Toro! DUKE OF PLAZA-TORO *Ib*

8 I stole the Prince, and I brought him here,
And left him gaily prattling
With a highly respectable gondolier. DON ALHAMBRA etc. *Ib*

9 Of that there is no manner of doubt—
No probable, possible shadow of doubt—
No possible doubt whatever. DON ALHAMBRA etc. *Ib*

10 A taste for drink, combined with gout,
Had doubled him up for ever. DON ALHAMBRA etc. *Ib*

11 When a merry maiden marries,
Sorrow goes and pleasure tarries. TESSA *Ib*

12 Rising early in the morning,
We proceed to light the fire,
Then our Majesty adorning
In its workaday attire,
We embark without delay
On the duties of the day. GIUSEPPE *Ib, Act 2*

13 But the privilege and pleasure
That we treasure beyond measure
Is to run on little errands for the Ministers of State. GIUSEPPE *Ib*

14 Take a pair of sparkling eyes. MARCO *Ib*

15 When every one is somebodee,
Then no one's anybody! DON ALHAMBRA *Ib*

16 Tripping hither, tripping thither,
Nobody knows why or whither. CHORUS OF FAIRIES *Iolanthe, Act 1*

1 Bow, bow, ye lower middle classes!
Bow, bow, ye tradesmen, bow, ye masses! CHORUS OF PEERS *Iolanthe, Act 1*

2 The Law is the true embodiment
Of everything that's excellent.
It has no kind of fault or flaw,
And I, my Lords, embody the Law. LORD CHANCELLOR *Ib*

3 A pleasant occupation for
A rather susceptible Chancellor! LORD CHANCELLOR *Ib*

4 When I went to the Bar as a very young man,
(Said I to myself—said I). LORD CHANCELLOR *Ib*

5 My learned profession I'll never disgrace
By taking a fee with a grin on my face,
When I haven't been there to attend to the case. LORD CHANCELLOR *Ib*

6 When all night long a chap remains
On sentry-go, to chase monotony
He exercises of his brains,
That is, assuming that he's got any. PRIVATE WILLIS *Ib, Act 2*

7 I am an intellectual chap,
And think of things that would astonish you. PRIVATE WILLIS *Ib*

8 I often think it's comical
How Nature always does contrive
That every boy and every gal
That's born into the world alive
Is either a little Liberal
Or else a little Conservative! PRIVATE WILLIS *Ib*

9 When in that House M.P.'s divide,
If they've a brain and cerebellum, too,
They've got to leave that brain outside,
And vote just as their leaders tell 'em to. PRIVATE WILLIS *Ib*

10 Yet Britain won her proudest bays
In good Queen Bess's glorious days! LORD MOUNTARARAT *Ib*

11 The House of Peers, throughout the war,
Did nothing in particular,
And did it very well. LORD MOUNTARARAT *Ib*

12 When you're lying awake with a dismal headache, and repose is taboo'd by anxiety,
I conceive you may use any language you choose to indulge in, without impropriety. LORD CHANCELLOR *Ib*

13 For you dream you are crossing the Channel, and tossing about in a steamer from Harwich—
Which is something between a large bathing machine and a very small second-class carriage. LORD CHANCELLOR *Ib*

14 Pooh-Bah (Lord High Everything Else) *The Mikado, Dramatis Personae*

15 If you want to know who we are,
We are gentlemen of Japan. CHORUS OF NOBLES *Ib, Act 1*

16 A wandering minstrel I—
A thing of shreds and patches,
Of ballads, songs and snatches,
And dreamy lullaby! NANKI-POO *Ib*

1 But if patriotic sentiment is wanted,
I've patriotic ballads cut and dried. NANKI-POO *The Mikado, Act 1*

2 I can trace my ancestry back to a protoplasmal primordial atomic globule.
POOH-BAH *Ib*

3 Taken from the county jail
By a set of curious chances. KO-KO *Ib*

4 As some day it may happen that a victim must be found,
I've got a little list—I've got a little list
Of society offenders who might well be underground,
And who never would be missed—who never would be missed!
There's the pestilential nuisances who write for autographs—
All people who have flabby hands and irritating laughs. KO-KO *Ib*

5 The idiot who praises, with enthusiastic tone,
All centuries but this, and every country but his own. KO-KO *Ib*

6 Three little maids from school are we,
Pert as a school-girl well can be,
Filled to the brim with girlish glee. YUM-YUM, PEEP-BO AND PITTI-SING
Ib

7 To sit in solemn silence in a dull, dark dock,
In a pestilential prison, with a life-long lock,
Awaiting the sensation of a short sharp shock,
From a cheap and chippy chopper on a big black block!
KO-KO, POOH-BAH AND PISH-TUSH *Ib*

8 Brightly dawns our wedding day;
Joyous hour, we give thee greeting! YUM-YUM, PITTI-SING, NANKI-POO
AND PISH-TUSH *Ib, Act 2*

9 Here's a how-de-do!
If I marry you,
When your time has come to perish,
Then the maiden whom you cherish
Must be slaughtered, too!
Here's a how-de-do! YUM-YUM *Ib*

10 My object all sublime
I shall achieve in time—
To let the punishment fit the crime—
The punishment fit the crime. MIKADO *Ib*

11 A source of innocent merriment! MIKADO *Ib*

12 On a cloth untrue,
With a twisted cue
And elliptical billiard balls! MIKADO *Ib*

13 I have a left shoulder-blade that is a miracle of loveliness. People come miles to see it. My right elbow has a fascination that few can resist.
KATISHA *Ib*

14 Something lingering, with boiling oil in it, I fancy. MIKADO *Ib*

15 The flowers that bloom in the spring,
Tra la,
Have nothing to do with the case.
I've got to take under my wing,
Tra la,

A most unattractive old thing,
Tra la,
With a caricature of a face. KO-KO *The Mikado, Act 2*

1 On a tree by a river a little tom-tit
Sang 'Willow, titwillow, titwillow!' KO-KO *Ib*

2 Twenty love-sick maidens we,
Love-sick all against our will. CHORUS *Patience, Act 1*

3 Now is not this ridiculous—and is not this preposterous?
A thorough-paced absurdity—explain it if you can.
CHORUS OF DRAGOONS *Ib*

4 If this young man expresses himself in terms too deep for *me*,
Why, what a very singularly deep young man this deep young man must be!
BUNTHORNE *Ib*

5 An attachment *à la* Plato for a bashful young potato, or a not-too-French
French bean! BUNTHORNE *Ib*

6 Prithee, pretty maiden, will you marry me?
(Hey, but I'm hopeful, willow willow waly!) GROSVENOR *Ib*

7 A greenery-yallery, Grosvenor Gallery,
Foot-in-the-grave young man! BUNTHORNE *Ib, Act 2*

8 We sail the ocean blue,
And our saucy ship's a beauty. CHORUS *H.M.S. Pinafore, Act 1*

9 For I'm called Little Buttercup—dear Little Buttercup,
Though I could never tell why,
But still I'm called Buttercup—poor Little Buttercup,
Sweet Little Buttercup I! LITTLE BUTTERCUP *Ib*

10 CAPTAIN CORCORAN: I am the Captain of the *Pinafore*;
ALL: And a right good captain, too! *Ib*

11 CAPTAIN: I'm never, never sick at sea!
ALL: What, never?
CAPTAIN: No, never!
ALL: What, *never*?
CAPTAIN: Hardly ever! *Ib*

12 Though 'Bother it' I may
Occasionally say,
I never use a big, big D. CAPTAIN CORCORAN *Ib*

13 Then give three cheers, and one cheer more,
For the well-bred Captain of the *Pinafore*! CREW *Ib*

14 And so do his sisters, and his cousins, and his aunts! CHORUS *Ib*

15 When I was a lad I served a term
As office boy to an Attorney's firm.
I cleaned the windows and I swept the floor,
And I polished up the handle of the big front door.
I polished up that handle so carefullee
That now I am the Ruler of the Queen's Navee! SIR JOSEPH PORTER
Ib

16 I grew so rich that I was sent
By a pocket borough into Parliament.
I always voted at my party's call,
And I never thought of thinking for myself at all.
I thought so little, they rewarded me
By making me the Ruler of the Queen's Navee! SIR JOSEPH PORTER *Ib*

1 Never mind the why and wherefore. CAPTAIN CORCORAN *H.M.S. Pinafore, Act 2*

2 For he himself has said it,
And it's greatly to his credit,
That he is an Englishman! BOATSWAIN *Ib*

3 For he might have been a Roosian,
A French, or Turk, or Proosian,
Or perhaps Itali-an! BOATSWAIN *Ib*

4 I am the very model of a modern Major-General,
I've information vegetable, animal, and mineral,
I know the kings of England, and I quote the fights historical,
From Marathon to Waterloo, in order categorical.
MAJOR-GENERAL STANLEY *The Pirates of Penzance, Act 1*

5 When the foeman bares his steel,
Tarantara! tarantara!
We uncomfortable feel. SERGEANT *Ib, Act 2*

6 When constabulary duty's to be done—
A policeman's lot is not a happy one. SERGEANT *Ib*

7 When the enterprising burglar's not a-burgling—
When the cut-throat isn't occupied in crime—
He loves to hear the little brook a-gurgling—
And listen to the merry village chime. SERGEANT *Ib*

8 Politics we bar,
They are not our bent;
On the whole we are
Not intelligent. ARAC *Princess Ida, Act 1*

9 We will hang you, never fear,
Most politely, most politely! HILDEBRAND *Ib*

10 Man's a ribald—Man's a rake,
Man is Nature's sole mistake! LADY PSYCHE *Ib, Act 2*

11 While Darwinian Man, though well-behaved,
At best is only a monkey shaved! LADY PSYCHE *Ib*

12 Hunger, I beg to state,
Is highly indelicate. LADY BLANCHE *Ib*

13 Oh, don't the days seem lank and long
When all goes right and nothing goes wrong,
And isn't your life extremely flat
With nothing whatever to grumble at! GAMA *Ib, Act 3*

14 Some word that teems with hidden meaning—like 'Basingstoke'.
MAD MARGARET *Ruddigore, Act 2*

15 She may very well pass for forty-three
In the dusk, with a light behind her! JUDGE *Trial by Jury*

16 The screw may twist and the rack may turn,
And men may bleed and men may burn. DAME CARRUTHERS
The Yeomen of the Guard, Act 1

17 Is life a boon?
If so, it must befall
That Death, whene'er he call,
Must call too soon. FAIRFAX *Ib*

1 POINT: I have a song to sing, O!
ELSIE: Sing me your song, O!
POINT: It is sung to the moon
By a love-lorn loon. *The Yeomen of the Guard, Act 1*

2 It's a song of a merryman, moping mum,
Whose soul was sad, and whose glance was glum,
Who sipped no sup, and who craved no crumb,
As he sighed for the love of a ladye. POINT *Ib*

3 For he who'd make his fellow-creatures wise
Should always gild the philosophic pill! POINT *Ib*

4 Were I thy bride,
Then all the world beside
Were not too wide
To hold my wealth of love—
Were I thy bride! PHOEBE *Ib*

5 Oh! a private buffoon is a light-hearted loon,
If you listen to popular rumour. POINT *Ib, Act 2*

6 It is purely a matter of skill,
Which all may attain if they will:
But every Jack,
He must study the knack
If he wants to make sure of his Jill! ELSIE, PHOEBE AND FAIRFAX *Ib*

GLADSTONE, William Ewart, 1809–1898

7 You cannot fight against the future. Time is on our side. *Speech on Reform Bill, 1866*

8 [*The Turks*] one and all, bag and baggage, shall, I hope, clear out from the province they have desolated and profaned. *Speech, House of Commons, 7 May 1877*

9 All the world over, I will back the masses against the classes. *Speech, Liverpool, 28 June 1886*

10 We are part of the community of Europe, and we must do our duty as such. *Speech, Carnarvon, 10 April 1888*

GLASSE, Hannah, 18th century

11 Take your hare when it is cased. *Art of Cookery (Often misquoted as 'First catch your hare' and wrongly attributed to Mrs. Beeton)*

GLENN, Colonel John Herschel, 1921—

12 It was hot in there. *Remark after return from orbit, 20 Feb. 1962*

GLOUCESTER, William Henry, Duke of, 1743–1805

13 Another damned, thick, square book! Always scribble, scribble, scribble! Eh! Mr. Gibbon? *Attributed*

GLOVER-KIND, John A., ?–1918

14 I do Like to be Beside the Seaside. *Title of Song*

GOERING, Hermann, 1893–1946

1 Guns will make us powerful; butter will only make us fat. *Broadcast, 1936*

GOETHE, Johann Wolfgang von, 1749–1832

2 *Ein unnütz Leben ist ein früher Tod.* A useless life is an early death. *Iphigenie, 1, 2*

3 *Mehr Licht!* More light! *Last words, attributed*

GOLDSMITH, Oliver, 1728?–1774

4 Sweet Auburn! loveliest village of the plain. *The Deserted Village, 1*

5 Ill fares the land, to hastening ills a prey,
Where wealth accumulates, and men decay. *Ib, 51*

6 A time there was, ere England's griefs began
When every rood of ground maintained its man. *Ib, 57*

7 How happy he who crowns in shades like these,
A youth of labour with an age of ease. *Ib, 99*

8 The watchdog's voice that bayed the whispering wind,
And the loud laugh that spoke the vacant mind. *Ib, 121*

9 A man he was to all the country dear,
And passing rich with forty pounds a year. *Ib, 141*

10 Truth from his lips prevailed with double sway,
And fools, who came to scoff, remained to pray. *Ib, 179*

11 The village master taught his little school;
A man severe he was, and stern to view;
I knew him well, and every truant knew;
Well had the boding tremblers learned to trace
The day's disasters in his morning face. *Ib, 196*

12 And still they gazed, and still the wonder grew,
That one small head could carry all he knew. *Ib, 215*

13 The chest contrived a double debt to pay,
A bed by night, a chest of drawers by day. *Ib, 229*

14 In all the silent manliness of grief. *Ib, 384*

15 Man wants but little here below,
Nor wants that little long. *Edwin and Angelina, 31*

16 The King himself has followed her,—
When she has walked before. *Elegy on Mrs. Mary Blaize, 19*

17 The doctors found, when she was dead,—
Her last disorder mortal. *Ib, 23*

18 Good people all, of every sort,
Give ear unto my song;
And if you find it wond'rous short,
It cannot hold you long. *Elegy on the Death of a Mad Dog, 1*

19 The dog, to gain some private ends,
Went mad and bit the man. *Ib, 19*

20 The man recovered of the bite,
The dog it was that died. *Ib, 31*

1 Here lies our good Edmund, whose genius was such,
We scarcely can praise it, or blame it too much;
Who, born for the Universe, narrowed his mind,
And to party gave up what was meant for mankind. [*Edmund Burke*]
Retaliation, 29

2 Too nice for a statesman, too proud for a wit:
For a patriot, too cool; for a drudge, disobedient;
And too fond of the *right* to pursue the *expedient*. [*Edmund Burke*] *Ib, 38*

3 Here lies David Garrick, describe me, who can,
An abridgement of all that was pleasant in man. *Ib, 93*

4 As a wit, if not first, in the very first line. [*Garrick*] *Ib, 96*

5 On the stage he was natural, simple, affecting;
'Twas only that when he was off he was acting. [*Garrick*] *Ib, 101*

6 I love everything that's old: old friends, old times, old manners, old books, old wine. HARDCASTLE *She Stoops to Conquer, Act 1, Scene 2*

7 It's a damned long, dark, boggy, dirty, dangerous way. TONY LUMPKIN
Ib, Act 1, Scene 2

8 This is Liberty Hall, gentlemen. HARDCASTLE *Ib, Act 2*

9 We are the boys
That fear no noise
Where the thundering cannons roar. TONY LUMPKIN *Ib*

10 Ask me no questions, and I'll tell you no fibs. TONY LUMPKIN
Ib, Act 3

11 Women and music should never be dated. MISS HARDCASTLE *Ib*

12 Remote, unfriended, melancholy, slow. *The Traveller, 1*

13 Where'er I roam, whatever realms to see,
My heart untravelled fondly turns to thee. *Ib, 7*

14 Such is the patriot's boast, where'er we roam,
His first, best country ever is, at home. *Ib, 73*

15 Where wealth and freedom reign, contentment fails,
And honour sinks where commerce long prevails. *Ib, 91*

16 Laws grind the poor, and rich men rule the law. *Ib, 386*

17 Still to ourselves in every place consigned,
Our own felicity we make or find. *Ib, 431*

18 A book may be amusing with numerous errors, or it may be very dull without a single absurdity. *The Vicar of Wakefield, Preface*

19 I was ever of opinion that the honest man who married and brought up a large family, did more service than he who continued single and only talked of population. *Ib, Ch. 1*

20 I . . . chose my wife, as she did her wedding gown, not for a fine glossy surface, but such qualities as would wear well. *Ib, Ch. 1*

21 Let us draw upon content for the deficiencies of fortune. *Ib, Ch. 3*

22 I find you want me to furnish you with argument and intellects, too.
Ib, Ch. 7

23 They would talk of nothing but high life, and high-lived company, with other fashionable topics, such as pictures, taste, Shakespeare, and the musical glasses. *Ib, Ch. 9*

1 When lovely woman stoops to folly,
And finds too late that men betray,
What charm can soothe her melancholy,
What art can wash her guilt away? *The Vicar of Wakefield, Song, Ch. 9*

2 There is no arguing with Johnson: for if his pistol misses fire, he knocks you down with the butt end of it. *1769, Boswell's Life of Johnson*

3 [*To Dr. Johnson*] If you were to make little fishes talk, they would talk like whales. *1773, Ib*

GOLDWYN, Samuel, 1882—1975

4 In two words: im - possible. *Quoted in Alva Johnson, The Great Goldwyn*

5 Include me out. *Attributed*

GORDON, Adam Lindsay, 1833–1870

6 Life is mostly froth and bubble,
Two things stand like stone,
Kindness in another's trouble,
Courage in your own. *Ye Wearie Wayfarer*

GOSCHEN, George Joachim, 1st Viscount, 1831–1907

7 We have stood alone in what is called isolation—our splendid isolation, as one of our Colonial friends was good enough to call it. *Speech, Lewes, 26 Feb. 1896 (see Sir George Foster)*

GRAHAM, Harry, 1874–1936

8 'There's been an accident,' they said,
'Your servant's cut in half; he's dead!'
'Indeed!' said Mr. Jones, 'and please,
Send me the half that's got my keys.' *Ruthless Rhymes, Mr. Jones*

9 I had written to Aunt Maud,
Who was on a trip abroad,
When I heard she'd died of cramp
Just too late to save the stamp. *Ib, Waste*

10 Billy, in one of his nice new sashes,
Fell in the fire and was burned to ashes;
Now, although the room grows chilly,
I haven't the heart to poke poor Billy. *Ib, Billy*

11 Weep not for little Leonie,
Abducted by a French *Marquis*!
Though loss of honour was a wrench,
Just think how it's improved her French. *Compensation*

GRAHAME, Kenneth, 1859–1932

12 There is nothing—absolutely nothing—half so much worth doing as simply messing about in boats. WATER RAT *The Wind in the Willows, Ch. 1*

13 The clever men at Oxford
Know all that there is to be knowed.
But they none of them know one half as much
As intelligent Mr. Toad. TOAD *Ib, Ch. 10*

GRANT, Ulysses Simpson, 1822–1885

1 No terms except an unconditional and immediate surrender can be accepted.
To General Buckner, 16 Feb. 1862

2 I know no method to secure the repeal of bad or obnoxious laws so effective as their stringent execution. *Inaugural Address, 4 Mar. 1869*

GRANVILLE, George, 1st Baron Lansdowne, 1667–1735

3 Of all the plagues with which the world is curst,
Of every ill, a woman is the worst. AMADIS *The British Enchanters, Act 2*

GRAVES, Alfred Perceval, 1846–1931

4 Of priests we can offer a charmin' variety,
Far renowned for larnin' and piety. *Father O'Flynn*

5 Checkin' the crazy ones, coaxin' unaisy ones,
Liftin' the lazy ones on wid the stick. *Ib*

GRAVES, John Woodcock, 1795–1886

6 D'ye ken John Peel with his coat so gay,
D'ye ken John Peel at the break of the day
D'ye ken John Peel when he's far, far away
With his hounds and his horn in the morning?

For the sound of his horn brought me from my bed,
And the cry of his hounds which he oft-times led;
Peel's view halloo would a-waken the dead,
Or a fox from his lair in the morning. *John Peel*

GRAVES, Robert, 1895—

7 Goodbye to All That. *Title of Book*

8 As you are woman, so be lovely:
As you are lovely, so be various,
Merciful as constant, constant as various,
So be mine, as I yours for ever. *Pygmalion to Galatea*

GRAY, Thomas, 1716–1771

9 'Twas on a lofty vase's side,
Where China's gayest art had dy'd
The azure flowers, that blow. *Ode on the Death of a Favourite Cat, 1*

10 What female heart can gold despise?
What Cat's averse to fish? *Ib, 23*

11 A Fav'rite has no friend! *Ib, 36*

12 Not all that tempts your wand'ring eyes
And heedless hearts, is lawful prize;
Nor all, that glisters, gold. *Ib, 40*

13 Where once my careless childhood stray'd,
A stranger yet to pain! *Ode on a Distant Prospect of Eton College, 13*

1 They hear a voice in every wind,
And snatch a fearful joy. *Ode on a Distant Prospect of Eton College, 39*

2 Where ignorance is bliss,
'Tis folly to be wise. *Ib, 99*

3 The Curfew tolls the knell of parting day,
The lowing herd winds slowly o'er the lea,
The plowman homeward plods his weary way,
And leaves the world to darkness and to me.
Elegy written in a Country Church-Yard, 1

4 Now fades the glimmering landscape on the sight,
And all the air a solemn stillness holds,
Save where the beetle wheels his droning flight,
And drowsy tinklings lull the distant folds. *Ib, 5*

5 Save that from yonder ivy-mantled tow'r
The moping owl does to the moon complain. *Ib, 9*

6 The rude Forefathers of the hamlet sleep. *Ib, 16*

7 Let not Ambition mock their useful toil,
Their homely joys, and destiny obscure;
Nor Grandeur hear with a disdainful smile,
The short and simple annals of the poor. *Ib, 29*

8 The boast of heraldry, the pomp of pow'r. *Ib, 33*

9 The paths of glory lead but to the grave. *Ib, 36*

10 Full many a gem of purest ray serene,
The dark unfathom'd caves of ocean bear:
Full many a flower is born to blush unseen,
And waste its sweetness on the desert air. *Ib, 53*

11 Some village-Hampden, that with dauntless breast
The little Tyrant of his fields withstood;
Some mute inglorious Milton here may rest,
Some Cromwell guiltless of his country's blood. *Ib, 57*

12 Far from the madding crowd's ignoble strife. *Ib, 73*

13 Here rests his head upon the lap of Earth
A Youth to Fortune and to Fame unknown.
Fair Science frown'd not on his humble birth,
And Melancholy mark'd him for her own. *Ib, The Epitaph, 117*

14 Large was his bounty, and his soul sincere,
Heav'n did a recompence as largely send:
He gave to Mis'ry all he had, a tear,
He gain'd from Heav'n ('twas all he wish'd) a friend. *Ib, 121*

15 No farther seek his merits to disclose,
Or draw his frailties from their dread abode,
(There they alike in trembling hope repose,)
The bosom of his Father and his God. *Ib, 125*

16 Daughter of Jove, relentless Power,
Thou Tamer of the human breast,
Whose iron scourge and tort'ring hour,
The Bad affright, afflict the Best! *Hymn to Adversity, 1*

1 Far from the sun and summer-gale,
In thy green lap was Nature's Darling laid. [*Shakespeare*]
The Progress of Poesy, 83

2 Yet shall he mount, and keep his distant way
Beyond the limits of a vulgar fate,
Beneath the Good how far—but far above the Great. [*Milton*] *Ib, 121*

3 Too poor for a bribe, and too proud to importune,
He had not the method of making a fortune. *Sketch of his own Character*

GREELEY, Horace, 1811–1872

4 Go West, young man, and grow up with the country. *Hints toward Reform*

GREENE, Robert, 1560?–1592

5 Weep not, my wanton, smile upon my knee;
When thou art old there's grief enough for thee. *Sephestia's Song*

6 For there is an upstart crow, beautified with our feathers, that with his tiger's heart wrapped in a player's hide, supposes he is as well able to bumbast out a blank verse as the best of you; and being an absolute *Iohannes fac totum* is in his own conceit the only shake-scene in a country. [*Reference probably to Shakespeare*] *A Groatsworth of Wit*

GREGORY 1, Pope, 540–604

7 *Non Angli, sed Angeli.* Not Angles, but angels. *Attributed (on seeing a group of English captives on sale at Rome)*

GREY OF FALLODON, Edward, 1st Viscount, 1862–1933

8 The lamps are going out all over Europe; we shall not see them lit again in our lifetime. *On the eve of war, 3 Aug. 1914*

GROSSMITH, George, 1847–1912, and GROSSMITH, Walter Weedon, 1854–1919

9 What's the good of a home, if you are never in it? *The Diary of a Nobody, Ch. 1*

GUINAN, Texas, 1884–1933

10 Fifty million Frenchmen can't be wrong. *Attributed*

HALE, Sarah Josepha, 1788–1879

11 Mary had a little lamb,
Its fleece was white as snow;
And everywhere that Mary went
The lamb was sure to go. *Mary's Little Lamb*

HALIFAX, George Savile, 1st Marquis of, 1633–1695

12 Men are not hanged for stealing horses, but that horses may not be stolen. *Political Thoughts and Reflections of Punishment*

HALL, Charles Sprague, 19th century

13 John Brown's body lies a mould'ring in the grave,
His soul is marching on! *John Brown's Body*

HAMMERSTEIN, Oscar, 1895–1960

1 The last time I saw Paris, her heart was young and gay,
I heard the laughter of her heart in every street café.
The Last Time I saw Paris

2 Ol' man river, dat ol' man river,
He must know sumpin', but don't say nothin',
He just keeps rollin', he keeps on rollin' along. *Ol' Man River*

HANDLEY, Thomas Reginald (Tommy), see KAVANAGH, Ted

HANFF, Minny Maud, c. 1900

3 Since then they called him Sunny Jim. *Advertisement for Force, a breakfast food*

HANKEY, Katherine, 1834–1911

4 Tell me the old, old story,
Of unseen things above. *Hymn*

HARCOURT, Sir William, 1827–1904

5 We are all Socialists now. *Speech*

HARDY, E. J., 1849–1910

6 How to be Happy though Married. *Title of book, 1910*

HARDY, Thomas, 1840–1928

7 My argument is that War makes rattling good history; but Peace is poor reading. *The Dynasts, Pt. 1*

8 A lover without indiscretion is no lover at all. *The Hand of Ethelberta, Ch. 20*

9 Good, but not religious-good. *Under the Greenwood Tree, Ch. 2*

10 This is the weather the cuckoo likes,
And so do I. *Weathers*

HARE, Maurice Evan, 1886—

11 There once was a man who said, 'Damn!
It is borne in upon me I am
An engine that moves
In determinate grooves,
I'm not even a bus but a tram.' *Limerick*

HARGREAVES, William, 1846–1919

12 I'm Burlington Bertie:
I rise at ten-thirty. *Burlington Bertie*

HARINGTON, Sir John, 1561–1612

13 Treason doth never prosper: what's the reason?
For if it prosper, none dare call it treason. *Epigrams, Of Treason*

HARRIS, Charles K., 1865–1930

1 Many a heart is aching, if you could read them all,
Many the hopes that have vanished, after the ball. *After the Ball*

HARTE, Francis Bret, 1836–1902

2 And on that grave where English oak and holly
And laurel wreaths entwine
Deem it not all a too presumptuous folly,—
This spray of Western pine! *Dickens in Camp*

3 He smiled a kind of sickly smile, and curled up on the floor,
And the subsequent proceedings interested him no more. *The Society upon the Stanislaus*

HAWKER, Robert Stephen, 1803–1875

4 And have they fixed the where and when?
And shall Trelawny die?
Here's twenty thousand Cornish men
Will know the reason why! *Song of the Western Men*

HAY, Ian (John Hay Beith), 1876–1952

5 Funny peculiar, or funny ha-ha? 'BUTTON' FARINGDON *Housemaster, Act 3*

HAYES, J. Milton, 1884–1940

6 There's a one-eyed yellow idol to the north of Khatmandu,
There's a little marble cross below the town,
There's a broken-hearted woman tends the grave of Mad Carew,
And the yellow god forever gazes down. *The Green Eye of the Yellow God*

HAZLITT, William, 1778–1830

7 His sayings are generally like women's letters; all the pith is in the postscript. [*Charles Lamb*] *Conversations of Northcote, Boswell Redivivus*

8 He [*Coleridge*] talked on for ever; and you wished him to talk on for ever. *Lectures on the English Poets, 8*

9 The English (it must be owned) are rather a foul-mouthed nation. *On Criticism*

10 No young man believes he shall ever die. *On the Feeling of Immortality in Youth, 1*

11 One of the pleasantest things in the world is going a journey; but I like to go by myself. *On Going a Journey*

12 There is not a more mean, stupid, dastardly, pitiful, selfish, spiteful, envious, ungrateful animal than the public. It is the greatest of cowards, for it is afraid of itself. *On Living to Oneself*

13 The art of pleasing consists in being pleased. *On Manner*

14 A nickname is the heaviest stone that the devil can throw at a man. *On Nicknames*

15 We never do anything well till we cease to think about the manner of doing it. *On Prejudice*

HEBER, Bishop Reginald, 1783–1826

1 From Greenland's icy mountains,
From India's coral strand,
Where Afric's sunny fountains,
Roll down their golden sand. *From Greenland's Icy Mountains*

2 Though every prospect pleases,
And only man is vile. *Ib*

3 Holy, Holy, Holy! all the Saints adore Thee. *Holy, Holy, Holy!*

HEMANS, Felicia Dorothea, 1793–1835

4 The boy stood on the burning deck,
Whence all but he had fled. *Casabianca*

5 The stately homes of England!
How beautiful they stand,
Amidst their tall ancestral trees,
O'er all the pleasant land. *The Homes of England*

HEMINGWAY, Ernest, 1898–1961

6 A Farewell to Arms. *Title of novel*

7 Bullfighting is the only art in which the artist is in danger of death and in which the degree of brilliance in the performance is left to the fighter's honour. *Death in the Afternoon, Ch. 9*

HENLEY, William Ernest, 1849–1903

8 Out of the night that covers me,
Black as the pit from pole to pole,
I thank whatever gods may be
For my unconquerable soul. *Invictus*

9 Under the bludgeonings of chance
My head is bloody, but unbowed. *Ib*

10 I am the master of my fate:
I am the captain of my soul. *Ib*

11 What have I done for you,
England, my England?
What is there I would not do,
England, my own? *Rhymes and Rhythms, 25, For England's Sake*

HENRI IV of France, 1553–1610

12 *Paris vaut bien une messe.* Paris is well worth a mass. *Attributed*

13 The wisest fool in Christendom. [*James I*] *Attributed*

HENRY II of England, 1133–1189

14 Will no one free me of this turbulent priest? [*Becket*] *Attributed*

HENRY, Matthew, 1662–1714

15 They that die by famine die by inches. *Commentaries, Psalms, 59, 15*

16 All this and heaven too. *Life of Philip Henry*

HENRY, O. (William Sydney Porter), 1862–1910

1 Life is made up of sobs, sniffles, and smiles, with sniffles predominating. *Gift of the Magi*

2 If men knew how women pass the time when they are alone, they'd never marry. *Memoirs of a Yellow Dog*

3 Turn up the lights; I don't want to go home in the dark. *Last words*

HENRY, Patrick, 1736–1799

4 I know not what course others may take; but as for me, give me liberty or give me death. *Speech in the Virginia Convention, 23 Mar. 1775*

HERBERT, Sir Alan Patrick, 1890–1971

5 Not huffy or stuffy, nor tiny or tall,
But fluffy, just fluffy, with no brains at all. *I Like them Fluffy*

6 This high official, all allow,
Is grossly overpaid,
There wasn't any board; and now
There isn't any trade. *On the President of the Board of Trade*

7 The Englishman never enjoys himself except for a noble purpose. *Uncommon Law*

8 Holy Deadlock. *Title of novel*

HERBERT, George, 1593–1633

9 Dare to be true: nothing can need a lie;
A fault, which needs it most, grows two thereby. *The Temple, The Church Porch*

10 Love bade me welcome; yet my soul drew back,
Guilty of dust and sin. *Ib, Love*

11 'You must sit down,' says Love, 'and taste My meat,'
So I did sit and eat. *Ib*

12 Sweet day, so cool, so calm, so bright,
The bridal of the earth and sky. *Ib, Virtue*

HERRICK, Robert, 1591–1674

13 Cherry ripe, ripe, ripe, I cry,
Full and fair ones; come and buy:
If so be, you ask me where
They do grow? I answer, there
Where my Julia's lips do smile;
There's the land, or cherry-isle. *Hesperides, Cherry Ripe*

14 A sweet disorder in the dress
Kindles in clothes a wantonness. *Ib, Delight in Disorder, 2*

15 A careless shoe-string, in whose tie
I see a wild civility:
Do more bewitch me, than when art
Is too precise in every part. *Ib*

1 Fair daffodils, we weep to see
You haste away so soon:
As yet the early-rising sun
Has not attain'd his noon. *Hesperides, To Daffodils*

2 I dare not ask a kiss;
I dare not beg a smile;
Lest having that, or this,
I might grow proud the while. *Ib, To Electra*

3 You say, to me-wards your affection's strong;
Pray love me little, so you love me long. *Ib, Love me little, love me long*

4 Night makes no difference 'twixt the Priest and Clerk;
Joan as my Lady is as good i' th' dark. *Ib, No difference i' th' dark*

5 Attempt the end, and never stand to doubt;
Nothing's so hard, but search will find it out. *Ib, Seek and find*

6 Whenas in silks my Julia goes,
Then, then (methinks) how sweetly flows
That liquefaction of her clothes. *Ib, Upon Julia's Clothes*

7 Gather ye rosebuds while ye may,
Old time is still a-flying:
And this same flower that smiles to-day
To-morrow will be dying. *Ib, To the Virgins, to make much of Time*

8 Then be not coy, but use your time;
And while ye may, go marry:
For having lost but once your prime,
You may for ever tarry. *Ib*

HEYWOOD, Thomas, 1574?–1641

9 Seven cities warred for Homer, being dead,
Who, living, had no roof to shroud his head.
Hierarchy of the Blessed Angels

10 A Woman Killed with Kindness. *Title of play*

HICKSON, William Edward, 1803–1870

11 If at first you don't succeed,
Try, try again. *Try and Try Again*

HILL, Rowland, 1744–1833

12 He did not see any good reasons why the devil should have all the good tunes. *E. W. Broome, Rev. Rowland Hill*

HIPPOCRATES, 460?–377? B.C.

13 *Ars longa, vita brevis.* Art is long, but life is short. *The Latin version of the Greek original*

HITLER, Adolf, 1889–1945

14 The Sudetenland is the last territorial claim I have to make in Europe.
Speech, 26 Sept. 1938

1 Germany will be either a world power or will not be at all. *Mein Kampf*

HOBBES, Thomas, 1588–1679

2 The condition of man . . . is a condition of war of everyone against everyone. *Leviathan, Pt. 1, Ch. 4*

3 No arts; no letters; no society; and which is worst of all, continual fear and danger of violent death; and the life of man, solitary, poor, nasty, brutish, and short. *Ib, Ch. 13*

4 I am about to take my last voyage, a great leap in the dark. *Last words*

HOCH, Edward Wallis, 1849–1925

5 There is so much good in the worst of us,
And so much bad in the best of us,
That it hardly becomes any of us
To talk about the rest of us. *Good and Bad*

HODGSON, Ralph, 1871–1962

6 Time, you old gypsy man,
Will you not stay,
Put up your caravan
Just for one day? *Time, you old Gypsy Man*

HOFFMANN, August Heinrich, von Fallersleben, 1798–1874

7 *Deutschland, Deutschland, über alles.* Germany, Germany above all. *Song*

HOFFMANN, Heinrich, 1809–1874

8 But one day, one cold winter's day,
He screamed out, 'Take the soup away!' *Struwwelpeter, Augustus*

9 Here is cruel Frederick, see!
A horrid wicked boy was he. *Ib, Cruel Frederick*

10 Look at little Johnny there,
Little Johnny Head-in-Air. *Ib, Johnny Head-In-Air*

11 Anything to me is sweeter
Than to see Shock-headed Peter. *Ib, Shock-headed Peter*

HOLMES, Oliver Wendell, 1809–1894

12 When the last reader reads no more. *The Last Reader*

13 And silence, like a poultice, comes
To heal the blows of sound. *The Music Grinders*

14 Wisdom has taught us to be calm and meek,
To take one blow, and turn the other cheek;
It is not written what a man shall do
If the rude caitiff smite the other too. *Non-Resistance*

1 Ay, tear her tattered ensign down!
Long has it waved on high,
And many an eye has danced to see
That banner in the sky. *Old Ironsides*

2 Man wants but little drink below,
But wants that little strong. *A Song of other Days*
(*Parody on Goldsmith, see 122:15*)

3 Man has his will,—but woman has her way.
The Autocrat of the Breakfast Table, Prologue

4 A thought is often original, though you have uttered it a hundred times.
Ib, Ch. 1

5 Build thee more stately mansions, O my soul,
As the swift seasons roll!
Leave thy low-vaulted past! *Ib, Ch. 4,*
The Chambered Nautilus

6 The world's great men have not commonly been great scholars, nor great scholars great men. *Ib, Ch. 6*

7 To be seventy years young is sometimes far more cheerful and hopeful than to be forty years old. *On the Seventieth Birthday of Julia Ward Howe*

HOMER, c. 900 B.C.

8 As the generation of leaves, so also is that of men. *Iliad, 6, 146*

9 Always to be best and distinguished above others. *Ib, 6, 208*

HOOD, Thomas, 1799–1845

10 One more Unfortunate,
Weary of breath,
Rashly importunate,
Gone to her death!

Take her up tenderly,
Lift her with care;
Fashion'd so slenderly,
Young, and so fair! *The Bridge of Sighs*

11 Ben Battle was a soldier bold,
And used to war's alarms;
But a cannon-ball took off his legs,
So he laid down his arms! *Faithless Nelly Gray*

12 For here I leave my second leg,
And the Forty-second Foot! *Ib*

13 His death, which happen'd in his berth,
At forty-odd befell:
They went and told the sexton, and
The sexton toll'd the bell. *Faithless Sally Brown*

14 I remember, I remember,
The house where I was born,
The little window where the sun
Came peeping in at morn. *I Remember, I Remember*

15 I remember, I remember,
The fir trees dark and high;

I used to think their slender tops
Were close against the sky. *I Remember, I Remember*

1 But evil is wrought by want of Thought,
As well as want of Heart! *The Lady's Dream*

2 When Eve upon the first of Men
The apple press'd with specious cant
Oh! what a thousand pities then
That Adam was not Adamant! *A Reflection*

3 With fingers weary and worn,
With eyelids heavy and red,
A woman sat, in unwomanly rags,
Plying her needle and thread—
Stitch! stitch! stitch!
In poverty, hunger, and dirt. *The Song of the Shirt*

4 Oh! God! that bread should be so dear,
And flesh and blood so cheap. *Ib*

HOOVER, Herbert Clark, 1874–1964

5 The American system of rugged individualism. *Speech, New York 22 Oct. 1928*

HOPKINS, Gerard Manley, 1844–1889

6 The world is charged with the grandeur of God. *God's Grandeur*

7 Glory be to God for dappled things—
For skies of couple-colour as a brinded cow;
For rose-moles all in stipple upon trout that swim. *Pied Beauty*

HORACE, Quintus Horatius Flaccus, 65–8 B.C.

8 *Brevis esse laboro,*
Obscurus fio.
I struggle to be brief, and become obscure. *Ars Poetica, 25*

9 *Grammatici certant et adhuc sub iudice lis est.*
Scholars dispute, and the case is still before the courts. *Ib, 78*

10 *Indignor, quandoque bonus dormitat Homerus.*
I think it shame when the worthy Homer nods. *Ib, 359*

11 *Si possis recte, si non, quocumque modo rem.*
By honest means, if you can, but by any means make money. *Epistles, 1, 1, 66*

12 *Pallida Mors aequo pulsat pede pauperum tabernas Regumque turris.*
Pale Death with impartial foot knocks at the doors of poor men's hovels and of King's palaces. *Odes 1, 4, 13*

13 *Carpe diem, quam minimum credula postero.*
Seize the present day, trusting the morrow as little as you can. *Ib, 1, 11, 8*

14 *Integer vitae scelerisque purus.*
The man of upright life unstained by guilt. *Ib, 1, 22, 1*

15 *Eheu fugaces, Postume, Postume,*
Labuntur anni.
Alas, Postumus, Postumus, the fleeting years are slipping by. *Ib, 2, 14, 1*

1 *Dulce et decorum est pro patria mori.*
It is a sweet and seemly thing to die for one's country. *Odes, 3, 2, 13*

HORNE, Kenneth, see MURDOCH, Richard

HOUSMAN, Alfred Edward, 1859–1936

2 The Grizzly Bear is huge and wild;
He has devoured the infant child.
The infant child is not aware
He has been eaten by the bear. *Infant Innocence*

3 We'll to the woods no more,
The laurels all are cut. *Last Poems*

4 And naked to the hangman's noose
The morning clocks will ring
A neck God made for other use
Than strangling in a string. *A Shropshire Lad, 9*

5 When I was one-and-twenty
I heard a wise man say,
'Give crowns and pounds and guineas
But not your heart away.' *Ib, 13*

6 Here of a Sunday morning
My love and I would lie,
And see the coloured counties,
And hear the larks so high
About us in the sky. *Ib, 21*

7 From far, from eve and morning
And yon twelve-winded sky,
The stuff of life to knit me
Blew hither: here am I. *Ib, 32*

8 With rue my heart is laden
For golden friends I had,
For many a rose-lipt maiden
And many a lightfoot lad. *Ib, 54*

9 Malt does more than Milton can
To justify God's ways to man. *Ib, 62*

HOWITT, Mary, 1799–1888

10 'Will you walk into my parlour?' said a spider to a fly;
''Tis the prettiest little parlour that ever you did spy.'
The Spider and the Fly

HOYLE, Edmond, 1672–1769

11 When in doubt, win the trick. *Hoyle's Games, Whist, Twenty-four Short Rules for Learners*

HUBBARD, Elbert, 1856–1915

12 Life is just one damned thing after another. *A Thousand and One Epigrams*

HUGHES, Thomas, 1822–1896

13 Life isn't all beer and skittles. *Tom Brown's Schooldays, Pt. 1, Ch. 2*

HUME, David, 1711–1776

1 Avarice, the spur of industry. *Essays, Of Civil Liberty*

2 Custom, then, is the great guide of human life. *Inquiry Concerning Human Understanding, 5, 1*

HUNGERFORD, Margaret, 1855?–1897

3 Beauty is altogether in the eye of the beholder. *Molly Bawn*

HUNT, George William, 1825–1904

4 We don't want to fight, but by jingo if we do,
We've got the ships, we've got the men, we've got the money too.
Music-Hall Song, 1878

HUNT, James Henry Leigh, 1784–1859

5 Abou Ben Adhem (may his tribe increase!)
Awoke one night from a deep dream of peace. *Abou Ben Adhem and the Angel*

6 Write me as one that loves his fellow-men. *Ib*

7 Jenny kissed me when we met,
Jumping from the chair she sat in. *Rondeau*

HUXLEY, Aldous Leonard, 1894–1963

8 The time of our Ford. *Brave New World, Ch. 3*

9 Ending is better than mending. *Ib*

10 The Ideal man is the non-attached man. *Ends and Means, Ch. 1*

11 I can sympathise with people's pains, but not with their pleasures. There is something curiously boring about somebody else's happiness. *Limbo, Cynthia*

12 There are not enough *bons mots* in existence to provide any industrious conversationalist with a new stock for every social occasion. *Point Counter Point, Ch. 7*

13 A bad book is as much a labour to write as a good one; it comes as sincerely from the author's soul. *Ib, Ch. 13*

14 A million million spermatozoa,
All of them alive:
Out of their cataclysm but one poor Noah
Dare hope to survive,
And among that billion minus one
Might have chanced to be
Shakespeare, another Newton, a new Donne—
But the One was Me. *The Fifth Philosopher's Song*

15 But when the wearied Band
Swoons to a waltz, I take her hand,
And there we sit in peaceful calm,
Quietly sweating palm to palm. *Frascati's*

HUXLEY, Thomas Henry, 1825–1895

1 It is the customary fate of new truths to begin as heresies and to end as superstitions. *The Coming of Age of the Origin of Species*

IBSEN, Henrik, 1828–1906

2 In that moment it burst upon me that I had been living here these eight years with a strange man, and had borne him three children. NORA HELMER *A Doll's House, Act 3*

3 The majority never has right on its side. Never I say! That is one of the social lies that a free, thinking man is bound to rebel against. Who makes up the majority in any given country? Is it the wise men or the fools? I think we must agree that the fools are in a terrible, overwhelming majority, all the wide world over. DR STOCKMANN *An Enemy of the People, Act 4*

4 A man should never put on his best trousers when he goes out to battle for freedom and truth. DR STOCKMANN *Ib, Act 5*

5 Mother, give me the sun. OSWALD ALVING *Ghosts, Act 3*

6 What's a man's first duty? The answer's brief: To be himself. PEER GYNT *Peer Gynt, Act 4, Scene 1*

INGE, William Ralph, 1860–1954

7 Literature flourishes best when it is half a trade and half an art. *The Victorian Age*

8 The nations which have put mankind and posterity most in their debt have been small states—Israel, Athens, Florence, Elizabethan England. *Marchant, Wit and Wisdom of Dean Inge*

INGERSOLL, Robert Green, 1833–1899

9 An honest God is the noblest work of man. *Gods, Part 1 (see also 203:8)*

IRVING, Washington, 1783–1859

10 Whenever a man's friends begin to compliment him about looking young, he may be sure that they think he is growing old. *Bracebridge Hall, Bachelors*

11 A woman's whole history is a history of the affections. *The Sketch Book, The Broken Heart*

12 A sharp tongue is the only edged tool that grows keener with constant use. *Ib, Rip Van Winkle*

13 The almighty dollar, that great object of universal devotion throughout our land, seems to have no genuine devotees in these peculiar villages. *Wolfert's Roost, The Creole Village*

JAMES I of England, 1566–1625

14 A custom loathsome to the eye, hateful to the nose, harmful to the brain, dangerous to the lungs, and in the black, stinking fume thereof nearest resembling the horrible Stygian smoke of the pit that is bottomless. *A Counterblast to Tobacco*

15 Dr. Donne's verses are like the peace of God: they pass all understanding. *Attributed*

1 No bishop, no King. *Attributed*

JAMES, Henry, 1843–1916

2 The deep well of unconscious cerebration. *The American, Preface*

3 The only obligation to which in advance we may hold a novel without incurring the accusation of being arbitrary, is that it be interesting. *The Art of Fiction, Partial Portraits*

4 It takes a great deal of history to produce a little literature. *Life of Nathaniel Hawthorne, Ch. 1*

5 He [*Thoreau*] was unperfect, unfinished, inartistic; he was worse than provincial—he was parochial. *Ib, Ch. 4*

JEFFERSON, Thomas, 1743–1826

6 We hold these truths to be self-evident: that all men are created equal; that they are endowed by their Creator with certain unalienable rights; that among these are life, liberty, and the pursuit of happiness. *Declaration of American Independence, 4 July 1776*

7 We mutually pledge to each other our lives, our fortunes, and our sacred honour. *Ib*

8 Error of opinion may be tolerated when reason is left free to combat it. *First Inaugural Address, 4 Mar. 1801*

9 Peace, commerce, and honest friendship with all nations, entangling alliances with none. *Ib*

10 The care of human life and happiness, and not their destruction, is the first and only legitimate object of good government. *To the Republican citizens of Washington County, Maryland, 1809*

11 Resistance to tyrants is obedience to God. *Epigrams*

12 Ignorance is preferable to error; and he is less remote from the truth who believes nothing, than he who believes what is wrong. *Notes on the state of Virginia*

13 I tremble for my country when I reflect that God is just. *Ib*

JEROME, Jerome Klapka, 1859–1927

14 Love is like the measles; we all have to go through with it. *Idle Thoughts of an Idle Fellow, On Being in Love*

15 It always does seem to me that I am doing more work than I should do. It is not that I object to the work, mind you; I like work; it fascinates me. I can sit and look at it for hours. I love to keep it by me; the idea of getting rid of it nearly breaks my heart. *Three Men in a Boat, Ch. 15*

16 The Passing of the Third Floor Back. *Title of Play*

JERROLD, Douglas William, 1803–1857

17 Religion's in the heart, not in the knees. *The Devil's Ducat, 1*

18 The best thing I know between France and England is the sea. *Wit and opinions of Douglas Jerrold*

JOAD, Cyril Edwin Mitchinson, 1891–1953

19 It all depends what you mean by . . . *B.B.C. Brains Trust, 1942 to 1948*

JOHNSON, Samuel, 1709–1784

1 When I took the first survey of my undertaking, I found our speech copious without order, and energetic without rules. *Dictionary of the English Language, Preface*

2 I am not yet so lost in lexicography, as to forget that words are the daughters of earth, and that things are the sons of heaven. *Ib*

3 Every quotation contributes something to the stability or enlargement of the language. *Ib*

4 I have protracted my work till most of those whom I wished to please have sunk into the grave, and success and miscarriage are empty sounds; I therefore dismiss it with frigid tranquillity, having little to fear or hope from censure or from praise. *Ib*

5 *Cricket.*—A sport, at which the contenders drive a ball with sticks in opposition to each other. *Ib, Definitions*

6 *Grubstreet.*—Originally the name of a street near Moorfields in London much inhabited by writers of small histories, dictionaries, and temporary poems. *Ib*

7 *Lexicographer.*—A harmless drudge. *Ib*

8 *Network.*—Any thing reticulated or decussated, at equal distances, with interstices between the intersections. *Ib*

9 *Oats.*—A grain, which in England is generally given to horses, but in Scotland supports the people. *Ib*

10 *Patron.*—Commonly a wretch who supports with insolence, and is paid with flattery. *Ib*

11 *Pension.*—An allowance made to any one without an equivalent. In England it is generally understood to mean pay given to a state hireling for treason to his country. *Ib*

12 When two Englishmen meet, their first talk is of the weather. *The Idler, 11*

13 Condemned to hope's delusive mine. *On the Death of Mr. Levet*

14 Officious, innocent, sincere,
Of every friendless name the friend. *Ib*

15 Of all the griefs that harass the distressed,
Sure the most bitter is a scornful jest. *London*

16 This mournful truth is ev'rywhere confessed
Slow rises worth, by poverty depressed. *Ib*

17 If the man who turnips cries,
Cry not when his father dies,
'Tis a proof that he had rather
Have a turnip than his father. *Burlesque of lines by Lope De Vega*

18 Long expected, one-and-twenty,
Lingering year, at length is flown. *One-and-twenty*

19 When learning's triumph o'er her barb'rous foes
First rear'd the stage, immortal Shakspear rose;
Each change of many-colour'd life he drew,
Exhausted worlds, and then imagin'd new:
Existence saw him spurn her bounded reign,
And panting time toil'd after him in vain. *Prologue at the Opening of the Theatre in Drury Lane, 1747*

1 For we that live to please, must please to live. *Prologue at the Opening of the Theatre in Drury Lane, 1747*

2 No place affords a more striking conviction of the vanity of human hopes, than a public library. *The Rambler, 23 March 1751*

3 Ye who listen with credulity to the whispers of fancy, and pursue with eagerness the phantoms of hope; who expect that age will perform the promises of youth, and that the deficiencies of the present day will be supplied by the morrow; attend to the history of Rasselas, prince of Abyssinia. *Rasselas, Ch. 1*

4 Some desire is necessary to keep life in motion, and he whose real wants are supplied, must admit those of fancy. *Ib, Ch. 8*

5 The business of a poet, said Imlac, is to examine, not the individual, but the species; to remark general properties and large appearances: he does not number the streaks of the tulip, or describe the different shades in the verdure of the forest. *Ib, Ch. 10*

6 Human life is every where a state in which much is to be endured, and little to be enjoyed. *Ib, Ch. 11*

7 The life of a solitary man will be certainly miserable, but not certainly devout. *Ib, Ch. 21*

8 To live without feeling or exciting sympathy, to be fortunate without adding to the felicity of others, or afflicted without tasting the balm of pity, is a state more gloomy than solitude: it is not retreat but exclusion from mankind. Marriage has many pains, but celibacy has no pleasures. *Ib, Ch. 26*

9 Let observation with extensive view,
Survey mankind from China to Peru;
Remark each anxious toil, each eager strife,
And watch the busy scenes of crowded life. *The Vanity of Human Wishes*

10 There mark what ills the scholar's life assail,
Toil, envy, want, the patron, and the jail. *Ib*

11 He left the name, at which the world grew pale,
To point a moral, or adorn a tale. *Ib*

12 Hides from himself his state, and shuns to know
That life protracted is protracted woe. *Ib*

13 Still raise for good the supplicating voice,
But leave to Heaven the measure and the choice. *Ib*

14 JOHNSON: I had no notion that I was wrong or irreverent to my tutor.
BOSWELL: That, Sir, was great fortitude of mind.
JOHNSON: No, Sir, stark insensibility. *Boswell's Life of Johnson, 1728*

15 If you call a dog Hervey, I shall love him. *Ib, 1737*

16 When asked how he felt upon the ill success of his tragedy [*Irene*], he replied, 'Like the Monument'. *Ib, 1750*

17 Johnson scolded him [*Langton*] for 'leaving his social friends to go and sit with a set of wretched un-idea'd girls'. *Ib, 1752*

18 This man [*Lord Chesterfield*] I thought had been a Lord among wits; but, I find, he is only a wit among Lords! *Ib, 1754*

19 They teach the morals of a whore, and the manners of a dancing-master. [*Lord Chesterfield's Letters*] *Ib*

1 Is not a Patron, my Lord, one who looks with unconcern on a man struggling for life in the water, and, when he has reached ground, encumbers him with help? The notice which you have been pleased to take of my labours, had it been early, had been kind; but it has been delayed till I am indifferent, and cannot enjoy it; till I am solitary, and cannot impart it; till I am known, and do not want it. *Boswell's Life of Johnson, Letter to Lord Chesterfield, 7 Feb. 1755*

2 When the messenger who carried the last sheet [*of Johnson's Dictionary*] to Millar returned, Johnson asked him, 'Well, what did he say?'—'Sir, (answered the messenger) he said, thank God I have done with him.' 'I am glad (replied Johnson, with a smile,) that he thanks God for any thing.' *Ib, 1755*

3 I respect Millar, Sir; he has raised the price of literature. *Ib*

4 Ignorance, Madam, pure ignorance. [*When asked why, in his Dictionary, he defined 'Pastern' as the 'knee of a horse'*] *Ib*

5 If a man does not make new acquaintances as he advances through life, he will soon find himself left alone. A man, Sir, should keep his friendship in constant repair. *Ib*

6 BOSWELL: I do indeed come from Scotland, but I cannot help it . . .
JOHNSON: That, Sir, I find, is what a very great many of your countrymen cannot help. *Ib, 1763*

7 The morality of an action depends on the motive from which we act. If I fling half a crown to a beggar with intention to break his head, and he picks it up and buys victuals with it, the physical effect is good; but, with respect to me, the action is very wrong. *Ib*

8 The noblest prospect which a Scotchman ever sees, is the high road that leads him to England. *Ib*

9 A man ought to read just as inclination leads him; for what he reads as a task will do him little good. *Ib*

10 In civilized society, personal merit will not serve you so much as money will. Sir, you may make the experiment. Go into the street, and give one man a lecture on morality, and another a shilling, and see which will respect you most. *Ib*

11 It is a sad reflection but a true one, that I knew almost as much at eighteen as I do now. *Ib*

12 Your levellers wish to level down as far as themselves; but they cannot bear levelling up to themselves. They would all have some people under them; why not then have some people above them? *Ib*

13 A woman's preaching is like a dog's walking on his hind legs. It is not done well; but you are surprised to find it done at all. *Ib*

14 I mind my belly very studiously, and very carefully; for I look upon it, that he who does not mind his belly, will hardly mind any thing else. *Ib*

15 This was a good dinner enough, to be sure; but it was not a dinner to ask a man to. *Ib*

16 A very unclubbable man. [*Sir John Hawkins*] *Ib, 1764*

17 The longer we live, and the more we think, the higher value we learn to put on the friendship and tenderness of parents and of friends. Parents we can have but once; and he promises himself too much, who enters life with the expectation of finding many friends. *Ib, 1766*

1 I cannot see that lectures can do so much good as reading the books from which the lectures are taken. *Boswell's Life of Johnson, 1766*

2 So far is it from being true that men are naturally equal, that no two people can be half an hour together, but one shall acquire an evident superiority over the other. *Ib*

3 JOHNSON: Well, we had good talk.
BOSWELL: Yes, Sir, you tossed and gored several persons. *Ib, 1768*

4 It matters not how a man dies, but how he lives. *Ib, 1769*

5 Now that you are going to marry, do not expect more from life, than life will afford. *Ib*

6 A gentleman who had been very unhappy in marriage, married immediately after his wife died: Johnson said, it was the triumph of hope over experience. *Ib, 1770*

7 I would not give half a guinea to live under one form of Government rather than another. It is of no moment to the happiness of an individual. *Ib, 1772*

8 The mass of every people must be barbarous where there is no printing. *Ib*

9 Much may be made of a Scotchman, if he be caught young. *Ib*

10 People seldom read a book which is given to them; and few are given. The way to spread a work is to sell it at a low price. No man will send to buy a thing that costs even sixpence, without an intention to read it. *Ib, 1773*

11 The Irish are not in a conspiracy to cheat the world by false representations of the merits of their countrymen. No, Sir; the Irish are a fair people;—they never speak well of one another. *Ib, 1775*

12 They [*the Americans*] are a race of convicts, and ought to be thankful for any thing we allow them short of hanging. *Ib*

13 There are few ways in which a man can be more innocently employed than in getting money. *Ib*

14 Fleet-street has a very animated appearance; but I think the full tide of human existence is at Charing-Cross. *Ib*

15 There may be other reasons for a man's not speaking in publick than want of resolution: he may have nothing to say. *Ib*

16 The greatest part of a writer's time is spent in reading, in order to write; a man will turn over half a library to make one book. *Ib*

17 Patriotism is the last refuge of a scoundrel. *Ib*

18 Being pressed upon this subject, and asked if he really was of opinion, that though, in general, happiness was very rare in human life, a man was not sometimes happy in the moment that was present, he answered, 'Never, but when he is drunk.' *Ib*

19 Knowledge is of two kinds. We know a subject ourselves, or we know where we can find information upon it. *Ib*

20 There is now less flogging in our great schools than formerly, but then less is learned there; so that what the boys get at one end they lose at the other. *Ib*

21 A ship is worse than a gaol. There is, in a gaol, better air, better company, better conveniency of every kind; and a ship has the additional disadvantage of being in danger. When men come to like a sea-life, they are not fit to live on land. *Ib, 1776*

1 There is no private house, (said he) in which people can enjoy themselves so well, as at a capital tavern. *Boswell's Life of Johnson, 1776*

2 Marriage is the best state for a man in general; and every man is a worse man, in proportion as he is unfit for the married state. *Ib*

3 It is commonly a weak man, who marries for love. *Ib*

4 Melancholy, indeed, should be diverted by every means but drinking. *Ib*

5 No man but a blockhead ever wrote, except for money. *Ib*

6 A man who has not been in Italy, is always conscious of an inferiority. *Ib*

7 If I had no duties, and no reference to futurity, I would spend my life in driving briskly in a post-chaise with a pretty woman. *Ib, 1777*

8 Depend upon it, Sir, when a man knows he is to be hanged in a fortnight, it concentrates his mind wonderfully. *Ib*

9 You find no man, at all intellectual, who is willing to leave London. No, Sir, when a man is tired of London, he is tired of life; for there is in London all that life can afford. *Ib*

10 I am willing to love all mankind, except an American. *Ib, 1778*

11 It is better to live rich than to die rich. *Ib*

12 I have always said, the first Whig was the Devil. *Ib*

13 Wine gives great pleasure; and every pleasure is of itself a good. It is a good, unless counterbalanced by evil. *Ib*

14 What I gained by being in France was, learning to be better satisfied with my own country. *Ib*

15 Claret is the liquor for boys; port for men; but he who aspires to be a hero must drink brandy. *Ib, 1779*

16 BOSWELL: Is not the Giant's-Causeway worth seeing?
JOHNSON: Worth seeing? Yes; but not worth going to see. *Ib*

17 Sir, I have two very cogent reasons for not printing any list of subscribers;—one, that I have lost all the names,—the other, that I have spent all the money. *Ib, 1781*

18 Clear your mind of cant. You may talk as other people do: you may say to a man, 'Sir, I am your most humble servant.' You are *not* his most humble servant. *Ib, 1783*

19 Let your imports be more than your exports, and you'll never go far wrong. *Ib*

20 No man is a hypocrite in his pleasures. *Ib, 1784*

21 I look upon every day to be lost, in which I do not make a new acquaintance. *Ib*

22 *Nullum quod tetigit non ornavit*—He touched nothing that he did not adorn. *Epitaph on Goldsmith*

23 There is no tracing the connection of ancient nations, but by language; and therefore I am always sorry when any language is lost, because languages are the pedigree of nations. *Boswell's Journal of a Tour to the Hebrides*

24 Difficult do you call it, Sir? I wish it were impossible. [*Of a violinist's performance*] *Anecdotes by William Seward*

25 What is written without effort is in general read without pleasure. *Ib*

26 The great source of pleasure is variety. *Lives of the English Poets, Butler*

1 But what are the hopes of man! I am disappointed by that stroke of death, which has eclipsed the gaiety of nations and impoverished the public stock of harmless pleasure. [*Garrick's death*] *Lives of the English Poets, Edmund Smith*

2 I have heard him assert, that a tavern chair was the throne of human felicity. *Hawkin's Life of Johnson*

3 A man is in general better pleased when he has a good dinner upon his table, than when his wife talks Greek. *Johnsonian Miscellanies*

4 You could not stand five minutes with that man [*Edmund Burke*] beneath a shed, while it rained, but you must be convinced you had been standing with the greatest man you had ever yet seen. *Attributed by Mrs Piozzi*

JONSON, Ben, 1573–1637

5 Our scene is London, 'cause we would make known,
No country's mirth is better than our own. *The Alchemist, Prologue*

6 Zeal-of-the-Land Busy. *Bartholomew Fair, name of character*

7 Drink to me only with thine eyes
And I will pledge with mine;
Or leave a kiss but in the cup
And I'll not look for wine. *To Celia*

8 Queen and Huntress, chaste and fair,
Now the sun is laid to sleep,
Seated in thy silver chair,
State in wonted manner keep:
Hesperus entreats thy light,
Goddess, excellently bright. HESPERUS *Cynthia's Revels, Act 5, Scene 3*

9 Still to be neat, still to be drest,
As you were going to a feast. SONG *Epicoene, Act 1, Scene 1*

10 Such sweet neglect more taketh me,
Than all the adulteries of art;
They strike mine eyes, but not my heart. SONG *Ib*

11 Soul of the Age!
The applause! delight! the wonder of our Stage.
To the Memory of William Shakespeare

12 Thou art a monument, without a tomb. *Ib*

13 How far thou didst our Lyly out-shine
Or sporting Kyd, or Marlowe's mighty line. *Ib*

14 Thou hadst small Latin, and less Greek. *Ib*

15 He was not of an age, but for all time! *Ib*

16 Sweet Swan of Avon! *Ib*

17 Good morning to the day: and, next, my gold!—
Open the shrine, that I may see my saint. VOLPONE
Volpone, Act 1, Scene 1

18 O, health! health! the blessing of the rich! the riches of the poor! who can buy thee at too dear a rate, since there is no enjoying the world without thee? VOLPONE *Ib, Act 2, Scene 1*

1 Come, my Celia, let us prove,
While we can, the sports of love,
Time will not be ours for ever,
He, at length, our good will sever. VOLPONE *Volpone, Act 3, Scene 6*

2 O rare Ben Jonson. *Epitaph in Westminster Abbey*

JORDAN, Dorothea, 1762–1816

3 'Oh! where, and Oh! where is your Highland Laddie gone?'
'He's gone to fight the French, for King George upon the throne,
And it's Oh! in my heart, how I wish him safe at home!'
The Blue Bells of Scotland

JOYCE, James, 1882–1941

4 A Portrait of the Artist as a Young Man. *Title of Book*

JUDGE, Jack, see WILLIAMS, Harry

JUNIUS, 18th century

5 The Liberty of the press is the *Palladium* of all the civil, political and religious rights of an Englishman. *Letters, Dedication*

6 To be acquainted with the merit of a ministry, we need only observe the condition of the people. *Letter 1, 21 Jan. 1769*

7 There is a holy, mistaken zeal in politics, as well as religion. By persuading others we convince ourselves. *Letter 35, 19 Dec. 1769*

JUVENAL, 60–130? A.D.

8 *Nemo repente fuit turpissimus.* No one ever became thoroughly bad in one step. *Satires, 2, 83*

9 *Quis custodiet ipsos*
Custodes?
Who is to guard the guards themselves? *Ib, 6, 347*

10 *Tenet insanabile multos*
Scribendi cacoethes et aegro in corde senescit.
An inveterate and incurable itch for writing besets many and grows old with their sick hearts. *Ib, 7, 51*

11 *Orandum est ut sit mens sana in corpore sano.*
Your prayer must be for a sound mind in a sound body. *Ib, 10, 356*

KARR, Alphonse, 1808–1890

12 *Plus ça change, plus c'est la même chose.* The more things change, the more they are the same. *Les Guêpes, Jan. 1849*

KAVANAGH, Ted, 1892–1958

13 Can I do you now, sir? MRS MOP *Itma, B.B.C. Radio Programme, 1939–1949, with Tommy Handley (1892–1949)*

14 Don't forget the diver. *Ib*

15 I don't mind if I do. COLONEL CHINSTRAP *Ib*

16 It's That Man Again. *Ib*

17 Wot, me? In my state of health? CHARLES ATLAS *Ib*

KEATS, John, 1795–1821

1 Season of mists and mellow fruitfulness,
Close bosom-friend of the maturing sun;
Conspiring with him how to load and bless
With fruit the vines that round the thatch-eves run. *To Autumn*

2 To set budding more,
And still more, later flowers for the bees,
Until they think warm days will never cease,
For Summer has o'er-brimm'd their clammy cells. *Ib*

3 Who hath not seen thee oft amid thy store?
Sometimes whoever seeks abroad may find
Thee sitting careless on a granary floor. *Ib*

4 Where are the songs of Spring? Ay, where are they?
Think not of them, thou hast thy music too. *Ib*

5 The red-breast whistles from a garden-croft;
And gathering swallows twitter in the skies. *Ib*

6 Bards of Passion and of Mirth,
Ye have left your souls on earth!
Have ye souls in heaven too,
Double lived in regions new? *Ode, Written on the blank page before Beaumont and Fletcher's 'The Fair Maid of the Inn'*

7 The imagination of a boy is healthy, and the mature imagination of a man is healthy; but there is a space of life between, in which the soul is in a ferment, the character undecided, the way of life uncertain, the ambition thick-sighted: thence proceeds mawkishness. *Endymion, Preface*

8 A thing of beauty is a joy for ever:
Its loveliness increases; it will never
Pass into nothingness. *Ib, Book 1, 1*

9 Pleasure is oft a visitant; but pain
Clings cruelly to us. *Ib, 906*

10 O Sorrow,
Why dost borrow
Heart's lightness from the merriment of May? *Ib, Book 4, 164*

11 It is a flaw
In happiness, to see beyond our bourn,—
It forces us in summer skies to mourn,
It spoils the singing of the Nightingale.
Epistle to John Hamilton Reynolds, 82

12 St. Agnes' Eve—Ah, bitter chill it was!
The owl, for all his feathers, was a-cold;
The hare limp'd trembling through the frozen grass,
And silent was the flock in woolly fold. *The Eve of St. Agnes, 1*

13 Upon the honey'd middle of the night. *Ib, 6*

14 And they are gone: aye, ages long ago
These lovers fled away into the storm. *Ib, 42*

15 The Beadsman, after thousand aves told,
For aye unsought for slept among his ashes cold. *Ib*

1 Fanatics have their dreams, wherewith they weave
A paradise for a sect. *The Fall of Hyperion, Book 1, 1*

2 The poet and the dreamer are distinct,
Diverse, sheer opposite, antipodes.
The one pours out a balm upon the World,
The other vexes it. *Ib, 199*

3 Ever let the fancy roam,
Pleasure never is at home. *Fancy, 1*

4 Deep in the shady sadness of a vale
Far sunken from the healthy breath of morn,
Far from the fiery noon, and eve's one star,
Sat gray-hair'd Saturn, quiet as a stone. *Hyperion, Book 1, 1*

5 No stir of air was there,
Not so much life as on a summer's day
Robs not one light seed from the feather'd grass,
But where the dead leaf fell, there did it rest. *Ib, 7*

6 As when, upon a tranced summer-night,
Those green-rob'd senators of mighty woods,
Tall oaks, branch-charmed by the earnest stars,
Dream, and so dream all night without a stir. *Ib, 72*

7 For as in theatres of crowded men
Hubbub increases more they call out 'Hush!' *Ib, 253*

8 For 'tis the eternal law
That first in beauty should be first in might. *Ib, Book 2, 228*

9 Knowledge enormous makes a God of me. *Ib, Book 3, 113*

10 Parting they seem'd to tread upon the air,
Twin roses by the zephyr blown apart
Only to meet again more close, and share
The inward fragrance of each other's heart. *Isabella, 10*

11 But, for the general award of love,
The little sweet doth kill much bitterness. *Ib, 13*

12 So the two brothers and their murder'd man
Rode past fair Florence. *Ib, 27*

13 O cruelty,
To steal my Basil-pot away from me! *Ib, 63*

14 Ah, what can ail thee, wretched wight,
Alone and palely loitering;
The sedge is wither'd from the lake,
And no birds sing. *La Belle Dame Sans Merci, 1*

15 I met a lady in the meads
Full beautiful, a faery's child;
Her hair was long, her foot was light,
And her eyes were wild. *Ib, 4*

16 She look'd at me as she did love,
And made sweet moan. *Ib, 6*

17 And sure in language strange she said,
I love thee true. *Ib, 7*

1 Love in a hut, with water and a crust,
Is—Love, forgive us!—cinders, ashes, dust;
Love in a palace is perhaps at last
More grievous torment than a hermit's fast. *Lamia, Part 2, 1*

2 Do not all charms fly
At the mere touch of cold philosophy? *Ib, 229*

3 Philosophy will clip an Angel's wings. *Ib, 234*

4 Souls of Poets dead and gone,
What Elysium have ye known,
Happy field or mossy cavern,
Choicer than the Mermaid Tavern?
Have ye tippled drink more fine
Than mine host's Canary wine? *Lines on the Mermaid Tavern, 1*

5 Ah! dearest love, sweet home of all my fears,
And hopes, and joys, and panting miseries. *Ode to Fanny, 2*

6 Thou still unravish'd bride of quietness,
Thou foster-child of silence and slow time. *Ode on a Grecian Urn, 1*

7 Heard melodies are sweet, but those unheard
Are sweeter; therefore, ye soft pipes, play on;
Not to the sensual ear, but, more endear'd,
Pipe to the spirit ditties of no tone. *Ib, 2*

8 She cannot fade, though thou hast not thy bliss,
For ever wilt thou love, and she be fair! *Ib*

9 For ever piping songs for ever new. *Ib, 3*

10 'Beauty is truth, truth beauty,'—that is all
Ye know on earth, and all ye need to know. *Ib, 5*

11 No, no, go not to Lethe, neither twist
Wolf's-bane, tight-rooted, for its poisonous wine. *Ode on Melancholy, 1*

12 She dwells with Beauty—Beauty that must die;
And Joy, whose hand is ever at his lips
Bidding adieu. *Ib, 3*

13 My heart aches, and a drowsy numbness pains
My sense, as though of hemlock I had drunk. *Ode to a Nightingale, 1*

14 O for a beaker full of the warm South,
Full of the true, the blushful Hippocrene,
With beaded bubbles winking at the brim,
And purple-stained mouth;
That I might drink, and leave the world unseen,
And with thee fade away into the forest dim. *Ib, 2*

15 Where youth grows pale, and spectre-thin, and dies
Where but to think is to be full of sorrow
And leaden-eyed despairs. *Ib, 3*

16 Away! away! for I will fly to thee,
Not charioted by Bacchus and his pards,
But on the viewless wings of Poesy,
Though the dull brain perplexes and retards:
Already with thee! tender is the night,
And haply the Queen-Moon is on her throne. *Ib, 4*

1 I cannot see what flowers are at my feet,
Nor what soft incense hangs upon the boughs. *Ode to a Nightingale, 5*

2 The murmurous haunt of flies on summer eves. *Ib*

3 Darkling I listen; and, for many a time
I have been half in love with easeful Death,
Call'd him soft names in many a mused rhyme,
To take into the air my quiet breath;
Now more than ever seems it rich to die,
To cease upon the midnight with no pain,
While thou art pouring forth thy soul abroad
In such an ecstasy! *Ib, 6*

4 Thou wast not born for death, immortal Bird!
No hungry generations tread thee down;
The voice I hear this passing night was heard
In ancient days by emperor and clown:
Perhaps the self-same song that found a path
Through the sad heart of Ruth, when, sick for home,
She stood in tears amid the alien corn;
The same that oft-times hath
Charm'd magic casements, opening on the foam
Of perilous seas, in faery lands forlorn. *Ib, 7*

5 Forlorn! the very word is like a bell
To toll me back from thee to my sole self! *Ib, 8*

6 Was it a vision, or a waking dream?
Fled is that music:—Do I wake or sleep? *Ib*

7 A bright torch, and a casement ope at night,
To let the warm Love in! *Ode to Psyche, 66*

8 What is more gentle than a wind in summer? *Sleep and Poetry, 1*

9 Stop and consider! life is but a day;
A fragile dew-drop on its perilous way
From a tree's summit. *Ib, 85*

10 O for ten years, that I may overwhelm
Myself in poesy; so I may do the deed
That my own soul has to itself decreed. *Ib, 96*

11 And can I ever bid these joys farewell?
Yes, I must pass them for a nobler life,
Where I may find the agonies, the strife
Of human hearts. *Ib, 122*

12 A drainless shower
Of light is poesy; 'tis the supreme of power;
'Tis might half slumb'ring on its own right arm. *Ib, 235*

13 The great end
Of poesy, that it should be a friend
To sooth the cares, and lift the thoughts of man. *Ib, 245*

14 Much have I travell'd in the realms of gold,
And many goodly states and kingdoms seen.
Sonnet, On First Looking into Chapman's Homer

15 Then felt I like some watcher of the skies
When a new planet swims into his ken;

Or like stout Cortez when with eagle eyes
He star'd at the Pacific—and all his men
Look'd at each other with a wild surmise—
Silent, upon a peak in Darien. *Sonnet, On First Looking into Chapman's Homer*

1 The poetry of earth is never dead:
When all the birds are faint with the hot sun,
And hide in cooling trees, a voice will run
From hedge to hedge about the new-mown mead.
Sonnet, On the Grasshopper and Cricket

2 Happy is England! I could be content
To see no other verdure than its own. *Sonnet, Happy is England*

3 Happy is England, sweet her artless daughters;
Enough their simple loveliness for me. *Ib*

4 Four seasons fill the measure of the year;
There are four seasons in the mind of man. *Sonnet, The Human Seasons*

5 Glory and loveliness have pass'd away. *Sonnet, To Leigh Hunt*

6 To one who has been long in city pent,
'Tis very sweet to look into the fair
And open face of heaven. *Sonnet, To one who has been long in City pent*

7 When I have fears that I may cease to be
Before my pen has glean'd my teeming brain.
Sonnet, When I have fears

8 Then on the shore
Of the wide world I stand alone, and think
Till love and fame to nothingness do sink. *Ib*

9 I am certain of nothing but of the holiness of the Heart's affections and the truth of Imagination—What the imagination seizes as Beauty must be truth—whether it existed before or not. *Letter to Benjamin Bailey, 22 Nov. 1817*

10 O for a Life of Sensations rather than of Thoughts! *Ib*

11 Negative Capability, that is, when a man is capable of being in uncertainties, mysteries, doubts, without any irritable reaching after fact and reason.
Letter to George and Thomas Keats, 28 Dec. 1817

12 I am quite perplexed in a world of doubts and fancies—there is nothing stable in the world; uproar's your only music.
Letter to George and Thomas Keats, 13 Jan. 1818

13 Poetry should be great and unobtrusive, a thing which enters into one's soul, and does not startle it or amaze it with itself, but with its subject.
Letter to J. H. Reynolds, 3 Feb. 1818

14 Poetry should surprise by a fine excess and not by Singularity—it should strike the Reader as a wording of his own highest thoughts, and appear almost a Remembrance. *Letter to John Taylor, 27 Feb. 1818*

15 If Poetry comes not as naturally as the Leaves to a tree it had better not come at all. *Ib*

16 Scenery is fine—but human nature is finer. *Letter to Benjamin Bailey, 13 March 1818*

1 I have not the slightest feel of humility towards the Public—or to anything in existence,—but the eternal Being, the Principle of Beauty, and the Memory of great Men. *Letter to J. H. Reynolds, 9 April 1818*

2 I find that I can have no enjoyment in the World but continual drinking of Knowledge. *Letter to John Taylor, 24 April 1818*

3 I compare human life to a large Mansion of Many Apartments, two of which I can only describe, the doors of the rest being as yet shut upon me. *Letter to J. H. Reynolds, 3 May 1818*

4 I would sooner fail than not be among the greatest. *Letter to J. A. Hessey, 9 Oct. 1818*

5 I think I shall be among the English Poets after my death. *Letter to George and Georgiana Keats, Oct. 1818*

6 Though the most beautiful Creature were waiting for me at the end of a Journey or a Walk . . . my Happiness would not be so fine, as my Solitude is sublime. Then instead of what I have described, there is a Sublimity to welcome me home. The roaring of the wind is my wife and the Stars through the window pane are my children. The mighty abstract Idea I have of Beauty in all things stifles the more divided and minute domestic happiness. *Ib*

7 A Man's life of any worth is a continual allegory, and very few eyes can see the Mystery of his life—a life like the scriptures, figurative—which such people can no more make out than they can the hebrew Bible. Lord Byron cuts a figure—but he is not figurative—Shakespeare led a life of Allegory: his works are the comments on it. *Letter to George and Georgiana Keats, 14 Feb. 1819*

8 I have two luxuries to brood over in my walks, your Loveliness and the hour of my death. O that I could have possession of them both in the same minute. *Letter to Fanny Brawne, 25 July 1819*

9 I equally dislike the favour of the public with the love of a woman—they are both a cloying treacle to the wings of independence. *Letter to John Taylor, 24 Aug. 1819*

10 Love is my religion—I could die for that. *Letter to Fanny Brawne, 13 Oct. 1819*

11 'If I should die,' said I to myself, 'I have left no immortal work behind me—nothing to make my friends proud of my memory—but I have lov'd the principle of beauty in all things, and if I had had time I would have made myself remember'd.' *Letter to Fanny Brawne, Feb. 1820*

12 You, I am sure, will forgive me for sincerely remarking that you might curb your magnanimity, and be more of an artist, and load every rift of your subject with ore. *Letter to P. B. Shelley, Aug. 1820*

13 Here lies one whose name was writ in water. *Epitaph*

KEMPIS, Thomas À, 1380–1471

14 Man proposes but God disposes. *The Imitation of Christ, 1, 19*

15 *Sic transit gloria mundi.* Thus the glory of the world passes away. *Ib, 3, 6*

16 It is much safer to obey than to rule. *Ib, 9, 1*

KENNEDY, John Fitzgerald, 1917–1963

1 Let the word go forth from this time and place, to friend and foe alike, that the torch has been passed to a new generation of Americans—born in this century, tempered by war, disciplined by a hard and bitter peace, proud of our ancient heritage. *Inaugural address, 20 Jan. 1961*

2 My fellow Americans: ask not what your country can do for you, ask what you can do for your country. My fellow citizens of the world: ask not what America will do for you, but what together we can do for the freedom of man. *Ib*

KESSELRING, Joseph, 1902–1967

3 Arsenic and Old Lace. *Title of play*

KETHE, William, ?–1608

4 All people that on earth do dwell
Sing to the Lord with cheerful voice. *All People that on Earth do Dwell*

5 For why, the Lord our God is good:
His mercy is for ever sure;
His truth at all times firmly stood,
And shall from age to age endure. *Ib*

KEY, Francis Scott, 1780–1843

6 O! say can you see, by the dawn's early light,
What so proudly we hailed at the twilight's last gleaming,
Whose broad stripes and bright stars, through the perilous fight,
O'er the ramparts we watched, were so gallantly streaming.
The Star-Spangled Banner

7 'Tis the star-spangled banner! O long may it wave,
O'er the land of the free, and the home of the brave. *Ib*

KHAYYÁM, Omar, see FITZGERALD, Edward

KINGSLEY, Charles, 1819–1875

1 Airly Beacon, Airly Beacon;
Oh the pleasant sight to see
Shires and towns from Airly Beacon,
While my love climbed up to me. *Airly Beacon*

2 Be good, sweet maid, and let who will be clever;
Do noble things, not dream them, all day long:
And so make life, death, and that vast for-ever
One grand, sweet song. *A Farewell, To C.E.G.*

3 For men must work, and women must weep,
And the sooner it's over, the sooner to sleep. *The Three Fishers*

4 When all the world is young, lad,
And all the trees are green. *Songs from the Water Babies, Young and Old*

5 Young blood must have its course, lad,
And every dog its day. *Ib*

6 He did not know that a keeper is only a poacher turned outside in, and a poacher is a keeper turned inside out. *The Water Babies, Ch. 1*

7 More ways of killing a cat than choking her with cream. *Westward Ho! Ch. 20*

KIPLING, Rudyard, 1865–1936

8 Oh, East is East, and West is West, and never the twain shall meet. *The Ballad of East and West*

9 Four things greater than all things are,—
Women and Horses and Power and War. *Ballad of the King's Jest*

10 And a woman is only a woman, but a good cigar is a smoke. *The Betrothed*

11 Boots—boots—boots—boots—movin' up an' down again! *Boots*

12 But the Devil whoops, as he whooped of old:
'It's clever, but is it art?' *The Conundrum of the Workshops*

13 And what should they know of England who only England know?

1 On the road to Mandalay
Where the flyin'-fishes play. *Mandalay*

2 Ship me somewhere East of Suez, where the best is like the worst,
Where there aren't no Ten Commandments, an' a man can raise a thirst. *Ib*

3 The tumult and the shouting dies—
The captains and the kings depart. *Recessional*

4 Lest we forget, lest we forget! *Ib*

5 Oh, it's Tommy this, an' Tommy that, an' 'Tommy, go away';
But it's 'Thank you, Mister Atkins,' when the band begins to play. *Tommy*

6 Take up the White Man's Burden. *The White Man's Burden*

7 This is too butch for be. *Just-so Stories, The Elephant's Child*

8 Led go! You are hurtig be! *Ib*

9 The camel's hump is an ugly lump
Which well you may see at the Zoo;
But uglier yet is the hump we get
From having too little to do. *Ib, How the Camel got his Hump*

10 A man of infinite—resource—and—sagacity. *Ib, How the Whale got his Throat*

11 The Light that Failed. *Title of novel*

KLINGER, Friedrich von, 1752–1831

12 *Sturm und Drang.* Storm and stress. *Title of play*

KNOX, John, 1505–1572

13 The First Blast of the Trumpet Against the Monstrous Regiment of Women. *Title of Pamphlet, 1558*

KNOX, Ronald Arbuthnot, 1888–1957

14 There once was a man who said, 'God
Must think it exceedingly odd
   If he finds that this tree
   Continues to be
When there's no one about in the Quad.' *Limerick*

15 A loud noise at one end and no sense of responsibility at the other. *Definition of a Baby*

KYD, Thomas, 1558?–1594?

16 In time the savage bull sustains the yoke,
In time all haggard hawks will stoop to lure,
In time small wedges cleave the hardest oak,
In time the flint is pierced with softest shower. LORENZO *The Spanish Tragedy, Act 2, Scene 1*

LABOUCHÈRE, Henry, 1831–1912

17 He [*Labouchère*] did not object, he once said, to Gladstone's always having the ace of trumps up his sleeve, but only to his pretence that God had put it there. *Quoted in Dictionary of National Biography, 1912–1921*

LAMB, Lady Caroline, 1785–1828

1 Mad, bad, and dangerous to know. [*Byron*] *Journal*

LAMB, Charles, 1775–1834

2 The human species, according to the best theory I can form of it, is composed of two distinct races, the men who borrow, and the men who lend. *Essays of Elia, The Two Races of Men*

3 Borrowers of books—those mutilators of collections, spoilers of the symmetry of shelves, and creators of odd volumes. *Ib*

4 'A clear fire, a clean hearth, and the rigour of the game.' This was the celebrated wish of old Sarah Battle (now with God) who, next to her devotions, loved a good game of whist. *Ib, Mrs. Battle's Opinions on Whist*

5 'Presents,' I often say, 'endear Absents.' *Ib, A Dissertation upon Roast Pig*

6 I love to lose myself in other men's minds. When I am not walking, I am reading; I cannot sit and think. Books think for me. *Last Essays of Elia, Detached Thoughts on Books and Reading*

7 To be strong-backed and neat-bound is the desideratum of a volume. Magnificence comes after. *Ib*

8 Newspapers always excite curiosity. No one ever lays one down without a feeling of disappointment. *Ib*

9 I have had playmates, I have had companions,
In my days of childhood, in my joyful schooldays—
All, all are gone, the old familiar faces. *The Old Familiar Faces*

LANDOR, Walter Savage, 1775–1864

10 George the First was always reckoned
Vile, but viler George the Second;
And what mortal ever heard
Any good of George the Third?
When from earth the Fourth descended
God be praised, the Georges ended. *Epigram*

11 I strove with none; for none was worth my strife;
Nature I loved and, next to Nature, Art:
I warmed both hands before the fire of life;
It sinks, and I am ready to depart. *Finis*

12 I loved him not; and yet now he is gone,
I feel I am alone.
I check'd him while he spoke: yet, could he speak,
Alas! I would not check. *The Maid's Lament*

13 Ah, what avails the sceptred race!
Ah, what the form divine! *Rose Aylmer*

LANE, George Martin, 1823–1897

14 The waiter roars it through the hall:
'We don't give bread with one fish-ball!' *One Fish-ball*

LANGBRIDGE, Frederick, 1849–1923

15 Two men look out through the same bars:
One sees the mud, and one the stars. *A Cluster of Quiet Thoughts*

LANGLAND, William, 1330?–1400?

1 In a somer seson, when soft was the sonne. *A Vision of William concerning Piers the Plowman, B Text, Prologue, 1*

LATIMER, Bishop Hugh, 1485?–1555

2 Be of good comfort, Master Ridley, and play the man; we shall this day light such a candle by God's grace in England, as I trust shall never be put out. *16 Oct. 1555, while Latimer and Ridley were being burned at the stake for heresy*

LAUDER, Sir Harry, 1870–1950

3 I love a lassie. *Song*

4 Just a wee doch-an'-dorris
Before we gang awa' . . .
If you can say, 'It's a braw, bricht, moonlicht nicht'
Ye're a' richt. *Song*

5 Keep right on to the end of the road,
Keep right on to the end.
'Though you're tired and weary still journey on. *Song*

6 O! it's nice to get up in the mornin'
But it's nicer to lie in bed. *Song*

7 Roamin' in the gloamin'. *Song*

LAWRENCE, David Herbert, 1885–1930

8 How beastly the bourgeois is
especially the male of the species. *How Beastly the Bourgeois is*

9 Nicely groomed, like a mushroom
Standing there so sleek and erect and eyeable—
and like a fungus, living on the remains of bygone life
sucking his life out of the dead leaves of greater life than his own. *Ib*

10 My love lies underground
With her face upturned to mine,
And her mouth unclosed in a last long kiss
That ended her life and mine. *Hymn to Priapus*

11 When I read Shakespeare I am struck with wonder
That such trivial people should muse and thunder
In such lovely language. *When I Read Shakespeare, 1*

LEACOCK, Stephen Butler, 1869–1944

12 If every day in the life of a school could be the last day but one, there would be little fault to find with it. *College Days, Memories and Miseries of a Schoolmaster*

13 Lord Ronald said nothing; he flung himself from the room, flung himself upon his horse and rode madly off in all directions. *Nonsense Novels, Gertrude the Governess*

14 Golf may be played on Sunday, not being a game within the view of the law, but being a form of moral effort. *Other Fancies, Why I refuse to play Golf*

15 The general idea, of course, in any first-class laundry is to see that no shirt or collar ever comes back twice. *Winnowed Wisdom, Ch. 6*

LEAR, Edward, 1812–1888

1 Who, or why, or which, or *what*, is the Akond of Swat?
The Akond of Swat

2 On the Coast of Coromandel
Where the early pumpkins blow,
In the middle of the woods
Lived the Yonghy-Bonghy-Bò.
The Courtship of the Yonghy-Bonghy-Bò

3 The Dong!—the Dong!
The wandering Dong through the forest goes!
The Dong!—the Dong!
The Dong with a luminous Nose! *The Dong with a Luminous Nose*

4 They went to sea in a sieve, they did
In a sieve they went to sea. *The Jumblies*

5 Far and few, far and few,
Are the lands where the Jumblies live;
Their heads are green, and their hands are blue,
And they went to sea in a sieve. *Ib*

6 'How pleasant to know Mr. Lear!'
Who has written such volumes of stuff!
Some think him ill-tempered and queer,
But a few think him pleasant enough. *Nonsense Songs, Preface*

7 The Owl and the Pussy-Cat went to sea
In a beautiful pea-green boat,
They took some honey, and plenty of money,
Wrapped up in a five-pound note. *The Owl and the Pussy-Cat*

8 They sailed away for a year and a day,
To the land where the Bong-tree grows,
And there in a wood a Piggy-wig stood,
With a ring at the end of his nose. *Ib*

9 They dined on mince and slices of quince,
Which they ate with a runcible spoon;
And hand in hand, on the edge of the sand
They danced by the light of the moon. *Ib*

10 He has gone to fish, for his Aunt Jobiska's
Runcible Cat with crimson whiskers. *The Pobble who has no Toes*

11 Two old Bachelors were living in one house;
One caught a Muffin, the other caught a Mouse. *The Two Old Bachelors*

12 There was an Old Man who said, 'Hush!
I perceive a young bird in this bush!'
When they said, 'Is it small?'
He replied, 'Not at all!
It is four times as big as the bush!' *The Old Man Who said 'Hush!'*

13 There was an Old Man with a beard,
Who said, 'It is just as I feared!—
Two Owls and a Hen,
Four Larks and a Wren,
Have all built their nests in my beard!' *The Old Man With a Beard*

LEE, Nathaniel, 1655?–1692

1 When Greeks joined Greeks, then was the tug of war. CLYTUS
The Rival Queens, Act 4, Scene 2

LELAND, Charles Godfrey, 1824–1903

2 Hans Breitmann gife a barty—
Where ish dat barty now? *Hans Breitmann's Barty*

LENIN, Nikolai, 1870–1924

3 It is true that liberty is precious—so precious that it must be rationed.
Attributed

LÉVIS, Duc de, 1764–1830

4 *Noblesse oblige.* Nobility imposes its own obligations. *Maximes et Réflexions*

LEYBOURNE, George, ?–1884

5 O, he flies through the air with the greatest of ease,
This daring young man on the flying trapeze. *The Man on the Flying Trapeze*

LINCOLN, Abraham, 1809–1865

6 If the good people in their wisdom shall see fit to keep me in the background, I have been too familiar with disappointments to be very much chagrined. *Speech, 9 March 1832*

7 No man is good enough to govern another man without that other's consent. *Speech, 1854*

8 The ballot is stronger than the bullet. *Speech, 19 May 1856*

9 We cannot be free men if this is, by our national choice, to be a land of slavery. Those who deny freedom to others, deserve it not for themselves. *Ib*

10 That is the issue that will continue in this country when these poor tongues of Judge Douglas and myself shall be silent. It is the eternal struggle between these two principles—right and wrong—throughout the world. They are the two principles that have stood face to face from the beginning of time, and will ever continue to struggle. *Speech, 15 Oct. 1858*

11 What is conservatism? Is it not adherence to the old and tried, against the new and untried? *Speech, 27 Feb. 1860*

12 I intend no modification of my oft-expressed personal wish that all men everywhere could be free. *Letter to Horace Greeley, 22 Aug. 1862*

13 That this nation, under God, shall have a new birth of freedom; and that government of the people, by the people, and for the people, shall not perish from the earth. *Address at Dedication of National Cemetery, Gettysburg, 19 Nov. 1863*

14 An old Dutch farmer, who remarked to a companion once that it was not best to swap horses in mid-stream. *Speech, 9 June 1864*

15 With malice toward none; with charity for all; with firmness in the right, as God gives us to see the right,—let us strive on to finish the work we are in: to bind up the nation's wounds; to care for him who shall have borne the battle, and for his widow and his orphan; to do all which may achieve and cherish a just and lasting peace among ourselves, and with all nations. *Second Inaugural Address, 1865*

1 You can fool some of the people all the time and all the people some of the time; but you can't fool all the people all the time. *Attributed*

2 People who like this sort of thing will find this is the sort of thing they like. *Criticism of book*

LITVINOV, Maxim, 1876–1951

3 Peace is indivisible. *Speech, Geneva, 1 July 1936*

LIVY, 59 B.C.–A.D. 17

4 *Vae victis.* Woe to the vanquished. *History, 5, 48*

LLOYD, Marie, 1870–1922

5 A little of what you fancy does you good. *Song*

6 I'm one of the ruins that Cromwell knocked about a bit. *Song*

7 Oh, mister porter, what shall I do?
I wanted to go to Birmingham, but they've carried me on to Crewe.
Song, words by Thomas Le Brunn

LLOYD, Robert, 1733–1764

8 Slow and steady wins the race. *The Hare and the Tortoise*

LLOYD GEORGE, David, 1st Earl, 1863–1945

9 What is our task? To make Britain a fit country for heroes to live in. *Speech, 24 Nov. 1918*

LONGFELLOW, Henry Wadsworth, 1807–1882

10 I shot an arrow into the air,
It fell to earth I knew not where. *The Arrow and the Song*

11 Thou, too, sail on, O Ship of State!
Sail on, O Union, strong and great!
Humanity with all its fears,
With all the hopes of future years
Is hanging breathless on thy fate! *The Building of the Ship*

12 The shades of night were falling fast,
As through an Alpine village passed
A youth, who bore, 'mid snow and ice,
A banner with the strange device,
Excelsior! *Excelsior*

13 A traveller, by the faithful hound,
Half-buried in the snow was found. *Ib*

14 Tell me not, in mournful numbers,
Life is but an empty dream!
For the soul is dead that slumbers,
And things are not what they seem.

Life is real! Life is earnest!
And the grave is not its goal;
Dust thou art, to dust returnest,
Was not spoken of the soul. *A Psalm of Life*

15 Art is long, and Time is fleeting,
And our hearts, though stout and brave,
Still, like muffled drums, are beating
Funeral marches to the grave. *Ib*

1 Lives of great men all remind us
We can make our lives sublime,
And, departing, leave behind us
Footprints on the sands of time. *A Psalm of Life*

2 Let us, then, be up and doing,
With a heart for any fate,
Still achieving, still pursuing,
Learn to labour and to wait. *Ib*

3 Though the mills of God grind slowly,
yet they grind exceeding small;
Though with patience He stands waiting,
with exactness grinds He all. *Retribution*
(translation from von Logau)

4 'Wouldst thou'—so the helmsman answered,—
'Learn the secret of the sea?
Only those who brave its dangers
Comprehend its mystery.' *The Secret of the Sea*

5 From the waterfall he named her,
Minnehaha, Laughing Water. *The Song of Hiawatha, 4*

6 As unto the bow the cord is,
So unto the man is woman,
Though she bends him, she obeys him,
Though she draws him, yet she follows,
Useless each without the other! *Ib, 10*

7 Ships that pass in the night, and speak each other in passing,
Only a signal shown and a distant voice in the darkness;
So on the ocean of life we pass and speak one another,
Only a look and a voice, then darkness again and a silence.
Tales of a Wayside Inn, 3, The Theologian's Tale

8 There was a little girl
Who had a little curl
Right in the middle of her forehead,
And when she was good
She was very, very good,
But when she was bad she was horrid. *There was a Little Girl*

9 Under a spreading chestnut-tree
The village smithy stands;
The smith, a mighty man is he,
With large and sinewy hands. *The Village Blacksmith*

10 He earns whate'er he can,
And looks the whole world in the face,
For he owes not any man. *Ib*

11 Something attempted, something done
Has earned a night's repose. *Ib*

12 It was the schooner Hesperus,
That sailed the wintry sea;
And the skipper had taken his little daughter,
To bear him company. *The Wreck of the Hesperus*

LOOS, Anita, 1893—

13 Gentlemen Prefer Blondes. *Title of Book*

1 Kissing your hand may make you feel very very good but a diamond and safire bracelet lasts forever. *Gentlemen Prefer Blondes, Ch. 4*

LOUIS XIV of France, 1638–1715

2 *L'État c'est moi.* I am the State. *Attributed*

3 *Il n'y a plus de Pyrénées.* The Pyrenees no longer exist. *Attributed*

LOUIS XVIII of France, 1755–1824

4 *L'exactitude est la politesse des rois.* Punctuality is the politeness of kings. *Attributed*

LOVELACE, Richard, 1618–1658

5 Stone walls do not a prison make,
Nor iron bars a cage. *To Althea, from Prison*

6 Tell me not, sweet, I am unkind,
That from the nunnery
Of thy chaste breast, and quiet mind,
To war and arms I fly. *To Lucasta, Going to the Wars*

7 I could not love thee, Dear, so much,
Loved I not Honour more. *Ib*

LOVELL, Maria Anne, 1803–1877

8 Two souls with but a single thought,
Two hearts that beat as one. *Ingomar the Barbarian (translated from German)*

LOVER, Samuel, 1797–1868

9 When once the itch of literature comes over a man, nothing can cure it but the scratching of a pen. *Handy Andy, Ch. 36*

LOWELL, James Russell, 1819–1891

10 An' you've got to get up airly
Ef you want to take in God. *The Biglow Papers, 1st series, No. 1*

11 I *don't* believe in princerple,
But O, I *du* in interest. *Ib, No. 6*

12 No man is born into the world, whose work
Is not born with him; there is always work,
And tools to work withal, for those who will:
And blessed are the horny hands of toil! *A Glance Behind the Curtain, 201*

13 The birch, most shy and ladylike of trees. *An Indian Summer Reverie*

14 Once to every man and nation comes the moment to decide,
In the strife of Truth with Falsehood, for the good or evil side. *The Present Crisis*

15 And what is so rare as a day in June?
Then, if ever, come perfect days;
Then Heaven tries earth if it be in tune,
And over it softly her warm ear lays. *The Vision of Sir Launfal, Part 1, Prelude*

16 A wise scepticism is the first attribute of a good critic. *Among My Books, Shakespeare Once More*

1 There is no good in arguing with the inevitable. The only argument available with an east wind is to put on your overcoat. *Democracy and Addresses*

LUTHER, Martin, 1483–1546

2 *Wer nicht liebt Wein, Weib und Gesang,*
Der bleibt ein Narr sein Lebelang.
Who loves not wine, woman and song,
Remains a fool his whole life long. *Attributed*

LYLY, John, 1554?–1606

3 Cupid and my Campaspe play'd
At cards for kisses—Cupid paid. *Campaspe, 3, 5*

4 O Love! has she done this to thee?
What shall, alas! become of me? *Ib*

LYTE, Henry Francis, 1793–1847

5 Abide with me; fast falls the eventide;
The darkness deepens; Lord, with me abide!
When other helpers fail, and comforts flee,
Help of the helpless, O abide with me. *Abide with Me*

6 Change and decay in all around I see;
O thou who changest not, abide with me. *Ib*

7 I fear no foe with thee at hand to bless;
Ills have no weight, and tears no bitterness.
Where is death's sting? where, grave, thy victory?
I triumph still, if thou abide with me. *Ib*

8 Praise, my soul, the King of heaven;
To his feet thy tribute bring. *Praise, my soul, the King of Heaven*

LYTTON, 1st Earl of, see MEREDITH, Owen

MACAULAY, Thomas Babington, 1st Baron, 1800–1859

9 Lars Porsena of Clusium
By the Nine Gods he swore
That the great house of Tarquin
Would suffer wrong no more. *Lays of Ancient Rome, Horatius, 1*

10 And how can man die better
Than facing fearful odds,
For the ashes of his fathers,
And the temples of his Gods? *Ib, 27*

11 Now who will stand on either hand,
And keep the bridge with me? *Ib, 29*

12 Then none was for a party;
Then all were for the state. *Ib, 32*

13 But those behind cried 'Forward!'
And those before cried 'Back!' *Ib, 50*

14 Oh, Tiber! father Tiber!
To whom the Romans pray,
A Roman's life, a Roman's arms,
Take thou in charge this day! *Ib, 59*

1 And even the ranks of Tuscany
Could scarce forbear to cheer. *Lays of Ancient Rome, Horatius, 60*

2 Every schoolboy knows who imprisoned Montezuma, and who strangled Atahualpa. *Essay in Edinburgh Review, Lord Clive*

3 The English Bible, a book which, if everything else in our language should perish, would alone suffice to show the whole extent of its beauty and power. *Ib, On John Dryden*

4 The gallery in which the reporters sit has become a fourth estate of the realm. *Ib, Hallam's Constitutional History*

5 The history of England is emphatically the history of progress. *Ib, Sir J. Mackintosh's History of the Revolution*

6 We know of no spectacle so ridiculous as the British public in one of its periodical fits of morality. *Ib, Moore's Life of Lord Byron*

7 The Puritan hated bear-baiting, not because it gave pain to the bear, but because it gave pleasure to the spectators. *History of England, Ch. 2*

McCRAE, John, 1872–1918

8 In Flanders fields the poppies blow
Between the crosses, row on row. *In Flanders Fields*

9 If ye break faith with us who die
We shall not sleep, though poppies grow
In Flanders fields. *Ib*

MACDONALD, George, 1824–1905

10 Here lie I, Martin Elginbrodde:
Hae mercy o' my soul, Lord God;
As I wad do, were I Lord God,
And ye were Martin Elginbrodde. *David Elginbrod, Book 1, Ch. 13*

MACMAHON, Maurice de, 1808–1893

11 *J'y suis, j'y reste.* Here I am, and here I stay. *Attributed at taking of Malakoff, 1855*

MACMILLAN, Harold, 1894—

12 Most of our people have never had it so good. Go around the country—go to the industrial towns, go to the farms—and you will see a state of prosperity such as we have never had in my lifetime, or indeed ever in the history of this country. *Speech, Bedford Football Ground, 20 July 1957*

13 The wind of change is blowing through the continent. Whether we like it or not, this growth of national consciousness is a political fact. *Speech, South African Parliament, Cape Town, 3 Feb. 1960*

MACNEICE, Louis, 1907–1963

14 It's no go the merrygoround, it's no go the rickshaw,
All we want is a limousine and a ticket for the peepshow. *Bagpipe Music*

15 It's no go my honey love, it's no go my poppet;
Work your hands from day to day, the winds will blow the profit.
The glass is falling hour by hour, the glass will fall for ever,
But if you break the bloody glass you won't hold up the weather. *Ib*

1 Between the enormous fluted Ionic columns
There seeps from heavily jowled or hawk-like foreign faces
The guttural sorrow of the refugees. *The British Museum Reading Room*

2 Time was away and somewhere else,
There were two glasses and two chairs
And two people with one pulse
(Somebody stopped the moving stairs):
Time was away and somewhere else. *Meeting Point*

MAISTRE, Joseph de, 1754–1821

3 *Toute nation a le gouvernement qu'elle mérite.* Every nation has the government it deserves. *Letter about Russia, 1811*

MALLET, David, 1705?–1765

4 O grant me, Heaven, a middle state,
Neither too humble nor too great;
More than enough, for nature's ends,
With something left to treat my friends. *Imitation of Horace*

MANDALE, W. R., 19th century

5 Up and down the City Road,
In and out the Eagle,
That's the way the money goes—
Pop goes the weasel! *Pop Goes the Weasel*

MANNERS, Lord John, see RUTLAND, 7th Duke of

MARIE-ANTOINETTE, Queen of France, 1755–1793

6 *Qu'ils mangent de la brioche.* Let them eat cake. *Attributed (Similar phrases date back to thirteenth century)*

MARLOWE, Christopher, 1564–1593

7 What doctrine call you this, *Che sera, sera,*
What will be, shall be? FAUSTUS *Doctor Faustus*

8 Was this the face that launch'd a thousand ships
And burnt the topless towers of Ilium?
Sweet Helen, make me immortal with a kiss.
Her lips suck forth my soul: see, where it flies!
Come, Helen, come, give me my soul again.
Here will I dwell, for heaven is in these lips,
And all is dross that is not Helena. FAUSTUS *Ib*

9 O, thou art fairer than the evening air
Clad in the beauty of a thousand stars. FAUSTUS *Ib*

10 Now hast thou but one bare hour to live,
And then thou must be damn'd perpetually!
Stand still, you ever-moving spheres of heaven,
That time may cease, and midnight never come. FAUSTUS *Ib*

11 Ugly hell, gape not! come not, Lucifer!
I'll burn my books! FAUSTUS *Ib*

1 Cut is the branch that might have grown full straight,
And burned is Apollo's laurel-bough,
That sometime grew within this learned man. CHORUS *Doctor Faustus*

2 My men, like satyrs grazing on the lawns,
Shall with their goat-feet dance an antic hay. GAVESTON
Edward the Second

3 I count religion but a childish toy,
And hold there is no sin but ignorance. MACHIAVEL *The Jew of Malta, Prologue*

4 And, as their wealth increaseth, so inclose
Infinite riches in a little room. BARABAS *Ib, Act 1*

5 FRIAR BARNARDINE: Thou hast committed—
BARABAS: Fornication: but that was in another country;
And beside the wench is dead. *Ib, Act 4*

6 Jigging veins of rhyming mother-wits. *Tamburlaine the Great, Pt. 1, Prologue*

7 Zenocrate, lovelier than the love of Jove,
Brighter than is the silver Rhodope,
Fairer than whitest snow on Scythian hills. TAMBURLAINE
Ib, Act 1, Scene 2

8 Accurs'd be he that first invented war. MYCETES *Ib, Act 2, Scene 4*

9 Is it not passing brave to be a king,
And ride in triumph through Persepolis? TAMBURLAINE
Ib, Act 2, Scene 5

10 Nature, that fram'd us of four elements
Warring within our breasts for regiment,
Doth teach us all to have aspiring minds:
Our souls, whose faculties can comprehend
The wondrous architecture of the world,
And measure every wandering planet's course,
Still climbing after knowledge infinite,
And always moving as the restless spheres,
Will us to wear ourselves, and never rest,
Until we reach the ripest fruit of all,
That perfect bliss and sole felicity,
The sweet fruition of an earthly crown. TAMBURLAINE
Ib, Act 2, Scene 7

11 Ah, fair Zenocrate!—divine Zenocrate!
Fair is too foul an epithet for thee. TAMBURLAINE *Ib, Act 5, Scene 1*

12 Holla, ye pamper'd jades of Asia!
What, can ye draw but twenty miles a-day? TAMBURLAINE
Ib, Pt. 2, Act 4, Scene 3

13 Tamburlaine, the scourge of God, must die. TAMBURLAINE
Ib, Act 5, Scene 3

14 It lies not in our power to love or hate,
For will in us is over-rul'd by fate. *Hero and Leander*

15 Where both deliberate, the love is slight:
Who ever lov'd, that lov'd not at first sight? *Ib*

1 Come live with me, and be my love;
And we will all the pleasures prove
That hills and valleys, dales and fields,
Woods or steepy mountain yields. *The Passionate Shepherd to his Love*

MARQUIS, Donald Robert, 1878–1937

2 its cheerio
my deario that
pulls a lady through *archy and mehitabel, cheerio my deario*

3 toujours gai archy
toujours gai *Ib*

4 so unlucky
that he runs into accidents
which started out to happen
to somebody else *archy's life of mehitabel, archy says*

MARRYAT, Frederick, 1792–1848

5 If you please, ma'am, it was a very little one. [*Of her illegitimate baby*] *Midshipman Easy, Ch. 3*

6 I never knows the children. It's just six of one and half-a-dozen of the other. *The Pirate, Ch. 4*

7 Every man paddle his own canoe. *Settlers in Canada, Ch. 8*

MARVELL, Andrew, 1621–1678

8 Where the remote Bermudas ride,
In the ocean's bosom unespied. *Bermudas, 1*

9 Echo beyond the Mexique Bay. *Ib, 36*

10 And all the way, to guide their chime,
With falling oars they kept the time. *Ib, 39*

11 Had we but world enough, and time,
This coyness, lady, were no crime. *To His Coy Mistress, 1*

12 My vegetable love should grow
Vaster than empires and more slow. *Ib, 11*

13 But at my back I always hear
Time's winged chariot hurrying near;
And yonder all before us lie
Deserts of vast eternity. *Ib, 21*

14 The grave's a fine and private place,
But none, I think, do there embrace. *Ib, 31*

15 Thus, though we cannot make our sun
Stand still, yet we will make him run. *Ib, 45*

16 My Love is of a birth as rare
As 'tis, for object, strange and high;
It was begotten by Despair
Upon Impossibility. *The Definition of Love, 1*

17 Therefore the love which us doth bind,
But fate so enviously debars,
Is the conjunction of the mind,
And opposition of the stars. *Ib, 29*

1 Annihilating all that's made
To a green thought in a green shade. *The Garden, 47*

2 Casting the body's vest aside,
My soul into the boughs does glide. *Ib, 51*

3 So restless Cromwell could not cease
In the inglorious arts of peace. *An Horatian Ode upon Cromwell's Return from Ireland, 9*

4 He nothing common did or mean,
Upon that memorable scene.
But with his keener eye
The axe's edge did try. [*Charles 1*] *Ib, 57*

5 Who can foretell for what high cause
This darling of the Gods was born? *The Picture of Little T.C. in a Prospect of Flowers, 9*

6 Gather the flowers, but spare the buds. *Ib, 35*

MARX, Karl, 1818–1883

7 From each according to his abilities, to each according to his needs. *Criticism of the Gotha Programme*

8 Religion . . . is the opium of the people. *Criticism of the Hegelian Philosophy of Right, Introduction*

9 The ruling ideas of each age have ever been the ideas of its ruling class. *Manifesto of the Communist Party, 2*

10 The workers have nothing to lose but their chains. They have a world to gain. Workers of the world, unite. *Ib, 4*

MARY TUDOR, Queen of England, 1516–1558

11 When I am dead and opened, you shall find 'Calais' lying in my heart. *Holinshed's Chronicles, 3, 1160*

MASEFIELD, John, 1878–1967

12 But the loveliest things of beauty God ever has showed to me,
Are her voice, and her hair, and eyes, and the dear red curve of her lips. *Beauty*

13 Quinquireme of Nineveh from distant Ophir
Rowing home to haven in sunny Palestine,
With a cargo of ivory,
And apes and peacocks,
Sandalwood, cedarwood, and sweet white wine. *Cargoes*

14 Dirty British coaster with a salt-caked smoke-stack
Butting through the Channel in the mad March days. *Ib*

15 I must down to the seas again, to the lonely sea and the sky,
And all I ask is a tall ship and a star to steer her by. *Sea Fever*

16 I must down to the seas again, for the call of the running tide
Is a wild call and a clear call that may not be denied. *Ib*

17 I must down to the seas again, to the vagrant gypsy life,
To the gull's way and the whale's way where the wind's like a whetted knife;
And all I ask is a merry yarn from a laughing fellow-rover,
And quiet sleep and a sweet dream when the long trick's over. *Ib*

1 It is good to be out on the road, and going one knows not where,
Going through meadow and village, one knows not whither nor why.
Tewkesbury Road

MASSINGER, Philip, 1583–1640

2 He that would govern others, first should be
The master of himself. *The Bondman, Act 1, Scene 3*

3 A New Way to Pay Old Debts. *Title of Play*

MAUGHAM, William Somerset, 1874—1965

4 People ask you for criticism, but they only want praise.
Of Human Bondage, Ch. 50

5 Impropriety is the soul of wit. *The Moon and Sixpence, Ch. 4*

6 I would sooner read a time-table or a catalogue than nothing at all. They are much more entertaining than half the novels that are written.
The Summing Up

7 Life is too short to do anything for oneself that one can pay others to do for one. *Ib*

MEARNS, Hughes, 1875–1965

8 As I was going up the stair
I met a man who wasn't there.
He wasn't there again today.
I wish, I wish he'd stay away. *The Psychoed*

MELBOURNE, William Lamb, 2nd Viscount, 1779–1848

9 I like the Garter; there is no damned merit in it.
On the Order of the Garter

10 Things have come to a pretty pass when religion is allowed to invade the sphere of private life. *Attributed*

11 I wish that I was as cocksure of anything as Tom Macaulay is of everything.
Attributed

MENCKEN, Henry Louis, 1880–1956

12 All successful newspapers are ceaselessly querulous and bellicose. They never defend anyone or anything if they can help it; if the job is forced upon them, they tackle it by denouncing someone or something else.
Prejudices, First Series

13 The average schoolmaster is and always must be essentially an ass, for how can one imagine an intelligent man engaging in so puerile an avocation?
Ib, Third Series

14 I've made it a rule never to drink by daylight and never to refuse a drink after dark. *Quoted in New York Post, 18 Sept. 1945*

MEREDITH, George, 1828–1909

15 Cynicism is intellectual dandyism. *The Egoist, Ch. 7*

16 The actors are, it seems, the usual three:
Husband, and wife, and lover. *Modern Love, Stanza 25*

1 We'll sit contentedly
And eat our pot of honey on the grave. *Modern Love, Stanza 29*

2 Ah, what a dusty answer gets the soul
When hot for certainties in this our life! *Ib, Stanza 50*

3 I expect that Woman will be the last thing civilized by Man. *The Ordeal of Richard Feverel, Ch. 1*

4 Kissing don't last: cookery do! *Ib, Ch. 28*

MEREDITH, Owen (Earl of Lytton), 1831–1891

5 Genius does what it must, and Talent does what it can. *Last Words of a Sensitive Second-Rate Poet*

MERRITT, Dixon Lanier, 1879–1954

6 A wonderful bird is the pelican,
His beak holds more than his belican.
He can take in his beak
Enough food for a week,
But I'm damned if I know how the helican! *The Pelican*

MIKES, George, 1912—

7 On the Continent people have good food; in England people have good table manners. *How to be an Alien*

8 Continental people have sex life; the English have hot-water bottles. *Ib*

9 An Englishman, even if he is alone, forms an orderly queue of one. *Ib*

MILL, John Stuart, 1806–1873

10 All good things which exist are the fruits of originality. *On Liberty, Ch. 3*

11 The worth of a State in the long run is the worth of the individuals composing it. *Ib*

12 That so few now dare to be eccentric marks the chief danger of the time. *Ib*

MILLAY, Edna St. Vincent, 1892–1950

13 My candle burns at both ends;
It will not last the night;
But, oh, my foes, and oh, my friends—
It gives a lovely light. *Figs from Thistles, First Fig*

14 What lips my lips have kissed, and where, and why,
I have forgotten, and what arms have lain
Under my head till morning; but the rain
Is full of ghosts tonight, that tap and sigh
Upon the glass and listen for reply. *Sonnet, What Lips My Lips Have Kissed*

15 I only know that summer sang in me
A little while, that in me sings no more. *Ib*

MILLIGAN, Spike, 1918—

16 'Do you come here often?'
'Only in the mating season.' *B.B.C. programme, The Goon Show, with Spike Milligan, Harry Secombe and Peter Sellers*

MILNE, Alan Alexander, 1882–1956

1 The more it snows
(Tiddely pom),
The more it goes
(Tiddely pom),
The more it goes
(Tiddely pom),
On snowing.
And nobody knows
(Tiddely pom),
How cold my toes
(Tiddely pom),
How cold my toes
(Tiddely pom),
Are growing. POOH *The House at Pooh Corner, Ch. 1*

2 Tiggers don't like honey. TIGGER *Ib, Ch. 2*

3 'Climbing trees is what they do best,' said Tigger. 'Much better than Poohs.' *Ib, Ch. 4*

4 King John was not a good man—
He had his little ways. *Now We Are Six, King John's Christmas*

5 No one can tell me,
Nobody knows,
Where the wind comes from,
Where the wind goes. *Ib. Wind on the Hill*

6 They're changing guard at Buckingham Palace—
Christopher Robin went down with Alice.
Alice is marrying one of the guard.
'A soldier's life is terrible hard,'
Says Alice. *When We Were Very Young, Buckingham Palace*

7 'Do you think the King knows all about me?'
'Sure to, dear, but it's time for tea,'
Says Alice. *Ib*

8 James James
Morrison Morrison
Weatherby George Dupree
Took great
Care of his Mother,
Though he was only three. *Ib, Disobedience*

9 You must never go down to the end of the town, if you don't go down with me. *Ib*

10 *What* is the matter with Mary Jane?
I've promised her sweets and a ride in the train,
And I've begged her to stop for a bit and explain—
What *is* the matter with Mary Jane? *Ib, Rice Pudding*

11 The King asked
The Queen, and
The Queen asked
The Dairymaid:
'Could we have some butter for
The Royal slice of bread?' *Ib, The King's Breakfast*

1 I do like a little bit of butter to my bread! *When We Were Very Young, The King's Breakfast*

2 Little Boy kneels at the foot of the bed,
Droops on the little hands little gold head.
Hush! Hush! Whisper who dares!
Christopher Robin is saying his prayers. *Ib, Vespers*

3 Isn't it funny
How a bear likes honey?
Buzz! Buzz! Buzz!
I wonder why he does? *Winnie-the-Pooh, Ch. 1*

4 'Well', said Owl, 'the customary procedure in such cases is as follows.' 'What does Crustimoney Proseedcake mean?' said Pooh. 'For I am a Bear of Very Little Brain, and long words Bother me.' *Ib, Ch. 4*

5 Eeyore, the old grey Donkey, stood by the side of the stream, and looked at himself in the water.
'Pathetic,' he said. 'That's what it is, Pathetic.' *Ib, Ch. 6*

6 Cottleston, Cottleston, Cottleston Pie.
A fly can't bird, but a bird can fly.
Ask me a riddle and I reply:
'Cottleston, Cottleston, Cottleston Pie.' POOH *Ib*

7 Time for a little something. POOH *Ib*

8 My spelling is Wobbly. It's good spelling but it Wobbles, and letters get in the wrong places. POOH *Ib*

9 A Useful Pot to put things in. POOH *Ib*

10 Sing Ho! for the life of a Bear. POOH *Ib, Ch. 8*

11 3 Cheers for Pooh!
(For Who?)
For Pooh—
(Why What did he do?)
I thought you knew;
He saved his friend from a wetting. ANXIOUS POOH SONG *Ib, Ch. 10*

MILTON, John, 1608–1674

12 Blest pair of Sirens, pledges of Heaven's joy,
Sphere-born harmonious sisters, Voice and Verse. *At a Solemn Music, 1*

13 Before the starry threshold of Jove's court
My mansion is. ATTENDANT SPIRIT *Comus: A Mask, 1*

14 Above the smoke and stir of this dim spot
Which men call Earth. ATTENDANT SPIRIT *Ib, 5*

15 What hath night to do with sleep? COMUS *Ib, 122*

16 Come, knit hands, and beat the ground
In a light fantastic round. COMUS *Ib, 143*

17 'Tis chastity, my brother, chastity:
She that has that, is clad in complete steel. ELDER BROTHER *Ib, 420*

18 How charming is divine Philosophy!
Not harsh and crabbed, as dull fools suppose.
But musical as is Apollo's lute,
And a perpetual feast of nectared sweets,
Where no crude surfeit reigns. SECOND BROTHER *Ib, 476*

1 That power
Which erring men call Chance. ELDER BROTHER *Comus: A Mask, 587*

2 Beauty is Nature's coin; must not be hoarded,
But must be current. COMUS *Ib, 739*

3 Sabrina fair,
Listen where thou art sitting
Under the glassy, cool, translucent wave,
In twisted braids of lilies knitting
The loose train of thy amber-dropping hair. ATTENDANT SPIRIT *Ib, 859*

4 Mortals, that would follow me,
Love Virtue, she alone is free.
She can teach ye how to climb
Higher than the sphery chime;
Or, if Virtue feeble were,
Heaven itself would stoop to her. ATTENDANT SPIRIT *Ib, 1018*

5 Hence, vain deluding Joys,
The brood of Folly without father bred! *Il Penseroso, 1*

6 But, hail! thou Goddess sage and holy
Hail, divinest Melancholy! *Ib, 11*

7 Thy rapt soul sitting in thine eyes. *Ib, 40*

8 Sweet bird, that shunn'st the noise of folly,
Most musical, most melancholy! *Ib, 61*

9 Where glowing embers through the room
Teach light to counterfeit a gloom,
Far from all resort of mirth,
Save the cricket on the hearth. *Ib, 79*

10 Where more is meant than meets the ear. *Ib, 120*

11 And storied windows richly dight,
Casting a dim religious light. *Ib, 159*

12 Till old experience do attain
To something like prophetic strain. *Ib, 173*

13 These pleasures, Melancholy, give;
And I with thee will choose to live. *Ib, 175*

14 Hence, loathed Melancholy,
Of Cerberus and blackest Midnight born
In Stygian cave forlorn
'Mongst horrid shapes, and shrieks, and sights unholy! *L'Allegro, 1*

15 So buxom, blithe, and debonair. *Ib, 24*

16 Haste thee, Nymph, and bring with thee
Jest, and youthful Jollity,
Quips and Cranks and wanton Wiles,
Nods and Becks and wreathed Smiles. *Ib, 25*

17 Sport that wrinkled Care derides,
And Laughter holding both his sides.
Come, and trip it as you go
On the light fantastic toe. *Ib, 31*

18 The mountain-nymph, sweet Liberty. *Ib, 36*

1 And, if I give thee honour due,
Mirth, admit me of thy crew,
To live with her, and live with thee,
In unreproved pleasures free. *L'Allegro, 37*

2 To hear the lark begin his flight,
And, singing, startle the dull night,
From his watch-tower in the skies,
Till the dappled dawn doth rise;
Then to come, in spite of sorrow,
And at my window bid good morrow,
Through the sweet-briar or the vine,
Or the twisted eglantine. *Ib, 41*

3 While the ploughman, near at hand,
Whistles o'er the furrowed land,
And the milkmaid singeth blithe,
And the mower whets his scythe,
And every shepherd tells his tale
Under the hawthorn in the dale. *Ib, 63*

4 Then to the spicy nut-brown ale. *Ib, 100*

5 Towered cities please us then,
And the busy hum of men. *Ib, 117*

6 Store of ladies, whose bright eyes
Rain influence, and judge the prize
Of wit or arms. *Ib, 121*

7 Such sights as youthful poets dream
On summer eves by haunted stream. *Ib, 129*

8 Or sweetest Shakespeare, Fancy's child,
Warble his native wood-notes wild. *Ib, 133*

9 Untwisting all the chains that tie
The hidden soul of harmony. *Ib, 143*

10 Such strains as would have won the ear
Of Pluto, to have quite set free
His half-regained Eurydice. *Ib, 148*

11 These delights if thou canst give,
Mirth, with thee I mean to live. *Ib, 151*

12 Yet once more, O ye laurels, and once more,
Ye myrtles brown, with ivy never sere,
I come to pluck your berries harsh and crude,
And with forced fingers rude
Shatter your leaves before the mellowing year. *Lycidas, 1*

13 He knew
Himself to sing, and build the lofty rhyme. *Ib, 10*

14 But, oh! the heavy change, now thou art gone,
Now thou art gone, and never must return! *Ib, 37*

15 Alas! what boots it with incessant care
To tend the homely, slighted, shepherd's trade,
And strictly meditate the thankless Muse? *Ib, 64*

16 To sport with Amaryllis in the shade,
Or with the tangles of Neaera's hair? *Ib, 68*

1 Fame is the spur that the clear spirit doth raise
(That last infirmity of noble mind)
To scorn delights, and live laborious days. *Lycidas, 70*

2 Fame is no plant that grows on mortal soil. *Ib, 78*

3 Blind mouths! that scarce themselves know how to hold
A sheep-hook. *Ib, 119*

4 And, when they list, their lean and flashy songs
Grate on their scrannel pipes of wretched straw;
The hungry sheep look up, and are not fed,
But, swoln with wind and the rank mist they draw,
Rot inwardly, and foul contagion spread. *Ib, 123*

5 Bring the rathe primrose that forsaken dies. *Ib, 142*

6 At last he rose, and twitched his mantle blue:
To-morrow to fresh woods, and pastures new. *Ib, 192*

7 This is the month, and this the happy morn. *On the Morning of Christ's Nativity, 1*

8 It was the winter wild,
While the Heaven-born Child
All meanly wrapt in the rude manger lies. *Ib, 29*

9 Time will run back and fetch the age of gold. *Ib, 135*

10 So when the sun in bed,
Curtained with cloudy red,
Pillows his chin upon an orient wave. *Ib, 229*

11 What needs my Shakespeare for his honoured bones,
The labour of an age in piled stones? *On Shakespeare, 1*

12 Dear son of memory, great heir of fame,
What need'st thou such weak witness of thy name? *Ib, 5*

13 Kings for such a tomb would wish to die. *Ib, 16*

14 Rhyme being no necessary adjunct or true ornament of poem or good verse, in longer works especially, but the invention of a barbarous age, to set off wretched matter and lame metre. *Paradise Lost, Preface, The Verse*

15 Of Man's first disobedience, and the fruit
Of that forbidden tree, whose mortal taste
Brought death into the World, and all our woe,
With loss of Eden, till one greater Man
Restore us, and regain the blissful seat,
Sing, Heavenly Muse. *Ib, Book 1, 1*

16 Things unattempted yet in prose or rhyme. *Ib, 1, 16*

17 What in me is dark
Illumine, what is low raise and support;
That, to the height of this great argument,
I may assert Eternal Providence,
And justify the ways of God to men. *Ib, 1, 22*

18 What though the field be lost?
All is not lost—the unconquerable will,
And study of revenge, immortal hate,
And courage never to submit or yield:
And what is else not to be overcome? *Ib, 1, 105*

1 To be weak is miserable,
Doing or suffering. *Paradise Lost, Book, 1, 157*

2 And out of good still to find means of evil. *Ib, 1, 165*

3 What reinforcement we may gain from hope,
If not, what resolution from despair. *Ib, 1, 190*

4 Farewell, happy fields,
Where joy for ever dwells! Hail, horrors! hail. *Ib, 1, 249*

5 A mind not to be changed by place or time.
The mind is its own place, and in itself
Can make a Heaven of Hell, a Hell of Heaven. *Ib, 1, 253*

6 To reign is worth ambition, though in Hell:
Better to reign in Hell than serve in Heaven. *Ib, 1, 262*

7 Awake, arise, or be for ever fallen! *Ib, 1, 330*

8 And when night
Darkens the streets, then wander forth the sons
Of Belial, flown with insolence and wine. *Ib, 1, 500*

9 Th' imperial ensign; which, full high advanced,
Shone like a meteor streaming to the wind. *Ib, 1, 536*

10 A shout that tore Hell's concave, and beyond
Frighted the reign of Chaos and old Night. *Ib, 1, 542*

11 His form had yet not lost
All her original brightness, nor appeared
Less than Archangel ruined, and the excess
Of glory obscured. *Ib, 1, 591*

12 Tears, such as Angels weep, burst forth. *Ib, 1, 620*

13 Who overcomes
By force hath overcome but half his foe. *Ib, 1, 648*

14 From morn
To noon he fell, from noon to dewy eve,
A summer's day, and with the setting sun
Dropped from the zenith, like a falling star. *Ib, 1, 742*

15 High on a throne of royal state, which far
Outshone the wealth of Ormus and of Ind,
Or where the gorgeous East with richest hand
Showers on her kings barbaric pearl and gold,
Satan exalted sat, by merit raised
To that bad eminence. *Ib, Book 2, 1*

16 My sentence is for open war. Of wiles,
More unexpert, I boast not. *Ib, 2, 51*

17 In our proper motion we ascend
Up to our native seat; descent and fall
To us is adverse. *Ib, 2, 75*

18 Though his tongue
Dropped manna, and could make the worse appear
The better reason. *Ib, 2, 112*

19 For who would lose,
Though full of pain, this intellectual being,
Those thoughts that wander through eternity,

To perish rather, swallowed up and lost
In the wide womb of uncreated Night,
Devoid of sense and motion? *Paradise Lost, Book, 2, 146*

1 Unrespited, unpitied, unreprieved,
Ages of hopeless end. *Ib, 2, 185*

2 Our torments also may, in length of time,
Become our elements. *Ib, 2, 274*

3 With grave
Aspect he rose, and in his rising seemed
A pillar of state; deep on his front engraven
Deliberation sat, and public care;
And princely counsel in his face yet shone,
Majestic, though in ruin. *Ib, 2, 300*

4 Another World, the happy seat
Of some new race, called Man, about this time
To be created like to us, though less
In power and excellence. *Ib, 2, 347*

5 Long is the way
And hard that out of Hell leads up to light. *Ib, 2, 432*

6 Others apart sat on a hill retired,
In thoughts more elevate, and reasoned high
Of Providence, Foreknowledge, Will, and Fate—
Fixed fate, free will, foreknowledge absolute—
And found no end, in wandering mazes lost. *Ib, 2, 557*

7 The other Shape—
If shape it might be called that shape had none. *Ib, 2, 666*

8 For Hot, Cold, Moist, and Dry, four champions fierce,
Strive here for mastery. *Ib, 2, 898*

9 Hail, holy Light, offspring of Heaven first-born! *Ib, Book 3, 1*

10 Thus with the year
Seasons return; but not to me returns
Day, or the sweet approach of even or morn,
Or sight of vernal bloom, or summer's rose,
Or flocks, or herds, or human face divine;
But cloud instead and ever-during dark
Surrounds me. *Ib, 3, 40*

11 Into a Limbo large and broad, since called
The Paradise of Fools; to few unknown. *Ib, 3, 495*

12 At whose sight all the stars
Hide their diminished heads. *Ib, Book 4, 34*

13 Me miserable! which way shall I fly
Infinite wrath and infinite despair?
Which way I fly is Hell; myself am Hell;
And, in the lowest deep, a lower deep
Still threat'ning to devour me opens wide,
To which the Hell I suffer seems a Heaven. *Ib, 4, 73*

14 So farewell hope, and, with hope, farewell fear,
Farewell remorse! All good to me is lost;
Evil, be thou my Good. *Ib, 4, 180*

1 Thence up he flew, and on the Tree of Life,
The middle tree and highest there that grew,
Sat like a cormorant. *Paradise Lost, Book 4, 194*

2 A Heaven on Earth. *Ib, 4, 208*

3 For contemplation he and valour formed,
For softness she and sweet attractive grace;
He for God only, she for God in him. *Ib, 4, 297*

4 Adam, the goodliest man of men since born
His sons; the fairest of her daughters Eve. *Ib, 4, 323*

5 Imparadised in one another's arms. *Ib, 4, 506*

6 Now came still Evening on, and Twilight grey
Had in her sober livery all things clad. *Ib, 4, 598*

7 God is thy law, thou mine: to know no more
Is woman's happiest knowledge, and her praise.
With thee conversing, I forget all time. *Ib, 4, 637*

8 Hail, wedded Love, mysterious law, true source
Of human offspring. *Ib, 4, 750*

9 Not to know me argues yourselves unknown. *Ib, 4, 830*

10 Abashed the Devil stood,
And felt how awful goodness is, and saw
Virtue in her shape how lovely. *Ib, 4, 846*

11 But wherefore thou alone? Wherefore with thee
Came not all Hell broke loose? *Ib, 4, 917*

12 Now Morn, her rosy steps in th' eastern clime
Advancing, sowed the earth with orient pearl. *Ib, Book 5, 1*

13 Good, the more
Communicated, more abundant grows. *Ib, 5, 71*

14 Best image of myself, and dearer half. *Ib, 5, 95*

15 Him first, him last, him midst, and without end. *Ib, 5, 165*

16 Nor jealousy
Was understood, the injured lover's hell. *Ib, 5, 449*

17 Midnight brought on the dusky hour
Friendliest to sleep and silence. *Ib, 5, 667*

18 Among the faithless, faithful only he. *Ib, 5, 897*

19 Servant of God, well done! Well hast thou fought
The better fight, who single hast maintained
Against revolted multitudes the cause
Of truth, in word mightier than they in arms. *Ib, Book 6, 29*

20 More safe I sing with mortal voice, unchanged
To hoarse or mute, though fallen on evil days,
On evil days though fallen, and evil tongues;
In darkness, and with dangers compassed round,
And solitude. *Ib, Book 7, 24*

21 God saw the light was good;
And light from darkness by the hemisphere
Divided: light the Day, and darkness Night,
He named. *Ib, 7, 249*

1 The Angel ended, and in Adam's ear
So charming left his voice that he a while
Thought him still speaking, still stood fixed to hear. *Paradise Lost, Book 8, 1*

2 To know
That which before us lies in daily life,
Is the prime wisdom. *Ib, 8, 192*

3 In solitude
What happiness? who can enjoy alone,
Or, all enjoying, what contentment find? *Ib, 8, 364*

4 Accuse not Nature! she hath done her part;
Do thou but thine. *Ib, 8, 561*

5 My unpremeditated verse. *Ib, Book 9, 24*

6 Since first this subject for heroic song
Pleased me, long choosing and beginning late. *Ib, 9, 25*

7 Revenge, at first though sweet,
Bitter ere long back on itself recoils. *Ib, 9, 171*

8 For solitude sometimes is best society,
And short retirement urges sweet return. *Ib, 9, 249*

9 As one who, long in populous city pent,
Where houses thick and sewers annoy the air. *Ib, 9, 445*

10 O fairest of creation, last and best
Of all God's works, creature in whom excelled
Whatever can to sight or thought be formed,
Holy, divine, good, amiable, or sweet!
How art thou lost! how on a sudden lost,
Defaced, deflowered, and now to death devote! *Ib, 9, 896*

11 Yet I shall temper so
Justice with mercy as may illustrate most
Them fully satisfied, and thee appease. *Ib, Book 10, 77*

12 A dismal universal hiss, the sound
Of public scorn. *Ib, 10, 508*

13 Demoniac frenzy, moping melancholy,
And moon-struck madness. *Ib, Book 11, 485*

14 Nor love thy life, nor hate; but what thou liv'st
Live well; how long or short permit to Heaven. *Ib, 11, 553*

15 A bevy of fair women, richly gay
In gems and wanton dress. *Ib, 11, 582*

16 An olive-leaf he brings, pacific sign. *Ib, 11, 860*

17 In me is no delay; with thee to go
Is to stay here; without thee here to stay
Is to go hence unwilling; thou to me
Art all things under Heaven, all places thou,
Who for my wilful crime art banished hence. *Ib, Book 12, 615*

18 The world was all before them, where to choose
Their place of rest, and Providence their guide:
They, hand in hand, with wandering steps and slow,
Through Eden took their solitary way. *Ib, 12, 646*

1 Most men admire
Virtue who follow not her lore. *Paradise Regained, Book 1, 482*

2 Beauty stands
In the admiration only of weak minds
Led captive. *Ib, Book 2, 220*

3 The childhood shows the man,
As morning shows the day. *Ib, Book 4, 220*

4 The first and wisest of them all professed
To know this only, that he nothing knew. *Ib, 4, 293*

5 Deep-versed in books and shallow in himself. *Ib, 4, 327*

6 He, unobserved,
Home to his mother's house private returned. *Ib, 4, 638*

7 Let us with a gladsome mind,
Praise the Lord, for He is kind,
For His mercies ay endure,
Ever faithful, ever sure. *Psalm 136*

8 A little onward lend thy guiding hand
To these dark steps, a little further on. SAMSON *Samson Agonistes, 1*

9 Ask for this great deliverer now, and find him
Eyeless in Gaza at the mill with slaves. SAMSON *Ib, 40*

10 O dark, dark, dark, amid the blaze of noon,
Irrecoverably dark, total eclipse,
Without all hope of day! SAMSON *Ib, 80*

11 The Sun to me is dark
And silent as the Moon,
When she deserts the night,
Hid in her vacant interlunar cave. SAMSON *Ib, 86*

12 Wisest men
Have erred, and by bad women been deceived. CHORUS *Ib, 210*

13 Just are the ways of God,
And justifiable to men,
Unless there be who think not God at all. CHORUS *Ib, 293*

14 Let me here,
As I deserve, pay on my punishment,
And expiate, if possible, my crime,
Shameful garrulity. SAMSON *Ib, 488*

15 But who is this, what thing of sea or land?
Female of sex it seems,
That, so bedecked, ornate, and gay,
Comes this way sailing,
Like a stately ship
Of Tarsus, bound for th' isles
Of Javan or Gadire,
With all her bravery on, and tackle trim,
Sails filled, and streamers waving,
Courted by all the winds that hold them play. CHORUS *Ib, 710*

16 Out, out, hyaena! These are thy wonted arts,
And arts of every woman false like thee. SAMSON *Ib, 748*

1 Weakness is thy excuse,
And I believe it; weakness to resist
Philistian gold. SAMSON *Samson Agonistes, 829*

2 At length, that grounded maxim,
So rife and celebrated in the mouths
Of wisest men, that to the public good
Private respects must yield, with grave authority
Took full possession of me, and prevailed. DALILA *Ib, 865*

3 In argument with men a woman ever
Goes by the worse, whatever be her cause. DALILA *Ib, 903*

4 Fame, if not double-faced, is double-mouthed,
And with contrary blast proclaims most deeds. DALILA *Ib, 971*

5 Yet beauty, though injurious, hath strange power,
After offence returning, to regain
Love once possessed. CHORUS *Ib, 1003*

6 He's gone, and who knows how he may report
Thy words by adding fuel to the flame? CHORUS *Ib, 1350*

7 All is best, though we oft doubt
What th' unsearchable dispose
Of Highest Wisdom brings about. CHORUS *Ib, 1745*

8 His servants he, with new acquist
Of true experience from this great event,
With peace and consolation hath dismissed,
And calm of mind, all passion spent. CHORUS *Ib, 1755*

9 How soon hath Time, the subtle thief of youth,
Stolen on his wing my three-and-twentieth year! *Sonnet, On being arrived at the age of twenty-three*

10 When I consider how my light is spent,
Ere half my days in this dark world and wide,
And that one talent which is death to hide
Lodged with me useless. *Sonnet, On his Blindness*

11 God doth not need
Either man's work or his own gifts. Who best
Bear his mild yoke, they serve him best: his state
Is kingly: thousands at his bidding speed,
And post o'er land and ocean without rest;
They also serve who only stand and wait. *Ib*

12 New Presbyter is but old Priest writ large. *Sonnet, On the new Forcers of Conscience under the Long Parliament*

13 Peace hath her victories
No less renowned than War. *Sonnet, To the Lord General Cromwell, May 1652*

14 For what can war but endless war still breed? *Sonnet, On the Lord General Fairfax*

15 Fly envious Time, till thou run out thy race,
Call on the lazy, leaden-stepping hours. *Sonnet, On Time*

16 Methought I saw my late espoused saint. *Sonnet, On his deceased wife*

1 He who would not be frustrate of his hope to write well hereafter in laudable things ought himself to be a true poem. *Apology for Smectymnuus*

2 Who kills a man kills a reasonable creature, God's image; but he who destroys a good book, kills reason itself, kills the image of God, as it were in the eye. *Areopagitica*

3 A good book is the precious life-blood of a master spirit, embalmed and treasured up on purpose to a life beyond life. *Ib*

4 I cannot praise a fugitive and cloistered virtue, unexercised and unbreathed, that never sallies out and sees her adversary, but slinks out of the race, where that immortal garland is to be run for, not without dust and heat. *Ib*

5 Our sage and serious poet Spenser, whom I dare be known to think a better teacher than Scotus or Aquinas. *Ib*

6 God sure esteems the growth and completing of one virtuous person more than the restraint of ten vicious. *Ib*

7 God is decreeing to begin some new and great period in His Church, even to the reforming of Reformation itself: what does He then but reveal Himself to His servants, and as His manner is, first to His Englishmen? *Ib*

8 Methinks I see in my mind a noble and puissant nation rousing herself like a strong man after sleep, and shaking her invincible locks. Methinks I see her as an eagle mewing her mighty youth, and kindling her undazzled eyes at the full midday beam. *Ib*

9 Give me the liberty to know, to utter, and to argue freely according to conscience, above all liberties. *Ib*

10 Let her and Falsehood grapple; who ever knew Truth put to the worse, in a free and open encounter? *Ib*

11 None can love freedom heartily, but good men; the rest love not freedom, but licence. *Tenure of Kings and Magistrates*

MIRABEAU, Comte de, 1749–1791

12 *La guerre est l'industrie nationale de la Prusse.* War is the national industry of Prussia. *Attributed*

MOLIÈRE (Jean Baptiste Poquelin), 1622–1673

13 *Par ma foi! il y a plus de quarante ans que je dis de la prose sans que j'en susse rien.* M. JOURDAIN
Good heavens! I have been talking prose for over forty years without realizing it. *Le Bourgeois Gentilhomme, Act 2, Scene 4*

14 *C'est une folie à nulle autre seconde,*
De vouloir se mêler à corriger le monde. PHILINTE
It is a stupidity second to none, to want to busy oneself with the correction of the world. *Le Misanthrope, Act 1, Scene 1*

15 *Ah! pour être dévot, je n'en suis pas moins homme!* TARTUFFE
Oh, I may be devout, but I am human all the same. *Tartuffe, Act 3, Scene 3*

16 *La scandale du monde est ce qui fait l'offense,*
Et ce n'est pas pécher que pécher en silence. TARTUFFE
It is a public scandal that gives offence, and it is no sin to sin in secret. *Ib, Act 4, Scene 5*

MONKHOUSE, William Cosmo, 1840–1901

1 There was an old party of Lyme,
Who married three wives at one time.
When asked, 'Why the third?'
He replied, 'One's absurd,
And bigamy, sir, is a crime!' *Limerick*

MONSELL, John Samuel Bewley, 1811–1875

2 Fight the good fight with all thy might,
Christ is thy strength, and Christ thy right;
Lay hold on life, and it shall be
Thy joy and crown eternally. *Fight the Good Fight*

MONTAIGNE, Michel de, 1533–1592

3 The greatest thing in the world is to know how to be self-sufficient. *Essays, 1, 39*

4 When I play with my cat, who knows whether she is not amusing herself with me more than I with her. *Ib, 2, 12*

5 Marriage is like a cage; one sees the birds outside desperate to get in, and those inside equally desperate to get out. *Ib, 3, 5*

6 It might well be said of me that here I have merely made up a bunch of other men's flowers, and provided nothing of my own but the string to tie them together. *Ib, 3, 12*

MONTGOMERY OF ALAMEIN, Bernard Law, 1st Viscount, 1887—

7 Anyone who votes Labour ought to be locked up. *Speech, Woodford, Essex, 1959*

MONTROSE, Percy, 19th century

8 In a cavern, in a canyon,
Excavating for a mine,
Dwelt a miner, Forty-niner,
And his daughter Clementine.
Oh my darling, oh my darling, oh my darling Clementine!
Thou art lost and gone for ever, dreadful sorry, Clementine. *Clementine*

9 Light she was and like a fairy,
And her shoes were number nine;
Herring boxes, without topses,
Sandals were for Clementine. *Ib*

10 How I missed her, how I missed her,
How I missed my Clementine!
But I kissed her little sister,
And forgot my Clementine. *Ib*

MOORE, Thomas, 1779–1852

11 The harp that once through Tara's halls
The soul of music shed,
Now hangs as mute on Tara's walls,
As if that soul were fled. *Irish Melodies, The Harp that once through Tara's Halls*

1 'Tis the last rose of summer
Left blooming alone;
All her lovely companions
Are faded and gone. *Irish Melodies, The Last Rose of Summer*

2 The Minstrel Boy to the war is gone,
In the ranks of death you'll find him;
His father's sword he has girded on,
And his wild harp slung behind him. *Ib, The Minstrel Boy*

3 'Come, Come,' said Tom's father, 'at your time of life,
There's no longer excuse for thus playing the rake—
It is time you should think, boy, of taking a wife'—
'Why, so it is, father—whose wife shall I take?' *A Joke Versified*

MORE, Sir Thomas, 1478–1535

4 I pray you, Master Lieutenant, see me safe up, and for coming down let me shift for myself. [*On mounting the scaffold*] *Roper, Life of Sir Thomas More*

5 Pluck up thy spirits, man, and be not afraid to do thine office; my neck is very short; take heed therefore thou strike not awry, for saving of thine honesty. [*To the executioner*] *Ib*

MORELL, Thomas, 1703–1784

6 See, the conquering hero comes!
Sound the trumpets, beat the drums! *Joshua, Pt. 3*

MORGAN, Augustus de, 1806–1871

7 Great fleas have little fleas upon their backs to bite 'em,
And little fleas have lesser fleas, and so *ad infinitum.*
A Budget of Paradoxes

MORLEY, Christopher Darlington, 1890–1957

8 The man who never in his life
Has washed the dishes with his wife
Or polished up the silver plate—
He still is largely celibate. *Washing the Dishes*

MORRIS, William, 1834–1896

9 Dreamer of dreams, born out of my due time,
Why should I strive to set the crooked straight? *The Earthly Paradise, An Apology*

10 Love is enough: though the world be a-waning,
And the woods have no voice but the voice of complaining.
Love is Enough, 1

MOTLEY, John Lothrop, 1814–1877

11 Give us the luxuries of life, and we will dispense with its necessities.
O. W. Holmes, The Autocrat of the Breakfast Table, Ch. 6

MOTTEUX, Peter Anthony, 1660–1718

1 The devil was sick, the devil a monk wou'd be;
The devil was well, and the devil a monk he'd be. *Translation of Rabelais, Gargantua and Pantagruel, Bk. 4, Ch. 24*

MUNRO, Hector Hugh, see 'SAKI'

MUNSTER, Ernst Friedrich Herbert, 1766–1839

2 Absolutism tempered by assassination. [*The Russian Constitution*] *Letter*

MURDOCH, Richard, 1907—, and HORNE, Kenneth, 1900–1969

3 Have you read any good books lately? *Much Binding in the Marsh, B.B.C. Radio Programme, 1945 to 1954*

MURPHY, C. W., 19th century

4 Has anybody here seen Kelly?
Kelly from the Isle of Man? *Has Anybody Here Seen Kelly?*

MUSSET, Alfred de, 1810–1857

5 *Il faut qu'une porte soit ouverte ou fermée.* A door must be either open or shut. *Title of Play*

6 *On ne badine pas avec l'amour.* One must not trifle with love. *Title of Play*

NAIRNE, Lady Carolina, 1766–1845

7 Charlie is my darling, my darling, my darling,
Charlie is my darling, the young Chevalier. *Charlie is my Darling*

8 Better lo'ed ye canna be,
Will ye no come back again? *Will ye no come back again?*

NAPIER, Sir Charles James, 1782–1853

9 *Peccavi.* [I have Sind]. *Despatch after victory of Hyderabad in Sind, 1843*

NAPOLEON, Bonaparte, 1769–1821

10 *Soldats, songez que, du haut de ces pyramides, quarante siècles vous contemplent.* —Think of it, soldiers, from the summit of these pyramids, forty centuries look down upon you. *Speech before Battle of the Pyramids, 1798*

11 *Du sublime au ridicule il n'y a qu'un pas.*—It is only a step from the sublime to the ridiculous. *After the retreat from Moscow, 1812*

12 *L'Angleterre est une nation de boutiquiers.*—England is a nation of shop-keepers. *Attributed, See Adam Smith*

13 *Tout soldat français porte dans sa giberne le bâton de maréchal de France.*— Every French soldier carries in his cartridge-pouch the baton of a marshal of France. *Attributed*

14 An army marches on its stomach. *Attributed*

NASH, Ogden, 1902–1971

1 A girl whose cheeks are covered with paint
Has an advantage with me over one whose ain't. *Biological Reflection*

2 One would be in less danger
From the wiles of the stranger
If one's own kin and kith
Were more fun to be with. *Family Court*

3 Home is heaven and orgies are vile
But you need an orgy, once in a while. *Home, 99 44/100% Sweet Home*

4 Beneath this slab
John Brown is stowed.
He watched the ads
And not the road. *Lather as You Go*

5 I have a bone to pick with fate,
Come here and tell me, girlie,
Do you think my mind is maturing late,
Or simply rotted early? *Lines on Facing Forty*

6 Children aren't happy with nothing to ignore,
And that's what parents were created for. *The Parent*

7 A bit of talcum
Is always walcum. *Reflection on Babies*

8 Candy
is dandy
But liquor
is quicker. *Reflection on Ice-Breaking*

9 I test my bath before I sit,
And I'm always moved to wonderment
That what chills the finger not a bit
Is so frigid upon the fundament. *Samson Agonistes*

10 I think that I shall never see
A billboard lovely as a tree.
Perhaps unless the billboards fall,
I'll never see a tree at all. *Song of the Open Road*

11 The turtle lives 'twixt plated decks
Which practically conceal its sex.
I think it clever of the turtle
In such a fix to be so fertile. *The Turtle*

NASHE, Thomas, 1567–1601

12 Brightness falls from the air;
Queens have died young and fair;
Dust hath closed Helen's eye. *In Time of Pestilence*

NEALE, John Mason, 1818–1866

13 Brief Life is here our portion;
Brief sorrow, short-lived care. *Brief Life is Here*

14 Good Christian men, rejoice
With heart, and soul, and voice. *Good Christian Men*

1 Good King Wenceslas looked out
On the Feast of Stephen;
When the snow lay round about,
Deep and crisp and even. *Good King Wenceslas*

2 Bring me flesh and bring me wine,
Bring me pine logs hither. *Ib*

3 In his master's steps he trod
Where the snow lay dinted. *Ib*

NELSON, Horatio, 1st Viscount, 1758–1805

4 Westminster Abbey or victory. *Remark at Battle of Cape St. Vincent*

5 England expects every man will do his duty. *Battle of Trafalgar*

6 Thank God, I have done my duty. *Ib*

7 Kiss me, Hardy. *Ib*

NERO (Nero Claudius Caesar), A.D. 37–68

8 *Qualis artifex pereo!* What an artist dies with me! *Last words, attributed*

NEWBOLT, Sir Henry John, 1862–1938

9 Drake he's in his hammock till the great Armadas come.
(Capten, art tha sleepin' there below?)
Slung atween the round shot, listenin' for the drum,
An' dreamin' arl the time o' Plymouth Hoe. *Drake's Drum*

10 Where the old trade's plying an' the old flag flyin'
They shall find him ware an' wakin', as they found him long ago! *Ib*

11 There's a breathless hush in the Close to-night—
Ten to make and the match to win—
A bumping pitch and a blinding light,
An hour to play and the last man in. *Vitai Lampada*

12 But his captain's hand on his shoulder smote—
'Play up! play up! and play the game!' *Ib*

NEWMAN, John Henry, Cardinal, 1801–1890

13 It is almost a definition of a gentleman to say that he is one who never inflicts pain. *The Idea of a University, Knowledge and Religious Duty*

14 Lead, Kindly Light, amid the encircling gloom,
Lead thou me on;
The night is dark, and I am far from home,
Lead thou me on. *Lead Kindly Light*

NICHOLAS I of Russia, 1796–1855

15 Russia has two generals in whom she can confide—Generals Janvier and Février. *Punch, 10 March 1853*

NORTH, Christopher (John Wilson), 1785–1854

16 His Majesty's dominions, on which the sun never sets.
Noctes Ambrosianae, No. 20, April 1829

17 Laws were made to be broken. *Ib, No. 24, May 1830*

NOYES, Alfred, 1880–1958

1 Go down to Kew in lilac-time, in lilac-time, in lilac-time,
  Go down to Kew in lilac-time (it isn't far from London!)
And you shall wander hand in hand with love in summer's wonderland;
  Go down to Kew in lilac-time (it isn't far from London!)

The Barrel Organ

2 Look for me by moonlight;
  Watch for me by moonlight;
I'll come to thee by moonlight, though hell should bar the way!

The Highwayman

NURSERY RHYMES

The Oxford Dictionary of Nursery Rhymes, edited by Iona and Peter Opie, gives the sources of over 500 nursery rhymes.

In many cases nursery rhymes have changed considerably since they first appeared in print. It seemed most useful, in the selection of familiar nursery rhymes below, to give the version most commonly in use to-day, together with title and date of the first known publication.

3 As I was going to St. Ives,
I met a man with seven wives.

Mother Goose's Quarto, c. 1825

4 Baa, baa, black sheep,
  Have you any wool?
Yes, sir, yes, sir,
  Three bags full;
One for the master,
  And one for the dame,
And one for the little boy
  Who lives down the lane.

Tommy Thumb's Pretty Song Book, c. 1744

5 Bobby Shafto's gone to sea,
  Silver buckles at his knee;
He'll come back and marry me,
  Bonny Bobby Shafto!

Songs for the Nursery, 1805

6 Boys and girls come out to play,
The moon doth shine as bright as day.

Useful Transactions in Philosophy, William King, 1708–9

7 Cock a doodle doo!
My dame has lost her shoe,
My master's lost his fiddlestick,
And knows not what to do.

The Most Cruel and Bloody Murder, 1606

8 Curly locks, Curly locks,
  Wilt thou be mine?
Thou shalt not wash dishes
  Nor yet feed the swine,
But sit on a cushion
  And sew a fine seam,
And feed upon strawberries,
  Sugar and cream.

Infant Institutes, 1797

9 Ding, dong, bell,
Pussy's in the well.
Who put her in?

Little Johnny Green.
Who pulled her out?
Little Tommy Stout. *Mother Goose's Melody, c. 1765*

1 Eena, meena, mina, mo,
Catch a nigger by his toe;
If he squeals, let him go,
Eena, meena, mina, mo. *Games and Songs of American Children, Newell, 1883*

2 A frog he would a-wooing go,
Heigh ho! says Rowley,
A frog he would a-wooing go,
Whether his mother would let him or no.
With a rowley, powley, gammon and spinach,
Heigh ho! says Anthony Rowley. *Melismata, Thomas Ravenscroft, 1611*

3 Georgie Porgie, pudding and pie,
Kissed the girls and made them cry;
When the boys came out to play,
Georgie Porgie ran away. *Nursery Rhymes, J. O. Halliwell, 1844*

4 Goosey, goosey gander,
Whither shall I wander?
Upstairs and downstairs
And in my lady's chamber. *Gammer Gurton's Garland, 1784*

5 Hey diddle diddle,
The cat and the fiddle,
The cow jumped over the moon;
The little dog laughed
To see such sport,
And the dish ran away with the spoon. *Mother Goose's Melody, c. 1765*

6 Hickory, dickory, dock,
The mouse ran up the clock.
The clock struck one,
The mouse ran down,
Hickory, dickory, dock. *Tommy Thumb's Pretty Song Book, c. 1744*

7 Hot cross buns!
Hot cross buns!
One a penny, two a penny,
Hot cross buns! *Christmas Box, 1797*

8 How many miles to Babylon?
Three score miles and ten.
Can I get there by candle-light?
Yes, and back again.
If your heels are nimble and light,
You may get there by candle-light. *Songs for the Nursery, 1805*

9 Humpty Dumpty sat on a wall,
Humpty Dumpty had a great fall.
All the king's horses,
And all the king's men,
Couldn't put Humpty together again. *Gammer Gurton's Garland, 1810*

10 Hush-a-bye, baby, on the tree top,
When the wind blows the cradle will rock;
When the bough breaks the cradle will fall,
Down will come baby, cradle, and all. *Mother Goose's Melody, c. 1765*

1 I had a little nut tree,
Nothing would it bear
But a silver nutmeg
And a golden pear;
The King of Spain's daughter
Came to visit me,
And all for the sake
Of my little nut tree.

Newest Christmas Box, c. 1797

2 I love sixpence, jolly little sixpence,
I love sixpence better than my life;
I spent a penny of it, I lent a penny of it,
And I took fourpence home to my wife.

Gammer Gurton's Garland, 1810

3 I'm the king of the castle,
Get down you dirty rascal.

Brand's Popular Antiquities, 1870

4 I saw three ships come sailing by,
Come sailing by, come sailing by,
I saw three ships come sailing by,
On Christmas day in the morning.

Bishoprick Garland, Sir Cuthbert Sharp, 1834

5 I see the moon,
And the moon sees me;
God bless the moon,
And God bless me.

Gammer Gurton's Garland, 1784

6 Jack and Jill went up the hill
To fetch a pail of water;
Jack fell down and broke his crown,
And Jill came tumbling after.

Mother Goose's Melody, c. 1765

7 Jack Sprat could eat no fat,
His wife could eat no lean,
And so between them both, you see,
They licked the platter clean.

Paroemiologia Anglo-Latina, John Clarke, 1639

8 Ladybird, ladybird,
Fly away home,
Your house is on fire
And your children all gone.

Tommy Thumb's Pretty Song Book, c. 1744

9 The lion and the unicorn
Were fighting for the crown;
The lion beat the unicorn
All round about the town.

Some gave them white bread,
And some gave them brown;
Some gave them plum cake
And drummed them out of town.

Useful Transactions in Philosophy, William King, 1708–9

10 Little Bo-peep has lost her sheep,
And can't tell where to find them;
Leave them alone, and they'll come home,
And bring their tails behind them.

Gammer Gurton's Garland, 1810

1 Little Boy Blue,
  Come blow your horn,
The sheep's in the meadow,
  The cow's in the corn. *Famous Tommy Thumb's Little Story Book, c. 1760*

2 Little Jack Horner
Sat in the corner,
Eating a Christmas pie;
He put in his thumb,
And pulled out a plum,
And said, What a good boy am I! *Namby Pamby, Henry Carey, 1725*

3 Little Miss Muffet
Sat on a tuffet,
Eating her curds and whey;
There came a big spider,
Who sat down beside her
And frightened Miss Muffet away. *Songs for the Nursery, 1805*

4 Little Tommy Tucker,
  Sings for his supper:
What shall we give him?
  White bread and butter.
How shall he cut it
  Without a knife?
How will he be married
  Without a wife? *Tommy Thumb's Pretty Song Book, c. 1744*

5 London Bridge is broken down,
  My fair lady. *Namby Pamby, Henry Carey, 1725*

6   The man in the moon
  Came down too soon,
And asked his way to Norwich;
  He went by the south,
  And burnt his mouth
With supping cold plum porridge. *Gammer Gurton's Garland, 1784*

7 Mary, Mary, quite contrary,
  How does your garden grow?
With silver bells and cockle shells,
  And pretty maids all in a row. *Tommy Thumb's Pretty Song Book, c. 1744*

8 Monday's child is fair of face,
Tuesday's child is full of grace,
Wednesday's child is full of woe,
Thursday's child has far to go,
Friday's child is loving and giving,
Saturday's child works hard for his living,
And the child that is born on the Sabbath day
Is bonny and blithe, and good and gay. *Traditions of Devonshire, A. E. Bray, 1838*

9 My mother said that I never should
Play with the gypsies in the wood;
If I did, she would say,
Naughty girl to disobey. *Come Hither, Walter de la Mare, 1922*

1 Old King Cole
Was a merry old soul,
And a merry old soul was he;
He called for his pipe,
And he called for his bowl,
And he called for his fiddlers three.

Useful Transactions in Philosophy, William King, 1708–9

2 Old Mother Hubbard
Went to the cupboard,
To fetch her poor dog a bone;
But when she got there
The cupboard was bare
And so the poor dog had none.

The Comic Adventures of Old Mother Hubbard and Her Dog, 1805

3 One, two,
Buckle my shoe;
Three, four,
Knock at the door.

Songs for the Nursery, 1805

4 Oranges and lemons,
Say the bells of St. Clement's.

You owe me five farthings,
Say the bells of St. Martin's.

When will you pay me?
Say the bells of Old Bailey.

When I grow rich,
Say the bells of Shoreditch.

When will that be?
Say the bells of Stepney.

I'm sure I don't know,
Says the great bell at Bow.

Here comes a candle to light you to bed,
Here comes a chopper to chop off your head.

Tommy Thumb's Pretty Song Book, c. 1744

5 Pat-a-cake, pat-a-cake, baker's man,
Bake me a cake as fast as you can;
Pat it and prick it, and mark it with B,
Put it in the oven for baby and me.

The Campaigners, Tom D'Urfey, 1698

6 Peter Piper picked a peck of pickled pepper;
A peck of pickled pepper Peter Piper picked;
If Peter Piper picked a peck of pickled pepper,
Where's the peck of pickled pepper Peter Piper picked?

Peter Piper's Practical Principles of Plain and Perfect Pronunciation, 1819

7 Pussy cat, pussy cat, where have you been?
I've been to London to look at the queen.
Pussy cat, pussy cat, what did you there?
I frightened a little mouse under her chair.

Songs for the Nursery, 1805

8 The Queen of Hearts
She made some tarts,

All on a summer's day;
  The Knave of Hearts
  He stole the tarts,
And took them clean away. *The European Magazine, April, 1782*

1 Ride a cock-horse to Banbury Cross,
To see a fine lady upon a white horse;
Rings on her fingers and bells on her toes,
And she shall have music wherever she goes. *Gammer Gurton's Garland, 1784*

2 Ring-a-ring o' roses,
A pocket full of posies,
  A-tishoo! A-tishoo!
We all fall down. *Mother Goose, Kate Greenaway, 1881*

3 See-saw, Margery Daw,
Jacky shall have a new master;
Jacky shall have but a penny a day,
Because he can't work any faster. *Mother Goose's Melody, c. 1765*

4 Simple Simon met a pieman,
  Going to the fair;
Says Simple Simon to the pieman,
  Let me taste your ware.
Says the pieman to Simple Simon,
  Show me first your penny;
Says Simple Simon to the pieman,
  Indeed I have not any. *Simple Simon (Chapbook Advertisement), 1764*

5 Sing a song of sixpence,
  A pocket full of rye;
Four and twenty blackbirds,
  Baked in a pie.

When the pie was opened,
  The birds began to sing;
Was not that a dainty dish,
  To set before the king?

The king was in his counting-house,
  Counting out his money;
The queen was in the parlour,
  Eating bread and honey.

The maid was in the garden,
  Hanging out the clothes,
There came a little blackbird,
  And snapped off her nose. *Tommy Thumb's Pretty Song Book, c. 1744*

6 Solomon Grundy,
Born on a Monday,
Christened on Tuesday,
Married on Wednesday,
Took ill on Thursday,
Worse on Friday,
Died on Saturday,
Buried on Sunday.
This is the end
Of Solomon Grundy. *Nursery Rhymes, J. O. Halliwell, 1842*

1 The first day of Christmas,
My true love sent to me
A partridge in a pear tree. *Mirth without Mischief, c. 1780*

2 The twelfth day of Christmas,
My true love sent to me
Twelve lords a-leaping,
Eleven ladies dancing,
Ten pipers piping,
Nine drummers drumming,
Eight maids a-milking,
Seven swans a-swimming,
Six geese a-laying,
Five gold rings,
Four colly birds,
Three French hens,
Two turtle doves, and
A partridge in a pear tree. *Ib*

3 There was a crooked man, and he walked a crooked mile,
He found a crooked sixpence against a crooked stile:
He bought a crooked cat, which caught a crooked mouse,
And they all lived together in a little crooked house. *Nursery Rhymes, J. O. Halliwell, 1842*

4 There was an old woman
Lived under a hill,

And if she's not gone
She lives there still. *Academy of Complements, 1714*

5 There was an old woman who lived in a shoe,
She had so many children she didn't know what to do;
She gave them some broth without any bread;
She whipped them all soundly and put them to bed. *Gammer Gurton's Garland, 1784*

6 Thirty days hath September,
April, June, and November;
All the rest have thirty-one,
Excepting February alone
And that has twenty-eight days clear
And twenty-nine in each leap year. *Abridgement of the Chronicles of England, Richard Grafton, 1570*

7 This little pig went to market,
This little pig stayed at home,
This little pig had roast beef,
This little pig had none,
And this little pig cried, Wee-wee-wee-wee-wee,
I can't find my way home. *The Famous Tommy Thumb's Little Story Book, c. 1760*

8 This is the farmer sowing his corn,
That kept the cock that crowed in the morn,
That waked the priest all shaven and shorn,
That married the man all tattered and torn,
That kissed the maiden all forlorn,

That milked the cow with the crumpled horn,
That tossed the dog,
That worried the cat,
That killed the rat,
That ate the malt,
That lay in the house that Jack built. *Nurse Truelove's New-Year's-Gift, 1755*

1 Three blind mice, see how they run!
They all run after the farmer's wife,
Who cut off their tails with a carving knife,
Did you ever see such a thing in your life,
As three blind mice? *Deuteromelia, Thomas Ravenscroft, 1609*

2 Tinker,
Tailor,
Soldier,
Sailor,
Rich man,
Poor man,
Beggarman,
Thief. *Popular Rhymes and Nursery Tales, J. O. Halliwell, 1849*

3 Tom, he was a piper's son,
He learnt to play when he was young,
And all the tune that he could play
Was 'Over the hills and far away'. *Tom, The Piper's Son, c. 1795*

4 Tom, Tom, the piper's son,
Stole a pig and away he run;
The pig was eat
And Tom was beat,
And Tom went howling down the street. *Ib*

5 Two little dicky birds,
Sitting on a wall;
One named Peter,
The other named Paul.
Fly away, Peter!
Fly away, Paul!
Come back, Peter!
Come back, Paul! *Mother Goose's Melody, c. 1765*

6 What are little boys made of?
What are little boys made of?
Frogs and snails
And puppy-dogs' tails,
That's what little boys are made of.
What are little girls made of?
What are little girls made of?
Sugar and spice
And all that's nice,
That's what little girls are made of. *Nursery Rhymes, J. O. Halliwell, 1844*

7 Where are you going to, my pretty maid?
I'm going a-milking, sir, she said. *Archaeologia Cornu-Britannica, William Pryce, 1790*

1 What is your fortune, my pretty maid?
My face is my fortune, sir, she said.

Then I can't marry you, my pretty maid.
Nobody asked you, sir, she said. *Archaeologia Cornu-Britannica, William Pryce, 1790*

2 Who killed Cock Robin?
I, said the Sparrow,
With my bow and arrow,
I killed Cock Robin.

Who saw him die?
I, said the Fly,
With my little eye,
I saw him die. *Tommy Thumb's Pretty Song Book, c. 1744*

3 All the birds of the air
Fell a-sighing and a-sobbing,
When they heard the bell toll
For poor Cock Robin. *Ib*

4 Yankee Doodle came to town,
  Riding on a pony;
He stuck a feather in his cap
  And called it macaroni. *Gammer Gurton's Garland, 1810*

For other nursery rhymes, see Thomas Ady (9:13), S. J. Hale (127:11), and Jane Taylor (311:5).

OAKELEY, Frederick, 1802–1880

5 O come, all ye faithful,
Joyful and triumphant,
O come ye, O come ye to Bethlehem. *Hymn translated from Latin, Adeste Fideles*

6 Sing, choirs of Angels,
Sing in exultation,
Sing, all ye citizens of heaven above. *Ib*

OATES, Lawrence Edward Grace, 1880–1912

7 I am just going outside, and may be some time. *Last words. Recorded in Captain R. F. Scott's Antarctic Diary, 16 March 1912*

O'CASEY, Sean, 1884–1964

8 The whole worl's in a state o' chassis. BOYLE *Juno and the Paycock, Act I*

OCHS, Adolph S., 1858–1935

9 All the news that's fit to print. *Motto of New York Times*

O'KEEFE, Patrick, 1872–1934

10 Say it with flowers. *Slogan for Society of American Florists*

OPIE, John, 1761–1807

11 I mix them with my brains, sir. *When asked with what he mixed his colours. Quoted in Samuel Smiles, Self Help, Ch. 4*

ORWELL, George, (Eric Blair) 1903–1950

1 All animals are equal but some animals are more equal than others. *Animal Farm, Ch. 10*

2 It was a bright cold day in April, and the clocks were striking thirteen. *Nineteen Eighty-Four, Pt. 1, Ch. 1*

3 Big Brother is watching you. *Ib*

4 War is Peace, Freedom is Slavery, Ignorance is Strength. *Ib*

5 Down with Big Brother. *Ib*

6 Doublethink means the power of holding two contradictory beliefs in one's mind simultaneously, and accepting both of them. *Ib, Pt. 2, Ch. 9*

OSBORNE, John, 1929—

7 But I have a go, lady, don't I? I 'ave a go. ARCHIE RICE *The Entertainer, No. 7*

8 Don't clap too hard—it's a very old building. ARCHIE RICE *Ib*

9 Yes, thank God we're normal,
Yes, this was our finest shower! ARCHIE RICE *Ib*

10 How I long for a little ordinary human enthusiasm. Just enthusiasm—that's all. I want to hear a warm, thrilling voice cry out Hallelujah! Hallelujah! I'm alive! JIMMY PORTER *Look Back in Anger, Act 1*

11 His knowledge of life and ordinary human beings is so hazy, he really deserves some sort of decoration for it—a medal inscribed 'For Vaguery in the Field'. JIMMY PORTER *Ib*

12 I don't think one 'comes down' from Jimmy's university. According to him, it's not even red brick, but white tile. ALISON PORTER *Ib, Act 2, Scene 1*

OTIS, James, 1725–1783

13 Taxation without representation is tyranny. *Watchword of the American Revolution*

OVID (Publius Ovidius Naso), 43 B.C.–17 A.D.

14 *Quae dant, quaeque negant, gaudent tamen esse rogatae.* Whether they give or refuse, women are glad to have been asked. *Ars Amatoria, 1*

15 *Inopem me copia fecit.* Plenty makes me poor. *Metamorphoses, 3*

16 *Tempus edax rerum.* Time, the devourer of things. *Ib, 15*

OWEN, Robert, 1771–1858

17 All the world is queer save thee and me, and even thou art a little queer. *Of his business partner, William Allen, 1828*

PAINE, Thomas, 1737–1809

18 The sublime and the ridiculous are often so nearly related that it is difficult to class them separately. One step above the sublime makes the ridiculous; and one step above the ridiculous makes the sublime again. *The Age of Reason, Part 2*

19 Government, even in its best state, is but a necessary evil; in its worst state, an intolerable one. *Common Sense, Ch. 1*

PALMERSTON, Henry John Temple, 3rd Viscount, 1784–1865

1 Die, my dear Doctor, that's the last thing I shall do! *Last words, attributed*

PARKER, Dorothy, 1893–1967

2 Men seldom make passes
At girls who wear glasses. *News Item*

3 Guns aren't lawful;
Nooses give;
Gas smells awful;
You might as well live. *Résumé*

PARKER, Ross, 1914—, and CHARLES, Hughie, 1907—

4 There'll always be an England
While there's a country lane,
Wherever there's a cottage small
Beside a field of grain. *There'll Always be an England*

PARKINSON, Cyril Northcote, 1909—

5 Work expands so as to fill the time available for its completion. General recognition of this fact is shown in the proverbial phrase 'It is the busiest man who has time to spare.' *Parkinson's Law*

6 The Law of Triviality. Briefly stated, it means that the time spent on any item of the agenda will be in inverse proportion to the sum involved. *Ib, High Finance or the Point of Vanishing Interest*

PASCAL, Blaise, 1623–1662

7 *Le nez de Cléopâtre: s'il eût été plus court, toute la face de la terre aurait changé.*—Had Cleopatra's nose been shorter, the whole history of the world would have been different. *Pensées, 2, 162*

8 *Le cœur a ses raisons que la raison ne connaît point.*—The heart has its reasons which reason does not know. *Ib, 4, 277*

PATER, Walter Horatio, 1839–1894

9 To burn always with this hard, gem-like flame, to maintain this ecstasy, is success in life. *The Renaissance, Conclusion*

PATERSON, Andrew, 1864–1941

10 Once a jolly swagman camped by a billabong,
Under the shade of a coolibah tree,
And he sang as he sat and waited till his billy boiled,
'You'll come a-waltzing, Matilda, with me.' *Waltzing Matilda*

PATMORE, Coventry Kersey Dighton, 1823–1896

11 'I saw you take his kiss!' 'Tis true,'
'O, modesty!' 'Twas strictly kept:
He thought me asleep; at least, I knew
He thought I thought he thought I slept.'
The Angel in the House, Bk. 2, 8

12 A woman is a foreign land,
Of which, though there he settle young,
A man will ne'er quite understand
The customs, politics, and tongue. *Ib, Bk. 2, 9*

PAUL, Leslie Allen, 1905—

1 Angry Young Man. *Title of Book, 1951*

PAYNE, John Howard, 1791–1852

2 Mid pleasures and palaces though we may roam,
Be it ever so humble, there's no place like home.
Clari, The Maid of Milan, Home, Sweet Home

PEACOCK, Thomas Love, 1785–1866

3 Respectable means rich, and decent means poor. I should die if I heard my family called decent. LADY CLARINDA *Crotchet Castle, Ch. 3*

4 A book that furnishes no quotations is, *me judice*, no book—it is a plaything. *Ib, Ch. 9*

5 There are two reasons for drinking: one is, when you are thirsty, to cure it; the other, when you are not thirsty, to prevent it . . . Prevention is better than cure. MR PORTPIPE *Melincourt, Ch. 16*

6 The mountain sheep are sweeter,
But the valley sheep are fatter;
We therefore deemed it meeter
To carry off the latter. *The Misfortunes of Elphin, Ch. 11, The War Song of Dinas Vawr*

PENN, William, 1644–1718

7 Men are generally more careful of the breed of their horses and dogs than of their children. *Reflexions and Maxims, Pt. 1, 85*

PEPYS, Samuel, 1633–1703

8 And so to bed. *Diary, 6 May 1660 and passim*

9 A silk suit, which cost me much money, and I pray God to make me able to pay for it. *Ib, 1 July 1660*

10 Strange to say what delight we married people have to see these poor fools decoyed into our condition. *Ib, 25 Dec. 1665*

11 Music and women I cannot but give way to, whatever my business is. *Ib, 9 Mar. 1666*

12 To church; and with my mourning, very handsome, and new periwig, make a great show. *Ib, 31 Mar. 1667*

13 And so I betake myself to that course, which is almost as much as to see myself go into my grave; for which, and all the discomforts that will accompany my being blind, the good God prepare me! *Ib, 31 May 1669 (final entry)*

PERRAULT, Charles, 1628–1703

14 She [*Cinderella*] was as good as she was beautiful. *Histoires ou Contes du Temps Passé, 1697. First English Translation by Robert Samber*

15 Sister Anne, sister Anne, do you see anyone coming? BLUE BEARD *Ib*

PÉTAIN, Marshal Henri Phillipe, 1856–1951

16 *Ils ne passeront pas.* They shall not pass. *Verdun, Feb. 1916*

PETRONIUS, ?–66? A.D.

1 *Cave canem.*—Beware of the dog. *Satyricon, 29, 1*

PHELPS, Edward John, 1822–1900

2 The man who makes no mistakes does not usually make anything. *Speech, Mansion House, London, 24 Jan. 1899*

PHILLIPS, Wendell, 1811–1884

3 One on God's side is a majority. *Speech, Brooklyn, 1 Nov. 1859*

4 Every man meets his Waterloo at last. *Ib*

PINDAR, 522?–442? B.C.

5 Water is best. *Olympian Odes, 1*

PITT, William, 1st Earl of Chatham, 1708–1778

6 The atrocious crime of being a young man . . . I shall neither attempt to palliate nor deny. *Speech, House of Commons, 27 Jan. 1741*

7 Unlimited power is apt to corrupt the minds of those who possess it. *Speech, House of Lords, 9 Jan. 1770*

PITT, William, 1759–1806

8 Necessity is the plea for every infringement of human freedom. It is the argument of tyrants; it is the creed of slaves. *Speech, House of Commons, 18 Nov. 1783*

9 England has saved herself by her exertions, and will, as I trust, save Europe by her example. *Speech, Guildhall, 1805*

10 Roll up that map; it will not be wanted these ten years. *On hearing of Napoleon's victory at the Battle of Austerlitz*

11 I think I could eat one of Bellamy's veal pies. *Last words, attributed*

12 Oh, my country! How I leave my country! [Or 'love' for 'leave'] *Last words, attributed*

PLATO, 429?–347? B.C.

13 The good is the beautiful. *Lysis*

14 Our object in the construction of the state is the greatest happiness of the whole, and not that of any one class. *Republic, 4*

PLAUTUS, 254–184 B.C.

15 *Miles gloriosus.*—The Boastful Soldier. *Title of Play*

PLINY, The Elder, 23–79

16 *Ex Africa semper aliquid novi.* There is always something new out of Africa. *Natural History, 2, 8, 42*

17 *In vino veritas.* Truth comes out in wine. *Ib, 14, 141*

POE, Edgar Allan, 1809–1849

18 The glory that was Greece
And the grandeur that was Rome. *To Helen*

19 Take thy beak from out my heart, and take thy form from off my door!
Quoth the Raven, 'Nevermore.' *The Raven*

POMPADOUR, Madame de, 1721–1764

1 *Après nous le déluge.* After us the deluge. *After Battle of Rossbach, 1757*

POPE, Alexander, 1688–1744

2 A wit with dunces, and a dunce with wits. *The Dunciad, 4, 90*

3 The right divine of kings to govern wrong. *Ib, 4, 188*

4 O Grave! where is thy Victory?
O Death! where is thy Sting? *The Dying Christian to his Soul*

5 What beckoning ghost along the moonlight shade
Invites my steps, and points to yonder glade. *Elegy to the Memory of an Unfortunate Lady, 1*

6 Is it, in heav'n, a crime to love too well? *Ib, 6*

7 Ambition first sprung from your blest abodes,
The glorious fault of angels and of gods. *Ib, 13*

8 Love, free as air, at sight of human ties,
Spreads his light wings, and in a moment flies. *Eloisa to Abelard, 75*

9 How happy is the blameless vestal's lot!
The world forgetting, by the world forgot. *Ib, 207*

10 Shut, shut the door, good John! fatigued, I said;
Tie up the knocker, say I'm sick, I'm dead. *Epistle to Dr. Arbuthnot, 1*

11 Is there a parson much bemused in beer,
A maudlin poetess, a rhyming peer,
A clerk, foredoom'd his father's soul to cross,
Who pens a stanza, when he should engross? *Ib, 15*

12 No creature smarts so little as a fool. *Ib, 84*

13 Why did I write? whose sin to me unknown
Dipt me in ink, my parents', or my own?
As yet a child, nor yet a fool to fame,
I lisp'd in numbers, for the numbers came. *Ib, 125*

14 The Muse but serv'd to ease some friend, not Wife,
To help me through this long disease, my Life. *Ib, 131*

15 And He, whose fustian's so sublimely bad,
It is not Poetry, but prose run mad. *Ib, 187*

16 Damn with faint praise, assent with civil leer,
And, without sneering, teach the rest to sneer. *Ib, 201*

17 Who but must laugh, if such a man there be?
Who would not weep, if Atticus were he? *Ib, 213*

18 Curst be the verse, how well so'er it flow,
That tends to make one worthy man my foe. *Ib, 283*

19 Wit that can creep, and pride that licks the dust. *Ib, 333*

20 Unlearn'd, he knew no schoolman's subtle art,
No language but the language of the heart. *Ib, 398*

21 Nature and Nature's Laws lay hid in Night:
God said, Let Newton be! and all was Light. *Epitaph, intended for Sir Isaac Newton*

22 In wit a man; simplicity a child. *Epitaph on Mr. Gay*

1 'Tis hard to say, if greater want of skill
Appear in writing or in judging ill. *An Essay on Criticism, 1*

2 'Tis with our judgments as our watches, none
Go just alike, yet each believes his own. *Ib, 9*

3 First follow Nature, and your judgment frame
By her just standard, which is still the same:
Unerring Nature, still divinely bright,
One clear, unchang'd, and universal light,
Life, force, and beauty, must to all impart,
At once the source, and end, and test of Art. *Ib, 58*

4 Of all the causes which conspire to blind
Man's erring judgment, and misguide the mind,
What the weak head with strongest bias rules,
Is Pride, the never-failing vice of fools. *Ib, 201*

5 A little learning is a dangerous thing;
Drink deep, or taste not the Pierian spring:
There shallow draughts intoxicate the brain,
And drinking largely sobers us again. *Ib, 215*

6 A perfect judge will read each work of Wit
With the same spirit that its author writ. *Ib, 233*

7 Whoever thinks a faultless piece to see,
Thinks what ne'er was, nor is, nor e'er shall be. *Ib, 253*

8 True wit is nature to advantage dress'd;
What oft was thought, but ne'er so well express'd. *Ib, 297*

9 As some to church repair,
Not for the doctrine, but the music there. *Ib, 342*

10 True ease in writing comes from art, not chance,
As those move easiest who have learn'd to dance.
'Tis not enough no harshness gives offence,
The sound must seem an echo to the sense. *Ib, 362*

11 Yet let not each gay turn thy rapture move,
For fools admire, but men of sense approve. *Ib, 390*

12 Some praise at morning what they blame at night,
But always think the last opinion right. *Ib, 430*

13 Fondly we think we honour merit then,
When we but praise ourselves in other men. *Ib, 454*

14 To err is human, to forgive, divine. *Ib, 525*

15 The bookful blockhead, ignorantly read,
With loads of learned lumber in his head. *Ib, 612*

16 For fools rush in where angels fear to tread. *Ib, 625*

17 Awake, my St. John! leave all meaner things
To low ambition, and the pride of kings.
Let us (since life can little more supply
Than just to look about us and to die)
Expatiate free o'er all this scene of man;
A mighty maze! but not without a plan. *An Essay on Man, Epistle 1, 1*

18 Laugh where we must, be candid where we can;
But vindicate the ways of God to Man. *Ib, 1, 15*

1 Hope springs eternal in the human breast;
Man never is, but always to be blest. *An Essay on Man, Epistle 1, 95*

2 Why has not man a microscopic eye?
For this plain reason, man is not a fly. *Ib, 1, 193*

3 All are but parts of one stupendous whole,
Whose body Nature is, and God the soul. *Ib, 1, 267*

4 All nature is but art, unknown to thee;
All chance, direction which thou canst not see;
All discord, harmony not understood;
All partial evil, universal good:
And, spite of pride, in erring reason's spite,
One truth is clear, whatever is, is right. *Ib, 1, 289*

5 Know then thyself, presume not God to scan,
The proper study of Mankind is Man. *Ib, Epistle 2, 1*

6 Vice is a master of so frightful mien,
As to be hated needs but to be seen;
Yet seen too oft, familiar with her face,
We first endure, then pity, then embrace. *Ib, 2, 217*

7 O happiness! our being's end and aim!
Good, pleasure, ease, content! whate'er thy name:
That something still which prompts th' eternal sigh,
For which we bear to live, or dare to die. *Ib, Epistle 4, 1*

8 An honest Man's the noblest work of God. *Ib, 4, 248*

9 If parts allure thee, think how Bacon shined,
The wisest, brightest, meanest of mankind:
Or, ravished with the whistling of a name,
See Cromwell, damned to everlasting fame. *Ib, 4, 281*

10 Formed by thy converse happily to steer
From grave to gay, from lively to severe. *Ib, 4, 379*

11 Thou wert my guide, philosopher, and friend. *Ib, 4, 390*

12 That true self-love and social are the same;
That virtue only makes our bliss below;
And all our knowledge is, ourselves to know. *Ib, 4, 396*

13 To observations which ourselves we make,
We grow more partial for th' observer's sake. *Moral Essays, Epistle 1, 11*

14 'Tis education forms the common mind,
Just as the twig is bent, the tree's inclined. *Ib, 1, 149*

15 Men, some to business, some to pleasure take;
But every woman is at heart a rake. *Ib, Epistle 2, 215*

16 See how the world its veterans rewards!
A youth of frolics, an old age of cards. *Ib, 2, 243*

17 And mistress of herself, though China fall. *Ib, 2, 268*

18 Woman's at best a contradiction still. *Ib, 2, 270*

19 The ruling passion, be it what it will,
The ruling passion conquers reason still. *Ib, Epistle 3, 153*

20 Happy the man, whose wish and care
A few paternal acres bound,
Content to breathe his native air,
In his own ground. *Ode on Solitude*

1 Thus let me live, unseen, unknown,
Thus unlamented let me die,
Steal from the world, and not a stone
Tell where I lie. *Ode on Solitude*

2 I am His Highness' dog at Kew;
Pray tell me sir, whose dog are you? *On the collar of a dog given to His Royal Highness, Frederick, Prince of Wales*

3 I know the thing that's most uncommon;
(Envy, be silent and attend!)
I know a reasonable woman,
Handsome and witty, yet a friend. *On a Certain Lady at Court*

4 Where'er you walk, cool gales shall fan the glade.
Trees where you sit shall crowd into a shade:
Where'er you tread, the blushing flowers shall rise,
And all things flourish where you turn your eyes. *Pastorals, Summer, 73*

5 What dire offence from am'rous causes springs,
What mighty contests rise from trivial things. *The Rape of the Lock, Canto 1, 1*

6 If to her share some female errors fall,
Look on her face, and you'll forget 'em all. *Ib, Canto 2, 17*

7 Fair tresses man's imperial race insnare,
And beauty draws us with a single hair. *Ib, 2, 27*

8 At ev'ry word a reputation dies. *Ib, Canto 3, 16*

9 The hungry judges soon the sentence sign,
And wretches hang that jury-men may dine. *Ib, 3, 21*

10 Coffee, which makes the politician wise,
And see through all things with his half-shut eyes. *Ib, 3, 117*

11 Charms strike the sight, but merit wins the soul. *Ib, Canto 5, 34*

PORSON, Richard, 1759–1808

12 When Dido found Aeneas would not come,
She mourn'd in silence, and was Di-do-dum. *Epigram on Latin Gerunds*

13 I went to Frankfort, and got drunk
With that most learned professor, Brunck;
I went to Worts, and got more drunken
With that more learn'd professor, Ruhnken. *Facetiae Cantabrigienses*

PORTER, William Sydney, see HENRY, O.

POTTER, Beatrix, 1866–1943

14 They [*the rabbits*] did not awake because the lettuces had been so soporific. *The Tale of the Flopsy Bunnies*

POTTER, Stephen, 1900–1969

15 Gamesmanship or The Art of Winning Games Without Actually Cheating. *Title of book*

16 *How to be one up*—how to make the other man feel that something has gone wrong, however slightly. *Lifemanship, Introduction*

17 We work from half a dozen centres co-ordinated, of course, from our 'H.Q.' at Station Road, Yeovil. *Ib*

1 'Yes, but not in the South', with slight adjustments will do for any argument about any place, if not about any person. *Lifemanship, The Canterbury Block*

POUND, Ezra Loomis, 1885–1972

2 Winter is icummen in,
Lhude sing Goddamm,
Raineth drop and staineth slop
And how the wind doth ramm!
Sing: Goddamm. *Ancient Music*

3 Bah! I have sung women in three cities,
But it is all the same;
And I will sing of the sun. *Cino*

PRESCOTT, William, 1726–1795

4 Don't fire until you see the whites of their eyes. *Bunker Hill, 1775*
(*Also attributed to Israel Putnam, 1718–1790*)

PRIOR, Matthew, 1664–1721

5 Be to her virtues very kind;
Be to her faults a little blind;
Let all her ways be unconfined;
And clap your padlock on her mind. *An English Padlock, 78*

6 The merchant to secure his treasure,
Conveys it in a borrowed name;
Euphelia serves to grace my measure;
But Chloe is my real flame. *Ode, The Merchant to Secure his Treasure*

7 From ignorance our comfort flows,
The only wretched are the wise. *To the Hon. C. Montague*

PROVERBS

In this selection of familiar proverbs mainly in the English language, the name and publication date of the Dictionary in which the proverb was first included has been given, or the century of the first recorded use of the proverb in literature. Most proverbs were obviously in common use for many years before they were included in a dictionary.

The abbreviations shown opposite proverbs refer to the following Dictionaries:

Bohn	*H. G. Bohn, A Handbook of Proverbs, 1855.*
Camden	*W. Camden, Remains Concerning Britain, 1614 or later edition.*
Clarke	*J. Clarke, Parœmiologia Anglo-Latina, 1639.*
Draxe	*T. Draxe, Bibliotheca Scholastica, 1616 or later edition.*
Fergusson	*D. Fergusson, Scottish Proverbs, 1641.*
Fuller	*T. Fuller, Gnomologia, 1732.*
Herbert	*G. Herbert, Outlandish Proverbs, 1640 or later edition.*
Heywood	*J. Heywood, A Dialogue containing . . . the Proverbs in the English Tongue, 1546 or later edition.*
Howell	*J. Howell, Proverbs, 1659.*
Kelly	*J. Kelly, A Complete Collection of Scottish Proverbs, 1721.*
Lean	*V. S. Lean, Collectanea, 1902–4.*
Ray	*J. Ray, A Collection of English Proverbs, 1670, 1678 or later edition.*

8 Absence sharpens love, presence strengthens it. *Fuller, 1732*

9 Absent are always in the wrong, The. *Herbert, 1640*

1	Abundance of money ruins youth, The.	*Ray, 1670*
2	Accidents will happen in the best-regulated families.	*19th c.*
3	Accounting for tastes, There is no.	*Latin*
4	Actions speak louder than words.	*20th c.*
5	Adversity makes a man wise, not rich.	*Ray, 1678*
6	Adversity, Many can bear/ but few contempt.	*Fuller, 1732*
7	Advise none to marry or go to war.	*Herbert, 1640*
8	After a storm comes a calm.	*16th c.*
9	Agree, for the law is costly.	*Camden, 1623*
10	All in the day's work, It is.	*18th c.*
11	All is fair in love and war.	*17th c.*
12	All is not gold that glitters.	*Latin*
13	All is over bar (but) the shouting.	*19th c.*
14	All is well that ends well.	*14th c.*
15	All my eye and Betty Martin.	*18th c.*
16	All sorts to make a world, It takes.	*17th c.*
17	Any port in a storm.	*18th c.*
18	Anything for a quiet life.	*17th c.*
19	Apple a day keeps the doctor away, An.	*19th c.*
20	Apple-cart, To upset the.	*18th c.*
21	Archer is not known by his arrows, but his aim, A good.	*16th c.*
22	Art has no enemy except ignorance.	*Latin*
23	Art lies in concealing art.	*Latin*
24	Ask no questions ana you will be told no lies.	*18th c.*
25	Ask thy purse what thou shouldst buy.	*Fuller, 1732*
26	Ass of oneself, To make an.	*19th c.*
27	*Audi alteram partem*—Hear the other side.	*Latin*
28	Aunt had been a man, If my/ she'd have been my uncle.	*Ray, 1813*
29	*Autres temps, autres moeurs*—Other times, other manners.	*French*
30	Axe to grind, To have an.	*19th c.*
31	Bachelors' fare: bread and cheese, and kisses.	*18th c.*
32	Back again, like a bad penny.	*19th c.*
33	Bad excuse is better than none, A.	*16th c.*
34	Bad workman quarrels with his tools, A.	*Herbert, 1640*
35	Bald as a coot, As.	*15th c.*
36	Bald heads are soon shaven.	*Ray, 1678*
37	Barber shaves so close but another finds work, No.	*Herbert, 1640*
38	Bark at the moon, To.	*15th c.*
39	Bark is worse than his bite, His.	*17th c.*
40	Bark up the wrong tree, To.	*19th c.*

1	Barking dogs seldom bite.	*16th c.*
2	Bats in the belfry, To have.	*20th c.*
3	Be sure before you marry of a house wherein to tarry.	*Italian*
4	Bear wealth, poverty will bear itself.	*Fergusson, 1641*
5	Beat about the bush, To.	*16th c.*
6	Beauty is but skin-deep.	*17th c.*
7	Beauty is potent, but money is omnipotent.	*Ray, 1670*
8	Beauty will buy no beef.	*Fuller, 1732*
9	Bee in one's bonnet, To have a.	*19th c.*
10	Before one can say Jack Robinson.	*18th c.*
11	Beggar can never be bankrupt, A.	*Clarke, 1639*
12	Beggars cannot be choosers.	*Heywood, 1546*
13	Believe, He does not/ that does not live according to his belief.	*Fuller, 1732*
14	Beloved, To be/ is above all bargains.	*Herbert, 1640*
15	Best foot forward, To put one's.	*16th c.*
16	Best of a bad job, To make the.	*16th c.*
17	Better a lean peace than a fat victory.	*17th c.*
18	Better an egg to-day than a hen to-morrow.	*Italian*
19	Better an open enemy than a false friend.	*17th c.*
20	Better be alone than in bad company.	*15th c.*
21	Better be born lucky than rich.	*Clarke, 1639*
22	Better be envied than pitied.	*Greek*
23	Better be happy than wise.	*Heywood, 1546*
24	Better be sure (safe) than sorry.	*19th c.*
25	Better be the head of a dog than the tail of a lion.	*16th c.*
26	Better buy than borrow.	*Fergusson, 1641*
27	Better die a beggar than live a beggar.	*Ray, 1670*
28	Better give a shilling than lend a half-crown.	*Howell, 1659*
29	Better go to heaven in rags than to hell in embroidery.	*Fuller, 1732*
30	Better late than never.	*Latin*
31	Better luck next time.	*19th c.*
32	Better never begin than never make an end.	*16th c.*
33	Better some of a pudding than none of a pie.	*Ray, 1670*
34	Better suffer ill than do ill.	*Clarke, 1639*
35	Better the devil you know than the devil you don't know.	*19th c.*
36	Better untaught than ill-taught.	*Ray, 1678*
37	Better wear out shoes than sheets.	*17th c.*
38	Between Scylla and Charybdis.	*Greek*
39	Between two stools one falls to the ground.	*Latin*
40	Between you and me and the (gate) post.	*19th c.*
41	Bird in hand is worth two in the bush, A.	*Latin*

1	Birds of a feather flock together.	*16th c.*
2	Bitter to endure may be sweet to remember, That which was.	*Latin*
3	Black as ink.	*16th c.*
4	Black as soot.	*15th c.*
5	Black as the devil.	*14th c.*
6	Black sheep in every flock, There are.	*19th c.*
7	Blessings are not valued till they are gone.	*Fuller, 1732*
8	Blind as a bat, As.	*16th c.*
9	Blind as those who won't see, None so.	*Heywood, 1546*
10	Blind in their own cause, Men are.	*Heywood, 1546*
11	Blind man will not thank you for a looking-glass, A.	*Fuller, 1732*
12	Blind, In the land of the/ the one-eyed man is king.	*Greek*
13	Blood is thicker than water.	*17th c.*
14	Blow one's own trumpet, To.	*16th c.*
15	Bone in one's leg, To have a.	*Greek*
16	Book that is shut is but a block, A.	*Fuller, 1732*
17	Books and friends should be few and good.	*Spanish*
18	Books, To be in a person's good (or bad).	*19th c.*
19	Boot is on the other leg, The.	*19th c.*
20	Born on the wrong side of the blanket.	*18th c.*
21	Born to be hanged, He that is/ shall never be drowned.	*16th c.*
22	Born with a silver spoon in his mouth, He was.	*Clarke, 1639*
23	Born within the sound of Bow Bells, To be.	*16th c.*
24	Born yesterday, I was not.	*19th c.*
25	Both ends meet, To make.	*Clarke, 1639*
26	Bow at all, If you/ bow low.	*Chinese*
27	Boys will be boys.	*17th c.*
28	Boys will be men.	*17th c.*
29	Bread is buttered on both sides, His.	*Ray, 1678*
30	Bull in a china shop, A.	*19th c.*
31	Bulls the cow must keep the calf, He that.	*16th c.*
32	Bully is always a coward, A.	*19th c.*
33	Burn one's boats, To.	*19th c.*
34	Burn the candle at both ends, To.	*Ray, 1678*
35	Burn the midnight oil, To.	*17th c.*
36	Bury the hatchet, To.	*18th c.*
37	Busiest men have the most leisure, The.	*19th c.*
38	Business is business.	*18th c.*
39	Business before pleasure.	*19th c.*
40	Busy, Who is more/ than he that hath least to do?	*Draxe, 1616*
41	Butter would not melt in his mouth.	*Heywood, 1546*

1 Buy a pig in a poke, To. *Heywood, 1546*
2 Buy and sell, and live by the loss, To. *Draxe, 1616*
3 Bygones be bygones, Let. *Heywood, 1546*

4 Calf love, half love; old love, cold love. *19th c.*
5 Call a spade a spade, To. *Latin*
6 Cap fits, If the/ wear it. *18th c.*
7 Care killed a cat. *16th c.*
8 Carry coals to Newcastle, To. *16th c.*
9 Cart before the horse, To put the. *Latin*
10 Cast ne'er a clout till May be out. *Fuller, 1732*
11 Castles in Spain, To build. *14th c.*
12 Castles in the air, To build. *Latin*
13 Cat has nine lives, A. *Heywood, 1546*
14 Cat jumps, To see which way the. *19th c.*
15 Cat on hot bricks, Like a. *17th c.*
16 *Caveat emptor*—Let the buyer beware. *Latin*
17 Chalk and cheese. *14th c.*
18 Chanceth in an hour, It/ that happeneth not in seven years. *Heywood, 1546*
19 Charity begins at home. *14th c.*
20 *Che sera, sera*—Whatever will be, will be. *Italian*
21 Children should be seen and not heard. *19th c.*
22 Chip of the old block, A. *17th c.*
23 Choose a horse made, and a wife to make. *Herbert, 1640*
24 Choose a wife rather by your ear than your eye. *Fuller, 1732*
25 Choose neither a woman nor linen by candle-light. *16th c.*
26 Chop and change, To. *16th c.*
27 Christmas comes but once a year
But when it comes it brings good cheer. *16th c.*
28 Circumstances alter cases. *19th c.*
29 Civility costs nothing. *19th c.*
30 Clean as a whistle, As. *19th c.*
31 Clean breast, To make a. *18th c.*
32 Cleanliness is next to godliness. *Hebrew*
33 Close mouth catcheth no flies, A. *Italian*
34 Cloud has a silver lining, Every. *19th c.*
35 Cloud, To be under a. *16th c.*
36 Coast is clear, The. *17th c.*
37 Cock-a-hoop, To be. *17th c.*
38 Cock-and-bull story, A. *17th c.*
39 Cold as charity. *14th c.*

1	Cold comfort.	*16th c.*
2	Cold hand and a warm heart, A.	*Lean, 1902*
3	Cold shoulder, To give the.	*19th c.*
4	Company makes the feast, The.	*17th c.*
5	Comparisons are odious.	*15th c.*
6	Confession is good for the soul.	*Kelly, 1721*
7	Constant guest is never welcome, A.	*Fuller, 1732*
8	Cook one's goose, To.	*19th c.*
9	Cook that cannot lick his own fingers, He is an ill.	*Heywood, 1546*
10	Cool one's heels, To.	*17th c.*
11	Costs more to do ill than to do well, It.	*Herbert, 1640*
12	Counsel be good, If the/ no matter who gave it.	*Fuller, 1732*
13	Count one's chickens before they are hatched, To.	*16th c.*
14	Couple is not a pair, Every.	*19th c.*
15	Courtesy on one side only lasts not long.	*Herbert, 1640*
16	Coventry, To send to.	*17th c.*
17	Creditors have better memories than debtors.	*Howell, 1659*
18	Crocodile tears.	*16th c.*
19	Crooked by nature is never made straight by education.	*Fuller, 1732*
20	Cross the bridge till you get to it, Don't.	*19th c.*
21	Crowd is not company, A.	*17th c.*
22	Cry for the moon, To.	*19th c.*
23	Cry 'Wolf', To.	*17th c.*
24	Crying over spilt milk, It is no use.	*Howell, 1659*
25	Cupboard love.	*17th c.*
26	Curate's egg, good in parts, Like the. (*See Punch, 232:4*)	*19th c.*
27	Curses are like chickens; they come home to roost.	*14th c.*
28	Custom without reason is but ancient error.	*16th c.*
29	Cut off one's nose to spite one's face, To.	*13th c.*
30	Cut off with a shilling, To.	*18th c.*
31	Cut the grass from under a person's feet, To.	*16th c.*
32	Cut your coat according to your cloth.	*Heywood, 1546*
33	Dally not with money or women.	*Herbert, 1640*
34	Daughter win, He that would the/must with the mother first begin.	*Ray, 1670*
35	Day is short and the work is long, The.	*15th c.*
36	*De gustibus non est disputandum*—There is no disputing about tastes.	*Latin*
37	*De mortuis nil nisi bonum*—Concerning the dead (say) nothing but good.	*Latin*
38	Dead as a door-nail, As.	*14th c.*

1 Dead men don't bite. *Greek*
2 Dead men tell no tales. *17th c.*
3 Deaf as a post. *16th c.*
4 Deaf as those who won't hear, None so. *Heywood, 1546*
5 Death devours lambs as well as sheep. *17th c.*
6 Death is the grand leveller. *Fuller, 1732*
7 Death pays all debts. *17th c.*
8 Debt is the worst poverty. *Fuller, 1732*
9 Deceives me once, If a man/ shame on him; if he deceives me twice, shame on me. *Italian*
10 Deceive oneself is very easy, To. *Herbert, 1640*
11 Deeds are males, and words are females. *16th c.*
12 Deepest water is the best fishing, In the. *Draxe, 1616*
13 Delays are dangerous. *14th c.*
14 Deserves not the sweet that will not taste the sour, He. *Latin*
15 Desires honour, He that/ is not worthy of honour. *17th c.*
16 Desperate diseases must have desperate remedies. *Latin*
17 Devil and the deep sea, Between the. *17th c.*
18 Devil is not so black as he is painted, The. *16th c.*
19 Devil take the hindmost, The. *17th c.*
20 Discreet women have neither eyes nor ears. *Herbert, 1640*
21 Discretion is the better part of valour. *16th c.*
22 *Divide et impera*—Divide and rule. *Latin*
23 Divine grace was never slow. *Herbert, 1640*
24 Do as you would be done by. *14th c.*
25 Do as you're bidden and you'll never bear blame. *Ray, 1678*
26 Dog does not eat dog. *18th c.*
27 Dog has his day, Every. *Heywood, 1546*
28 Dog will not howl if you beat him with a bone, A. *Howell, 1659*
29 Dogs that bark at a distance never bite. *Camden, 1623*
30 Done by night appears by day, What is. *14th c.*
31 Done cannot be undone, Things. *Heywood, 1546*
32 Door may be shut but death's door, Every. *Italian*
33 Draw the line somewhere, One must. *19th c.*
34 Drink wine, and have the gout; drink no wine, and have the gout too. *16th c.*
35 Drowning man will catch at a straw, A. *17th c.*
36 Drunk as a fish, As. *17th c.*
37 Drunk as a lord, As. *17th c.*
38 Drunk as a mouse, As. *14th c.*
39 Drunk as a wheelbarrow, As. *Ray, 1678*
40 Drunken folks seldom take harm. *17th c.*

1 Drunken night makes a cloudy morning, A. *Fuller, 1732*

2 Dry as dust, As. *16th c.*

3 Ducks and drakes of, To make. *16th c.*

4 Dull as ditchwater, As. *18th c.*

5 Dumb men get no lands. *14th c.*

6 Dying duck in a thunderstorm, Like a. *18th c.*

7 Ears burn, If your/ someone is talking about you. *Heywood, 1546*

8 Early bird catches the worm, The. *Camden, 1636*

9 Early to bed and early to rise,
Makes a man healthy, wealthy and wise. *Clarke, 1639*

10 Easier said than done. *15th c.*

11 East or west, home is best. *Bohn, 1855*

12 Easy come, easy go. *19th c.*

13 Easy to be wise after the event, It is. *17th c.*

14 Eat, and welcome; fast, and heartily welcome. *Ray, 1678*

15 Eat one's words, To. *16th c.*

16 Eat to live, but do not live to eat. *Latin*

17 Eat your cake and have it, You cannot. *Heywood, 1546*

18 Education begins a gentleman, conversation completes him. *Fuller, 1732*

19 Eggs in one basket, Do not put all your. *18th c.*

20 Eleventh Commandment: The/ thou shalt not be found out. *19th c.*

21 Empty purse that is full of other men's money, That is but an. *Ray, 1678*

22 Empty vessels make the most noise. *16th c.*

23 End justifies the means, The. *17th c.*

24 England is the paradise of women, the hell of horses, and the purgatory of servants. *16th c.*

25 English never know when they are beaten, The. *19th c.*

26 Englishman's house (home) is his castle, An. *17th c.*

27 Enough is as good as a feast. *15th c.*

28 Enough is enough. *Heywood, 1546*

29 Evening crowns the day, The. *17th c.*

30 Every little helps. *18th c.*

31 Every man for himself, and God for us all. *Heywood, 1562*

32 Every man has his faults. *16th c.*

33 Every man is best known to himself. *Draxe, 1616*

34 Every man to his taste. *16th c.*

35 Everybody's business is nobody's business. *17th c.*

36 Everything comes to him who waits. *16th c.*

37 Everything hath an end, and a pudding hath two. *16th c.*

38 Everything is the worse for wearing. *Clarke, 1639*

39 Everything must have a beginning. *14th c.*

1 Evils, Of two/ choose the least. *14th c.*
2 Example is better than precept. *Latin*
3 Exception proves the rule, The. *17th c.*
4 Experience is good, if not bought too dear. *Kelly, 1721*
5 *Experientia docet*—Experience teaches. *Latin*
6 Extremes meet. *18th c.*
7 Eye sees not, What the/ the heart rues not. *Heywood, 1546*

8 Failing to trust everybody, It is an equal/ and to trust nobody. *Fuller, 1732*
9 Faint heart never won fair lady. *16th c.*
10 Fair and softly goes far. *14th c.*
11 Fair exchange is no robbery, A. *16th c.*
12 Fair face and a foul heart, A. *Howell, 1659*
13 Fair face is half a fortune, A. *Draxe, 1616*
14 Fair play's a jewel. *19th c.*
15 Fairer the hostess, the fouler the reckoning, The. *Howell, 1659*
16 Familiarity breeds contempt. *Latin*
17 Far from eye, far from heart. *14th c.*
18 Fast bind, fast find. *Heywood, 1546*
19 Fat is in the fire, The. *Heywood, 1546*
20 Faults are theirs that commit them, The first/ the second theirs that permit them. *Fuller, 1732*
21 Faults are thick where love is thin. *Howell, 1659*
22 Few lawyers die well, few physicians live well. *16th c.*
23 Few words are best. *Ray, 1678*
24 *Fiat justitia, ruat coelum*—Let justice be done, though heaven fall. *Latin*
25 Fiddle while Rome is burning, To. *17th c.*
26 Finding's keeping. *19th c.*
27 Finger in the pie, To have a. *17th c.*
28 Fire is a good servant but a bad master. *17th c.*
29 First blow is half the battle, The. *18th c.*
30 First catch your hare and then cook it. *18th c.*
31 First come, first served. *16th c.*
32 First impressions are most lasting. *19th c.*
33 First think, and then speak. *Clarke, 1639*
34 Fish out of water, Like a. *Latin*
35 Fish to fry, I have other. *17th c.*
36 Fit as a fiddle, As. *17th c.*
37 Flat as a pancake, As. *16th c.*
38 Fling dirt enough, and some will stick. *Latin*
39 Flog a dead horse, To. *19th c.*

1 Follow the river and you'll get to the sea. *Fuller, 1732*
2 Fool and his money are soon parted, A. *16th c.*
3 Fool like an old fool, No. *Heywood, 1546*
4 Fool that forgets himself, He is a. *14th c.*
5 Fool that is not melancholy once a day, He is a. *Ray, 1678*
6 Fool to the market, Send a/ and a fool he'll return. *16th c.*
7 Fool wanders, The/ the wise man travels. *Fuller, 1732*
8 Fools went not to market, If/ bad wares would not be sold. *Herbert, 1640*
9 Forewarned, forearmed. *Latin*
10 Forgive and forget. *Heywood, 1546*
11 Fortune favours fools. *Latin*
12 Fortune is blind. *16th c.*
13 Fortune knocks, When/open the door. *17th c.*
14 Foul water will quench fire. *Heywood, 1546*
15 Four eyes see more than two. *Latin*
16 Fox knows much, The/ but more he that catcheth him. *Herbert, 1640*
17 Friend at court, A. *17th c.*
18 Friend in need is a friend indeed, A. *Latin*
19 Friend to thyself, Be a/ and others will befriend thee. *Kelly, 1721*
20 Friend to everybody is a friend to nobody, A. *17th c.*
21 Friends are thieves of time. *17th c.*
22 Friends both in heaven and hell, It is good to have some. *Herbert, 1640*
23 Friends (The best of friends) must part. *17th c.*
24 Friends, Have but few/ though many acquaintances. *Howell, 1659*
25 Friendship should not be all on one side. *17th c.*
26 Frying-pan into the fire, Out of the. *Heywood, 1546*
27 Full of courtesy, full of craft. *16th c.*

28 Game is not worth the candle, The. *17th c.*
29 Geese are swans, All his. *16th c.*
30 Gift horse in the mouth, Look not a. *Latin*
31 Give a dog a bad name and hang him. *Kelly, 1721*
32 Give him an inch and he'll take an ell. *Heywood, 1546*
33 Give the devil his due. *16th c.*
34 Gives to all, denies all, Who. *Herbert, 1640*
35 Gives twice who gives quickly, He. *Latin*
36 Giving much to the poor doth increase a man's store. *Herbert, 1640*
37 Glass houses, People who live in/ should never throw stones. *Herbert, 1640*
38 Gluttony kills more than the sword. *16th c.*
39 Go down the ladder when thou marriest a wife; go up when thou choosest a friend. *Ray, 1678*
40 Go farther and fare worse. *Heywood, 1546*

1 Go to bed with the lamb, and rise with the lark. *16th c.*
2 God comes at last when we think he is furthest off. *Italian*
3 God defend me from my friends; from my enemies I can defend myself. *17th c.*
4 God heals, and the doctor takes the fee. *Herbert, 1640*
5 God help the poor, for the rich can help themselves. *Kelly, 1721*
6 God help the rich, the poor can beg. *Howell, 1659*
7 God helps them that help themselves. *Herbert, 1640*
8 God send me a friend that will tell me of my faults. *Fuller, 1732*
9 God send you joy, for sorrow will come fast enough. *Draxe, 1616*
10 God sends fortune to fools. *Heywood, 1546*
11 God tempers the wind to the shorn lamb. *French*
12 God's mill grinds slow but sure. *Greek*
13 Good against evil, Set. *Herbert, 1640*
14 Good and quickly seldom meet. *Herbert, 1640*
15 Good beginning makes a good ending, A. *14th c.*
16 Good example is the best sermon, A. *Fuller, 1732*
17 Good face needs no paint, A. *Fuller, 1732*
18 Good judgement that relieth not wholly on his own, He hath a. *Fuller, 1732*
19 Good life is the only religion, A. *Fuller, 1732*
20 Good to want and to have, It is not. *Fergusson, 1641*
21 Good turn deserves another, One. *15th c.*
22 Good wife and health are a man's best wealth, A. *Fuller, 1732*
23 Good wife makes a good husband, A. *Heywood, 1546*
24 Good wine needs no bush. *16th c.*
25 Good workmen are seldom rich. *Herbert, 1640*
26 Grasp all, lose all. *14th c.*
27 Great minds think alike. *20th c.*
28 Great ones if there were no little ones, There would be no. *Herbert, 1640*
29 Great talkers are great liars. *French*
30 Great trees are good for nothing but shade. *Herbert, 1640*
31 Greater the truth, The/ the greater the libel. *18th c.*
32 Greatest hate springs from the greatest love, The. *16th c.*
33 Greek to me, It is. *16th c.*
34 Grist to the mill, To bring. *16th c.*

35 Hail fellow well met, To be. *16th c.*
36 Half a loaf is better than no bread. *Heywood, 1546*
37 Half the world knows not how the other half lives. *Herbert, 1640*
38 Half-seas over, To be. *18th c.*
39 Halves, Never do things by. *18th c.*
40 Hand and glove. *17th c.*

1 Handful of good life is better than a bushel of learning, A. *Herbert, 1640*
2 Hands, Many/ make light work. *Latin*
3 Handsome at twenty, He that is not/ nor strong at thirty, nor rich at forty, nor wise at fifty, will never be handsome, strong, rich or wise. *Herbert, 1640*
4 Handsome is that handsome does. *Ray, 1670*
5 Hanged for a sheep as a lamb, As good be. *Ray, 1678*
6 Hanging and wiving go by destiny. *Heywood, 1546*
7 Happiness takes no account of time. *18th c.*
8 Happy is he that is happy in his children. *Fuller, 1732*
9 Happy is the country which has no history. *19th c.*
10 Happy is the child whose father goes to the devil. *16th c.*
11 Hard as a Flint (stone), As. *14th c.*
12 Hard cases make bad law. *Lean, 1902*
13 Hard cheese. *19th c.*
14 Hard nut to crack, A. *16th c.*
15 Haste, The more/ the less speed. *Heywood, 1546*
16 Hatred is blind, as well as love. *Fuller, 1732*
17 Hatch, match and despatch. *19th c.*
18 Haul over the coals, To. *16th c.*
19 Head, He that hath no/ needs no hat. *Herbert, 1640*
20 Heads I win, tails you lose. *17th c.*
21 Health is better than wealth. *16th c.*
22 Health is not valued till sickness come. *Fuller, 1732*
23 Hear all parties. *15th c.*
24 Hear twice before you speak once. *19th c.*
25 Heard a pin drop, You might have. *19th c.*
26 Heart is in his mouth, His. *16th c.*
27 Heavy purse makes a light heart, A. *17th c.*
28 Hell and Chancery are always open. *Fuller, 1732*
29 Hell is paved with good intentions. (The road to) *18th c.*
30 Hell, Hull and Halifax, From/ good Lord deliver us. *16th c.*
31 Higher up, The/ the greater the fall. *16th c.*
32 History repeats itself. *19th c.*
33 Hit the nail on the head, To. *16th c.*
34 Hobson's choice. *17th c.*
35 Hoist with his own petard. *17th c.*
36 Hold a candle to the devil, To. *15th c.*
37 Honest man's word is as good as his bond, An. *17th c.*
38 Honest men marry soon, wise ones not at all. *Ray, 1670*
39 Honesty is the best policy. *16th c*
40 *Honi soit qui mal y pense*—Evil be to him who evil thinks. *French*

1 Honour among thieves, There is. *18th c.*

2 Hook or by crook, By. *14th c.*

3 Hope for the best and prepare for the worst. *16th c.*

4 Hope is as cheap as despair. *Fuller, 1732*

5 Hot love is soon cold. *16th c.*

6 Hour in the morning is worth two in the evening, An *19th c.*

7 Hour of pain is as long as a day of pleasure, An. *Fuller, 1732*

8 Hour to-day, One/ is worth two to-morrow. *Fuller, 1732*

9 Hour's sleep before midnight, One/ is worth three after. *Herbert, 1640*

10 House on fire, Like a. *19th c.*

11 *Humanum est errare*—To err is human. *Latin*

12 Hypocrisy is a homage that vice pays to virtue. *Fuller, 1732*

13 Idle that might be better employed, He is. *Fuller, 1732*

14 If Ifs and Ans were pots and pans
There'd be no trade for tinkers. *19th c.*

15 *Il faut reculer pour mieux sauter*—One must draw back in order to leap better. *French*

16 Ill doers are ill thinkers. *16th c.*

17 Ill gotten, ill spent. *Latin*

18 Ill news comes too soon. *16th c.*

19 Ill wind that blows nobody good, It is an. *Heywood, 1546*

20 In at one ear and out at the other. *14th c.*

21 In for a penny, in for a pound. *17th c.*

22 Insult to injury, To add. *Latin*

23 Iron entered his soul, The. *Latin*

24 Iron hand in a velvet glove, An. *French*

25 Irons in the fire, To have many. *16th c.*

26 Jack has his Jill, Every. *17th c.*

27 Jack of all trades and master of none. *18th c.*

28 Joan is as good as my lady, in the dark. *17th c.*

29 Jolly (happy) as a sandboy, As. *19th c.*

30 Judge from appearances, Never. *16th c.*

31 Keep a dog and bark yourself, Do not. *16th c.*

32 Keep a thing seven years and you will find a use for it *17th c.*

33 Keep one's tongue between one's teeth, To. *17th c.*

34 Keep up with the Joneses, To. *20th c.*

35 Keep your eyes wide open before marriage and half shut afterwards. *18th c.*

36 Keep your mouth shut and your eyes open. *18th c.*

37 Kill not the goose that lays the golden eggs. *15th c.*

38 Kill two birds with one stone, To. *17th c.*

1	King can do no wrong, The.	*17th c.*
2	King never dies, The.	*Latin*
3	King's favour is no inheritance, The.	*Fuller, 1732*
4	Kiss and be friends.	*14th c.*
5	Kiss the mistress, If you can/ never kiss the maid.	*Ray, 1670*
6	Knaves and fools divide the world.	*Ray, 1670*
7	Knocked me down with a feather, You might have.	*19th c.*
8	Know on which side one's bread is buttered, To.	*Heywood, 1546*
9	Know the ropes, To.	*19th c.*
10	Know the worth of water till the well is dry, We never.	*Kelly, 1721*
11	Know which way the wind blows, To.	*Heywood, 1546*
12	Knowledge is power.	*17th c.*
13	Knows how many beans make nine, He.	*19th c.*
14	Knows little, He that/ soon repeats it.	*18th c.*
15	Knows nothing, He that/ doubts nothing.	*Herbert, 1640*

16	*Laborare est orare*—To work is to pray.	*Latin*
17	Large as life, As.	*18th c.*
18	Last but not least.	*16th c.*
19	Last legs, To be on one's.	*16th c.*
20	Last straw breaks the camel's back, The.	*17th c.*
21	Laughs best who laughs last, He.	*18th c.*
22	Law is a bottomless pit.	*18th c.*
23	Law for the rich, One/ and another for the poor.	*19th c.*
24	Law makers should not be law breakers.	*14th c.*
25	Laws, The more/ the more offenders.	*Latin*
26	Lawyers' houses are built on the heads of fools.	*Herbert, 1640*
27	Lay it on with a trowel, To.	*16th c.*
28	Lead a horse to the water, A man may/ but he cannot make him drink.	*Heywood, 1546*
29	Lean as a rake, As.	*14th c.*
30	Learning makes a good man better and an ill man worse.	*17th c.*
31	Least foolish is wise, The.	*Herbert, 1640*
32	Least said, soonest mended.	*15th c.*
33	Leave in the lurch, To.	*16th c.*
34	Leave no stone unturned, To.	*Greek*
35	Lend I am a friend, When I/ when I ask I am a foe.	*16th c.*
36	Lend your money and lose your friend.	*17th c.*
37	Let sleeping dogs lie.	*14th c.*
38	Let the cat out of the bag, To.	*18th c.*
39	Liar is not believed when he speaks the truth, A.	*Latin*
40	Liars should have good memories.	*Latin*

1	Lick into shape, To.	*15th c.*
2	Lie begets a lie, A.	*Fuller, 1732*
3	Lies upon the ground, He that/ can fall no lower.	*Latin*
4	Life is half spent before we know what it is.	*Herbert, 1640*
5	Life is sweet.	*14th c.*
6	Life, While there is/ there is hope.	*Latin*
7	Lifeless that is faultless, He is.	*Heywood, 1546*
8	Light cares speak, great ones are dumb.	*Latin*
9	Light purse makes a heavy heart, A.	*16th c.*
10	Lightly come, lightly go.	*16th c.*
11	Like father, like son.	*Latin*
12	Like it, If you don't/ you can (may) lump it.	*19th c.*
13	Like master, like man.	*Latin*
14	Line one's pockets, To.	*16th c.*
15	Lion is not so fierce as he is painted, The.	*17th c.*
16	Listeners hear no good of themselves.	*17th c.*
17	Little and often fills the purse.	*17th c.*
18	Little things please little minds.	*Latin*
19	Live and learn.	*Clarke, 1639*
20	Live and let live.	*Dutch*
21	Live without our friends, We can/ but not without our neighbours.	*Kelly, 1721*
22	Lock, stock, and barrel.	*19th c.*
23	Lombard Street to a China orange, All.	*18th c.*
24	Long absent, soon forgotten.	*Draxe, 1616*
25	Long spoon, He should have a/ that sups with the devil.	*14th c.*
26	Longest day must have an end, The.	*17th c.*
27	Look before you leap.	*14th c.*
28	Look (at) on the bright side.	*19th c.*
29	Lookers-on see most of the game.	*16th c.*
30	Losers are always in the wrong.	*Spanish*
31	Losers seekers, finders keepers.	*19th c.*
32	Lost his taste, To him that has/ sweet is sour.	*Draxe, 1616*
33	Love and a cough cannot be hid.	*Latin*
34	Love and business teach eloquence.	*Herbert, 1640*
35	Love begets love.	*Latin*
36	Love best, Whom we/ to them we can say least.	*16th c.*
37	Love comes in at the window and goes out at the door.	*Camden, 1614*
38	Love is blind.	*14th c.*
39	Love is sweet in the beginning but sour in the ending.	*Draxe, 1616*
40	Love lives in cottages as well as in courts.	*16th c.*

1 Love makes one fit for any work. *Herbert, 1640*
2 Love makes the world go round. *17th c.*
3 Love me little, love me long. *Heywood, 1546*
4 Love me, love my dog. *Latin*
5 Love of money and the love of learning rarely meet, The. *Herbert, 1651*
6 Love too much that die for love, They. *17th c.*
7 Love will find a way. *16th c.*

8 Mad as a hatter. *19th c.*
9 Mad as a March hare, As. *14th c.*
10 Maidens should be meek until they be married. *Fergusson, 1641*
11 Main chance, Have an eye to the. *16th c.*
12 Make hay while the sun shines. *Heywood, 1546*
13 Man can only die once, A. *16th c.*
14 Man in the moon. *14th c.*
15 Man in the street, The. *19th c.*
16 Man loveth his fetters, No/ be they made of gold. *Heywood, 1546*
17 Man is as old as he feels, and a woman as old as she looks, A. *20th c.*
18 Man is known by the company he keeps, A. *17th c.*
19 Man lives, As a/ so shall he die. *16th c.*
20 Man or mouse. *16th c.*
21 Man proposes, God disposes. *Latin*
22 Many a little makes a mickle. *13th c.*
23 March comes in like a lion and goes out like a lamb. *Ray, 1670*
24 Mare's nest, To find a. *16th c.*
25 Marriage is a lottery. *17th c.*
26 Marriages are made in heaven. *16th c.*
27 Marries for wealth, He that/ sells his liberty. *Herbert, 1640*
28 Marries late, He that/ marries ill. *16th c.*
29 Marrieth for love without money, Who/ hath good nights and sorry days. *Ray, 1670*
30 Marry first and love will follow. *17th c.*
31 Marry in haste and repent at leisure. *16th c.*
32 Marry late or never, It is good to. *Clarke, 1639*
33 Marry your daughters betimes, lest they marry themselves. *16th c.*
34 Marry your son when you will, your daughter when you can. *Herbert, 1640*
35 Measure in all things, There is a. *14th c.*
36 Measure thrice before you cut once. *Italian*
37 Meat, One man's/ is another man's poison. *Latin*
38 Meet troubles half-way, Don't. *16th c.*
39 Men who make a city, It is the. *Greek*

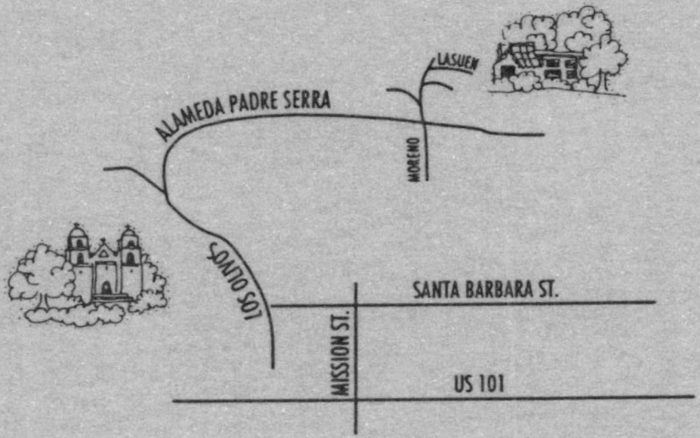
ALAMEDA PADRE SERRA
LASUEN
MORENO
LOS OLIVOS
SANTA BARBARA ST.
MISSION ST.
US 101

1731 Lasuen

Exit US 101 (northbound) at Mission Street turning right toward the Riviera. Turn left onto Santa Barbara St. then right onto Los Olivos. Continue on Los Olivos past the Mission. Keeping to the right, proceed up the hill on Alameda Padre Serra (past the El Encanto turn-off) to the 4-way stop. Turn left onto Moreno; keeping to the right, Lasuen will be the second right. Valet Parking.

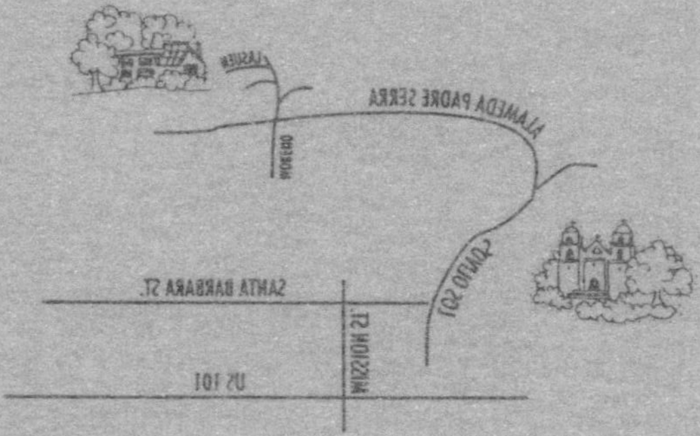
LASUEN
ALAMEDA PADRE SERRA
MORENO
LOS OLIVOS
SANTA BARBARA ST.
MISSION ST.
US 101

1731 Lasuen

Exit US 101 (northbound) at Mission Street turning right toward the Riviera. Turn left onto Santa Barbara St. then right onto Los Olivos. Continue on Los Olivos past the Mission. Keeping to the right, proceed up the hill on Alamedo Padre Serra (past the El Encanto turn-off) to the 4-way stop. Turn left onto Moreno; keeping to the right, Lasuen will be the second right. Valet Parking.

1 Meekness of Moses is better than the strength of Samson, The. *Fuller, 1732*
2 Merry as a cricket, As. *Heywood, 1546*
3 Might is right. *14th c.*
4 Mind your own business. *Clarke, 1639*
5 Mirror, The best/ is an old friend. *Herbert, 1640*
6 Misfortunes never come singly. *14th c.*
7 Miss is as good as a mile, A. *19th c.*
8 Mob has many heads, but no brains, The. *Fuller, 1732*
9 Money be not thy servant, If/ it will be thy master. *17th c.*
10 Money begets money. *Italian*
11 Money is a good servant, but a bad master. *17th c.*
12 Money makes marriage. *Fuller, 1732*
13 Money makes the man. *Greek*
14 Money or your life! Your. *19th c.*
15 Money talks. *17th c.*
16 More the merrier, The/ the fewer the better cheer. *Heywood, 1546*
17 Mother, Like/ like daughter. *16th c.*
18 Mother-in-law remembers not that she was a daughter-in-law, The. *Howell, 1659*
19 Mountain out of a molehill, To make a. *16th c.*
20 Much law, but little justice. *Fuller, 1732*
21 Murder will out. *14th c.*

22 Natural folly is bad enough, but learned folly is intolerable. *Fuller, 1732*
23 Necessity hath no law. *Latin*
24 Necessity is the mother of invention. *16th c.*
25 Neck or nothing. *Ray, 1678*
26 Need makes the old wife trot. *15th c.*
27 Needle in a haystack, To look for a. *15th c.*
28 Needs must when the devil drives. *15th c.*
29 Never a bad day that hath a good night, It is. *17th c.*
30 Never ask pardon before you are accused. *Bohn, 1855*
31 Never put off till to-morrow what may be done to-day. *14th c.*
32 Never refuse a good offer. *Ray, 1670*
33 Never say die. *19th c.*
34 Never too late to mend, It is. *17th c.*
35 Never too old to learn. *17th c.*
36 Never trouble trouble till trouble troubles you. *19th c.*
37 New broom sweeps clean, A. *Heywood, 1546*
38 No fire without some smoke. *Heywood, 1546*
39 No man's religion ever survives his morals. *Fuller, 1722*

1	No mischief but a woman or a priest is at the bottom of it.	*Latin*
2	No money, no swiss.	*17th c.*
3	No names, no pack drill.	*20th c.*
4	No news is good news.	*Italian*
5	No pleasure without pain.	*16th c.*
6	No rose without a thorn.	*15th c.*
7	No smoke without some fire.	*15th c.*
8	No sunshine but has some shadow.	*Ray, 1678*
9	No taxation without representation.	*18th c.*
10	Nose to the grindstone, To keep one's.	*16th c.*
11	Nothing costs so much as what is given us.	*Fuller, 1732*
12	Nothing for nothing.	*18th c.*
13	Nothing is certain but uncertainty.	*Latin*
14	Nothing is ours, but time.	*Fuller, 1732*
15	Nothing questioneth, He that/ nothing learneth.	*16th c.*
16	Nothing seek, nothing find.	*16th c.*
17	Nothing succeeds like success.	*French*
18	Nothing that is violent is permanent.	*16th c.*
19	Nothing venture, nothing win.	*15th c.*
20	Nowadays truth is the greatest news.	*Fuller, 1732*
21	Obedience is much more seen in little things than in great.	*Fuller, 1732*
22	Oil upon the waters, To pour.	*19th c.*
23	Old as the hills, As.	*19th c.*
24	Old friends and old wine are best.	*Herbert, 1640*
25	Old head on young shoulders, An.	*Clarke, 1639*
26	Old poacher makes a good game-keeper, An.	*14th c.*
27	Once bitten, twice shy.	*19th c.*
28	One foot in the grave, To have.	*16th c.*
29	Opportunity makes the thief.	*13th c.*
30	Ounce of discretion is worth a pound of learning, An.	*17th c.*
31	Out of sight, out of mind.	*13th c.*
32	P's and Q's, To mind one's.	*17th c.*
33	Painters and poets have leave to lie.	*16th c.*
34	Past cure, past care.	*16th c.*
35	Patience is a flower that grows not in everyone's garden.	*Ray, 1670*
36	Patience, money and time bring all things to pass.	*Herbert, 1640*
37	Pay a person in his own coin, To.	*16th c.*
38	Pay through the nose, To.	*17th c.*
39	Pays the piper may call the tune, He who.	*17th c.*
40	Peace makes plenty.	*15th c.*

1 Penny and penny laid up will be many. *Clarke, 1639*
2 Penny for your thoughts, A. *Heywood, 1546*
3 Penny wise, pound foolish. *17th c.*
4 Pension never enriched a young man. *Herbert, 1640*
5 Pigs might fly, but they are very unlikely birds. *19th c.*
6 Pillar to post, From. *15th c.*
7 Plain as a pike-staff, As. *16th c.*
8 Play first (or second) fiddle, To. *19th c.*
9 Plays best (well) that wins, He. *Heywood, 1555*
10 Pleased as Punch, As. *19th c.*
11 Pleased ourselves, When we are/ we begin to please others. *Fuller, 1732*
12 Pleasure, There is more/ in loving than in being loved. *Fuller, 1732*
13 Pleasure, To overcome/ is the greatest pleasure. *Fuller, 1732*
14 Pleasure of what we enjoy is lost by coveting more, The. *Fuller, 1732*
15 Poor as Job, As. *14th c.*
16 Poor heart that never rejoices, It is a. *19th c.*
17 Possession is nine points of the law. *Draxe, 1616*
18 Pot calls the kettle black, The. *17th c.*
19 Poverty breeds strife. *Ray, 1678*
20 Poverty is no sin. *Herbert, 1640*
21 Poverty is not a shame, but the being ashamed of it is. *Fuller, 1732*
22 Practice makes perfect. *Latin*
23 Practise what you preach. *14th c.*
24 Praise makes good men better and bad men worse. *Fuller, 1732*
25 Preaches well that lives well, He. *17th c.*
26 Prevention is better than cure. *Latin*
27 Pride will have a fall. *16th c.*
28 Promises too much, He that/ means nothing. *Draxe, 1616*
29 Proof of the pudding is in the eating, The. *Camden, 1623*
30 Prospect is often better than possession. *Fuller, 1732*
31 Prosperity has damned more souls than all the devils together. *Fuller, 1732*
32 Proud as Lucifer, As. *14th c.*
33 Proud as a peacock, As. *14th c.*
34 Put on one's thinking cap, To. *17th c.*
35 Pull down than to build, It is easier to. *16th c.*
36 Purse-strings are the most common ties of friendship, The. *Fuller, 1732*
37 Put that in your pipe and smoke it. *19th c.*
38 Put your shoulder to the wheel. *17th c.*

39 Queen Anne is dead. *18th c.*
40 *Quos Deus vult perdere, prius dementat*—Whom God wishes to destroy, he first makes mad. *Latin*

1 Rain before seven: fine before eleven. *19th c.*
2 Rain, rain, go to Spain: fair weather come again. *Howell, 1659*
3 Rains but it pours, It never. *18th c.*
4 Rainy day, Lay it up for a. *16th c.*
5 Rats desert a sinking ship. *17th c.*
6 Red as a rose, As. *14th c.*
7 Red rag to a bull, Like a. *16th c.*
8 Redemption from hell, There is no. *17th c.*
9 Religion an ill man is of, It matters not what. *Fuller, 1732*
10 Religion is the best armour in the world, but the worst cloak. *Fuller, 1732*
11 Remedy for all things but death, There is a. *16th c*
12 Repentance comes too late. *15th c.*
13 Resolves to deal with none but honest men, He that/ must leave off dealing. *Fuller, 1732*
14 Respects not is not respected, He that. *Herbert, 1640*
15 Revenge is sweet. *16th c.*
16 Revenge never repairs an injury. *Fuller, 1732*
17 Rich men have no faults. *Fuller, 1732*
18 Rich that is satisfied, He is. *Fuller, 1732*
19 Riches of the mind only that make a man rich and happy, It is. *Fuller, 1732*
20 Ridicule than commend, It is easier to. *Fuller, 1732*
21 Right as rain, As. *19th c.*
22 Roads lead to Rome, All. *14th c.*
23 Roar like a bull, To. *16th c.*
24 Rob Peter to pay Paul, To. *14th c.*
25 Rod for his own back, He makes a. *14th c.*
26 Rolling stone gathers no moss, A. *Heywood, 1546*
27 Rome was not built in a day. *Latin*
28 Room to swing a cat, Not. *18th c.*
29 Rope enough and he'll hang himself, Give a thief. *Ray, 1670*
30 Rough with the smooth, Take the. *15th c.*
31 Rule the roast (roost), To. *15th c.*
32 Rule youth well, for age will rule itself. *Fergusson, 1641*
33 Run with the hare and hunt with the hounds, To. *Heywood, 1546*

34 Sadness and gladness succeed each other. *Clarke, 1639*
35 Sail near the wind, To. *19th c.*
36 Same boat, To be all in the. *16th c.*
37 Sauce for the goose is sauce for the gander, What is. *Ray, 1670*
38 Save one's bacon, To. *17th c.*
39 Say Bo(o) to a goose, He cannot. *16th c.*
40 Say no ill of the year till it be past. *Herbert, 1640*

1 Saying is one thing and doing another. *Heywood, 1550*
2 Scot-free, To go. *16th c.*
3 Scratch, To come up to (the). *19th c.*
4 Scratch my back and I'll scratch yours, You. *17th c.*
5 Screw loose somewhere, There is a. *19th c.*
6 Second thoughts are best. *Latin*
7 See Naples and die. *Italian*
8 See the wood for the trees, You cannot. *Heywood, 1546*
9 See what we shall see, We shall. *19th c.*
10 Seeing is believing. *Clarke, 1639*
11 Seeks trouble, He that/ never misses. *Herbert, 1640*
12 Self-praise is no recommendation. *17th c.*
13 Self-preservation is the first law of nature. *17th c.*
14 Set the Thames on fire, To. *18th c.*
15 Share and share alike. *17th c.*
16 Shoe pinches, To know where the. *14th c.*
17 Short and sweet. *16th c.*
18 Shortest answer is doing, The. *Herbert, 1640*
19 Short life and a merry one, A. *17th c.*
20 Short pleasure, long lament. *15th c.*
21 Sickness is better than sadness. *Fuller, 1732*
22 Sight for sore eyes, A. *19th c.*
23 Silence gives consent. *14th c.*
24 Silk purse out of a sow's ear, You cannot make a. *16th c.*
25 Six hours' sleep for a man, seven for a woman, and eight for a fool. *18th c.*
26 Six of one and half a dozen of the other. *19th c.*
27 Sixes and sevens, To be at. *14th c.*
28 Skin of one's teeth, By the. *16th c.*
29 Slept well, He hath/ that remembers not he hath slept ill. *Fuller, 1732*
30 Slippery as an eel, As. *15th c.*
31 Slow but sure. *Clarke, 1639*
32 Small profits and quick returns. *19th c.*
33 Smell a rat, To. *16th c.*
34 Snake in the grass, There is a. *Latin*
35 Sneezed at, Not to be. *19th c.*
36 So far, so good. *Kelly, 1721*
37 Soberness conceals, What/ drunkenness reveals. *Latin*
38 Some are wise and some are otherwise. *Howell, 1659*
39 Soon as a man is born he begins to die, As. *Latin*
40 Soon got, soon spent. *Heywood, 1546*
41 Soon hot, soon cold. *15th c.*

1	Soon ripe, soon rotten.	*Latin*
2	Sorrow comes unsent for.	*Latin*
3	Soup and love, Of/ the first is the best.	*Spanish*
4	Sour grapes can ne'er make sweet wine.	*Fuller, 1732*
5	Speak not of my debts unless you mean to pay them.	*Herbert, 1640*
6	Speak well of your friend, of your enemy say nothing.	*18th c.*
7	Speak when you are spoken to.	*16th c.*
8	Speaks ill of his wife, He that/ dishonours himself.	*Fuller, 1732*
9	Speech is silver, silence is golden.	*Persian*
10	Spick and span.	*16th c.*
11	Split hairs, To.	*16th c.*
12	Spoke in one's wheel, To put a.	*17th c.*
13	Sprat to catch a mackerel (whale), To throw a.	*19th c.*
14	Spur a free horse, Do not.	*Latin*
15	Spur of the moment, On the.	*19th c.*
16	Stepmother, Take heed of a/ the very name of her sufficeth.	*Herbert, 1651*
17	Stew (fry) in one's own juice (grease), To.	*14th c.*
18	Sticks and stones may break my bones, but words will never hurt me.	*19th c.*
19	Stiff as a poker.	*18th c.*
20	Stiff upper lip, To keep a.	*19th c.*
21	Still waters run deep.	*14th c.*
22	Sting is in the tail, The.	*16th c.*
23	Sting of a reproach is the truth of it, The.	*Fuller, 1732*
24	Stir up a hornets' nest, To.	*Latin*
25	Stitch in time saves nine, A.	*Fuller, 1732*
26	Stone that lieth not in your way need not offend you, The.	*Fuller, 1732*
27	Storm in a tea-cup, A.	*19th c.*
28	Straight trees have crooked roots.	*16th c.*
29	Strike while the iron is hot.	*14th c.*
30	Subtlety is better than force.	*Draxe, 1616*
31	Sun shines upon all alike, The.	*16th c.*
32	Sure as eggs is eggs, As.	*17th c.*
33	Swallow, One/ does not make a summer.	*Greek*
34	Sweet discourse makes short days and nights.	*Herbert, 1640*
35	Sweet tooth, To have a.	*16th c.*
36	Swine, women, and bees cannot be turned.	*Ray, 1678*
37	Take a farthing away from a thousand pounds, it will be a thousand pounds no longer.	*18th c.*
38	Take a leaf out cf one's book, To.	*19th c.*
39	Take away my good name and take away my life.	*Ray, 1670*

1 Take care of the pence and the pounds will take care of themselves. *18th c.*
2 Take one down a peg or two, To. *16th c.*
3 Take the bull by the horns, To. *19th c.*
4 Take the gilt off the gingerbread, To. *19th c.*
5 Take the law into one's own hands, To. *17th c.*
6 Take the wind out of one's sails, To. *19th c.*
7 Take things as you find them. *Lean, 1902*
8 Tales out of school, To tell. *16th c.*
9 Talk the hind leg off a donkey, To. *19th c.*
10 Talk of the devil, and he is sure to appear. *17th c.*
11 Talk without thinking, To/ is to shoot without aiming. *Fuller, 1732*
12 Talkers, The greatest/ are (always) the least doers. *16th c.*
13 Talks to himself, He that/ speaks to a fool. *Kelly, 1721*
14 Tarred with the same brush, All. *19th c.*
15 Taste of the kitchen is better than the smell, The. *19th c.*
16 Teach an old dog tricks, It is hard to. *16th c.*
17 Teach your grandmother to suck eggs. *18th c.*
18 Teacheth ill, He/ who teacheth all. *Howell, 1659*
19 Tell that to the Marines. *19th c.*
20 Tell the truth and shame the devil. *16th c.*
21 Tells his wife news, He that/ is but newly married. *Herbert, 1640*
22 *Tempus fugit*—Time flies. *Latin*
23 Tenterhooks, To be on. *18th c.*
24 There's many a slip 'twixt the cup and the lip. *Greek*
25 Thick as thieves, As. *19th c.*
26 Thief to catch a thief, Set a. *Ray, 1670*
27 Thin end of the wedge is to be feared, The. *19th c.*
28 Things are difficult before they are easy, All. *Fuller, 1732*
29 Things at the worst will mend. *17th c.*
30 Think today and speak tomorrow. *Bohn, 1855*
31 Think well of all men. *Howell, 1659*
32 Think with the wise, but talk with the vulgar. *Greek*
33 Thinking is very far from knowing. *18th c.*
34 Though I say it that should not. *16th c.*
35 Thought is free. *14th c.*
36 Thousand pounds of law, In a/ there's not an ounce of love. *Ray, 1670*
37 Threadneedle Street, The old lady of. *19th c.*
38 Threatened men live long. *16th c.*
39 Three may keep counsel if two be away. *Heywood, 1546*
40 Three women and a goose make a market. *Italian*
41 Throw good money after bad, To. *19th c.*

1 Time and thinking tame the strongest grief. *Ray, 1670*
2 Time and tide wait for no man. *16th c.*
3 Time for all things, There is a. *14th c.*
4 Time like the present, No. *18th c.*
5 To-day, One/ is worth two to-morrows. *17th c.*
6 Tomorrow never comes. *Ray, 1678*
7 Tomorrow is a new day. *16th c.*
8 Tongue, One/ is enough for a woman. *Ray, 1678*
9 Tongue is not steel, yet it cuts, The. *Heywood, 1546*
10 Tongue of idle people is never idle, The. *Fuller, 1732*
11 Too big for one's boots, To be. *19th c.*
12 Too clever by half. *19th c.*
13 Too many cooks spoil the broth. *16th c.*
14 Touch him with a pair of tongs, I would not. *Ray, 1670*
15 Touch wood. *20th c.*
16 *Tout passe, tout casse, tout lasse.* Everything passes, everything perishes, everything palls. *French*
17 Translators, traitors. *Italian*
18 Travels far, He that/ knows much. *Clarke, 1639*
19 Tread on a worm and it will turn. *Heywood, 1546*
20 Tree is known by its fruit, A. *14th c.*
21 True blue will never stain. *Howell, 1659*
22 True word is spoken in jest, Many a. *14th c.*
23 Trust not a new friend nor an old enemy. *Kelly, 1721*
24 Truth fears no colours. *Ray, 1678*
25 Truth is stranger than fiction. *19th c.*
26 Truth is the daughter of God. *Fuller, 1732*
27 Truth never grows old. *Fuller, 1732*
28 Truth, The/ the whole truth, and nothing but the truth. *17th c.*
29 Turn an honest penny, To. *Heywood, 1546*
30 Turn in his grave, To make a person. *19th c.*
31 Turn over a new leaf, To. *Heywood, 1546*
32 Turn the tables, To. *17th c.*
33 Turn up one's nose, To. *16th c.*
34 Turn up trumps, To. *17th c.*
35 Twist round one's little finger, To. *19th c.*
36 Two bites of a cherry, To make. *French*
37 Two blacks do not make a white. *Kelly, 1721*
38 Two can play at that game. *19th c.*
39 Two dogs strive for a bone, and a third runs away with it. *16th c.*

1 Two heads are better than one. *Heywood, 1546*
2 Two is company, three is none. *19th c.*
3 Two negatives make an affirmative. *16th c.*
4 Two sides to every question, There are. *19th c.*
5 Two strings to one's bow, To have. *15th c.*
6 Two to make a quarrel, It takes. *19th c.*
7 Two wrongs don't make a right. *19th c.*

8 Ugly as sin, As. *19th c.*
9 Uncertainty of the law, The glorious. *19th c.*
10 Under the blanket the black one is as good as the white. *Fuller, 1732*
11 Unforeseen (unexpected) that always happens, It is the. *Latin*
12 Unity is strength. *French*

13 Variety is pleasing. *Greek*
14 Vengeance, The noblest/is to forgive. *16th c.*
15 Venom to that of the tongue, There is no. *Howell, 1659*
16 *Verbum sapienti sat est*—A word is enough to the wise. *Latin*
17 Virtue dwells not in the tongue but in the heart. *Fuller, 1732*
18 Virtue is its own reward. *Latin*
19 Virtue never grows old. *Herbert, 1640*
20 Virtue of necessity, Make a. *Latin*
21 Vows made in storms are forgotten in calm. *Fuller, 1732*

22 Wait and see. *19th c.*
23 Walls have ears. *17th c.*
24 Want a thing well done, If you/ do it yourself. *Draxe, 1616*
25 Want of wit is worse than want of wealth. *Kelly, 1721*
26 War begins, When/ hell opens. *Herbert, 1651*
27 Wars bring scars. *Clarke, 1639*
28 Warm the cockles of the heart, To. *17th c.*
29 Wash dirty linen in public, To. *19th c.*
30 Wash your hands often, your feet seldom, and your head never. *Ray, 1670*
31 Waste not, want not. *18th c.*
32 Watched pot never boils, A. *19th c.*
33 Water in a sieve, To carry. *Latin*
34 Water off a duck's back, Like. *19th c.*
35 Water (blood) out of a stone, To get. *Latin*
36 Way to an Englishman's heart is through his stomach, The. *19th c.*
37 Way to be safe is never to be secure, The. *Fuller, 1732*
38 Weakest goes to the wall, The. *16th c.*
39 Wealth, The greatest/ is contentment with a little. *Ray, 1670*

1	Wear one's heart on one's sleeve, To.	*17th c.*
2	Wear the breeches (pants), To.	*15th c.*
3	Wedlock is a padlock.	*Ray, 1678*
4	Welcome is the best cheer.	*Greek*
5	Well begun is half done.	*Latin*
6	Wet one's whistle, To.	*14th c.*
7	What can't be cured must be endured.	*14th c.*
8	What is worth doing is worth doing well.	*18th c.*
9	What's yours is mine, and what's mine is my own.	*18th c.*
10	Wheels within wheels, There are.	*17th c.*
11	When in doubt, leave out.	*20th c.*
12	When the cat is away the mice will play.	*16th c.*
13	Whispering, Where there is/ there is lying.	*Ray, 1678*
14	Widows are always rich.	*Ray, 1678*
15	Wife, He that has a/ has a master.	*Kelly, 1721*
16	Wild oats, To sow one's.	*16th c.*
17	Will, Where there's a/ there's a way.	*Herbert, 1640*
18	Will, Where there's a/ there's trouble.	*20th c.*
19	Wine and wenches empty men's purses.	*Clarke, 1639*
20	Wine in the bottle does not quench thirst, The.	*Herbert, 1640*
21	Wine in, truth out.	*16th c.*
22	Wisdom like silence, No.	*Greek*
23	Wise child that knows its own father, It is a.	*16th c.*
24	Wise man, He is not a/ who cannot play the fool on occasion.	*16th c.*
25	Wise men learn by other men's mistakes; fools by their own.	*Latin*
26	Wish is father to the thought, The.	*Latin*
27	Wive and thrive both in a year, It is hard to.	*15th c.*
28	Wives must be had, be they good or bad.	*Clarke, 1639*
29	Wolf from the door, To keep the.	*Heywood, 1546*
30	Woman conceals what she knows not, A.	*16th c.*
31	Woman's work is never done, A.	*16th c.*
32	Women and geese, Where there are/ there wants no noise.	*Draxe, 1616*
33	Women are always in extremes.	*Clarke, 1639*
34	Women are necessary evils.	*16th c.*
35	Women look in their glass, The more/ the less they look to their house.	*Herbert, 1640*
36	Women must have their wills while they live, because they make none when they die.	*17th c.*
37	Women must have the last word.	*16th c.*
38	Wonders will never cease.	*18th c.*
39	Wool over a person's eyes, To pull the.	*19th c.*
40	Work and no play makes Jack a dull boy, All.	*Ray, 1670*

1 World and his wife, All the. *18th c.*

2 Worse things happen at sea. *19th c.*

3 Worth his weight in gold, He is. *16th c.*

4 Worth of a thing is best known by the want, The. *17th c.*

5 Wrong never comes right. *19th c.*

6 Young man should not marry yet, A/ an old man not at all. *16th c.*

7 Young men may die, old men must. *16th c.*

8 Young men think old men fools, and old men know young men to be so. *16th c.*

9 Young saint, old devil. *15th c.*

10 Youth and age will never agree. *16th c.*

11 Youth will be served. *19th c.*

12 Youth will have its course (or swing, or fling). *16th c.*

13 Zeal is fit only for wise men, but is found mostly in fools. *Fuller, 1732*

14 Zeal, when it is a virtue, is a dangerous one. *Fuller, 1732*

15 Zeal without knowledge is fire without light. *Fuller, 1732*

PUDNEY, John, 1909—

16 Do not despair
For Johnny head-in-air;
He sleeps as sound
As Johnny underground. *For Johnny*

PUNCH

17 Advice to persons about to marry.—'Don't.' *Vol. 8, Page 1, 1845*

18 You pays your money and you takes your choice. *Vol. 10, 16, 1846*

19 What is better than Presence of Mind in a Railway accident?—Absence of Body. *Vol. 16, 231, 1849*

20 Never do today what you can put off till tomorrow. *Vol. 17, 241, 1849*

21 What is Matter?—Never Mind.
What is Mind?—No Matter. *Vol. 29, 19, 1855*

22 Why are Trafalgar Square fountains like Government Clerks?—Because they play from 10 till 4. *Vol. 35, 21, 1858*

23 Mun, a had no' been the-erre abune two hours when—bang—went saxpence!!! *Vol. 55, 235, 1868*

24 Nothink for nothink 'ere, and precious little for sixpence. *Vol. 57, 152, 1869*

25 Go directly—see what she's doing, and tell her she mustn't. *Vol. 63, 202, 1872*

26 Here was an old owl liv'd in an oak,
The more he heard the less he spoke:
The less he spoke, the more he heard,
O, if men were all like that wise bird. *Vol. 68, 155, 1875*

1 I never read books—I *write* them. *Vol. 74, 210, 1878*

2 I used your soap two years ago: since then I have used no other. *Vol. 86, 197, 1884*

3 Nearly all our best men are dead! Carlyle, Tennyson, Browning, George Eliot! I'm not feeling very well myself! *Vol. 104, 210, 1893*

4 I'm afraid you've got a bad egg, Mr. Jones.
Oh no, my Lord, I assure you! Parts of it are excellent. *Vol. 109, 222, 1895*

5 Look here, Steward, if this is coffee, I want tea; but if this is tea, then I wish for coffee. *Vol. 123, 44, 1902*

QUESNAY, François, 1694–1774

6 *Laissez faire, laissez passer.*—No interference, and complete freedom of movement. *[Of Government interference] Attributed*

RABELAIS, François, 1494?–1553?

7 *L'appétit vient en mangeant.* Appetite comes with eating. *Gargantua, 1, 5*

8 *Tirez le rideau, la farce est jouée.* Ring down the curtain, the farce is over. *Last words, attributed*

9 *Je m'en vais chercher un grand peut-être.* I am going in search of a great perhaps. *Last words, attributed*

RACINE, Jean, 1639–1699

10 *Elle flotte, elle hésite; en un mot, elle est femme.* She wavers, she hesitates; in a word, she is a woman. MATHAN *Athalie, Act 3, Scene 3*

RALEIGH, Sir Walter, 1552?–1618

11 Even such is Time, that takes in trust
Our youth, our joys, our all we have,
And pays us but with age and dust;
Who in the dark and silent grave,
When we have wandered all our ways,
Shuts up the story of our days;
But from this earth, this grave, this dust,
My God shall raise me up, I trust. *Written the night before his death*

12 Give me my scallop-shell of quiet,
My staff of faith to walk upon,
My scrip of joy, immortal diet,
My bottle of salvation,
My gown of glory, hope's true gage,
And thus I'll take my pilgrimage. *The Passionate Man's Pilgrimage*

13 So the heart be right, it is no matter which way the head lies. *On laying his head on the block*

14 If all the world and love were young,
And truth in every shepherd's tongue,
These pretty pleasures might me move
To live with thee, and be thy love. *The Nymph's Reply to the Passionate Shepherd*

RALEIGH, Sir Walter Alexander, 1861–1922

1 I wish I loved the Human Race;
I wish I loved its silly face;
I wish I liked the way it walks;
I wish I liked the way it talks;
And when I'm introduced to one
I wish I thought *What Jolly Fun*! *The Wishes of an Elderly Man*

RANKIN, Jeremiah Eames, 1828–1904

2 God be with you till we meet again. *Hymn*

RANSOME, Arthur, 1884–1969

3 Grab a chance and you won't be sorry for a might-have-been.
COMMANDER WALKER *We Didn't Mean To Go to Sea*

READE, Charles, 1814–1884

4 *Courage, mon ami, le diable est mort.* Courage, my friend, the devil is dead.
The Cloister and the Hearth, Ch. 24

5 Make 'em laugh; make 'em cry; make 'em wait. *Advice to young author on writing novels*

REED, Henry, 1914—

6 To-day we have naming of parts. Yesterday,
We had daily cleaning. And to-morrow morning
We shall have what to do after firing. But to-day,
To-day we have naming of parts. *Naming of Parts*

REMARQUE, Erich Maria, 1898–1970

7 *Im Westen nichts Neues.* All Quiet on the Western Front. *Title of Novel*

REYNOLDS, Frederic, 1764–1841

8 [*Taking out his watch*] How goes the *enemy*? ENNUI *The Dramatist, Act 1*

REYNOLDS, Sir Joshua, 1723–1792

9 If you have great talents, industry will improve them: if you have but moderate abilities, industry will supply their deficiency. *Discourses, 2*

RHODES, Cecil John, 1853–1902

10 So little done, so much to do. *Last words*

11 Educational relations make the strongest tie. *Will, endowing Rhodes Scholarships*

RICE, Grantland, 1880–1954

12 For when the one Great Scorer comes
To write against your name,
He marks—not that you won or lost—
But how you played the game. *Alumnus Football*

RIPLEY, Robert Leroy, 1893–1949

13 Believe it or not. *Title of newspaper feature*

ROCHE, Sir Boyle, 1743–1807

1 My love for England and Ireland is so great that I would have the two sisters embrace like one brother. *Reported in Irish Parliamentary Register, 11, 294*

2 What has posterity done for us? *Speech in Irish Parliament, 1780*

3 Mr Speaker, I smell a rat; I see him forming in the air and darkening the sky; but I'll nip him in the bud. *Attributed*

ROCHEFOUCAULD, Duc de la, 1613–1680

4 We have all enough strength to bear the misfortunes of others. *Les Maximes, 19*

5 Everyone complains of his memory, but no one complains of his judgment. *Ib, 89*

6 The intellect is always fooled by the heart. *Ib, 102*

7 Hypocrisy is the homage paid by vice to virtue. *Ib, 218*

8 The height of cleverness is to conceal one's cleverness. *Ib, 245*

9 In the misfortunes of our best friends, we find something that is not displeasing. *Maximes supprimées, 583*

ROCHEFOUCAULD-LIANCOURT, Duc de La, 1747–1827

10 LOUIS XVI: *C'est une révolte?* Is it a revolt?
THE DUKE: *Non, sire, c'est une révolution.* No, sire, it is a revolution. *On hearing of the Fall of the Bastille, 1789*

ROCHESTER, John Wilmot, 2nd Earl of, 1647–1680

11 Here lies our sovereign lord the King,
Whose word no man relies on;
He never said a foolish thing,
Nor ever did a wise one. *Epitaph on Charles II*

ROGERS, E. W., 1864–1913

12 Ev'ry member of the force
Has a watch and chain, of course;
If you want to know the time,
Ask a P'liceman. *Ask a P'liceman*

ROGERS, Samuel, 1763–1855

13 When a new book is published, read an old one. *Attributed*

14 Think nothing done while aught remains to do. *Human Life, 49*

15 Sheridan was listened to with such attention that you might have heard a pin drop. *Table Talk*

ROLAND, Madame Marie Jeanne Philipon, 1754–1793

16 *O Liberté! O Liberté! que de crimes on commet en ton nom!* O liberty, liberty, what crimes are committed in your name! *Remark from the scaffold, on viewing the Statue of Liberty*

ROOSEVELT, Franklin Delano, 1882–1945

17 I pledge you, I pledge myself, to a new deal for the American people. *Speech accepting nomination for Presidency, Democratic National Convention, Chicago, 2 July 1932*

18 The only thing we have to fear is fear itself. *First Inaugural Address, 4 March 1933*

1 In the field of world policy, I would dedicate this nation to the policy of a good neighbour. *First Inaugural Address, 4 March, 1933*

2 I see one third of a nation ill-housed, ill-clad, ill-nourished. *Second Inaugural Address, 20 Jan. 1937*

3 A radical is a man with both feet firmly planted in the air. *Broadcast, 26 Oct. 1939*

4 We look forward to a world founded upon four essential human freedoms. The first is freedom of speech and expression—everywhere in the world. The second is freedom of every person to worship God in his own way—everywhere in the world. The third is freedom from want . . . everywhere in the world. The fourth is freedom from fear . . . anywhere in the world. *Speech to Congress, 6 Jan. 1941*

5 We all know that books burn—yet we have the greater knowledge that books cannot be killed by fire. People die, but books never die. No man and no force can abolish memory . . . In this war, we know, books are weapons. *Message to American Booksellers Association, 23 April 1942*

6 More than an end to war, we want an end to the beginnings of all wars. *Speech written for broadcast, 13 April 1945 (the day after his death)*

ROOSEVELT, Theodore, 1858–1919

7 I wish to preach, not the doctrine of ignoble ease, but the doctrine of the strenuous life. *Speech, Chicago, 10 April 1899*

8 The first requisite of a good citizen in this Republic of ours is that he shall be able and willing to pull his weight. *Speech, New York, 11 Nov. 1902*

9 A man who is good enough to shed his blood for his country is good enough to be given a square deal afterwards. More than that no man is entitled to, and less than that no man shall have. *Speech, Springfield, Illinois, 4 July 1903*

10 There is no room in this country for hyphenated Americanism. *Speech, New York, 12 Oct. 1915*

11 No man is justified in doing evil on the ground of expediency. *The Strenuous Life*

ROSEBERY, Archibald Philip Primrose, 5th Earl of, 1847–1929

12 The Empire is a Commonwealth of Nations. *Speech, Adelaide, 18 Jan. 1884*

13 It is beginning to be hinted that we are a nation of amateurs. *Rectorial Address, Glasgow, 16 Nov. 1900*

ROSS, Alan Strode Campbell, 1907—

14 U and Non-U, An Essay in Sociological Linguistics. *Title of Essay included in Noblesse Oblige, 1956*

ROSSETTI, Christina Georgina, 1830–1894

15 In the bleak mid-winter
Frosty wind made moan,
Earth stood hard as iron,
Water like a stone;
Snow had fallen, snow on snow,
Snow on snow,
In the bleak mid-winter,
Long ago. *Mid-Winter*

1 Remember me when I am gone away,
Gone far away into the silent land. *Remember*

2 Better by far you should forget and smile
Than that you should remember and be sad. *Ib*

3 'Does the road wind up-hill all the way?'
'Yes, to the very end.'
'Will the day's journey take the whole long day?'
'From morn to night, my friend.' *Up-Hill*

4 When I am dead, my dearest
Sing no sad songs for me. *When I am Dead*

5 And if thou wilt, remember,
And if thou wilt, forget. *Ib*

ROSSETTI, Dante Gabriel, 1828–1882

6 A sonnet is a moment's monument,—
Memorial from the Soul's eternity
To one dead deathless hour. *The House of Life, Part 1, Introduction*

7 The hour when you too learn that all is vain
And that Hope sows what Love shall never reap.
Ib, 44, Cloud and Wind

8 My name is Might-Have-Been;
I am also called No-More, Too-Late, Farewell. *Ib, Part 2, 97*
A Superscription

9 Unto the man of yearning, thought
And aspiration, to do nought
Is in itself almost an act. *Soothsay*

10 I have been here before.
But when or how I cannot tell:
I know the grass beyond the door,
The sweet keen smell,
The sighing sound, the lights around the shore. *Sudden Light, 1*

ROUGET DE LISLE, Claude Joseph, 1760–1836

11 *Allons, enfants de la patrie,*
Le jour de gloire est arrivé.
Come, children of our native land, the day of glory has arrived.
La Marseillaise

ROUSSEAU, Jean-Jaques, 1712–1778

12 *L'homme est né libre, et partout il est dans les fers.* Man was born free and everywhere he is in chains. *Du Contrat Social, Ch. 1*

ROUTH, Martin Joseph, 1755–1854

13 Always verify your references. *Attributed*

'RED ROWLEY', 20th century

14 Mademoiselle from Armenteers,
Hasn't been kissed for forty years,
Hinky dinky, parley-voo. *Mademoiselle from Armentières*

RUNYON, Damon, 1884–1946

15 More than somewhat. *Passim*

RUSKIN, John, 1819–1900

1 All travelling becomes dull in exact proportion to its rapidity. *Modern Painters*

2 If a book is worth reading, it is worth buying. *Sesame and Lilies*

3 Remember that the most beautiful things in the world are the most useless; peacocks and lilies for instance. *The Stones of Venice*

4 The purest and most thoughtful minds are those which love colour the most. *Ib*

5 Fine art is that in which the hand, the head, and the heart of man go together. *The Two Paths*

6 There is no wealth but life. *Unto this Last*

RUSSELL, John, 1st Earl, 1792–1878

7 If peace cannot be maintained with honour, it is no longer peace. *Speech, Greenock, 19 Sept. 1853*

RUSSELL, Bertrand Arthur William, 3rd Earl, 1872–1970

8 Men are capable, not only of fear and hate, but also of hope and benevolence. If the populations of the world can be brought to see and to realize in imagination the hell to which hate and fear must condemn them on the one hand, and, on the other, the comparative heaven which hope and benevolence can create by means of new skills, the choice should not be difficult, and our self-tormented species should allow itself a life of joy such as the past has never known. *Common Sense and Nuclear Warfare, 1959*

9 Mathematics possesses not only truth, but supreme beauty—a beauty cold and austere, like that of sculpture. *The Study of Mathematics*

RUTLAND, John, 7th Duke of, 1818–1906

10 Let wealth and commerce, laws and learning die,
But leave us still our old nobility. *England's Trust, 3, 227*

'SAKI' (Hector Hugh Munro), 1870–1916

11 He's simply got the instinct for being unhappy highly developed. *Chronicles of Clovis, The Match-Maker*

12 The cook was a good cook, as cooks go; and as cooks go she went. *Reginald on Besetting Sins*

SALINGER, Jerome David, 1919—

13 If you really want to hear about it, the first thing you'll probably want to know is where I was born, and what my lousy childhood was like, and how my parents were occupied and all before they had me, and all that David Copperfield kind of crap, but I don't feel like going into it. *The Catcher in the Rye, opening words*

SALISBURY, Robert Cecil, 3rd Marquis of, 1830–1903

14 By office boys for office boys. *Remark about the Daily Mail*

SALLUST, 86–34 B.C.

15 *Idem velle atque idem nolle, ea demum firma amicitia est.* To like and dislike the same things, that is indeed true friendship. *Catiline, 20*

1 *Pro patria, pro liberis, pro aris atque focis suis.* On behalf of their country, their children, their altars, and their hearths. *Catiline, 59*

SAMUEL, Herbert Louis, 1st Viscount, 1870–1963

2 It takes two to make a marriage a success and only one a failure. *A Book of Quotations*

3 A truism is on that account none the less true. *Ib*

SANDBURG, Carl, 1878–1967

4 The fog comes
on little cat feet.
It sits looking
over the harbor and city
on silent haunches
and then moves on. *Fog*

5 Pile the bodies high at Austerlitz and Waterloo.
Shovel them under and let me work—
I am the grass; I cover all. *Grass*

6 Look out how you use proud words,
When you let proud words go, it is not easy to call them back. *Primer Lesson*

7 Homestead, Braddock, Birmingham, they make their steel with men,
Smoke and blood is the mix of steel. *Smoke and Steel*

SARGENT, Epes, 1813–1880

8 A life on the ocean wave,
A home on the rolling deep. *A Life on the Ocean Wave*

SASSOON, Siegfried, 1886–1967

9 And when the war is done and youth stone dead
I'd toddle safely home and die—in bed. *Base Details*

10 Everyone suddenly burst out singing. *Everyone Sang*

SAYERS, Henry, 1855–1932

11 Ta-ra-ra-boom-de-ay! *Title of song*

SCHILLER, Friedrich von, 1759–1805

12 *Alle Menschen werden Brüder Wo dein sanfter Flügel weilt.* In the shade of your soft wings, all men will be brothers. *An die Freude*

13 *Die Weltgeschichte ist das Weltgericht.* World history is the world's judgment. *Lecture, Jena, 26 May 1789*

SCHNECKENBURGER, Max, 1819–1849

14 *Die Wacht am Rhein.* The Watch on the Rhine. *Title of song*

SCOTT, Charles Prestwich, 1846–1932

15 Neither in what it gives, nor in what it does not give, nor in the mode of presentation, must the unclouded face of truth suffer wrong. Comment is free but facts are sacred. *Manchester Guardian, 6 May 1926*

SCOTT, Robert Falcon, 1868–1912

1 Great God! this is an awful place. [*The South Pole*] *Journal, 17 Jan. 1912*

2 For God's sake look after our people. *Ib, 25 March 1912*

3 Had we lived, I should have had a tale to tell of the hardihood, endurance, and courage of my companions which would have stirred the hearts of every Englishman. These rough notes and our dead bodies must tell the tale. *Message to the Public*

SCOTT, Sir Walter, 1771–1832

4 Come fill up my cup, come fill up my can,
Come saddle your horses, and call up your men;
Come open the West Port, and let me gang free,
And it's room for the bonnets of Bonny Dundee.
Bonny Dundee, The Doom of Devorgoil, 2, 3

5 But answer came there none. *Bridal of Triermain, 3, 10*

6 The stag at eve had drunk his fill,
Where danced the moon on Monan's rill. *The Lady of the Lake, 1, 1*

7 Forward and frolic glee was there,
The will to do, the soul to dare. *Ib, 1, 21*

8 Yet seem'd that tone, and gesture bland,
Less used to sue than to command. *Ib*

9 Soldier, rest! thy warfare o'er,
  Sleep the sleep that knows not breaking;
Dream of battled fields no more,
  Days of danger, nights of waking. *Ib, 1, 31*

10 Like the dew on the mountain,
  Like the foam on the river,
Like the bubble on the fountain,
  Thou art gone, and for ever! *Ib, 3, 16*

11 The way was long, the wind was cold,
The Minstrel was infirm and old;
His wither'd cheek, and tresses grey,
Seem'd to have known a better day.
The Lay of the Last Minstrel, Introduction, 1

12 If thou would'st view fair Melrose aright,
Go visit it by the pale moonlight. *Ib, 2, 1*

13 Love rules the court, the camp, the grove,
And men below, and saints above;
For love is heaven, and heaven is love. *Ib, 3, 2*

14 Call it not vain; they do not err,
  Who say, that when the Poet dies,
Mute Nature mourns her worshipper,
  And celebrates his obsequies. *Ib, 5, 1*

15 True love's the gift which God has given
To man alone beneath the heaven. *Ib, 5, 13*

16 Breathes there the man, with soul so dead,
Who never to himself hath said,
  This is my own, my native land! *Ib, 6, 1*

1 The wretch, concentred all in self,
Living, shall forfeit fair renown,
And, doubly dying, shall go down
To the vile dust, from whence he sprung,
Unwept, unhonour'd, and unsung. *The Lay of the Last Minstrel, 6, 1*

2 That day of wrath, that dreadful day,
When heaven and earth shall pass away. *Ib, 6, 31, Hymn for the Dead*

3 November's sky is chill and drear,
November's leaf is red and sear. *Marmion, 1, Introduction*

4 And come he slow or come he fast,
It is but Death who comes at last. *Ib, 2, 30*

5 O, young Lochinvar is come out of the west,
Through all the wide Border his steed was the best. *Ib, 5, 12, Lochinvar*

6 So faithful in love, and so dauntless in war,
There never was Knight like the young Lochinvar. *Ib*

7 And dar'st thou then
To beard the lion in his den,
The Douglas in his hall? *Ib, 6, 14*

8 O what a tangled web we weave,
When first we practise to deceive! *Ib, 6, 17*

9 O Woman! in our hours of ease,
Uncertain, coy, and hard to please,
And variable as the shade,
By the light quivering aspen made;
When pain and anguish wring the brow,
A ministering angel thou! *Ib, 6, 30*

10 He shook the fragment of his blade,
And shouted 'Victory!
Charge, Chester, charge! On, Stanley, on!'
Were the last words of Marmion. *Ib, 6, 32*

11 MRS BERTRAM: That sounds like nonsense, my dear.
MR BERTRAM: May be so, my dear; but it may be very good law for all that.
Guy Mannering, Ch. 9

12 The hour is come, but not the man. *The Heart of Midlothian, Ch. 4, Heading*

SCOTT, William, 1st Baron Stowell, 1745–1836

13 A dinner lubricates business. *Boswell's Life of Johnson, 1781*

SEARS, Edmund Hamilton, 1810–1876

14 It came upon the midnight clear,
That glorious song of old. *That Glorious Song of Old*

SEEGER, Alan, 1888–1916

15 I have a rendezvous with Death
At some disputed barricade. *I have a Rendezvous with Death*

SELDEN, John, 1584–1654

1 Old friends are best. King James used to call for his old shoes; they were easiest for his feet. *Table Talk*

2 There is not anything in the world so much abused as this sentence, Salus populi suprema lex esto. *Ib*

3 Philosophy is nothing but discretion. *Ib*

4 Preachers say, Do as I say, not as I do. *Ib*

5 A king is a thing men have made for their own sakes, for quietness' sake. Just as if in a family one man is appointed to buy the meat. *Ib*

6 Every law is a contract between the king and the people, and therefore to be kept. *Ib*

SELLAR, Walter Carruthers, 1898–1951, and YEATMAN, Robert Julian, 1897— 1968

7 1066 And All That. *Title of Book*

8 The Roman Conquest was, however, a *Good Thing*, since the Britons were only natives at that time. *1066 And All That, Ch. 1*

9 Has it never occurred to you that the Romans *counted backwards*? (Be honest.) *Ib, Test Paper 1*

10 Finding, however, that he was not memorable, he very patriotically abdicated in favour of Henry IV, Part II. *Ib, Ch. 26*

11 Shortly after this the cruel Queen died and a post-mortem examination revealed the word 'CALLOUS' engraved on her heart. *Ib, Ch. 32*

12 Williamanmary: England Ruled by an Orange. *Ib, Heading to Ch. 38*

13 Napoleon's armies always used to march on their stomachs, shouting: 'Vive l'intérieur!' *Ib, Ch. 48*

14 Do not on any account attempt to write on both sides of the paper at once. *Ib, Test Paper 5*

SERVICE, Robert William, 1874–1958

15 This is the Law of the Yukon, that only the strong shall thrive;
That surely the weak shall perish, and only the Fit survive.
The Law of the Yukon

16 When we, the Workers, all demand: 'What are we fighting for?' . . .
Then, then we'll end that stupid crime, that devil's madness—War.
Michael

SEWARD, William Henry, 1801–1872

17 There is a higher law than the Constitution. *Speech, U.S. Senate, 11 March 1850*

SHADWELL, Thomas, 1642?–1692

18 Words may be false and full of art,
Sighs are the natural language of the heart. CUPID *Psyche, Act 3*

19 He's a wise man that marries a harlot; he's on the surest side. Who but an ass would marry an uncertainty? SIR POSITIVE AT-ALL *The Sullen Lovers, Act 5*

20 I'll do't instantly, in the twinkling of a bed-staff. SIR SAMUEL HEARTY *The Virtuoso, Act 1*

SHAKESPEARE, William, 1564–1616

All's Well that Ends Well

1 Love all, trust a few,
Do wrong to none; be able for thine enemy
Rather in power than use, and keep thy friend
Under thy own life's key; be check'd for silence,
But never tax'd for speech. COUNTESS OF ROUSILLON *Act 1, Scene 1, Line 57*

2 Our remedies oft in ourselves do lie,
Which we ascribe to heaven. HELENA *1, 1, 202*

3 My friends were poor, but honest. HELENA *1, 3, 186*

4 A young man married is a man that's marr'd. PAROLLES *2, 3, 291*

5 No legacy is so rich as honesty. MARIANA *3, 5, 12*

6 The web of our life is of a mingled yarn, good and ill together. 2ND LORD *4, 3, 67*

7 Praising what is lost
Makes the remembrance dear. KING OF FRANCE *5, 3, 19*

8 Th' inaudible and noiseless foot of Time. KING OF FRANCE *5, 3, 41*

Antony and Cleopatra

9 The triple pillar of the world transform'd
Into a strumpet's fool. PHILO *1, 1, 12*

10 There's beggary in the love that can be reckon'd. ANTONY *1, 1, 15*

11 The nature of bad news infects the teller. MESSENGER *1, 2, 92*

12 Where's my serpent of old Nile? CLEOPATRA *1, 5, 25*

13 My salad days,
When I was green in judgment. CLEOPATRA *1, 5, 73*

14 The barge she sat in, like a burnish'd throne,
Burn'd on the water. The poop was beaten gold;
Purple the sails, and so perfumed that
The winds were love-sick with them; the oars were silver,
Which to the tune of flutes kept stroke, and made
The water which they beat to follow faster,
As amorous of their strokes. For her own person,
It beggar'd all description. ENOBARBUS *2, 2, 195*

15 Age cannot wither her, nor custom stale
Her infinite variety. Other women cloy
The appetites they feed, but she makes hungry
Where most she satisfies. ENOBARBUS *2, 2, 239*

16 Though it be honest, it is never good
To bring bad news. CLEOPATRA *2, 5, 85*

17 I will praise any man that will praise me. ENOBARBUS *2, 6, 88*

18 He will to his Egyptian dish again. ENOBARBUS *2, 6, 121*

19 Celerity is never more admir'd
Than by the negligent. CLEOPATRA *3, 7, 24*

20 He wears the rose
Of youth upon him. ANTONY *3, 13, 20*

1 Let's have one other gaudy night. ANTONY *Antony and Cleopatra* *3, 13, 183*

2 To business that we love we rise betime,
And go to't with delight. ANTONY *4, 4, 20*

3 O infinite virtue, com'st thou smiling from
The world's great snare uncaught? CLEOPATRA *4, 8, 18*

4 Unarm, Eros; the long day's task is done,
And we must sleep. ANTONY *4, 14, 35*

5 I am dying, Egypt, dying; only
I here importune death awhile, until
Of many thousand kisses the poor last
I lay upon thy lips. ANTONY *4, 15, 18*

6 O, wither'd is the garland of the war,
The soldier's pole is fall'n! Young boys and girls
Are level now with men. The odds is gone,
And there is nothing left remarkable
Beneath the visiting moon. CLEOPATRA *4, 15, 64*

7 The bright day is done,
And we are for the dark. IRAS *5, 2, 192*

8 His biting is immortal; those that do die of it do seldom or never recover. CLOWN *5, 2, 246*

9 I wish you joy o' th' worm. CLOWN *5, 2, 277*

10 I have
Immortal longings in me. CLEOPATRA *5, 2, 278*

11 Dost thou not see my baby at my breast
That sucks the nurse asleep? CLEOPATRA *5, 2, 307*

As You Like It

12 Fleet the time carelessly, as they did in the golden world. CHARLES *1, 1, 108*

13 Well said; that was laid on with a trowel. CELIA *1, 2, 94*

14 Beauty provoketh thieves sooner than gold. ROSALIND *1, 3, 106*

15 Sweet are the uses of adversity;
Which, like the toad, ugly and venomous,
Wears yet a precious jewel in his head;
And this our life, exempt from public haunt,
Finds tongues in trees, books in the running brooks,
Sermons in stones, and good in everything. DUKE SENIOR *2, 1, 12*

16 Sweep on, you fat and greasy citizens. 1ST LORD (quoting Jaques) *2, 1, 55*

17 Unregarded age in corners thrown. ADAM *2, 3, 42*

18 Therefore my age is as a lusty winter,
Frosty, but kindly. ADAM *2, 3, 52*

19 O good old man, how well in thee appears
The constant service of the antique world,
When service sweat for duty, not for meed!
Thou art not for the fashion of these times,
Where none will sweat but for promotion. ORLANDO *2, 3, 56*

1 I had rather bear with you than bear you. TOUCHSTONE *As You Like It, 2, 4, 9*

2 Ay, now am I in Arden; the more fool I; when I was at home I was in a better place; but travellers must be content. TOUCHSTONE *2, 4, 13*

3 If thou remembr'est not the slightest folly
That ever love did make thee run into,
Thou hast not lov'd. SILVIUS *2, 4, 31*

4 Under the greenwood tree
Who loves to lie with me,
And turn his merry note
Unto the sweet bird's throat,
Come hither, come hither, come hither.
Here shall he see
No enemy
But winter and rough weather. AMIENS *2, 5, 1*

5 I can suck melancholy out of a song, as a weasel sucks eggs.
JAQUES *2, 5, 12*

6 Who doth ambition shun,
And loves to live i' th' sun,
Seeking the food he eats,
And pleas'd with what he gets. AMIENS, ETC. *2, 5, 34*

7 I'll rail against all the first-born of Egypt. JAQUES *2, 5, 56*

8 A fool! I met a fool i' th' forest,
A motley fool. JAQUES *2, 7, 12*

9 And so, from hour to hour, we ripe and ripe,
And then, from hour to hour, we rot and rot;
And thereby hangs a tale. JAQUES *2, 7, 26*

10 Whate'er you are
That in this desert inaccessible,
Under the shade of melancholy boughs,
Lose and neglect the creeping hours of time. ORLANDO *2, 7, 109*

11 All the world's a stage,
And all the men and women merely players;
They have their exits and their entrances;
And one man in his time plays many parts,
His acts being seven ages. At first the infant,
Mewling and puking in the nurse's arms;
Then the whining school-boy, with his satchel
And shining morning face, creeping like snail
Unwillingly to school. And then the lover,
Sighing like furnace, with a woeful ballad
Made to his mistress' eyebrow. Then a soldier,
Full of strange oaths, and bearded like the pard,
Jealous in honour, sudden and quick in quarrel,
Seeking the bubble reputation
Even in the cannon's mouth. And then the justice,
In fair round belly with good capon lin'd,
With eyes severe and beard of formal cut,
Full of wise saws and modern instances;
And so he plays his part. The sixth age shifts
Into the lean and slipper'd pantaloon,

With spectacles on nose and pouch on side,
His youthful hose, well sav'd, a world too wide
For his shrunk shank; and his big manly voice,
Turning again toward childish treble, pipes
And whistles in his sound. Last scene of all,
That ends this strange eventful history,
Is second childishness and mere oblivion;
Sans teeth, sans eyes, sans taste, sans every thing. JAQUES *As You Like It*, *2, 7, 139*

1 Blow, blow, thou winter wind,
Thou art not so unkind
As man's ingratitude;
Thy tooth is not so keen,
Because thou art not seen,
Although thy breath be rude.
Heigh-ho! sing heigh-ho! unto the green holly.
Most friendship is feigning, most loving mere folly. AMIENS *2, 7, 174*

2 Run, run, Orlando; carve on every tree,
The fair, the chaste, and unexpressive she. ORLANDO *3, 2, 9*

3 He that wants money, means, and content, is without three good friends. CORIN *3, 2, 23*

4 Let us make an honourable retreat; though not with bag and baggage, yet with scrip and scrippage. TOUCHSTONE *3, 2, 150*

5 O wonderful, wonderful, and most wonderful wonderful, and yet again wonderful, and after that, out of all whooping! CELIA *3, 2, 177*

6 Do you not know I am a woman? When I think, I must speak. ROSALIND *3, 2, 234*

7 I do desire we may be better strangers. ORLANDO *3, 2, 243*

8 Time travels in divers paces with divers persons. I'll tell you who Time ambles withal, who Time trots withal, who Time gallops withal, and who he stands still withal. ROSALIND *3, 2, 290*

9 Truly, I would the gods had made thee poetical. TOUCHSTONE *3, 3, 13*

10 The truest poetry is the most feigning. TOUCHSTONE *3, 3, 16*

11 I am not a slut, though I thank the gods I am foul. AUDREY *3, 3, 34*

12 Men have died from time to time, and worms have eaten them, but not for love. ROSALIND *4, 1, 94*

13 Men are April when they woo, December when they wed: maids are May when they are maids, but the sky changes when they are wives. ROSALIND *4, 1, 130*

14 No sooner met but they look'd; no sooner look'd but they lov'd; no sooner lov'd but they sigh'd; no sooner sigh'd but they ask'd one another the reason; no sooner knew the reason but they sought the remedy. ROSALIND *5, 2, 29*

15 O, how bitter a thing it is to look into happiness through another man's eyes! ORLANDO *5, 2, 40*

16 It was a lover and his lass,
With a hey, and a ho, and a hey nonino,
That o'er the green corn-field did pass
In the spring time, the only pretty ring time,

When birds do sing, hey ding a ding, ding.
Sweet lovers love the spring. TWO PAGES *As You Like It, 5, 3, 14*

1 An ill-favour'd thing, sir, but mine own. TOUCHSTONE *5, 4, 55*

2 I will name you the degrees. The first, the Retort Courteous; the second, the Quip Modest; the third, the Reply Churlish; the fourth, the Reproof Valiant; the fifth, the Countercheck Quarrelsome; the sixth, the Lie with Circumstance; the seventh, the Lie Direct. TOUCHSTONE *5, 4, 86*

3 Your If is the only peace-maker; much virtue in If. TOUCHSTONE *5, 4, 97*

4 If it be true that good wine needs no bush, 'tis true that a good play needs no epilogue. ROSALIND *Epilogue, 3*

The Comedy of Errors

5 They brought one Pinch, a hungry lean-fac'd villain,
A mere anatomy, a mountebank,
A threadbare juggler, and a fortune-teller,
A needy, hollow-ey'd, sharp-looking wretch,
A living dead man. ANTIPHOLUS OF EPHESUS *5, 1, 237*

Coriolanus

6 My gracious silence, hail! CORIOLANUS *2, 1, 166*

7 Bid them wash their faces
And keep their teeth clean. CORIOLANUS *2, 3, 59*

8 Custom calls me to't.
What custom wills, in all things should we do't,
The dust on antique time would lie unswept,
And mountainous error be too highly heap'd
For truth to o'erpeer. CORIOLANUS *2, 3, 114*

9 Hear you this Triton of the minnows? Mark you
His absolute 'shall'? CORIOLANUS *3, 1, 89*

10 His nature is too noble for the world:
He would not flatter Neptune for his trident,
Or Jove for's power to thunder. His heart's his mouth;
What his breast forges, that his tongue must vent. MENENIUS *3, 1, 255*

11 Like a dull actor now
I have forgot my part and I am out,
Even to a full disgrace. CORIOLANUS *5, 3, 40*

12 If you have writ your annals true, 'tis there
That, like an eagle in a dove-cote, I
Flutter'd your Volscians in Corioli.
Alone I did it. CORIOLANUS *5, 6, 114*

Cymbeline

13 Hark, hark! the lark at heaven's gate sings,
And Phoebus 'gins arise,
His steeds to water at those springs
On chalic'd flow'rs that lies;
And winking Mary-buds begin
To ope their golden eyes.

With everything that pretty bin,
  My lady sweet, arise;
    Arise, arise! SONG — *Cymbeline, 2, 3, 19*

1 There be many Caesars
Ere such another Julius. Britain is
A world by itself, and we will nothing pay
For wearing our own noses. CLOTEN — *3, 1, 11*

2 O for a horse with wings! IMOGEN — *3, 2, 47*

3 O, this life
Is nobler than attending for a check,
Richer than doing nothing for a bribe,
Prouder than rustling in unpaid-for silk. BELARIUS — *3, 3, 21*

4 I have not slept one wink. PISANIO — *3, 4, 99*

5 Hath Britain all the sun that shines? IMOGEN — *3, 4, 135*

6 Society is no comfort
To one not sociable. IMOGEN — *4, 2, 12*

7 Though mean and mighty rotting
Together have one dust, yet reverence—
That angel of the world—doth make distinction
Of place 'tween high and low. BELARIUS — *4, 2, 247*

8 Thersites' body is as good as Ajax',
When neither are alive. GUIDERIUS — *4, 2, 253*

9 Fear no more the heat o' th' sun
  Nor the furious winter's rages;
Thou thy worldly task hast done,
  Home art gone, and ta'en thy wages.
Golden lads and girls all must,
As chimney-sweepers, come to dust. GUIDERIUS — *4, 2, 259*

10 All lovers young, all lovers must
Consign to thee and come to dust. GUIDERIUS AND ARVIRAGUS — *4, 2, 275*

11 Quiet consummation have,
And renowned be thy grave! GUIDERIUS AND ARVIRAGUS — *4, 2, 281*

12 He that sleeps feels not the toothache. GAOLER — *5, 4, 171*

Hamlet

13 For this relief much thanks. 'Tis bitter cold,
And I am sick at heart. FRANCISCO — *1, 1, 8*

14 What, has this thing appear'd again to-night? HORATIO — *1, 1, 21*

15 We do it wrong, being so majestical,
To offer it the show of violence. MARCELLUS — *1, 1, 143*

16 But look, the morn, in russet mantle clad,
Walks o'er the dew of yon high eastward hill. HORATIO — *1, 1, 166*

17 The memory be green. CLAUDIUS — *1, 2, 2*

18 A little more than kin, and less than kind. HAMLET — *1, 2, 65*

19 Not so, my lord; I am too much in the sun. HAMLET — *1, 2, 67*

20 Thou know'st 'tis common—all that lives must die,
Passing through nature to eternity. GERTRUDE — *1, 2, 72*

1 But I have that within which passes show—
These but the trappings and the suits of woe. HAMLET *Hamlet, 1, 2, 85*

2 O, that this too too solid flesh would melt,
Thaw, and resolve itself into a dew!
Or that the Everlasting had not fix'd
His canon 'gainst self-slaughter! O God! God!
How weary, stale, flat, and unprofitable,
Seem to me all the uses of this world! HAMLET *1, 2, 129*

3 So excellent a king that was to this
Hyperion to a satyr. HAMLET *1, 2, 139*

4 Why, she would hang on him
As if increase of appetite had grown
By what it fed on. HAMLET *1, 2, 143*

5 Frailty, thy name is woman! HAMLET *1, 2, 146*

6 It is not, nor it cannot come to good. HAMLET *1, 2, 158*

7 A truant disposition, good my lord. HORATIO *1, 2, 169*

8 Thrift, thrift, Horatio! The funeral bak'd-meats
Did coldly furnish forth the marriage tables. HAMLET *1, 2, 180*

9 'A was a man, take him for all in all,
I shall not look upon his like again. HAMLET *1, 2, 187*

10 A countenance more in sorrow than in anger. HORATIO *1, 2, 231*

11 Give it an understanding, but no tongue. HAMLET *1, 2, 249*

12 All is not well.
I doubt some foul play. HAMLET *1, 2, 254*

13 The chariest maid is prodigal enough
If she unmask her beauty to the moon. LAERTES *1, 3, 36*

14 Do not, as some ungracious pastors do,
Show me the steep and thorny way to heaven,
Whiles, like a puff'd and reckless libertine,
Himself the primrose path of dalliance treads
And recks not his own rede. OPHELIA *1, 3, 47*

15 And these few precepts in thy memory
Look thou character. Give thy thoughts no tongue,
Nor any unproportion'd thought his act.
Be thou familiar, but by no means vulgar.
Those friends thou hast, and their adoption tried,
Grapple them to thy soul with hoops of steel. POLONIUS *1, 3, 58*

16 Beware
Of entrance to a quarrel; but, being in,
Bear't that th' opposed may beware of thee.
Give every man thy ear, but few thy voice;
Take each man's censure, but reserve thy judgment.
Costly thy habit as thy purse can buy,
But not express'd in fancy; rich, not gaudy;
For the apparel oft proclaims the man. POLONIUS *1, 3, 65*

17 Neither a borrower nor a lender be;
For loan oft loses both itself and friend,

And borrowing dulls the edge of husbandry.
This above all—to thine own self be true,
And it must follow, as the night the day,
Thou canst not then be false to any man. POLONIUS *Hamlet, 1, 3, 75*

1 Be something scanter of your maiden presence. POLONIUS *1, 3, 121*

2 But to my mind, though I am native here
And to the manner born, it is a custom
More honour'd in the breach than the observance. HAMLET *1, 4, 14*

3 Angels and ministers of grace defend us!
Be thou a spirit of health or goblin damn'd,
Bring with thee airs from heaven or blasts from hell,
Be thy intents wicked or charitable,
Thou com'st in such a questionable shape
That I will speak to thee. HAMLET *1, 4, 39*

4 I do not set my life at a pin's fee;
And for my soul, what can it do to that,
Being a thing immortal as itself? HAMLET *1, 4, 65*

5 Something is rotten in the state of Denmark. MARCELLUS *1, 4, 90*

6 I am thy father's spirit,
Doom'd for a certain term to walk the night. GHOST *1, 5, 9*

7 But that I am forbid
To tell the secrets of my prison-house,
I could a tale unfold whose lightest word
Would harrow up thy soul, freeze thy young blood,
Make thy two eyes, like stars, start from their spheres,
Thy knotted and combined locks to part,
And each particular hair to stand on end,
Like quills upon the fretful porpentine.
But this eternal blazon must not be
To ears of flesh and blood. List, list, O, list! GHOST *1, 5, 13*

8 Revenge his foul and most unnatural murder. GHOST *1, 5, 25*

9 Murder most foul, as in the best it is;
But this most foul, strange, and unnatural. GHOST *1, 5, 27*

10 O my prophetic soul! My uncle! HAMLET *1, 5, 40*

11 O Hamlet, what a falling off was there. GHOST *1, 5, 47*

12 There are more things in heaven and earth, Horatio,
Than are dreamt of in your philosophy. HAMLET *1, 5, 166*

13 To put an antic disposition on. HAMLET *1, 5, 172*

14 The time is out of joint. O cursed spite,
That ever I was born to set it right! HAMLET *1, 5, 189*

15 Brevity is the soul of wit. POLONIUS *2, 2, 90*

16 More matter with less art. GERTRUDE *2, 2, 95*

17 That he's mad, 'tis true: 'tis true 'tis pity;
And pity 'tis 'tis true. POLONIUS *2, 2, 97*

18 POLONIUS: Do you know me, my lord?
HAMLET: Excellent well; you are a fishmonger. *2, 2, 172*

1 To be honest, as this world goes, is to be one man pick'd out of ten thousand. HAMLET *Hamlet, 2, 2, 177*

2 POLONIUS: What do you read, my Lord?
HAMLET: Words, words, words. *2, 2, 190*

3 Though this be madness, yet there is method in't. POLONIUS *2, 2, 204*

4 HAMLET: What news?
ROSENCRANTZ: None, my lord, but that the world's grown honest.
HAMLET: Then is doomsday near. *2, 2, 235*

5 There is nothing either good or bad, but thinking makes it so. HAMLET *2, 2, 248*

6 What a piece of work is a man! How noble in reason! how infinite in faculties! in form and moving, how express and admirable! in action, how like an angel! in apprehension, how like a god! the beauty of the world! the paragon of animals! And yet, to me, what is this quintessence of dust? Man delights not me—no, nor woman neither. HAMLET *2, 2, 303*

7 He that plays the king shall be welcome. HAMLET *2, 2, 317*

8 I am but mad north-north-west; when the wind is southerly I know a hawk from a handsaw. HAMLET *2, 2, 374*

9 The best actors in the world, either for tragedy, comedy, history, pastoral, pastoral-comical, historical-pastoral, tragical-historical, tragical-comical-historical-pastoral, scene individable, or poem unlimited. POLONIUS *2, 2, 392*

10 The play, I remember, pleas'd not the million; 'twas caviare to the general. HAMLET *2, 2, 429*

11 The mobled queen. 1st PLAYER *2, 2, 496*

12 Let them be well used; for they are the abstract and brief chronicles of the time. HAMLET *2, 2, 517*

13 Use every man after his desert, and who shall scape whipping? HAMLET *2, 2, 523*

14 O, what a rogue and peasant slave am I! HAMLET *2, 2, 543*

15 What's Hecuba to him or he to Hecuba,
That he should weep for her? HAMLET *2, 2, 552*

16 A dull and muddy-mettl'd rascal. HAMLET *2, 2, 561*

17 But I am pigeon-liver'd and lack gall
To make oppression bitter. HAMLET *2, 2, 572*

18 This is most brave,
That I, the son of a dear father murder'd,
Prompted to my revenge by heaven and hell,
Must, like a whore, unpack my heart with words,
And fall a-cursing like a very drab. HAMLET *2, 2, 578*

19 The play's the thing
Wherein I'll catch the conscience of the King. HAMLET *2, 2, 600*

20 To be, or not to be—that is the question;
Whether 'tis nobler in the mind to suffer
The slings and arrows of outrageous fortune,

Or to take arms against a sea of troubles,
And by opposing end them? To die, to sleep—
No more; and by a sleep to say we end
The heart-ache and the thousand natural shocks
That flesh is heir to. 'Tis a consummation
Devoutly to be wish'd. To die, to sleep;
To sleep, perchance to dream. Ay, there's the rub;
For in that sleep of death what dreams may come,
When we have shuffled off this mortal coil,
Must give us pause. There's the respect
That makes calamity of so long life;
For who would bear the whips and scorns of time,
Th' oppressor's wrong, the proud man's contumely,
The pangs of despis'd love, the law's delay,
The insolence of office, and the spurns
That patient merit of th' unworthy takes,
When he himself might his quietus make
With a bare bodkin? Who would fardels bear,
To grunt and sweat under a weary life,
But that the dread of something after death—
The undiscover'd country, from whose bourn
No traveller returns—puzzles the will,
And makes us rather bear those ills we have
Than fly to others that we know not of?
Thus conscience does make cowards of us all;
And thus the native hue of resolution
Is sicklied o'er with the pale cast of thought,
And enterprises of great pith and moment,
With this regard, their currents turn awry
And lose the name of action. HAMLET *Hamlet, 3, 1, 56*

1 For to the noble mind
Rich gifts wax poor when givers prove unkind. OPHELIA *3, 1, 100*

2 Get thee to a nunnery. HAMLET *3, 1, 121*

3 Be thou as chaste as ice, as pure as snow, thou shalt not escape calumny. HAMLET *3, 1, 135*

4 I have heard of your paintings too, well enough; God hath given you one face, and you make yourselves another. HAMLET *3, 1, 142*

5 O, what a noble mind is here o'erthrown!
The courtier's, soldier's, scholar's, eye, tongue, sword;
Th' expectancy and rose of the fair state,
The glass of fashion and the mould of form,
Th' observ'd of all observers—quite, quite down! OPHELIA *3, 1, 150*

6 Madness in great ones must not unwatch'd go. CLAUDIUS *3, 1, 188*

7 Speak the speech, I pray you, as I pronounc'd it to you, trippingly on the tongue; but if you mouth it, as many of our players do, I had as lief the town-crier spoke my lines. Nor do not saw the air too much with your hand, thus, but use all gently. HAMLET *3, 2, 1*

8 It out-herods Herod. HAMLET *3, 2, 14*

9 Suit the action to the word, the word to the action; with this special observance, that you o'erstep not the modesty of nature. HAMLET *3, 2, 17*

1 Give me that man
That is not passion's slave, and I will wear him
In my heart's core, ay, in my heart of heart,
As I do thee. HAMLET *Hamlet, 3, 2, 69*

2 Here's metal more attractive. HAMLET *3, 2, 106*

3 OPHELIA: 'Tis brief, my lord.
HAMLET: As woman's love. *3, 2, 148*

4 The lady doth protest too much, methinks. GERTRUDE *3, 2, 225*

5 We that have free souls, it touches us not. Let the galled jade wince, our withers are unwrung. HAMLET *3, 2, 235*

6 The proverb is something musty. HAMLET *3, 2, 334*

7 Very like a whale. POLONIUS *3, 2, 372*

8 'Tis now the very witching time of night,
When churchyards yawn, and hell itself breathes out
Contagion to this world. HAMLET *3, 2, 378*

9 Let me be cruel, not unnatural:
I will speak daggers to her, but use none. HAMLET *3, 2, 385*

10 O, my offence is rank, it smells to heaven. CLAUDIUS *3, 3, 36*

11 My words fly up, my thoughts remain below.
Words without thoughts never to heaven go. CLAUDIUS *3, 3, 97*

12 How now! a rat? Dead, for a ducat, dead! HAMLET *3, 4, 23*

13 A king of shreds and patches. HAMLET *3, 4, 102*

14 Assume a virtue, if you have it not. HAMLET *3, 4, 160*

15 I must be cruel only to be kind. HAMLET *3, 4, 178*

16 Diseases desperate grown
By desperate appliance are reliev'd,
Or not at all. CLAUDIUS *4, 3, 9*

17 How all occasions do inform against me,
And spur my dull revenge! What is a man,
If his chief good and market of his time
Be but to sleep and feed? A beast, no more! HAMLET *4, 4, 32*

18 Some craven scruple
Of thinking too precisely on th' event. HAMLET *4, 4, 40*

19 Rightly to be great
Is not to stir without great argument,
But greatly to find quarrel in a straw,
When honour's at the stake. HAMLET *4, 4, 53*

20 Come, my coach! Good night, ladies; good night, sweet ladies, good night, good night. OPHELIA *4, 5, 69*

21 When sorrows come, they come not single spies,
But in battalions! CLAUDIUS *4, 5, 75*

22 There's such divinity doth hedge a king
That treason can but peep to what it would. CLAUDIUS *4, 5, 120*

23 There's rosemary, that's for remembrance; pray you, love, remember. And there is pansies, that's for thoughts. OPHELIA *4, 5, 172*

24 A very riband in the cap of youth. CLAUDIUS *4, 7, 77*

1 There is a willow grows aslant the brook
That shows his hoar leaves in the glassy stream. GERTRUDE *Hamlet, 4, 7, 167*

2 Alas, poor Yorick! I knew him, Horatio: a fellow of infinite jest, of most excellent fancy. HAMLET *5, 1, 179*

3 Lay her i' th' earth;
And from her fair and unpolluted flesh
May violets spring! I tell thee, churlish priest,
A minist'ring angel shall my sister be
When thou liest howling. LAERTES *5, 1, 232*

4 Sweets to the sweet; farewell! GERTRUDE *5, 1, 237*

5 Let Hercules himself do what he may,
The cat will mew, and dog will have his day. HAMLET *5, 1, 285*

6 There's a divinity that shapes our ends,
Rough-hew them how we will. HAMLET *5, 2, 10*

7 A hit, a very palpable hit. OSRIC *5, 2, 273*

8 Report me and my cause aright. HAMLET *5, 2, 331*

9 If thou didst ever hold me in thy heart,
Absent thee from felicity awhile,
And in this harsh world draw thy breath in pain,
To tell my story. HAMLET *5, 2, 338*

10 The rest is silence. HAMLET *5, 2, 350*

11 Now cracks a noble heart. Good night, sweet prince,
And flights of angels sing thee to thy rest! HORATIO *5, 2, 351*

12 For he was likely, had he been put on,
To have prov'd most royal. FORTINBRAS *5, 2, 389*

King Henry the Fourth, Part One

13 So shaken as we are, so wan with care. HENRY IV *1, 1, 1*

14 To chase these pagans in those holy fields
Over whose acres walk'd those blessed feet
Which fourteen hundred years ago were nail'd
For our advantage on the bitter cross. HENRY IV *1, 1, 24*

15 See riot and dishonour stain the brow
Of my young Harry. HENRY IV *1, 1, 85*

16 Shall there be gallows standing in England when thou art king? FALSTAFF *1, 2, 56*

17 O, thou hast damnable iteration, and art indeed able to corrupt a saint. FALSTAFF *1, 2, 88*

18 Why, Hal, 'tis my vocation, Hal; 'tis no sin for a man to labour in his vocation. FALSTAFF *1, 2, 101*

19 There's neither honesty, manhood, nor good fellowship in thee. FALSTAFF *1, 2, 133*

20 I know you all, and will awhile uphold
The unyok'd humour of your idleness. PRINCE *1, 2, 188*

21 If all the year were playing holidays,
To sport would be as tedious as to work. PRINCE *1, 2, 197*

1 A certain lord, neat, and trimly dress'd,
Fresh as a bridegroom, and his chin new reap'd
Show'd like a stubble-land at harvest-home.
He was perfumed like a milliner,
And 'twixt his finger and his thumb he held
A pouncet-box, which ever and anon
He gave his nose and took't away again. HOTSPUR *Henry the Fourth, Part One, 1, 3, 33*

2 He made me mad
To see him shine so brisk, and smell so sweet,
And talk so like a waiting-gentlewoman
Of guns, and drums, and wounds—God save the mark!—
And telling me the sovereignest thing on earth
Was parmaceti for an inward bruise. HOTSPUR *1, 3, 53*

3 O, the blood more stirs
To rouse a lion than to start a hare! HOTSPUR *1, 3, 197*

4 By heaven, methinks it were an easy leap
To pluck bright honour from the pale-fac'd moon;
Or dive into the bottom of the deep,
Where fathom-line could never touch the ground,
And pluck up drowned honour by the locks. HOTSPUR *1, 3, 201*

5 I know a trick worth two of that. FIRST CARRIER *2, 1, 36*

6 I am bewitch'd with the rogue's company. If the rascal have not given me medicines to make me love him, I'll be hang'd. FALSTAFF *2, 2, 16*

7 Have you any levers to lift me up again, being down? FALSTAFF *2, 2, 33*

8 It would be argument for a week, laughter for a month, and a good jest for ever. PRINCE *2, 2, 91*

9 Falstaff sweats to death
And lards the lean earth as he walks along. PRINCE *2, 2, 104*

10 Out of this nettle, danger, we pluck this flower, safety. HOTSPUR *2, 3, 10*

11 Constant you are,
But yet a woman; and for secrecy,
No lady closer; for I well believe
Thou wilt not utter what thou dost not know. HOTSPUR *2, 3, 105*

12 I am not yet of Percy's mind, the Hotspur of the north; he that kills me some six or seven dozen of Scots at a breakfast, washes his hands, and says to his wife 'Fie upon this quiet life! I want work'. PRINCE *2, 4, 97*

13 A plague of all cowards, I say. FALSTAFF *2, 4, 109*

14 There lives not three good men unhang'd in England, and one of them is fat and grows old. FALSTAFF *2, 4, 123*

15 I have pepper'd two of them; two I am sure I have paid—two rogues in buckram suits. I tell thee what, Hal, if I tell thee a lie, spit in my face, call me horse. Thou knowest my old ward: here I lay, and thus I bore my point. Four rogues in buckram let drive at me. FALSTAFF *2, 4, 183*

16 O monstrous! eleven buckram men grown out of two! PRINCE *2, 4, 212*

17 A plague of sighing and grief! it blows a man up like a bladder. FALSTAFF *2, 4, 322*

1 That reverend vice, that grey iniquity, that father ruffian, that vanity in years. PRINCE *Henry the Fourth, Part One, 2, 4, 437*

2 Banish plump Jack, and banish all the world. FALSTAFF *2, 4, 462*

3 O monstrous! but one halfpenny-worth of bread to this intolerable deal of sack! PRINCE *2, 4, 521*

4 I am not in the roll of common men. GLENDOWER *3, 1, 43*

5 GLENDOWER: I can call spirits from the vasty deep.
HOTSPUR: Why, so can I, or so can any man;
But will they come when you do call for them? *3, 1, 53*

6 I had rather be a kitten and cry mew
Than one of these same metre ballad-mongers. HOTSPUR *3, 1, 129*

7 Mincing poetry.
'Tis like the forc'd gait of a shuffling nag. HOTSPUR *3, 1, 134*

8 I understand thy kisses, and thou mine,
And that's a feeling disputation. MORTIMER *3, 1, 204*

9 Swear me, Kate, like a lady as thou art,
A good mouth-filling oath. HOTSPUR *3, 1, 254*

10 He was but as the cuckoo is in June,
Heard, not regarded. HENRY IV *3, 2, 75*

11 Do I not bate? Do I not dwindle? Why, my skin hangs about me like an old lady's loose gown. FALSTAFF *3, 3, 2*

12 Company, villainous company, hath been the spoil of me. FALSTAFF *3, 2, 10*

13 I have more flesh than another man, and therefore more frailty. FALSTAFF *3, 3, 167*

14 Doomsday is near; die all, die merrily. HOTSPUR *4, 1, 134*

15 I have misused the King's press damnably. FALSTAFF *4, 2, 11*

16 The cankers of a calm world and a long peace. FALSTAFF *4, 2, 30*

17 To the latter end of a fray and the beginning of a feast
Fits a dull fighter and a keen guest. FALSTAFF *4, 2, 77*

18 For nothing can seem foul to those that win. HENRY IV *5, 1, 8*

19 Rebellion lay in his way, and he found it. FALSTAFF *5, 1, 28*

20 I would 'twere bed-time, Hal, and all well. FALSTAFF *5, 1, 125*

21 Honour pricks me on. Yea, but how if honour prick me off when I come on? How then? Can honour set to a leg? No. Or an arm? No. Or take away the grief of a wound? No. Honour hath no skill in surgery, then? No. What is honour? A word. What is in that word? Honour. What is that honour? Air. A trim reckoning! Who hath it? He that died o' Wednesday. Doth he feel it? No. Doth he hear it? No. 'Tis insensible, then? Yea, to the dead. But will it not live with the living? No. Why? Detraction will not suffer it. Therefore I'll none of it. Honour is a mere scutcheon. And so ends my catechism. FALSTAFF *5, 1, 129*

22 The time of life is short!
To spend that shortness basely were too long. HOTSPUR *5, 2, 82*

23 Two stars keep not their motion in one sphere. PRINCE *5, 4, 65*

1 But thoughts, the slaves of life, and life, time's fool,
And time, that takes survey of all the world,
Must have a stop. HOTSPUR *Henry the Fourth, Part One, 5, 4, 81*

2 What, old acquaintance! Could not all this flesh
Keep in a little life? Poor Jack, farewell!
I could have better spar'd a better man. PRINCE *5, 4, 102*

3 The better part of valour is discretion; in the which better part I have saved my life. FALSTAFF *5, 4, 120*

4 Lord, Lord, how this world is given to lying! FALSTAFF *5, 4, 143*

5 I'll purge, and leave sack, and live cleanly, as a nobleman should do. FALSTAFF *5, 4, 163*

King Henry the Fourth, Part Two

6 This man's brow, like to a title-leaf,
Foretells the nature of a tragic volume. NORTHUMBERLAND *1, 1, 60*

7 Yet the first bringer of unwelcome news
Hath but a losing office, and his tongue
Sounds ever after as a sullen bell,
Rememb'red tolling a departing friend. NORTHUMBERLAND *1, 1, 100*

8 The brain of this foolish-compounded clay, man, is not able to invent anything that tends to laughter, more than I invent or is invented on me. I am not only witty in myself, but the cause that wit is in other men. I do here walk before thee like a sow that hath overwhelm'd all her litter but one. FALSTAFF *1, 2, 7*

9 My lord, I was born about three of the clock in the afternoon, with a white head and something a round belly. For my voice—I have lost it with hallooing and singing of anthems. FALSTAFF *1, 2, 176*

10 Well, I cannot last ever; but it was alway yet the trick of our English nation, if they have a good thing, to make it too common. FALSTAFF *1, 2, 200*

11 I would to God my name were not so terrible to the enemy as it is. FALSTAFF *1, 2, 204*

12 I can get no remedy against this consumption of the purse; borrowing only lingers and lingers it out, but the disease is incurable. FALSTAFF *1, 2, 223*

13 O thoughts of men accurs'd!
Past and to come seems best; things present, worst. ARCHBISHOP *1, 3, 107*

14 Away, you scullion! you rampallian! you fustilarian! I'll tickle your catastrophe. FALSTAFF *2, 1, 57*

15 He hath eaten me out of house and home. HOSTESS *2, 1, 71*

16 Now, the Lord lighten thee! Thou art a great fool. CHIEF JUSTICE *2, 1, 187*

17 He was indeed the glass
Wherein the noble youth did dress themselves. LADY PERCY *2, 3, 21*

18 Hollow pamper'd jades of Asia. PISTOL *2, 4, 155*

19 Is it not strange that desire should so many years outlive performance? POINS *2, 4, 250*

20 Now comes in the sweetest morsel of the night, and we must hence, and leave it unpick'd. FALSTAFF *2, 4, 354*

1 You see, my good wenches, how men of merit are sought after; the undeserver may sleep, when the man of action is call'd on. FALSTAFF
Henry the Fourth, Part Two, 2, 4, 361

2 How many thousands of my poorest subjects
Are at this hour asleep! O sleep, O gentle sleep,
Nature's soft nurse, how have I frighted thee,
That thou no more wilt weigh my eyelids down,
And steep my senses in forgetfulness? HENRY IV *3, 1, 4*

3 Canst thou, O partial sleep, give thy repose
To the wet sea-boy in an hour so rude;
And in the calmest and most stillest night,
With all appliances and means to boot,
Deny it to a king? Then, happy low, lie down!
Uneasy lies the head that wears a crown. HENRY IV *3, 1, 26*

4 O God! that one might read the book of fate. HENRY IV *3, 1, 45*

5 There is a history in all men's lives,
Figuring the natures of the times deceas'd. WARWICK *3, 1, 80*

6 Death, as the Psalmist saith, is certain to all; all shall die. How a good yoke of bullocks at Stamford fair? SHALLOW *3, 2, 36*

7 We have heard the chimes at midnight. FALSTAFF *3, 2, 210*

8 I care not; a man can die but once; we owe God a death. FEEBLE *3, 2, 228*

9 Care I for the limb, the thews, the stature, bulk, and big assemblance of a man! Give me the spirit. FALSTAFF *3, 2, 251*

10 Lord, Lord, how subject we old men are to this vice of lying! FALSTAFF *3, 2, 294*

11 Against ill chances men are ever merry;
But heaviness foreruns the good event. ARCHBISHOP *4, 2, 81*

12 A peace is of the nature of a conquest;
For then both parties nobly are subdu'd,
And neither party loser. ARCHBISHOP *4, 2, 89*

13 I may justly say with the hook-nos'd fellow of Rome—I came, saw, and overcame. FALSTAFF *4, 3, 40*

14 He hath a tear for pity and a hand
Open as day for melting charity. HENRY IV *4, 4, 31*

15 Most subject is the fattest soil to weeds. HENRY IV *4, 4, 54*

16 O polish'd perturbation! golden care!
That keep'st the ports of slumber open wide
To many a watchful night! PRINCE *4, 5, 23*

17 This sleep is sound indeed; this is a sleep
That from this golden rigol hath divorc'd
So many English kings. PRINCE *4, 5, 35*

18 Thy wish was father, Harry, to that thought. HENRY IV *4, 5, 93*

19 Commit
The oldest sins the newest kind of ways. HENRY IV *4, 5, 126*

20 This is the English, not the Turkish court;
Not Amurath an Amurath succeeds,
But Harry Harry. HENRY V *5, 2, 47*

1 Under which king, Bezonian?
Speak, or die. PISTOL *Henry the Fourth, Part Two, 5, 3, 112*

2 Let us take any man's horses: the laws of England are at my commandment.
FALSTAFF *5, 3, 134*

3 I know thee not, old man. Fall to thy prayers.
How ill white hairs become a fool and jester!
I have long dreamt of such a kind of man,
So surfeit-swell'd, so old, and so profane. HENRY V *5, 5, 48*

4 Master Shallow, I owe you a thousand pound. FALSTAFF *5, 5, 74*

King Henry the Fifth

5 O for a Muse of fire, that would ascend
The brightest heaven of invention. CHORUS *Prologue, 1*

6 Can this cockpit hold
The vasty fields of France? Or may we cram
Within this wooden O the very casques
That did affright the air at Agincourt? CHORUS *Prologue, 11*

7 Turn him to any cause of policy,
The Gordian knot of it he will unloose,
Familiar as his garter; that, when he speaks,
The air, a charter'd libertine, is still. ARCHBISHOP OF CANTERBURY
1, 1, 45

8 For so work the honey bees,
Creatures that by a rule in nature teach
The act of order to a peopled kingdom.
They have a king, and officers of sorts,
Where some like magistrates correct at home;
Others like merchants venture trade abroad;
Others like soldiers, armed in their stings,
Make boot upon the summer's velvet buds,
Which pillage they with merry march bring home
To the tent-royal of their emperor;
Who, busied in his majesty, surveys
The singing masons building roofs of gold,
The civil citizens kneading up the honey,
The poor mechanic porters crowding in
Their heavy burdens at his narrow gate,
The sad-ey'd justice, with his surly hum,
Delivering o'er to executors pale
The lazy yawning drone. ARCHBISHOP OF CANTERBURY *1, 2, 187*

9 Now all the youth of England are on fire,
And silken dalliance in the wardrobe lies;
Now thrive the armourers, and honour's thought
Reigns solely in the breast of every man;
They sell the pasture now to buy the horse,
Following the mirror of all Christian kings
With winged heels, as English Mercuries.
For now sits Expectation in the air. CHORUS *2, Prologue, 1*

10 I dare not fight; but I will wink and hold out mine iron. NYM *2, 1, 6*

11 Though patience be a tired mare, yet she will plod. NYM *2, 1, 24*

1 He's in Arthur's bosom, if ever man went to Arthur's bosom. 'A made a finer end, and went away an it had been any christom child; 'a parted ev'n just between twelve and one, ev'n at the turning o' th' tide. HOSTESS
Henry the Fifth, 2, 3, 9

2 His nose was as sharp as a pen, and 'a babbl'd of green fields. HOSTESS
2, 3, 17

3 Once more unto the breach, dear friends, once more;
Or close the wall up with our English dead.
In peace there's nothing so becomes a man
As modest stillness and humility;
But when the blast of war blows in our ears,
Then imitate the action of the tiger:
Stiffen the sinews, summon up the blood,
Disguise fair nature with hard-favour'd rage. HENRY V *3, 1, 1*

4 On, on, you noblest English,
Whose blood is fet from fathers of war-proof. HENRY V *3, 1, 17*

5 I see you stand like greyhounds in the slips,
Straining upon the start. The game's afoot:
Follow your spirit; and upon this charge
Cry 'God for Harry, England, and Saint George!' HENRY V *3, 1, 31*

6 Men of few words are the best men. BOY *3, 2, 36*

7 I know the disciplines of war. FLUELLEN *3, 2, 132*

8 Now entertain conjecture of a time
When creeping murmur and the poring dark
Fills the wide vessel of the universe.
From camp to camp, through the foul womb of night,
The hum of either army stilly sounds,
That the fix'd sentinels almost receive
The secret whispers of each other's watch. CHORUS *4, Prologue, 1*

9 The King's a bawcock and a heart of gold,
A lad of life, an imp of fame;
Of parents good, of fist most valiant.
I kiss his dirty shoe, and from heart-string
I love the lovely bully. PISTOL *4, 1, 44*

10 I think the King is but a man as I am: the violet smells to him as it doth to me. HENRY V *4, 1, 101*

11 Every subject's duty is the King's; but every subject's soul is his own.
HENRY V *4, 1, 175*

12 O that we now had here
But one ten thousand of those men in England
That do no work to-day! WESTMORELAND *4, 3, 16*

13 If we are mark'd to die, we are enow
To do our country loss; and if to live,
The fewer men, the greater share of honour. HENRY V *4, 3, 20*

14 But if it be a sin to covet honour,
I am the most offending soul alive. HENRY V *4, 3, 28*

15 This day is call'd the feast of Crispian.
He that outlives this day, and comes safe home,
Will stand a tip-toe when this day is nam'd,
And rouse him at the name of Crispian. HENRY V *4, 3, 40*

1 Old men forget; yet all shall be forgot,
But he'll remember, with advantages,
What feats he did that day. HENRY V *Henry the Fifth, 4, 3, 49*

2 We few, we happy few, we band of brothers;
For he to-day that sheds his blood with me
Shall be my brother; be he ne'er so vile,
This day shall gentle his condition;
And gentlemen in England now a-bed
Shall think themselves accurs'd they were not here,
And hold their manhoods cheap whiles any speaks
That fought with us upon Saint Crispin's day. HENRY V *4, 3, 60*

3 There is occasions and causes why and wherefore in all things. FLUELLEN *5, 1, 3*

4 For these fellows of infinite tongue, that can rhyme themselves into ladies' favours, they do always reason themselves out again. HENRY V *5, 2, 157*

King Henry the Sixth, Part One

5 Hung be the heavens with black, yield day to night! BEDFORD *1, 1, 1*

6 Unbidden guests
Are often welcomest when they are gone. BEDFORD *2, 2, 55*

7 She's beautiful, and therefore to be woo'd;
She is a woman, therefore to be won. SUFFOLK *5, 3, 78*

King Henry the Sixth, Part Two

8 Smooth runs the water where the brook is deep. SUFFOLK *3, 1, 53*

9 I will make it felony to drink small beer. JACK CADE *4, 2, 64*

10 The first thing we do, let's kill all the lawyers. DICK *4, 2, 73*

11 Thou hast most traitorously corrupted the youth of the realm in erecting a grammar school; and whereas, before, our forefathers had no other books but the score and the tally, thou hast caused printing to be us'd, and, contrary to the King, his crown, and dignity, thou hast built a paper-mill. It will be proved to thy face that thou hast men about thee that usually talk of a noun and a verb, and such abominable words as no Christian ear can endure to hear. JACK CADE *4, 7, 30*

12 Away with him, away with him! He speaks Latin. JACK CADE *4, 7, 54*

King Henry the Sixth, Part Three

13 O God! methinks it were a happy life
To be no better than a homely swain;
To sit upon a hill, as I do now,
To carve out dials quaintly, point by point,
Thereby to see the minutes how they run—
How many makes the hour full complete,
How many hours brings about the day,
How many days will finish up the year,
How many years a mortal man may live. HENRY VI *2, 5, 21*

14 Gives not the hawthorn bush a sweeter shade
To shepherds looking on their silly sheep,
Than doth a rich embroider'd canopy
To kings that fear their subjects' treachery? HENRY VI *2, 5, 42*

1 Suspicion always haunts the guilty mind:
The thief doth fear each bush an officer. GLOUCESTER *Henry the Sixth, Part Three, 5, 6, 11*

2 Down, down to hell; and say I sent thee thither. GLOUCESTER *5, 6, 67*

King Henry the Eighth

3 Heat not a furnace for your foe so hot
That it do singe yourself. We may outrun
By violent swiftness that which we run at,
And lose by over-running. NORFOLK *1, 1, 140*

4 I swear 'tis better to be lowly born
And range with humble livers in content
Than to be perk'd up in a glist'ring grief
And wear a golden sorrow. ANNE *2, 3, 19*

5 I would not be a queen
For all the world. ANNE *2, 3, 45*

6 Orpheus with his lute made trees,
And the mountain tops that freeze,
Bow themselves when he did sing. SONG *3, 1, 3*

7 Heaven is above all yet: there sits a Judge
That no king can corrupt. QUEEN KATHARINE *3, 1, 100*

8 I have touch'd the highest point of all my greatness,
And from that full meridian of my glory
I haste now to my setting. I shall fall
Like a bright exhalation in the evening,
And no man see me more. WOLSEY *3, 2, 223*

9 Farewell, a long farewell, to all my greatness!
This is the state of man: to-day he puts forth
The tender leaves of hopes; to-morrow blossoms
And bears his blushing honours thick upon him;
The third day comes a frost, a killing frost,
And when he thinks, good easy man, full surely
His greatness is a-ripening, nips his root,
And then he falls, as I do. WOLSEY *3, 2, 351*

10 Vain pomp and glory of this world, I hate ye;
I feel my heart new open'd. O, how wretched
Is that poor man that hangs on princes' favours!
There is betwixt that smile we would aspire to,
That sweet aspect of princes, and their ruin
More pangs and fears than wars or women have;
And when he falls, he falls like Lucifer,
Never to hope again. WOLSEY *3, 2, 365*

11 A peace above all earthly dignities,
A still and quiet conscience. WOLSEY *3, 2, 379*

12 Love thyself last; cherish those hearts that hate thee;
Corruption wins not more than honesty. WOLSEY *3, 2, 443*

13 Had I but serv'd my God with half the zeal
I serv'd my King, he would not in mine age
Have left me naked to mine enemies. WOLSEY *3, 2, 455*

14 So may he rest; his faults lie gently on him! KATHARINE *4, 2, 31*

1 Men's evil manners live in brass: their virtues
We write in water. GRIFFITH *Henry the Eighth, 4, 2, 45*

2 He was a scholar, and a ripe and good one;
Exceeding wise, fair-spoken, and persuading;
Lofty and sour to them that lov'd him not,
But to those men that sought him sweet as summer. GRIFFITH *4, 2, 51*

3 Love and meekness, lord,
Become a churchman better than ambition. CRANMER *5, 3, 62*

Julius Caesar

4 You blocks, you stones, you worse than senseless things! MARULLUS *1, 1, 36*

5 Beware the ides of March. SOOTHSAYER *1, 2, 18*

6 Well, honour is the subject of my story.
I cannot tell what you and other men
Think of this life; but, for my single self,
I had as lief not be as live to be
In awe of such a thing as I myself. CASSIUS *1, 2, 92*

7 Ye gods! it doth amaze me
A man of such a feeble temper should
So get the start of the majestic world,
And bear the palm alone. CASSIUS *1, 2, 128*

8 Why, man, he doth bestride the narrow world
Like a Colossus, and we petty men
Walk under his huge legs, and peep about
To find ourselves dishonourable graves.
Men at some time are masters of their fates:
The fault, dear Brutus, is not in our stars,
But in ourselves, that we are underlings. CASSIUS *1, 2, 135*

9 Let me have men about me that are fat;
Sleek-headed men, and such as sleep o' nights.
Yond Cassius has a lean and hungry look;
He thinks too much. Such men are dangerous. CAESAR *1, 2, 192*

10 'Tis very like. He hath the falling sickness. BRUTUS *1, 2, 253*

11 For mine own part, it was Greek to me. CASCA *1, 2, 283*

12 And yesterday the bird of night did sit,
Even at noon-day, upon the market-place,
Hooting and shrieking. CASCA *1, 3, 26*

13 Between the acting of a dreadful thing
And the first motion, all the interim is
Like a phantasma or a hideous dream.
The Genius and the mortal instruments
Are then in council; and the state of man,
Like to a little kingdom, suffers then
The nature of an insurrection. BRUTUS *2, 1, 63*

14 Let's carve him as a dish fit for the gods. BRUTUS *2, 1, 173*

15 Cowards die many times before their deaths:
The valiant never taste of death but once. CAESAR *2, 2, 32*

1 How hard it is for women to keep counsel! PORTIA *Julius Caesar, 2, 4, 9*

2 Et tu, Brute? CAESAR *3, 1, 77*

3 Why, he that cuts off twenty years of life
Cuts off so many years of fearing death. CASSIUS *3, 1, 102*

4 How many ages hence
Shall this our lofty scene be acted over
In states unborn and accents yet unknown! CASSIUS *3, 1, 112*

5 O mighty Caesar! dost thou lie so low?
Are all thy conquests, glories, triumphs, spoils,
Shrunk to this little measure? MARK ANTONY *3, 1, 149*

6 The choice and master spirits of this age. MARK ANTONY *3, 1, 164*

7 O, pardon me, thou bleeding piece of earth,
That I am meek and gentle with these butchers!
Thou art the ruins of the noblest man
That ever lived in the tide of times. MARK ANTONY *3, 1, 255*

8 Cry 'Havoc!' and let slip the dogs of war. MARK ANTONY *3, 1, 274*

9 Not that I lov'd Caesar less, but that I lov'd Rome more. BRUTUS *3, 2, 20*

10 As Caesar lov'd me, I weep for him; as he was fortunate, I rejoice at it; as he was valiant, I honour him; but—as he was ambitious, I slew him. There is tears for his love; joy for his fortune; honour for his valour; and death for his ambition. Who is here so base that would be a bondman? If any, speak; for him have I offended. BRUTUS *3, 2, 24*

11 Friends, Romans, countrymen, lend me your ears;
I come to bury Caesar, not to praise him.
The evil that men do lives after them;
The good is oft interred with their bones. MARK ANTONY *3, 2, 73*

12 For Brutus is an honourable man;
So are they all, all honourable men. MARK ANTONY *3, 2, 82*

13 Ambition should be made of sterner stuff. MARK ANTONY *3, 2, 92*

14 But yesterday the word of Caesar might
Have stood against the world: now lies he there,
And none so poor to do him reverence. MARK ANTONY *3, 2, 118*

15 The will, the will! We will hear Caesar's will. PLEBEIANS *3, 2, 139*

16 If you have tears, prepare to shed them now. MARK ANTONY *3, 2, 169*

17 See what a rent the envious Casca made. MARK ANTONY *3, 2, 175*

18 This was the most unkindest cut of all. MARK ANTONY *3, 2, 183*

19 O, what a fall was there, my countrymen! MARK ANTONY *3, 2, 190*

20 For I have neither wit, nor words, nor worth,
Action, nor utterance, nor the power of speech,
To stir men's blood; I only speak right on. MARK ANTONY *3, 2, 221*

21 Tear him for his bad verses, tear him for his bad verses! 4TH PLEBEIAN *3, 3, 30*

22 You yourself
Are much condemn'd to have an itching palm. BRUTUS *4, 3, 9*

23 I had rather be a dog and bay the moon
Than such a Roman. BRUTUS *4, 3, 27*

1 Away, slight man! BRUTUS *Julius Caesar, 4, 3, 37*

2 A friend should bear his friend's infirmities,
But Brutus makes mine greater than they are. CASSIUS *4, 3, 85*

3 There is a tide in the affairs of men
Which, taken at the flood, leads on to fortune;
Omitted, all the voyage of their life
Is bound in shallows and in miseries.
On such a full sea are we now afloat,
And we must take the current when it serves,
Or lose our ventures. BRUTUS *4, 3, 216*

4 For ever and for ever farewell, Cassius!
If we do meet again, why, we shall smile;
If not, why then this parting was well made. BRUTUS *5, 1, 116*

5 O that a man might know
The end of this day's business ere it come! BRUTUS *5, 1, 122*

6 This was the noblest Roman of them all.
All the conspirators save only he
Did that they did in envy of great Caesar. MARK ANTONY *5, 5, 68*

7 His life was gentle; and the elements
So mix'd in him that Nature might stand up
And say to all the world 'This was a man!' MARK ANTONY *5, 5, 73*

King John

8 A strange beginning—'borrowed majesty'! ELINOR *1, 1, 5*

9 Lord of thy presence and no land beside. ELINOR *1, 1, 137*

10 For courage mounteth with occasion. AUSTRIA *2, 1, 82*

11 Saint George, that swing'd the dragon, and e'er since
Sits on's horse back at mine hostess' door. BASTARD *2, 1, 288*

12 Mad world! mad kings! mad composition! BASTARD *2, 1, 561*

13 That smooth-fac'd gentleman, tickling commodity,
Commodity, the bias of the world. BASTARD *2, 1, 573*

14 Well, whiles I am a beggar, I will rail
And say there is no sin but to be rich;
And being rich, my virtue then shall be
To say there is no vice but beggary. BASTARD *2, 1, 593*

15 Here I and sorrows sit;
Here is my throne, bid kings come bow to it. CONSTANCE *3, 1, 73*

16 Bell, book, and candle, shall not drive me back,
When gold and silver becks me to come on. BASTARD *3, 3, 12*

17 Life is as tedious as a twice-told tale
Vexing the dull ear of a drowsy man. LEWIS *3, 4, 108*

18 Heat me these irons hot. HUBERT *4, 1, 1*

19 To gild refined gold, to paint the lily,
To throw a perfume on the violet,
To smooth the ice, or add another hue
Unto the rainbow, or with taper-light
To seek the beauteous eye of heaven to garnish,
Is wasteful and ridiculous excess. SALISBURY *4, 2, 11*

1 And oftentimes excusing of a fault
Doth make the fault the worse by th' excuse. PEMBROKE *King John 4, 2, 30*

2 How oft the sight of means to do ill deeds
Make deeds ill done! KING JOHN *4, 2, 219*

3 I beg cold comfort. KING JOHN *5, 7, 42*

4 This England never did, nor never shall,
Lie at the proud foot of a conqueror,
But when it first did help to wound itself. BASTARD *5, 7, 112*

5 Nought shall make us rue,
If England to itself do rest but true. BASTARD *5, 7, 117*

King Lear

6 Nothing will come of nothing. Speak again. LEAR *1, 1, 89*

7 LEAR: So young and so untender?
CORDELIA: So young, my lord, and true. *1, 1, 105*

8 A still-soliciting eye. CORDELIA *1, 1, 231*

9 These late eclipses in the sun and moon portend no good to us. GLOUCESTER *1, 2, 99*

10 This is the excellent foppery of the world, that, when we are sick in fortune, often the surfeits of our own behaviour, we make guilty of our disasters the sun, the moon, and stars. EDMUND *1, 2, 112*

11 My cue is villainous melancholy, with a sigh like Tom o' Bedlam. EDMUND *1, 2, 129*

12 KENT: You have that in your countenance which I would fain call master.
LEAR: What's that?
KENT: Authority. *1, 4, 28*

13 LEAR: Dost thou call me fool, boy?
FOOL: All thy other titles thou hast given away; that thou wast born with. *1, 4, 147*

14 Ingratitude, thou marble-hearted fiend,
More hideous when thou show'st thee in a child
Than the sea-monster! LEAR *1, 4, 259*

15 How sharper than a serpent's tooth it is
To have a thankless child. LEAR *1, 4, 288*

16 Striving to better, oft we mar what's well. ALBANY *1, 4, 347*

17 O, let me not be mad, not mad, sweet heaven!
Keep me in temper; I would not be mad! LEAR *1, 5, 43*

18 Thou whoreson zed! thou unnecessary letter! KENT *2, 2, 58*

19 I have seen better faces in my time
Than stands on any shoulder that I see
Before me at this instant. KENT *2, 2, 88*

20 Fortune, good night; smile once more; turn thy wheel. KENT *2, 2, 168*

21 Hysterica passio—down, thou climbing sorrow,
Thy element's below. LEAR *2, 4, 56*

22 You are old;
Nature in you stands on the very verge
Of her confine. REGAN *2, 4, 144*

1 LEAR: I gave you all.
REGAN: And in good time you gave it. *King Lear, 2, 4, 248*

2 O, reason not the need! Our basest beggars
Are in the poorest thing superfluous.
Allow not nature more than nature needs,
Man's life is cheap as beast's. LEAR *2, 4, 263*

3 And let not women's weapons, water-drops,
Stain my man's cheeks! LEAR *2, 4, 276*

4 No, I'll not weep.
I have full cause of weeping; but this heart
Shall break into a hundred thousand flaws
Or ere I'll weep. O fool, I shall go mad! LEAR *2, 4, 282*

5 Who's there, besides foul weather? KENT *3, 1, 1*

6 Blow, winds, and crack your cheeks; rage, blow.
You cataracts and hurricanoes, spout
Till you have drench'd our steeples, drown'd the cocks. LEAR *3, 2, 1*

7 Rumble thy bellyful. Spit, fire; spout, rain.
Nor rain, wind, thunder, fire, are my daughters.
I tax not you, you elements, with unkindness. LEAR *3, 2, 14*

8 Here I stand, your slave,
A poor, infirm, weak and despis'd old man. LEAR *3, 2, 19*

9 For there was never yet fair woman but she made mouths in a glass.
FOOL *3, 2, 35*

10 Things that love night
Love not such nights as these. KENT *3, 2, 42*

11 I am a man
More sinn'd against than sinning. LEAR *3, 2, 59*

12 O, that way madness lies; let me shun that. LEAR *3, 4, 21*

13 Poor naked wretches, wheresoe'er you are,
That bide the pelting of this pitiless storm,
How shall your houseless heads and unfed sides,
Your loop'd and window'd raggedness, defend you
From seasons such as these? LEAR *3, 4, 28*

14 Take physic, pomp;
Expose thyself to feel what wretches feel. LEAR *3, 4, 33*

15 'Tis a naughty night to swim in. FOOL *3, 4, 109*

16 Poor Tom's a-cold. EDGAR *3, 4, 143*

17 Child Rowland to the dark tower came,
His word was still 'Fie, foh, and fum,
I smell the blood of a British man'. EDGAR *3, 4, 178*

18 Out vile jelly!
Where is thy lustre now? CORNWALL *3, 7, 82*

19 The worst is not
So long as we can say 'This is the worst'. EDGAR *4, 1, 28*

20 As flies to wanton boys are we to th' gods—
They kill us for their sport. GLOUCESTER *4, 1, 37*

21 Wisdom and goodness to the vile seem vile;
Filths savour but themselves. ALBANY *4, 2, 38*

1 It is the stars,
The stars above us, govern our conditions. KENT *King Lear, 4, 3, 32*

2 How fearful
And dizzy 'tis to cast one's eyes so low!
The crows and choughs that wing the mid-way air
Show scarce so gross as beetles. EDGAR *4, 6, 11*

3 Ay, every inch a king. LEAR *4, 6, 107*

4 The wren goes to't, and the small gilded fly
Does lecher in my sight. LEAR *4, 6, 112*

5 Give me an ounce of civet, good apothecary, to sweeten my imagination.
LEAR *4, 6, 129*

6 Through tatter'd clothes small vices do appear;
Robes and furr'd gowns hide all. LEAR *4, 6, 164*

7 Get thee glass eyes,
And, like a scurvy politician, seem
To see the things thou dost not. LEAR *4, 6, 170*

8 When we are born, we cry that we are come
To this great stage of fools. LEAR *4, 6, 183*

9 Mine enemy's dog,
Though he had bit me, should have stood that night
Against my fire. CORDELIA *4, 7, 36*

10 Thou art a soul in bliss; but I am bound
Upon a wheel of fire, that mine own tears
Do scald like molten lead. LEAR *4, 7, 46*

11 I am a very foolish fond old man,
Fourscore and upward, not an hour more nor less;
And, to deal plainly,
I fear I am not in my perfect mind. LEAR *4, 7, 60*

12 Men must endure
Their going hence, even as their coming hither:
Ripeness is all. EDGAR *5, 2, 9*

13 Come, let's away to prison.
We two alone will sing like birds i' th' cage;
When thou dost ask me blessing, I'll kneel down
And ask of thee forgiveness; so we'll live,
And pray, and sing, and tell old tales, and laugh
At gilded butterflies, and hear poor rogues
Talk of court news; and we'll talk with them too—
Who loses and who wins; who's in, who's out—
And take upon's the mystery of things
As if we were God's spies. LEAR *5, 3, 8*

14 The gods are just, and of our pleasant vices
Make instruments to plague us:
The dark and vicious place where thee he got
Cost him his eyes. EDGAR *5, 3, 170*

15 The wheel is come full circle. EDMUND *5, 3, 174*

1 But his flaw'd heart—
Alack, too weak the conflict to support!—
'Twixt two extremes of passion, joy and grief,
Burst smilingly. EDGAR *King Lear, 5, 3, 196*

2 Howl, howl, howl, howl! O, you are men of stones!
Had I your tongues and eyes, I'd use them so
That heaven's vault should crack. LEAR *5, 3, 257*

3 Her voice was ever soft,
Gentle, and low—an excellent thing in woman. LEAR *5, 3, 272*

4 And my poor fool is hang'd! No, no, no life!
Why should a dog, a horse, a rat have life,
And thou no breath at all? Thou'lt come no more,
Never, never, never, never, never.
Pray you undo this button. LEAR *5, 3, 305*

5 Vex not his ghost. O, let him pass! He hates him
That would upon the rack of this tough world
Stretch him out longer. KENT *5, 3, 313*

Love's Labour's Lost

6 Spite of cormorant devouring Time. KING *1, 1, 4*

7 Why, all delights are vain; but that most vain
Which, with pain purchas'd, doth inherit pain. BEROWNE *1, 1, 72*

8 Small have continual plodders ever won,
Save base authority from others' books. BEROWNE *1, 1, 86*

9 At Christmas I no more desire a rose
Than wish a snow in May's new-fangled shows. BEROWNE *1, 1, 105*

10 Remuneration! O, that's the Latin word for three farthings. COSTARD *3, 1, 129*

11 He hath never fed of the dainties that are bred in a book; he hath not eat paper, as it were; he hath not drunk ink; his intellect is not replenished. SIR NATHANIEL *4, 2, 22*

12 For where is any author in the world
Teaches such beauty as a woman's eye?
Learning is but an adjunct to ourself. BEROWNE *4, 3, 308*

13 And when Love speaks, the voice of all the gods
Make heaven drowsy with the harmony. BEROWNE *4, 3, 340*

14 From women's eyes this doctrine I derive.
They sparkle still the right Promethean fire;
They are the books, the arts, the academes,
That show, contain, and nourish, all the world. ROSALINE *4, 3, 346*

15 A world-without-end bargain. PRINCESS *5, 2, 777*

16 A jest's prosperity lies in the ear
Of him that hears it, never in the tongue
Of him that makes it. BEROWNE *5, 2, 849*

17 When daisies pied and violets blue
And lady-smocks all silver-white
And cuckoo-buds of yellow hue
Do paint the meadows with delight,

The cuckoo then on every tree
Mocks married men, for thus sings he:
'Cuckoo;
Cuckoo, cuckoo'—O word of fear,
Unpleasing to a married ear! SPRING *Love's Labour's Lost, 5, 2, 881*

1 When icicles hang by the wall,
And Dick the shepherd blows his nail,
And Tom bears logs into the hall,
And milk comes frozen home in pail,
When blood is nipp'd, and ways be foul,
Then nightly sings the staring owl:
'Tu-who;
Tu-whit, Tu-who'—A merry note,
While greasy Joan doth keel the pot.

When all aloud the wind doth blow,
And coughing drowns the parson's saw,
And birds sit brooding in the snow,
And Marian's nose looks red and raw,
When roasted crabs hiss in the bowl. WINTER *5, 2, 899*

2 The words of Mercury are harsh after the songs of Apollo. ARMADO *5, 2, 917*

Macbeth

3 1ST WITCH: When shall we three meet again?
In thunder, lightning, or in rain?
2ND WITCH: When the hurlyburly's done,
When the battle's lost and won. *1, 1, 1*

4 Fair is foul, and foul is fair:
Hover through the fog and filthy air. THREE WITCHES *1, 1, 10*

5 What bloody man is that? DUNCAN *1, 2, 1*

6 So foul and fair a day I have not seen. MACBETH *1, 3, 38*

7 What are these,
So wither'd, and so wild in their attire,
That look not like th' inhabitants o' th' earth,
And yet are on't? BANQUO *1, 3, 39*

8 If you can look into the seeds of time
And say which grain will grow and which will not,
Speak then to me, who neither beg nor fear
Your favours nor your hate. BANQUO *1, 3, 58*

9 This supernatural soliciting
Cannot be ill; cannot be good. MACBETH *1, 3, 130*

10 Come what come may,
Time and the hour runs through the roughest day. MACBETH *1, 3, 146*

11 Nothing in his life
Became him like the leaving it: he died
As one that had been studied in his death
To throw away the dearest thing he ow'd
As 'twere a careless trifle. MALCOLM *1, 4, 7*

12 Stars, hide your fires. MACBETH *1, 4, 50*

1 Yet do I fear thy nature;
It is too full o' th' milk of human kindness
To catch the nearest way. LADY MACBETH *Macbeth, 1, 5, 13*

2 Come, thick night,
And pall thee in the dunnest smoke of hell. LADY MACBETH *1, 5, 47*

3 O, never
Shall sun that morrow see!
Your face, my thane, is as a book where men
May read strange matters. LADY MACBETH *1, 5, 57*

4 If it were done when 'tis done, then 'twere well
It were done quickly. MACBETH *1, 7, 1*

5 That but this blow
Might be the be-all and the end-all here—
But here upon this bank and shoal of time—
We'd jump the life to come. MACBETH *1, 7, 4*

6 I have no spur
To prick the sides of my intent, but only
Vaulting ambition, which o'er-leaps itself,
And falls on th' other. MACBETH *1, 7, 25*

7 MACBETH: If we should fail?
LADY MACBETH: We fail!
But screw your courage to the sticking place,
And we'll not fail. *1, 7, 59*

8 False face must hide what the false heart doth know. MACBETH *1, 7, 82*

9 Is this a dagger which I see before me,
The handle toward my hand? MACBETH *2, 1, 33*

10 The bell invites me.
Hear it not, Duncan, for it is a knell
That summons thee to heaven or to hell. MACBETH *2, 1, 62*

11 Methought I heard a voice cry 'Sleep no more;
Macbeth does murder sleep'—the innocent sleep,
Sleep that knits up the ravell'd sleave of care,
The death of each day's life, sore labour's bath,
Balm of hurt minds, great nature's second course,
Chief nourisher in life's feast. MACBETH *2, 2, 35*

12 Will all great Neptune's ocean wash this blood
Clean from my hand? No; this my hand will rather
The multitudinous seas incarnadine,
Making the green one red. MACBETH *2, 2, 60*

13 I had thought to have let in some of all professions that go the primrose way to th' everlasting bonfire. PORTER *2, 3, 18*

14 It provokes the desire, but it takes away the performance. Therefore much drink may be said to be an equivocator with lechery. PORTER *2, 3, 28*

15 Had I but died an hour before this chance,
I had liv'd a blessed time; for, from this instant,
There's nothing serious in mortality—
All is but toys. MACBETH *2, 3, 89*

16 Where we are,
There's daggers in men's smiles; the near in blood,
The nearer bloody. DONALBAIN *2, 3, 138*

1 Ay, in the catalogue ye go for men;
As hounds, and greyhounds, mongrels, spaniels, curs,
Shoughs, water-rugs, and demi-wolves, are clept
All by the name of dogs. MACBETH *Macbeth, 3, 1, 91*

2 I am one, my liege,
Whom the vile blows and buffets of the world
Hath so incens'd that I am reckless what
I do to spite the world. 2ND MURDERER *3, 1, 107*

3 Nought's had, all's spent,
Where our desire is got without content.
'Tis safer to be that which we destroy,
Than by destruction dwell in doubtful joy. LADY MACBETH *3, 2, 4*

4 Duncan is in his grave;
After life's fitful fever he sleeps well. MACBETH *3, 2, 22*

5 Things bad begun make strong themselves by ill. MACBETH *3, 2, 55*

6 I had else been perfect,
Whole as the marble, founded as the rock,
As broad and general as the casing air,
But now I am cabin'd, cribb'd, confin'd, bound in
To saucy doubts and fears. MACBETH *3, 4, 21*

7 Now good digestion wait on appetite,
And health on both! MACBETH *3, 4, 38*

8 The time has been
That when the brains were out the man would die,
And there an end. MACBETH *3, 4, 78*

9 Stand not upon the order of your going,
But go at once. LADY MACBETH *3, 4, 119*

10 I am in blood
Stepp'd in so far that, should I wade no more,
Returning were as tedious as go o'er. MACBETH *3, 4, 136*

11 Double, double toil and trouble;
Fire burn, and cauldron bubble. THREE WITCHES *4, 1, 10*

12 Ditch-deliver'd by a drab. 3RD WITCH *4, 1, 31*

13 How now, you secret, black, and midnight hags! MACBETH *4, 1, 47*

14 A deed without a name. THREE WITCHES *4, 1, 49*

15 Be bloody, bold, and resolute; laugh to scorn
The pow'r of man, for none of woman born
Shall harm Macbeth. SECOND APPARITION *4, 1, 79*

16 But yet I'll make assurance double sure,
And take a bond of fate. MACBETH *4, 1, 83*

17 What, will the line stretch out to th' crack of doom? MACBETH *4, 1, 117*

18 I think our country sinks beneath the yoke;
It weeps, it bleeds; and each new day a gash
Is added to her wounds. MALCOLM *4, 3, 39*

19 Stands Scotland where it did? MACDUFF *4, 3, 164*

1 The night is long that never finds the day. MALCOLM *Macbeth, 4, 3, 240*

2 Out, damned spot! out, I say! LADY MACBETH *5, 1, 33*

3 Here's the smell of the blood still. All the perfumes of Arabia will not sweeten this little hand. LADY MACBETH *5, 1, 48*

4 To bed, to bed; there's knocking at the gate. Come, come, come, come, give me your hand. What's done cannot be undone. LADY MACBETH *5, 1, 64*

5 I have liv'd long enough. My way of life
Is fall'n into the sear, the yellow leaf;
And that which should accompany old age,
As honour, love, obedience, troops of friends,
I must not look to have. MACBETH *5, 3, 22*

6 Canst thou not minister to a mind diseas'd,
Pluck from the memory a rooted sorrow,
Raze out the written troubles of the brain,
And with some sweet oblivious antidote
Cleanse the stuff'd bosom of that perilous stuff
Which weighs upon the heart? MACBETH *5, 3, 40*

7 I will not be afraid of death and bane
Till Birnam Forest come to Dunsinane. MACBETH *5, 3, 59*

8 Hang out our banners on the outward walls;
The cry is still 'They come'. MACBETH *5, 5, 1*

9 I have supp'd full with horrors. MACBETH *5, 5, 13*

10 She should have died hereafter;
There would have been a time for such a word.
To-morrow, and to-morrow, and to-morrow,
Creeps in this petty pace from day to day
To the last syllable of recorded time,
And all our yesterdays have lighted fools
The way to dusty death. Out, out, brief candle!
Life's but a walking shadow, a poor player,
That struts and frets his hour upon the stage,
And then is heard no more; it is a tale
Told by an idiot, full of sound and fury,
Signifying nothing. MACBETH *5, 5, 17*

11 I gin to be aweary of the sun,
And wish th' estate o' th' world were now undone.
Ring the alarum bell. Blow wind, come wrack;
At least we'll die with harness on our back. MACBETH *5, 5, 49*

12 MACBETH: I bear a charmed life, which must not yield
To one of woman born.
MACDUFF: Despair thy charm;
And let the angel whom thou still hast serv'd
Tell thee Macduff was from his mother's womb
Untimely ripp'd. *5, 8, 12*

13 Live to be the show and gaze o' th' time. MACDUFF *5, 8, 24*

14 Lay on, Macduff;
And damn'd be him that first cries 'Hold, enough!' MACBETH *5, 8, 33*

Measure for Measure

1 'Tis one thing to be tempted, Escalus,
Another thing to fall. I not deny
The jury, passing on the prisoner's life,
May in the sworn twelve have a thief or two
Guiltier than him they try. ANGELO *2, 1, 17*

2 Some rise by sin, and some by virtue fall. ESCALUS *2, 1, 38*

3 This will last out a night in Russia,
When nights are longest there. ANGELO *2, 1, 128*

4 No ceremony that to great ones longs,
Not the king's crown nor the deputed sword,
The marshal's truncheon nor the judge's robe,
Become them with one half so good a grace
As mercy does. ISABELLA *2, 2, 59*

5 The law hath not been dead, though it hath slept. ANGELO *2, 2, 90*

6 O, it is excellent
To have a giant's strength! But it is tyrannous
To use it like a giant. ISABELLA *2, 2, 107*

7 But man, proud man,
Dress'd in a little brief authority,
Most ignorant of what he's most assur'd,
His glassy essence, like an angry ape,
Plays such fantastic tricks before high heaven
As makes the angels weep. ISABELLA *2, 2, 117*

8 That in the captain's but a choleric word
Which in the soldier is flat blasphemy. ISABELLA *2, 2, 130*

9 The miserable have no other medicine
But only hope. CLAUDIO *3, 1, 2*

10 Ay, but to die, and go we know not where;
To lie in cold obstruction, and to rot;
This sensible warm motion to become
A kneaded clod; and the delighted spirit
To bathe in fiery floods or to reside
In thrilling region of thick-ribbed ice. CLAUDIO *3, 1, 119*

11 The weariest and most loathed worldly life
That age, ache, penury, and imprisonment,
Can lay on nature is a paradise
To what we fear of death. CLAUDIO *3, 1, 130*

12 Take, O, take those lips away,
That so sweetly were forsworn;
And those eyes, the break of day,
Lights that do mislead the morn;
But my kisses bring again, bring again;
Seals of love, but seal'd in vain, seal'd in vain. SONG *4, 1, 1*

13 I am a kind of burr; I shall stick. LUCIO *4, 3, 173*

14 Haste still pays haste, and leisure answers leisure;
Like doth quit like, and Measure still for Measure. DUKE *5, 1, 408*

15 What's mine is yours, and what is yours is mine. DUKE *5, 1, 535*

The Merchant of Venice

1 I hold the world but as the world, Gratiano—
A stage, where every man must play a part,
And mine a sad one. ANTONIO *1, 1, 77*

2 There are a sort of men whose visages
Do cream and mantle like a standing pond. GRATIANO *1, 1, 88*

3 As who should say 'I am Sir Oracle,
And when I ope my lips let no dog bark'. GRATIANO *1, 1, 93*

4 In Belmont is a lady richly left,
And she is fair and, fairer than that word,
Of wondrous virtues. BASSANIO *1, 1, 161*

5 By my troth, Nerissa, my little body is aweary of this great world. PORTIA *1, 2, 1*

6 If to do were as easy as to know what were good to do, chapels had been churches, and poor men's cottages princes' palaces. PORTIA *1, 2, 11*

7 How like a fawning publican he looks!
I hate him for he is a Christian;
But more for that in low simplicity
He lends out money gratis, and brings down
The rate of usance here with us in Venice.
If I can catch him once upon the hip,
I will feed fat the ancient grudge I bear him. SHYLOCK *1, 3, 36*

8 The devil can cite Scripture for his purpose. ANTONIO *1, 3, 93*

9 Many a time and oft
In the Rialto you have rated me. SHYLOCK *1, 3, 101*

10 Still have I borne it with a patient shrug,
For suff'rance is the badge of all our tribe;
You call me misbeliever, cut-throat dog,
And spit upon my Jewish gaberdine. SHYLOCK *1, 3, 104*

11 I like not fair terms and a villain's mind. BASSANIO *1, 3, 174*

12 It is a wise father that knows his own child. LAUNCELOT GOBBO *2, 2, 69*

13 There is some ill a-brewing towards my rest,
For I did dream of money-bags to-night. SHYLOCK *2, 5, 17*

14 But love is blind, and lovers cannot see
The pretty follies that themselves commit. JESSICA *2, 6, 36*

15 The ancient saying is no heresy:
Hanging and wiving goes by destiny. NERISSA *2, 9, 82*

16 Let him look to his bond. SHYLOCK *3, 1, 39*

17 Hath not a Jew eyes? Hath not a Jew hands, organs, dimensions, senses, affections, passions, fed with the same food, hurt with the same weapons, subject to the same diseases, healed by the same means, warmed and cooled by the same winter and summer, as a Christian is? If you prick us, do we not bleed? If you tickle us, do we not laugh? If you poison us, do we not die? And if you wrong us, shall we not revenge? SHYLOCK *3, 1, 49*

18 Tell me where is fancy bred,
Or in the heart or in the head,
How begot, how nourished? SONG *3, 2, 63*

1 The quality of mercy is not strain'd;
It droppeth as the gentle rain from heaven
Upon the place beneath. It is twice blest:
It blesseth him that gives and him that takes.
'Tis mightiest in the mightiest; it becomes
The throned monarch better than his crown;
His sceptre shows the force of temporal power,
The attribute to awe and majesty,
Wherein doth sit the dread and fear of kings;
But mercy is above this sceptred sway,
It is enthroned in the hearts of kings,
It is an attribute to God himself;
And earthly power doth then show likest God's
When mercy seasons justice. Therefore, Jew,
Though justice be thy plea, consider this—
That in the course of justice none of us
Should see salvation; we do pray for mercy,
And that same prayer doth teach us all to render
The deeds of mercy. PORTIA *The Merchant of Venice, 4, 1, 179*

2 Wrest once the law to your authority;
To do a great right do a little wrong. BASSANIO *4, 1, 210*

3 A Daniel come to judgment! Yea, a Daniel! SHYLOCK *4, 1, 218*

4 'Tis not in the bond. SHYLOCK *4, 1, 257*

5 A pound of that same merchant's flesh is thine.
The court awards it and the law doth give it. PORTIA *4, 1, 294*

6 You take my house when you do take the prop
That doth sustain my house; you take my life
When you do take the means whereby I live. SHYLOCK *4, 1, 370*

7 He is well paid that is well satisfied. PORTIA *4, 1, 410*

8 How sweet the moonlight sleeps upon this bank!
Here will we sit and let the sounds of music
Creep in our ears; soft stillness and the night
Become the touches of sweet harmony.
Sit, Jessica. Look how the floor of heaven
Is thick inlaid with patines of bright gold;
There's not the smallest orb which thou behold'st
But in his motion like an angel sings,
Still quiring to the young-ey'd cherubins;
Such harmony is in immortal souls,
But whilst this muddy vesture of decay
Doth grossly close it in, we cannot hear it. LORENZO *5, 1, 54*

9 I am never merry when I hear sweet music. JESSICA *5, 1, 69*

10 The man that hath no music in himself,
Nor is not mov'd with concord of sweet sounds,
Is fit for treasons, stratagems, and spoils. LORENZO *5, 1, 83*

11 How far that little candle throws his beams!
So shines a good deed in a naughty world. PORTIA *5, 1, 90*

12 For a light wife doth make a heavy husband. PORTIA *5, 1, 130*

The Merry Wives of Windsor

1 I will make a Star Chamber matter of it. SHALLOW *1, 1, 1*

2 I had rather than forty shillings I had my Book of Songs and Sonnets here. SLENDER *1, 1, 179*

3 Here will be an old abusing of God's patience and the King's English. MISTRESS QUICKLY *1, 4, 5*

4 Why, then the world's mine oyster,
Which I with sword will open. PISTOL *2, 2, 4*

5 I cannot tell what the dickens his name is. MRS PAGE *3, 2, 15*

6 O, what a world of vile ill-favour'd faults
Looks handsome in three hundred pounds a year! ANNE PAGE *3, 4, 32*

7 I'll no pullet-sperm in my brewage. FALSTAFF *3, 5, 27*

8 They say there is divinity in odd numbers, either in nativity, chance, or death. FALSTAFF *5, 1, 3*

A Midsummer Night's Dream

9 To live a barren sister all your life,
Chanting faint hymns to the cold fruitless moon. THESEUS *1, 1, 72*

10 For aught that I could ever read,
Could ever hear by tale or history,
The course of true love never did run smooth. LYSANDER *1, 1, 132*

11 O hell! to choose love by another's eyes. HERMIA *1, 1, 140*

12 Love looks not with the eyes, but with the mind;
And therefore is wing'd Cupid painted blind. HELENA *1, 1, 234*

13 'The most Lamentable Comedy and most Cruel Death of Pyramus and Thisby.' QUINCE *1, 2, 10*

14 A part to tear a cat in, to make all split. BOTTOM *1, 2, 24*

15 I am slow of study. SNUG *1, 2, 59*

16 Over hill, over dale,
Thorough bush, thorough brier,
Over park, over pale,
Thorough flood, thorough fire. FAIRY *2, 1, 2*

17 Ill met by moonlight, proud Titania. OBERON *2, 1, 60*

18 Since once I sat upon a promontory,
And heard a mermaid on a dolphin's back
Uttering such dulcet and harmonious breath
That the rude sea grew civil at her song,
And certain stars shot madly from their spheres
To hear the sea-maid's music. OBERON *2, 1, 149*

19 I'll put a girdle round about the earth
In forty minutes. PUCK *2, 1, 175*

20 I know a bank whereon the wild thyme blows,
Where oxlips and the nodding violet grows,
Quite over-canopied with luscious woodbine,
With sweet musk-roses, and with eglantine. OBERON *2, 1, 249*

21 A lion among ladies is a most dreadful thing; for there is not a more fearful wild-fowl than your lion living. BOTTOM *3, 1, 27*

1 A calendar, a calendar! Look in the almanack; find out moonshine, find out moonshine. BOTTOM *A Midsummer Night's Dream, 3, 1, 46*

2 Bless thee, Bottom, bless thee! Thou art translated. QUINCE *3, 1, 109*

3 Lord, what fools these mortals be! PUCK *3, 2, 115*

4 I have a reasonable good ear in music. Let's have the tongs and the bones. BOTTOM *4, 1, 26*

5 The lunatic, the lover, and the poet,
Are of imagination all compact. THESEUS *5, 1, 7*

6 The poet's eye, in a fine frenzy rolling,
Doth glance from heaven to earth, from earth to heaven;
And as imagination bodies forth
The forms of things unknown, the poet's pen
Turns them to shapes, and gives to airy nothing
A local habitation and a name. THESEUS *5, 1, 12*

7 Very tragical mirth. THESEUS *5, 1, 57*

8 The iron tongue of midnight hath told twelve.
Lovers, to bed; 'tis almost fairy time. THESEUS *5, 1, 352*

Much Ado About Nothing

9 A victory is twice itself when the achiever brings home full numbers. LEONATO *1, 1, 7*

10 He wears his faith but as the fashion of his hat. BEATRICE *1, 1, 62*

11 BEATRICE: I wonder that you will still be talking, Signior Benedick; nobody marks you.
BENEDICK: What, my dear Lady Disdain! Are you yet living? *1, 1, 99*

12 Would you have me speak after my custom, as being a professed tyrant to their sex? BENEDICK *1, 1, 144*

13 Benedick the married man. BENEDICK *1, 1, 232*

14 What need the bridge much broader than the flood? DON PEDRO *1, 1, 278*

15 Friendship is constant in all other things
Save in the office and affairs of love. CLAUDIO *2, 1, 154*

16 She speaks poniards, and every word stabs. BENEDICK *2, 1, 220*

17 Silence is the perfectest herald of joy: I were but little happy if I could say how much. CLAUDIO *2, 1, 275*

18 DON PEDRO: Will you have me, lady?
BEATRICE: No, my lord, unless I might have another for working-days; your Grace is too costly to wear every day. *2, 1, 293*

19 I was born to speak all mirth and no matter. BEATRICE *2, 1, 297*

20 There was a star danc'd, and under that was I born. BEATRICE *2, 1, 302*

21 Sigh no more, ladies, sigh no more,
Men were deceivers ever,
One foot in sea and one on shore,
To one thing constant never. BALTHASAR *2, 3, 57*

22 Doth not the appetite alter? A man loves the meat in his youth that he cannot endure in his age. BENEDICK *2, 3, 215*

1 The world must be peopled. When I said I would die a bachelor, I did not think I should live till I were married. BENEDICK *Much Ado About Nothing, 2, 3, 219*

2 Disdain and scorn ride sparkling in her eyes. HERO *3, 1, 51*

3 Are you good men and true? DOGBERRY *3, 3, 1*

4 To be a well-favoured man is the gift of fortune; but to write and read comes by nature. DOGBERRY *3, 3, 13*

5 You are thought here to be the most senseless and fit man for the constable of the watch. DOGBERRY *3, 3, 19*

6 For the watch to babble and to talk is most tolerable and not to be endured. DOGBERRY *3, 3, 32*

7 I thank God I am as honest as any man living that is an old man and no honester than I. VERGES *3, 5, 13*

8 Comparisons are odorous. DOGBERRY *3, 5, 16*

9 A good old man, sir, he will be talking; as they say 'When the age is in the wit is out'. DOGBERRY *3, 5, 32*

10 Our watch, sir, have indeed comprehended two aspicious persons. DOGBERRY *3, 5, 42*

11 O, what men dare do! What men may do! What men daily do, not knowing what they do! CLAUDIO *4, 1, 18*

12 For it so falls out
That what we have we prize not to the worth
Whiles we enjoy it, but being lack'd and lost,
Why, then we rack the value, then we find
The virtue that possession would not show us
Whiles it was ours. FRIAR FRANCIS *4, 1, 217*

13 Write down that they hope they serve God; and write God first; for God defend but God should go before such villains! DOGBERRY *4, 2, 17*

14 Flat burglary as ever was committed. DOGBERRY *4, 2, 46*

15 O villain! thou wilt be condemn'd into everlasting redemption for this. DOGBERRY *4, 2, 52*

16 O that he were here to write me down an ass! DOGBERRY *4, 2, 70*

17 For there was never yet philosopher
That could endure the toothache patiently. LEONATO *5, 1, 35*

18 They have committed false report; moreover, they have spoken untruths; secondarily, they are slanders; sixth and lastly, they have belied a lady; thirdly, they have verified unjust things; and to conclude, they are lying knaves. DOGBERRY *5, 1, 204*

19 Done to death by slanderous tongues. CLAUDIO *5, 3, 3*

Othello

20 But I will wear my heart upon my sleeve
For daws to peck at. IAGO *1, 1, 65*

21 Rude am I in my speech,
And little blest with the soft phrase of peace;
For since these arms of mine had seven years' pith,
Till now some nine moons wasted, they have us'd
Their dearest action in the tented field. OTHELLO *1, 3, 81*

1 I will a round unvarnish'd tale deliver
Of my whole course of love. OTHELLO *Othello, 1, 3, 90*

2 My story being done,
She gave me for my pains a world of sighs;
She swore, in faith, 'twas strange, 'twas passing strange;
'Twas pitiful, 'twas wondrous pitiful.
She wish'd she had not heard it; yet she wish'd
That heaven had made her such a man. She thank'd me;
And bade me, if I had a friend that lov'd her,
I should but teach him how to tell my story,
And that would woo her. Upon this hint I spake;
She lov'd me for the dangers I had pass'd;
And I lov'd her that she did pity them.
This only is the witchcraft I have us'd. OTHELLO *1, 3, 158*

3 To mourn a mischief that is past and gone
Is the next way to draw new mischief on. DUKE *1, 3, 204*

4 The robb'd that smiles steals something from the thief. DUKE *1, 3, 208*

5 Look to her, Moor, if thou hast eyes to see:
She has deceiv'd her father, and may thee. BRABANTIO *1, 3, 292*

6 Put money in thy purse. IAGO *1, 3, 338*

7 For I am nothing if not critical. IAGO *2, 1, 119*

8 To suckle fools and chronicle small beer. IAGO *2, 1, 159*

9 But men are men; the best sometimes forget. IAGO *2, 3, 233*

10 Reputation, reputation, reputation! O, I have lost my reputation! I have lost the immortal part of myself, and what remains is bestial. CASSIO *2, 3, 254*

11 Good wine is a good familiar creature if it be well us'd. IAGO *2, 3, 299*

12 How poor are they that have not patience!
What wound did ever heal but by degrees? IAGO *2, 3, 358*

13 Thereby hangs a tail. CLOWN *3, 1, 8*

14 Excellent wretch! Perdition catch my soul
But I do love thee; and when I love thee not
Chaos is come again. OTHELLO *3, 3, 91*

15 Good name in man and woman, dear my lord,
Is the immediate jewel of their souls:
Who steals my purse steals trash; 'tis something, nothing;
'Twas mine, 'tis his, and has been slave to thousands;
But he that filches from me my good name
Robs me of that which not enriches him
And makes me poor indeed. IAGO *3, 3, 159*

16 O, beware, my lord, of jealousy;
It is the green-ey'd monster which doth mock
The meat it feeds on. IAGO *3, 3, 169*

17 O curse of marriage,
That we can call these delicate creatures ours,
And not their appetites! I had rather be a toad,
And live upon the vapour of a dungeon,
Than keep a corner in the thing I love
For others' uses. OTHELLO *3, 3, 272*

1 He that is robb'd, not wanting what is stol'n,
Let him not know't, and he's not robb'd at all. OTHELLO *Othello, 3, 3, 346*

2 O, now for ever
Farewell the tranquil mind! farewell content!
Farewell the plumed troops, and the big wars
That makes ambition virtue! O, farewell!
Farewell the neighing steed and the shrill trump,
The spirit-stirring drum, th' ear-piercing fife,
The royal banner, and all quality,
Pride, pomp, and circumstance, of glorious war! OTHELLO *3, 3, 351*

3 They are not ever jealous for the cause,
But jealous for they are jealous. EMILIA *3, 4, 161*

4 But yet the pity of it, Iago! O, Iago, the pity of it, Iago! OTHELLO *4, 1, 191*

5 But, alas, to make me
The fixed figure for the time of scorn
To point his slow unmoving finger at. OTHELLO *4, 2, 54*

6 O thou weed
Who art so lovely fair and smell'st so sweet
That the sense aches at thee!
Would thou had'st never been born! OTHELLO *4, 2, 67*

7 'Tis neither here nor there. EMILIA *4, 3, 57*

8 If Cassio do remain,
He hath a daily beauty in his life
That makes me ugly. IAGO *5, 1, 18*

9 This is the night
That either makes me or fordoes me quite. IAGO *5, 1, 128*

10 It is the cause, it is the cause, my soul—
Let me not name it to you, you chaste stars—
It is the cause. OTHELLO *5, 2, 1*

11 Put out the light, and then put out the light.
If I quench thee, thou flaming minister,
I can again thy former light restore,
Should I repent me; but once put out thy light,
Thou cunning'st pattern of excelling nature,
I know not where is that Promethean heat
That can thy light relume. When I have pluck'd thy rose,
I cannot give it vital growth again. OTHELLO *5, 2, 7*

12 Not Cassio kill'd! Then murder's out of tune,
And sweet revenge grows harsh. OTHELLO *5, 2, 118*

13 Here is my journey's end, here is my butt,
And very sea-mark of my utmost sail. OTHELLO *5, 2, 270*

14 Soft you; a word or two before you go.
I have done the state some service, and they know't—
No more of that. I pray you, in your letters,
When you shall these unlucky deeds relate,
Speak of me as I am; nothing extenuate,
Nor set down aught in malice. Then must you speak
Of one that lov'd not wisely, but too well;
Of one not easily jealous, but, being wrought,

Perplexed in the extreme; of one whose hand,
Like the base Indian, threw a pearl away
Richer than all his tribe; of one whose subdu'd eyes,
Albeit unused to the melting mood,
Drops tears as fast as the Arabian trees
Their med'cinable gum. Set you down this:
And say besides that in Aleppo once,
Where a malignant and a turban'd Turk
Beat a Venetian and traduc'd the state,
I took by th' throat the circumcised dog,
And smote him—thus. OTHELLO *Othello, 5, 2, 341*

1 I kiss'd thee ere I kill'd thee. No way but this—
Killing my self, to die upon a kiss. OTHELLO *5, 2, 361*

Pericles

2 See where she comes, apparell'd like the spring. PERICLES *1, 1, 12*

3 Few love to hear the sins they love to act. PERICLES *1, 1, 92*

4 Kings are earth's gods; in vice their law's their will. PERICLES *1, 1, 103*

5 3RD FISHERMAN: Master, I marvel how the fishes live in the sea.
1ST FISHERMAN: Why, as men do a-land—the great ones eat up the little ones. *2, 1, 27*

King Richard the Second

6 Old John of Gaunt, time-honoured Lancaster. RICHARD II *1, 1, 1*

7 Let's purge this choler without letting blood. RICHARD II *1, 1, 153*

8 The purest treasure mortal times afford
Is spotless reputation; that away,
Men are but gilded loam or painted clay.
A jewel in a ten-times barr'd-up chest
Is a bold spirit in a loyal breast.
Mine honour is my life; both grow in one;
Take honour from me, and my life is done. MOWBRAY *1, 1, 177*

9 We were not born to sue, but to command. RICHARD II *1, 1, 196*

10 That which in mean men we entitle patience
Is pale cold cowardice in noble breasts. DUCHESS OF GLOUCESTER *1, 2, 33*

11 This must my comfort be—
That sun that warms you here shall shine on me. BOLINGBROKE *1, 3, 144*

12 How long a time lies in one little word!
Four lagging winters and four wanton springs
End in a word: such is the breath of Kings. BOLINGBROKE *1, 3, 213*

13 Things sweet to taste prove in digestion sour. GAUNT *1, 3, 236*

14 All places that the eye of heaven visits
Are to a wise man ports and happy havens.
Teach thy necessity to reason thus:
There is no virtue like necessity. GAUNT *1, 3, 275*

1 O, who can hold a fire in his hand
By thinking on the frosty Caucasus?
Or cloy the hungry edge of appetite
By bare imagination of a feast?
Or wallow naked in December snow
By thinking on fantastic summer's heat?
O, no! the apprehension of the good
Gives but the greater feeling to the worse. BOLINGBROKE
Richard the Second, 1, 3, 295

2 Pray God we may make haste, and come too late! RICHARD II *1, 4, 64*

3 More are men's ends mark'd than their lives before.
The setting sun, and music at the close,
As the last taste of sweets, is sweetest last,
Writ in remembrance more than things long past. GAUNT *2, 1, 11*

4 Methinks I am a prophet new inspir'd,
And thus expiring do foretell of him:
His rash fierce blaze of riot cannot last,
For violent fires soon burn out themselves;
Small showers last long, but sudden storms are short;
He tires betimes that spurs too fast betimes. GAUNT *2, 1, 31*

5 This royal throne of kings, this sceptred isle,
This earth of majesty, this seat of Mars,
This other Eden, demi-paradise,
This fortress built by Nature for herself
Against infection and the hand of war,
This happy breed of men, this little world,
This precious stone set in the silver sea,
Which serves it in the office of a wall,
Or as a moat defensive to a house,
Against the envy of less happier lands;
This blessed plot, this earth, this realm, this England,
This nurse, this teeming womb of royal kings,
Fear'd by their breed, and famous by their birth. GAUNT *2, 1, 40*

6 England, bound in with the triumphant sea,
Whose rocky shore beats back the envious siege
Of wat'ry Neptune, is now bound in with shame,
With inky blots and rotten parchment bonds;
That England, that was wont to conquer others,
Hath made a shameful conquest of itself.
Ah, would the scandal vanish with my life,
How happy then were my ensuing death! GAUNT *2, 1, 61*

7 Can sick men play so nicely with their names? RICHARD II *2, 1, 84*

8 I count myself in nothing else so happy
As in a soul rememb'ring my good friends. BOLINGBROKE *2, 3, 46*

9 Grace me no grace, nor uncle me no uncle. YORK *2, 3, 87*

10 The caterpillars of the commonwealth. BOLINGBROKE *2, 3, 166*

11 Things past redress are now with me past care. YORK *2, 3, 171*

12 Eating the bitter bread of banishment. BOLINGBROKE *3, 1, 21*

1 I weep for joy
To stand upon my kingdom once again.
Dear earth, I do salute thee with my hand,
Though rebels wound thee with their horses' hoofs. RICHARD II
Richard the Second, *3*, *2*, *4*

2 Not all the water in the rough rude sea
Can wash the balm off from an anointed king;
The breath of worldly men cannot depose
The deputy elected by the Lord. RICHARD II *3*, *2*, *54*

3 O, call back yesterday, bid time return. SALISBURY *3*, *2*, *69*

4 Cry woe, destruction, ruin, and decay—
The worst is death, and death will have his day. RICHARD II *3*, *2*, *102*

5 Of comfort no man speak.
Let's talk of graves, of worms, and epitaphs;
Make dust our paper, and with rainy eyes
Write sorrow on the bosom of the earth.
Let's choose executors and talk of wills. RICHARD II *3*, *2*, *144*

6 For God's sake let us sit upon the ground
And tell sad stories of the death of kings:
How some have been depos'd, some slain in war,
Some haunted by the ghosts they have depos'd,
Some poison'd by their wives, some sleeping kill'd,
All murder'd—for within the hollow crown
That rounds the mortal temples of a king
Keeps Death his court; and there the antic sits,
Scoffing his state and grinning at his pomp;
Allowing him a breath, a little scene,
To monarchize, be fear'd, and kill with looks;
Infusing him with self and vain conceit,
As if this flesh which walls about our life
Were brass impregnable; and, humour'd thus,
Comes at the last, and with a little pin
Bores through his castle wall, and farewell, king! RICHARD II *3*, *2*, *155*

7 What must the King do now? Must he submit?
The King shall do it. Must he be depos'd?
The King shall be contented. Must he lose
The name of king? A God's name, let it go.
I'll give my jewels for a set of beads,
My gorgeous palace for a hermitage,
My gay apparel for an almsman's gown,
My figur'd goblets for a dish of wood,
My sceptre for a palmer's walking staff,
My subjects for a pair of carved saints,
And my large kingdom for a little grave,
A little little grave, an obscure grave. RICHARD II *3*, *3*, *143*

8 And if you crown him, let me prophesy—
The blood of English shall manure the ground,
And future ages groan for this foul act;
Peace shall go sleep with Turks and infidels. CARLISLE *4*, *1*, *136*

1 Did they not sometime cry 'All hail!' to me?
So Judas did to Christ; but he, in twelve,
Found truth in all but one; I, in twelve thousand, none.
God save the King! Will no man say amen?
Am I both priest and clerk? Well then, amen. RICHARD II
Richard the Second, 4, 1, 169

2 I give this heavy weight from off my head,
And this unwieldy sceptre from my hand,
The pride of kingly sway from out my heart;
With mine own tears I wash away my balm,
With mine own hands I give away my crown. RICHARD II *4, 1, 204*

3 The woe's to come; the children yet unborn
Shall feel this day as sharp to them as thorn. CARLISLE *4, 1, 322*

4 I am sworn brother, sweet,
To grim Necessity; and he and I
Will keep a league till death. RICHARD II *5, 1, 19*

5 As in a theatre the eyes of men
After a well-grac'd actor leaves the stage
Are idly bent on him that enters next,
Thinking his prattle to be tedious. YORK *5, 2, 23*

6 I have been studying how I may compare
This prison where I live unto the world. RICHARD II *5, 5, 1*

7 How sour sweet music is
When time is broke and no proportion kept!
So is it in the music of men's lives. RICHARD II *5, 5, 42*

King Richard the Third

8 Now is the winter of our discontent
Made glorious summer by this sun of York. GLOUCESTER *1, 1, 1*

9 Our stern alarums chang'd to merry meetings,
Our dreadful marches to delightful measures. GLOUCESTER *1, 1, 7*

10 Deform'd, unfinish'd, sent before my time
Into this breathing world scarce half made up,
And that so lamely and unfashionable
That dogs bark at me as I halt by them. GLOUCESTER *1, 1, 20*

11 In this weak piping time of peace. GLOUCESTER *1, 1, 24*

12 I am determined to prove a villain. GLOUCESTER *1, 1, 30*

13 Was ever woman in this humour woo'd?
Was ever woman in this humour won? GLOUCESTER *1, 2, 227*

14 And thus I clothe my naked villainy
With odd old ends stol'n forth of holy writ,
And seem a saint when most I play the devil. GLOUCESTER *1, 3, 336*

15 O, I have pass'd a miserable night,
So full of fearful dreams, of ugly sights,
That, as I am a Christian faithful man,
I would not spend another such a night
Though 'twere to buy a world of happy days—
So full of dismal terror was the time! CLARENCE *1, 4, 2*

1 O Lord, methought what pain it was to drown,
What dreadful noise of waters in my ears,
What sights of ugly death within my eyes!
Methoughts I saw a thousand fearful wrecks,
A thousand men that fishes gnaw'd upon,
Wedges of gold, great anchors, heaps of pearl,
Inestimable stones, unvalued jewels,
All scatt'red in the bottom of the sea;
Some lay in dead men's skulls, and in the holes
Where eyes did once inhabit there were crept,
As 'twere in scorn of eyes, reflecting gems,
That woo'd the slimy bottom of the deep
And mock'd the dead bones that lay scatt'red by. CLARENCE
Richard the Third, 1, 4, 21

2 So wise so young, they say, do never live long. GLOUCESTER *3, 1, 79*

3 My lord of Ely, when I was last in Holborn
I saw good strawberries in your garden there. GLOUCESTER *3, 4, 32*

4 Talk'st thou to me of ifs? Thou art a traitor.
Off with his head! GLOUCESTER *3, 4, 77*

5 High-reaching Buckingham grows circumspect. RICHARD III *4, 2, 31*

6 But I am in
So far in blood that sin will pluck on sin. RICHARD III *4, 2, 65*

7 I am not in the giving vein to-day. RICHARD III *4, 2, 120*

8 Their lips were four red roses on a stalk,
And in their summer beauty kiss'd each other. TYRREL *4, 3, 12*

9 An honest tale speeds best being plainly told. QUEEN ELIZABETH *4, 4, 358*

10 Harp not on that string. RICHARD III *4, 4, 364*

11 Is the chair empty? Is the sword unsway'd?
Is the King dead, the empire unpossess'd? RICHARD III *4, 4, 470*

12 True hope is swift and flies with swallow's wings;
Kings it makes gods, and meaner creatures kings. RICHMOND *5, 2, 23*

13 The King's name is a tower of strength. RICHARD III *5, 3, 12*

14 I have not that alacrity of spirit
Nor cheer of mind that I was wont to have. RICHARD III *5, 3, 73*

15 My conscience hath a thousand several tongues,
And every tongue brings in a several tale,
And every tale condemns me for a villain. RICHARD III *5, 3, 193*

16 A horse! a horse! my kingdom for a horse! RICHARD III *5, 4, 7*

Romeo and Juliet

17 A pair of star-cross'd lovers. CHORUS *Prologue, 6*

18 The two hours' traffic of our stage. CHORUS *Prologue, 12*

19 Saint-seducing gold. ROMEO *1, 1, 213*

20 For I am proverb'd with a grandsire phrase;
I'll be a candle-holder and look on. ROMEO *1, 4, 37*

1 O, then I see Queen Mab hath been with you.
She is the fairies' midwife, and she comes
In shape no bigger than an agate stone
On the fore-finger of an alderman,
Drawn with a team of little atomies
Athwart men's noses as they lie asleep. MERCUTIO *Romeo and Juliet, 1, 4, 53*

2 For you and I are past our dancing days. CAPULET *1, 5, 29*

3 O, she doth teach the torches to burn bright!
It seems she hangs upon the cheek of night
As a rich jewel in an Ethiop's ear—
Beauty too rich for use, for earth too dear! ROMEO *1, 5, 42*

4 For I ne'er saw true beauty till this night. ROMEO *1, 5, 51*

5 My only love sprung from my only hate! JULIET *1, 5, 136*

6 He jests at scars that never felt a wound.
But, soft! What light through yonder window breaks?
It is the east, and Juliet is the sun. ROMEO *2, 2, 1*

7 See how she leans her cheek upon her hand!
O that I were a glove upon that hand,
That I might touch that cheek! ROMEO *2, 2, 23*

8 O Romeo, Romeo! wherefore art thou Romeo? JULIET *2, 2, 33*

9 What's in a name? That which we call a rose
By any other name would smell as sweet. JULIET *2, 2, 43*

10 O, swear not by the moon, th' inconstant moon,
That monthly changes in her circled orb,
Lest that thy love prove likewise variable. JULIET *2, 2, 109*

11 This bud of love, by summer's ripening breath,
May prove a beauteous flow'r when next we meet. JULIET *2, 2, 121*

12 Love goes toward love as school-boys from their books;
But love from love, toward school with heavy looks. ROMEO *2, 2, 156*

13 How silver-sweet sound lovers' tongues by night,
Like softest music to attending ears! ROMEO *2, 2, 166*

14 Good night, good night! Parting is such sweet sorrow
That I shall say good night till it be morrow. JULIET *2, 2, 185*

15 Wisely and slow; they stumble that run fast. FRIAR LAWRENCE *2, 3, 94*

16 O flesh, flesh, how art thou fishified! MERCUTIO *2, 4, 37*

17 I am the very pink of courtesy. MERCUTIO *2, 4, 56*

18 Therefore love moderately: long love doth so;
Too swift arrives as tardy as too slow. FRIAR LAWRENCE *2, 6, 14*

19 A plague o' both your houses!
They have made worms' meat of me. MERCUTIO *3, 1, 103*

20 O, I am fortune's fool! ROMEO *3, 1, 133*

21 Come, civil night,
Thou sober-suited matron, all in black. JULIET *3, 2, 10*

22 Night's candles are burnt out, and jocund day
Stands tiptoe on the misty mountain tops. ROMEO *3, 5, 9*

1 Thank me no thankings, nor proud me no prouds. CAPULET
Romeo and Juliet, 3, 5, 152

2 'Tis an ill cook that cannot lick his own fingers. SERVINGMAN *4, 2, 6*

3 Beauty's ensign yet
Is crimson in thy lips and in thy cheeks,
And death's pale flag is not advanced there. ROMEO *5, 3, 94*

4 O, here
Will I set up my everlasting rest,
And shake the yoke of inauspicious stars
From this world-wearied flesh. Eyes, look your last.
Arms, take your last embrace. ROMEO *5, 3, 109*

The Taming of the Shrew

5 Look in the chronicles: we came in with Richard Conqueror.
CHRISTOPHER SLY *Induction, 1, 4*

6 No profit grows where is no pleasure ta'en;
In brief, sir, study what you most affect. TRANIO *1, 1, 39*

7 There's small choice in rotten apples. HORTENSIO *1, 1, 131*

8 Kiss me, Kate. PETRUCHIO *2, 1, 316*

9 Thereby hangs a tale. GRUMIO *4, 1, 50*

10 This is a way to kill a wife with kindness. PETRUCHIO *4, 1, 192*

11 Our purses shall be proud, our garments poor;
For 'tis the mind that makes the body rich;
And as the sun breaks through the darkest clouds,
So honour peereth in the meanest habit. PETRUCHIO *4, 3, 167*

12 A woman mov'd is like a fountain troubled—
Muddy, ill-seeming, thick, bereft of beauty. KATHERINA *5, 2, 142*

The Tempest

13 He hath no drowning mark upon him; his complexion is perfect gallows.
GONZALO *1, 1, 28*

14 The wills above be done, but I would fain die a dry death. GONZALO
1, 1, 63

15 What seest thou else
In the dark backward and abysm of time? PROSPERO *1, 2, 49*

16 Your tale, sir, would cure deafness. MIRANDA *1, 2, 106*

17 My library
Was dukedom large enough. PROSPERO *1, 2, 109*

18 From the still-vex'd Bermoothes. ARIEL *1, 2, 229*

19 You taught me language, and my profit on't
Is, I know how to curse. The red plague rid you
For learning me your language! CALIBAN *1, 2, 363*

20 Come unto these yellow sands,
And then take hands. ARIEL *1, 2, 375*

1 Full fathom five thy father lies;
  Of his bones are coral made;
Those are pearls that were his eyes;
  Nothing of him that doth fade
But doth suffer a sea-change
Into something rich and strange. ARIEL *The Tempest, 1, 2, 396*

2 This swift business
I must uneasy make, lest too light winning
Make the prize light. PROSPERO *1, 2, 450*

3 He receives comfort like cold porridge. SEBASTIAN *2, 1, 10*

4 I' th' commonwealth I would by contraries
Execute all things. GONZALO *2, 1, 141*

5 While you here do snoring lie,
Open-ey'd conspiracy
  His time doth take. ARIEL *2, 1, 291*

6 When they will not give a doit to relieve a lame beggar, they will lay out ten to see a dead Indian. TRINCULO *2, 2, 29*

7 Misery acquaints a man with strange bedfellows. TRINCULO *2, 2, 38*

8 Well, here's my comfort. (*Drinks*) STEPHANO *2, 2, 43*

9 The master, the swabber, the boatswain, and I,
The gunner, and his mate,
Lov'd Mall, Meg, and Marian, and Margery,
But none of us car'd for Kate. STEPHANO *2, 2, 44*

10 'Ban 'Ban, Ca—Caliban,
Has a new master—Get a new man. CALIBAN *2, 2, 173*

11 They say there's but five upon this isle: we are three of them; if th' other two be brain'd like us, the state totters. TRINCULO *3, 2, 4*

12 He that dies pays all debts. STEPHANO *3, 2, 126*

13 Be not afeard. The isle is full of noises,
Sounds, and sweet airs, that give delight, and hurt not. CALIBAN *3, 2, 130*

14 Travellers ne'er did lie,
Though fools at home condemn 'em. ANTONIO *3, 3, 26*

15 You fools! I and my fellows
Are ministers of Fate; the elements
Of whom your swords are temper'd may as well
Wound the loud winds, or with bemock'd-at stabs
Kill the still-closing waters, as diminish
One dowle that's in my plume. ARIEL *3, 3, 60*

16 Our revels now are ended. These our actors,
As I foretold you, were all spirits, and
Are melted into air, into thin air;
And, like the baseless fabric of this vision,
The cloud-capp'd towers, the gorgeous palaces,
The solemn temples, the great globe itself,
Yea, all which it inherit, shall dissolve,
And, like this insubstantial pageant faded,
Leave not a rack behind. We are such stuff
As dreams are made on; and our little life
Is rounded with a sleep. PROSPERO *4, 1, 148*

1 Wit shall not go unrewarded while I am king of this country. STEPHANO
The Tempest, 4, 1, 240

2 With foreheads villainous low. CALIBAN *4, 1, 248*

3 The rarer action is
In virtue than in vengeance. PROSPERO *5, 1, 27*

4 Ye elves of hills, brooks, standing lakes, and groves;
And ye that on the sands with printless foot
Do chase the ebbing Neptune, and do fly him
When he comes back. PROSPERO *5, 1, 33*

5 I'll break my staff,
Bury it certain fathoms in the earth,
And deeper than did ever plummet sound
I'll drown my book. PROSPERO *5, 1, 54*

6 Where the bee sucks, there suck I;
In a cowslip's bell I lie;
There I couch when owls do cry.
On the bat's back I do fly
After summer merrily.
Merrily, merrily shall I live now
Under the blossom that hangs on the bough. ARIEL *5, 1, 88*

7 How beauteous mankind is! O brave new world
That has such people in't! MIRANDA *5, 1, 183*

8 Retire me to my Milan, where
Every third thought shall be my grave. PROSPERO *5, 1, 310*

Timon of Athens

9 'Tis not enough to help the feeble up,
But to support him after. TIMON *1, 1, 110*

10 I wonder men dare trust themselves with men. APEMANTUS *1, 2, 42*

11 Uncover, dogs, and lap. TIMON *3, 6, 85*

Titus Andronicus

12 Sweet mercy is nobility's true badge. TAMORA *1, 1, 119*

13 She is a woman, therefore may be woo'd;
She is a woman, therefore may be won;
She is Lavinia, therefore must be lov'd.
What, man! more water glideth by the mill
Than wots the miller of; and easy it is
Of a cut loaf to steal a shive, we know. DEMETRIUS *2, 1, 82*

14 If one good deed in all my life I did,
I do repent it from my very soul. AARON *5, 3, 189*

Troilus and Cressida

15 Women are angels, wooing:
Things won are done; joy's soul lies in the doing.
That she belov'd knows nought that knows not this:
Men prize the thing ungain'd more than it is. CRESSIDA *1, 2, 278*

1 The heavens themselves, the planets, and this centre,
Observe degree, priority, and place,
Insisture, course, proportion, season, form,
Office, and custom, in all line of order. ULYSSES *Troilus and Cressida, 1, 3, 85*

2 O, when degree is shak'd,
Which is the ladder of all high designs,
The enterprise is sick! ULYSSES *1, 3, 101*

3 Take but degree away, untune that string,
And hark what discord follows! ULYSSES *1, 3, 109*

4 I would thou didst itch from head to foot and I had the scratching of thee. THERSITES *2, 1, 26*

5 To be wise and love
Exceeds man's might. CRESSIDA *3, 2, 152*

6 Time hath, my lord, a wallet at his back,
Wherein he puts alms for oblivion,
A great-siz'd monster of ingratitudes. ULYSSES *3, 3, 145*

7 One touch of nature makes the whole world kin. ULYSSES *3, 3, 175*

8 There's language in her eye, her cheek, her lip,
Nay, her foot speaks; her wanton spirits look out
At every joint and motive of her body. ULYSSES *4, 5, 55*

9 Lechery, lechery! Still wars and lechery! Nothing else holds fashion. THERSITES *5, 2, 193*

Twelfth Night

10 If music be the food of love, play on,
Give me excess of it, that, surfeiting,
The appetite may sicken and so die.
That strain again! It had a dying fall;
O, it came o'er my ear like the sweet sound
That breathes upon a bank of violets,
Stealing and giving odour! Enough, no more;
'Tis not so sweet now as it was before. DUKE ORSINO *1, 1, 1*

11 Speaks three or four languages word for word without book. SIR TOBY BELCH *1, 3, 24*

12 Is it a world to hide virtues in? SIR TOBY BELCH *1, 3, 123*

13 Many a good hanging prevents a bad marriage. FESTE *1, 5, 18*

14 A plague o' these pickle-herring! SIR TOBY BELCH *1, 5, 114*

15 Make me a willow cabin at your gate,
And call upon my soul within the house;
Write loyal cantons of contemned love
And sing them loud even in the dead of night;
Halloo your name to the reverberate hills,
And make the babbling gossip of the air
Cry out 'Olivia!' VIOLA *1, 5, 252*

16 Farewell, fair cruelty. VIOLA *1, 5, 272*

17 Not to be abed after midnight is to be up betimes. SIR TOBY BELCH *2, 3, 1*

1 O mistress mine, where are you roaming?
O, stay and hear; your true love's coming,
That can sing both high and low.
Trip no further, pretty sweeting;
Journeys end in lovers meeting,
Every wise man's son doth know. FESTE *Twelfth Night 2, 3, 38*

2 What is love? 'Tis not hereafter;
Present mirth hath present laughter;
What's to come is still unsure.
In delay there lies no plenty,
Then come kiss me, sweet and twenty;
Youth's a stuff will not endure. FESTE *2, 3, 46*

3 He does it with a better grace, but I do it more natural.
SIR ANDREW AGUECHEEK *2, 3, 79*

4 Is there no respect of place, persons, nor time, in you? MALVOLIO
2, 3, 89

5 Dost thou think, because thou art virtuous, there shall be no more cakes and ale? SIR TOBY BELCH *2, 3, 109*

6 Come away, come away, death;
And in sad cypress let me be laid;
Fly away, fly away, breath,
I am slain by a fair cruel maid.
My shroud of white, stuck all with yew,
O, prepare it!
My part of death no one so true
Did share it. FESTE *2, 4, 50*

7 She never told her love,
But let concealment, like a worm i' th' bud,
Feed on her damask cheek. She pin'd in thought;
And with a green and yellow melancholy
She sat like Patience on a monument,
Smiling at grief. VIOLA *2, 4, 109*

8 I am all the daughters of my father's house,
And all the brothers too. VIOLA *2, 4, 119*

9 Some are born great, some achieve greatness, and some have greatness thrust upon 'em. MALVOLIO (reading letter) *2, 5, 129*

10 Remember who commended thy yellow stockings, and wish'd to see thee ever cross-garter'd. MALVOLIO (reading letter) *2, 5, 135*

11 O world, how apt the poor are to be proud! OLIVIA *3, 1, 124*

12 Love sought is good, but given unsought is better. OLIVIA *3, 1, 153*

13 Why, this is very midsummer madness. OLIVIA *3, 4, 53*

14 If this were play'd upon a stage now, I could condemn it as an improbable fiction. FABIAN *3, 4, 121*

15 More matter for a May morning. FABIAN *3, 4, 136*

16 Still you keep o' th' windy side of the law. FABIAN *3, 4, 156*

17 Out of my lean and low ability
I'll lend you something. VIOLA *3, 4, 328*

1 I hate ingratitude more in a man
Than lying, vainness, babbling drunkenness,
Or any taint of vice whose strong corruption
Inhabits our frail blood. VIOLA *Twelfth Night, 3, 4, 338*

2 And thus the whirligig of time brings in his revenges. FESTE *5, 1, 363*

3 When that I was and a little tiny boy,
With hey, ho, the wind and the rain,
A foolish thing was but a toy,
For the rain it raineth every day. FESTE *5, 1, 375*

The Two Gentlemen of Verona

4 Home-keeping youth have ever homely wits. VALENTINE *1, 1, 2*

5 I have no other but a woman's reason:
I think him so, because I think him so. LUCETTA *1, 2, 23*

6 O, how this spring of love resembleth
The uncertain glory of an April day. PROTEUS *1, 3, 84*

7 Dumb jewels often in their silent kind
More than quick words do move a woman's mind. VALENTINE *3, 1, 90*

8 Who is Silvia? What is she,
That all our swains commend her?
Holy, fair, and wise is she. SONG *4, 2, 38*

9 Is she kind as she is fair?
For beauty lives with kindness. SONG *4, 2, 43*

10 How use doth breed a habit in a man! VALENTINE *5, 4, 1*

11 O heaven, were man
But constant, he were perfect! PROTEUS *5, 4, 110*

The Winter's Tale

12 Two lads that thought there was no more behind
But such a day to-morrow as to-day,
And to be boy eternal. POLIXENES *1, 2, 63*

13 A sad tale's best for winter. I have one
Of sprites and goblins. MAMILLIUS *2, 1, 25*

14 What's gone and what's past help
Should be past grief. PAULINA *3, 2, 219*

15 *Exit, pursued by a bear.* STAGE DIRECTION *3, 3, 58*

16 I would there were no age between ten and three and twenty, or that youth would sleep out the rest; for there is nothing in the between but getting wenches with child, wronging the ancientry, stealing, fighting. SHEPHERD *3, 3, 59*

17 When daffodils begin to peer,
With heigh! the doxy over the dale,
Why, then comes in the sweet o' the year,
For the red blood reigns in the winter's pale. AUTOLYCUS *4, 3, 1*

18 A snapper-up of unconsidered trifles. AUTOLYCUS *4, 3, 26*

19 Jog on, jog on, the footpath way,
And merrily hent the stile-a;
A merry heart goes all the day,
Your sad tires in a mile-a. AUTOLYCUS *4, 3, 118*

1 For you there's rosemary and rue; these keep
Seeming and savour all the winter long. PERDITA *The Winter's Tale*, *4, 4, 74*

2 What you do
Still betters what is done. When you speak, sweet,
I'd have you do it ever. When you sing,
I'd have you buy and sell so; so give alms;
Pray so; and, for the ord'ring your affairs,
To sing them too. FLORIZEL *4, 4, 135*

3 Lawn as white as driven snow. AUTOLYCUS *4, 4, 215*

4 The self-same sun that shines upon his court. PERDITA *4, 4, 436*

5 Prosperity's the very bond of love,
Whose fresh complexion and whose heart together
Affliction alters. CAMILLO *4, 4, 565*

6 Though I am not naturally honest, I am so sometimes by chance. AUTOLYCUS *4, 4, 701*

7 Let me have no lying; it becomes none but tradesmen. AUTOLYCUS *4, 4, 711*

8 Though authority be a stubborn bear, yet he is oft led by the nose with gold. CLOWN *4, 4, 790*

Sonnets

9 To the onlie begetter of these insuing sonnets. *Dedication*

10 From fairest creatures we desire increase,
That thereby beauty's rose might never die. *Sonnet 1*

11 Look in thy glass, and tell the face thou viewest. *Sonnet 3*

12 But wherefore do not you a mightier way
Make war upon this bloody tyrant Time? *Sonnet 16*

13 Shall I compare thee to a summer's day?
Thou art more lovely and more temperate.
Rough winds do shake the darling buds of May,
And summer's lease hath all too short a date. *Sonnet 18*

14 But thy eternal summer shall not fade. *Sonnet 18*

15 So long as men can breathe or eyes can see,
So long lives this, and this gives life to thee. *Sonnet 18*

16 A woman's face, with Nature's own hand painted,
Hast thou, the Master Mistress of my passion. *Sonnet 20*

17 For thy sweet love rememb'red such wealth brings
That then I scorn to change my state with kings. *Sonnet 29*

18 When to the sessions of sweet silent thought
I summon up remembrance of things past,
I sigh the lack of many a thing I sought,
And with old woes new wail my dear time's waste. *Sonnet 30*

19 But if the while I think on thee, dear friend,
All losses are restor'd, and sorrows end. *Sonnet 30*

20 So true a fool is love that in your will,
Though you do anything, he thinks no ill. *Sonnet 57*

1 Like as the waves make towards the pebbled shore,
So do our minutes hasten to their end. *Sonnet 60*

2 Some glory in their birth, some in their skill,
Some in their wealth, some in their body's force;
Some in their garments, though new-fangled ill;
Some in their hawks and hounds, some in their horse. *Sonnet 91*

3 For sweetest things turn sourest by their deeds:
Lilies that fester smell far worse than weeds. *Sonnet 94*

4 How like a winter hath my absence been
From thee, the pleasure of the fleeting year!
What freezings have I felt, what dark days seen! *Sonnet 97*

5 From you have I been absent in the spring,
When proud-pied April, dress'd in all his trim,
Hath put a spirit of youth in every thing. *Sonnet 98*

6 When in the chronicle of wasted time
I see descriptions of the fairest wights. *Sonnet 106*

7 For we, which now behold these present days,
Have eyes to wonder, but lack tongues to praise. *Sonnet 106*

8 Let me not to the marriage of true minds
Admit impediments. Love is not love
Which alters when it alteration finds,
Or bends with the remover to remove.
O, no! it is an ever-fixed mark,
That looks on tempests and is never shaken. *Sonnet 116*

9 Love alters not with his brief hours and weeks,
But bears it out even to the edge of doom.
If this be error, and upon me prov'd,
I never writ, nor no man ever lov'd. *Sonnet 116*

10 'Tis better to be vile than vile esteemed,
When not to be receives reproach of being. *Sonnet 121*

11 Th' expense of spirit in a waste of shame
Is lust in action; and till action, lust
Is perjur'd, murd'rous, bloody, full of blame,
Savage, extreme, rude, cruel, not to trust;
Enjoy'd no sooner but despised straight. *Sonnet 129*

12 All this the world well knows; yet none knows well
To shun the heaven that leads men to this hell. *Sonnet 129*

13 My mistress' eyes are nothing like the sun;
Coral is far more red than her lips' red. *Sonnet 130*

14 And yet, by heaven, I think my love as rare
As any she belied with false compare. *Sonnet 130*

15 When my love swears that she is made of truth,
I do believe her, though I know she lies. *Sonnet 138*

16 Two loves I have, of comfort and despair,
Which like two spirits do suggest me still;
The better angel is a man right fair,
The worser spirit a woman colour'd ill. *Sonnet 144*

Poems

1 Crabbed age and youth cannot live together:
Youth is full of pleasance, age is full of care;
Youth like summer morn, age like winter weather;
Youth like summer brave, age like winter bare. *The Passionate Pilgrim 12*

2 Age, I do abhor thee; youth, I do adore thee. *Ib*

3 The first heire of my invention. *Venus and Adonis, Dedication*

4 Hunting he lov'd, but love he laugh'd to scorn. *Ib, 1, 4*

5 Beauty itself doth of itself persuade
The eyes of men without an orator. *The Rape of Lucrece, 1, 29*

SHAW, George Bernard, 1856–1950

6 Breakages, Limited, the biggest industrial corporation in the country. BALBUS *The Apple Cart, Act 1*

7 You can always tell an old soldier by the inside of his holsters and cartridge boxes. The young ones carry pistols and cartridges: the old ones grub. BLUNTSCHLI *Arms and the Man, Act 1*

8 You are a very poor soldier: a chocolate cream soldier! RAINA *Ib, Act 1*

9 It is enough that there *is* a beyond. LILITH *Back to Methuselah, Part 5, Last words*

10 When a stupid man is doing something he is ashamed of, he always declares that it is his duty. APOLLODORUS *Caesar and Cleopatra, Act 3*

11 We have no more right to consume happiness without producing it than to consume wealth without producing it. MORELL *Candida, Act 1*

12 The overpaying instinct is a generous one: better than the underpaying instinct, and not so common. MORELL *Ib, Act 1*

13 Im only a beer teetotaller, not a champagne teetotaller. PROSERPINE *Ib, Act 3*

14 Martyrdom . . . is the only way in which a man can become famous without ability. BURGOYNE *The Devil's Disciple, Act 3*

15 SWINDON: What will History say?
BURGOYNE: History, sir, will tell lies, as usual. *Ib, Act 3*

16 Stimulate the phagocytes. B. B. *The Doctor's Dilemma, Act 1*

17 Go anywhere in England where there are natural, wholesome, contented, and really nice English people; and what do you always find? That the stables are the real centre of the house-hold. LADY UTTERWORD *Heartbreak House, Act 3*

18 Tell me all me faults as man to man. I can stand anything but flattery. TIM *John Bull's Other Island, Act 1*

19 The more a man knows, and the further he travels, the more likely he is to marry a country girl afterwards. KEEGAN *Ib, Act 2*

20 My way of joking is to tell the truth. Its the funniest joke in the world. KEEGAN *Ib*

1 I am a Millionaire. That is my religion. UNDERSHAFT *Major Barbara, Act 2*

2 Wot prawce selvytion nah? BILL WALKER *Ib*

3 A lifetime of happiness! No man alive could bear it: it would be hell on earth. TANNER *Man and Superman, Act 1*

4 There is no love sincerer than the love of food. TANNER *Ib*

5 The true artist will let his wife starve, his children go barefoot, his mother drudge for his living at seventy, sooner than work at anything but his art. TANNER *Ib*

6 It is a womans business to get married as soon as possible, and a mans to keep unmarried as long as he can. TANNER *Ib, Act 2*

7 An Englishman thinks he is moral when he is only uncomfortable. THE DEVIL *Ib, Act 3*

8 There are two tragedies in life. One is to lose your hearts desire. The other is to gain it. MENDOZA *Ib, Act 4*

9 Any person under the age of thirty, who, having any knowledge of the existing social order, is not a revolutionist, is an inferior. *Ib, The Revolutionist's Handbook, Foreword*

10 We learn from history that we learn nothing from history. *Ib*

11 The golden rule is that there are no golden rules. *Ib, Maxims for Revolutionists*

12 Liberty means responsibility. That is why most men dread it. *Ib*

13 He who can, does. He who cannot, teaches. *Ib*

14 Marriage is popular because it combines the maximum of temptation with the maximum of opportunity. *Ib*

15 Ladies and gentlemen are permitted to have friends in the kennel, but not in the kitchen. *Ib*

16 Every man over forty is a scoundrel. *Ib*

17 There is only one religion, though there are a hundred versions of it. *Plays Pleasant, Preface*

18 Remember that you are a human being with a soul and the divine gift of articulate speech: that your native language is the language of Shakespear and Milton and The Bible: and dont sit there crooning like a bilious pigeon. HIGGINS *Pygmalion, Act 1*

19 I dont want to talk grammar. I want to talk like a lady. ELIZA *Ib, Act 2*

20 Time enough to think of the future when you havent any future to think of. HIGGINS *Ib*

21 Im one of the undeserving poor: thats what I am. Think of what that means to a man. It means that he's up agen middle class morality all the time. DOOLITTLE *Ib*

22 My aunt died of influenza: so they said . . . But its my belief they done the old woman in. ELIZA *Ib, Act 3*

23 Walk! Not bloody likely. ELIZA *Ib*

24 No eggs! No eggs!! Thousand thunders, man, what do you mean by no eggs? ROBERT *Saint Joan, Scene 1*

1 We want a few mad people now. See where the sane ones have landed us! POULENGEY *Saint Joan, Scene 1*

2 I hear voices telling me what to do. They come from God. JOAN *Ib*

3 A miracle, my friend, is an event which creates faith. That is the purpose and nature of miracles. ARCHBISHOP *Ib, Scene 2*

4 Do not think you can frighten me by telling me that I am alone. France is alone; and God is alone; and what is my loneliness before the loneliness of my country and my God? JOAN *Ib, Scene 5*

5 THE EXECUTIONER: You have heard the last of her.
WARWICK: The last of her? Hm! I wonder! *Ib, Scene 6*

6 All dress is fancy dress, is it not, except our natural skins? DUNOIS *Ib, Epilogue*

7 Well, sir, you never can tell. Thats a principle in life with me, sir, if youll excuse my having such a thing, sir. WAITER *You Never Can Tell, Act 2*

8 With the single exception of Homer, there is no eminent writer, not even Sir Walter Scott, whom I can despise so entirely as I despise Shakespeare when I measure my mind against his. *Dramatic Opinions and Essays, Vol. 2, 52*

SHELLEY, Percy Bysshe, 1792–1822

9 I weep for Adonais—he is dead!
O, weep for Adonais! though our tears
Thaw not the frost which binds so dear a head! *Adonais, 1*

10 Ah, woe is me! Winter is come and gone,
But grief returns with the revolving year. *Ib, 154*

11 Through wood and stream and field and hill and Ocean
A quickening life from the Earth's heart has burst
As it has ever done, with change and motion,
From the great morning of the world when first
God dawned on Chaos. *Ib, 163*

12 Alas! that all we loved of him should be,
But for our grief, as if it had not been,
And grief itself be mortal! *Ib, 181*

13 The Pilgrim of Eternity, whose fame
Over his living head like Heaven is bent,
An early but enduring monument. *Ib, 264*

14 A pardlike Spirit beautiful and swift. *Ib, 280*

15 Live thou, whose infamy is not thy fame!
Live! fear no heavier chastisement from me,
Thou noteless blot on a remembered name! *Ib, 325*

16 He has outsoared the shadow of our night;
Envy and calumny and hate and pain,
And that unrest which men miscall delight,
Can touch him not and torture not again;
From the contagion of the world's slow stain
He is secure, and now can never mourn
A heart grown cold, a head grown gray in vain. *Ib, 352*

17 He lives, he wakes—'tis Death is dead, not he. *Ib, 361*

1 He is a portion of the loveliness
Which once he made more lovely. *Adonais, 379*

2 The One remains, the many change and pass;
Heaven's light forever shines, Earth's shadows fly;
Life, like a dome of many-coloured glass,
Stains the white radiance of Eternity. *Ib, 460*

3 The soul of Adonais, like a star,
Beacons from the abode where the Eternal are. *Ib, 494*

4 I bring fresh showers for the thirsting flowers,
From the seas and the streams. *The Cloud, 1*

5 I wield the flail of the lashing hail,
And whiten the green plains under,
And then again I dissolve it in rain,
And laugh as I pass in thunder. *Ib, 9*

6 I am the daughter of Earth and Water,
And the nursling of the Sky;
I pass through the pores of the ocean and shores;
I change, but I cannot die. *Ib, 73*

7 How wonderful is Death,
Death and his brother Sleep! *The Daemon of the World, 1, 1*

8 I never was attached to that great sect,
Whose doctrine is, that each one should select
Out of the crowd a mistress or a friend,
And all the rest, though fair and wise, commend
To cold oblivion. *Epipsychidion, 149*

9 True Love in this differs from gold and clay,
That to divide is not to take away. *Ib, 160*

10 Good-night? ah! no; the hour is ill
Which severs those it should unite;
Let us remain together still,
Then it will be good night. *Good-Night, 1*

11 The world's great age begins anew,
The golden years return,
The earth doth like a snake renew
Her winter weeds outworn:
Heaven smiles, and faiths and empires gleam,
Like wrecks of a dissolving dream. *Hellas, 1060*

12 Thou Paradise of exiles, Italy! *Julian and Maddalo, 57*

13 I met Murder on the way—
He had a mask like Castlereagh. *The Mask of Anarchy, 5*

14 Shake your chains to earth like dew
Which in sleep had fallen on you—
Ye are many—they are few. *Ib, 153*

15 Swiftly walk o'er the western wave,
Spirit of Night!
Out of the misty eastern cave,
Where, all the long and lone daylight,
Thou wovest dreams of joy and fear. *To Night, 1*

1 I ask of thee, belovèd Night—
Swift be thine approaching flight,
Come soon, soon! *To Night, 33*

2 A glorious people vibrated again
The lightning of the nations. *Ode to Liberty, 1*

3 O Wild West Wind, thou breath of Autumn's being,
Thou, from whose unseen presence the leaves dead
Are driven, like ghosts from an enchanter fleeing,
Yellow, and black, and pale, and hectic red,
Pestilence-stricken multitudes. *Ode to the West Wind, 1*

4 Wild Spirit, which art moving everywhere;
Destroyer and preserver; hear, oh, hear! *Ib, 13*

5 Oh, lift me as a wave, a leaf, a cloud!
I fall upon the thorns of life! I bleed!
A heavy weight of hours has chained and bowed
One too like thee: tameless, and swift, and proud. *Ib, 53*

6 Scatter, as from an unextinguished hearth
Ashes and sparks, my words among mankind!
Be through my lips to unawakened earth
The trumpet of a prophecy! O, Wind,
If Winter comes, can Spring be far behind? *Ib, 66*

7 I met a traveller from an antique land
Who said: Two vast and trunkless legs of stone
Stand in the desert. *Ozymandias, 1*

8 And on the pedestal these words appear:
'My name is Ozymandias, king of kings:
Look on my works, ye Mighty, and despair!'
Nothing beside remains. Round the decay
Of that colossal wreck, boundless and bare
The lone and level sands stretch far away. *Ib, 9*

9 Hell is a city much like London—
A populous and a smoky city. *Peter Bell the Third, Part 3, Hell, 1*

10 Crucified 'twixt a smile and whimper. *Ib, 196*

11 But from these create he can
Forms more real than living man,
Nurslings of immortality! *Prometheus Unbound, 1, 747*

12 Yet all love is sweet,
Given or returned. Common as light is love,
And its familiar voice wearies not ever. *Ib, 2, 5, 39*

13 Familiar acts are beautiful through love. *Ib, 4, 403*

14 A Sensitive Plant in a garden grew,
And the young winds fed it with silver dew,
And it opened its fan-like leaves to the light,
And closed them beneath the kisses of Night. *The Sensitive Plant, 1, 1*

15 It is a modest creed, and yet
Pleasant if one considers it,
To own that death itself must be,
Like all the rest, a mockery. *Ib, Conclusion, 126*

16 For love, and beauty, and delight,
There is no death nor change. *Ib, Ib, 134*

1 Hail to thee, blithe Spirit!
Bird thou never wert,
That from Heaven, or near it,
Pourest thy full heart
In profuse strains of unpremeditated art. *To a Skylark, 1*

2 We look before and after,
And pine for what is not:
Our sincerest laughter
With some pain is fraught;
Our sweetest songs are those that tell of saddest thought. *Ib, 86*

3 Teach me half the gladness
That thy brain must know,
Such harmonious madness
From my lips would flow
The world should listen then—as I am listening now. *Ib, 101*

4 Rarely, rarely, comest thou,
Spirit of Delight! *Song, Rarely, Rarely, Comest Thou*

5 An old, mad, blind, despised, and dying king. *Sonnet, England in 1819*

6 Music, when soft voices die,
Vibrates in the memory—
Odours, when sweet violets sicken,
Live within the sense they quicken.
Rose leaves, when the rose is dead,
Are heaped for the belovèd's bed;
And so thy thoughts, when thou art gone,
Love itself shall slumber on. *To —, Music, When Soft Voices Die*

7 I fear thy kisses, gentle maiden,
Thou needest not fear mine;
My spirit is too deeply laden
Ever to burthen thine. *To —, I Fear Thy Kisses*

8 The desire of the moth for the star,
Of the night for the morrow,
The devotion to something afar
From the sphere of our sorrow. *To —, One Word is too often Profaned*

9 Poetry lifts the veil from the hidden beauty of the world, and makes familiar objects be as if they were not familiar. *A Defence of Poetry*

10 Poetry is the record of the best and happiest moments of the happiest and best minds. *Ib*

11 Poets are the unacknowledged legislators of the world. *Ib*

SHENSTONE, William, 1714–1763

12 Whoe'er has travell'd life's dull round,
Where'er his stages may have been,
May sigh to think he still has found
The warmest welcome, at an inn. *Written at an Inn at Henley*

SHERIDAN, Philip Henry, 1831–1888

13 The only good Indian is a dead Indian. *Attributed*

SHERIDAN, Richard Brinsley, 1751–1816

1 Yes, sir, puffing is of various sorts; the principal are, the puff direct, the puff preliminary, the puff collateral, the puff collusive, and the puff oblique, or puff by implication. PUFF *The Critic, Act 1, Scene 2*

2 No scandal about Queen Elizabeth I hope. SNEER *Ib, Act 2, Scene 1*

3 An oyster may be crossed in love. TILBURINA *Ib, Act 3, Scene 1*

4 Thought does not become a young woman. MRS MALAPROP *The Rivals, Act 1, Scene 2*

5 Illiterate him, I say, quite from your memory. MRS MALAPROP *Ib*

6 'Tis safest in matrimony to begin with a little aversion. MRS MALAPROP *Ib*

7 A circulating library in a town is as an ever-green tree of diabolical knowledge! It blossoms through the year. SIR ANTHONY ABSOLUTE *Ib*

8 A progeny of learning. MRS MALAPROP *Ib*

9 A supercilious knowledge in accounts. MRS MALAPROP *Ib*

10 If I reprehend any thing in this world it is the use of my oracular tongue and a nice derangement of epitaphs. MRS MALAPROP *Ib, Act 3, Scene 3*

11 As headstrong as an allegory on the banks of the Nile. MRS MALAPROP *Ib*

12 Too civil by half. ACRES *Ib, Act 3, Scene 4*

13 You shall see them on a beautiful quarto page, where a neat rivulet of text shall meander through a meadow of margin. SIR BENJAMIN BACKBITE *School for Scandal, Act 1, Scene 1*

14 Though I can't make her love me, there is great satisfaction in quarrelling with her. SIR PETER TEAZLE *Ib, Act 2, Scene 1*

15 There is the whole set! a character dead at every word. SIR PETER TEAZLE *Ib, Act 2, Scene 2*

16 I'm called away by particular business. But I leave my character behind me. SIR PETER TEAZLE *Ib*

17 Here's to the maiden of bashful fifteen;
Here's to the widow of fifty;
Here's to the flaunting extravagant quean,
And here's to the housewife that's thrifty.
Let the toast pass,—
Drink to the lass,
I'll warrant she'll prove an excuse for a glass. SIR HARRY BUMPER *Ib, Act 3, Scene 3*

18 What is principle against the flattery of a handsome, lively young fellow? SIR PETER TEAZLE *Ib, Act 4, Scene 2*

19 The Right Honourable gentleman is indebted to his memory for his jests, and to his imagination for his facts. *Reply to Mr. Dundas, House of Commons*

SHERMAN, General William Tecumseh, 1820–1891

20 There is many a boy here to-day who looks on war as all glory, but, boys, it is all hell. *Speech, 1880*

SIDNEY, Algernon, 1622–1683

1 Liars ought to have good memories. *Discourses on Government, Ch. 2, 15*

SIDNEY, Sir Philip, 1554–1586

2 My true love hath my heart, and I have his,
By just exchange one for another given:
I hold his dear, and mine he cannot miss,
There never was a better bargain driven. *The Arcadia, 3*

3 Biting my truant pen, beating myself for spite:
'Fool!' said my Muse to me, 'look in thy heart and write.'
Astrophel and Stella, Sonnet 1

4 With how sad steps, O Moon, thou climb'st the skies!
How silently, and with how wan a face! *Ib, Sonnet 31*

5 With a tale forsooth he cometh unto you, with a tale which holdeth children from play, and old men from the chimney corner. *The Defence of Poesy*

6 Certainly, I must confess mine own barbarousness, I never heard the old song of Percy and Douglas, that I found not my heart moved more than with a trumpet. *Ib*

7 Thy necessity is greater than mine. *On giving his water-bottle to a dying soldier at Zutphen, 1586*

SIMS, George Robert, 1847–1922

8 It is Christmas Day in the Workhouse. *Christmas Day in the Workhouse*

SITWELL, Edith, 1887–1964

9 Still falls the Rain—
Dark as the world of man, black as our loss—
Blind as the nineteen hundred and forty nails
Upon the Cross. *Still Falls the Rain*

SITWELL, Sir Osbert, 1892–1969

10 The British Bourgeoisie
Is not born,
And does not die,
But, if it is ill,
It has a frightened look in its eyes. *At the House of Mrs Kinfoot*

SKELTON, John, 1460?–1529

11 For though my ryme be ragged,
Tattered and jagged,
Rudely rayne beaten,
Rusty and mothe eaten;
If ye take well therwith,
It hath in it some pyth. *Colyn Cloute, 2, 53*

12 With solace and gladness,
Much mirth and no madness,
All good and no badness. *To Mistress Margaret Hussey*

SMART, Christopher, 1722–1771

13 Glorious the northern lights astream;
Glorious the song, when God's the theme;
Glorious the thunder's roar. *Song to David, 85*

1 And now the matchless deed's achieved,
Determined, dared, and done! *Song to David, 86*

SMEDLEY, Francis Edward, 1818–1864

2 You are looking as fresh as paint. *Frank Fairleigh, Ch. 41*

SMITH, Adam, 1723–1790

3 No society can surely be flourishing and happy, of which the far greater part of the members are poor and miserable. *The Wealth of Nations, 1, 8*

4 To found a great empire for the sole purpose of raising up a people of customers, may at first sight appear a project fit only for a nation of shopkeepers. It is, however, a project altogether unfit for a nation of shopkeepers; but extremely fit for a nation that is governed by shopkeepers. *Ib, 2, 4*

SMITH, Logan Pearsall, 1865–1946

5 Happiness is a wine of the rarest vintage, and seems insipid to a vulgar taste. *Afterthoughts, 1, Life and Human Nature*

6 There are few sorrows, however poignant, in which a good income is of no avail. *Ib*

7 The wretchedness of being rich is that you live with rich people. *Ib, 4, In the World*

8 People say that Life is the thing, but I prefer Reading. *Ib, 6, Myself*

9 Thank heavens, the sun has gone in, and I don't have to go out and enjoy it. *Last words*

SMITH, Samuel Francis, 1808–1895

10 My country, 'tis of thee,
Sweet land of liberty,
Of thee I sing. *America*

SMITH, Sydney, 1771–1845

11 Poverty is no disgrace to a man, but it is confoundedly inconvenient. *His Wit and Wisdom*

12 No furniture so charming as books. *Lady Holland, Memoir, Vol. 1, Ch. 9*

13 How can a bishop marry? How can he flirt? The most he can say is, 'I will see you in the vestry after the service.' *Ib*

14 As the French say, there are three sexes,—men, women, and clergymen. *Ib*

15 Praise is the best diet for us, after all. *Ib*

16 I never read a book before reviewing it; it prejudices a man so. *H. Pearson, The Smith of Smiths, Ch. 3*

17 I am convinced digestion is the great secret of life. *Letter to Arthur Kinglake, 30 Sept. 1837*

18 I have no relish for the country; it is a kind of healthy grave. *Letter to Miss G. Harcourt, 1838*

SMOLLETT, Tobias George, 1721–1771

19 Hark ye, Clinker, you are a most notorious offender. You stand convicted of sickness, hunger, wretchedness, and want. *Humphrey Clinker*

20 Some folk are wise, and some are otherwise. *Roderick Random, Ch. 6*

1 I consider the world as made for me, not me for the world. It is my maxim therefore to enjoy it while I can, and let futurity shift for itself.
Roderick Random, Ch. 45

2 True patriotism is of no party. *Sir Launcelote Greaves*

3 That great Cham of literature, Samuel Johnson. *Letter to John Wilkes, 16 March 1759, quoted in Boswell's Life of Johnson*

SNAGGE, John, 1904—

4 I can't see who's ahead—it's either Oxford or Cambridge.
B.B.C. Commentary on Boat Race, 1949

SOCRATES, 469–399 B.C.

5 I am a citizen, not of Athens or Greece, but of the world.
Plutarch, De Exilio

6 Other men live to eat, whereas I eat to live. *Plutarch, Moralia*

SOLON, 640?–558? B.C.

7 Call no man happy until he dies; he is at best fortunate.
Herodotus, Histories, 1, 32

SOMERVILLE, William, 1675–1742

8 The chase, the sport of kings;
Image of war, without its guilt. *The Chase, 1, 13*

SOULE, John Babsone Lane, 1815–1891

9 Go west, young man. *Terre Haute Express, Indiana, 1851*

SOUTHEY, Robert, 1774–1843

10 My days among the Dead are past:
Around me I behold,
Where'er these casual eyes are cast,
The mighty minds of old. *My Days among the Dead*

11 Yet leaving here a name, I trust,
That will not perish in the dust. *Ib*

12 It was a summer's evening,
Old Kaspar's work was done. *The Battle of Blenheim*

13 And by him sported on the green
His little grandchild Wilhelmine. *Ib*

14 But what they fought each other for,
I could not well make out. *Ib*

15 'And everybody praised the Duke
Who this great fight did win.'
'But what good came of it at last?'
Quoth little Peterkin.
'Why that I cannot tell,' said he,
'But 'twas a famous victory.' *Ib*

SPENCER, Herbert, 1820–1903

16 Time: that which man is always trying to kill, but which ends in killing him.
Definitions

1 Science is organised knowledge. *Education, Ch. 2*

2 The Republican form of Government is the highest form of government; but because of this it requires the highest type of human nature—a type nowhere at present existing. *Essays, The Americans*

3 Survival of the fittest. *Principles of Biology*

4 We all decry prejudice, yet are all prejudiced. *Social Statics, Part 2*

5 Education has for its object the formation of character. *Ib*

6 Hero-worship is strongest where there is least regard for human freedom. *Ib, Part 3*

SPENSER, Edmund, 1552?–1599

7 The woods shall to me answer and my Echo ring. *Epithalamion, 18*

8 Ah! when will this long weary day have end,
And lend me leave to come unto my love? *Ib, 278*

9 Fierce wars and faithful loves shall moralize my song. *The Faerie Queen, Book 1, Introduction, Stanza 1*

10 A gentle knight was pricking on the plain. *Ib, Book 1, Canto 1, 1*

11 Sleep after toil, port after stormy seas,
Ease after war, death after life does greatly please. *Ib, Book 1, Canto 9, 40*

12 And as she looked about, she did behold,
How over that same door was likewise writ,
Be bold, be bold, and everywhere Be bold. *Ib, Book 3, Canto 11, 54*

13 Dan Chaucer, well of English undefiled,
On Fame's eternal beadroll worthy to be filed. *Ib, Book 4, Canto 2, 32*

14 The gentle mind by gentle deeds is known,
For a man by nothing is so well bewrayed
As by his manners. *Ib, Book 6, Canto 3, 1*

15 Calm was the day, and through the trembling air,
Sweet breathing Zephyrus did softly play. *Prothalamion, 1*

16 Sweet Thames! run softly, till I end my Song. *Ib, 18*

17 So now they have made our English tongue a gallimaufry or hodgepodge of all other speeches. *The Shepherd's Calendar, Letter to Gabriel Harvey*

SPOONER, Rev. William Archibald, 1844–1930

18 Kinquering Congs their titles take. *Announcing the hymn in New College Chapel, Oxford, 1879 (See 78:12)*

19 Sir, you have tasted two whole worms; you have hissed all my mystery lectures and been caught fighting a liar in the quad; you will leave by the next town drain. *Attributed*

20 Let us drink to the queer old Dean. *Attributed*

21 I remember your name perfectly, but I just can't think of your face. *Attributed*

SPRING-RICE, Sir Cecil Arthur, 1858–1918

22 I vow to thee, my country—all earthly things above—
Entire and whole and perfect, the service of my love.
I Vow to Thee, My Country

1 I am the Dean of Christ Church, Sir,
This is my wife—look well at her.
She is the Broad: I am the High:
We are the University. *The Masque of Balliol*

SQUIRE, Sir John Collings, 1884–1958

2 It did not last: the Devil howling 'Ho,
Let Einstein be,' restored the status quo. *In Continuation of Pope on Newton (see 201:21)*

3 But I'm not so think as you drunk I am. *Ballade of Soporific Absorption*

STANLEY, Sir Henry Morton, 1841–1904

4 Dr. Livingstone, I presume? *On meeting Livingstone in Ujiji, Central Africa, 10 Nov. 1871*

STANTON, Frank Lebby, 1857–1927

5 Sweetest li'l feller, everybody knows;
Dunno what to call him, but he's mighty lak' a rose. *Mighty Lak' a Rose*

STEELE, Sir Richard, 1672–1729

6 Among all the diseases of the mind there is not one more epidemical or more pernicious than the love of flattery. *The Spectator, No. 238*

7 There are so few who can grow old with a good grace. *Ib, No. 263*

8 Reading is to the mind what exercise is to the body. *The Tatler, No. 147*

STEPHEN, James Kenneth, 1859–1892

9 Two voices are there: one is of the deep . . .
And one is of an old half-witted sheep
Which bleats articulate monotony
And indicates that two and one are three. *Lapsus Calami, Sonnet (Parody of Wordsworth, see 333:10)*

10 When the Rudyards cease from kipling
And the Haggards ride no more. *Ib, To R.K.*

STERNE, Laurence, 1713–1768

11 They order, said I, this matter better in France. *A Sentimental Journey, Opening words*

12 As an Englishman does not travel to see Englishmen, I retired to my room. *Ib, Preface*

13 I pity the man who can travel from Dan to Beersheba, and cry, 'tis all barren. *Ib, In the Street, Calais*

14 There are worse occupations in the world than feeling a woman's pulse. *Ib, The Pulse*

15 'God tempers the wind,' said Maria, 'to the shorn lamb.' *Ib, Maria*

16 So that when I stretched out my hand, I caught hold of the fille de chambre's—. *Ib, Last words*

17 'Our armies swore terribly in Flanders,' cried my Uncle Toby, 'but nothing to this.' *Tristram Shandy, Book 3, Ch. 11*

1 Love, 'an please your honour, is exactly like war in this; that a soldier, though he has escaped three weeks complete o' Saturday night,—may nevertheless be shot through his heart on Sunday morning.
Tristram Shandy, Book 8, Ch. 21

2 'L--d!' said my mother, 'what is all this story about?'
'A Cock and a Bull,' said Yorick. *Ib, Last words*

STEVENSON, Robert Louis, 1850–1894

3 Sing me a song of a lad that is gone,
Say, could that lad be I?
Merry of soul he sailed on a day
Over the sea to Skye. *Songs of Travel, 42*

4 Fifteen men on the dead man's chest—
Yo-ho-ho and a bottle of rum!
Drink and the devil had done for the rest. SONG *Treasure Island, Ch. 1*

5 Many's the long night I've dreamed of cheese—toasted, mostly.
BEN GUNN *Ib, Ch. 15*

6 This be the verse you grave for me:
'Here he lies where he longed to be;
Home is the sailor, home from sea,
And the hunter home from the hill.' *Underwoods, Book 1, 21, Requiem*

7 Even if we take matrimony at its lowest, even if we regard it as no more than a sort of friendship recognised by the police. *Virginibus Puerisque, Part 1*

8 Extreme busyness, whether at school or college, kirk or market, is a symptom of deficient vitality. *Ib, An Apology for Idlers*

9 There is no duty we so much underrate as the duty of being happy. *Ib*

10 To travel hopefully is a better thing than to arrive, and the true success is to labour. *Ib, El Dorado*

STEVENSON, William, 1530?–1575

11 I cannot eat but little meat
My stomach is not good;
But sure I think that I can drink
With him that wears a hood. SONG *Gammer Gurton's Needle, Act 2*

12 I stuff my skin, so full within,
Of jolly good ale and old. SONG *Ib*

STONE, Samuel John, 1839–1900

13 The Church's one foundation
Is Jesus Christ her Lord;
She is His new creation
By water and the Word. *The Church's One Foundation*

STOWE, Harriet Elizabeth Beecher, 1811–1896

14 'Never had any mother? What do you mean? Where were you born?' 'Never was born!' persisted Topsy; 'never had no father, nor mother, nor nothin'. I was raised by a speculator.' *Uncle Tom's Cabin, Ch. 20*

1 'Do you know who made you?' 'Nobody, as I knows on,' said the child, [*Topsy*] with a short laugh . . . 'I 'spect I grow'd. Don't think nobody never made me.' *Uncle Tom's Cabin, Ch. 20*

SUCKLING, Sir John, 1609–1642

2 Out upon it, I have loved
Three whole days together;
And am like to love three more,
If it prove fair weather. *A Poem with the Answer*

SUETONIUS, 75?–150? A.D.

3 *Festina lente.* Hasten slowly. *Augustus, 25*

4 *Ave, Imperator, morituri te salutant.* Hail, Emperor, those about to die salute you. *Claudius, 21*

SURTEES, Robert Smith, 1803–1864

5 The only infallible rule we know is, that the man who is always talking about being a gentleman never is one. *Ask Mamma, Ch. 1*

6 Hellish dark, and smells of cheese! *Handley Cross, Ch. 50*

7 Three things I never lends—my 'oss, my wife, and my name. *Hillingdon Hall, Ch. 33*

8 Women never look so well as when one comes in wet and dirty from hunting. *Mr. Sponge's Sporting Tour, Ch. 21*

9 He was a gentleman who was generally spoken of as having nothing a-year, paid quarterly. *Ib, Ch. 24*

10 There is no secret so close as that between a rider and his horse. *Ib, Ch. 31*

SWIFT, Jonathan, 1667–1745

11 The two noblest of things, which are sweetness and light. *The Battle of the Books, Preface*

12 'Tis an old maxim in the schools,
That flattery's the food of fools;
Yet now and then your men of wit
Will condescend to take a bit. *Cadenus and Vanessa*

13 Yet malice never was his aim;
He lash'd the vice, but spared the name;
No individual could resent,
Where thousands equally were meant. *On the Death of Dr. Swift, 512*

14 He put this engine [*a watch*] to our ears, which made an incessant noise like that of a water-mill; and we conjecture it is either some unknown animal, or the god that he worships. *Gulliver's Travels, Voyage to Lilliput, Ch. 2*

15 Big-endians and small-endians. *Ib, Ch. 4*

16 I cannot but conclude the bulk of your natives to be the most pernicious race of little odious vermin that nature ever suffered to crawl upon the surface of the earth. *Ib, Voyage to Brobdingnag, Ch. 6*

1 Whoever could make two ears of corn or two blades of grass to grow upon a spot of ground where only one grew before would deserve better of mankind and do more essential service to his country than the whole race of politicians put together. *Gulliver's Travels, Voyage to Brobdingnag, Ch. 7*

2 Proper words in proper places make the true definition of a style.
Letter to a young clergyman, 9 Jan. 1720

3 Hail fellow, well met,
All dirty and wet:
Find out, if you can,
Who's master, who's man. *My Lady's Lamentation*

4 So, naturalists observe, a flea
Hath smaller fleas that on him prey,
And these have smaller fleas to bite 'em,
And so proceed *ad infinitum.* *On Poetry, 337*

5 Promises and pie-crust are made to be broken. *Polite Conversation, 1*

6 The sight of you is good for sore eyes. *Ib*

7 What though his head be empty, provided his common-place book be full.
A Tale of a Tub, Digression in Praise of Digression

8 We have just enough religion to make us hate, but not enough to make us love one another. *Thoughts on Various Subjects*

9 Few are qualified to shine in company; but it is in most men's power to be agreeable. *Ib*

10 A nice man is a man of nasty ideas. *Ib*

11 *Ubi saeva indignatio ulterius cor lacerare nequit*—Where burning indignation no longer lacerates his heart. *Swift's Epitaph*

12 I shall be like that tree, I shall die at the top. *Attributed*

13 Good God! What a genius I had when I wrote that book.
[*A Tale of a Tub*] *Attributed*

SWINBURNE, Algernon Charles, 1837–1909

14 When the hounds of spring are on winter's traces,
The mother of months in meadow or plain
Fills the shadows and windy places
With lisp of leaves and ripple of rain. *Atalanta in Calydon*

15 Before the beginning of years
There came to the making of man
Time, with a gift of tears,
Grief, with a glass that ran. *Ib*

16 Shall I strew on thee rose or rue or laurel,
Brother, on this that was the veil of thee? *Ave Atque Vale*

17 Could you hurt me, sweet lips, though I hurt you?
Men touch them, and change in a trice
The lilies and languors of virtue
For the raptures and roses of vice. *Dolores*

18 I am tired of tears and laughter,
And men that laugh and weep;
Of what may come hereafter
For men that sow to reap. *The Garden of Proserpine*

1 From too much love of living,
From hope and fear set free,
We thank with brief thanksgiving
Whatever gods may be
That no life lives for ever;
That dead men rise up never;
That even the weariest river
Winds somewhere safe to sea. *The Garden of Proserpine*

2 Glory to Man in the Highest! for Man is the master of things. *Hymn of Man*

3 I have lived long enough, having seen one thing, that love hath an end;
Goddess and maiden and queen, be near me now and befriend.
Hymn to Proserpine

4 Laurel is green for a season, and love is sweet for a day;
But love grows bitter with treason, and laurel outlives not May. *Ib*

5 Rise ere the dawn be risen;
Come, and be all souls fed;
From field and street and prison
Come, for the feast is spread;
Live, for the truth is living; wake, for night is dead. *A Marching Song*

6 I will go back to the great sweet mother,
Mother and lover of men, the sea.
I will go down to her, I and no other,
Close with her, kiss her and mix her with me. *The Triumph of Time*

SYNGE, John Millington, 1871–1909

7 When I was writing 'The Shadow of the Glen' I got more aid than any learning could have given me from a chink in the floor of the old Wicklow house where I was staying, that let me hear what was being said by the servant girls in the kitchen. *The Playboy of the Western World, Preface*

TACITUS, 55?–117? A.D.

8 *Ubi solitudinem faciunt pacem appellant.*—They create desolation and call it peace. *Agricola, 30*

9 *Proprium humani ingenii est odisse quem laeseris.*—It is human nature to hate the man whom you have hurt. *Ib*

TALLEYRAND, Charles Maurice de, 1754–1838

10 *C'est le commencement de la fin.*—It is the beginning of the end.
Remark to Napoleon, 1813

11 *Noir comme le diable,*
Chaud comme l'enfer,
Pur comme un ange,
Doux comme l'amour.

Black as the devil,
Hot as hell,
Pure as an angel,
Sweet as love. *Recipe for coffee*

12 *Ils n'ont rien appris, ni rien oublié.*—They have learnt nothing, and forgotten nothing. *Attributed*

1 *La parole a été donnée à l'homme pour déguiser sa pensée.*—Speech was given to man to disguise his thoughts. *Attributed*

2 *Pas trop de zèle.*—Not too much zeal. *Attributed*

3 War is much too serious a thing to be left to military men. *Attributed*

TATE, Nahum, 1652–1715

4 While shepherds watched their flocks by night,
All seated on the ground,
The Angel of the Lord came down,
And glory shone around.

'Fear not,' said he, for mighty dread
Had seized their troubled mind;
'Glad tidings of great joy I bring
To you and all mankind'. *While Shepherds Watched*

TAYLOR, Jane, 1783–1827

5 Twinkle, twinkle, little star,
How I wonder what you are!
Up above the world so high,
Like a diamond in the sky. *The Star*

TENNYSON, Alfred, 1st Baron, 1809–1892

6 O for the touch of a vanish'd hand,
And the sound of a voice that is still! *Break, Break, Break*

7 A happy bridesmaid makes a happy bride. *The Bridesmaid, 4*

8 For men may come and men may go
But I go on for ever. *The Brook, 33*

9 Half a league, half a league,
Half a league onward,
All in the valley of Death
Rode the six hundred. *The Charge of the Light Brigade, 1*

10 'Forward, the Light Brigade!'
Was there a man dismay'd? *Ib, 2*

11 Their's not to make reply,
Their's not to reason why,
Their's but to do and die. *Ib, 2*

12 Into the jaws of Death
Into the mouth of Hell. *Ib, 3*

13 Sunset and evening star,
And one clear call for me!
And may there be no moaning of the bar
When I put out to sea. *Crossing the Bar*

14 The spacious times of great Elizabeth
With sounds that echo still. *A Dream of Fair Women, 7*

15 A daughter of the gods, divinely tall,
And most divinely fair. *Ib, 87*

1 He clasps the crag with crooked hands;
Close to the sun in lonely lands,
Ring'd with the azure world, he stands.

The wrinkled sea beneath him crawls;
He watches from his mountain walls,
And like a thunderbolt he falls. *The Eagle*

2 God made the woman for the man,
And for the good and increase of the world. *Edwin Morris, 43*

3 Then she rode forth, clothed on with chastity. *Godiva, 53*

4 His honour rooted in dishonour stood,
And faith unfaithful kept him falsely true. *Idylls of the King, Lancelot and Elaine, 871*

5 He makes no friend who never made a foe. *Ib, 1082*

6 For men at most differ as Heaven and Earth,
But women, worst and best, as Heaven and Hell. *Ib, Merlin and Vivien, 812*

7 The days darken round me, and the years,
Among new men, strange faces, other minds. *Ib, The Passing of Arthur, 405*

8 And slowly answer'd Arthur from the barge:
'The old order changeth, yielding place to new,
And God fulfils himself in many ways.' *Ib, 407*

9 Pray for my soul. More things are wrought by prayer
Than this world dreams of. *Ib, 415*

10 Our little systems have their day;
They have their day and cease to be. *In Memoriam A.H.H., Prologue*

11 Men may rise on stepping-stones
Of their dead selves to higher things. *Ib, 1*

12 For words, like Nature, half reveal
And half conceal the Soul within. *Ib, 5*

13 I hold it true, whate'er befall;
I feel it, when I sorrow most;
'Tis better to have loved and lost
Than never to have loved at all. *Ib, 27*

14 Be near me when my light is low,
When the blood creeps, and the nerves prick
And tingle; and the heart is sick,
And all the wheels of Being slow. *Ib, 50*

15 Oh yet we trust that somehow good
Will be the final goal of ill. *Ib, 54*

16 Are God and Nature then at strife
That Nature lends such evil dreams?
So careful of the type she seems,
So careless of the single life. *Ib, 55*

17 Nature, red in tooth and claw. *Ib, 56*

18 Fresh from brawling courts
And dusty purlieus of the law. *Ib, 89*

1 There lives more faith in honest doubt,
Believe me, than in half the creeds. *In Memoriam, A.H.H., 96*

2 He seems so near and yet so far. *Ib, 97*

3 Ring out, wild bells, to the wild sky. *Ib, 106*

4 Ring out the old, ring in the new,
Ring, happy bells, across the snow:
The year is going, let him go;
Ring out the false, ring in the true. *Ib, 106*

5 Ring out a slowly dying cause,
And ancient forms of party strife;
Ring in the nobler modes of life,
With sweeter manners, purer laws. *Ib, 106*

6 Ring out the thousand wars of old,
Ring in the thousand years of peace. *Ib, 106*

7 Ring in the valiant man and free,
The larger heart, the kindlier hand;
Ring out the darkness of the land,
Ring in the Christ that is to be. *Ib, 106*

8 And thus he bore without abuse
The grand old name of gentleman,
Defamed by every charlatan,
And soil'd with all ignoble use. *Ib, 111*

9 One God, one law, one element,
And one far-off divine event,
To which the whole creation moves. *Ib, 131*

10 Kind hearts are more than coronets,
And simple faith than Norman blood. *Lady Clara Vere de Vere*

11 On either side the river lie
Long fields of barley and of rye,
That clothe the wold and meet the sky;
And thro' the field the road runs by
To many-tower'd Camelot. *The Lady of Shalott, 1*

12 Willows whiten, aspens quiver,
Little breezes dusk and shiver. *Ib*

13 'The curse is come upon me,' cried
The Lady of Shalott. *Ib, 3*

14 Comrades, leave me here a little, while as yet 'tis early morn:
Leave me here, and when you want me, sound upon the bugle-horn.
Locksley Hall, 1

15 In the Spring a young man's fancy lightly turns to thoughts of love.
Ib, 20

16 For I dipt into the future, far as human eye could see,
Saw the Vision of the world, and all the wonder that would be. *Ib, 116*

17 Till the war-drum throbb'd no longer, and the battle-flags were furl'd
In the Parliament of man, the Federation of the world. *Ib, 127*

18 Knowledge comes, but wisdom lingers. *Ib, 141*

19 Woman is the lesser man, and all thy passions, match'd with mine
Are as moonlight unto sunlight, and as water unto wine. *Ib, 151*

1 They came upon a land
In which it seemed always afternoon. *The Lotos-Eaters*

2 Music that gentlier on the spirit lies,
Than tir'd eyelids upon tir'd eyes. *Ib*

3 Come into the garden, Maud,
For the black bat, night, has flown,
Come into the garden, Maud,
I am here at the gate alone. *Maud, Part 1, 22*

4 There has fallen a splendid tear
From the passion-flower at the gate.
She is coming, my dove, my dear;
She is coming, my life, my fate. *Ib, 22*

5 O that 'twere possible
After long grief and pain
To find the arms of my true love
Round me once again! *Ib, Part 2, 4*

6 You must wake and call me early, call me early, mother dear. *The May Queen*

7 For I'm to be Queen of the May. *Ib*

8 Follow the Gleam. *Merlin and the Gleam*

9 The last great Englishman is low. *Ode on the Death of the Duke of Wellington, 3*

10 O fall'n at length that tower of strength
Which stood four-square to all the winds that blew! *Ib*

11 Not once or twice in our rough island-story,
The path of duty was the way to glory. *Ib, 8*

12 With prudes for proctors, dowagers for deans,
And sweet girl-graduates in their golden hair. *The Princess, Prologue, 141*

13 Sweet and low, sweet and low,
Wind of the Western Sea. *Ib, 3, Song*

14 The splendour falls on castle walls
And snowy summits old in story. *Ib, 4, Song*

15 Blow, bugle, blow, set the wild echoes flying,
Blow, bugle; answer, echoes, dying, dying, dying. *Ib*

16 Tears, idle tears, I know not what they mean,
Tears from the depth of some divine despair. *Ib, 2nd Song*

17 Man is the hunter; woman is his game:
The sleek and shining creatures of the chase,
We hunt them for the beauty of their skins. *Ib, 5, 147*

18 Man for the field and woman for the hearth:
Man for the sword and for the needle she:
Man with the head and woman with the heart:
Man to command and woman to obey:
All else confusion. *Ib, 5, 427*

19 My strength is as the strength of ten,
Because my heart is pure. *Sir Galahad*

TERENCE, 190?–159? B.C.

1 *Hinc illae lacrimae.*—Hence these tears. *Andria, 126*

2 *Amantium irae amoris integratio est.*—Lovers' quarrels are the renewal of love. *Ib, 555*

3 *Fortis fortuna adiuvat.*—Fortune favours the brave. *Phormio, 203*

4 *Quot homines tot sententiae.*—So many men, so many opinions. *Ib, 454*

THACKERAY, William Makepeace, 1811–1863

5 It is impossible, in our condition of society, not to be sometimes a Snob. *The Book of Snobs, Ch. 3*

6 'Tis not the dying for a faith that's so hard, Master Harry—every man of every nation has done that—'tis the living up to it that is difficult. RICHARD STEELE *Henry Esmond, Bk. 1, Ch. 6*

7 'Tis strange what a man may do, and a woman yet think him an angel. *Ib, Ch. 7*

8 The *Pall Mall Gazette* is written by gentlemen for gentlemen. *Pendennis, Ch. 32*

9 A woman with fair opportunities and without a positive hump, may marry whom she likes. *Vanity Fair, Ch. 4*

10 Whenever he met a great man he grovelled before him and my-lorded him as only a free-born Englishman can do. *Ib, Ch. 13*

11 Them's my sentiments. FRED BULLOCK *Ib, Ch. 21*

12 I think I could be a good woman if I had five thousand a year. BECKY SHARP *Ib, Ch. 36*

THOMAS, Brandon, 1857–1914

13 I'm Charley's aunt from Brazil, where the nuts come from. LORD FANCOURT BABERLEY *Charley's Aunt, Act 1*

THOMAS, Dylan, 1914–1953

14 And death shall have no dominion.
Dead men naked they shall be one
With the man in the wind and the west moon.
And Death shall have no Dominion

15 Do not go gentle into that good night,
Old age should burn and rave at close of day;
Rage, rage, against the dying of the light.
Do not go gentle into that good night

16 The force that through the green fuse drives the flower
Drives my green age. *The Force that through the green Fuse drives the Flower*

17 The hand that signed the treaty bred a fever,
And famine grew, and locusts came;
Great is the hand that holds dominion over
Man by a scribbled name. *The Hand that Signed the Paper*

18 Light breaks where no sun shines;
Where no sea runs, the waters of the heart
Push in their tides. *Light Breaks where no Sun Shines*

1 After the first death, there is no other. *A Refusal to Mourn the Death, by Fire, of a Child in London*

2 It is spring, moonless night in the small town, starless and bible-black. FIRST VOICE *Under Milk Wood*

3 It is night neddying among the snuggeries of babies. FIRST VOICE *Ib*

4 You're thinking, you're no better than you should be, Polly, and that's good enough for me. Oh, isn't life a terrible thing, thank God? POLLY GARTER *Ib*

5 Praise the Lord! We are a musical nation. REV. ELI JENKINS *Ib*

6 Organ Morgan, you haven't been listening to a word I said. It's organ organ all the time with you. MRS ORGAN MORGAN *Ib*

THOMPSON, Francis, 1859–1907

7 For the field is full of shades as I near the shadowy coast,
And a ghostly batsman plays to the bowling of a ghost,
And I look through my tears on a soundless-clapping host
As the run-stealers flicker to and fro,
To and fro:—
O my Hornby and my Barlow long ago! *At Lord's*

8 Nothing begins, and nothing ends,
That is not paid with moan;
For we are born in other's pain,
And perish in our own. *Daisy*

9 I fled Him, down the nights and down the days;
I fled Him, down the arches of the years. *The Hound of Heaven*

10 'Tis ye, 'tis your estrangèd faces,
That miss the many-splendour'd thing. *The Kingdom of God*

11 Look for me in the nurseries of Heaven. *To my Godchild*

THOMSON, James, 1700–1748

12 When Britain first, at Heaven's command,
Arose from out the azure main,
This was the charter of the land,
And guardian angels sung this strain:
'Rule, Britannia, rule the waves;
Britons never will be slaves.' *Alfred: A Masque, Act 2, Scene 5*

13 An elegant sufficiency, content,
Retirement, rural quiet, friendship, books,
Ease and alternate labour, useful life,
Progressive virtue, and approving Heaven! *The Seasons, Spring, 1161*

THOMSON, Roy Herbert, 1st Lord, 1894—

14 It is as good as having a Government licence to print money. *Remark on the profitability of commercial television in Great Britain, made during an interview in Canada*

THOREAU, Henry David, 1817–1862

15 The mass of men lead lives of quiet desperation. *Walden, Economy*

1 Our life is frittered away by detail . . . Simplify, simplify.
Walden, Where I Lived and What I Lived For

2 The government of the world I live in was not framed, like that of Britain, in after-dinner conversations over the wine. *Ib, Conclusion*

3 It takes two to speak the truth,—one to speak, and another to hear.
A Week on the Concord and Merrimack Rivers, Wednesday

4 Not that the story need be long, but it will take a long while to make it short.
Letter

THUCYDIDES, c. 471–c. 400 B.C.

5 It is great glory in a woman to show no more weakness than is natural to her sex, and not to be talked of, either for good or evil by men.
History, 2, 45, 2

THURBER, James, 1894–1961

6 Early to rise and early to bed makes a male healthy and wealthy and dead.
Fables for Our Time, The Shrike and the Chipmunks

7 All right, have it your way—you heard a seal bark. *Title of cartoon*

8 Well, if I called the wrong number, why did you answer the phone?
Title of cartoon

9 The War between Men and Women. *Title of series of cartoons*

TILZER, Harry, 1878–1956

10 Come, Come, Come and have a drink with me
Down at the old 'Bull and Bush'. *Song*

11 Come, Come, Come and make eyes at me. *Ib*

TOBIN, John, 1770–1804

12 The man that lays his hand upon a woman,
Save in the way of kindness, is a wretch
Whom 'twere gross flattery to name a coward. *The Honeymoon, Act 2, Scene 1*

TOLSTOY, Leo, 1828–1910

13 All happy families resemble one another, each unhappy family is unhappy in its own way. *Anna Karenina, 1, Ch. 1*

14 Pure and complete sorrow is as impossible as pure and complete joy.
War and Peace, 15, Ch. 1

TOPLADY, Augustus Montague, 1740–1778

15 Rock of Ages, cleft for me,
Let me hide myself in Thee. *Rock of Ages*

TRAHERNE, Thomas, 1637?–1674

16 You will never enjoy the world aright, till the sea itself floweth in your veins, till you are clothed with the heavens, and crowned with the stars.
Centuries of Meditation, 1, 29

17 The corn was orient and immortal wheat, which never should be reaped, nor was ever sown. I thought it had stood from everlasting to everlasting.
Ib, 3, 3

TRAPP, Joseph, 1679–1747

1 The King, observing with judicious eyes,
The state of both his universities,
To Oxford sent a troop of horse, and why?
That learned body wanted loyalty;
To Cambridge books, as very well discerning,
How much that loyal body wanted learning. *On George I's donation of a library to Cambridge University (For reply, see 60:4)*

TROLLOPE, Anthony, 1815–1882

2 It's dogged as does it. It ain't thinking about it. *Last Chronicle of Barset, Ch. 61*

3 Three hours a day will produce as much as a man ought to write. *Autobiography, Ch. 15*

TUER, Andrew White, 1838–1900

4 English as she is Spoke. *Title of Portuguese-English Conversation Guide*

TUSSER, Thomas, 1524?–1580

5 At Christmas play and make good cheer,
For Christmas comes but once a year. *Five Hundred Points of Good Husbandry, Ch. 12*

TWAIN, Mark (Samuel Langhorne Clemens), 1835–1910

6 There was things which he stretched, but mainly he told the truth. *The Adventures of Huckleberry Finn, Ch. 1*

7 *Pilgrim's Progress,* about a man that left his family, it didn't say why. I read considerable in it now and then. The statements was interesting but tough. *Ib, Ch. 17*

8 Deep down in me I knowed it was a lie, and He knowed it. You can't pray a lie—I found that out. *Ib, Ch. 21*

9 All Kings is mostly rapscallions. *Ib, Ch. 23*

10 There are three kinds of lies: lies, damned lies, and statistics. *Autobiography*

11 Soap and education are not as sudden as a massacre, but they are more deadly in the long run. *The Facts concerning the Recent Resignation*

12 I must have a prodigious quantity of mind; it takes me as much as a week, sometimes, to make it up. *The Innocents Abroad, Ch. 7*

13 They spell it Vinci and pronounce it Vinchy; foreigners always spell better than they pronounce. *Ib, Ch. 19*

14 Familiarity breeds contempt—and children. *Notebooks*

15 Adam was but human—this explains it all. He did not want the apple for the apple's sake, he wanted it only because it was forbidden. *Pudd'nhead Wilson's Calendar, Ch. 2*

16 Training is everything. The peach was once a bitter almond; cauliflower is nothing but cabbage with a college education. *Ib, Ch. 5*

17 One of the most striking differences between a cat and a lie is that a cat has only nine lives. *Ib, Ch. 7*

18 When angry, count four; when very angry, swear. *Ib, Ch. 10*

1 Nothing so needs reforming as other people's habits. *Pudd'nhead Wilson's Calendar, Ch. 15*

2 A classic is something that everybody wants to have read and nobody wants to read. *Speech, The Disappearance of Literature*

3 There ain't-a-going to *be* no core. *Tom Sawyer Abroad, Ch. 1*

4 Reports of my death are greatly exaggerated. *Cable to the Associated Press*

UNITED NATIONS

5 WE THE PEOPLES OF THE UNITED NATIONS DETERMINED

to save succeeding generations from the scourge of war, which twice in our lifetime has brought untold sorrow to mankind, and

to reaffirm faith in fundamental human rights, in the dignity and worth of the human person, in the equal rights of men and women and of nations large and small, and

to establish conditions under which justice and respect for the obligations arising from treaties and other sources of international law can be maintained, and

to promote social progress and better standards of life in larger freedom,

AND FOR THESE ENDS

to practise tolerance and live together in peace with one another as good neighbours and

to unite our strength to maintain international peace and security, and

to ensure, by the acceptance of principles and the institution of methods, that armed force shall not be used, save in the common interest, and

to employ international machinery for the promotion of the economic and social advancement of all peoples,

HAVE RESOLVED TO COMBINE OUR EFFORTS TO ACCOMPLISH THESE AIMS.

Preamble to United Nations Charter, 1945

UNWIN, Sir Stanley, 1884–1968

6 Much is written of the power of the Press, a power which may last but a day; by comparison, little is heard of the power of books, which may endure for generations. *The Truth about Publishing*

UPTON, Ralph R., 20th century

7 Stop; look; listen. *Notice at American railway crossings, 1912*

USTINOV, Peter, 1921—

8 THE PHOTOGRAPHER: The prisoners have been brought in, Your Excellency.

THE MARSHAL: Question them, promise them life, and then kill them. Let us have the honour of honourable men. Give them hope before you blacken their world. Lift them high in the air before you drop them.

The Moment of Truth, Act 3

9 You will find us only on the very best atlases, because we are the smallest country left in Europe . . . a self-respecting country which deserves and sometimes achieves a colour of its own on the map—usually a dyspeptic mint green, which misses the outline of the frontier by a fraction of an inch, so that one can almost hear the printer saying damn. THE GENERAL

Romanoff and Juliet, Act 1

1 As for being a General, well, at the age of four with paper hats and wooden swords we're all Generals. Only some of us never grow out of it.
THE GENERAL *Romanoff and Juliet, Act 1*

2 A diplomat these days is nothing but a head-waiter who's allowed to sit down occasionally. THE GENERAL *Ib*

VANBRUGH, Sir John, 1664–1726

3 The want of a thing is perplexing enough, but the possession of it is intolerable. CLARISSA *The Confederacy, Act 1, Scene 3*

4 Much of a muchness. JOHN MOODY *The Provok'd Husband, Act 1*

VAUGHAN, Henry, 1622–1695

5 They are all gone into the world of light,
And I alone sit lingering here. *Ascension Hymn*

6 Man is the shuttle, to whose winding quest
And passage through these looms
God order'd motion, but ordain'd no rest. *Man*

7 My soul, there is a country
Far beyond the stars. *Peace*

VEGETIUS, 4th century

8 *Qui desiderat pacem, praeparet bellum.*—Let him who desires peace, prepare for war. *De re mil., 3, Prologue*

VERLAINE, Paul, 1844–1896

9 *Et tout le reste est littérature.*—All the rest is just literature. *L'Art Poétique*

10 *Il pleure dans mon cœur*
Comme il pleut sur la ville.—Tears fall in my heart like rain on the town.
Romances sans paroles, 3

VICTORIA, Queen, 1819–1901

11 We are not amused. *Notebooks of a Spinster Lady, 2 Jan. 1900*

12 He [*Gladstone*] speaks to Me as If I was a public meeting. *Russell, Collections and Recollections, Ch. 14*

VIGNY, Alfred de, 1797–1863

13 *Hélas je suis, Seigneur, puissant et solitaire.*—Alas, Lord, I am powerful but alone. *Moïse*

14 *Seul le silence est grand; tout le reste est faiblesse.*—Only silence is great; all else is weakness. *La Mort du Loup*

VILLON, François, 1431–1485

15 *Mais où sont les neiges d'antan?*—But where are the snows of yesteryear?
Ballade des Dames du Temps Jadis

VIRGIL, 70–19 B.C.

16 *Arma virumque cano.* Arms and the man I sing. *Aeneid, 1, 1*

17 *Furor arma ministrat.* Anger supplies the arms. *Ib, 1, 150*

1 *Forsan et haec olim meminisse iuvabit.* Perhaps even these things will some day be pleasant to remember. *Aeneid, 1, 203*

2 *Timeo Danaos et dona ferentes.* I fear the Greeks, even when they bring gifts. *Ib, 2, 49*

3 *Varium et mutabile semper*
Femina.
Woman is always fickle and changing. *Ib, 4, 569*

4 *Facilis descensus Averni.* The way down to Hell is easy. *Ib, 6, 126*

5 *Omnia vincit amor, et nos cedamus amori.* Love conquers all, and we too succumb to love. *Ib, 10, 69*

6 *Labor omnia vicit*
Improbus et duris urgens in rebus egestas.
Persistent labour overcame all things, and the stress of need in a hard life. *Georgics, 1, 145*

7 *Felix qui potuit rerum cognoscere causas.* Happy is he who has been able to learn the causes of things. *Ib, 2, 490*

8 *Sed fugit interea, fugit inreparabile tempus.* Meanwhile, time is flying—flying, never to return. *Ib, 3, 284*

VOLTAIRE, François Marie Arouet, 1694–1778

9 *Tout est pour le mieux dans le meilleur des mondes possibles.* All is for the best in the best of possible worlds. *Candide, Ch. 1*

10 *Dans ce pays-ci il est bon de tuer de temps en temps un amiral pour encourager les autres.* In this country [*England*] it is good to kill an admiral from time to time, to encourage the others. *Ib, Ch. 23*

11 *Cela est bien dit, répondit Candide, mais il faut cultiver notre jardin.* 'That is well said,' replied Candide, 'but we must cultivate our garden.' *Ib, Ch. 30*

12 *Ils ne se servent de la pensée que pour autoriser leurs injustices, et n'emploient les paroles que pour déguiser leurs pensées.* Men use thought only to justify their wrong-doing, and words only to conceal their thoughts. *Dialogue 14, Le Chapon et la Poularde*

13 *Le mieux est l'ennemi du bien.* The best is the enemy of the good. *Dictionnaire Philosophique, Art Dramatique*

14 *Si Dieu n'existait pas, il faudrait l'inventer.* If God did not exist, it would be necessary to invent Him. *Épîtres, 96, A L'Auteur du livre des Trois Imposteurs*

15 *L'histoire des grands événements de ce monde n'est guère que l'histoire des crimes.* The history of the great events of this world is scarcely more than the history of crimes. *Essai sur les Mœurs et L'Esprit des Nations, 23*

16 *Ce corps qui s'appelait et qui s'appelle encore le saint empire romain n'était en aucune manière ni saint, ni romain, ni empire.* This agglomeration which was called and which still calls itself the Holy Roman Empire was neither holy, nor Roman, nor an empire. *Ib, 70*

17 *On dit que Dieu est toujours pour les gros bataillons.* It is said that God is always for the big battalions. *Letter to M. le Riche, 1770*

18 I disapprove of what you say, but I will defend to the death your right to say it. *Attributed*

WALLER, Edmund, 1606–1687

1 Go, lovely Rose!
Tell her that wastes her time and me,
That now she knows
When I resemble her to thee,
How sweet and fair she seems to be. *Go, Lovely Rose*

2 Poets that lasting marble seek
Must carve in Latin or in Greek. *Of English Verse*

WALPOLE, Sir Robert, 1st Earl of Orford, 1676–1745

3 The balance of power. *Speech, House of Commons, 1741*

4 All those men have their price. *W. Coxe, Memoirs of Walpole*

5 Anything but history, for history must be false. *Walpoliana*

WALPOLE, Horace, 4th Earl of Orford, 1717–1797

6 It is charming to totter into vogue. *Letter to G. A. Selwyn, 1765*

7 The world is a comedy to those who think, a tragedy to those who feel. *Letter to Sir Horace Mann, 1769*

8 Prognostics do not always prove prophecies,—at least the wisest prophets make sure of the event first. *Letter to Thomas Walpole, 1785*

WALTON, Izaak, 1593–1683

9 We may say of angling as Dr Boteler said of strawberries, 'Doubtless God could have made a better berry, but doubtless God never did.' *The Compleat Angler, Ch. 5*

WARD, Artemus (Charles Farrar Browne), 1834–1867

10 My pollertics, like my religion, being of an exceedin' accommodatin' character. *Artemus Ward His Book, The Crisis*

11 Did you ever have the measels, and if so how many? *Ib, The Census*

12 I prefer temperance hotels—although they sell worse kinds of liquor than any other kind of hotels. *Artemus Ward's Lecture*

13 Why is this thus? What is the reason of this thusness? *Ib*

14 I am happiest when I am idle. I could live for months without performing any kind of labour, and at the expiration of that time I should feel fresh and vigorous enough to go right on in the same way for numerous more months. *Pyrotechny*

15 Let us all be happy and live within our means, even if we have to borrer the money to do it with. *Science and Natural History*

WASHINGTON, George, 1752–1799

16 It is our true policy to steer clear of permanent alliances with any portion of the foreign world. *Farewell Address, 17 Sept. 1796*

17 Associate yourself with men of good quality if you esteem your own reputation; for 'tis better to be alone than in bad company. *Rules of Civility*

18 Father, I cannot tell a lie. I did it with my little hatchet. *Attributed*

WATTS, Isaac, 1674–1748

1 How doth the little busy bee
Improve each shining hour,
And gather honey all the day
From every opening flower. *Against Idleness*

2 For Satan finds some mischief still
For idle hands to do. *Ib*

3 Birds in their little nests agree;
And 'tis a shameful sight,
When children of one family
Fall out, and chide, and fight. *Love between Brothers and Sisters*

4 O God, our help in ages past,
Our hope for years to come,
Our shelter from the stormy blast,
And our eternal home. *O God, our help in ages past*

5 A thousand ages in thy sight
Are like an evening gone,
Short as the watch that ends the night
Before the rising sun. *Ib*

6 Time, like an ever-rolling stream,
Bears all its sons away;
They fly forgotten, as a dream
Dies at the opening day. *Ib*

7 'Tis the voice of the sluggard, I heard him complain:
'You have waked me too soon, I must slumber again.' *The Sluggard*

WEBB, Sidney, 1st Baron Passfield, 1859–1947

8 The inevitability of gradualness. *Presidential Address to Labour Party Conference, 1923*

WEBSTER, Daniel, 1782–1852

9 Let our object be our country, our whole country and nothing but our country. *Speech, Bunker Hill, 17 June 1825*

10 Liberty and Union, now and for ever, one and inseparable. *Speech, 26 Jan. 1830*

11 I was born an American; I will live an American; I shall die an American. *Speech, 17 July 1850*

12 There is always room at the top. *When advised not to become a lawyer, as there were already too many*

WEBSTER, John, 1580?–1625?

13 I am Duchess of Malfi still. *The Duchess of Malfi, Act 4, Scene 2*

14 Glories, like glow-worms, afar off shine bright,
But looked to near, have neither heat nor light. BOSOLA *Ib*

15 Other sins only speak; murder shrieks out. BOSOLA *Ib*

16 Cover her face: mine eyes dazzle: she died young. FERDINAND *Ib*

17 We are merely the stars' tennis balls, struck and bandied
Which way please them. BOSOLA *Ib, Act 5, Scene 4*

1 Is not old wine wholesomest, old pippins toothsomest, old wood burn brightest, old linen wash whitest? Old soldiers, sweethearts, are surest, and old lovers are soundest. BIRDLIME *Westward Hoe, Act 2, Scene 2*

2 I saw him even now going the way of all flesh, that is to say towards the kitchen. BIRDLIME *Ib*

3 Call for the robin redbreast, and the wren,
Since o'er shady groves they hover,
And with leaves and flowers do cover
The friendless bodies of unburied men. CORNELIA *The White Devil, Act 5, Scene 4*

4 My soul, like to a ship in a black storm,
Is driven, I know not whither. VITTORIA *Ib, Scene 6*

5 I have caught
An everlasting cold; I have lost my voice
Most irrecoverably. FLAMINEO *Ib*

WELLINGTON, Arthur Wellesley, 1st Duke of, 1769–1852

6 Nothing except a battle lost can be half so melancholy as a battle won. *Dispatch, 1815*

7 I used to say of him [*Napoleon*] that his presence on the field made the difference of forty thousand men. *Stanhope, Notes of Conversations with the Duke of Wellington, 2 Nov. 1831*

8 Ours [*our army*] is composed of the scum of the earth. *Ib, 4 Nov. 1831*

9 Up, Guards, and at 'em. *Waterloo, 18 June 1815, Attributed*

10 The battle of Waterloo was won on the playing fields of Eton. *Attributed*

11 Publish and be damned. *Attributed*

WELLS, Herbert George, 1866–1946

12 He [*Mr. Polly*] broke into a quavering song: Roöötten Beëëastly Silly Hole! *The History of Mr. Polly, Ch. 1, 2*

13 'Sesquippledan,' he would say. 'Sesquippledan verboojuice.' *Ib, Ch. 1, 5*

14 I was thinking jest what a Rum Go everything is. *Kipps, Bk. 2, Ch. 3, 8*

15 In England we have come to rely upon a comfortable time-lag of fifty years or a century intervening between the perception that something ought to be done and a serious attempt to do it. *The Work, Wealth and Happiness of Mankind, Ch. 11*

16 The Shape of Things to Come. *Title of Book*

WESKER, Arnold, 1932—

17 God in heaven, Mother, you live in the country but you got no—no—no majesty. You spend your time among green fields, you grow flowers and you breathe fresh air and you got no majesty. You go on and you go on talking and talking so your mind's cluttered up with nothing and you shut out the world. What kind of life did you give me? BEATIE BRYANT *Roots, Act 2, Scene 2*

18 Education ent only books and music—it's asking questions, all the time. There are millions of us, all over the country and no one, not one of us, is asking questions, we're all taking the easiest way out. Everyone I ever worked with took the easiest way out. We don't fight for anything, we're so mentally lazy we might as well be dead! BEATIE BRYANT *Ib, Act 3*

WESLEY, Charles, 1707–1788

1 Gentle Jesus, meek and mild,
Look upon a little child;
Pity my simplicity,
Suffer me to come to thee. *Gentle Jesus, Meek and Mild*

2 Hark! the herald Angels sing
Glory to the new-born King;
Peace on earth and mercy mild,
God and sinners reconciled. *Hark! the Herald Angels sing*

3 Love Divine, all loves excelling,
Joy of heaven, to earth come down,
Fix in us thy humble dwelling,
All thy faithful mercies crown.
Jesu, thou art all compassion,
Pure unbounded love thou art;
Visit us with thy salvation,
Enter every trembling heart. *Love Divine, All Loves Excelling*

WESLEY, John, 1703–1791

4 I look upon all the world as my parish. *Journal, 11 June 1739*

WEST, Mae, 1893—

5 Come up and see me sometime. *Diamond Lil*

WHISTLER, James Abbott McNeill, 1834–1903

6 I am not arguing with you—I am telling you. *The Gentle Art of Making Enemies*

7 OSCAR WILDE: I wish I had said that.
WHISTLER: You will, Oscar, you will. *L. C. Ingleby, Oscar Wilde*

WHITE, E. B., 1899—

8 Commuter—one who spends his life
In riding to and from his wife;
A man who shaves and takes a train,
And then rides back to shave again. *The Commuter*

WHITMAN, Walt, 1819–1892

9 Women sit or move to and fro, some old, some young,
The young are beautiful—but the old are more beautiful than the young.
Beautiful Women

10 I hear it was charged against me that I sought to destroy institutions,
But really I am neither for nor against institutions.
I Hear it was Charged Against Me

11 If anything is sacred the human body is sacred. *I Sing the Body Electric, 8*

12 O Captain! my Captain! our fearful trip is done,
The ship has weather'd every rack, the prize we sought is won,
The port is near, the bells I hear, the people all exulting.
O Captain! My Captain!

13 I celebrate myself, and sing myself,
And what I assume you shall assume. *Song of Myself, 1*

1 I loafe and invite my soul. *Song of Myself, 1*

2 I think I could turn and live with animals, they're so placid and self-contain'd,
I stand and look at them long and long. *Ib, 32*

3 Behold, I do not give lectures or a little charity,
When I give I give myself. *Ib, 40*

4 I have said that the soul is not more than the body,
And I have said that the body is not more than the soul,
And nothing, not God, is greater to one than one's self is. *Ib, 48*

5 Do I contradict myself?
Very well then I contradict myself,
(I am large, I contain multitudes). *Ib, 51*

WHITTIER, John Greenleaf, 1807–1892

6 Oh, rank is good, and gold is fair,
And high and low mate ill;
But love has never known a law
Beyond its own sweet will! *Amy Wentworth*

7 'Shoot, if you must, this old gray head,
But spare your country's flag,' she said. *Barbara Frietchie*

8 For all sad words of tongue or pen,
The saddest are these: 'It might have been!' *Maud Muller*

WILCOX, Ella Wheeler, 1850–1919

9 Laugh, and the world laughs with you;
Weep, and you weep alone,
For the sad old earth must borrow its mirth,
But has trouble enough of its own. *Solitude*

10 Feast, and your halls are crowded;
Fast, and the world goes by. *Ib*

11 So many gods, so many creeds,
So many paths that wind and wind,
When just the art of being kind
Is all this sad world needs. *The World's Need*

WILDE, Oscar Fingall O'Flahertie Wills, 1856–1900

12 Yet each man kills the thing he loves,
By each let this be heard,
Some do it with a bitter look,
Some with a flattering word.
The coward does it with a kiss,
The brave man with a sword! *The Ballad of Reading Gaol, 1, 7*

13 Something was dead in each of us,
And what was dead was Hope. *Ib, 3, 31*

14 For he who lives more lives than one
More deaths than one must die. *Ib, 3, 37*

15 I know not whether Laws be right
Or whether Laws be wrong;
All that we know who live in gaol

Is that the wall is strong;
And that each day is like a year,
A year whose days are long. *The Ballad of Reading Gaol, 5, 1*

1 The man who sees both sides of a question is a man who sees absolutely nothing at all. *The Critic as Artist, Part 2*

2 A little sincerity is a dangerous thing, and a great deal of it is absolutely fatal. *Ib*

3 Ah! don't say you agree with me. When people agree with me I always feel that I must be wrong. *Ib*

4 There is no sin except stupidity. *Ib*

5 To love oneself is the beginning of a lifelong romance. LORD GORING *An Ideal Husband, Act 3*

6 Really, if the lower orders don't set us a good example, what on earth is the use of them? ALGERNON *The Importance of Being Earnest, Act 1*

7 The truth is rarely pure and never simple. Modern life would be very tedious if it were either, and modern literature a complete impossibility! ALGERNON *Ib, 1*

8 I have invented an invaluable permanent invalid called Bunbury, in order that I may be able to go down into the country whenever I choose. ALGERNON *Ib, 1*

9 The amount of women in London who flirt with their own husbands is perfectly scandalous. It looks so bad. It is simply washing one's clean linen in public. ALGERNON *Ib, 1*

10 In married life three is company and two is none. ALGERNON *Ib, 1*

11 I do not approve of anything that tampers with natural ignorance. Ignorance is like a delicate exotic fruit; touch it, and the bloom is gone. LADY BRACKNELL *Ib, 1*

12 To lose one parent, Mr. Worthing, may be regarded as a misfortune; to lose both looks like carelessness. LADY BRACKNELL *Ib, 1*

13 JACK: In a hand-bag.
LADY BRACKNELL: A hand-bag?
JACK: Yes, Lady Bracknell. It was in a hand-bag—a somewhat large, black leather hand-bag, with handles to it—an ordinary hand-bag in fact. *Ib, 1*

14 LADY BRACKNELL: The cloak-room at Victoria Station?
JACK: Yes. The Brighton line.
LADY BRACKNELL: The line is immaterial. *Ib, 1*

15 Memory, my dear Cecily, is the diary we all carry about with us. MISS PRISM *Ib, Act 2*

16 I never travel without my diary. One should always have something sensational to read in the train. GWENDOLEN FAIRFAX *Ib, 2*

17 No woman should ever be quite accurate about her age. It looks so calculating. LADY BRACKNELL *Ib, Act 3*

18 It is a terrible thing for a man to find out suddenly that all his life he has been speaking nothing but the truth. JACK *Ib, 3*

19 Please do not shoot the pianist. He is doing his best. *Impressions of America, Leadville*

1 It is absurd to divide people into good and bad. People are either charming or tedious. LORD DARLINGTON *Lady Windermere's Fan, Act 1*

2 I can resist everything except temptation. LORD DARLINGTON *Ib, 1*

3 Scandal is gossip made tedious by morality. CECIL GRAHAM *Ib, Act 3*

4 CECIL GRAHAM: What is a cynic?
LORD DARLINGTON: A man who knows the price of everything and the value of nothing. *Ib, 3*

5 All Art is quite useless. *The Picture of Dorian Gray, Preface*

6 There is only one thing in the world worse than being talked about, and that is not being talked about. *Ib, 1*

7 The only way to get rid of a temptation is to yield to it. *Ib, 2*

8 MRS ALLONBY: They say, Lady Hunstanton, that when good Americans die they go to Paris.
LADY HUNSTANTON: Indeed? And when bad Americans die, where do they go?
LORD ILLINGWORTH: Oh, they go to America.
A Woman of No Importance, Act 1

9 The youth of America is their oldest tradition. It has been going on now for three hundred years. LORD ILLINGWORTH *Ib, 1*

10 One knows so well the popular idea of health. The English country gentleman galloping after a fox—the unspeakable in full pursuit of the uneatable. LORD ILLINGWORTH *Ib, 1*

11 We in the House of Lords are never in touch with public opinion. That makes us a civilised body. LORD ILLINGWORTH *Ib, 1*

12 One should never trust a woman who tells one her real age. A woman who would tell one that, would tell one anything. LORD ILLINGWORTH *Ib, 1*

13 LORD ILLINGWORTH: People's mothers always bore me to death. All women become like their mothers. That is their tragedy.
MRS ALLONBY: No man does. That is his. *Ib, 2*

14 Moderation is a fatal thing, Lady Hunstanton. Nothing succeeds like excess. LORD ILLINGWORTH *Ib, 3*

15 No woman should have a memory. Memory in a woman is the beginning of dowdiness. LORD ILLINGWORTH *Ib, 3*

16 I have nothing to declare except my genius. *At New York Custom House*

17 I suppose that I shall have to die beyond my means. [*When asked a large fee for an operation*] *Sherard, Life of Wilde*

18 Work is the curse of the drinking classes. *Attributed*

WILLIAM III of England, 1650–1702

19 I will die in the last ditch. *Quoted in Hume's History of England*

20 Every bullet has its billet. *John Wesley, Journal, 6 June 1765*

WILLIAM OF WYKEHAM, 1324–1404

21 Manners maketh man. *Motto of his foundations, Winchester College and New College, Oxford*

WILLIAMS, Harry, 1874–1924, and JUDGE, Jack, 1878–1938

1 It's a long way to Tipperary, it's a long way to go;
It's a long way to Tipperary, to the sweetest girl I know!
Good-bye, Piccadilly, farewell, Leicester Square,
It's a long, long way to Tipperary, but my heart's right there! *Tipperary*

WILLIAMS, W., 1717–1791

2 Guide me, O thou great Redeemer,
Pilgrim through this barren land;
I am weak, but thou art mighty,
Hold me with thy powerful hand:
Bread of heaven,
Feed me till I want no more. *Guide me, O thou great Redeemer*

WILLS, William Gorman, 1828–1891

3 I'll sing thee songs of Araby,
And Tales of fair Cashmere. *Lalla Rookh*

WILSON, Charles Erwin, 1890–1961

4 I thought what was good for the country was good for General Motors and vice versa. *Statement to U.S. Congressional Committee, 23 Jan. 1953*

WILSON, Harriette, 1789–1846

5 I shall not say why and how I became, at the age of fifteen, the mistress of the Earl of Craven. *Memoirs, Opening words*

WILSON, John, see NORTH, Christopher

WILSON, Sandy, 1924—

6 I could be happy with you. *The Boy Friend, Title of Song*

WILSON, Thomas Woodrow, 1856–1924

7 There is such a thing as a man being too proud to fight. *Speech, 10 May 1915*

8 America cannot be an ostrich with its head in the sand. *Speech, 1 Feb. 1916*

9 The world must be made safe for democracy. *Speech, 2 April 1917*

WITHER, George, 1588–1667

10 I loved a lass, a fair one,
As fair as e'er was seen;
She was indeed a rare one,
Another Sheba Queen. *I Loved a Lass*

11 Shall I, wasting in despair,
Die because a woman's fair?
Or make pale my cheeks with care,
'Cause another's rosy are? *The Lover's Resolution*

1 If she love me, this believe,
I will die ere she shall grieve;
If she slight me when I woo;
I can scorn and let her go;
For if she be not for me,
What care I for whom she be? *The Lover's Resolution*

WODEHOUSE, Pelham Grenville, 1881—1975

2 He spoke with a certain what-is-it in his voice, and I could see that, if not actually disgruntled, he was far from being gruntled. *The Code of the Woosters*

WOLFE, Charles, 1791–1823

3 Not a drum was heard, not a funeral note,
As his corse to the rampart we hurried;
Not a soldier discharged his farewell shot
O'er the grave where our hero we buried. *The Burial of Sir John Moore at Corunna, 1*

4 We carved not a line, and we raised not a stone,
But we left him alone with his glory. *Ib, 31*

WOLFE, James, 1727–1759

5 I would rather have written that poem, [*Gray's Elegy*], gentlemen, than take Quebec. *The night before he was killed in battle at Quebec*

WOLSEY, Thomas, Cardinal, 1475?–1530

6 Had I but served God as diligently as I have served the king, he would not have given me over in my gray hairs. *To Sir William Kingston*

WOOD, Mrs Henry, 1814–1887

7 Dead! and . . . never called me mother. *East Lynne, dramatized version*

WOOLCOTT, Alexander, 1887–1943

8 I must get out of these wet clothes and into a dry Martini. *Attributed*
(*Also attributed to Robert Benchley and Billy Wilder*)

WOOLF, Virginia, 1882–1941

9 A Room of One's Own. *Title of Book*

WORDSWORTH, Elizabeth, 1840–1932

10 If all the good people were clever,
And all clever people were good,
The world would be wiser than ever
We thought that it possibly could.
But somehow 'tis seldom or never
The two hit it off as they should;
The good are so harsh to the clever,
The clever so rude to the good! *Good and Clever*

WORDSWORTH, William, 1770–1850

11 Give all thou canst; high Heaven rejects the lore
Of nicely-calculated less or more. *Ecclesiastical Sonnets, Pt. 3, 43, King's College Chapel*

1 The light that never was, on sea or land,
The consecration, and the Poet's dream. *Elegiac Stanzas suggested by a Picture of Peele Castle in a storm, 15*

2 A deep distress hath humanised my Soul. *Ib, 36*

3 On Man, on Nature, and on Human Life,
Musing in solitude. *The Excursion, Preface, 1*

4 Oh, Sir! the good die first,
And they whose hearts are dry as summer dust
Burn to the socket. *Ib, 1, 500*

5 Think you, 'mid all this mighty sum
Of things for ever speaking,
That nothing of itself will come,
But we must still be seeking? *Expostulation and Reply, 25*

6 I travelled among unknown men,
In lands beyond the sea;
Nor, England! did I know till then
What love I bore to thee. *I travelled among unknown men*

7 I wandered lonely as a cloud
That floats on high o'er vales and hills,
When all at once I saw a crowd,
A host, of golden daffodils;
Beside the lake, beneath the trees,
Fluttering and dancing in the breeze. *I wandered lonely as a Cloud, 1*

8 Continuous as the stars that shine
And twinkle on the milky way. *Ib, 7*

9 Ten thousand saw I at a glance,
Tossing their heads in sprightly dance. *Ib, 11*

10 A poet could not but be gay,
In such a jocund company. *Ib, 15*

11 For oft, when on my couch I lie
In vacant or in pensive mood,
They flash upon that inward eye
Which is the bliss of solitude. *Ib, 19*

12 There was a time when meadow, grove, and stream,
The earth, and every common sight,
To me did seem
Apparelled in celestial light,
The glory and the freshness of a dream. *Ode, Intimations of Immortality from Recollections of Early Childhood, Stanza 1*

13 The Rainbow comes and goes,
And lovely is the Rose. *Ib, Stanza 2*

14 The sunshine is a glorious birth;
But yet I know, where'er I go,
That there hath past away a glory from the earth. *Ib*

15 While the young lambs bound
As to the tabor's sound. *Ib, Stanza 3*

16 Whither is fled the visionary gleam?
Where is it now, the glory and the dream? *Ib, Stanza 4*

1 Our birth is but a sleep and a forgetting:
The Soul that rises with us, our life's Star,
Hath had elsewhere its setting,
And cometh from afar:
Not in entire forgetfulness,
And not in utter nakedness,
But trailing clouds of glory do we come
From God, who is our home:
Heaven lies about us in our infancy!
Shades of the prison-house begin to close
Upon the growing Boy. *Ode, Intimations of Immortality from Recollections of Early Childhood, Stanza 5*

2 The Youth, who daily farther from the east
Must travel, still is Nature's Priest,
And by the vision splendid
Is on his way attended;
At length the Man perceives it die away,
And fade into the light of common day. *Ib*

3 Behold the Child among his new-born blisses,
A six years' Darling of a pigmy size! *Ib, Stanza 7*

4 O joy! that in our embers
Is something that doth live,
That nature yet remembers
What was so fugitive! *Ib, Stanza 9*

5 And O, ye Fountains, Meadows, Hills, and Groves,
Forebode not any severing of our loves! *Ib, Stanza 11*

6 To me the meanest flower that blows can give
Thoughts that do often lie too deep for tears. *Ib*

7 I heard a thousand blended notes,
While in a grove I sate reclined,
In that sweet mood when pleasant thoughts
Bring sad thoughts to the mind. *Lines written in early Spring, 1*

8 Have I not reason to lament
What man has made of man? *Ib, 23*

9 I chanced to see at break of day
The solitary child. *Lucy Gray, 3*

10 The sweetest thing that ever grew
Beside a human door! *Ib, 7*

11 Meantime Luke began
To slacken in his duty; and, at length,
He in the dissolute city gave himself
To evil courses. *Michael, 442*

12 There is a comfort in the strength of love;
'Twill make a thing endurable, which else
Would overset the brain, or break the heart. *Ib, 448*

13 Nuns fret not at their convent's narrow room;
And hermits are contented with their cells. *Miscellaneous Sonnets, Pt. 1, 1*

14 'Twas pastime to be bound
Within the Sonnet's scanty plot of ground. *Ib*

1 Surprised by joy—impatient as the Wind
I turned to share the transport. *Miscellaneous Sonnets, Pt. 1, 27*

2 It is a beauteous evening, calm and free,
The holy time is quiet as a Nun
Breathless with adoration. *Ib, 1, 30*

3 The world is too much with us; late and soon,
Getting and spending, we lay waste our powers:
Little we see in Nature that is ours. *Ib, 1, 33*

4 Great God! I'd rather be
A Pagan suckled in a creed outworn;
So might I, standing on this pleasant lea,
Have glimpses that would make me less forlorn;
Have sight of Proteus rising from the sea;
Or hear old Triton blow his wreathèd horn. *Ib*

5 Scorn not the Sonnet; Critic, you have frowned,
Mindless of its just honours; with this key
Shakespeare unlocked his heart. *Ib, Pt. 2, 1*

6 Earth has not anything to show more fair:
Dull would he be of soul who could pass by
A sight so touching in its majesty:
This City now doth, like a garment, wear
The beauty of the morning; silent, bare,
Ships, towers, domes, theatres, and temples lie
Open unto the fields, and to the sky;
All bright and glittering in the smokeless air. *Ib, 2, 36*

7 Dear God! the very houses seem asleep;
And all that mighty heart is lying still! *Ib*

8 My heart leaps up when I behold
A rainbow in the sky. *My Heart leaps up*

9 The Child is father of the Man;
And I could wish my days to be
Bound each to each by natural piety. *Ib*

10 Two Voices are there; one is of the sea,
One of the mountains; each a mighty Voice:
In both from age to age thou didst rejoice,
They were thy chosen music, Liberty! *National Independence and Liberty, Pt. 1, 12, Thought of a Briton on the Subjugation of Switzerland*

11 Plain living and high thinking are no more:
The homely beauty of the good old cause
Is gone; our peace, our fearful innocence,
And pure religion breathing household laws. *Ib, 1, 13, Written in London, Sept. 1802*

12 Milton! thou shouldst be living at this hour:
England hath need of thee: she is a fen
Of stagnant waters. *Ib, 1, 14, London, 1802*

13 Thy soul was like a Star, and dwelt apart;
Thou hadst a voice whose sound was like the sea:
Pure as the naked heavens, majestic, free,
So didst thou travel on life's common way,
In cheerful godliness; and yet thy heart
The lowliest duties on herself did lay. *Ib*

1 We must be free or die, who speak the tongue
That Shakespeare spake; the faith and morals hold
Which Milton held. *National Independence and Liberty, Pt. 1, 16*

2 Another year!—another deadly blow!
Another mighty Empire overthrown!
And We are left, or shall be left, alone. *Ib, 1, 27*

3 Stern Daughter of the Voice of God!
O Duty! if that name thou love
Who art a light to guide, a rod
To check the erring, and reprove. *Ode to Duty, 1*

4 Give unto me, made lowly wise,
The spirit of self-sacrifice. *Ib, 54*

5 Bliss was it in that dawn to be alive,
But to be young was very Heaven! *The Prelude, 11, 108*

6 There is
One great society alone on earth:
The noble Living and the noble Dead. *Ib, 11, 393*

7 There was a roaring in the wind all night;
The rain came heavily and fell in floods. *Resolution and Independence, 1*

8 I thought of Chatterton, the marvellous Boy,
The sleepless Soul that perished in his pride. *Ib, 7*

9 Still glides the Stream, and shall for ever glide;
The Form remains, the Function never dies. *The River Duddon, 34, After-Thought*

10 Through love, through hope, and faith's transcendent dower,
We feel that we are greater than we know. *Ib*

11 She dwelt among the untrodden ways
Beside the springs of Dove,
A Maid whom there were none to praise
And very few to love. *She Dwelt among the Untrodden Ways*

12 She was a Phantom of delight
When first she gleamed upon my sight. *She was a Phantom of Delight, 1*

13 I saw her upon nearer view,
A Spirit, yet a Woman too! *Ib, 11*

14 A perfect Woman, nobly planned,
To warn, to comfort, and command;
And yet a Spirit still, and bright
With something of angelic light. *Ib, 27*

15 No motion has she now, no force;
She neither hears nor sees;
Rolled round in earth's diurnal course,
With rocks, and stones, and trees. *A Slumber did my Spirit seal*

16 Behold her, single in the field,
Yon solitary Highland Lass! *The Solitary Reaper, 1*

17 Will no one tell me what she sings?—
Perhaps the plaintive numbers flow
For old, unhappy, far-off things,
And battles long ago. *Ib, 17*

1 I listened, motionless and still;
And, as I mounted up the hill,
The music in my heart I bore,
Long after it was heard no more. *The Solitary Reaper, 29*

2 Strange fits of passion have I known:
And I will dare to tell. *Strange Fits of Passion, 1*

3 What fond and wayward thoughts will slide
Into a Lover's head!
'O mercy!' to myself I cried,
'If Lucy should be dead!' *Ib, 25*

4 Up! up! my Friend, and quit your books;
Or surely you'll grow double. *The Tables Turned, 1*

5 Books! 'tis a dull and endless strife:
Come, hear the woodland linnet,
How sweet his music! on my life,
There's more of wisdom in it. *Ib, 9*

6 Come forth into the light of things,
Let Nature be your Teacher. *Ib, 15*

7 One impulse from a vernal wood
May teach you more of man,
Of moral evil and of good,
Than all the sages can. *Ib, 21*

8 Come forth, and bring with you a heart
That watches and receives. *Ib, 31*

9 Three years she grew in sun and shower,
Then Nature said, 'A lovelier flower
On earth was never sown;
This Child I to myself will take;
She shall be mine, and I will make
A Lady of my own.' *Three Years she Grew, 1*

10 That best portion of a good man's life,
His little, nameless, unremembered, acts
Of kindness and of love. *Lines composed a few miles above Tintern Abbey, 33*

11 That blessed mood,
In which the burthen of the mystery,
In which the heavy and the weary weight
Of all this unintelligible world,
Is lightened. *Ib, 37*

12 We are laid asleep
In body, and become a living soul:
While with an eye made quiet by the power
Of harmony, and the deep power of joy,
We see into the life of things. *Ib, 45*

13 How oft, in spirit, have I turned to thee,
O sylvan Wye! *Ib, 55*

14 I have learned
To look on nature, not as in the hour
Of thoughtless youth; but hearing often-times
The still, sad music of humanity. *Ib, 88*

1 Nature never did betray
The heart that loved her. *Lines composed a few miles above Tintern Abbey, 122*

2 O Blithe New-comer! I have heard,
I hear thee and rejoice.
O Cuckoo! shall I call thee Bird,
Or but a wandering Voice? *To the Cuckoo, 1*

3 Thrice welcome, darling of the Spring! *Ib, 13*

4 O blessèd Bird! the earth we pace
Again appears to be
An unsubstantial, faery place;
That is fit home for Thee! *Ib, 29*

5 'And where are they? I pray you tell.'
She answered, 'Seven are we;
And two of us at Conway dwell,
And two are gone to sea.' *We are Seven, 17*

6 'You run about, my little Maid,
Your limbs they are alive;
If two are in the church-yard laid,
Then ye are only five.' *Ib, 33*

7 Poetry is the spontaneous overflow of powerful feelings: it takes its origin from emotion recollected in tranquillity. *Lyrical Ballads, Preface*

WORK, Henry Clay, 1832–1884

8 But it stopped short—never to go again—
When the old man died. *Grandfather's Clock*

9 Bring the good old bugle, boys, we'll sing another song:
Sing it with a spirit that will start the world along,
Sing it as we used to sing it—fifty thousand strong,
As we were marching through Georgia. *Marching through Georgia*

10 'Hurrah! hurrah! we bring the Jubilee!
Hurrah! hurrah! the flag that makes you free!'
So they sang the chorus from Atlanta to the sea
As we were marching through Georgia. *Ib, Chorus*

WOTTON, Sir Henry, 1568–1639

11 An Ambassador is an honest man sent to lie abroad for his country. *Written in Mr. Christopher Fleckamore's Album*

12 He first deceased; she for a little tried
To live without him, liked it not, and died. *Upon the Death of Sir Albertus Morton's wife*

13 How happy is he born and taught,
That serveth not another's will;
Whose armour is his honest thought,
And simple truth his utmost skill! *The Character of a Happy Life*

WREN, Sir Christopher, 1632–1723

1 *Si monumentum requiris, circumspice.* If you seek my monument, look around you. *Inscription in St. Paul's Cathedral, London, written by his son*

WYKEHAM, William of, see WILLIAM OF WYKEHAM

XENOPHON, 435?–354? B.C.

2 The sea! the sea! *Anabasis, 4, 7*

YEATMAN, Robert Julian, see SELLAR, Walter Carruthers

YEATS, William Butler, 1865–1939

3 When I was young,
I had not given a penny for a song
Did not the poet sing it with such airs
That one believed he had a sword upstairs. *All Things can Tempt Me*

4 I will arise and go now, and go to Innisfree,
And a small cabin build there, of clay and wattles made;
Nine bean rows will I have there, a hive for the honey bee,
And live alone in the bee-loud glade. *The Lake Isle of Innisfree*

5 And I shall have some peace there, for peace comes dropping slow,
Dropping from the veils of the morning to where the cricket sings. *Ib*

6 The land of faery,
Where nobody gets old and godly and grave,
Where nobody gets old and crafty and wise,
Where nobody gets old and bitter of tongue. *The Land of Heart's Desire*

7 All things uncomely and broken, all things worn out and old,
The cry of a child by the roadway, the creak of a lumbering cart,
The heavy steps of the ploughman, splashing the wintry mould,
Are wronging your image that blossoms a rose in the deeps of my heart.
The Lover Tells of the Rose in his Heart

8 When I was a boy with never a crack in my heart.
The Meditation of the Old Fisherman

9 A pity beyond all telling
Is hid in the heart of love. *The Pity of Love*

10 When you are old and grey and full of sleep
And, nodding by the fire, take down this book,
And slowly read, and dream of the soft look
Your eyes had once, and of their shadows deep. *When You are Old*

YOUNG, Edward, 1683–1765

11 Some for renown, on scraps of learning dote,
And think they grow immortal as they quote. *Love of Fame, 1, 89*

12 Be wise with speed,
A fool at forty is a fool indeed. *Ib, 2, 281*

13 Be wise today; 'tis madness to defer. *Night Thoughts, Night 1, 390*

14 Procrastination is the thief of time. *Ib, 393*

1 At thirty man suspects himself a fool;
Knows it at forty, and reforms his plan;
At fifty chides his infamous delay,
Pushes his prudent purpose to resolve:
In all the magnanimity of thought
Resolves; and re-resolves; then dies the same. *Night Thoughts, Night 1, 417*

2 Man wants but little, nor that little, long. *Ib, Night 4, 118*

ZOLA, Émile, 1840–1902

3 *J'accuse.* I accuse. *Title of open letter to French President about Dreyfus Case, 1898*

Index

NOTE TO INDEX

The overriding aims in compiling the index have been to refresh memories by providing fingerposts to half-remembered quotations, and to furnish useful quotations related to given subjects. This being so, in many cases brief and pregnant passages have received particularly thorough analysis.

'A' and 'the' have frequently been omitted from the beginnings of quoted phrases when their presence did not seem essential. The object has been to quote what are, in each case, the most informative words in a phrase. 'Your', 'yours', 'would', 'could', 'should' are the principal abbreviated words; any other isolated abbreviations have been made only when they are unmistakable.

References in the index after a quotation are to the page and to the place on the page. Thus 95:6 after a quotation refers to page 95, quotation 6

Index

Abandon hope, all ye who enter 95:6
Abbot: bishop and a. and prior 24:4
Abducted by a French Marquis 124:11
Abdul the Bulbul Amir 16:15
Abed: not ... a. after midnight 290:17
Abhor: age, I do a. thee 295:2
Abide: a. with me ... Lord, with me a.! 163:5
no where did a. 86:12
others a. our question 19:2
Abideth: and now a. faith, hope, charity 48:8
Abilities: from each according to his a. 168:7
if you have but moderate a. 233:9
Ability: out of my lean and low a. 291:17
studies serve for delight ... a. 23:5
Able: be a. for thine enemy 242:1
Abner ... smote him 34:13
Abode: frailties from their dread a. 126:15
Abou Ben Adhem (may his tribe increase!) 137:5
Abraham: certainly rough on A. 12:6
safe at last on A.'s breast 12:6
Abridgement of all that was pleasant 123:3
Abroad: pouring ... thy soul a. 150:3
when he next doth ride a. 92:13
who was on a trip a. 124:9
Absalom: O A., my son! 34:14
Absence: *a. est à l'amour* 67:13
a. is to love ... wind is to fire 67:13
a. makes the heart grow fonder 14:8, 25:5
a. of occupation is not rest 93:4
a. sharpens love 205:8
like a winter hath my a. been 294:4
Absent: a. are always ... wrong 205:9
a. thee from felicity awhile 253:9
I have been a. in the spring 294:5
long a., soon forgotten 219:24
Absents: *see* Presents
Absolute: a. power corrupts absolutely 9:1
Grape that can with Logic a. 110:10
through ... realms of Nonsense a. 104:13
Absolutism tempered by assassination 185:2
Absurde: nihil tam a. ... quod non dicatur 84:1
Absurdity: a thorough-paced a. 119:3
book ... dull without a single a. 123:18
Abundance: if thou hast a., give alms 51:8
one that hath ... shall have a. 44:28
Abuse: bore without a. ... the ... name 313:8
the more dangerous the a. 64:20
Abused: not anything so much a. 241:2
Abusing: an old a. of God's patience 276:3
Abysm: dark backward and a. of time 287:15
Abyssinia: Rasselas, prince of A. 141:3
Academes: the books, the arts, the a. 268:14
Accents: states unborn and a. yet unknown 263:4
Accepting: contradictory beliefs ... a. both 197:6
Accident: there's been an a., they said 124:8
Accidents: a. which started out to happen 167:4
a. will happen 206:2
Accidents (*continued*)
a. will occur in the best-regulated families 98:1
Accommodating: my pollertics ... religion ... exceedin' a. 322:10
Accurate: quite a. about her age 327:17
Accursed: a. ... that first invented war 166:8
think themselves a. ... not here 260:2
Accuse: a. not Nature! 179:4
I a. 338:3
J.'a. 338:3
Accused: defence ... apology ... before you be a. 78:13
never ask pardon before ... a. 221:30
Ace of trumps up [Gladstone's] sleeve 155:17
Ache, penury and imprisonment 273:11
Aches: the sense a. at thee 280:6
Achieve: my object ... shall a. in time 118:10
Achieving: still a., still pursuing 161:2
Aching: an a. void 92:14
Achitophel: of these the false A. was first 102:16
A-cold: owl, for all his feathers, was a. 147:12
Acquaintance: day ... lost ... do not make a new a. 144:21
hope our a. ... a long 'un 99:2
shd. auld a., be forgot 65:12
what, old a.! ... all this flesh! 256:2
Acquaintances: few friends though many a. 214:24
if a man does not make new a. 142:5
Acquist: he with new a. 181:8
Acres: a few paternal a. 203:20
over whose a. walked those blessed feet 253:14
three a. and a cow 88:6
Act: between the motion and the a. 106:8
every prudent a. ... barter 64:7
future ages groan for this foul a. 283:8
hear the sins they love to a. 281:3
is in itself almost an a. 236:9
unproportion'd thought his a. 248:15
Acting: only ... when ... off he was a. 123:5
Action: a. nor utterance 263:20
dearest a. in the tented field 278:21
I cannot forecast ... the a. of Russia 82:10
in a., how like an angel! 250:6
lose the name of a. 250–1:20
lust in a., and till a., lust 294:11
man of a. is called on 257:1
rarer a. is in virtue 289:3
suit the a. to the word 251:9
Actions speak louder than words 206:4
Actor: after a well-graced a. leaves 284:5
like a dull a. ... I have forgot 246:11
Actors: best a. ... for tragedy, comedy 250:9
our a. ... were all spirits 288:16
the a. are ... the usual three 169:16
Acts: desires but a. not 57:2

Acts (*continued*)
familiar a. are beautiful 299:13
his a. being seven ages 244:11
little, nameless, unremembered a. 335:10
Ad infinitum: and so proceed *a.* 309:4
Adam: A. the goodliest man 178:4
A. was but human 318:15
A. was not Adamant! 135:2
in A.'s ear so charming ... his voice 179:1
the old A. in this child 53:10
when A. and Eve were dispossessed 57:11
when A. delved and Eve span 24:2
Adamant: Adam was not A. 135:2
Add: a. insult to injury 217:22
God shall a. ... the plagues 51:4
Adder: deaf a. that stoppeth her ear 36:17
Addington: Pitt is to A. 72:17
Adieu: a. a.! my native shore 69:1
joy ... is ever ... bidding a. 149:12
Adjunct: learning is but an a. to ourself 268:12
Admiral: kill an a. from time to time 321:10
Admiration only of weak minds 180:2
Admire: fools a., but men of sense approve 202:11
Admiring: an a. bog 99:14
Admittance: no a. till ... week after next 77:9
Adonais: O, weep for A.! 297:9
the soul of A. like a star 298:3
Adoption: friends ... and their a. tried 248:15
Adoration: breathless with a. 333:2
Adore: Youth, I do a. thee 295:2
Adorn: nothing that he did not a. 144:22
Adriatic: in the A., an iron curtain 83:11
Adullam: David ... escaped to the cave A. 34:8
Adulteries: all the a. of art 145:10
Adultery: men call gallantry and gods a. 69:10
thou shalt not commit a. 32:6
Advance: retrograde if it does not a. 116:4
Advancement: economic and social a. of all peoples 319:5
Advantage: a. of doing one's praising 68:10
for our a. on the bitter cross 253:14
Advantages: remember, with a., what feats 260:1
Adventure: death ... the most beautiful a. 113:7
to die will be an awfully big a. 24:13
Adversary: never ... sees her a. 182:4
Adversity: a. ... blessing of the New 21:13
a. doth best discover virtue 21:15
a. is not without comforts 21:14
a. makes ... wise, not rich 206:5
many can bear a. 206:6
of fortune's sharp a. 80:5
sweet are the uses of a. 243:15
Advice: a woman seldom asks a. 9:10
a. is seldom welcome 80:12
Afar: and cometh from a. 332:1
the devotion to something a. 300:8
Affair: had an a. with a darky 13:2
Affairs: for the ord'ring yr. a., to sing 293:2
tide in the a. of men 264:3
tide in the a. of women 70:3
Affect: study what you most a. 287:6
Affection: to me-wards your a.'s strong 132:3
Affections: hath not a Jew ... a.? 274:17
woman's ... history is ... of the a. 138:11
Affirmative: two negatives make an a. 229:3
Afflicted: any ways a., or distressed 52:29
Affliction: prosperity ... whose heart ... a. alters 293:5
Afflictions: happy issue out of ... a. 52:30
Affluent: The A. Society 114:12
Affront: a moral ... man will not a. me 92:4
Afraid: a. you've got a bad egg 232:4
be not a. to do thine office 184:5
I will not be a. of death 272:7
it [public] is a. of itself 129:12
not be a. for the terror by night 36:26
see all, nor be a. 62:9
Afric's sunny fountains 130:1
Africa: always something new out of A. 200:16
ex A. semper aliquid novi 200:16
silent over A. 61:5
After his head was cut off 14:2
Afternoon: seemed always a. 314:1
Afternoons: slant of light on winter a. 99:16
Afton: flow gently, sweet A. 65:11
Agag came delicately 34:4
Again: and then rides back to shave a. 325:8
I do it a. and a. 74:3
we'll fight ... conquer a. an a. 115:1
Against: hand a. every man, every ... hand a. 31:1
he said he was a. it [sin] 90:11
neither for nor a. institutions 325:10
streams ... a. the wind 69:7
to live ... all reason is a. it 68:8
who can be a. us? 47:21
Agate: no bigger than an a. stone 286:1
Age: a. cannot wither her 242:15
a., I do abhor thee 295:2
a. is full of care 295:1
a. is in the wit is out 278:9
a. like winter bare 295:1
a. shall not weary them 54:5
a. will not be defied 22:23
a. will rule itself 224:32
but the a. of chivalry is gone 64:11
choice and master spirits of this a. 263:6
crabbed a. and youth 295:1
drives my green a. 315:16
fetch the a. of gold 175:9
from a. to a. endure 153:5
labour of an a. in piled stones 175:11
lady of a certain a. 70:4
let a. approve of youth 62:10
most loathed ... life, that a., ache 273:11
my a. is as a lusty winter 243:18
not of an a. but for all time 145:15
old a. a regret 100:9
old a. shd. burn and rave 315:15
prefer old a. to the alternative 81:15
quite accurate about her a. 327:17
rhyme ... invention of a barbarous a. 175:14
that which should accompany old a. 272:5
unregarded a. in corners thrown 243:17
when a., disease, or sorrows strike 84:14
woman who tells one her real a. 328:12
world's great a. begins anew 298:11
youth of labour ... a. of ease 122:7
Aged: 'certain age' ... certainly a. 70:4
Ages: a thousand a. in thy sight 323:5
a. of hopeless end 177:1
future a. groan for this foul act 283:8
gone: aye, a. long ago 147:14
his acts being seven a. 244:11

Ages (*continued*)
how many a. hence 263:4
Rock of A., cleft for me 317:15
Agglomeration: this a. ... Holy Roman Empire 321:16
Agincourt: did affright the air at A. 258:6
A-gley: gang aft a. 66:12
Agony: dreadful is the check—intense the a. 58:15
my soul in a. 86:10
Agree: a., for the law is costly 206:9
all colours will a. 21:11
you and I shall never a. 14:11
Agreeable: in most men's power to be a. 309:9
the problems of victory are more a. 83:8
Agreed: a. to have a battle 75:14
except they be a. 42:15
Aide-toi, le ciel t'aidera 111:7
Ail: what can a. thee, wretched wight 148:14
Aim: malice never was his a. 308:13
Aims: sick hurry, its divided a. 18:21
Ain't: as it isn't, it a. 75:15
Air: affright the a. at Agincourt 258:6
A. A trim reckoning! 255:21
all the a. a solemn stillness holds 126:4
babbling gossip of the a. 290:15
both feet firmly planted in the a. 235:3
breathing English a. 59:6
broad and general as the casing a. 271:6
castles in the a. 209:12
diet, humour, a. 59:14
do not saw the a. too much 251:7
fairer than the evening a. 165:9
glittering in the smokeless a. 333:6
I see him forming in the a. 234:3
melted into a., into thin a. 288:16
no stir of a. was there 148:5
seemed to tread upon the a. 148:10
take into the a. my quiet breath 150:3
the a., a charter'd libertine, is still 258:7
the fog and filthy a. 269:4
we shall fight ... on the seas ... in the a. 82:13
wing the mid-way a. 267:2
Airly: A. Beacon, A. Beacon 154:1
shires and towns from A. Beacon 154:1
Airs: a. from heaven or blasts from hell 249:3
said his father, Don't give yourself a. 74:4
sing it with such a. 337:3
Airy: gives to a. nothing 277:6
up the a. mountain 10:9
Ajalon: Moon, in the valley of A. 33:12
Ajax: Thersites' body is as good as A. 247:8
Akond of Swat 158:1
Alarms (Alarums): dwell in the midst of a. 93:15
our stern a. ... to merry meetings 284:9
used to war's a. 134:11
Alas, poor Yorick! 253:2
Albatross: I shot the a. 86:3
Alderman: on the fore-finger of an a. 286:1
Aldershot: burnish'd by A. sun 29:12
Ale: if at the Church ... some a. 56:4
jolly good a. and old 307:12
no more cakes and a.? 291:5
then to the spicy nut-brown a. 174:4
Aleppo: in A. once ... took by th' throat 280–1:14
Alexander: some talk of A. 16:14
Alibi: vy worn't there a a.! 99:9
Alice: a soldier's life is ... hard, says A. 171:6
A. is marrying one of the guard 171:6
A.-Mutton; Mutton-A. 77:10
March Hare said to A. 74:10
stuff and nonsense! said A. 75:8
the lion looked at A. wearily 77:6
time for tea, says A. 171:7
Alike: men's natures are a. 89:2
million of faces ... none a. 59:15
Alive: a. a. O! 15:10
bliss ... in that dawn to be a. 334:5
born into the world a. 117:8
if I shouldn't be a. 99:18
officiously to keep a. 84:16
All: ain't it a. a bleedin' shame? 16:13
a. for one and one for a. 105:3
a. is best 181:7
a. is but toys 270:15
a. is for the best 321:9
a. knowledge ... my province 23:14
a. she loves is love 69:17
a. things are artificial 59:13
a. were for the state 163:12
a. ye know on earth 149:10
gives to a., denies a. 214:34
Goodbye to A. That 125:7
grasp a., lose a. 215:26
Lord God made them a. 10:4
made and loveth a. 87:4
nor a. that glistens, gold 125:12
ripeness is a. 267:12
teacheth ill, who teacheth a. 227:18
1066 and A. That 241:7
we are a. Socialists now 128:5
Allegory: an a. on the banks of the Nile 301:11
life ... a continual a. 152:7
Shakespeare led a life of a. 152:7
Alliances: entangling a. with none 139:9
steer clear of permanent a. 322:16
Alluring: nothing is more a. than a levee 89:15
Almanack: look in the a.; find out moonshine 277:1
Almighty: an arrow from the A.'s bow 55:5
the a. dollar, that great object 138:13
Almond: peach was ... a bitter a. 318:16
Alms: a. for oblivion 290:6
if thou hast abundance, give a. 51:8
so give a.; pray so 293:2
Almsman: gay apparel for an a.'s gown 283:7
Alone: all we ask is to be let a. 96:4
a., a., all, all a. 86:10
a. and palely loitering 148:14
a. I did it 246:12
as I was walking all a. 11:16
bear the palm a. 262:7
better be a. than in bad company 207:20, 322:17
but wherefore thou a.? 178:11
France is a.; and God is a. 297:4
here at the gate a. 314:3
how women pass the time when ... a. 131:2
I a. sit lingering here 320:5
I am powerful but a. 320:13
I feel I am a. 156:12
I want to be a. 114:15

Alone (*continued*)
leave them a., and they'll come home 190:10
left him a. with his glory 330:4
not good that the man shd. be a. 30:7
we are left, or shall be left, a. 334:2
we two a. will sing like birds 267:13
weep, and you weep a. 326:9
who can enjoy a.? 179:3
Alph the sacred river ran 87:11
Alpha: I am A. and Omega 50:15
Alphabet: got to the end of the a. 99:3
Alpine: through an A. village passed 160:12
Altars: on behalf of ... their a. ... their hearths 238:1
Alteration: alters when it a. finds 294:8
Alternative: prefer old age to the a. 81:15
Alters: a. when it alteration finds 294:8
love a. not 294:9
Always (Alway): I am with you a. 45:4
it seemed a. afternoon 314:1
Am: by the grace of God I a. what I a. 48:12
here I a., and here I stay 164:11
I a. that I a. 31:19
I think, therefore I a. 97:7
Amami: Friday night is A. night 11:3
Amaryllis: sport with A. in the shade 174:16
Amateurs: hinted that we are a nation of a. 235:13
Amaze: Ye gods! it doth a. me 262:7
Ambassador: an a. is an honest man sent to lie 336:11
Ambiguity: Seven Types of A. 108:24
Ambition: a. first sprung from yr. blest abodes 201:7
a. shd. be made of sterner stuff 263:13
a. thick-sighted 147:7
become a churchman better than a. 262:3
death for his a. 263:10
let not a. mock 126:7
love ... not with a. join'd 89:14
meaner things to low a. 202:17
to reign is worth a. 176:6
vaulting a. which o'erleaps itself 270:6
wars that makes a. virtue 280:2
who doth a. shun 244:6
Ambitious: as he was a., I slew him 263:10
Amen: will no man say a.? 284:1
America: A. cannot be an ostrich 329:8
A. ... country of young men 108:21
A.! God shed His grace 25:4
ask not what A. will do for you 153:2
O my A.!, my new-found-land 101:3
Oh, they go to A. 328:8
the youth of A. 328:9
wake up, A. 114:16
American: a new deal for the A. people 234:17
A. system of rugged individualism 135:5
born an A.; I will live an A. 323:11
love all mankind, except an A. 144:10
retreat of the A. Army to our line 83:10
Americanism: no room ... for hyphenated A. 235:10
Americans: a new generation of A. 153:1
my fellow A., ask not 153:2
when good A. die 328:8
Amiral: tuer de temps en temps un a. 321:10
Ammunition: Praise the Lord and pass the a. 111:13
Amor: a. che muove il sole 95:8
a. vincit insomnia 114:6
omnia vincit a. 321:5
Amoris: amantium irae a. integratio est 315:2
Amorous: water ... a. of their strokes 242:14
Amour: absence est à l'a. 67:13
doux comme l'a. 310:11
on ne badine pas avec l'a. 185:6
Amurath: not A. an A. succeeds 257:20
Amused: we are not a. 320:11
Amusing herself [my cat] more with me 183:4
Anatomy: a mere a., a mountebank 246:5
Ancestral voices prophesying war 87:14
Ancestry: I can trace my a. back 118:2
mule without pride of a. 101:9
Anchors: great a., heaps of pearl 285:1
Ancient: a. nobility ... act of time 22:7
a. of days 42:6
did those feet in a. time 55:8
fear thee, a. Mariner 86:9
from a. melody have ceased 56:13
have you left the a. love 56:14
it is an a. mariner 85:11
Ancientry: wronging the a., stealing 292:16
Anderson: John A. my jo 66:5
Ange: pur comme un a. 310:11
Angel: a beautiful and ineffectual a. 19:9
a minist'ring a. ... my sister be 253:3
a ministering a. thou 240:9
A. of the Lord came down 311:4
a. whom thou still hast serv'd 272:12
clip an A.'s wings 149:3
in action, how like an a.! 250:6
is man an ape or an a.? 100:5
like an a. sings 275:8
reverence—that a. of the world 247:7
she drew an a. down. 103:15
sword of an a. king 55:5
the A. ended 179:1
the A. of Death has been abroad 58:8
the better a. is a man 294:16
who wrote like an a. 115:2
woman yet think him an a. 315:7
Angelic: something of a. light 334:14
Angels: a. and ministers of grace defend us 249:3
a band of a. coming 17:1
fantastic tricks ... as makes the a. weep 273:7
flights of a. sing thee to thy rest 253:11
guardian a. sung this strain 316:12
I ... am on the side of the a. 100:5
made him a little lower than the a. 35:19
sing, choirs of A. 196:5
tears, such as A. weep 176:12
the glorious fault of a. 201:7
the herald a. sing 325:2
where a. fear to tread 202:16
women are a., wooing 289:15
Anger: a. supplies the arms 320:17
more in sorrow than in a. 248:10
Angles: not A. but Angels 127:7
Angleterre est une nation de boutiquiers 185:12
Angli: non A. sed Angeli 127:7
Angling: ... say of a. as Dr. Boteler said of strawberries 322:9
Anglo-Saxon: he's an A. Messenger 77:4
those are A. attitudes 77:4
Angry: a. for the gourd 42:20

Angry (*continued*)
A. Young Man 199:1
be ye a., and sin not 48:24
his glassy essence, like an a. ape 273:7
when a., count four, when very a. 318:18
Anguish: when pain and a. wring the brow 240:9
Animal: are you a.—or vegetable—or mineral? 77:6
man is a noble a. 60:3
man is ... a political a. 18:5
man is ... a religious a. 64:12
man is a tool-making a. 113:4
spiteful, envious ... a. ... the public 129:12
we conjecture ... unknown a. ... or the god 308:14
Animals: all a. are equal but some ... more equal 197:1
a. are such agreeable friends 105:16
cd. ... live with a., they're so placid 326:2
Ann(e) (ie): for bonnie A. Laurie 101:10
Queen A. is dead 223:39
sister A., do you see anyone? 199:15
Annals: if you have writ yr. a. true 246:12
short and simple a. of the poor 126:7
Annihilating all that's made 168:1
Annoy: he only does it to a. 74:6
sewers a. the air 179:9
Annoyance: to his extreme a. tempted him 27:8
Annoys: pernicious weed ... the fair a. 92:5
Annual income twenty pounds ... happiness 97:16
Another: can I see a.'s woe? 56:12
have a. for working-days 277:18
he who wd. do good to a. 55:6
hell! to choose love by a.'s eyes 276:11
no man truly knows a. 59:16
one religion as true as a. 67:11
who ... king ... that's quite a. thing 68:15
you make yourselves a. [face] 251:4
Answer: blow, bugle, a., echoes 314:15
but a. came there none 76:6, 239:5
give me your a. do 95:4
here is the a. ... to President Roosevelt 83:2
sent an a. back to me 77:2
shortest a. is doing 225:18
soft a. turneth away wrath 38:16
the woods shall ... a. 305:7
wd. not stay for an a. 21:8
Ant: go to the a., thou sluggard 38:4
Anthems: hallooing and singing of a. 256:9
loud a. will always be ringing 12:1
Anthony Rowley: Heigh ho! says A. 189:2
Antic: and there the a. sits 283:6
dance an a. hay 166:2
put an a. disposition on 249:13
Antidote: and with some sweet oblivious a. 272:6
she is the a. to desire 90:2
Antipathy: no a. ... in diet, humour 59:14
Antipodes: sheer opposite, a. 148:2
Anybody: is there a. there? said the Traveller 96:14
no one's a.! 116:15
Anything: a. but history 322:5
a. that tampers with ... ignorance 327:11
Earth has not a. ... more fair 333:6
if a. is sacred ... body is 325:11
though you do a., he thinks no ill 293:20
Apart: love is of man's life a thing a. 69:14
others a. sat 177:6
Ape: glassy essence, like an angry a. 273:7
is man an a. or an angel? 100:5
Apes: ivory, and a. and peacocks 168:13
Apollo: after the songs of A. 269:2
burned is A.'s laurel-bough 166:1
musical as is A.'s lute 172:18
Apollos watered 47:32
Apology before you be accused 78:13
Apostles: Cristes lore, and his a. twelve 79:18
Apothecary: an ounce of civet, good a. 267:5
Apparel: a. oft proclaims the man 248:16
gay a. for an almsman's gown 283:7
Apparelled in celestial light 331:12
Appeal: I a. unto Caesar 47:11
Appearance: judge not according to the a. 46:23
man looketh on the outward a. 34:5
never judge from a. 217:30
Appears: done by night a. by day 211:30
God a., and God is light 55:1
Appétit vient en mangeant 232:7
Appetite: a. comes with eating 232:7
as if increase of a. had grown 248:4
cloy the hungry edge of a. 282:1
doth not the a. alter? 277:22
now good digestion wait on a. 271:7
surfeiting the a. may sicken 290:10
Appetites: cloy the a. they feed 242:15
creatures ours, and not their a.! 279:17
Applause: the a.! delight! ... of our Stage 145:11
Apple: an a. a day ... doctor away 206:19
a. for the a.'s sake 318:15
kept him as the a. of his eye 33:6
my a. trees will never get across 113:13
the a. press'd with specious cant 135:2
Apple-cart: upset the a. 206:20
Apples: comfort me with a. 40:6
Kent ... a., cherries, hops and women 98:18
small choice in rotten a. 287:7
Appliance: by desperate a. are reliev'd 252:16
Appliances: all a. and means to boot 257:3
Apprehension: a. of the good gives ... feeling 282:1
in a., how like a god! 250:6
Approach: sweet a. of even or morn 177:10
Approve: let age a. of youth 62:10
Approves all forms of competition 84:17
April: a bright cold day in A. 197:2
and after A. 61:2
A. is the cruellest month 107:3
A., June, and November 194:6
A. with his shoures sote 79:1
men are A. when they woo 245:13
now that A.'s there 61:1
proud-pied A. 294:5
uncertain glory of an A. day 292:6
Aprons: made themselves a. 30:12
Aquinas: better teacher than ... A. 182:5
Arabia: all the perfumes of A. 272:3
Arabian trees their med'cinable gum 280–1:14
Araby: I'll sing thee songs of A. 329:3
Aram: how Eugene A., though a thief 72:3
Ararat: upon the mountains of A. 30:21
Arbitrary: accusation of being a. 139:3
Arcadia: et in A. ego 17:12

Arcadia (*continued*)
I too am in A. 17:12
Archangel: nor appeared less than A. ruined 176:11
Arches: fled Him down the a. of the years 316:9
Architecture: the wondrous a. of the world 166:10
Arden: am in A.; the more fool I 244:2
Arguing: I am not a. ... I am telling 325:6
no a. with Johnson 124:2
no good in a. with the inevitable 163:1
Argument: any a. about any place 205:1
a. for a week 254:8
furnish ... a. and intellects 123:22
height of this great a. 175:17
in a. with men a woman 181:3
not to stir without great a. 252:19
Tories ... no a. but force 60:4
Whigs ... no force but a. 60:4
Arise: I will a. and go now 337:4
my lady sweet, a. 246–7:13
Aristotle: bokes ... of A. and his philosophye 79:9
Arithmetic: branches of A.—Ambition, Distraction 74:15
Ark: a. rested in the seventh month 30:21
unto Noah into the a. 30:20
Arm: human on my faithless a. 20:2
I bit my a., I sucked the blood 86:7
Arma: a. virumque cano 320:16
cedant a. togae ... laurea laudi 84:4
Armadas: till the great A. come 187:9
Armageddon: a place called ... A. 50:27
Armies: our a. swore terribly 306:17
Armour: put on ... a. of God 48:26
religion is the best a. 224:10
whose a. is his honest thought 336:13
Armourers: now thrive the a. 258:9
Arms: anger supplies the a. 320:17
a. against a sea of troubles 250–51:20
a. and the man I sing 105:1, 320:16
a. of mine had seven years' pith 278:21
a., take your last embrace 287:4
imparadised in one another's a. 178:5
so he laid down his a. 134:11
the a. of my true love 314:5
underneath are the everlasting a. 33:9
what a. ... under my head 170:14
Army: an a. marches on its stomach 185:14
hum of either a. stilly sounds 259:8
noble a. of Martyrs 52:15
terrible as an a. with banners 40:13
Arrive: a better thing than to a. 307:10
Arrow: an a. from the Almighty's bow 55:5
I shot an a. into the air 160:10
the a. that flieth by day 36:26
Arrows: my a. of desire 55:8
Ars longa, vita brevis 132:13
Arse upon which everyone has sat 94:12
Arsenic and Old Lace 153:3
Art: all a. is quite useless 328:5
all nature is but a. 203:4
all the adulteries of a. 145:10
a. for a.'s sake 91:4
a. has no enemy except ignorance 206:22
a. is a jealous mistress 108:1
A. is long, and Time is fleeting 160:15
a. is long, but l. is short 132:13
a. is too precise in every part 131:15
Art (*continued*)
a. lies in concealing a. 206:23
a. of being kind 326:11
a. of drawing sufficient conclusions 68:6
a. pour l'a. 91:4
aspires ... to the condition of a. 90:7
China's gayest a. had dyed 125:9
clever, but is it a.? 154:12
fine a. ... hand ... head ... heart 237:5
half a trade and half an a. 138:7
more matter with less a. 249:16
nature is the a. of God 59:13
next to Nature, A. 156:11
source, and end, and test, of A. 202:3
squandering ... his peculiar a. 103:5
strains of unpremeditated a. 300:1
true ease in writing ... a., not chance 202:10
what a. can wash her guilt 124:1
Arthur: he's in A.'s bosom 259:1
slowly answered A. from the barge 312:8
Article: snuff'd out by an a. 70:6
these a. subscribed ... I may ... dwindle into a wife 89:18
Artifex: qualis a. pereo! 187:8
Artificial: all things are a. 59:13
Artisan: merchant, and a., without ... meddling 9:6
to give employment to the a. 27:6
Artist: a. is in danger of death 130:7
be more of an a. 152:12
true a. will let his wife starve 296:5
what an a. dies with me! 187:8
Arts: a. of every woman false 180:16
in the inglorious a. of peace 168:3
the books, the a., the academes 268:14
Ash on an old man's sleeve 106:10
Ashamed: naked ... and were not a. 30:10
she that maketh a. 38:12
Ashes: a. and sparks, my words among mankind 299:6
a. to a., dust to dust 53:30
for the a. of his fathers 163:10
man ... splendid in a. 60:3
slept among his a. cold 147:15
to give ... beauty for a. 41:11
Asia: hollow pamper'd jades of A. 256:18
ye pamper'd jades of A.! 166:12
Ask: we a. and a. 19:2
Asked: nobody a. you, sir, she said 196:1
women are glad to have been a. 197:14
Askelon: in the streets of A. 34:10
Asleep: he thought me a. 198:11
old ships sail like swans a. 111:3
the very houses seem a. 333:7
we are laid a. in body 335:12
Aspect: meet in her a. and her eyes 71:2
sweet a. of princes 261:10
with grave a. he rose 177:3
Aspen: shade ... light quivering a. made 240:9
Aspens: willows whiten, a. quiver 313:12
Aspicious: comprehended two a. persons 278:10
Ass: an a. wd. marry an uncertainty 241:19
a. [knoweth] his master's crib 40:16
average schoolmaster ... essentially an a. 169:13
bridle for ... a., a rod for the fool's back 38:30
make an a. of oneself 206:26
write me down an a. 278:16

Assassination: absolutism tempered with a. 185:2
Assay: th' a. so hard 80:4
Assert: I may a. Eternal Providence 175:17
Asset: healthy citizens are the greatest a. 83:9
Assume: a. a virtue, if you have it not 252:14
what I a. you shall a. 325:13
Assuming that he's got any [brains] 117:6
Assurance: I'll make a. double sure 271:16
Assured: most ignorant of what he's most a. 273:7
Astonish: things that wd a. you 117:7
Astonished: a. at my own moderation 84:11
a. Mayor and Corporation 62:2
Asunder: let no man put a. 53:25
Atahualpa: knows ... who strangled A. 164:2
Atheism: a little philosophy inclineth ... to a. 22:11
Athens: a citizen, not of A. 304:5
Israel, A., Florence 138:8
maid of A. 71:1
Atkins: it's Thank You, Mr. A. 155:5
Atlanta: from A. to the sea 336:10
Atlases: only on the very best a. 319:9
Atomies: drawn with a team of little a. 286:1
Attached: decidedly and conscientiously a. 94:6
Attachment à la Plato 119:5
Attack: dared a. my Chesterton 27:12
situation excellent. I shall a. 111:5
Attempt: serious a. to do it 324:15
Attempted: something a., something done 161:11
Attentions: these pleasing a. 21:1
Attic: beauty crieth in an a. 68:9
mellow glory of the A. stage 18:14
Atticus: if A. were he! 201:17
Attire: in its workaday a. 116:12
so wild in their a. 269:7
Attitudes: Anglo-Saxon a. 77:4
Attorney: office boy to an A.'s firm 119:15
Attraction and repulsion 56:15
Attribute: an a. to God himself 275:1
a. to awe and majesty 275:1
grandest moral a. of a Scotsman 25:1
Auburn: sweet A.! loveliest village 122:4
Audace: de l'a., ... toujours de l'a. 95:9
Audi alteram partem 206:27
Audible: illiberal ... ill-bred as a. laughter 80:13
August: to recommence [winter] in A. 70:8
Augustus: Fleckno ... like A., young was called 104:13
Auld: a. acquaintance 65:12
a. lang syne 65:13
the a. wife sat 71:16
Aunt: if my a. had been a man 206:28
I'm Charley's a. from Brazil 315:13
my a. died of influenza 296:22
written to A. Maud 124:9
Aunts: his cousins and his a. 119:14
Austerlitz: pile the bodies high at A. 238:5
Austin: laboure, as A. bit 79:6
let A. have his swink 79:6
Austria: Don John of A. is going to the war 81:5
Author: as sincerely from the a.'s soul 137:13
a. ... of all good things 53:6
a. who speaks about his own books 100:6
where is any a. in the world 268:12
Authority: a man under a. 44:10
a. be a stubborn bear 293:8
base a. from others' books 268:8
dress'd in a little brief a. 273:7
in your countenance ... a. 265:12
nothing destroys a. so much 22:15
wrest ... the law to your a. 275:2
Autographs: nuisances who write for a. 118:4
Autres temps, autres moeurs 206:29
Autumn: thou breath of A.'s being 299:3
Autumnal: grace ... in one a. face 101:1
Availeth: say not the struggle naught a. 85:1
Avails: what a. the sceptred race! 156:13
Avarice, the spur of industry 137:1
Ave: a. in perpetuum ... a. atque vale 77:17
Averni: facilis descensus A. 321:4
Aversion: in matrimony to begin with a little a. 301:6
Aves: after thousand a. told 147:15
Avocation: engaging in so puerile an a. 169:13
Avon: sweet Swan of A. 145:16
Awake: a.! for Morning in the Bowl of Night 109:13
a. my heart, to be loved 58:3
a., my St. John! 202:17
lying a. with a dismal headache 117:12
smiles a. you 96:11
Award: general a. of love 148:11
Aware: England bore, shaped, made a. 59:6
Away: a.! a.! for I will fly to thee 149:16
a. with him! He speaks Latin 260:12
a., you rolling river 16:9
come, dear children, let us a. 18:11
I wish, I wish he'd stay a. 169:8
spotless reputation; that a. 281:8
the little less, and what worlds a. 60:15
to bear my soul a. 9:13
were t'other dear charmer a. 115:7
Awe: attribute to a. and majesty 275:1
in a. of such a thing as I 262:6
Awful: felt how a. goodness is 178:10
nothing ... nobody ... it's a.! 25:11
that men might shun the a. shops 81:10
Awoke: I a. ... and found myself famous 71:7
so I a., and behold ... a dream 63:12
Awry: their currents turn a. 250–1:20
Axe: an a. to grind 206:30
Lizzie Borden took an a. 14:3
the a.'s edge did try 168:4
Axiom: long been an a. of mine 101:12
Axis: soft under-belly of the A. 83:7
Azure: arose from out the a. main 316:12
ring'd with the a. world 312:1
robes the mountain in ... a. hue 72:9
the a. flowers that blow 125:9

Baa, b., black sheep 188:4
Babble: watch to b. and to talk 278:6
Babbled: a' b. of green fields 259:2
Babe: find the b. ... in a manger 45:21
Babel: name of it called B. 30:27
Babes: out of the mouth of b. 35:17
Babies: bit the b. in the cradles 61:17
putting milk into b. 83:9
the snuggeries of b. 316:3
Baby: a Mother laid her B. 10:6
b., cradle, and all 189:10
every b. born ... finer than the last 98:10

Baby (*continued*)
hush-a-bye b., on the tree top 189:10
in the oven for b. and me 192:5
see my b. at my breast? 243:11
when the first b. laughed 24:11
Babylon: by the rivers of B. ... we sat 37:22
how many miles to B.? 189:8
king of B. ... at the parting 41:22
Bacchus: not charioted by B. 149:16
Bachelor: I wd. die a b. 278:1
now I am a b. 16:3
Bachelors: two old b. ... in one house 158:11
Back: at my b. I always hear 167:13
die with harness on our b. 272:11
his wife looked b. from behind 31:4
mermaid on a dolphin's b. 276:18
one who never turned his b. 60:12
rod for his own b. 224:25
those before cried 'B.!' 163:13
Background: see fit to keep me in the b. 159:6
Backward: dark b. and abysm of time 287:15
I b. cast my e'e 66:13
look b. to with pride 113:10
Bacon: think how B. shined 203:9
to save one's b. 224:38
when their lordships asked B. 29:7
Bad: altogether irreclaimably b. 73:11
became ... b. in one step 146:8
hope ... good breakfast ... b. supper 23:13
how sad and b. and mad 60:16
mad, b., and dangerous 156:1
so much b. in the best of us 133:5
swans sing ... 'twere no b. thing 87:10
the b. affright 126:16
things b. begun make strong themselves 271:5
truth told with b. intent 54:14
when she was b. she was horrid 161:8
Badine: on ne b. pas avec l'amour 185:6
Badness: all good and no b. 302:12
Baffled to fight better 60:12
Bag: cat out of the b. 218:38
not with b. and baggage 245:4
one and all, b. and baggage, ... clear out 121:8
Bags: three b. full 188:4
Baked: you have b. me too brown 75:4
Baker Street: the B. irregulars 102:4
Balance: redress the b. of the Old 72:15
the b. of power 322:3
Bald: b. as a coot 206:35
b. heads are soon shaven 206:36
go up thou b. head 34:23
Ball: after the b. 129:1
contenders drive a b. with sticks 140:5
Ballad: woeful b. made to ... eyebrow 244:11
Ballad-mongers: these same metre b. 255:6
Ballads: of b., songs and snatches 117:16
patriotic b. cut and dried 118:1
Ballot is stronger than the bullet 159:8
Balls: the stars' tennis b. 323:17
Balm: a b. upon the world 148:2
b. of hurt minds 270:11
is there no b. in Gilead? 41:13
wash the b. off ... anointed king 283:2
with ... tears I wash away my b. 284:2
without tasting the b. of pity 141:8
Baltic: from Stettin in the B. 83:11
Banbury: cock-horse to B. Cross 193:1
to B. came I 58:2
Band: wearied b. swoons to a waltz 137:15
when the b. begins to play 155:5
Bands: with b. of love 42:10
Bane: I will not be afraid of death and b. 272:7
Bang: b. went saxpence! 231:23
not with a b. but a whimper 106:9
Banish plump Jack and b. all the world 255:2
Banishing: worst effect is b. for hours 92:5
Banishment: the bitter bread of b. 282:12
Bank: as I sat on a sunny b. 14:10
b. and shoal of time 270:5
b. whereon the wild thyme blows 276:20
moonlight sleeps upon this b. 275:8
Bankrupt: b. of life yet prodigal of ease 103:1
beggar can never be b. 207:11
Banks: bonnie b. o' Loch Lomon' 16:10
ye b. and braes 67:5
Banner: b. with the strange device 160:12
his b. over me was love 40:5
that b. in the sky 134:1
the royal b. and all quality 280:2
thy b., torn, but flying 69:7
Banners: hang out our b. on the outward walls 272:8
Bar: no moaning at the b. 311:13
when I went to the B. 117:4
Barabbas was a publisher 72:11
Barbara Allen 11:12
Barbarian: dancing? ... certainly a B. exercise 65:4
Barbarians, Philistines, Populace 19:6
Barbarous: mass of ... people must be b. 143:8
Barbarousness: I must confess my own b. 302:6
Barber: no b. shaves so close but 206:37
Bards: ancient love that b. of old enjoy'd 56:14
B. of Passion and of Mirth 147:6
Bare: the cupboard was b. 192:2
Bargain: a world-without-end b. 268:15
never was a better b. driven 302:2
Bargains: be beloved is above all b. 207:14
here's the rule for b. 98:6
Barge: answer'd Arthur from the b. 312:8
the b. she sat in, like a ... throne 242:14
Bark: all right ... you heard a seal b. 317:7
b. at a distance never bite 211:29
b. at the moon 206:38
b. up the wrong tree 206:40
b. ... worse than his bite 206:39
keep a dog and b. yourself 217:31
when I ope my lips let no dog b. 274:3
Barkis: 'as true,' said Mr. B., 'as taxes is' 97:19
B. is willin' 97:14
Barley: long fields of b. and of rye 313:11
Barlow: Councillor B. 28:7
Barrel: lock, stock and b. 219:22
Barren: a b. sister all your life 276:9
and cry, 'tis all b. 306:13
nature is b. 57:6
Barricade: at some disputed b. 240:15
Bars: look out through the same b. 156:15
nor iron b. a cage 162:5
Barter: founded on compromise and b. 64:7
Base: so b. that wd. be a bondman 263:10
Bashful: maiden of b. fifteen 301:17
Basia: da mi b. mille 77:15
Basil: steal my B.-pot 148:13

Basingstoke: word ... like B. 120:14
Basket: all yr. eggs in one b. 212:19
Bat: black b., night, has flown 314:3
blind as a b. 208:8
twinkle, twinkle, little b. 74:8
Bataillons: *Dieu est ... pour les gros b.* 321:17
Bate: do I not b.? ... dwindle? 255:11
Bath: I test my b. before I sit 186:9
sore labour's b. 270:11
Bathe: spirit to b. in fiery floods 273:10
Bathing: caught the Whigs b. 100:3
Bathing machine: between a large b. 117:13
Baton of a marshal of France 185:13
Bats: have b. in the belfry 207:2
suspicions ... like b. amongst birds 22:24
Batsman: a ghostly b. plays 316:7
Battalions: God is ... for the big b. 321:17
not single spies, but in b. 252:21
Battle: agreed to have a b. 75:14
b. [is not] to the strong 39:23
b. of Waterloo was won 324:10
Ben B. was a soldier bold 134:11
care for him who shall have borne the b. 159:15
first blow is half the b. 213:29
melancholy as a b. won 324:6
nothing except a b. lost 324:6
the b. and the breeze 72:10
the b. day is past 107:16
to b. for freedom and truth 138:4
when the b.'s lost and won 269:3
Battle-flags: till ... the b. were furl'd 313:17
Battles long ago 334:17
Bauble: what shall we do with this b.? 94:8
Bays: Britain won her proudest b. 117:10
Bay-tree: flourishing like a green b. 36:10
Be: ain't-a-going to b. no core 319:3
b. not solitary, b. not idle 67:12
b. strong and of a good courage 33:10
fears that I may cease to b. 151:7
Germany ... will not b. at all 133:1
God said, Let Newton b.! 201:21
Ho, let Einstein b.! 306:2
lest we shd. b. by and by 10:3
ne'er was, nor is, nor e'er shall b. 202:7
nobody is healthy ... nobody can b. 20:8
this tree continues to b. 155:14
to b. or not to b. 250:20
what will b., shall b. 165:7
whatever will b., will b. 209:20
when will that b.? say the bells 192:4
ye shall b. as gods 30:11
Be-all and the end-all 270:5
Beach: I shall ... walk upon the b. 106:16
Beaches: we shall fight on the b. 82:13
Beachy Head: to Birmingham by way of B. 81:7
Beacons from the abode ... Eternal are 298:3
Beadle: a b. on boxin' day 99:5
Beads: jewels for a set of b. 283:7
Beadsman: the B., after thousand aves 147:15
Beak: b. holds more than his belican 170:6
take thy b. from out my heart 200:19
Beaker full of the warm South 149:14
Beale: Miss B. and Miss Buss 14:4
Beam: at the full midday b. 182:8
Beamish: my b. boy! 75:11
Beams: little candle throws his b.! 275:11
Bean: home of the b. and the cod 57:10
nine b. rows 337:4
Bean (*continued*)
not-too-French French b. 119:5
Beans: how many b. make nine 218:13
Bear: a B. of Very Little Brain 172:4
authority be a stubborn b. 293:8
b. those ills we have 250–1:20
because it gave pain to the b. 164:7
exit, pursued by a b. 292:15
funny how a b. likes honey? 172:3
grizzly b. is huge and wild 136:2
he has been eaten by the b. 136:2
nothing wd. it b. 190:1
rather b. with you than b. you 244:1
sing Ho! for the life of a b. 172:10
Bear-baiting: the Puritan hated b. 164:7
Beard: b. of formal cut 244:11
b. the lion in his den 240:7
by thy long grey b. 85:11
Old Man with a b. 158:13
singed the Spanish king's b. 102:7
Bearded like the pard 244:11
Bears it out ... to the edge of doom 294:9
Beast: a b., but a just b. 13:6
a b., no more! 252:17
a wild b. or a god 22:21
both man and bird and b. 87:3
man's life is cheap as b.'s 266:2
wee ... cow'rin', tim'rous [beastie] 66:10
when people call this b. to mind 27:1
Beastly: don't let's be B. to the Germans 91:9
how b. the bourgeois is 157:8
Beasts: brute b. that have no understanding 53:19
Beat: b. him when he sneezes 74:6, 7
lion b. the unicorn 190:9
shall b. ... swords into plowshares 40:18
to b. about the bush 207:5
Tom was b. 195:4
ye b. my people to pieces 40:19
Beaten: English never know when ... b. 212:25
Beating: almost hear the b. of his wings 58:8
b. myself for spite 302:3
Beats: truth ... with bad intent b. all the lies 54:14
Beauteous: a b. evening, calm and free 333:2
Beautified with our feathers 127:6
Beautiful: all heiresses are b. 104:10
as good as she was b. 199:14
b. Soup! 75:5
full b., a faery's child 148:15
how b. upon the mountains 41:4
most b. things ... are the most useless 237:3
old are more b. than the young 325:9
see, not feel, how b. 87:8
she's b. and ... to be woo'd 260:7
stately homes ... how b. they stand 130:5
the good is the b. 200:13
the many men, so b. 86:11
Beauty: a b. cold and austere 237:9
a daily b. in his life 280:8
a thing of b. is a joy for ever 147:8
abstract Idea ... of B. 152:6
as a b. I'm not a ... star 109:1
as b. must be truth 151:9
b. crieth in an attic 68:9
b. draws us with a single hair 204:7
b. is but skin-deep 207:6

Beauty (*continued*)
b. is ... in the eye of the beholder 137:3
b. is nature's coin; must not be hoarded 173:2
b. is potent 207:7
b. is truth, truth b. 149:10
b. itself doth of itself persuade 295:5
b. lives with kindness 292:9
b. of a thousand stars 165:9
b. provoketh thieves 243:14
b. stands in the admiration 180:2
b. though injurious, hath strange power 181:5
b. too rich for use 286:3
b. will buy no beef 207:8
b.'s ensign ... crimson in thy lips 287:3
dress her b. at yr. eyes 96:1
dwells with B.—B. that must die 149:12
extent of its b. and power 164:3
exuberance is b. 57:5
first in b. ... first in might 148:8
have loved the principle of b. 152:11
her B. and her Chivalry 69:3
hidden b. of the world 300:9
homely b. of the good old cause 333:11
humility towards ... Principle of B. 152:1
in their summer b. kiss'd 285:8
Isle of B., fare thee well 25:5
like a garment wear the b. 333:6
love built on b., soon as b. dies 100:19
more inviting than b. unadorn'd 26:13
muddy, ill-seeming, ... bereft of b. 287:12
needs not June for b.'s heightening 19:4
ne'er saw true b. till this night 286:4
no Spring, nor Summer b. hath such grace 101:1
our saucy ship's a b. 119:8
she walks in b., like the night 71:2
teaches such b. as a woman's eye 268:12
that ... b.'s rose might never die 293:10
the b. of the world! 250:6
to give unto them b. for ashes 41:11
unmask her b. to the moon 248:13
Because: b. he knows, a frightful fiend 86:16
b. I do not hope to turn 106:1
b. we're here b. we're here b. 17:6
we cannot do it, Sir, b. 77:2
Bechstein: if ... we pawn the B. Grand 91:6
Becomes: in peace ... nothing so b. a man 259:3
it hardly b. any of us 133:5
Bed: a b. by night, a chest ... by day 122:13
a manger for His b. 10:6
and so to b. 199:8
b. be blest that I lie on 9:13
candle to light you to b. 192:4
early to b. and early to rise 212:9
early to b. makes a male ... dead 317:6
four angels to my b. 9:13
nicer to lie in b. 157:6
she whipped them ... put them to b. 194:5
to b., to b., there's knocking 272:4
took her into b. and covered up her head 16:4
welcome to yr. gory b. 67:1
Bedecked, ornate and gay 180:15
Bedfellows: misery acquaints ... with strange b. 288:7
Bed-time, Hal, and all well 255:20
Bee: a b. in one's bonnet 207:9
the little busy b. 323:1
where the b. sucks 289:6
Beef: beauty will buy no b. 207:8
roast b. of England 109:9
this little pig had roast b. 194:7
Been: shd. be ... as if it had not b. 297:12
Beer: felony to drink small b. 260:9
life isn't all b. and skittles 136:13
parson, much bemused in b. 201:11
suckle fools and chronicle small b. 279:8
Beer-sheba: from Dan even to B. 33:23
travel from Dan to B. 306:13
Bees: late flowers for the b. 147:2
so work the honey b. 258:8
swine, women and b. cannot be turned 226:36
Beethoven's Fifth Symphony ... most sublime noise 112:1
Beetle wheels his droning flight 126:4
Beetles: scarce so gross as b. 267:2
Before: b. behind, between 101:3
b. you are on with the new 16:1
I have been here b. 236:10
those b. cried 'Back!' 163:13
Befriend: be near me now and b. 310:3
Beg: the poor can b. 215:6
to b. I am ashamed 46:5
Begetter: onlie b. of these ... sonnets 293:9
Beggar: b. can never be bankrupt 207:11
better die a b. than live a b. 207:27
made a b. by banqueting 51:23
not ... a doit to relieve a ... b. 288:6
whiles I am a b. I will rail 264:14
Beggared: her own person it b. all description 242:14
Beggars: basest b. are in ... thing superfluous 266:2
b. cannot be choosers 207:12
Beggary: b. in the love 242:10
no vice but b. 264:14
Begin: b. with certainties ... end in doubts 23:12
content to b. with doubts 23:12
Beginning: as it was in the b. 52:14
before the b. of years 309:15
b. of a feast fits ... keen guest 255:17
b. of a lifelong romance 327:5
everything must have a b. 212:39
good b. makes a good ending 215:15
I am ... the b. and the ending 50:15
in the b. God created 30:1
in the b. was the Word 46:14
it is the b. of the end 310:10
long choosing and b. late 179:6
memory ... the b. of dowdiness 328:15
strange b.—'borrowed majesty' 264:8
that was the b. of fairies 24:11
Beginnings: end to the b. of all wars 235:6
Begins: charity b. at home 209:19
nothing b. and nothing ends 316:8
Begone dull care ... b. from me 14:11
Begot: how b., how nourished? 274:18
Begun: well b. is half done 230:5
Behaviour: often the surfeits of our own b. 265:10
Behest: darkness falls at thy b. 107:17
Behind: and, departing, leave b. us 161:1
bring their tails b. them 190:10
fiend doth close b. him tread 86:16
get thee b. me, Satan 44:18
lads that thought there was no more b. 292:12

Behind (*continued*)
led his regiment from b. 116:6
my work is left b. 28:2
those b. cried 'Forward!' 163:13
Behold: as she looked ... she did b. 305:12
b. her, single in the field 334:16
b., this dreamer cometh 31:11
mortality, b. and fear 25:8
Being: all the wheels of B. slow 312:14
eternal B., the Principle of Beauty 152:1
live and move and have our b. 47:6
receives reproach of b. 294:10
who wd. lose ... this intellectual b.? 176:19
Belfry: bats in the b. 207:2
Belgium's capital had gathered then 69:3
Belial: sons of B., flown with insolence 176:8
sons of B. had a Glorious Time 103:7
Belied: they have b. a lady 278:18
Belief: does not live according to his b. 207:13
Beliefs: holding two contradictory b. 197:6
home of ... forsaken b. 19:7
Believe: b. a woman or an epitaph 70:14
b. it or not 233:13
I do b. her ... know she lies 294:15
I don't b. in fairies 24:12
say quick that you b. 24:14
some b. they've none [soul] 68:2
Believed: have not seen, yet have b. 46:35
liar is not b. ... speaks the truth 218:39
Believes: he who b. what is wrong 139:12
less remote ... who b. nothing 139:12
none go ... alike, yet each b. his own 202:2
Believing: seeing is b. 225:10
Bell: b. book and candle shall not drive 264:16
b. toll for poor Cock Robin 196:3
for whom the b. tolls 101:8
in a cowslip's b. I lie 289:6
ring the alarum b. Blow wind, come wrack 272:11
says the great b. at Bow 192:4
sexton toll'd the b. 134:13
the B. at Edmonton 92:7
the b. invites me. Hear it not, Duncan 270:10
tongue sounds ... as a sullen b. 256:7
very word is like a b. 150:5
why people ... do not ring the b. 23:21
Bells: ring, happy b., across the snow 313:4
ring out, wild b. 313:3
say the b. of St. Clement's 192:4
silver b. and cockle shells 191:7
the b. of hell go ting-a-ling-a-ling 14:12
the port is near, the b. I hear 325:12
up so floating many b. down 94:13
Belly: b. (*see also* Under-belly): born ... with something a round b. 256:9
fair round b. with good capon lin'd 244:11
I mind my b. very studiously 142:14
whose God is their b. 48:29
wd. fain have filled his b. 46:3
Bellyful: rumble thy b. 266:7
Belmont: In B. is a lady richly left 274:4
Beloved: be b. ... is above all bargains 207:14
heaped for the b.'s bed 300:6
Oh sleep! ... b. from pole to pole! 86:13
Below: down and away b. 18:11
Bends: he who b. himself a joy 55:4
though she b. him, she obeys 161:6
Benedick: B. the married man 277:13
Signior B., nobody marks you 277:11
Benevolence: comparative heaven ... b. can create 237:8
Bent: politics ... are not our b. 120:8
though on pleasure she was b. 92:8
Bermoothes: the still-vex'd B. 287:18
Bermudas: remote B. ride 167:8
Berries: pluck your b. harsh and crude 174:12
Berry: God, cd. have made a better b. 322:9
O sweeter than the b. 115:4
Berth: his death ... happened in his b. 134:13
Beset: idols which b. men's minds 23:16
Best: all is for the b. 321:9
all that's b. of dark and bright 71:2
b. and distinguished above others 134:9
b. is ... enemy of the good 321:13
b. is yet to be 62:9
b. of friends must part 17:4
b. of life is but intoxication 69:15
b. of possible worlds 321:9
b. portion of a good man's life 335:10
b. thing ... between France and England 139:18
b. to be off with the old love 16:1
b. words in their b. order 88:3
hope for the b. 217:3
make the b. of a bad job 207:16
past and to come seems b. 256:13
prayeth b. who loveth b. 87:4
so much bad in the b. of us 133:5
stolen sweets are b. 83:16
tort'ring hour ... afflict the b. 126:16
where the b. is like the worst 155:2
Bestial: what remains is b. 279:10
Bestride: he doth b. the narrow world 262:8
Bet: I b. my money on de bob-tail 112:4
three ... farmers once b. a pound 97:2
Bethlehem: O come ye to B. 196:5
O little town of B. 59:8
Betimes: he tires b. that spurs too fast b. 282:4
Better: a far, far b. thing ... I do 99:12
baffled to fight b. 60:12
b. ... alone than in bad company 322:17
b. book ... b. sermon ... b. mouse-trap 108:23
b. is a dinner of herbs 38:18
b. man than I am, Gunga Din 154:16
b. part of valour is discretion 256:3
b. rest ... I go to 99:12
b. than a play 78:17
b. that ten guilty ... escape 54:11
b. to err with Pope 70:15
b. to have loved and lost 68:12, 312:13
b. to have no opinion 22:12
b. to marry than to burn 48:3
b. to wear out than to rust out 94:11
ending is b. than mending 137:9
for b. for worse 53:22
former days ... b. than these 39:20
good name ... b. than precious ointment 39:18
how can man die b.? 163:10
he is no b. ... much the same 21:6
I am getting b. and b. 91:3
I cd. have b. spar'd a b. man 256:2
if you knows of a b. 'ole 23:22
it is b. to trust in the Lord 37:12
nae b. than he shd. be 65:17

Better (*continued*)
no b. than you shd. be, Polly 316:4
open rebuke is b. than secret love 39:2
poetry ... had b. not come at all 151:15
seen b. faces in my time 265:19
striving to b. ... mar what's well 265:16
thy love is b. than wine 40:2
to a b. land I know 112:10
wd. deserve b. of mankind 309:1
you shall now give place to b. men 94:9
Betters: order myself lowly ... to all my b. 53:13
still b. what is done 293:2
Between: no age b. ten and three and twenty 292:16
Bevy: a b. of fair women 179:15
Beware: b. the fury of a patient man 103:9
b. the Ides of March 262:5
Bewitched with the rogue's company 254:6
Beyond: enough that there *is* a b. 295:9
Bezonian: under which king, B.? 258:1
Bias: commodity, the b. of the world 264:13
what the weak head with ... b. rules 202:4
Bible: his studie was but litel on the b. 79:13
make out ... the hebrew B. 152:7
the English B. ... wd. alone suffice 164:3
Bible-black: starless and b. 316:2
Bicycle made for two 95:4
Bigamy, sir, is a crime! 183:1
Billet: every bullet has its b. 328:20
Billiard balls: and elliptical b. 118:12
Billion: among that b. minus one 137:14
Billows: make the b. smooth and bright 75-6:16
Bills: inflammation of his weekly b. 69:20
Billy: B. in one of his nice new sashes 124:10
poke poor B. 124:10
waited till his b. boiled 198:10
Bind: fast b., fast find 213:18
Biographies: history ... essence of innumerable b. 73:10
Biography: B. is about chaps 29:2
b. is different from Geography 29:2
history ... is but the b. of great men 73:8
there is ... no history: only b. 108:6
Birch, most shy and ladylike 162:13
Bird: a b. in hand ... two in the bush 207:41
a young b. in this bush 158:12
all like that wise b. 231:26
b. of night did sit 262:12
B., or but a wandering voice 336:2
b. thou never wert 300:1
both man and b. and beast 87:3
early b. catches the worm 212:8
fly can't b., but a b. can fly 172:6
not born for death, immortal B.! 150:4
O, blessèd B.! the earth we pace 336:4
speed ... like a b. on the wing 57:12
sweet b. that shunn'st the noise 173:8
the B. of Time has ... little way to fly 109:14
unto the sweet b.'s throat 244:4
Birds: all the b. are faint 151:1
all the b. of the air fell a-sighing 196:3
b. began to sing 193:5
b. in their little nests agree 323:3
b. in their ... nests agree with Chinamen 27:11
b. of a feather flock together 208:1
Birds (*continued*)
b. outside desperate to get in 183:5
b. sit brooding in the snow 269:1
four colly b. 194:2
how can ye chant, ye little b.? 67:5
kill two b. with one stone 217:38
pigs ... are very unlikely b. 223:5
sedge is wither'd ... no b. sing 148:14
she was one of the early b. 90:5
suspicions ... like bats amongst b. 22:24
two little dicky b. 195:5
will sing like b. i' th' cage 267:13
words that frightened the b. 12:11
Birmingham: I wanted to go to B. 160:7
to B. by way of Beachy Head 81:7
Birnam: ... till B. Forest come to Dunsinane 272:7
Birth: b., and copulation, and death 107:2
my love is of a b. as rare 167:16
our b. ... a sleep and a forgetting 332:1
royal kings ... famous by their b. 282:5
some glory in their b. 294:2
sunshine is a glorious b. 331:14
Birthright: sold his b. unto Jacob 31:6
Bishop: b. and abbot and prior 24:4
how can a b. marry? 303:13
no b., no King 139:1
Bit: b. the babies in their cradles 61:17
condescend to take a b. 308:12
I b. my arm, I sucked the blood 86:7
mine enemy's dog, though he had b. me 267:9
went mad and b. the man 122:19
Bite: bark at a distance never b. 211:29
bark worse than his b. 206:39
b. some other of my generals 115:14
b. the hand that fed them 64:16
dead men don't b. 211:1
smaller fleas to b. 'em 309:4
the man recovered of the b. 122:20
upon their backs to b. 'em 184:7
Bites: make two b. of a cherry 228:36
Biting: his b. is immortal 243:8
Bitten: once b., twice shy 222:27
Bitter: and shed a b. tear 76:3
b. groan of a martyr's woe 55:5
b. ... on itself [revenge] recoils 179:7
b. to endure ... sweet to remember 208:2
children ... make misfortunes more b. 21:18
eating the b. bread of banishment 282:12
lack gall to make oppression b. 250:17
love grows b. with treason 310:4
old and b. of tongue 337:6
peach was once a b. almond 318:16
sadden after none or b. fruit 110:8
Bitterness: ills have no weight, and tears no b. 163:7
little sweet doth kill much b. 148:11
no hatred or b. towards anyone 78:1
Black: b. as ink 208:3
b. as soot 208:4
b. as the devil 208:5
b. as the devil, hot as hell 310:11
b. as the pit from pole to pole 130:8
b. one ... good as the white 229:10
b. sheep in every flock 208:6
dark as the world ... b. as our loss 302:9
hung be the heavens with b. 260:5
I am b. but comely 40:3

Black (*continued*)
I am b. ... my soul is white 56:10
not so b. as he is painted 211:18
one b., and one white, and two khaki 13:2
pot calls the kettle b. 223:18
ravens ... as b. as they might be 11:15
secret, b., and midnight hags! 271:13
ship in a b. storm 324:4
sober-suited matron all in b. 286:21
two lovely b. eyes 85:6
Blackbird: there came a little b. 193:5
Blackbirds: four-and-twenty b. 193:5
Bladder: blows a man up like a b. 254:17
Blade: shook the fragment of his b. 240:10
vorpal b. went snicker-snack! 75:10
Blame: murd'rous, bloody, full of b. 294:11
poor wot gets the b. 16:13
scarcely can ... b. it too much 123:1
what they b. at night 202:12
Blanket: under the b. the black ... as good 229:10
wrong side of the b. 208:20
Blasphemy: in the soldier is flat b. 273:8
Blast: our shelter from the stormy b. 323:4
with contrary b. proclaims most deeds 181:4
Blaze: his rash fierce b. of riot cannot last 282:4
Blazon: this eternal b. must not be 249:7
Bleats articulate monotony 306:9
Bleed: if you prick us, do we not b.? 274:17
upon the thorns of life! I b.! 299:5
Bleeding: thou b. piece of earth 263:7
Bleeds: our country ... weeps it b. 271:18
Bless: b. the turf that wraps their clay 88:11
God b. the moon and God b. me 190:5
'God b. us every one!' said Tiny Tim 97:12
with thee at hand to b. 163:7
Blessed: b. are the horny hands of toil 162:12
judge none b. before his death 51:21
more b. to give 47:8
Blesseth: it b. him that gives ... that takes 275:1
Blessing: a boon and a b. to men 11:8
b. of the Old Testament 21:13
God bless—no harm in b. 68:15
prophetick b.—Be thou dull 103:10
set before you ... b. and cursing 33:5
when thou dost ask me b. 267:13
Blessings: all the b. of this life 53:1
b. are not valued till ... gone 208:7
Blest: always to be b. 203:1
thou art b. compared with me 66:13
Blind: be to her faults a little b. 205:5
b. as a bat 208:8
b. as the nineteen hundred and forty nails 302:9
b., despised, and dying king 300:5
b. man will not thank you 208:11
b. mouths! that scarce ... know how 175:3
Cupid painted b. 276:12
discomforts ... accompany my being b. 199:13
hatred is b. 216:16
if the b. lead the b. 44:15
in the land of the b. 208:12
love is b. 219:38, 274:14
men are b. in their own cause 208:10
none so b. as those who won't see 208:9
Blind (*continued*)
the maimed, and the halt, and the b. 46:1
three b. mice 195:1
Blindly: never lov'd so b. 65:10
Bliss: b. was it in that dawn to be alive 334:5
inward eye ... the b. of solitude 331:11
perfect b. and sole felicity 166:10
thou art a soul in b. 267:10
though thou hast not thy b. 149:8
virtue only makes our b. below 203:12
where ignorance is b. 126:2
Blisses: child among his new-born b. 332:3
Blithe: no lark more b. than he 54:1
O b. Newcomer ... O Cuckoo! 336:2
Block: a chip of the old b. 209:22
big black b. 118:7
he was ... the old b. itself 64:9
Blockhead: bookful b., ignorantly read 202:15
no man but a b. ever wrote 144:5
Blockheads of all ages 89:8
Blocks: you b., you stones! 262:4
Blood: all great Neptune's ocean wash this b. 270:12
b. and iron 54:8
b. is fet from fathers of war-proof 259:4
b. is nipp'd and ways be foul 269:11
b. is thicker than water 208:13
b. of English shall manure the ground 283:8
b. of this just person 45:3
b. out of a stone 229:35
by man shall his b. be shed 30:24
corruption inhabits our frail b. 292:1
freeze thy young b. 249:7
guiltless of his country's b. 126:11
here's the smell of the b. still 272:3
he today that sheds his b. with me 260:2
I am in b. stepp'd in so far 271:10
I smell the b. of a British man 266:17
I sucked the b. 86:7
in so far in b. that sin will pluck 285:6
nothing to offer but b., toil, tears and sweat 82:11
O, the b. more stirs 254:3
purge this choler without letting b. 281:7
red b. reigns ... winter's pale 292:17
simple faith than Norman b. 313:10
smoke and b. is the mix of steel 238:7
some moment when the moon was b. 81:1
speech to stir men's b. 263:20
summon up the b. 259:3
sunset ran one glorious b.-red 61:4
the b. of Jesus whispers peace 54:4
the near in b. the nearer bloody 270:16
who thicks man's b. with cold 86:8
whoso sheddeth man's b. 30:24
young b. must have its course 154:5
Bloody: be b., bold and resolute 271:15
if you break the b. glass 164:15
my head is b. but unbowed 130:9
often wipe a b. nose 115:11
walk! not b. likely 296:23
what b. man is that? 269:5
wrong with our b. ships 25:6
Bloom: how can ye b. sae fresh and fair? 67:5
you seize the flow'r, its b. is shed 67:4
Blooming: last rose ... left b. alone 184:1
like a b. Eastern bride 103:11
Blossom that hangs on the bough 289:6

Blot: noteless b. on a remembered name 297:15
Blots: inky b. and rotten parchment bonds 282:6
Blow: another deadly b.! 334:2
b., b., thou winter wind 245:1
b., bugle, b., set ... echoes flying 314:15
b. out, you bugles, over the rich Dead 59:1
b. wind, come wrack 272:11
b. your pipe ... till you burst 62:5
hear old Triton b. his wreathed horn 333:4
liberty's in every b. 67:2
that but this b. might be the be-all 270:5
to take one b. and turn 133:14
Blows: heal the b. of sound 133:13
the wild thyme b. 276:20
Bludgeonings: under the b. of chance 130:9
Blue: Little Boy B. 191:1
their hands are b. 158:5
true b. will never stain 228:21
Blunder: wonder at so grotesque a b. 29:6
youth is a b. 100:9
Blunders: one of Nature's agreeable b. 91:14
Blush: wd. it bring a b.? 98:16
Blushing: bears his b. honours 261:9
Blut und Eisen 54:8
Board: wasn't any b. ... isn't any trade 131:6
Boards: all the b. did shrink 86:6
Boast of heraldry ... pomp of power 126:7
Boasts two soul-sides 61:14
Boat: all in the same b. 224:36
beautiful pea-green b. 158:7
Boatman do not tarry 72:8
Boats: burn one's b. 208:33
messing about in b. 124:12
Boatswain and I, the gunner and his mate 288:9
Bobby Shafto: bonny B. 188:5
Bodies: friendless b. of unburied men 324:3
pile the b. high 238:5
rough notes and our dead b. 239:3
their b. are buried in peace 52:8
Bodkin: quietus make with a bare b. 250–1:20
Body: absent in b., ... present in spirit 47:33
asleep in b., ... become a living soul 335:12
b. is not more than the soul 326:4
b. of a ... feeble woman 107:13
carry ... b. around ... its sentimental value 114:1
every joint and motive of her b. 290:8
fretted the pigmy b. to decay 102:17
gin a b. meet a b. 65:15
mind that makes the b. rich 287:11
my little b. is aweary 274:5
need a b. cry? 65:15
perfect little b., without fault 58:6
Presence of Mind ... Absence of B. 231:19
reading is to ... mind what exercise ... to the b. 306:8
some in their b.'s force 294:2
soul not more than the b. 326:4
sound mind in a sound b. 146:11
that learned b. wanted loyalty 318:1
the corruptible b. 51:13
Thersites' b. is as good as Ajax' 247:8
we ... are one b. in Christ 47:22
we therefore commit his b. 53:30
with my b. I thee worship 53:24
Bog: tell your name ... to an admiring b. 99:14
Boil: we b. at different degrees 108:20
Bold: be bloody, b. and resolute 271:15
be b., be b., ... everywhere Be b. 305:12
Boldness, and again b., and always b. 95:9
Bond: let him look to his b. 274:16
take a b. of fate 271:16
'tis not in the b. 275:4
the very b. of love 293:5
word is as good as his b. 216:37
Bondage: out of the house of b. 31:29
Bondman: so base that wd. be a b.? 263:10
Bonds: inky blots and rotten parchment b. 282:6
Bone: a b. to pick with fate 186:5
beat him with a b. 211:28
b. of my bones 30:9
fetch her poor dog a b. 192:2
have a b. in one's leg 208:15
two dogs strive for a b. 228:39
Bones: as rottenness in his b. 38:12
good ... interred with their b. 263:11
let's have the tongs and the b. 277:4
mock'd the dead b. ... scatt'red by 285:1
my Shakespeare for his honoured b. 175:11
o ye dry b., hear the word 41:23
of his b. are coral made 288:1
Bonfire: primrose way to th' everlasting b. 270:13
Bong-tree: land where the B. grows 158:8
Bonnet: a bee in one's b. 207:9
Bonnets: the b. of Bonny Dundee 239:4
Bonnie (Bonny): b., b. banks o' Loch Lomon' 16:10
braes o' b. Doon 67:5
bring back my B. 16:2
for b. Annie Laurie 101:10
is b. and blithe and good 191:8
my B. is over the ocean 16:2
Bons mots: not enough b. in existence 137:12
Bonum: *Summum b.* 84:3
Bo(o): cannot say B. to a goose 224:39
Booby: give her b. for another 115:10
Book: a bad b. is as much labour 137:13
a b. ... amusing with numerous errors 123:18
a b.'s a b. although 70:12
a good b. is the precious life-blood 182:3
a leaf out of one's b. 226:38
bell, b. and candle shall not drive me back 264:16
b. ... shut is but a block 208:16
b. that furnishes no quotations 199:4
but where's the b.? 82:3
dainties ... bred in a b. 268:11
damned, thick, square b.! 121:13
do not throw this b. about 26:14
go, litel b. 80:6
half a library to make one b. 143:16
he who destroys a good b. 182:2
his common-place b. ... full 309:7
if a b. is worth reading ... worth buying 237:2
I'll drown my b. 289:5
is no b.—it is a plaything 199:4
my B. of Songs and Sonnets 276:2
never read a b. before reviewing 303:16
never read ... b. ... not a year old 108:17
seldom read a b. ... given to them 143:10
take down this b. 337:10
that one might read the b. of fate! 257:4
upon a b. in cloistre ... to poure 79:6

Book (*continued*)
use of a b. without pictures? 73:14
what genius ... when I wrote that b. 309:13
when a new b. is published 234:13
word for word without b. 290:11
write a better b. 108:23
your face, my thane, is as a b. 270:3
Books: as school-boys from their b. 286:12
at his beddes heed twenty b. 79:9
author who speaks about his own b. 100:6
base authority from others' b. 268:8
b. and friends ... few and good 208:17
b. cannot always please 93:17
b. cannot be killed by fire 235:5
b. from which the lectures are taken 143:1
b. in the running brooks 243:15
b. think for me 156:6
b.! 'tis a dull and endless strife 335:5
borrowers of b. 156:3
deep-versed in b. and shallow 180:5
his sins ... scarlet ... his b. ... read 27:5
I keep my b. at the British Museum 68:4
I never read b.—I *write* them 232:1
I'll burn my b.! 165:11
in a person's bad [good] b. 208:18
in this war, ... b. are weapons 235:5
learning ... gained most by those b. 114:10
needed not the spectacles of b. 104:4
no furniture so charming as b. 303:12
of making many b. ... is no end 39:28
old b. maken us memorie 80:1
old b., old wine 123:6
quit your b. 335:4
read any good b. lately? 185:3
read of in b., or dreamt of 24:5
rural quiet, friendship, b. 316:13
some b. are to be tasted 23:7
the b., the arts, the academes 268:14
to Cambridge b. 318:1
to Cambridge b. he sent 60:4
true University ... collection of b. 73:9
we all know that b. burn 235:5
Boom: strong gongs groaning ... guns b. far 81:5
Boon: a b. and a blessing to men 11:8
is life a b.? 120:17
Boot: b. is on the other leg 208:19
make b. upon the summer's ... buds 258:8
Boots: b., b., b. 154:11
too big for one's b. 228:11
what b. it with incessant care? 174:15
Bo-peep has lost her sheep 190:10
Border: through all the wide B. 240:5
Bore: every hero ... a b. at last 108:16
people's mothers ... b. me 328:13
Bored: two mighty tribes, the *Bores* and *B.* 70:9
Boring: something ... b. about somebody else's happiness 137:11
Born: a sucker b. every minute 24:10
better to be lowly b. 261:4
b., bred, and hanged ... same parish 12:5
b. for the Universe 123:1
b. out of my due time 184:9
b. to be hanged 208:21
b. to speak all mirth 277:19
b. with silver spoon 208:22
b. within the sound of Bow Bells 208:23
b. ... wrong side of the blanket 208:20
I was b. about three of the clock 256:9
Born (*continued*)
I was not b. yesterday 208:24
is not b., and does not die 302:10
man that is b. of a woman 53:28
native here, and to the manner b. 249:2
'Never was b.!' persisted Topsy 307:14
none of woman b. shall harm Macbeth 271:15
not b. to sue, but to command 281:9
one b. out of due time 48:11
powerless to be b. 18:15
some are b. great 291:9
that ever I was b. to set it right 249:14
then surely I was b. 81:1
under that [star] I was b. 277:20
we are b. in other's pain 316:8
when we are b. we cry 267:8
who are b. of thee 28:10
wd. thou had'st never been b. 280:6
ye must be b. again 46:19
yield to one of woman b. 272:12
Borne it with a patient shrug 274:10
Borogoves: mimsy were the b. 75:9
Borrow: better buy than b. 207:26
earth must b. its mirth 326:9
even if we have to b. 322:15
Sorrow, why dost b.? 147:10
the men who b. 156:2
Borrower: neither a b. nor a lender be 248:17
Borrowers of books—those mutilators 156:3
Borrowing: beggar by banqueting upon b. 51:23
b. dulls the edge of husbandry 248–9:17
b. only ... lingers it out 256:12
Bosom: b. of his Father and his God 126:15
cleanse the stuff'd b. 272:6
Bosom-friend: close b. of the maturing sun 147:1
Bosoms: to men's business, and b. 21:7
Boston: and this is good old B. 57:10
readers of the B. Evening Transcript 106:2
Boteler: as Dr. B. said of strawberries 322:9
Both: money ... life; women require b. 68:13
much might be said on b. sides 9:8
to lose b. [parents] ... carelessness 327:12
Bottle: my b. of salvation 232:12
she found a little b. on it 73:15
Bottles: new wine into old b. 45:25
Bottom: bless thee, B. ... thou art translated 277:2
Bottomless: the b. pit 50:24
Bough: blossom that hangs on the b. 289:6
when the b. breaks 189:10
Boughs: incense hangs upon the b. 150:1
lowest b. and the brushwood sheaf 61:1
my soul into the b. does glide 168:2
shade of melancholy b. 244:10
Bought: until she has b. her wedding clothes 9:10
Boulogne: a young man of B. 12:11
Bound upon a wheel of fire 267:10
Bounty: large was his b. 126:14
Bourgeois: how beastly the b. is 157:8
Bourgeoisie: British B. is not born 302:10
Bourn: from whose b. no traveller returns 250–1:20
to see beyond our b. 147:11
Boutiquiers: une nation de b. 185:12
Bow: arrow from the Almighty's b. 55:5
as unto the b. the cord is 161:6

Bow (*continued*)
b., b., ye lower middle classes! 117:1
b. themselves when he did sing 261:5
bring me my b. of burning gold 55:8
if you b. ... b. low 208:26
my throne, bid kings come b. 264:15
says the great bell at B. 192:4
set my b. in the cloud 30:25
two strings to one's b. 229:5
with my b. and arrow 196:2
Bow Bells: within the sound of B. 208:23
Bowed: b. himself with all his might 33:22
I have not ... b. to its idolatries 69:5
Bowels: beseech you, in the b. of Christ 94:7
his b. of compassion 50:11
Bower: Lime-tree B. my prison 87:17
Bowl: crabs hiss in the b. 269:1
fill the flowing b. 14:14
he called for his b. 192:1
inverted b. we call the sky 110:13
love in a golden b. 55:2
Box: worth a guinea a b. 11:10
Boy: a horrid, wicked b. was he 133:9
and to be b. eternal 292:12
being read to by a b. 106:5
b. stood on the burning deck 130:4
b. who lives down the lane 188:4
b. with never a crack in my heart 337:8
boys when I was a b. 28:4
Chatterton, the marvellous b. 334:8
every b. and every gal 117:8
imagination of a b. is healthy 147:7
let the b. win his spurs 105:9
little B. Blue 191:1
my beamish b.! 75:11
said, what a good b. am I 191:2
shades ... close upon the growing b. 332:1
speak roughly to your little b. 74:6
was and a little tiny b. 292:3
Boys: all the little b. and girls 62:6
as flies to wanton b. 266:20
b. and girls come out to play 188:6
b. will be b. 208:27
b. will be men 208:28
by office b. for office b. 237:14
Christian b. I can scarcely ... make 19:13
claret is the liquor for b. 144:15
guns with b., are never valued 94:1
mealy b., and beef-faced b. 98:14
men that were b. when I was 28:4
only know two sorts of b. 98:14
till the b. come home 111:12
we are the b. that fear no noise 123:9
what are little b. made of? 195:6
when the b. came out to play 189:3
young b. ... are level now with men 243:6
Brace: let us ... b. ourselves to our duties 82:14
Braces: damn b. Bless relaxes 57:4
Bradshaw: the vocabulary of B. is nervous 102:6
Brain: b. [begins] to think again 58:15
b. of ... man is not able 256:8
dull b. perplexes and retards 149:16
gladness ... thy b. must know 300:3
glean'd my teeming b. 151:7
got to leave that b. outside 117:9
I feared it might injure the b. 74:3
let my b. lie also 61:13
like madness in the b. 87:7
Brain (*continued*)
overset the b. or break the heart 332:12
shallow draughts intoxicate the b. 202:5
written troubles of the b. 272:6
Brains: fluffy, with no b. at all 131:5
he exercises of his b. 117:6
I mix them with my b., sir 196:11
mob has ... heads but no b. 221:8
when the b. were out the man would die 271:8
Brand plucked out of the fire 43:2
Brandy: some are fou o' b. 66:4
to be a hero must drink b. 144:15
Brass: as if this flesh ... were b. impregnable 283:6
asked ... where he carried his b. 28:9
men's evil manners live in b. 262:1
Brave: b. that are no more 93:1
b. who sink to rest 88:10
fortune favours the b. 315:3
is it not passing b. to be a king? 166:9
none but the b. deserves the fair 103:12
O b. new world! 289:7
sons of the prophet were b. 16:15
toll for the b. 93:1
Bravery: all her b. on and tackle trim 180:15
Bravest: the b. by far in the ranks 16:15
Bray: I will be the Vicar of B. 15:13
Brazil, where the nuts come from 315:13
Breach: more honoured in the b. 249:2
once more unto the b. 259:3
Bread: a Loaf of B. beneath the Bough 109:15
bitter b. of banishment 282:12
b. and cheese and kisses 206:31
b. eaten in secret is pleasant 38:7
b. is buttered on both sides 208:29
b. of heaven, feed me 329:2
b. which the Lord hath given 31:28
b. with one fish-ball 156:14
but one halfpenny-worth of b. 255:3
cast thy b. upon the waters 39:24
did eat b. to the full 31:27
God! that b. shd. be so dear 135:4
in the sweat ... shalt thou eat b. 30:13
looked to government for b. 64:16
man doth not live by b. only 32:23
neither yet b. to the wise 39:23
nor his seed begging b. 36:9
not live by b. alone 43:13
some gave them white b. 190:9
thine enemy ... give him b. 38:28
this day our daily b. 43:24
to eat the b. of sorrows 37:20
trees were b. and cheese 14:1
which side one's b. is buttered 218:8
white b. and butter 191:4
Break: never doubted clouds wd. b. 60:12
Breakages Ltd., the biggest ... corporation 295:6
Breakfast: b., dinner, lunch and tea 27:4
b., supper, dinner, luncheon 62:4
hope is a good b. 23:13
kills me ... Scots at a b. 254:12
where shall we our b. take? 11:15
Breaking: sleep that knows not b. 239:9
Breast: bold spirit in a loyal b. 281:8
charms to soothe a savage b. 89:5
earth's sweet flowing b. 153:8
make a clean b. 209:31
nunnery of thy chaste b. 162:6

Breast (*continued*)
one who ... marched b. forward 60:12
panic's in thy b. [breastie] 66:10
safe ... on Abraham's b. 12:6
Tamer of the human b. 126:16
that with dauntless b. 126:11
what his b. forges ... tongue must vent 246:10
Breasts: cowardice in noble b. 281:10
Breath: allowing him a b., a little scene 283:6
although thy b. be rude 245:1
and thou no b. at all? 268:4
b. of worldly men 283:2
draw thy b. in pain 253:9
fly away, b. 291:6
not flatter'd its rank b. 69:5
such dulcet and harmonious b. 276:18
such is the b. of kings 281:12
summer's ripening b. 286:11
take into the air my quiet b. 150:3
thou b. of Autumn's being 299:3
Breathe: so long as men can b. or eyes can see 293:15
Breathes: b. ... man, with soul so dead 239:16
b. upon a bank of violets 290:10
Breathing: rifle all the b. spring 88:8
Breathless: a nun b. with adoration 333:2
hanging b. on thy fate! 160:11
Bred: where is fancy b. 274:18
Breeches: to wear the b. 230:2
Breed: b. of their horses and dogs 199:7
fear'd by their b. 282:5
this happy b. of men, this little world 282:5
Breeding lilacs out of the dead land 107:3
Breeze: fair b. blew, the white foam flew 86:4
fluttering and dancing in the b. 331:7
the battle and the b. 72:10
Breezes: little b. dusk and shiver 313:12
Brent: yr. bonnie brow was b. 66:5
Brethren: b. to dwell together in unity 37:21
least of these my b. 44:30
Brevis esse laboro, obscurus fio 135:8
Brevity is the soul of wit 249:15
Brewage: no pullet-sperm in my b. 276:7
Brewery: O take me to a b. 15:9
Bribe: doing nothing for a b. 247:3
too poor for a b. 127:3
Bribes: how many b. he had taken 29:7
Brick: straw to make b. 31:20
Bricks: a cat on hot b. 209:15
Bridal: the b. of the earth and sky 131:12
Bride: b. hath paced into the hall 86:1
happy bridesmaid ... happy b. 311:7
Jerusalem ... as a b. adorned 51:2
sate like a blooming Eastern b. 103:11
still unravish'd b. of quietness 149:6
were I thy b.! 121:4
Bridegroom: fresh as a b. 254:1
Bridesmaid: happy b., happy bride 311:7
Bridge: don't cross the b. till you get to it 210:20
keep the b. with me 163:11
on the b. at midnight 16:12
on the B. of Sighs 69:6
what need the b. much broader? 277:14
women, and champagne and b. 27:7
Brief: b. life is here our portion 186:13
b., my lord, as woman's love 252:3
dress'd in a little b. authority 273:7
Brief (*continued*)
I struggle to be b., and become obscure 135:8
out, out, b. candle! 272:10
Brigands demand ... women require 68:13
Bright: all things b. and beautiful 10:4
best of dark and b. 71:2
goddess, excellently b. 145:8
look, the land is b. 85:3
moon be still as b. 71:3
Sun came up ... and he shone b. 85:13
young lady named B. 63:1
Brightness: all her original b. 176:11
b. falls from the air 186:12
Brighton: yes, the B. line 327:14
Brilliance: degree of b. ... left to fighter's honour 130:7
Brillig: 'twas b. and the slithy toves 75:9
Bring: b. back my Bonnie to me 16:2
b. me flesh and b. me wine 187:2
b. me my bow ... arrows ... spear 55:8
b. the good old bugle, boys 336:9
Bringer: first b. of unwelcome news 256:7
Brioche: qu'ils mangent de la b. 165:6
Britain: B. a fit country for heroes 160:9
B. is a world by itself 247:1
B. won her proudest bays 117:10
government ... framed, like that of B. 317:2
hath B. all the sun? 247:5
that B. would fight on alone 83:4
when B. first, at Heaven's command 316:12
British: B. Bourgeoisie ... if it is ill 302:10
B. Empire ... last for a thousand years 82:14
dirty B. coaster 168:14
I keep my books at the B. Museum 68:4
liquidation of the B. Empire 83:6
maxim of the B. ... 'Business as usual' 82:8
no spectacle so ridiculous as the B. 164:6
smell the blood of a B. man 266:17
tow, ... row, row, for the B. Grenadier 16:14
Britons: B. never will be slaves 316:12
B. were only natives 241:8
Broad: she is the B.: I am the High 306:1
Broken: a b. spirit: a b. ... contrite heart 36:15
laws were made to be b. 187:17
Broken-hearted: half b. to sever for years 71:5
we had ne'er been b. 65:10
Brood of Folly without father bred 173:5
Brook: a willow grows aslant the b. 253:1
hear the little b. a-gurgling 120:7
where the b. is deep 260:8
Brooks: books in the running b. 243:15
golden sands, and crystal b. 100:17
Broom: new b. sweeps clean 221:37
Broth: gave them ... b. without any bread 194:5
too many cooks spoil the b. 228:13
Brother: am I my b.'s keeper? 30:16
be my b.; be he ne'er so vile 260:2
Big B. is watching you 197:3
Death and his b. Sleep 298:7
down with Big B. 197:5
sworn b. ... to grim Necessity 284:4
two sisters embrace like one b. 234:1
Brotherhood: crown thy good with b. 25:4
Brotherly: let b. love continue 49:23

Brothers: all men will be b. 238:12
and all the b. too 291:8
two b. and their murder'd man 148:12
Brow: b. like to a title-leaf 256:6
on Ida's shady b. 56:13
yr. bonnie b. was brent 66:5
Brown: baked me too b. 75:4
Bruce: Scots whom B. has ... led 67:1
Brüder: alle Menschen werden B. 238:12
Bruise: parmaceti for an inward b. 254:2
Brunck: most learned professor, B. 204:13
Brush: all tarred with the same b. 227:14
Brute beasts that have no understanding 53:19
Brute: et tu, B.? 71:14, 263:2
Brutish: life ... nasty, b., and short 133:3
Brutus: for B. is an honourable man 263:12
the fault, dear B. 262:8
you too, B.? 71:14
Bubble: fire burn and cauldron b. 271:11
like the b. on the fountain 239:10
seeking the b. reputation 244:11
Bubbles: beaded b. winking 149:14
Bucket: nations are as a drop of a b. 41:1
Buckingham Palace: changing the guard at B. 171:6
high-reaching B. grows circumspect 285:5
Buckram: rogues in b. 254:15
Bud: concealment, like a worm i' th' b. 291:7
this b. of love 286:11
Buds: gather the flowers, but spare the b. 168:6
shake the darling b. of May 293:13
Buffets: blows and b. of the world 271:2
Buffoon: a private b. 121:5
statesman and b. 103:4
Bugle: blow, b.; answer, echoes 314:15
bring the good old b., boys 336:9
Bugles: blow out, you b., over the rich Dead 59:1
Build: easier to pull down than to b. 223:35
except the Lord b. the house 37:19
on this rock ... b. my church 44:16
Building: don't clap too hard ... very old b. 197:8
Built: houses are b. to live in 23:3
Rome was not b. in a day 224:27
Bulbul: Abdul the B. Amir 16:15
Bull: b. in a china shop 208:30
in time the savage b. 155:16
red rag to a b. 224:7
roar like a b. 224:23
take the b. by the horns 227:3
Bull and Bush: down at the old B. 317:10
Bullet: ballot is stronger than the b. 159:8
every b. has its billet 328:20
Bullfighting is the only art in which 130:7
Bullocks: good yoke of b. at Stamford 257:6
he ... whose talk is of b. 52:4
Bulls the cow must keep the calf 208:31
Bully: I love the lovely b. 259:9
Bumbast out a blank verse 127:6
Bunbury: a ... permanent invalid called B. 327:8
Bunk: Gert's poems are b. 13:4
history is b. 111:9
Buns: hot cross b.! 189:7
Burden: take up the White Man's B. 155:6
Burdens: bear ye one another's b. 48:22
heavy b. at his narrow gate 258:8
Burglar: enterprising b.'s not a-burgling 120:7
Burglary: flat b. as ever was committed 278:14
Buried: half-b. in the snow was found 160:13
the old Adam ... so b. 53:10
Burlington: I'm B. Bertie 128:12
Burn: better to marry than to b. 48:3
b. ... candle at both ends 208:34
b. one's boats 208:33
b. the midnight oil 208:35
hearts are dry ... b. to the socket 331:4
I'll b. my books! 165:11
old age shd. b. and rave 315:15
violent fires soon b. out 282:4
we all know that books b. 235:5
Burned: bush b. with fire 31:17
Burning: b. indignation no longer lacerates 309:11
my bow of b. gold 55:8
stood on the b. deck 130:4
tiger, tiger, b. bright 56:5
where b. Sappho loved and sung 69:21
Burnt: ash the b. roses leave 106:10
Burr: a kind of b., I shall stick 273:13
Burst: blow your pipe ... till you b. 62:5
his flaw'd heart ... b. smilingly 268:1
she b. while drinking 12:4
the first that ... b. into that ... sea 86:4
Burthen: b. of the mystery 335:11
spirit ... too ... laden ever to b. thine 300:7
Bury: I come to bury C. 263:11
to b. the hatchet 208:36
Bus: a b. bound for Ealing 13:3
Hitler has missed the b. 78:11
I'm not even a b. but a tram 128:11
Bush: beat about the b. 207:5
b. burned with fire 31:17
fear each b. an officer 261:1
four times as big as the b. 158:12
good wine needs no b. 215:24
true that good wine needs no b. 246:4
two in the b. 207:41
Busier: semed b. than he was 79:11
Business: a dinner lubricates b. 240:13
b. before pleasure 208:39
b. is b. 208:38
b. ... may bring money 20:10
b. of consequence, *do it yourself* 24:3
called away by particular b. 301:16
do b. in great waters 37:4
everybody's b. is nobody's b. 212:35
if everybody minded their own b. 74:5
it is the b. of the wealthy man 27:6
love and b. teach eloquence 219:34
men, some to b., some to pleasure 203:15
mind yr. own b. 221:4
servants of b. 22:2
that's the true b. precept 98:6
the end of this day's b. 264:5
the maxim ... is 'B. as usual' 82:8
to b. that we love we rise 243:2
to men's b. and bosoms 21:7
Buss: Miss B. and Miss Beale 14:4
Busy: b. ... hath least to do 208:40
no-wher so b. a man 79:11
Busyness: extreme b. ... deficient vitality 307:8

Butch: too b. for be 155:7
Butchers: I am ... gentle with these b. 263:7
Butt: here is my b. and ... sea-mark 280:13
Butter: a little bit of b. to my bread 172:1
b. and eggs and ... cheese 71:16
b. for the royal slice 171:11
b. in a lordly dish 33:15
b. will only make us fat 122:1
b. wd. not melt in his mouth 208:41
white bread and b. 191:4
Buttercup: I'm called Little B. 119:9
Butterflies: laugh at gilded b. 267:13
Button: pray you undo this b. 268:4
Buxom: so b., blithe, and debonair 173:15
Buy: ask thy purse what thou shdst. b. 206:25
better b. than borrow 207:26
cherries grow, which none may b. 72:14
I'd have you b. and sell so 293:2
stop me and b. one 11:7
to b. a world of happy days 284:15
Buyer: let the b. beware 209:16
naught, saith the b. ... then he boasteth 38:24
Buzz, b., I wonder why he does? 172:3
Bygones: let b. be b. 209:3
Byron: Lord B. cuts a figure 152:7
Byzantium: and the Soldan of B. is smiling 81:4

Cabbage with a college education 318:16
Cabbages: of c. and kings 76:4
Cabin: a small c. build there 337:4
make me a willow c. at yr. gate 290:15
Cabined: but now I am c., cribb'd 271:6
Cabots talk only to God 57:10
Cacoethes: tenet insanabile ... scribendi c. 146:10
Cadiz: sunset ... reeking into C. Bay 61:4
Caesar: as C. loved me, I weep 263:10
C.'s wife ... above suspicion 71:15
hast thou appealed unto C.? 47:12
I appeal unto C. 47:11
I come to bury C. 263:11
in envy of great C. 264:6
not that I lov'd C. less 263:9
O mighty C., dost thou lie so low? 263:5
regions C. never knew 92:2
unto C. shalt thou go 47:12
unto C. the things which are C.'s 44:25
Caesars: there be many C. 247:1
Café: laughter ... in every street c. 128:1
Cage: a robin redbreast in a c. 54:13
marriage is like a c. 183:5
nor iron bars a c. 162:5
will sing like birds i' th' c. 267:13
Cain: the first city C. [made] 91:12
the Lord set a mark upon C. 30:17
Caitiff: rude c. smite the other too 133:14
Cake: bake me a c. 192:5
eat yr. c. and have it 212:17
let them eat c. 165:6
some gave them plum c. 190:9
Cakes: no more c. and ale? 291:5
Calais: find C. lying in my heart 168:11
Calamity: makes c. of so long life 250–1:20
Calamus saevior ense patet 67:9
Calculated: nicely-c. less or more 330:11
Calculating: accurate about her age. It looks so c. 327:17
Calculation of the expense of ... bow-windows 97:15
Calculators: age of ... sophisters ... c. 64:11
Calendar: a c., a c.! ... find out moonshine! 277:1
Calf: bring hither the fatted c. 46:4
c. love, half love 209:4
c. ... young lion ... fatling together 40:24
Caliban: 'ban, 'ban, Ca-C. 288:10
Call: a wild c. and a clear c. 168:16
c. me early, mother dear 314:6
c. of the running tide 168:16
Death ... must c. too soon 120:17
dost thou c. me fool, boy? 265:13
go, for they c. you, Shepherd 18:18
I can c. spirits from the ... deep 255:5
one clear c. for me! 311:13
that ... I wd. fain c. master 265:12
Called: he c. for his pipe ... his bowl 192:1
Callooh! Callay! 75:11
Callous engraved on her heart 241:11
Calm of mind, all passion spent 181:8
Calumny: envy and c. and hate 297:16
thou shalt not escape c. 251:3
Camberwell: a long way east of C. 28:1
Cambridge: to C. books, as ... wanted learning 318:1
to C., books he sent 60:4
who's ahead ... either Oxford or C. 304:4
Came: for yr. pleasure you c. here 92:12
I c., I saw, I conquered 71:13
I c. like Water, and like Wind I go 110:5
I c., saw, and overcame 257:13
tell them I c. and no one answered 96:15
Camel: c. ... through the eye of a needle 44:23
last straw breaks the c.'s back 218:20
strain at a gnat and swallow a c. 44:26
Camelot: many-tower'd C. 313:11
Camp: from c. to c., through ... night 259:8
love rules ... court ... c. ... grove 239:13
Campbells are coming 14:13
Can: fill up my cup ... my c. 239:4
he who c., does ... cannot, teaches 296:13
Canary: mine host's C. wine 149:4
Cancel: lure it back to c. half a line 110:12
Cancels: debt which c. all others 89:1
Candid: be c. where we can 202:18
save me from the c. friend 72:16
Candide: '...Well said,' replied C. 321:11
Candle: bell, book and c. shall not drive me back 264:16
burn the c. at both ends 208:34
c. to light you to bed 192:4
game is not worth the c. 214:28
hold a c. to the devil 216:36
little c. throws his beams 275:11
my c. burns at both ends 170:13
out, out, brief c.! 272:10
this day light such a c. 157:2
Candle-holder: I'll be a c. and look on 285:20
Candle-light: can I get there by c.? 189:8
choose ... woman nor linen by c. 209:25
Candles: night's c. are burnt out 286:22
Candy is dandy 186:8
Cankered: heart ... grief hath c. 72:1
Cankers: the c. of a calm world 255:16
Cannon: even in the c.'s mouth 244:11
Cannon-ball: a c. took off his legs 134:11
Cannons: where the thundering c. roar 123:9
Canoe: paddle his own c. 167:7

Canon: his c. 'gainst self-slaughter 248:2
Canopy: rich embroider'd c. to kings 260:14
Canossa: nach C. gehen wir nicht 54:7
We will not go to C. 54:7
Cant: apple press'd with specious c. 135:2
clear yr. mind of c. 144:18
Cantons: loyal c. of contemned love 290:15
Cap: if the c. fits 209:6
put on one's thinking c. 223:34
riband in the c. of youth 252:24
stuck a feather in his c. 196:4
Capability: Negative C. 151:11
Capon: belly with good c. lined 244:11
Captain: a right good c., too! 119:10
a train-band c. eke was he 92:6
C., art tha sleepin' there below? 187:9
c.'s hand on his shoulder smote 187:12
in the c.'s but a choleric word 273:8
O C.! my C.! 325:12
the c. of my soul 130:10
Captains: the c. and the kings depart 155:3
Captive: weak minds led c. 180:2
Caravan: put up yr. c. just for one day 133:6
Cardinal: C. Lord Archbishop of Rheims 24:5
jackdaw sat on the C.'s chair 24:4
Cards: an old age of c. 203:16
can pack the c. ... cannot play 22:16
played at c. for kisses 163:3
Care: begone, dull c. 14:11
c. killed a cat 209:7
I c. for nobody 54:2
I c. not whether a man is good 55:7
nor for itself hath any c. 56:2
past my help is past my c. 25:9
past redress ... with me past c. 282:11
polish'd perturbation! golden c.! 257:16
ravell'd sleave of c. 270:11
sae weary, fu' o' c. 67:5
so shaken ... wan with c. 253:13
sport that wrinkled C. derides 173:17
this life if full of c. 96:2
what boots it with incessant c. 174:15
what c. I for whom she be? 330:1
Career: which might damage his c. 25:1
Careful: be very c. o' vidders ... Sammy 98:24
Careless: first fine c. rapture 61:3
sitting c. on a granary floor 147:3
so c. of the single life 312:16
Cares: if no one c. for me 54:2
light c. speak, great ones are dumb 219:8
Carew: the grave of Mad C. 129:6
Cargo of ivory and apes 168:13
Caricature of a face 118–9:15
Carlyle, Tennyson, Browning 232:3
Carouse: for ... marriage I did make c. 110:9
Carpe diem, quam minimum ... postero 135:13
Carpenter: Walrus and the C. 76:2–6
Carriage: a very small second-class c. 117:13
I can't afford a c. 95:4
the c. held but just ourselves 99:17
Cart: creak of a lumbering c. 337:7
put the c. before the horse 209:9
Carthago: delenda est C. 77:13
Carve: c. on every tree the fair ... she 245:2
c. out dials quaintly 260:13
let's c. him as a dish 262:14
must c. in Latin or in Greek 322:2
Carved: we c. not a line 330:4
Casca: the envious C. 263:17
Case: c. is still before the courts 135:9
nothing to do with the c. 118:15
there to attend to the c. 117:5
Cased: yr. hare when it is c. 121:11
Casement ope at night 150:7
Casements: magic c. opening on the foam 150:4
Cases: circumstances alter c. 209:28
hard c. make bad law 216:12
Cash: he takes yr c., but where's the book? 82:3
Cashmere: tales of fair C. 329:3
Casques: within this wooden O the very c. 258:6
Cassio: if C. do remain 280:8
not C. kill'd! 280:12
Cassius: for ever ... farewell, C. 264:4
yond C. has a lean and hungry look 262:9
Cast: I backward c. my e'e 66:13
pale c. of thought 250–1:20
the die is c. 71:12
Castle: a c. called Doubting C. 63:11
a man's house is his c. 85:8
Englishman's house is his c. 212:26
I'm the king of the c. 190:3
splendour falls on c. walls 314:14
the rich man in his c. 10:5
Castlereagh: a mask like C. 298:13
Castles: build c. in Spain 209:11
c. in the air 209:12
Cat: a c. and a lie 318:17
care killed a c. 209:7
c. has nine lives 209:13
c. is away the mice will play 230:12
c. out of the bag 218:38
c. will mew, and dog will have his day 253:5
fog comes on little c. feet 238:4
hanging of his c. 58:2
he bought a crooked c. 194:3
like a c. on hot bricks 209:15
more ways of killing a c. 154:7
part to tear a c. in 276:14
room to swing a c. 224:28
runcible c. with crimson whiskers 158:10
the c. and the fiddle 189:5
what c.'s averse to fish? 125:10
when I play with my c. 183:4
which way the c. jumps 209:14
Cataclysm: out of their c. but one poor Noah 137:14
Catalogue: in the c. ye go for men 271:1
Cataracts: you c. and hurricanoes, spout 266:6
Catastrophe: I'll tickle yr. c. 256:14
Catch: c. a falling star 101:5
c. a nigger by his toe 189:1
c. him once upon the hip 274:7
perdition c. my soul 279:14
set a thief to c. a thief 227:26
Catechism: and so ends my c. 255:21
Categorical: in order c. 120:4
Caterpillars of the commonwealth 282:10
Cats: killed the c. and bit the babies 61:17
Caucasus: thinking on the frosty C. 282:1
Caught: maidens ... are ever c. by glare 68:18
one c. a Muffin, the other c. a Mouse 158:11
Cauldron: fire burn and c. bubble 271:11
Causas: felix qui potuit rerum cognoscere c. 321:7

Cause: an effect whose c. is God 93:11
beauty of the good old c. 333:11
blind in their own c. 208:10
great c. of cheering us all up 28:7
it is the c., it is the c., my soul 280:10
jealous for the c. 280:3
know c., or just impediment 53:18
report me and my c. aright 253:8
ring out a slowly dying c. 313:5
'what great c. ... identified with?' 28:7
Causes: able to learn the c. of things 321:7
c. why and wherefore in all 260:3
home of lost c. ... beliefs 19:7
of all the c. which conspire 202:4
Cavaliero: he was a perfect c. 68:16
Cave canem 200:1
Cave: her vacant interlunar c. 180:11
Idols of the C. 23:16
in Stygian c. forlorn 173:14
out of the misty eastern c. 298:15
Cave (of) Adullam: escaped to the C. 34:8
retired into ... his political C. 58:10
Caveat emptor 209:16
Cavern: happy field or mossy c. 149:4
in a c. in a canyon 183:8
Caverns measureless to man 87:11
Caves: dark unfathom'd c. of ocean 126:10
pleasure-dome with c. of ice 87:15
Caviare to the general 250:10
Cavity: filling his last c. 12:7
Cease: I will not c. from mental fight 55:8
poor shall never c. 33:3
seedtime ... harvest ... shall not c. 30:23
warm days will never c. 147:2
Ceases: love c. to be a pleasure 26:11
Ceiling: stood up and spat on the c. 13:3
Celebrate: I celebrate myself 325:13
Celerity ... admir'd ... by the negligent 242:19
Celia: come, my C. 146:1
Celibacy has no pleasures 141:8
Celibate: he still is largely c. 184:8
Cells: hermits ... contented with their c. 332:13
o'er-brimm'd their clammy c. 147:2
Censure: every trade save c. 70:13
little to fear ... from c. ... praise 140:4
no man can ... c. or condemn 59:16
take each man's c. 248:16
Centre: mon c. cède, ma droite recule 111:5
Centuries: forty c. look down upon you 185:10
praises ... all c. but this 118:5
Cerberus: of C. and ... Midnight born 173:14
Cerebration: deep well of unconscious c. 139:2
Ceremony: no c. that to great ones longs 273:4
Certain: death ... is c. to all 257:6
however c. our expectation 107:11
I am c. of nothing but 151:9
nothing is c. but death and taxes 113:3
nothing is c. but uncertainty 222:13
of a 'c. age' ... certainly aged 70:4
one thing is c. ... Rest is Lies 110:4
Certainly miserable, but not c. devout 141:7
Certainties: if a man will begin with c. 23:12
when hot for c. 170:2
Certainty: the c. of power 96:6
Cesspool: London, that great c. 102:5
Chaffinch sings on the orchard bough 61:1
Chain: flesh to feel the c. 58:15
Chains: c. that tie ... soul of harmony 174:9
nothing to lose but their c. 168:10
shake yr. c. to earth 298:14
Chair: give Dayrolles a c. 80:19
is the c. empty? 285:11
little mouse under her c. 192:7
seated in thy silver c. 145:8
tavern c. ... throne of ... felicity 145:2
Chaise: all in a c. and pair 92:7
Chalk and cheese 209:17
Cham: that great C. of literature 304:3
Chamber: and in my lady's c. 189:4
Chambers: in the c. of the East 56:13
the c. of the sun 56:13
Champagne: goes with women, and c., and bridge 27:7
I'm ... not a c. teetotaller 295:13
Champions: four c. ... strive ... for mastery 177:8
Chance: all c., direction ... thou canst not see 203:4
an hour before this c. 270:15
eye to the main c. 220:11
grab a c. 233:3
happiness in marriage ... matter of c. 20:18
I am ... [honest] sometimes by c. 293:6
in nativity, c., or death 276:8
power which erring men call C. 173:1
time and c. happeneth to ... all 39:23
under the bludgeonings of c. 130:9
Chancellor: a rather susceptible C.! 117:3
Chancery: hell and C. are always open 216:28
Chances: a set of curious c. 118:3
against ill c. men are ... merry 257:11
Change: c. and decay in all around 163:6
c. we think we see in life 113:9
doth suffer a sea-c. 288:1
heavy c., now thou art gone 174:14
I c. but I cannot die 298:6
plus ça c., plus ... même chose 146:12
the more things c. the more ... the same 146:12
the wind of c. is blowing 164:13
what a c. of flesh is here 25:8
Changes: monthly c. in her circled orb 286:10
Changest: O thou who c. not 163:6
Channel: butting through the C. 168:14
dream you are crossing the C. 117:13
Chant: how can ye c., ye little birds? 67:5
Chaos: reign of C. and old Night 176:10
when first God dawned on C. 297:11
when I love thee not C. is come 279:14
Chapel: Devil ... builds a c. there 96:9
Chapels had been churches ... cottages ... palaces 274:6
Chaps: biography is about c. 29:2
Character: a c. dead at every word 301:15
education ... formation of c. 305:5
I leave my c. behind me 301:16
precepts ... look thou c. 248:15
she gave me a good c. 75:7
Characteristics: vanity and love; ... their universal c. 80:16
Charge: c. Chester, c.! 240:10
take thou in c. this day 163:14
Charged with the grandeur of God 135:6
Charing-Cross: full tide of ... existence is at C. 143:14
Chariot: bring me my c. of fire 55:8
swing low, sweet c. 17:1

Chariot (*continued*)
Time's winged c. hurrying near 167:13
Charioted: not c. by Bacchus 149:16
Chariots: some trust in c., and some in horses 35:26
Charity: c. begins at home 209:19
c. shall cover ... sins 50:7
cold as c. 209:39
doings without c. are nothing worth 53:3
greatest of these is c. 48:8
hand open as day for melting c. 257:14
I do not give ... c., ... I give myself 326:3
in c. there is no excess 22:5
living need c. more than the dead 18:8
with c. for all 159:15
Charity-boy: as the c. said 99:3
Charlatan: defamed by every c. 313:8
Charles the First: King C. walked and talked 14:2
Charm: despair thy c. 272:12
what c. can soothe her melancholy? 124:1
Charmed: I bear a c. life, which must not yield 272:12
Charmer: were t'other dear c. away 115:7
Charming: c. to totter into vogue 322:6
how c. is divine Philosophy! 172:18
people are either c. or tedious 328:1
the rabbit has a c. face 14:6
Charms: c. strike the sight, but merit wins 204:11
do not all c. fly? 149:2
music has c. to soothe 89:5
solitude! Where are the c.? 93:15
Charter: this was the c. of the land 316:12
Charybdis: between Scylla and C. 207:38
Chase: the c., the sport of kings 304:8
Chasing the wild deer 66:14
Chassis: whole worl's in a state of c. 196:8
Chaste: be thou as c. as ice 251:3
Chasteneth: c. his son, so the Lord ... c. thee 32:24
loveth him c. him betimes 38:14
whom the Lord loveth he c. 49:22
Chastisement: fear no heavier c. from me 297:15
Chastity: c. and continence, but not yet 20:5
clothed on with c. 312:3
'tis c., my brother, c. 172:17
Chatterton, the marvellous Boy 334:8
Chaucer: Dan C., well of English undefiled 305:13
Che sera sera 209:20
Che sera sera: what doctrine ... *C.*? 165:7
Cheap: flesh and blood so c. 135:4
man's life is c. as beast's 266:2
Cheating: Winning Games Without Actually C. 204:15
Check: alas! I wd. not c. 156:12
O dreadful is the c. 58:15
Checked: I c. him while he spoke 156:12
Cheek: bring a blush to the c. 98:16
feed on her damask c. 291:7
leans her c. upon her hand 286:7
pale grew thy c. and cold 71:5
she hangs upon the c. of night 286:3
smite thee on thy right c. 43:19
take one blow and turn the other c. 133:14
that I might touch that c.! 286:7
there's language in her eye, her c. 290:8
wither'd c. and tresses grey 239:11
Cheeks: beauty's ensign ... crimson ... in thy c. 287:3
blow winds, and crack yr. c. 266:6
make pale my c. with care 329:11
rosy c. and flaxen curls 62:6
stain my man's c. 266:3
Cheer: Christmas ... brings good c. 209:27
cd. scarce forbear to c. 164:1
cups that c. 93:10
so I piped with merry c. 56:8
the fewer the better c. 221:16
welcome is the best c. 230:4
Cheerful: God loveth a c. giver 48:16
merry heart ... c. countenance 38:17
more c. ... than to be forty 134:7
Cheerfully: how c. he seems to grin 73-4:17
Cheerfulness was always breaking in 105:11
Cheering: great cause of c. us all up 28:7
Cheerio my deario 167:2
Cheers: three c. and one cheer more 119:13
Cheese: chalk and c. 209:17
dreamed of c.—toasted mostly 307:5
hard c. 216:13
hellish dark, and smells of c.! 308:6
Cheltenham: killed by drinking C. waters 11:17
Chemist (Chymist): was c., fiddler, statesman 103:4
Chequer-board: a c. of Nights and Days 110:11
Cherish: c. those hearts that hate thee 261:12
to love and to c., till death 53:22
to love, c., and to obey 53:23
Cherries: c. ... which none may buy 72:14
Kent ... apples, c., hops 98:18
Cherry: c. ripe, ripe ... I cry 131:13
make two bites of a c. 228:36
ruddier than the c. 115:4
there's the land, or c.-isle 131:13
till 'C. Ripe' themselves do cry 72:14
Cherubins: quiring to the young-ey'd c. 275:8
Chess: life's too short for c. 71:8
Chest: a c. of drawers by day 122:13
on the dead man's c. 307:4
ten-times barred-up c. 281:8
Chester: charge, C., charge! 240:10
Chesterton: dared attack my C. 27:12
Chestnut-tree: under a spreading c. 161:9
Chevalier: the young C. 185:7
Chewing little bits of string 27:2
Chicken: Some c.! Some neck 83:4
Chickens: count one's c. before ... hatched 210:13
curses are like c. ... home to roost 210:27
Chides: at fifty c. his infamous delay 338:1
Chief: brilliant c., irregularly great 63:2
Child: a little c. shall lead them 40:24
an it had been any christom c. 259:1
at break of day the solitary c. 332:9
C. among his new-born blisses 332:3
C.! do not throw this book 26:14
C. Rowland to the dark tower came 266:17
c. says 'I don't believe in fairies' 24:12
c. whose father goes to the devil 216:10
divide the ... c. in two 34:16
even a c. is known by his doings 38:23
get with c. a mandrake root 101:5
has devoured the infant c. 136:2

Child (*continued*)
Heaven-born C. all meanly wrapt 175:8
Jesus Christ her little c. 10:6
Monday's c. is fair of face 191:8
more hideous ... in a c. 265:14
on a cloud I saw a c. 56:7
the cry of a c. by the roadway 337:7
the old Adam in this c. 53:10
this c. I to myself will take 335:9
to have a thankless c. 265:15
train up a c. in the way 38:27
unto us a c. is born 40:23
wise c. ... knows its own father 230:23
wise father ... knows his own c. 274:12
with that the wretched c. expires 27:4
Childhood: companions, in my days of c. 156:9
my careless c. stray'd 125:13
the c. shows the man 180:3
what my lousy c. was like 237:13
Childishness: second c. and mere oblivion 244–5:11
Children: artist will let ... his c. go barefoot 296:5
as c. fear ... the dark 21:9
become as little c. 44:19
c., dear, was it yesterday? 18:12
c. of one family fall out 323:3
c. of this world ... wiser ... c. of light 46:6
c. shd. be seen and not heard 209:21
c.'s teeth are set on edge 41:16
c. sweeten labours 21:18
c. ... with nothing to ignore 186:6
c. yet unborn shall feel this day 284:3
come, c. of our native land 236:11
come, dear c., let us away 18:11
do you hear the c. weeping? 60:7
familiarity breeds ... c. 318:14
father pitieth his c. 36:28
had borne him three c. 138:2
happy ... that is happy in his c. 216:8
he that hath wife and c. 21:19
men ... c. of a larger growth 104:1
more careful of ... dogs than ... c. 199:7
Rachel weeping for her c. 43:9
she had so many c. 194:5
stars ... are my c. 152:6
tale which holdeth c. from play 302:5
voices of c. are heard on the green 56:11
your c. all gone 190:8
Chill: Ah, bitter c. it was 147:12
Chills the finger not a bit 186:9
Chilly: although the room grows c. 124:10
Chime: higher than the sphery c. 173:4
merry village c. 120:7
Chimes: heard the c. at midnight 257:7
Chimney: old men from the c. corner 302:5
Chimney-sweepers: as c., come to dust 247:9
Chin: his c. new reap'd 254:1
his c. upon an orient wave 175:10
China: bull in a c. shop 208:30
C.'s gayest art had dyed 125:9
mistress of herself, though C. fall 203:17
China orange: Lombard Street to a C. 219:23
Chinamen: birds in ... nests agree with C. 27:11
Chink: aid ... from a c. in the floor 310:7
Chip: a c. of the old block 209:22
not merely a c. of the old block 64:9
Chirche-dore: housbondes at c. 79:15
Chivalry: age of c. is gone 64:11
her Beauty and her C. 69:3
Chloe: but C. is my real flame 205:6
Chocolate cream soldier 295:8
Choice: Hobson's c. 216:34
pays yr. money ... takes yr. c. 231:18
small c. in rotten apples 287:7
Choir: sweet singing in the c. 15:8
Choler: purge ... c. without letting blood 281:7
Choleric: in the captain's but a c. word 273:8
Choose: c. life, that ... thy seed may live 33:5
to c. love by another's eyes 276:11
to c. time is to save time 22:19
where to c. their place of rest 179:18
Choosing: subject for ... song ... long c. 179:6
Chop and change 209:26
Chopper: cheap and chippy c. 118:7
here comes a c. 192:4
Chops and Tomata sauce ... Pickwick 99:7
Chortled in his joy 75:11
Chorus: a c.-ending from Euripides 60:13
Chosen: many are called, but few are c. 44:24
Choughs: the crows and c. that wing 267:2
Christ: beseech you, in the bowels of C. 94:7
C. is thy strength ... thy right 183:2
so Judas did to C. 284:1
the C. that is to be 313:7
we ... are one body in C. 47:22
Christ Church: I am the Dean of C., Sir 306:1
Christendom: the wisest fool in C. 130:13
Christian: a C. faithful man 284:15
assume the honourable style of C. 59:12
good C. men, rejoice 186:14
hate him for he is a C. 274:7
if possible ... C. men for C. boys 19:13
in what peace a C. can die 9:12
mirror of all C. kings 258:9
persuadest me to be a C. 47:14
warmed and cooled ... as a C. is 274:17
words ... no C. ear can endure 260:11
Christians: C. awake, salute 68:14
profess and call themselves C. 52:28
Christmas: at C. I no more desire a rose 268:9
C. comes but once a year 209:27, 318:5
C. Day in the Workhouse 302:8
eating a C. pie 191:2
on C. Day in the morning 14:10, 190:4
the first day of C. 194:1
the twelfth day of C. 194:2
Christopher Robin: C. is saying his prayers 172:2
C. went down with Alice 171:6
Chronicle: in the c. of wasted time 294:6
suckle fools and c. small beer 279:8
Chronicles: abstract and brief c. 250:12
look in the c.: we came in 287:5
Church: if at the C. ... give us some ale 56:4
new and great period in His C. 182:7
some to c. repair, ... for ... the music 202:9
the C.'s one foundation 307:13
the C.'s Restoration in 1883 29:11
wish from the C. to stray 56:4
Churches: chapels had been c. 274:6
let yr. women keep silence in the c. 48:9
Churchman: become a c. better than ambition 262:3
Church-yard: if two are in the c. laid 336:6
Churchyards: when c. yawn 252:8

Cigar: a good cigar is a smoke 154:10
Circle: weave a c. round him thrice 87:16
wheel is come full c. 267:15
Circumcised: took by th' throat the c. dog 280–1:14
Circumlocution office was beforehand 98:4
Circumspect: high-reaching Buckingham grows c. 285:5
Circumstances alter cases 209:28
Cities: sung women in three c. 205:3
towered c. please us then 174:5
Citizen: c. of no mean city 47:9
first requisite of a good c. 235:8
I am a c. ... of the world 304:5
John Gilpin was a c. 92:6
Citizens: civil c. kneading up the honey 258:8
healthy c. are the greatest asset 83:9
my fellow c. of the world 153:2
sing, all ye c. of heaven 196:6
you fat and greasy c. 243:16
City: a populous and a smoky c. 299:9
c. now doth like a garment wear 333:6
c. with her dreaming spires 19:4
he in the dissolute c. 332:11
in Dublin's fair c. 15:10
it is the men who make a c. 220:39
long in c. pent 151:6
once in royal David's c. 10:6
one ... in populous c. pent 179:9
rose-red c. half as old as time 64:3
the first c. Cain [made] 91:12
without a c. wall 10:7
City Road: up and down the C. 165:5
Civet: an ounce of c. 267:5
Civil: over violent or over c. 103:5
too c. by half 301:12
Civilises: the sex whose presence c. ours 92:5
Civility costs nothing 209:29
I see a wild c. 131:15
Civilized: woman will be the last thing c. 170:3
Civis Romanus sum 84:7
Clad: she that has [chastity] is c. in ... steel 172:17
Clap: don't c. too hard 197:8
if you believe, c. yr. hands 24:14
Claret is the liquor for boys 144:15
Class: not [happiness] of any one c. 200:14
Classes: the masses against the c. 121:9
the three great c. ... our society 19:6
to prove the upper c. 91:5
Classic: a c. ... nobody wants to read 319:2
Clay: as the c. is in the potter's hand 41:15
cabin ... of c. and wattles made 337:4
men ... gilded loam or painted c. 281:8
tenement of c. 102–3:17
turf that wraps their c. 88:11
Clean: as c. as a whistle 209:30
halo? ... one more thing to keep c. 114:2
make a c. breast 209:31
Cleaning: yesterday, we had daily c. 233:6
Cleanliness is next to godliness 209:32
Cleanly: thus so c. I myself can free 102:12
Cleanse the stuff'd bosom 272:6
Cleared: if this were only c. away 76:2
Clearing-house of the world 78:7
Clementine: oh my darling C. 183:8
Cleopatra: had C.'s nose been shorter 198:7
Cléopâtre: le nez de C. 198:7
Clergy: as the c. are, or are not 20:11
Clergymen: three sexes—men, women, and c. 303:14
Clerk: am I both priest and c.? 284:1
c. foredoom'd his father's soul to cross 201:11
Clerks: fountains like Government C.? 231:22
Clever: c. of the turtle 186:11
c. so rude to the good 330:10
if all the good people were c. 330:10
it's c., but is it art? 154:12
let who will be c. 154:2
our c. young poets 88:3
too c. by half 228:12
Cleverness: height of c. ... to conceal one's c. 234:8
Climate: common where the c.'s sultry 69:10
Climax: that c. of all human ills 69:20
Climb: teach you how to c. 173:4
Climbing after knowledge infinite 166:10
Climbs: sun c. slow, how slowly 85:3
Clive: what I like about C. 29:4
Cloak: religion is ... the worst c. 224:10
Cloakroom: the c. at Victoria Station 327:14
Clock: mouse ran up the c. 189:6
stand the church c. at ten to three? 59:4
Clocks: morning c. will ring 136:4
the c. were striking thirteen 197:2
Clod: warm motion to become a kneaded c. 273:10
Cloke: Knyf under the c. 79:20
Close: breathless hush in the C. tonight 187:11
c. yr. eyes with holy dread 87:16
fiend doth c. behind him tread 86:16
no barber shaves so c. but 206:37
now ... c. the shutters fast 93:10
porpoise c. behind us 75:2
the setting sun, and music at the c. 282:3
Closet: one by one back in the c. lays 110:11
Cloth: cut yr. coat according to ... c. 210:32
on a c. untrue 118:12
Clothe: long fields ... that c. the wold 313:11
Clothed: she rode ... c. on with chastity 312:3
Clothes: fine c., rich furniture 26:13
hanging out the c. 193:5
kindles in c. a wantonness 131:14
out of ... wet c. and into a dry Martini 330:8
that liquefaction of her c. 132:6
through tatter'd c. small vices 267:6
walked away with their c. 100:3
Clothing: false prophets ... in sheep's c. 44:9
Cloud: a fiend hid in a c. 56:3
but c. instead ... surrounds me 177:10
every c. has a silver lining 209:34
I wandered lonely as a c. 331:7
on a c. I saw a child 56:7
set my bow in the c. 30:25
there ariseth a little c. 34:20
through the dark c. shining 111:12
to be under a c. 209:35
turn the dark c. inside out 111:12
Clouds: never doubted c. wd. break 60:12
O c., unfold! 55:8
sun breaks through the darkest c. 287:11
trailing c. of glory do we come 332:1
Clout: cast ne'er a c. 209:10
Clown: heard ... by emperor and c. 150:4

Cloy the hungry edge of appetite 282:1
Clutching the inviolable shade 19:1
Coals: carry c. to Newcastle 209:8
haul over the c. 216:18
heap c. of fire 38:28
Coarse: one of them is rather c. 13:11
Coast: the c. is clear 209:36
Coaster: dirty British c. 168:14
Coat: a riband to stick in his c. 61:8
c. of many colours 31:10
cut yr. c. according to yr. cloth 210:32
Cock: a C. and a Bull, said Yorick 307:2
before the c. crow twice 45:17
C. a doodle doo! 188:7
c. that crowed in the morn 194:8
Cock Robin: heard the bell toll for poor C. 196:3
I killed C. 196:2
Cock-a-hoop: to be c. 209:37
Cock-and-bull story 209:38
Cockles: c. and mussels ... alive O! 15:10
warm the c. of the heart 229:28
Cockpit: can this c. hold ... fields of France? 258:6
Cocks: drench'd our steeples, drown'd the c. 266:6
Cocksure ... as Tom Macaulay 169:11
Cod: home of the bean and the c. 57:10
Coeur: le c. a ses raisons 198:8
Coffee: c. which makes the politicians wise 204:10
if this is c., I want tea 232:5
Cogito ergo sum 97:7
Coil: shuffled off this mortal c. 250–1:20
Coin: beauty is nature's c. 173:2
pay ... in his own c. 222:37
Cold: caught an everlasting c. 324:5
c. comfort 210:1
comfort like c. porridge 288:3
I beg c. comfort 265:3
pale grew thy cheek and c. 71:5
poor Tom's a-c. 266:16
seedtime ... harvest ... c. and heat 30:23
slept among his ashes c. 147:15
'tis bitter c. and I am sick at heart 247:13
to lie in c. obstruction 273:10
to shelter me from the c. 28:3
we called a c. a c. 28:6
who thicks man's blood with c. 86:8
Colder thy kiss 71:5
Coliseum: when falls the C. 69:8
while stands the C. 69:8
College: I am Master of this C. 26:6
Colossus: bestride the ... world like a C. 262:8
Colour: a c. of its own on the map 319:9
purest ... minds ... love c. the most 237:4
Coloured: see the c. counties 136:6
worser spirit a woman c. ill 294:16
Colours: all c. will agree in the dark 21:11
coat of many c. 31:10
truth fears no c. 228:24
Column: urn throws up a steamy c. 93:10
Columns: enormous fluted Ionic c. 165:1
Combine: love and marriage rarely can c. 69:18
Come: but will they c. when you do call? 255:5
c., and trip it as you go 173:17
c. back, Peter! C. back, Paul! 195:5
Come (*continued*)
c., c. and have a drink 317:10
c., c. and make eyes at me 317:11
c., c., give me yr. hand 272:4
c. forth into the light of things 335:6
c. he slow or c. he fast 240:4
c., Helen, give me my soul 165:8
c. here often? ... in the mating season 170:16
c. into the garden, Maud 314:3
c., knit hands 172:16
c., landlord, fill the flowing bowl 14:14
c., lasses and lads 14:15
c., let's away to prison 267:13
c., my coach! 252:20
c. not, Lucifer! 165:11
c. up and see me sometime 325:5
easy c., easy go 212:12
lightly c., lightly go 219:10
nothing of itself will c. 331:5
O c., all ye faithful ... c. ye 196:5
rise up, my love ... c. away 40:7
suffer me to c. to thee 325:1
the cry is still 'They c.' 272:8
thou'lt c. no more 268:4
will ye no c. back again? 185:8
Comedies: all c. are ended by a marriage 69:19
Comedy: most Lamentable C. ... of Pyramus 276:13
world is a c. to those who think 322:7
Comes: c. from the heart, goes to the heart 88:5
c. silent, flooding in, the main 85:2
here she c. ... full sail ... fan spread 89:10
knowledge c. but wisdom lingers 313:18
nobody c., nobody goes 25:11
repentance c. too late 224:12
tomorrow never c. 228:6
when daylight c., c. in the light 85:3
Cometh: behold, this dreamer c. 31:11
Comfort: cold c. 210:1
c. in the strength of love 332:12
c. me with apples 40:6
c.'s a cripple and comes ... slow 102:10
from ignorance our c. flows 205:7
here's my c. 288:8
I beg cold c. 265:3
no c. to one not sociable 247:6
of c., no man speak 283:5
receives c. like cold porridge 288:3
this must my c. be 281:11
to warm, to c., and command 334:14
two loves ... of c. and despair 294:16
Comfortably: liv'd c. so long together 115:5
Comforters: miserable c. are ye all 35:6
Comforts: not without c. and hopes 21:14
Comical: I often think it's c. 117:8
Coming: Campbells are c. 14:13
c. through the rye 65:15
I'm c., I'm c. 112:11
she is c., my dove, my dear 314:4
their going ... even as their c. 267:12
thy going out and thy c. in 37:17
Command: less used to sue than to c. 239:8
man to c. and woman to obey 314:18
not born to sue but to c. 281:9
not in mortals to c. success 9:4
to warn, to comfort, and c. 334:14
Commanded: nature, to be c., must be obeyed 23:17

Commandment: laws of England are at my c. 258:2
Commandments: aren't no Ten C. 155:2
fear God, and keep his c. 40:1
Commencement de la fin 310:10
Commend: all our swains c. her 292:8
easier to ridicule than c. 224:20
Commended: who c. thy yellow stockings 291:10
Comment is free but facts are sacred 238:15
Commerce: honour sinks where c. ... prevails 123:15
Commit: c. his body to the ground 53:30
pretty follies that themselves c. 274:14
Committed: they have c. false report 278:18
Commodity, the bias of the world 264:13
Common: earth and every c. sight 331:12
fade into the light of c. day 332:2
have a good thing to make it too c. 256:10
more c. where the climate's sultry 69:10
nothing c. did or mean 168:4
Common-place: his c. book be full 309:7
Commonwealth: caterpillars of the c. 282:10
if the ... C. last for a thousand years 82:14
i' th' c. I wd. ... execute 288:4
The Empire is a C. of Nations 235:12
Communicated: good, the more c., more abundant 178:13
Communist: a c.? One who has yearnings 107:18
Community: no finer investment for any c. 83:9
part of the c. of Europe 121:10
Commuter—one who spends his life 325:8
Compact: of imagination all c. 277:5
Companions: I have had c. 156:9
lovely c. are faded and gone 184:1
wives ... c. for middle age 21:20
Company: better ... alone than in bad c. 207:20
c. makes the feast 210:4
c., villainous c. 255:12
crowd is not c. 210:21
crowds without c. 116:2
his little daughter, to bear him c. 161:12
in married life three is c. 327:10
in such a jocund c. 331:10
known by the c. he keeps 220:18
qualified to shine in c. 309:9
take the tone of the c. 80:11
tell me what c. thou keepest 78:6
two is c., three is none 229:2
withouten other c. in youthe 79:15
Compare: belied with false c. 294:14
c. thee to a summer's day? 293:13
how I may c. this prison 284:6
Comparisons: c. are odious 210:5
c. are odorous 278:8
Compassion: shutteth up his bowels of c. 50:11
thou art all c. 325:3
Compassions: his c. fail not ... new every morning 41:19
Competition: tradition approves all forms of c. 84:17
Complain: moping owl ... to the moon c. 126:5
sluggard, I heard him c. 323:7
Complaining: woods have no voice but ... c. 184:10
Complete: let ... death c. the same 62:10
Complexion: his c. is perfect gallows 287:13
that schoolgirl c. 11:6
whose fresh c. and whose heart 293:5
Complies against his will 68:1
Comprehended: our watch ... have indeed c. 278:10
Compromise: All ... founded on c. and barter 64:7
Comrades, leave me here a little 313:14
Conceal: cleverness is to c. one's cleverness 234:8
knowing anything, shd. c. it 20:15
use ... words ... to c. ... thoughts 321:12
Concealment, like a worm i' th' bud 291:7
Conceit: infusing him with self and vain c. 283:6
Conceits: wise in yr. own c. 47:25
Concentrates: it c. his mind wonderfully 144:8
Concessions of the weak, ... c. of fear 64:4
Conclusions: life ... art of drawing ... c. 68:6
Condemn: age shall not weary ... years c. 54:5
travellers ... fools at home c. 'em 288:14
Condemned: much c. to have an itching palm 263:22
Condemns: Johnson c. whatever he disapproves 65:6
Condescend: your men of wit will c. 308:12
Condition: the c. of man ... c. of war 133:2
Conditions: stars above us, govern our c. 267:1
Cones: eat the c. under his pines 113:13
Conference [maketh] a ready man 23:8
Confession is good for the soul 210:6
Confidence: we shall fight with growing c. 82:13
Confident: never glad c. morning again 61:9
Conflict: never in the field of human c. 82:15
too weak the c. to support 268:1
Confound: Lord did ... c. the language 30:27
Confusion: all else, c. 314:18
c. to his enemies 15:6
levee from a couch in some c. 89:15
Congregation: latter has the largest c. 96:9
Conjecture: now entertain c. of a time 259:8
we c. ... animal or ... god 308:14
Conjunction: is the c. of the mind 167:17
Conquer: England ... wont to c. others 282:6
we'll c. again and again 115:1
Conquered: I came, I saw, I c. 71:13
nation ... perpetually to be c. 64:5
Conquering: see the c. hero comes 184:6
so sharp the c. 80:4
went forth c., and to conquer 50:21
Conqueror: came in with Richard C. 287:5
lie at the proud foot of a c. 265:4
Conquers: love c. all and we too succumb 321:5
Conquest: a shameful c. of itself 282:6
peace is of the nature of a c. 257:12
Conquests: all thy c., glories, triumphs, spoils 263:5
Conscience: a still and quiet c. 261:11
argue freely according to c. 182:9
catch the c. of the king 250:19
c. does make cowards of us all 250–1:20
my c. hath a thousand ... tongues 285:15
Consciousness: this growth of national c. 164:13

Consecration: the c. and the poet's dream 331:1
Consent: govern another man without ... c. 159:7
'I will ne'er c.'—consented 69:11
silence gives c. 225:23
Consented: whispering 'I will ne'er consent' —c. 69:11
Consequence: business of c., *do it yourself* 24:3
Conservatism: what is c.? 159:11
Conservative: a c. government ... organised hypocrisy 100:4
or else a little C. 117:8
with more propriety be called the C. 94:6
Consider: though justice be thy plea, c. 275:1
Considereth: blessed is he that c. the poor 36:12
Consign to thee and come to dust 247:10
Consolation: with peace and c. ... dismissed 181:8
Consorts: constitution ... c. ... with all things 59:14
Conspiracy: a c. to cheat the world 143:11
open-ey'd c. his time doth take 288:5
Conspirators: all the c. save only he 264:6
Conspiring ... how to load and bless with fruit 147:1
Constable: fit man for the c. of the watch 278:5
Constabulary duty's to be done 120:6
Constancy: c. lives in realms above 87:7
hope c. in wind 70:14
in c. follow the Master 63:13
Constant: a woman c. ... argues a decay 89:9
c. you are, but yet a woman 254:11
friendship is c. in all ... things 277:15
merciful as c., c. as various 125:8
to one thing c. never 277:21
were man but c. 292:11
Constitution: higher law than the C. 241:17
I am of a c. so general 59:14
our C. is in ... operation 113:3
principle of the English c. 54:10
Consul: Rome, born when I was c. 84:8
Consults: neither c. ... nor trusts [women] 80:14
Consume: no more right to c. happiness 295:11
Consumed: bush burned ... was not c. 31:17
Consummation: a c. devoutly to be wish'd 250–1:20
quiet c. have 247:11
Consumption: remedy against ... c. of the purse 256:12
Contagion: breathes out c. to this world 252:8
c. of the world's slow stain 297:16
rot inwardly, and foul c. spread 175:4
Contemplate: let us c. existence 98:5
Contemplation: for c. he 178:3
left for c. not what ... used to be 29:11
Contempt: familiarity breeds c. 213:16
familiarity breeds c. ... children 318:14
few [can bear] c. 206:6
means ... for c. too high 91:13
Content: be c. with yr. wages 45:23
but if I'm c. with a little 54:3
c. to breathe his native air 203:20
c. to have them ... course by course 82:9
farewell c.! 280:2
in whatsoever state ... to be c. 49:2
Content (*continued*)
let us draw upon c. 123:21
where our desire is got without c. 271:3
Contented: hermits are c. with their cells 332:13
Contentment: all enjoying, what c. find? 179:3
where wealth and freedom ... c. fails 123:15
Contests: what mighty c. rise from trivial things 204:5
Continence: chastity and c., but not yet 20:5
Continent: every man ... a piece of the c. 101:7
Continued: how long so ever ... c. ... no force in law 85:7
Continuous as the stars that shine 331:8
Contract between the king and the people 241:6
Contradict: very well, ... I c. myself 326:5
Contradiction: woman's at best a c. still 203:18
Contraries: without c. is no progression 56:15
wd. by c. execute all things 288:4
'Contrariwise', continued Tweedledee 75:15
Contrary (Contrairy): everythink goes c. with me 97:13
Mary, Mary, quite c. 191:7
Contrive to write so even 20:19
Contumely: the proud man's c. 250–1:20
Convent's narrow room 332:13
Conversation: our c. is in heaven 48:30
Conversationalist: to provide any industrious c. 137:12
Conversations: after-dinner c. over the wine 317:2
Converse: formed by thy c. 203:10
Conversing: with thee c. I forget all time 178:7
Converted: except ye be c. 44:19
Convicted of sickness, hunger 303:19
Convicts: they [Americans] are a race of c. 143:12
Convince: persuading others we c. ourselves 146:7
Cook: ill c. ... cannot lick his own fingers 210:9, 287:2
to c. one's goose 210:8
Cookery: kissing don't last: c. do! 170:4
Cooking: no c., or washing, or sewing 12:1
Cooks: as c. go she went 237:12
too many c. spoil the broth 228:13
Coolibah: shade of a c. tree 198:10
Coot: bald as a c. 206:35
Copulation: birth, and c., and death 107:2
Coral: c. is far more red 294:13
of his bones are c. made 288:1
Corbies: twa c. making a mane 11:16
Cord: a threefold c. is not quickly broken 39:15
Cords of a man, with bands of love 42:10
Corioli: flutter'd yr. Volscians in C. 246:12
Cormorant: c. devouring Time 268:6
sat like a c. 178:1
Corn: as soon ... hope ... c. in chaff 70:14
c. in Egypt 31:12
c. was orient and immortal wheat 317:17
cow's in the c. 191:1
farmer sowing his c. 194:8
in tears amid the alien c. 150:4

Corn (*continued*)
readers ... sway ... like ... ripe c. 106:2
when he treadeth out the c. 33:4
Corner: Jack Horner sat in the c. 191:2
keep a c. in the thing I love 279:17
some c. of a foreign field 59:5
Corners: unregarded age in c. thrown 243:17
Cornfield: down in de c. 112:6
o'er the green c. did pass 245:16
Cornish men: here's twenty thousand C. 129:4
Coromandel: on the Coast of C. 158:2
Coronets: kind hearts are more than c. 313:10
Corpse: he'd make a lovely c. 98:7
Correct: like magistrates, c. at home 258:8
Correcteth: whom the Lord loveth he c. 38:2
Corrupt: a people generally c. 64:19
art ... able to c. a saint 253:17
judge that no king can c. 261:6
power tends to c. 9:1
unlimited power is apt to c. 200:7
Corrupted the youth of the realm 260:11
Corrupteth: wanton love c. 22:1
Corruption: c. wins not more than honesty 261:12
vice whose ... c. inhabits 292:1
Corse: his c. to the rampart we hurried 330:3
Cortez: like stout C. 150–1:15
Cost: defend our island, whatever the c. may be 82:13
Costly: c. thy habit 248:16
Your Grace is too c. 277:18
Costs: nothing c. so much as what is given 222:11
victory at all c. 82:12
Cottage: wherever there's a c. small 198:4
Cottages: love lives in c. ... courts 219:40
poor men's c. princes' palaces 274:6
Cottleston, C. Pie 172:6
Cotton: from the c. fields away 112:10
Couch: a levee from a c. 89:15
oft, when on my c. I lie 331:11
there I c. when owls do fly 289:6
Cough cannot be hid 219:33
Coughing drowns the parson's saw 269:1
Counsel: hard ... for women to keep c. 263:1
if the c. be good 210:12
justice, c., and treasure 22:8
princely c. in his face yet shone 177:3
three may keep c. if two be away 227:39
Counsellers: in the multitude of c. ... safety 38:10
Counsels: close designs and crooked c. 102:16
Count one's chickens before ... hatched 210:13
Countenance: knight of the sorrowful c. 78:2
the Lord lift up his c. 32:18
you have that in yr. c. 265:12
Countercheck: fifth, the c. Quarrelsome 246:2
Counties: and see the coloured c. 136:6
Counting-house: the king was in his c. 193:5
Country: better satisfied with my own c. 144:14
but spare yr. c.'s flag, she said 326:7
by all their c.'s wishes blest! 88:10
fit c. for heroes to live in 160:9
go West ... grow up with the c. 127:4
God made the c. 93:6
good for the c. ... good for General Motors 329:4
Country (*continued*)
happy is the c. ... has no history 216:9
his first, best c. ever is at home 123:14
I have no relish for the c. 303:18
I loathe the c. 89:16
I love thee still, my c. 93:7
I tremble for my c. 139:13
I vow to thee, my c. 305:22
left our c. for our c.'s good 25:2
Mother, you live in the c. 324:17
my c.! How I leave [love] my c.! 200:12
my c., 'tis of thee 303:10
my soul, there is a c. 320:7
not what yr. c. can do for you 153:2
not without honour save ... own c. 44:14
on behalf of ... c., ... children, ... altars 238:1
our c., right or wrong 96:7
our c. sinks beneath the yoke 271:18
our c., ... whole c. and nothing but our c. 323:9
[praises] every c. but his own 118:5
she is my c. still 82:1
some Cromwell, guiltless of his c.'s blood 126:11
sweet and seemly ... to die for one's c. 136:1
the loneliness of my c. 297:4
undiscover'd country from whose bourn 250–1:20
walking ... 'tis a c. diversion 89:16
Countrymen: friends, Romans, c. 263:11
the merits of their c. 143:11
what a fall ... my c. 263:19
Couple: every c. is not a pair 210:14
Courage: be strong and of a good c. 33:10
c. in yr. own [trouble] 124:6
c. mounteth with occasion 264:10
c. never to submit or yield 175:18
endurance and c. of my companions 239:3
screw yr. c. to the sticking place 270:7
Course: content to have them ... c. by c. 82:9
c. of true love never ... smooth 276:10
c., proportion, season 290:1
earth's diurnal c. 334:15
Courses: gave himself to evil c. 332:11
stars in their c. fought 33:14
Court: c. awards it ... law doth give it 275:5
friend at c. 214:17
starry threshold of Jove's c. 172:13
sun that shines upon his c. 293:4
the English, not the Turkish c. 257:20
within the ... crown ... keeps Death his c. 283:6
Courted by all the winds 180:15
Courteous: gracious and c. to strangers 22:6
Courtesy: by c. a man 21:5
c. on one side only 210:15
full of c., full of craft 214:27
I am the very pink of c. 286:17
Courtier's, soldier's, scholar's 251:5
Courting: I heard a linnet c. 58:4
Courts: brawling c. and dusty purlieus 312:18
white founts ... in the C. of the sun 81:4
Cousins: his sisters, and his c., and his aunts! 119:14
Coventry: send to C. 210:16
Cover: c. her face: mine eyes dazzle 323:16
c. thee with his feathers 36:25
with leaves and flowers do c. 324:3

Covet: thou shalt not c.; but tradition 84:17
Coveting: pleasure ... is lost by c. 223:14
Cow: couple-colour as a brindled c. 135:7
c. jumped over the moon 189:5
c.'s in the corn 191:1
c. with the crumpled horn 194–5:8
I never saw a Purple C. 64:1
I wrote the 'Purple C.' 64:2
three acres and a c. 88:6
Coward: bully is always a c. 208:32
c. does it with a kiss 326:12
gross flattery to name a c. 317:12
no c. soul is mine 58:12
Cowardice: pale cold c. in noble breasts 281:10
Cowards: a plague of all c. 254:13
conscience does make c. of us all 250–1:20
c. die many times before ... deaths 262:15
it [public] is the greatest of c. 129:12
though c. flinch, and traitors jeer 90:3
Cowslip: in a c.'s bell I lie 289:6
Coy: be not c. but use yr. time 132:8
Coyness: this c., lady, were no crime 167:11
Crabs: roasted c. hiss in the bowl 269:1
Crack: stretch out to th' c. of doom? 271:17
that heaven's vault shd. c. 268:2
winds ... c. yr. cheeks 266:6
Cracked: it c. and growled and roared 86:2
Crackling of thorns under a pot 39:19
Cracks: now c. a noble heart 253:11
Cradle: the c. will rock 189:10
Cradles: bit the babies in the c. 61:17
Craft: c. so long to lerne 80:4
gentlemen of the gentle c. 96:12
Cramp: when I heard she'd died of c. 124:9
Cravat: the one [robin] in red c. 99:18
Crawling: whereunder c. coop't we live 110:13
Crazy: checkin' the c. ones 125:5
I'm half c. 95:4
Creak of a lumbering cart 337:7
Cream: choking her with c. 154:7
visages do c. and mantle 274:2
Created: about ... to be c. like to us 177:4
c. man in his own image 30:3
God c. the heaven 30:1
Creation: O fairest of c. 179:10
our c., preservation 53:1
she is His new c. 307:13
to which the whole c. moves 313:9
Creature: God's first c., which was light 23:15
lone lorn c. 97:13
she is an excellent c., but 100:14
though the most beautiful C. ... waiting 152:6
wine is a good familiar c. 279:11
Creatures: all c. great and small 10:4
call these delicate c. ours 279:17
from fairest c. we desire 293:10
the meanest of his c. 61:14
true hope ... makes ... meaner c. kings 285:12
Credit: citizen of c. and renown 92:6
my c. in men's eyes 110:15
stories ... not to thy c. 72:4
to his c. ... is an Englishman! 120:2
Creditors have better memories 210:17
Creed: a modest c. and yet 299:15
Creeds: honest doubt ... than in half the c. 313:1
so many gods, so many c. 326:11
Creeds *(continued)*
vain are the thousand c. 58:13
Creeks: far back through c. and inlets 85:2
Creep: let the sounds of music c. 275:8
Creeping like snail ... to school 244:11
Creeps: when the blood c. ... nerves prick 312:14
Crew: Mirth, admit me of thy c. 174:1
we were a ghastly c. 86:14
Cricket: c.—a sport at which the contenders 140:5
merry as a c. 221:2
save the c. on the hearth 173:9
to where the c. sings 337:5
Crime: atrocious c. of being ... young 200:6
bigamy, sir, is a c.! 183:1
cut-throat isn't occupied in c. 120:7
for my wilful c. art banished 179:17
in heaven, a c. to love too well? 201:6
no c.'s so great as ... to excel 82:2
nor any c. so shameful as poverty 109:3
the Napoleon of c. 101:16
the punishment fit the c. 118:10
this coyness, lady, were no c. 167:11
treason was no c. 103:7
Crimes: c., follies and misfortunes of mankind 116:3
history of the great events ... history of c. 321:15
l'histoire des c. 321:15
liberté, que de c. ... en ton nom 234:16
liberty, what c. ... in yr. name 234:16
Crimson in thy lips and in thy cheeks 287:3
Cripple: comfort's a c. 102:10
Crispian: this day is call'd the feast of Crispian 259:15
Critic: first attribute of a good c. 162:16
scorn not the sonnet; C., you have frowned 333:5
Critical: I am nothing if not c. 279:7
Criticism: ask ... for c. ... only want praise 169:4
my own definition of c. 19:8
Criticisms: animals ... pass no c. 105:16
Critics: before you trust in c. 70:14
c. all are ready made 70:13
Crocodile: c. tears 210:18
how doth the little c. 73:17
Cromek: O! Mr. C., how do ye do? 56:1
Cromwell: restless C. cd. not cease 168:3
ruins that C. knocked about 160:6
see C., damned to everlasting fame 203:9
some C. guiltless 126:11
Crooked: c. by nature is never ... straight 210:19
straight trees have c. roots 226:28
strive to set the c. straight? 184:9
there was a c. man 194:3
Crop: a-watering the last year's c. 105:14
Cross: a little marble c. below the town 129:6
blind as the ... nails upon the C. 302:9
c. the bridge ... get to it 210:20
e'en though it be a c. 9:3
for our advantage on the bitter c. 253:14
one more river to c. 14:9
with the C. of Jesus 24:9
Cross-bow: with my c. I shot the albatross 86:3
Crosses: between the c., row on row 164:8
Cross-gartered: wished to see thee ever c. 291:10

Crow: there is an upstart c. 127:6
Crowd: all at once I saw a c. 331:7
c. is not company 210:21
madding c.'s ignoble strife 126:12
out of the c. a mistress or a friend 298:8
trees ... shall c. into a shade 204:4
Crowded: feast, and yr. halls are c. 326:10
Crowds without company 116:2
Crowed: cock that c. in the morn 194:8
Crown: all thy faithful mercies c. 325:3
c. thy good with brotherhood 25:4
fighting for the c. 190:9
I give away my c. 284:2
I will give thee a c. of life 50:16
if you c. him, let me prophesy 283:8
let us c. ourselves with rosebuds 51:10
not the king's c. ... deputed sword 273:4
sweet fruition of an earthly c. 166:10
the holly bears the c. 15:8
this I count the glory of my c. 107:14
throned monarch better than his c. 275:1
uneasy ... head that wears a c. 257:3
virtuous woman ... c. to her husband 38:12
within the ... c. ... keeps Death his court 283:6
Crowns: evening c. the day 212:29
give c. and pounds and guineas 136:5
who c. ... a youth of labour 122:7
Crows: the c. and choughs that wing 267:2
Crucified: c. 'twixt a smile and a whimper 299:10
the dear Lord was c. 10:7
Crucify him 45:18
Cruel: I must be c. only to be kind 252:15
let me be c., not unnatural 252:9
more c. the pen is than the sword 67:9
Cruelly: I am c. used 21:2
Cruelty: farewell, fair c. 290:16
O c., to steal my Basil-pot 148:13
Crumb: a memorial c. 99:18
who craved no c. 121:2
Crumbs ... from the rich man's table 46:8
Cruse: neither shall the c. of oil fail 34:18
Crustimoney Proseedcake: what does C. mean? 172:4
Cry: c. for the moon 210:22
c. 'Havoc!' 263:8
c. not when his father dies 140:17
c. out 'Olivia!' 290:15
c. woe, destruction, ruin 283:4
c. 'Wolf' 210:23
did they not sometime c. 'All hail'? 284:1
kissed the girls and made them c. 189:3
need a body c.? 65:15
the c. is still 'They come' 272:8
Crying over spilt milk 210:24
Cuckoo: but as the c. is in June 255:10
c., c.—O word of fear 268–9:17
lhude sing c. 14:7
O C., shall I call thee bird? 336:2
the c. then on every tree 268–9:17
the weather the c. likes 128:10
Cuckoo-buds of yellow hue 268:17
Cue: my c. is villainous melancholy 265:11
with a twisted c. 118:12
Cultivate: we must c. our garden 321:11
Cultiver: il faut c. notre jardin 321:11
Culture, the acquainting ourselves with the best 19:11
Cunning: my right hand forget her c. 37:26
Cup: ah, fill the C. 110:7
C. that clears TO-DAY of past Regrets 110:2
kiss but in the c. 145:7
'twixt the c. and the lip 227:24
we'll tak' a c. o' kindness 65:13
Cupboard: c. love 210:25
Mother Hubbard went to the c. 192:2
Cupid: C. and my Campaspe 163:3
C. painted blind 276:12
C.'s darts do not feel 14:4
Cups that cheer but not inebriate 93:10
Curate: like the C.'s egg 210:26
Curb: you might c. yr. magnanimity 152:12
Curds: eating her c. and whey 191:3
Cure: past c., past care 222:34
prevention is better than c. 223:26
there is no c. for this disease 27:3
Cured: can't be c. must be endured 230:7
Curfew tolls the knell of parting day 126:3
Curiosity: newspapers always excite c. 156:8
Curious: that was the c. incident 102:1
'Curiouser and c.!' cried Alice 73:16
Curled: he ... c. up on the floor 129:3
Curls: rosy cheeks and flaxen c. 62:6
Curly locks, c. 188:8
Current: take the c. when it serves 264:3
Currents: their c. turn awry 250–1:20
Curs: mongrels, spaniels, c. 271:1
Curse: I know how to c. 287:19
O c. of marriage 279:17
the c. is come upon me! 313:13
work ... c. of the drinking classes 328:18
Curses are like chickens 210:27
Cursing: fall a-c. like a very drab 250:18
Curst be the verse 201:18
Curtain: ring down the c., the farce is over 232:8
Curtained with cloudy red 175:10
Curtains: let fall the c., wheel the sofa 93:10
Curve: dear red c. of her lips 168:12
Custodiet: quis c. ipsos custodes? 146:9
Custom: a c., loathsome ... hateful ... harmful 138:14
c. calls me to't 246:8
c. without reason ... ancient error 210:28
what c. wills ... shd. we do 246:8
Customary: said Owl, the c. procedure 172:4
Customers: a people of c. 303:4
Customs: the c., politics, and tongue 198:12
Cut: c. is the branch that might have grown 166:1
c. it without a knife? 191:4
easy ... of a c. loaf to steal 289:13
most unkindest c. of all 263:18
the flash c. him 11:18
Cuts: he that c. off twenty years 263:3
tongue is not steel yet it c. 228:9
Cut-throat: call me misbeliever, c. dog 274:10
Cutting all the pictures out 26:14
Cynara: faithful to thee, C.! 101:11
Cynic: what is a c.? 328:4
Cynicism is intellectual dandyism 169:15
Cypress: in sad c. let me be laid 291:6

D: never use a big, big D. 119:12
Dads: get leave of yr. d. 14:15
Daffodils: a host of golden d. 331:7
fair d., we weep to see 132:1
when d. begin to peer 292:17

Dagger: is this a d. ... I see before me? 270:9
Daggers: I will speak d. to her 252:9
there's d. in men's smiles 270:16
Daisies pied and violets blue 268:17
Daisy, Daisy, give me yr. answer, do 95:4
Dale: heigh! the doxy over the d. 292:17
over hill, over d. 276:16
through wood and d. the sacred river 87:13
Dalliance: primrose path of d. 248:14
silken d. in the wardrobe lies 258:9
Damage: which might d. his career 25:1
Dame: my d. has lost her shoe 188:7
one for the d. 188:4
Damn: a man who said 'D.!' 128:11
almost hear the printer saying d. 319:9
d. with faint praise 201:16
Damned: and d. be him that first cries 'Hold!' 272:14
another d., thick ... book! 121:13
d. from here to Eternity 154:15
d. if I know how the helican 170:6
d. to everlasting fame 203:9
life ... one d. thing after another 136:12
out, d. spot! 272:2
prosperity has d. more ... than ... devils 223:31
publish, and be d. 324:11
she cried, she d. near died 16:4
thou must be d. perpetually 165:10
what those d. dots meant 82:6
Damsel: to every man a d. or two 33:16
Dan: can travel from D. to Beersheba 306:13
from D. even to Beer-sheba 33:23
Danaos: timeo D. et dona ferentes 321:2
Dance: each d. the others wd. off the ground 97:2
move easiest who have learn'd to d. 202:10
on with the d.! 69:4
will you join the d.? 75:3
Danced: d. by the light of the moon 158:9
sang his didn't he d. his did 94:13
Dancing: d.? Oh, dreadful! 65:4
you and I are past our d. days 286:2
Dancing-master: teach ... the manners of a d. 141:19
Danger: continual ... d. of violent death 133:3
d. from the wiles of a stranger 186:2
out of this nettle d. 254:10
pleas'd with the d. 102–3:17
the chief d. of the time 170:12
when we conquer without d. 90:14
Dangerous: a little learning is a d. thing 202:5
boggy, dirty, d. way 123:7
greater the power, the more d. the abuse 64:20
he thinks too much; such men are d. 262:9
Dangers: brave its d. comprehend its mystery 161:4
lov'd me for the d. I had passed 279:2
with d. compassed round 178:20
Daniel: a D. come to judgment! Yea, a D.! 275:3
brought D., ... cast him into the den 42:5
O D., ... greatly beloved 42:7
Dant: quae d. ... negant gaudent ... esse rogatae 197:14
Dante, who loved ... hated 61:12
Dappled: glory be to God for d. things 135:7
Dare: d. to be true 131:9
I d. ... assume ... style of Christian 59:12
Dare (*continued*)
I d. not ask a kiss 132:2
O, what men d. do! ... may do! 278:11
we d. n't go a-hunting 10:9
Dared attack my Chesterton 27:12
Darien: silent, upon a peak in D. 150–1:15
Darjeeling: there was an old man from D. 13:3
Dark: a great leap in the d. 133:4
all colours will agree in the d. 21:11
all that's best of d. and bright 71:2
as children fear to go in the d. 21:9
creeping murmur and the poring d. 259:8
d. as the world of man 302:9
d. backward and abysm of time 287:15
don't want to go home in the d. 131:3
ever-during d. 177:10
good as my lady in the d. 217:28
hellish d. and smells of cheese 308:6
in the morning's d. 96:5
Joan as my Lady is as good i' th' d. 132:4
never to refuse a drink after d. 169:14
O d., d., d., amid the blaze 180:10
the sun to me is d. 180:11
we are for the d. 243:7
what in me is d. illumine 175:17
Darken: the days d. round me 312:7
Darkeneth: who is this that d. counsel? 35:12
Darkling I listen 150:3
Darkly: see through a glass, d. 48:7
Darkness: a distant voice in the d. 161:7
and d. Night be named 178:21
and light from d. ... divided 178:21
d. again and a silence 161:7
d. falls at thy behest 107:17
d. which may be felt 31:23
in d. and with dangers compassed 178:20
leaves the world to d. and to me 126:3
lighten our d. 52:20
men loved d. rather than light 46:22
pestilence that walketh in d. 36:27
ring out the d. of the land 313:7
rulers of the d. of this world 48:27
the d. deepens; Lord, with me abide! 163:5
the d. silvers away 58:3
the people that walked in d. 40:22
Darling: Charlie is my d. 185:7
d. buds of May 293:13
d. of the Spring 336:3
in thy green lap was Nature's d. 127:1
oh my d. Clementine 183:8
Six years' d. of a pigmy size 332:3
the d. of my heart 73:3
Darts: Cupid's d. do not feel 14:4
Dated: women and music shd. never be d. 123:11
Daughter: d. of Earth and Water 298:6
d. of Jove, relentless Power 126:16
d. of the gods divinely tall 311:15
D. of the Vine to Spouse 110:9
don't put your d. on the stage 91:10
he that wd. the d. win 210:34
like mother, like d. 221:17
marry ... yr. d. ... when you can 220:3
skipper had taken his little d. 161:12
stern D. of the Voice of God 334:3
the King of Spain's d. 190:1
truth is the d. of God 228:26

Daughter-in-law: remembers not ... she was a d. 221:18
Daughters: all the d. of my father's house 291:8
d. of the Philistines rejoice 34:10
d. of the uncircumcised triumph 34:10
here lie I and my four d. 11:17
marry yr. d. betimes 220:33
nor rain, wind ... are my d. 266:7
sweet her artless d. 151:3
the fairest of her d. Eve 178:4
words are the d. of earth 140:2
David: D. ... escaped to the cave Adullam 34:8
D. [hath slain] his ten thousands 34:7
D. took an harp and played 34:6
once in royal D.'s city 10:6
D. Copperfield kind of crap 237:13
Davy: Sir Humphrey D. detested gravy 29:5
Dawn: till the dappled d. doth rise 174:2
Daws: heart ... for d. to peck at 278:20
Day: a thousand years as one d. 50:10
a tip-toe when this d. is named 259:15
ah! when will this long weary d. 305:8
and those eyes, the break of d. 273:12
arrow that flieth by d. 36:26
as morning shows the d. 180:3
calm was the d. 305:15
chanced to see at break of d. 332:9
compare thee to a summer's d. 293:13
d. and night shall not cease 30:23
d. as sharp to them as thorn 284:3
d. for a man to afflict his soul 41:10
d. is short and the work is long 210:35
d. of death ... d. of ... birth 39:18
d. of Empires has come 78:8
d. of wrath, that dreadful d. 240:2
d. returns too soon 71:4
d.'s at the morn 62:7
d.'s journey take the whole long d.? 236:3
d.'s out and the labour done 60:5
d. thou gavest, Lord, is ended 107:17
d. unto d. uttereth speech 35:23
death of each d.'s life 270:11
death will have his d. 283:4
deficiencies of the present d. 141:3
dies at the opening d. 323:6
dog will have his d. 253:5
drinka pinta milka d. 11:2
dwell in realms of d. 55:1
each d. is like a year 326–7:15
eclipse without all hope of d.! 180:10
every d., in every way ... better 91:3
every d. to be lost 144:21
every dog has his d. 211:27
every dog its d. 154:5
from this d. forward, for better for worse 53:22
good morning to the d. ... my gold! 145:17
he that outlives this d. 259:15
how many hours bring about the d. 260:13
if every d. ... last d. but one 157:12
in the d. of judgement 52:25
in the shade on a fine d. 20:12
jocund d. stands tiptoe 286:22
known a better d. 239:11
lay it up for a rainy d. 224:4
light the D. ... He named 178:21
live to fight another d. 13:8
longest d. ... have an end 219:26
merry heart goes all the d. 292:19

Day (*continued*)
murmur of a summer's d. 18:19
never a bad d. ... hath a good night 221:29
night is long that never finds the d. 272:1
not to me returns d. 177:10
now the d. is over 24:8
O frabjous d.! 75:11
old age ... at close of d. 315:15
one d. is with the Lord as a thousand years 50:10
our little systems have their d. 312:10
power of the press ... last but a d. 319:6
rain it raineth every d. 292:3
remember the sabbath d. 32:3
Rome was not built in a d. 224:27
sailed ... for a year and a d. 158:8
seize the present d. 135:13
sing ... pray all the livelong d. 56:4
so foul and fair a d. 269:6
so rare as a d. in June? 162:15
sufficient unto the d. ... evil thereof 44:4
sweet d., so cool, so calm 131:12
the bright d. is done 243:7
the d. of small things 43:3
the light of common d. 332:2
this d. our daily bread 43:24
time ... runs through the roughest d. 269:10
uncertain glory of an April d. 292:6
until the d. break, ... shadows flee 40:11
yield d. to night! 260:5
Daylight: all the long and lone d. 298:15
when d. comes, comes in the light 85:3
Days: all the d. of Methuselah 30:18
Ancient of d. 42:6
as thy d. ... thy strength 33:8
chequer-board of nights and d. 110:11
d. of danger, nights of waking 239:9
d. seem lank and long 120:13
ere half my d. in this dark world 181:10
former d. ... better than these 39:20
good nights and sorry d. 220:29
how many d. will finish ... year 260:13
in good Queen Bess's glorious d. 117:10
in the belly of the fish three d. 42:19
in the mad March d. 168:14
King Charles's golden d. 15:12
loved three whole d. 308:2
my d. among the dead 304:10
my salad d. 242:13
now behold these present d. 294:7
of few d. and full of trouble 35:5
past our dancing d. 286:2
shalt find it after many d. 39:24
six d. shalt thou labour 32:3
teach us to number our d. 36:24
that has twenty-eight d. clear 194:6
that thy d. may be long 32:4
the d. of our years 36:23
then, if ever, come perfect d. 162:15
think warm d. will never cease 147:2
though fallen on evil d. 178:20
what dark d. seen! 294:4
while the evil d. come not 39:26
world of happy d. 284:15
year whose d. are long 326–7:15
Dazzle: mine eyes d.: she died young 323:16
Dead: a character d. at every word 301:15
and they all d. did lie 86:11
beside the wench is d. 166:5
blow ... bugles, over the rich D. 59:1

Dead (*continued*)
concerning the d. [say] ... good 210:37
courage ... the devil is d. 233:4
d.! and never called me mother! 330:7
d. as a door-nail 210:38
d. for a ducat, d.! 252:12
dew on the face of the d. 26:10
doctors found when she was d. 122:17
down among the d. men 105:7
faith without works is d. 49:25
great deal to be said for being d. 29:4
healthy and wealthy and d. 317:6
it struck him d.: and serve him right 27:6
just as d. as if he'd been wrong 12:8
little fairy ... falls down d. 24:12
my days among the d. 304:10
nearly all our best men are d.! 232:3
need charity more than the d. 18:8
on stepping-stones of their d. selves 312:11
Queen Anne is d. 223:39
say I'm sick, I'm d. 201:10
something ... d. in each of us 326:13
soul is d. that slumbers 160:14
that d. men rise up never 310:1
the law hath not been d. 273:5
the noble D. 334:6
'tis Death is d., not he 297:17
to see a d. Indian 288:6
two worlds, one d. 18:15
view halloo wd. awaken the d. 125:6
wake, for night is d. 310:5
we might as well be d. 324:18
weep for Adonais, he is d. 297:9
when I am d. and opened 168:11
when I am d., my dearest 236:4
Deadener: habit is a great d. 26:2
Deadlock: Holy D. 131:8
Deadly: soap ... more d. in the long run 318:11
Deaf: d. as a post 211:3
none so d. as those who won't hear 211:4
Deafness: your tale ... wd. cure d. 287:16
Deal: a new d. for the American people 234:17
d. with none but honest men 224:13
good enough to be given a square d. 235:9
Dean: I am the D. of Christ Church 306:1
queer old D. 305:20
Deans: with ... dowagers for d. 314:12
Dear: a man ... to all the country d. 122:9
beauty ... for earth too d. 286:3
d. to me as light and life 66:3
God! that bread shd. be so d.! 135:4
Plato is d. to me 18:7
the d. God who loveth us 87:4
Dearie: flew o'er me and my d. 66:3
Deario: its cheerio my d. 167:2
Death: a rendezvous with D. 240:15
a sunset-touch, a fancy ... some one's d. 60:13
after the first d. ... no other 316:11
all in the valley of D. 311:9
all tragedies are finished by a d. 69:19
and d. complete the same 62:10
and d. shall have no dominion 315:14
and now to d. devote 179:10
Angel of D. has been abroad 58:8
any man's d. diminishes me 101:8
as one that had been studied in his d. 269:11
Death (*continued*)
be thou faithful unto d. 50:16
because I cd. not stop for D. 99:17
birth, and copulation, and d. 107:2
brood over ... the hour of my d. 152:8
come away, d. 291:6
day of d. [is better] 39:18
d. after life does greatly please 305:11
d., as the Psalmist saith, is certain 257:6
d., be not proud 101:4
d. devours lambs as well 211:5
d. for his ambition 263:10
d. hath no more dominion 47:17
d. is an ende of every ... sore 79:21
d. is the grand leveller 211:6
d. ... like all the rest, a mockery 299:15
d. of each day's life 270:11
d. pays all debts 211:7
d.'s pale flag is not advanced 287:3
D., whene'er he call ... too soon 120: 17
die not, poor d. 101:4
die the d. of the righteous 32:20
disappointed by that stroke of d. 145:1
dread of something after d. 250–1:20
every door ... shut but d.'s door 211:32
fear and danger of violent d. 133:3
for love, and beauty ... no d. 299:16
give me liberty or give me d. 131:4
half in love with easeful D. 150:3
happy ... were my ensuing d. 282:6
his d., which happened in his berth 134:13
how wonderful ... D. and ... Sleep! 298:7
I have set before you life and d. 33:5
I here importune d. awhile 243:5
I will not be afraid of d. and bane 272:7
I'll ... condemn you to d. 74:1
if ought but d. part 33:26
in nativity, chance, or d. 276:8
in that sleep of d. what dreams? 250–1:20
in the hour of d. 52:25
in the ranks of d. 184:2
in their d. ... not divided 34:11
into the jaws of D. 311:12
it is but D. who comes at last 240:4
judge none blessed before his d. 51:21
keep a league till d. 284:4
love is strong as d. 40:14
men fear d., as children ... dark 21:9
midst of life we are in d. 53:29
most cruel d. of Pyramus 276:13
my part of d. no one so true 291:6
never taste of d. but once 262:15
no one till his d. ... unhappy 60:5
nothing is certain but d. and taxes 113:3
O D., where is thy sting? 48:13, 201:4
pale D. with impartial foot 135:12
pale horse ... that sat on him was D. 50:22
paradise to what we fear of d. 273:11
precious ... the d. of his saints 37:11
rashly importunate, gone to her d. 134:10
remedy for all ... but d. 224:11
reports of my d. ... exaggerated 319:4
sad stories of the d. of kings 283:6
so many years of fearing d. 263:3
the way to dusty d. 272:10
there is d. in the pot 34:24
there shall be no more d. 51:3
thou wast not born for d. 150:4
through envy of the devil came d. 51:11
till d. us do part 53:22

Death (*continued*)
'tis D. is dead, not he 297:17
useless life is an early d. 122:2
valley of the shadow of d. 35:29
vasty Hall of D. 18:17
wages of sin is d. 47:18
we owe God a d. 257:8
Webster ... much possessed by d. 107:6
what sights of ugly d. 285:1
when d. to either shall come 58:7
where is d.'s sting? 163:7
whose mortal taste brought d. 175:15
within the hollow crown keeps D. his court 283:6
worst is d. and d. will have his day 283:4
wd. fain die a dry d. 287:14
Deaths: cowards die many times before ... d. 262:15
more d. than one must die 326:14
Debate: Rupert of D. 63:2
Debonair: so buxom, blithe and d. 173:15
Debt: contrived a double d. to pay 122:13
d. is the worst poverty 211:8
the d. which cancels all others 89:1
Debts: and forgive us our d. 43:24
death pays all d. 211:7
he that dies pays all d. 288:12
speak not of my d. unless 226:5
Decay: be sincere ... argues a d. 89:9
d. of that colossal wreck 299:8
energies of our system will d. 23:23
fretted the ... body to d. 102:17
this muddy vesture of d. 275:8
wealth accumulates, and men d. 122:5
Deceased: he first d.; she for a little tried 336:12
Deceive: Oh, don't d. me 15:1
to d. oneself is very easy 211:10
when first we practise to d. 240:8
Deceived: by bad women been d. 180:12
d. her father, and may thee 279:5
Deceivers: men were d. ever 277:21
Deceives me once ... d. me twice 211:9
December: as soon seek roses in D. 70:14
D. when they are wed 245:13
wallow naked in D. snow 282:1
Decent: d. godless people 107:1
d. means poor 199:3
Decently: things done d. and in order 48:10
Deck: boy stood on the burning d. 130:4
Declare: nothing to d. except my genius 328:16
Decoration: deserves some sort of d. 197:11
Decoyed into our condition 199:10
Decreed: soul has to itself d. 150:10
Dee: lived on the river D. 54:1
Deed: a d. without a name 271:14
a good d. in a naughty world 275:11
if one good d. ... I did 289:14
now the matchless d.'s achieved 303:1
so I may do the d. ... my soul ... decreed 150:10 :
Deeds: d. are males, and words are females 211:11
means to do ill d. ... d. ill done 265:2
these unlucky d. relate 280:14
turn sourest by their d. 294:3
Deep: call spirits from the vasty d. 255:5
d. and crisp and even 187:1
in the lowest d., a lower d. 177:13
Deep (*continued*)
thoughts ... too d. for tears 332:6
two voices ... one is of the d. 306:9
very singularly d. young man 119:4
Deeper than did ever plummet sound 289:5
Deer: in the Highlands, a-chasing the d. 66:14
the running of the d. 15:8
Defaced, deflowered 179:10
Defamed by every charlatan 313:8
Defeat: in D.: Defiance 83:13
the problems of victory ... of d. 83:8
Defect: chief d. of Henry King 27:2
Defence or apology before ... accused 78:13
Defend: d. ... yr. right to say it 321:18
from my enemies ... d. myself 215:3
they [newspapers] never d. anyone 169:12
we shall d. our island 82:13
Defender: I mean the Faith's D. 68:15
Defiance: in Defeat: D. 83:13
Defied: age will not be d. 22:23
Definition: true d. of a style 309:2
Definitions: homely d. of prose and poetry 88:3
Deflowered: defaced, d. 179:10
Deformed, unfinish'd, sent before my time 284:10
Degree: a d. of delight ... in ... misfortunes 65:1
O, when d. is shak'd 290:2
observe d., priority and place 290:1
people ... a d. or two lower 20:6
take but d. away 290:3
Degrees: did ever heal but by d.? 279:12
we boil at different d. 108:20
Delay: in d. ... lies no plenty 291:2
in me is no d. 179:17
Delayed till ... I cannot enjoy ... impart it 142:1
Delays are dangerous 211:13
Deliberate: where both d., the love is slight 166:15
Deliberates: woman that d. 9:5
Deliberation: deep on his front engraven d. sat 177:3
Delicate: we can call these d. creatures ours 279:17
Delicately: Agag came ... d. 34:4
Delight: a Phantom of d. 334:12
d. ... in ... misfortunes ... of others 65:1
d. ... ornament ... ability 23:5
energy is eternal d. 56:16
go to't with d. 243:2
I sing this song for your d. 76:11
my d. on a shining night 16:6
paint the meadows with d. 268:17
rarely comest ... Spirit of D. 300:4
sounds ... give d. and hurt not 288:13
unrest which men miscall d. 297:16
Delights: man d. not me 250:6
scorn d. and live laborious days 175:1
these d. if thou canst give 174:11
Deliver: d. me from myself 60:2
from ... ghosties ... beasties ... d. us 13:7
Delos: where D. rose 69–70:21
Deluge: after us, the d. 201:1
Déluge: après nous le d. 201:1
Delusion: a d., a mockery, and a snare 97:4
Delved: when Adam d. 24:2
Dementat: quos Deus vult perdere ... d. 223:40

de Mille: Cecil B. d. ... was persuaded 29:8
Democracy: d. resumed her reign 27:7
two cheers for D. 112:2
world ... made safe for d. 329:9
Democratic Party is like a mule 101:9
Demon-lover: wailing for her d. 87:12
Den: ye have made it a d. of thieves 45:14
Denmark: something is rotten in the state of D. 249:5
Denouncing someone or something else 169:12
Deny: he that will this health d. 105:7
those who d. freedom to others 159:9
thou shalt d. me thrice 45:17
Departed: minds me o' d. joys 67:6
Depends: it all d. what you mean by 139:19
Depth in philosophy bringeth ... to religion 22:11
Deputy elected by the Lord 283:2
Derangement: a nice d. of epitaphs 301:10
Descent and fall to us is adverse 176:17
Descriptions of the fairest wights 294:6
Desert: in this d. inaccessible 244:10
legs of stone stand in the d. 299:7
nothing ... unrewarded but d. 103:5
rats d. a sinking ship 224:5
use every man after his d. 250:13
waste its sweetness on the d. air 126:10
Deserts: d. of vast eternity 167:13
moon when she d. the night 180:11
Deserve: d. not [freedom] for themselves 159:9
Sempronius, we'll d. it 9:4
wd. d. better of mankind 309:1
Deserves: has the government it d. 165:3
Designs: close d. and crooked counsels 102:16
Desire: d. of the moth for the star 300:8
d. shd. so ... outlive performance? 256:19
few things to d. 22:14
from what I've tasted of d. 113:12
provokes the d. ... takes away the performance 270:14
she is the antidote to d. 90:2
some d. is necessary 141:4
universal ... d. ... to live beyond ... income 68:7
where our d. is got without content 271:3
Desired: more to be d. ... than gold 35:24
Desires: he who d. but acts not 57:2
Desolation: create d. and call it peace 310:8
Despair: a heaven in hell's d. 56:2
begotten by D. upon Impossibility 167:16
hope is as cheap as d. 217:4
look on my works ... and d. 299:8
loves ... of comfort and d. 294:16
owner whereof was Giant D. 63:11
shall I, wasting in d. 329:11
some divine d. 314:16
what resolution from d. 176:3
where Seraphs might d. 68:18
Despairs: leaden-eyed d. 149:15
Desperate: diseases d. grown 252:16
Desperation: lives of quiet d. 316:15
Despise ... as I d. Shakespeare 297:8
Despised: d. and rejected of men 41:5
enjoy'd no sooner but d. 294:11
Despond: name of the slough was D. 63:7
Destiny: d. with Men for Pieces plays 110:11
hanging and wiving goes by d. 274:15
Destiny (*continued*)
homely joys and d. obscure 126:7
Destroy: doth the wingèd life d. 55:4
I sought to d. institutions 325:10
'tis safer to be that which we d. 271:3
whom God wishes to d. 223:40
Destroyer and preserver; hear, oh, hear! 299:4
Destruction: by d. dwell in doubtful joy 271:3
d. that wasteth at noonday 36:27
pride goeth before d. 38:19
Detail: our life is frittered away by d. 317:1
Determined, dared and done! 303:1
Detest: but they d. at leisure 70:7
Detraction will not suffer it 255:21
Deutschland über alles 133:7
Device: banner with the strange d. 160:12
miracle of rare d. 87:15
Devil: abashed the D. stood 178:10
better the d. you know 207:35
between the d. and the deep sea 211:17
black as the d. 208:5, 310:11
courage ... the d. is dead 233:4
d. ... builds a chapel 96:9
d. can cite Scripture 274:8
d., having nothing else to do 27:8
d. is not so black 211:18
d. shd. have all the good tunes 132:12
d.'s walking parody 81:2
d. take the hindmost 211:19
d. was sick ... a monk wd. be 185:1
d. was well ... a monk he'd be 185:1
d. whoops, as he whooped 154:12
drink and the d. had done for 307:4
every man ... god or d. 103:5
first Whig was the D. 144:12
give the d. his due 214:33
he ... that sups with the d. 219:25
heaviest stone ... d. can throw 129:14
hold a candle to the d. 216:36
needs must when the d. drives 221:28
renounce the d. ... his works 53:11
resist the d. and he will flee 50:2
saint when most I play the d. 284:14
shame the d. 227:20
talk of the d. ... sure to appear 227:10
the D., howling Ho! 306:2
the world, the flesh, and the d. 52:24
through envy of the d. came death 51:11
who cleft the d.'s foot 101:5
young saint, old d. 231:9
your adversary the d., as a roaring lion 50:8
Devils: prosperity has damned more ... than ... d. 223:31
Devoir: faites votre d. et laissez faire aux dieux 90:15
Devon, glorious D. 57:11
Dévot: pour être d. ... pas moins homme! 182:15
Devotion: dollar ... object of universal d. 138:13
the d. to something afar 300:8
Devour: threat'ning to d. me opens wide 177:13
Devout: d. but ... human 182:15
miserable, but not ... d. 141:7
Dew: d. on the face of the dead 26:19
foggy, foggy d. 16:4

Dew (*continued*)
hill-side's d.-pearled 62:7
like the d. on the mountain 239:10
resolve itself into a d. 248:2
walks o'er the d. of yon ... hill 247:16
Dew-drop: fragile d. on its perilous way 150:9
Diable: courage ... le d. est mort 233:4
noir comme le d. 310:11
Dials: carve out d. quaintly 260:13
Diamond: d. and safire bracelet lasts 162:1
like a d. in the sky 311:5
Diana of the Ephesians 47:7
Diary: I never travel without my d. 327:16
memory ... is the d. 327:15
Dick the shepherd blows his nail 269:1
Dickens: what the d. his name is 276:5
Dictate: not presume to d., but broiled fowl 98:17
Dictator: the German d., instead of snatching 82:9
Did: d. nothing ... d. it very well 117:11
d. that they d. in envy of great Caesar 264:6
nor ever d. a wiser one 234:11
sang his didn't he danced his d. 94:13
Dido found Aeneas wd. not come 204:12
Di-do-dum: Dido ... was D. 204:12
Die: a man can d. but once 257:8
and shall Trelawny d.? 129:4
appointed unto men once to d. 49:19
as a man lives, so shall he d. 220:19
as natural to d. 21:10
beauty's rose might never d. 293:10
beauty that must d. 149:12
beneath its shade we'll live and d. 90:3
break faith with us who d. 164:9
cowards d. many times 262:15
crawling coop't we live and d. 110:13
d. a dry death 287:14
d. all, d. merrily 255:14
d. and go we know not where 273:10
d. because a woman's fair 329:11
d. beyond my means 328:17
d. in the last ditch 65:3
d. not, poor death 101:4
d. ... the last thing I shall do! 198:1
do d. of it do seldom ... recover 243:8
how can man d. better? 163:10
I shall d. at the top 309:12
I will d. ere she shall grieve 330:1
I will d. in the last ditch 328:19
if I shd. d. think only this 59:5
if we are mark'd to d. 259:13
in what peace a Christian can d. 9:12
lay me down and d. 101:10
leave me there to d. 15:9
let me d. the death of the righteous 32:20
let us do or d. 67:2
look about us and to d. 202:17
love her till I d. 17:2
love too much ... d. for love 220:6
lovers ... d. as soon as one pleases 89:13
man can only d. once 220:13
more deaths than one must d. 326:14
never say d. 221:33
no young man believes he shall ... d. 129:10
Oh, Sir! the good d. first 331:4
people d., but books never d. 235:5
said I wd. d. a bachelor 278:1
Die (*continued*)
see Naples and d. 225:7
seemly ... to d. for one's country 136:1
seems it rich to d. 150:3
shd. certain persons d. before they sing 87:10
soon as ... born, he begins to d. 225:39
swans sing before they d. 87:10
Tamburlaine ... must d. 166:13
the d. is cast 71:12
the Man perceives it d. away 332:2
theirs but to do and d. 311:11
they ... d. by famine, d. by inches 130:15
those about to d. salute you 308:4
to d. ... awfully big adventure 24:13
to d., to sleep 250–1:20
to d. upon a kiss 281:1
toddle ... home and d. in bed 238:9
we must be free or d. 334:1
when good ... bad ... Americans d. 328:8
who wd. wish to d.? 57:8
with my little eye, I saw him d. 196:2
you asked this man to d. 19:16
young men may d., old men must 231:7
Died: d. maintaining his right of way 12:8
d. when his prospects ... brightening 11:18
in the odour of sanctity d. 24:6
laugh! I thought I shd. have d. 81:13
liked it not, and d. 336:12
men have d. ... but not for love 245:12
queens have d. young and fair 186:12
she damned near d. 16:4
she had d. of cramp 124:9
she shd. have d. hereafter 272:10
since Maurice d. 58:5
stopped short ... when the old man d. 336:8
the dog it was that d. 122:20
to the North-west d. away 61:4
who d. to save us all 10:7
wd. God I had d. for thee 34:14
wd. to God we had d. ... in ... Egypt 31:27
Dies: flower ... once has blown for ever d. 110:4
he that d. pays all debts 288:12
light of the bright world d. 57:13
love ... soon as beauty d. 100:19
no man happy until he d. 304:7
not how a man d., but how he lives 143:4
person who either marries or d. 20:9
say that when the Poet d. 239:14
the king never d. 54:9, 218:2
what an artist d. with me! 187:8
Diet: all necessaries ... d. unparalleled 98:9
no ... idiosyncrasy in d. 59:14
praise is the best d. 303:15
Dieu: D. est ... pour les gros bataillons 321:17
si D. n'existait pas 321:14
Differ: men ... d. as Heaven and Earth 312:6
Different: how d. from us, Miss Beale 14:4
Difficult: all things are d. before ... easy 227:28
d. ..., Sir? I wish it were impossible 144:24
problems of victory ... no less d. 83:8
Dig: I cannot d.; to beg I am ashamed 46:5
Digest: mark, learn, and inwardly d. 53:2
Digestion: d. ... great secret of life 303:17
now good d. wait on appetite 271:7
things sweet ... prove in d. sour 281:13
Diggeth: whoso d. a pit shall fall 39:1

Dignities: peace above all earthly d. 261:11
Dignity and worth of the human person 319:5
Diminish one dowle ... in my plume 288:15
Diminished: stars hide their d. heads 177:12
Diminishes: any man's death d. me 101:8
Dimmed: glory of the sun will be d. 23:23
Dine: and go to inns to d. 81:10
I shd. d. at Ware 92:11
if wife shd. d. at Edmonton 92:11
Noah ... when he sat down to d. 81:11
'whar shall we ... d. the day?' 11:16
Dined on mince and ... quince 158:9
Ding: d. dong, bell 188:9
sing hey d. a d. d. 245–6:16
Dinner: a d. lubricates business 240:13
d. of herbs where love is 38:18
good d. enough, to be sure 142:13
good d. upon his table 145:1
people who want d. do not ring 23:21
Diplomat these days ... a head-waiter 320:2
Direction: all chance, d. 203:4
Directions: rode madly off in all d. 157:13
Dirge: by forms unseen their d. is sung 88:11
Dirt: fling d. enough ... will stick 213:38
Dirty: hail fellow ... all d. and wet 309:3
Disadvantage: ship has ... d. of ... danger 143:21
Disappointments: I have been too familiar with d. 159:6
Disapprove: I d. ... but will defend ... yr. right 321:18
Disapproves: condemns whatever he d. 65:6
Disaster: meet with Triumph and D. 154:19
valiant ... 'gainst all d. 63:13
Disasters: day's d. in his morning face 122:11
we make guilty of our d. 265:10
Disbelief: willing suspension of d. 87:19
Disciplines: I know the d. of war 259:7
Discobolus: the D. standeth ... dusty ... maimed 68:9
Discommendeth: he who d. others 59:11
Discontent: winter of our d. 284:8
Discord: all d., harmony not understood 203:4
hark what d. follows! 290:3
Discount: sells us life at a d. 114:3
Discouragement: no d. shall make him ... relent 63:13
Discover: doth ... d. vice ... d. virtue 21:15
Discretion: an ounce of d. is worth 222:30
being now come to the years of d. 53:17
better part of valour is d. 256:3
d. is the better part of valour 211:21
fair woman ... without d. 38:11
philosophy ... nothing but d. 241:3
Disdain: d. and scorn ride sparkling 278:2
what, my dear Lady D.! 277:11
Disease: d. [consumption of purse] is incurable 256:12
remedy ... worse than the d. 22:10
strange d. of modern life 18:21
'There is no cure for this d.' 27:3
this long d., my Life 201:14
when age, d., or sorrows strike him 84:14
Diseases: among all the d. of the mind 306:6
desperate d. ... desperate remedies 211:16
d. desperate grown 252:16
subject to the same d. 274:17
Disgrace: am out, even to a full d. 246:11
Disgrace (*continued*)
its private life is a d. 14:6
my learned profession ... never d. 117:5
Disgruntled: if not ... d., ... far from ... gruntled 330:2
Dish: a d. fit for the gods 262:14
butter in a lordly d. 33:15
d. ran away with the spoon 189:5
goblets for a d. of wood 283:7
he will to his Egyptian d. 242:18
was not that a dainty d. 193:5
Dishes: no washing of d. 12:1
thou shalt not wash d. 188:8
washed the d. with his wife 184:8
Dishonour: d. stain the brow of my young Harry 253:15
his honour rooted in d. 312:4
Dishonourable: find ourselves d. graves 262:8
Dislike what I fancy I feel 12:9
Dismay: let nothing you d. 15:3
Dismayed: was there a man d.? 311:10
Disobedience: of Man's first d. 175:15
Disobedient: for a drudge, d. 123:2
not d. unto the heavenly vision 47:13
Disobey: naughty girl to d. 191:9
Disorder: a sweet d. in the dress 131:14
her last d. mortal 122:17
Dispose: unsearchable d. of Highest Wisdom 181:7
Disposes: man proposes, God d. 220:21
Disposition: a truant d. 248:7
put an antic d. on 249:13
Disputation: a feeling d. 255:8
Dispute: my right there is none to d. 93:14
Dissimulation: let love be without d. 47:23
Dissipation without pleasure 116:2
Dissolute: in the d. city 332:11
Dissolve: all which it inherit shall d. 288:16
and then ... I d. it in rain 298:5
Distance: d. lends enchantment 72:9
sixty seconds' worth of d. 154:20
Distinction: reverence ... doth make d. 247:7
Distress: a deep d. hath humanised 331:2
Distressed: mind quite vacant is a mind d. 93:4
Distributed: dollars ... will not be d. 84:10
Ditch: both shall fall into the d. 44:15
die in the last d. 65:3
I will die in the last d. 328:19
Ditchwater: as dull as d. 212:4
Ditties of no tone 149:7
Dive into the bottom of the deep 254:4
Diver: don't forget the d. 146:14
Diverse, sheer opposite 148:2
Diversion: walking ... a country d. 89:16
Divide et impera 211:22
Divide: d. and rule 211:22
d. the living child in two 34:16
to d. is not to take away 298:9
Divine: depth of some d. despair 314:16
one far-off d. event 313:9
study the past ... d. the future 89:3
Divinely tall and most d. fair 311:15
Divinity: by these we reach d. 100:18
d. in odd numbers 276:8
d. that shapes our ends 253:6
such d. doth hedge a king 252:22
Divorced old barren Reason 110:9
Dizzy 'tis to cast one's eyes 267:2
Do: as I wad d., were I Lord God 164:10

Do (*continued*)
business of consequence, d. it yourself 24:3
can I d. you now, sir? 146:13
d. as I say, not as I d. 241:4
d. as you're bidden 211:25
d. as you wd. be done by 211:24
d. nothing ... damage his career 25:1
d. other men ... they wd. d. you 98:6
d. ... that one can pay others to d. 169:7
d. thou but thine 179:4
d. what seemeth him good 33:29
d. ye even so to them 44:7
from having too little to d. 155:8
I am to d. what I please 113:6
I don't mind if I d. 146:15
knows not what to d. 188:7
let us d. or die 67:2
never d. today what you can put off 231:20
the Lord d. so to me 33:26
we never d. anything well till 129:15
what men dare d. ... daily d. 278:11
what you can d. for yr. country 153:2
Doch-an'-dorris 157:4
Dock: in a dull, dark d. 118:7
Doctor: God heals ... d. takes the fee 215:4
Doctrine: d. is that each one shd. select 298:8
d. of a strenuous life 235:7
from women's eyes this d. I derive 268:14
not for the d., but the music 202:9
Doctrines: makes all d. plain and clear 67:17
Dodger: sobriquet of 'The artful D.' 98:13
Dog: as a d. returneth to his vomit 38:31
beware of the d. 200:1
d. did nothing in the night-time 102:1
d. does not eat d. 211:26
d. is turned to his own vomit 50:9
d. it was that died 122:20
d.'s walking on his hind legs 142:13
d., to gain some private ends 122:19
d. will have his day 253:5
d. will not howl if you beat 211:28
every d. has his d. 211:27
every d. its day 154:5
fetch her poor d. a bone 192:2
give a d. a bad name 214:31
I am His Highness' d. at Kew 204:2
if you call a d. Hervey 141:15
keep a d. and bark yourself 217:31
let no d. bark 274:3
love me, love my d. 220:4
mine enemy's d., though he had bit me 267:9
misbeliever, cut-throat d. 274:10
pray tell me sir, whose d. are you? 204:2
rather be a d. and bay the moon 263:23
teach an old d. tricks 227:16
the little d. laughed 189:5
the young man's d. with them 51:9
they grin like a d., and run 36:18
took by th' throat the circumcised d. 280–1:14
when a d. bites a man 95:5
why should a d. ... have life? 268:4
Dogged: it's d. as does it 318:2
Dogs: barking d. seldom bite 207:1
clept all by the name of d. 271:1
d. bark at me as I halt 284:10
fought the d. and killed the cats 61:17
let sleeping d. lie 218:37
let slip the d. of war 263:8
Dogs (*continued*)
mad d. and Englishmen 91:8
two d. strive ... a third runs ... with [bone] 228:39
uncover, d., and lap 289:11
Doing: joy's soul lies in the d. 289:15
let us then be up and d. 161:2
nothing—half so much worth d. 124:12
saying is one thing and d. another 225:1
see what she's d. and tell her she mustn't 231:25
shortest answer is d. 225:18
what was he d. ... god Pan? 60:9
worth d. at all is worth d. well 80:9
worth d. is worth d. well 230:8
Doings: all our d. without charity 53:3
even a child is known by his d. 38:23
Doit: a d. to relieve a lame beggar 288:6
Dollar: almighty d. ... object of ... devotion 138:13
Dollars: however plenty ... d. may become 84:10
Dolore: nessun maggior d. che ricordarsi 95:7
Dolphin: a mermaid on a d.'s back 276:18
Dome: a d. of many-coloured glass 298:2
Dominion: death hath no more d. 47:17
death shall have no d. 315:14
hand that holds d. over man 315:17
I'm truly sorry man's d. 66:11
Dominions on which the sun never sets 187:16
Don: remote and ineffectual d. 27:12
Done: do as you wd. be d. by 211:24
d. those things ... we ought not 52:13
easier said than d. 212:10
nothing d. while aught remains to do 234:14
put off ... what may be d. today 221:31
so little d., so much to do 233:10
something ought to be d. 324:15
surprised to find it d. 142:13
thank God I have d. with him 142:2
they d. the old woman in 296:22
things d. cannot be undone 211:31
to have loved ... thought ... d. 18:10
'twere well it were d. quickly 270:4
well begun is half d. 230:5
what have I d. for you, England? 130:11
what's d. cannot be undone 272:4
Dong with a luminous Nose 158:3
Donkey: talk the hind leg off a d. 227:9
Donne: another Newton, a new D. 137:14
D.'s verses ... the peace of God 138:15
Doom: even to the edge of d. 294:9
stretch out to th' crack of d. 271:17
Doomed for a ... term to walk the night 249:6
Doomsday: d. is near; die ... merrily 255:14
then is d. near 250:4
Doon: banks and braes o' bonnie D. 67:5
Door: a beaten path to his d. 108:23
a d. must be ... open or shut 185:5
a D. to which ... no key 110:6
at her ivied d. 71:16
every d. ... shut but death's d. 211:32
fortune knocks, open the d. 214:13
keep the d. of my lips 37:29
keep the wolf from the d. 230:29
knocking at Preferment's d. 18:20
knocking on the moonlit d. 96:14
love ... goes out at the d. 219:37

Door (*continued*)
stand at the d., and knock 50:20
three, four, knock at the d. 192:3
thy form from off my d. 200:19
Doorkeeper: I had rather be a d. 36:21
Doors: d. ... being as yet shut upon me 152:3
pale Death ... knocks at the d. 135:12
Dotheboys Hall: at ... D. Youth are boarded 98:9
Dots: what those damned d. meant 82:6
Double: d., d., toil and trouble 271:11
surely you'll grow d. 335:4
Double entendre: the horrible d. 12:11
Doubled him up for ever 116:10
Doublethink means ... two contradictory beliefs 197:6
Doubt: 'I d. it,' said the Carpenter 76:3
more faith in honest d. 313:1
new philosophy calls all in d. 100:16
no probable ... possible d. whatever 116:9
when in d., leave out 230:11
when in d., win the trick 136:11
Doubted: never d. clouds wd. break 60:12
Doubtful: by destruction dwell in d. joy 271:3
Doubting: a castle called D. Castle 63:11
Doubts: begin with d., ... end in certainties 23:12
he shall end in d. 23:12
knows nothing, d. nothing 218:15
saucy d. and fears 271:6
Douglas: Judge D. and myself 159:10
old song of Percy and D. 302:6
the D. in his hall 240:7
Dove: beside the springs of D. 334:11
d. came ... in the evening 30:22
my d., my dear ... my life 314:4
Oh that I had wings like a d.! 36:16
Dove-cote: like an eagle in a d. 246:12
Doves: grass is as soft as the breast of d. 90–1:16
Dowagers: with ... d. for deans 314:12
Dowdiness: memory ... beginning of d. 328:15
Dower: faith's transcendent d. 334:10
Down: d., d. to hell 261:2
d. will come baby, cradle 189:10
easier to pull d. than to build 223:35
get d. you dirty rascal 190:3
he that is d. ... fear no fall 63:15
I don't think one 'comes d.' 197:12
levers to lift me ... being d. 254:7
never go d. to the end of the town 171:9
quite, quite d. 251:5
Downstairs: be off, or I'll kick you d. 74:4
Doxy over the dale 292:17
Drab: a-cursing like a very d. 250:18
ditch-deliver'd by a d. 271:12
Dragon: Saint George, that swing'd the d. 264:11
Drain: leave by the next town d. 305:19
Drake he's in his hammock 187:9
Draughts: shallow d. intoxicate the brain 202:5
Draw: d. back ... to leap better 217:15
d. but twenty miles a-day? 166:12
must d. the line somewhere 211:33
Drawers: hewers of wood and d. of water 33:11
Dread: close your eyes with holy d. 87:16
Dread (*continued*)
doth walk in fear and d. 86:16
d. and fear of kings 275:1
d. of something after death 250–1:20
Dreadful: dancing? Oh, d. 65:4
death ... mighty and d. 101:4
O! d. is the check 58:15
the acting of a d. thing 262:13
Dream: a sight to d. of 87:6
a vision or a waking d.? 150:6
and slowly read, and d. 337:10
awoke ... from a deep d. of peace 137:5
behold it was a d. 63:12
consecration, and the poet's d. 331:1
d. of battled fields no more 239:9
d. of money-bags to-night 274:13
d. you are crossing the Channel 117:13
fly, forgotten, as a d. dies 323:6
glory and the freshness of a d. 331:12
if you can d. 154:18
life is but an empty d. 160:14
lust of fame was but a d. 58:14
not d. them, all day long 154:2
oaks ... d., and so d. all night 148:6
old men shall d. dreams 42:13
perchance to d. Ay, there's the rub 250–1:20
phantasma or a hideous d. 262:13
the glory and the d. 331:16
they d. of home 111:12
wrecks of a dissolving d. 298:11
Dreamed: d. of cheese—toasted, mostly 307:5
I d. that Greece might ... be free 70:1
Dreamer: behold, this d. cometh 31:11
d. of dreams 184:9
poet and the d. 148:2
Dreaming: city with her d. spires 19:4
d. arl the time o' Plymouth Hoe 187:9
Dreams: fanatics have their d. 148:1
into the land of my d. 153:11
more things ... than this world d. 312:9
nature lends such evil d. 312:16
not make d. yr. master 154:18
read of ... or dreamt of in d. 24:5
so full of fearful d. 284:15
such stuff as d. are made on 288:16
wovest d. of joy and fear 298:15
Dreamt: d. of in yr. philosophy 249:12
d. that I dwelt in marble halls 63:4
I have long d. of such a ... man 258:3
read of ... or d. of 24:5
Dreary: how d. to be somebody 99:14
world am sad and d. 112:9
Drenched with dew, Old Nod the shepherd 97:1
Dress: a sweet disorder in the d. 131:14
all d. is fancy d. 297:6
noble youths did d. themselves 256:17
Drill: no names, no pack d. 222:3
Drink: a rule never to d. by daylight 169:14
d. and the devil had done for the rest 307:4
d. 'a pinta milka day 11:2
d. deep, or taste not the Pierian spring 202:5
'D. ME' beautifully printed 73:15
d. no longer water 49:12
d. to me only with thine eyes 145:7
d. with him that wears a hood 307:11
five reasons we shd. d. 10:3

Drink (*continued*)
lead a horse ... cannot make him d. 218:28
man wants but little d. 134:2
much d. ... equivocator with lechery 270:14
nor any drop to d. 86:6
shall sit and d. with me 28:4
taste for d., combined with gout 116:10
that I might d., and leave the world 149:14
what shd. we do for d.? 14:1
Drinking: continual d. of Knowledge 152:2
diverted by every means but d. 144:4
d. Cheltenham waters 11:17
d. is the soldier's pleasure 103:14
d. largely sobers us again 202:5
d. the blude red wine 11:13
there are two reasons for d. 199:5
Drinks his wine 'mid laughter free 17:3
Driven: soul ... d., I know not whither 324:4
Drives the flower .. d. my green age 315:16
Driving: d. of Jehu ... he driveth furiously 34:25
spend my life in d. briskly 144:7
Drone: the lazy, yawning d. 258:8
Drop: every d. of the Thames 65:7
nor any d. to drink 86:6
raineth d. and staineth slop 205:2
Drops: little d. of water 73:13
women's weapons, water-d. 266:3
Dross: all is d. that is not Helena 165:8
Drought of Marche hath perced 79:1
Drown: I'll d. my book 289:5
what pain ... to d. 285:1
Drowned: drench'd our steeples, d. the cocks 266:6
d. in the depth of the sea 44:20
d. my Honour in a shallow Cup 110:15
pluck up d. honour by the locks 254:4
Drowning: d. man ... catch at a straw 211:35
no d. mark upon him 287:13
Drowns things weighty and solid 23:10
Drudge: for a d., disobedient 123:2
lexicographer—a harmless d. 140:7
Drum: listenin' for the d. 187:9
not a d. was heard 330:3
the spirit-stirring d. 280:2
war-d. throbbed no longer 313:17
Drummed them out of town 190:9
Drummers: nine d. drumming 194:2
Drums: hearts ... like muffled d. are beating 160:15
sound the trumpets, beat the d. 103:13
Drunk: d. as a fish 211:36
d. as a lord 211:37
d. as a mouse 211:38
d. as a wheelbarrow 211:39
d. the milk of Paradise 87:16
man ... must get d. 69:15
never [happy] but when he is d. 143:18
not so think as you d. 306:3
stag at eve had d. his fill 239:6
this meeting is d. 99:6
Drunkard: the rolling English d. made the rolling English road 81:6
Drunken: do with the d. sailor 17:7
d. folks seldom take harm 211:40
d. night ... cloudy morning 212:1
went to Worts and got more d. 204:13
Drunkenness: babbling d. 292:1
Dry: a d. brain in a d. season 106:6
as d. as dust 212:2
but oh, I am so d. 15:9
die a d. death 287:14
hearts ... d. as summer dust 331:4
old man in a d. month 106:5
Dublin: in D.'s fair city 15:10
Duchess: I am D. of Malfi still 323:13
the D.! Oh, my dear paws! 74:2
the D. said, in a hoarse growl 74:5
Duck: dying d. in a thunderstorm 212:6
water off a d.'s back 229:34
Duckling: The Ugly D. 10:11
Ducks and drakes: to make d. of 212:3
Due: give the devil his d. 214:33
one born out of d. time 48:11
Duke: became a most important d. 28:1
everybody praised the D. 304:15
Dukedom: library was d. large enough 287:17
Dulce et decorum est pro patria mori 136:1
Dull: as d. as ditchwater 212:4
d. in himself, ... cause of dullness 11:8
d. wd. he be of soul 333:6
prophetick blessing—Be thou d. 103:10
Dullness: Shadwell ... mature in d. 104:14
Dumb: d. men get no lands 212:5
great [cares] are d. 219:8
Duncan is in his grave 271:4
Dunce: a d. ... kept at home 93:2
a d. ... sent to roam 93:2
a d. with wits 201:2
Dundee: bonnets of Bonny D. 239:4
Dunfermline: king sits in D. town 11:13
Dungeon: live upon the vapour of a d. 279:17
Dunsinane: till Birnam Forest come to D. 272:7
Dusk: in the d. ... light behind her 120:15
little breezes d. and shiver 313:12
Dust: a d. whom England bore 59:6
all lovers must ... come to d. 247:10
as chimney-sweepers, come to d. 247:9
as dry as d. 212:2
ashes to ashes, d. to d. 53:30
before we too into the D. descend 110:3
cinders, ashes, d. 149:1
d. hath closed Helen's eye 186:12
d. in the air suspended 106:10
D. into D., and under D. to lie 110:3
d. on antique time wd. lie unswept 246:8
d. thou art, and unto d. 30:14
d. thou art, to d. returnest 160:14
guilty of d. and sin 131:10
hearts are dry as summer d. 331:4
make d. our paper 283:5
name ... not perish in the d. 304:11
not without d. and heat 182:4
pays us but with age and d. 232:11
pride that licks the d. 201:19
rotting together have one d. 247:7
vile d. from whence he sprung 240:1
what is the quintessence of d.? 250:6
Dust-heap: great d. called history 54:6
Dusty: d. cobweb-covered, maimed 68:9
the way to d. death 272:10
what a d. answer gets the soul 170:2
Dutch: my dear old D. 81:14
Duties: embark ... on the d. of the day 116:12
let us ... brace ourselves to our d. 82:14
lowliest d. on herself did lay 333:13
property has its d. 102:13

Duty: ashamed of ... declares it is his d. 295:10
do yr. d. and leave the rest to the Gods 90:15
every man will do his d. 187:5
man's first d.? ... To be himself 138:6
my d. in that state of life 53:15
no d. we so ... underrate 307:9
O D.! if that name thou love 334:3
picket's off d. forever 26:10
Thank God, I have done my d. 187:6
the path of d. was the way 314:11
the whole d. of man 40:1
when constabulary d.'s to be done 120:6
when service sweat for d. 243:19
Dwell: poor souls who d. in night 55:1
those who d. in realms of day 55:1
Dwelling: fix in us thy humble d. 325:3
Dwelt: she d. among the untrodden ways 334:11
Dwindle into a wife 89:18
Dying: a most unconscionable time d. 78:14
a slowly d. cause 313:5
doubly d. shall go down 240:1
echoes, d., d., d. 314:15
I am d., Egypt, d. 243:5
it had a d. fall 290:10
'tis not the d. for a faith 315:6
to-morrow will be d. 132:7
truth sits upon the lips of d. men 19:3
unmoved see thee d. ... frog! 98:21

Eagle: an e. mewing her mighty youth 182:8
does the E. know? 55:2
in and out the E. 165:5
like an e. in a dove-cote 246:12
the way of an e. 39:7
Eagles: where his e. never flew 92:2
Ealing: boarded a bus bound for E. 13:3
Ear: a rich jewel in an Ethiop's e. 286:3
choose a wife ... by yr. e. 209:24
deaf adder that stoppeth her e. 36:17
every man thy e., but few thy voice 248:16
give e. unto my song 122:18
in at one e. and out at the other 217:20
more is meant than meets the e. 173:10
not to the sensual e. 149:7
O, it came o'er my e. 290:10
reasonable good e. in music 277:4
silk purse out of a sow's e. 225:24
softly her warm e. lays 162:15
vexing the dull e. of a drowsy man 264:17
when the e. begins to hear 58:15
wd. have won the e. of Pluto 174:10
Earl: an e. by right, by courtesy a man 21:5
Earl of Craven: mistress of the E. 329:5
Early: call me e., mother dear 314:6
e. one morning, just as the sun 15:1
e. to bed and e. to rise 212:9
e. to rise ... wealthy and dead 317:6
get up e. ... to take in God 162:10
she was one of the e. birds 90:5
vain ... to rise up e. 37:20
Earnest: Life is real, Life is e. 160:14
Earnings: equal division of unequal e. 107:18
Earns: he e. whate'er he can 161:10
Ears: e. burn, someone is talking 212:7
have e., but they hear not 37:9
he that hath e. to hear 45:8
lend me your e. 263:11
make two e. of corn ... to grow 309:1
music creep in our e. 275:8
Ears (*continued*)
noise of waters in my e. 285:1
put this engine to our e. 308:14
softest music to attending e. 286:13
there was a shout about my e. 81:3
to e. of flesh and blood 249:7
walls have e. 229:23
Earth: a girdle round about the e. 276:19
a Heaven on E. 178:2
a ladder set up on the e. 31:9
a new heaven and a new e. 51:1
all people that on e. do dwell 153:4
created the heaven and the e. 30:1
daughter of E. and Water 298:6
dear e., I do salute thee 283:1
differ as Heaven and E. 312:6
dim spot which men call E. 172:14
e. has not anything ... more fair 333:6
e. is the Lord's, and the fulness 36:1
e.'s diurnal course 334:15
e.'s sweet flowing breast 153:8
e.'s the right place for love 113:8
e. to e., ashes to ashes 53:30
e. was without form, and void 30:1
firm place ... I will move the e. 18:3
from this e., this grave, this dust 232:11
heaven to e., from e. to heaven 277:6
Heaven tries e. if it be in tune 162:15
Judge of all the e. 31:2
kings are e.'s gods 281:4
lards the lean e. as he walks 254:9
lay her i' th' e. 253:3
multiply and replenish the e. 30:4
old sad e. must borrow its mirth 326:9
past away a glory from the e. 331:14
poetry of e. is never dead 151:1
shall not perish from the e. 159:13
the e. abideth for ever 39:11
the e. and every common sight 331:12
the e. ... appear ... [a] faery place 336:4
the e. doth like a snake renew 298:11
the e., tideless and inert 23:23
the meek shall inherit the e. 36:8
there were giants in the e. 30:19
this e. of majesty, this seat of Mars 282:5
this e., this realm, this England 282:5
thou bleeding piece of e. 263:7
through my lips to unawakened e. 299:6
while the e. remaineth, seedtime 30:23
write sorrow on the bosom of the e. 283:5
yours is the E. and everything 154:20
Ease: bankrupt of life, ... prodigal of e. 103:1
done with so much e. 102:15
for another gives its e. 56:2
not the doctrine of ignoble e. 235:7
O Woman! in our hours of e. 240:9
through the air with the greatest of e. 159:5
true e. in writing comes from art 202:10
youth of labour ... age of e. 122:7
Easiest: the e. way out 324:18
Easy come, e. go 212:12
East: a long way e. of Camberwell 28:1
E. is E., and West is West 154:8
gorgeous E. with richest hand 176:15
in the chambers of the E. 56:13
it is the e. and Juliet is the sun 286:6
somewhere E. of Suez 155:2
we have seen his star in the e. 43:8
Eastern: like a blooming E. bride 103:11
not by e. windows only 85:3

Eat: dare to e. a peach 106:16
did e. bread to the full 31:27
dog does not e. dog 211:26
e. and welcome 212:14
e. one's words 212:15
e. to live ... not live to e. 212:16
e. yr. cake and have it 212:17
great ones e. up the little ones 281:5
I always e. peas with honey 13:10
I cannot e. but little meat 307:11
let us e. and drink; for tomorrow we ... die 40:27
my apple trees will never ... e. 113:13
so I did sit and e. 131:11
some ... canna e., ... some wad e. 67:3
we hae meat and we can e. 67:3
where they don't e. ... no ... dishes 12:1
whereas I e. to live 304:6
wd. not work, neither shd. he e. 49:8
ye shall e. the fat of the land 31:13
Eaten: e. me out of house and home 256:15
he has been e. by the bear 136:2
they'd e. every one 76:6
Eater: out of the e. came forth meat 33:19
Eating: appetite comes with e. 232:7
proof ... is in the e. 223:29
Eccentric: so few ... dare to be e. 170:12
Echo: e. beyond the Mexique Bay 167:9
sound ... an e. to the sense 202:10
sounds that e. still 311:14
woods shall ... answer ... E. ring 305:7
Echoes: answer, e., dying, dying 314:15
set the wild e. flying 314:15
Eclipse without all hope of day 180:10
Eclipses: late e. in the sun and moon 265:9
Ecstasy: pouring ... thy soul ... in such an e. 150:3
to maintain this e., is success 198:9
Eden: garden of E. to dress it 30:6
this other E., demi-paradise 282:5
through E. took their solitary way 179:18
with loss of E. 175:15
Edge: cloy the hungry e. of appetite 282:1
Edmonton: if wife shd. dine at E. 92:11
repair unto the Bell at E. 92:7
Edmund [Burke]: good E., whose genius was such 123:1
Education: cabbage with a college e. 318:16
e. begins a gentleman 212:18
e. ent only books and music 324:18
e. has for its object 305:5
never made straight by e. 210:19
soap and e. ... are more deadly 318:11
'tis e. forms the common mind 203:14
travel ... part of e. 22:13
Educational relations make the strongest tie 233:11
Eel: as slippery as an e. 225:30
Eena, meena, mina, mo 189:1
Eeyore, the old grey Donkey 172:5
Effect: nature is ... name for an e. 93:11
worst e. is banishing for hours 92:5
Effort: written without e. ... read without pleasure 144:25
Efforts: have resolved to combine our e. 319:5
Egestas: improbus et duris ... rebus e. 321:6
Egg: bad e. ... parts ... are excellent 232:4
better an e. today 207:18
like the curate's e. 210:26
Eggs: all yr. e. in one basket 212:19
as a weasel sucks e. 244:5
as sure as e. is e. 226:32
goose that lays the golden e. 217:37
teach yr. grandmother to suck e. 227:17
what do you mean by no e.? 296:24
Eglantine: musk-roses and with e. 276:20
or the twisted e. 174:2
Egypt: a new king over E. 31:15
brought thee out of ... E. 31:29
firstborn in the land of E. 31:25
I am dying, E., dying 243:5
rail against ... first-born of E. 244:7
saw that there was corn in E. 31:12
strangers in the land of E. 33:2
wd. to God we had died ... in ... E. 31:27
Egyptian: to his E. dish again 242:18
Eheu fugaces, Postume ... labuntur anni 135:15
Eighteen: knew almost as much at e. 142:11
Einstein: Ho, let E. be 306:2
Either: how happy I cd. be with e. 115:7
Elbow: my ... e. has a fascination 118:13
Elder: the e. unto the elect lady 50:14
Elders: miss not ... discourse of the e. 51:17
Electric: across the wires the e. message 21:6
Lord Finchley tried to mend the e. light 27:6
Elegant: an e. sufficiency 316:13
Element: e. of fire is ... put out 100:16
one God, one law, one e. 313:9
thy e.'s below 265:21
'Elementary,' said he [Holmes] 101:15
Elements: e. of whom yr. swords are temper'd 288:15
framed us of four e. 166:10
I tax not you, you e. 266:7
our torments also may ... become our e. 177:2
the e. so mix'd in him 264:7
Eleven: e. buckram men ... out of two 254:16
rain before seven, fine before e. 224:1
Eleventh Commandment ... not be found out 212:20
Elf: a servant's ... an impudent e. 24:3
Elijah ... cast his mantle 34:22
Eliminated: when you have e. the impossible 102:3
Elinor: 'I am afraid,' replied E. 21:3
Elizabeth: no scandal about Queen E. 301:2
spacious times of great E. 311:14
Eloquence: love and business teach e. 219:34
Elsewhere: when e., live as they live e. 10:10
Elves of hills, brooks, ... groves 289:4
Ely: my Lord of E., when I was ... in Holborn 285:3
Elysium: what E. have ye known? 149:4
Embarras des richesses 10:8
Embarrassing: the e. young 115:3
Embers: glowing e. through the room 173:9
O joy! that in our e. ... doth live 332:4
Embodiment: the Law is the true e. 117:2
Embody: I, my Lords, e. the Law 117:2
Embrace: arms, take your last e. 287:4
none, I think, do there e. 167:14
Eminence: by merit raised to that bad e. 176:15
Emotion recollected in tranquillity 336:7
Emperor: heard ... by e. and clown 150:4
to the tent-royal of their e. 258:8
Empire: all the loungers of the E. 102:5

Empire *(continued)*
another mighty E. overthrown! 334:2
how is the E.? 115:16
if the British E. ... last for a thousand years 82:14
King dead, the e. unpossess'd? 285:11
Mother E. stands splendidly isolated 112:3
neither holy, nor Roman, nor an e. 321:16
preside over the liquidation of the British E. 83:6
the E. is a Commonwealth of Nations 235:12
to found a great e. 303:4
young was called to E. 104:13
Empires: day of E. has come 78:8
vaster than e. and more slow 167:12
Employment: give e. to the artisan 27:6
the pleasantness of an e. 21:3
Empty vessels make the most noise 212:22
Enchanted: as holy and e. 87:12
Enchanter: ghosts from an e. fleeing 299:3
Enchantment: lends e. to the view 72:9
Encourage: kill an admiral ... to e. the others 321:10
Encourager: pour e. les autres 321:10
Encumbers: Patron ... e. him with help 142:1
End: a loud noise at one e. 155:15
'a made a finer e. 259:1
ages of hopeless e. 177:1
attempt the e. 132:5
beginning of the e. 310:10
big e.-ians and small e.-ians 308:15
boys get at one e. ... lose at the other 143:20
e. justifies the means 212:23
everything hath an e. 212:37
found no e., in wandering mazes lost 177:6
four ... winters ... springs e. in a word 281:12
he shall e. in certainties 23:12
long weary day have e. 305:8
longest day must have an e. 219:26
Lord, make me to know mine e. 36:11
more than an e. to war, we want 235:6
my last e. be like his! 32:20
not even the beginning of the e. ... but ... the e. of the beginning 83:5
our minutes hasten to their e. 294:1
seen one thing, that love hath an e. 310:3
the e. of this day's business 264:5
the man would die ... and there an e. 271:8
the right true e. of love 101:2
Sans Wine ... Song ... E.! 110:3
vegetate and wish ... an e. 65:5
yes, to the very e. 236:3
Endeavour: a disinterested e. to learn 19:8
Ending: e. is better than mending 137:9
love is ... sour in the e. 219:39
Endowed by their Creator with ... rights. 139:6
Ends: divinity that shapes our e. 253:6
dog, to gain some private e. 122:19
make both e. meet 208:25
odd old e. stol'n forth of holy writ 284:14
to serve our private e. 82:3
Endurable: love [will] make a thing e. 332:12
Endure: cannot e. in his age 277:22
cd. e. the toothache patiently 278:17
first e., then pity, then embrace 203:6
from age to age e. 153:5
youth's a stuff will not e. 291:2
Endured: can't be cured, must be e. 230:7
much is to be e. 141:6
tolerable and not to be e. 278:6
Enemies: confusion to his e. 15:6
left me naked to mine e. 261:13
love your e. 43:20
Enemy: best ... e. of the good 321:13
better an open e. 207:19
here shall he see no e. 244:4
how goes the *e.*? 233:8
if thine e. be hungry 38:28
mine e.'s dog 267:9
my name ... terrible to the e. 256:11
of yr e. say nothing 226:6
the e. faints not 85:1
trust not ... an old e. 228:23
Energetic: our speech ... e. without rules 140:1
Energies of our system will decay 23:23
Energy: e. is eternal delight 56:16
reason and e., love and hate 56:15
Enfants: les e. terribles 115:3
Enfer: chaud comme l'e. 310:11
Engine: e. that moves in determinate grooves 128:11
put this e. to our ears 308:14
England: a body of E.'s, breathing English air 59:6
a dust whom E. bore 59:6
a time there was, ere E.'s griefs 122:6
be E. what she will 82:1
between France and E. is the sea 139:18
E., bound in with the triumphant sea 282:6
E. expects every man 187:5
E. has saved herself ... save Europe 200:9
E. hath need of thee 333:12
E. ... hell for horses 67:10, 212:24
E. is a nation of shop-keepers 185:12
E. is the mother of parliaments 58:9
E. is the paradise of women 67:10, 111:4, 212:24
E., my E.? E. my own 130:11
E.'s green and pleasant land 55:8
E. will have her neck wrung 83:4
E., with all thy faults 93:7
E. ... wont to conquer others 282:6
Florence, Elizabethan E. 138:8
for E.'s the one land 59:3
foreign field ... forever E. 59:5
gallows standing in E. when thou art king? 253:16
gentlemen in E., now abed 260:2
Happy is E.! I cd. be content 151:2
heart and stomach of ... King of E. 107:13
high road that leads him to E. 142:8
history of E. is ... history of progress 164:5
I know the kings of E. 120:4
if E. to itself do rest but true 265:5
in E.—now! 61:1
in E. we ... rely on ... time-lag 324:15
know of E. who only E. know? 154:13
laws of E. are at my commandment 258:2
light such a candle ... in E. 157:2
men in E. that do no work today 259:12
my love for E. and Ireland 234:1
nor, E., did I know till then 331:6
not three good men unhang'd in E. 254:14
Oats.—... in E. ... given to horses 140:9

England (*continued*)
Oh, to be in E. 61:1
on E.'s pleasant pastures seen 55:8
people of E. that never have spoken yet 81:9
roast beef of E. 109:9
Stately Homes of E. 91:5,6
stately homes of E.! 130:5
there'll always be an E. 198:4
this earth, this realm, this E. 282:5
this E. never did ... lie at the ... foot 265:4
'Tis for the honour of E. 89:8
wake up, E. 115:15
walk upon E.'s mountains 55:8
ye mariners of E. 72:10
youth of E. are on fire 258:9
English: a body of England's, breathing E. air 59:6
be among the E. Poets after my death 152:5
blood of E. shall manure the ground 283:8
Chaucer, well of E. undefiled 305:13
E. are ... the least ... pure philosophers 23:20
E. as she is Spoke 318:4
E. never know when ... beaten 212:25
E. winter—ending in July 70:8
grave where E. oak and holly 129:2
on, on, you noblest E. 259:4
our E. tongue a gallimaufry 305:17
principle of the E. constitution 54:10
the E. ... a foul-mouthed nation 129:9
the E. country gentleman 328:10
the E. have hot-water bottles 170:8
the rolling E. drunkard made the rolling E. road 81:6
the sort of E. up with which 83:12
trick of our E. nation 256:10
under an E. heaven 59:7
wholesome ... really nice E. people 295:17
winged heels, as E. Mercuries 258:9
with our E. dead 259:3
Englishman: an E., even ... alone, forms a ... queue 170:9
an E. thinks he is moral 296:7
E. does not travel to see Englishmen 306:12
E. ... enjoys himself ... for a noble purpose 131:7
E.'s home is his castle 212:26
my-lorded as only a free-born E. can 315:10
rights of an E. 146:5
stirred the hearts of every E. 239:3
the last great E. is low 314:9
to his credit ... an E.! 120:2
way to an E.'s heart 229:36
Englishmen: mad dogs and E. 91:8
reveal Himself ... first to his E. 182:7
when two E. meet ... talk of the weather 140:12
Engross: pens a stanza when he shd. e. 201:11
Enigma: a riddle wrapped in a mystery inside an e. 82:10
Enjoy: can thoroughly e. the pepper 74:7
e. themselves so well, as at ... tavern 144:1
prize not ... whiles we e. it 278:12
who can e. alone? 179:3
you will never e. the world 317:16
Enjoyed: e. no sooner but despised 294:11
Enjoyed (*continued*)
human life ... little to be e. 141:6
that bards of old e. 56:14
to have e. the sun 18:10
what peaceful hours I once e. 92:14
Enjoyment: variety is the mother of e. 100:13
Enjoys: the Englishman never e. himself 131:7
Enough: e. is as good as a feast 54:3, 212:28
e. is e. 212:28
e. that there *is* a beyond 295:9
grant me ... more than e. 165:4
wore e. for modesty 62:13
Enriched: pension never e. a young man 223:4
Enriches: robs me ... not e. him 279:15
Ense: calamus saevior e. patet 67:9
Ensign: beauty's e. yet is crimson 287:3
tear her tattered e. down 134:1
th' imperial e. ... high advanced 176:9
Enter: abandon hope all ye who e. 95:6
e. ye in at ... strait gate 44:8
ye shall not e. into ... Kingdom 44:19
Enterprise: the e. is sick 290:2
Enterprises: e. of great pith and moment 250–1:20
impediments to great e. 21:19
Entertaining: more e. than half the novels 169:6
Enthroned in the hearts of kings 275:1
Enthusiasm: considering that e. moves the world 24:1
long for a little ordinary e. 197:10
nothing great ... without e. 108:3
Enthusiasts: so few e. ... speak the truth 24:1
Entire and whole and perfect 305:22
Entrance: beware of e. to a quarrel 248:16
Entrances: have their exits and their e. 244:11
Envied: better be e. than pitied 207:22
Envious: rent the e. Casca made 263:17
Envy: e. and calumny and hate and pain 297:16
e., hatred, and malice 52:23
in e. of great Caesar 264:6
means ... too low for e. 91:13
the e. of less happier lands 282:5
Ephesians: Diana of the E. 47:7
Epilogue: a good play needs no e. 246:4
Epitaph: believe a woman or an e. 70:14
Epitaphs: a nice derangement of e. 301:10
graves and worms and e. 283:5
Epithet: fair is too foul an e. for thee 166:11
Epitome: all mankind's e. 103:4
Eppur si muove 114:14
Epsom Salts: had we but stuck to E. 11:17
Equal: all animals are e. but some are more e. 197:1
e. division of unequal earnings 107:18
far from ... true ... naturally e. 143:2
inferiors revolt ... be e. 18:6
that all men are created e. 139:6
Equals [revolt] that they may be superior 18:6
Eros: unarm, E.; the ... task is done 243:4
Err: better to e. with Pope 70:15
not e., who say ... when the Poet dies 239:14
the most may e. as grossly 103:8
to e. is human 217:11
to e. is human, to forgive divine 202:14
Errand: in thy joyous e. reach the spot 111:1

Errands for the Ministers of State 116:13
Erred: we have e. and strayed 52:12
Erring: a rod to check the e. 334:3
Error: custom without reason ... ancient e. 210:28
e. of opinion may be tolerated 139:8
gross e. held in schools 115:12
if this be e. and upon me prov'd 294:9
ignorance is preferable to e. 139:12
mountainous e. ... highly heap'd 246:8
Errors: amusing with numerous e. [book] 123:18
e., like straws, upon the surface 103:16
if to her share some female e. 204:6
Esau: E. my brother ... a hairy man 31:7
the hands of E. 31:8
Escape: e. me?—never 61:7
thou shalt not e. calumny 251:3
who shall e. whipping? 250:13
Essence: his glassy e., like an angry ape 273:7
Estate: become a fourth e. of the realm 164:4
ordered their e. 10:5
Esteem: riches I hold in light e. 58:14
Esteemed: better to be vile than vile e. 294:10
Esther: loved E. above all ... women 34:27
État: l'É. c'est moi 162:2
Eternal: abode where the E. are 298:3
condition ... liberty ... e. vigilance 95:3
energy is e. delight 56:16
e. summer gilds them yet 69–70:21
on Fame's e. beadroll 305:13
thought ... to be boy e. 292:12
Eternity: damned from here to E. 154:15
deserts of vast e. 167:13
e. in an hour 54:12
lives in e.'s sunrise 55:4
make the mighty ages of e. 73:13
memorial from the soul's e. 236:6
passing through nature to e. 247:20
stains the white radiance of E. 298:2
thoughts that wander through e. 176:19
Etherised: evening is spread out ... like a patient e. 106:11
Ethiop: a rich jewel in an E.'s ear 286:3
Ethiopian: can the E. change his skin? 41:14
Eton: Waterloo ... won on the playing fields of E. 324:10
Euphelia serves to grace my measure 205:6
Euripides: a chorus-ending from E. 60:13
Europe: all E. shd. know that we have blockheads 89:8
glory of E. is extinguished 64:11
lamps are going out all over E. 127:8
last territorial claim ... in E. 132:14
part of the community of E. 121:10
save E. by her example 200:9
Soviet power into heart of Western E. 83:10
splendidly isolated in E. 112:3
we are ... smallest country left in E. 319:9
Eurydice: half-regained E. 174:10
Eve: fairest of her daughters E. 178:4
from noon to dewy e. 176:14
when Adam delved and E. span 24:2
when E. upon the first of Men 135:2
Even: contrive to write so e. 20:19
Événements: l'histoire des grands é. 321:15
Evening: bright exhalation in the e. 261:8
e. crowns the day 212:29
Evening (*continued*)
e. is spread out against the sky 106:11
I light my lamp in the e. 28:2
it is a beauteous e. 33:2
It was a summer's e. 304:12
like an e. gone 323:5
now came still e. on 178:6
shadows of the e. steal 24:8
the winter e. settles down 106:19
who turns as I, this e. 61:5
Event: heaviness foreruns the good e. 257:11
one far-off divine e. 313:9
wise after the e. 212:13
wisest prophets make sure of the e. 322:8
Ever: but I go on for e. 311:8
do nothing for e. and e. 12:1
for e. and for e. farewell, Cassius! 264:4
for e. hold his peace 53:20
if for e., still for e. 70:16
left lonely for e. 18:13
that no life lives for e. 310:1
thou art gone, and for e. 239:10
what, *never*? Hardly e.! 119:11
wished him to talk on for e. 129:8
Everlasting: caught an e. cold 324:5
condemn'd into e. redemption 278:15
had stood [wheat] from e. to e. 317:17
primrose way to th' e. bonfire 270:13
that the E. had not fix'd 248:2
Everybody: e. praised the Duke 304:15
e. wants to have read 319:2
friend to e. ... friend to nobody 214:20
Everyman, I will go with thee 13:5
Everyone: e. ... put his whole wit 25:7
e. suddenly burst out singing 238:10
war of e. against e. 133:2
Everything: a smattering of e. 99:11
can resist e. except temptation 328:2
e. by starts and nothing long 103:4
e.'s got a moral 74:12
God saw e. ... he had made 30:5
sans taste, sans e. 244–5:11
sermons in stones, and good in e. 243:15
with e. that pretty bin 246–7:13
Everywhere: e. be bold 305:12
e. that Mary went 127:11
water, water e. 86:6
Eves: on summer e. by haunted stream 174:7
Evidence of things not seen 49:21
Evil: abhor that which is e. 47:23
all partial e., universal good 203:4
be not overcome of e. 47:27
care not whether ... good or e. 55:7
decide ... for the good or e. side 162:14
deliver us from e. 43:24
doing e. on the ground of expediency 235:11
E., be thou my Good 177:14
e. be to him who e. thinks 216:40
e. is wrought by want of Thought 135:1
e. that men do lives after them 263:11
e. which I wd. not, that I do 47:19
government ... a necessary e. 197:19
I will fear no e. 35:29
knowing good and e. 30:11
love of money ... root of all e. 49:14
loved darkness ... their deeds were e. 46:22
Luke ... gave himself to e. courses 332:11
maketh ... sun to rise on the e. 43:21
nature lends such e. dreams 312:16

Evil (*continued*)
of moral e. and of good 335:7
on e. days ... fallen, and e. tongues 178:20
out of good ... find means of e. 176:2
overcome e. with good 47:27
purer eyes than to behold e. 42:25
resist not e. 43:19
root of all e. The want of money 68:3
set good against e. 215:13
supernatural source of e. 90:9
the tongue ... is an unruly e. 50:1
them that call e. good 40:20
Evils: he ... must expect new e. 22:18
of two e. choose the least 213:1
women are necessary e. 230:34
Exact: an e. man 23:8
Exactitude ... politesse des rois 162:4
Exactness: with e. grinds he all 161:3
Exaggerated: reports of my death ... e. 319:4
Exalteth: righteousness e. a nation 38:15
Examination: post-mortem e. revealed ... 'Callous' 241:11
Examinations are formidable even to the best 88:20
Example: e. is better than precept 213:2
e. is the school of mankind 64:15
good e. is the best sermon 215:16
Excavating for a mine 183:8
Exceed: reach shd. e. his grasp 60:11
Excel: daring to e. 82:2
unstable ... thou shalt not e. 31:14
Excellent: an e. thing in woman 268:3
embodiment of everything ... e. 117:2
e. to have a giant's strength 273:6
Excels: how much a dunce ... e 93:2
Excelsior: the strange device, E.! 160:12
Exception proves the rule 213:3
Excess: e. leads to wisdom 57:1
e. of glory obscured 176:11
give me e. of it 290:10
in charity there is no e. 22:5
nothing in e. 17:10
nothing succeeds like e. 328:14
surprise by a fine e. 151:14
wasteful and ridiculous e. 264:19
Exchange: by just e. one for another given 302:2
fair e. is no robbery 213:11
novels gain by the e. 70:10
Exciting: he found it less e. 116:6
Exclamation: 'fifty thousand!' was the e. 62:2
Excommunicate: unbaptized, or e. 53:27
Excuse: a bad e. is better than none 206:33
make the fault the worse by the e. 265:1
no longer e. for ... playing the rake 184:3
she'll prove an e. for a glass 301:17
Execution: their [of laws] stringent e. 125:2
Executioner: I am mine own e. 101:6
Executors: delivering o'er to e. pale 258:8
let's choose e. and talk of wills 283:5
Exercise: dancing? ... a barbarian e. 65:4
what e. is to the body 306:8
Exhalation: I shall fall like some bright e. 261:8
Exhausted worlds ... imagin'd new 140:19
Exiles: thou Paradise of e., Italy 298:12
Exist: if God did not e. 321:14
Existence: contraries ... are necessary to ... e. 56:15
E. saw him spurn her ... reign 140:19
Existence (*continued*)
love ... 'tis woman's whole e. 69:14
Exits: they have their e. and their entrances 244:11
Expands: work e. ... to fill the time available 198:5
Expatiate free o'er all this scene of man 202:17
Expectancy and rose of the fair state 251:5
Expectation: however certain our e. 107:11
now sits E. in the air 258:9
Expediency: doing evil on the ground of e. 235:11
Expedient: all things ... lawful ... but ... not e. 48:2
too fond of the *right* to pursue the *e.* 123:2
Expense: at the e. of two [Gods] 84:15
Expensive: did ... from e. sins refrain 103:6
Experience: an e. of women which extends 102:2
e. ... if not bought too dear 213:4
e. teaches 213:5
till old e. do attain ... prophetic 173:12
travel ... part of e. 22:13
triumph of hope over e. 143:6
true e. from this great event 181:8
Experientia docet 213:5
Expires: with that the Wretched Child e. 27:4
Expiring: thus e. do foretell of him 282:4
Expose thyself to feel what wretches feel 266:14
Expressed: oft was thought, but ne'er so well e. 202:8
Expresses himself in terms too deep 119:4
Extensive: knowledge of London ... e. and peculiar 98:23
Extent of [our language's] beauty and power 164:3
Extenuate: speak ... as I am; nothing e. 280:14
Extinguished: glory of Europe is e. 64:11
nature is ... seldom e. 22:26
Extinguishes the small, ... inflames the great 67:13
Extremes: e. meet 213:6
two e. of passion, joy and grief 268:1
women are always in e. 230:33
Extremity: a daring pilot in e. 102–3:17
Exuberance: e. is beauty 57:5
e. of his own verbosity 100:8
Exulting: the people all e. 325:12
Eye: a custom loathsome to the e. 138:14
a still-soliciting e. 265:8
all my e. and Betty Martin 206:15
all places that the e. of heaven visits 281:14
an e. for an e. 43:18
an e. made quiet by ... harmony 335:12
as the apple of his e. 33:6
camel ... through the e. of a needle 44:23
courtier's, soldier's, scholar's e. 251:5
e. for e., tooth for tooth 32:10
e. sees not, ... heart rues not 213:7
e. to the main chance 220:11
far from e., far from heart 213:17
flash upon that inward e. 331:11
has not man a microscopic e.? 203:2
holds him with his glittering e. 85:12
I backward cast my e. 66:13
if thine e. offend thee 44:21
in the c. of the beholder 137:3

Eye (*continued*)
keep me as the apple of the e. 35:21
long grey beard and glittering e. 85:11
many an e. has danced to see 134:1
my credit in men's e. 110:15
now mine e. seeth thee 35:15
poet's e. in a fine frenzy rolling 277:6
teaches such beauty as a woman's e. 268:12
the e. begins to see 58:15
the ... e. of heaven to garnish 264:19
there's language in her e. 290:8
what immortal hand or e. 56:5
with his keener e. the axe's edge 168:4
with my little e., I saw him die 196:2
Eyebrow: ballad ... to his mistress' e. 244:11
Eyeless in Gaza 180:9
Eyelids: no more wilt weigh my e. down 257:2
tir'd e. upon tir'd eyes 314:2
with e. heavy and red 135:3
Eyes: and her e. were wild 148:15
and those e., the break of day 273:12
as in a theatre the e. of men 284:5
as 'twere in scorn of e. 285:1
choose love by another's e. 276:11
close yr. e. with holy dread 87:16
cost him his e. 267:14
discreet women ... neither e. nor ears 211:20
disdain and scorn ride ... in her e. 278:2
dress her beauty at yr. e. 96:1
drink to me only with thine e. 145:7
e. have they but they see not 37:8
e., look your last 287:4
e. of all wait upon thee 37:30
e. wide open before marriage 217:35
flourish where you turn yr. e. 204:4
four e. see more than two 214:15
from women's e. this doctrine 268:14
get thee glass e. 267:7
golden slumbers kiss your e. 96:11
had I your tongues and e. 268:2
handkerchief before his streaming e. 76:5
happiness through another man's e. 245:15
have e. to wonder but lack tongues 294:7
her aspect and her e. 71:2
holes where e. did once inhabit 285:1
how fearful ... to cast one's e. so low 267:2
I was e. to the blind 35:10
if thou hast e. to see 279:5
justice ... with e. severe 244:11
kindling her undazzled e. 182:8
love looks not with the e. 276:12
make thy two e. ... start from ... spheres 249:7
mine e. dazzle 323:16
my mistress' e. ... nothing like the sun 294:13
night has a thousand e. 57:13
not all that tempts yr. wand'ring e. 125:12
one whose subdu'd e. ... drops tears 280–1:14
pearls that were his e. 288:1
pull the wool over ... e. 230:39
rapt soul sitting in thine e. 173:7
right in his own e. 33:24
see through all things with his half-shut e. 204:10
set my e. on sweet Molly Malone 15:10
sight for sore e. 225:22
sight ... good for sore e. 309:6

Eyes (*continued*)
sights of ... death within my e. 285:1
so long as ... e. can see 293:15
soft look your e. had once 337:10
sparkling e., ... teeth like pearls 62:6
stout Cortez ... with eagle e. 150–1:15
strike mine e. but not my heart 145:10
take a pair of sparkling e. 116:14
thou art of purer e. 42:25
tired eyelids upon tired e. 314:2
to ope their golden e. 246:13
two lovely black e. 85:6
until you see the whites of their e. 205:4
very few e. can see the Mystery 152:7
where'er these casual e. are cast 304:10
whose bright e. rain influence 174:6
with e. up-rais'd, as one inspired 88:13
with rainy e. write sorrow 283:5
yr. mouth shut and yr. e. open 217:36

Fabric: baseless f. of this vision 288:16
Face: a caricature of a f. 118–9:15
a garden in her f. 72:13
and with how wan a f.! 302:4
but then f. to f. 48:7
cover her f.: mine eyes dazzle 323:16
dew on the f. of the dead 26:10
disasters in his morning f. 122:11
Discobolus ... turneth his f. to the wall 68:9
f. that launch'd a thousand ships 165:8
f. with nature's own hand painted 293:16
fair and open f. of heaven 151:6
fair f. ... foul heart 213:12
fair f. ... half a fortune 213:13
false f. must hide 270:8
God hath given you one f. 251:4
good f. needs no paint 215:17
grace, ... seen in one autumnal f. 101:1
grace to get ... red in the f. 29:7
honour the f. of the old man 32:17
human f. divine 177:10
I wish I loved its silly f. 233:1
in the sweat of thy f. 30:13
just can't think of yr. f. 305:21
look on her f. and you'll forget 204:6
looks the whole world in the f. 161:10
Monday's child is fair of f. 191:8
my f.—I don't mind it 109:1
my f. is my fortune, sir 196:1
never f. so pleased my mind 17:2
painting a f. and not washing 114:7
princely counsel in his f. yet shone 177:3
principles ... f. to f. from ... beginning 159:10
satchel and shining morning f. 244:11
seen too oft, familiar with her f. 203:6
smile on the f. of the tiger 12:10
tell the f. thou viewest 293:11
the air on his f. unkind 96:5
the unclouded f. of truth 238:15
with her f. upturned 157:10
your f., my thane ... a book 270:3
Faces: grind the f. of the poor 40:19
heavily jowled or hawk-like ... f. 165:1
seen better f. in my time 265:19
so many millions of f. ... none alike 59:15
strange f., other minds 312:7
the old familiar f. 156:9
'tis ye, 'tis yr. estranged f. 316:10
Facilis descensus Averni 321:4

Facing: Mr. F.-both-ways 63:10
Facts: all the f. when ... brass tacks 107:2
f. are sacred 238:15
indebted to ... imagination for his f. 301:19
irritable reaching after f. 151:11
Faculties: our souls, whose f. can comprehend 166:10
Fade: f. away into the forest dim 149:14
f. into the light of common day 332:2
old soldiers ... only f. away 16:7
she cannot f. 149:8
thy eternal summer shall not f. 293:14
Faded: like this insubstantial pageant f. 288:16
Fades: now f. the glimmering landscape 126:4
Faery: full beautiful, a f.'s child 148:15
in f. lands forlorn 150:4
the land of f. 337:6
Faiblesse: tout le reste est f. 320:14
Fail: if we shd. f.? We f.! 270:7
neither shall ... cruse of oil f. 34:18
sooner f. than not be among the greatest 152:4
we shall not flag or f. 82:13
Failed: The Light that F. 155:11
Faileth: enemy faints not, nor f. 85:1
Failing: f. to trust everybody ... nobody 213:8
true ... she had one f. 66:6
Failure: only one [to make a marriage] a f. 238:2
Faint, yet pursuing 33:17
Faints: the enemy f. not 85:1
Fair: all is f. in love and war 206:11
brave deserves the f. 103:12
f. is foul and foul is f. 269:4
f. is too foul an epithet for thee 166:11
f. stood the wind for France 102:9
for ever shalt thou love and she be f. 149:8
holy, f. and wise is she 292:8
how sweet and f. she seems to be 322:1
is she kind as she is f.? 292:9
like not f. terms and a villain's mind 274:11
most divinely f. 311:15
pernicious weed! ... the f. annoys 92:5
she is f. and, fairer 274:4
she is not f. to outward view 85:10
so foul and f. a day 269:6
Fair play's a jewel 213:14
Fairer: and f. than that word 274:4
I can't say no f. than that 98:2
thou art f. than the evening air 165:9
Fairest: O, f. of creation 179:10
Fairies: do you believe in f.? 24:14
f. at the bottom of our garden 114:11
I don't believe in f. 24:12
she is the f. midwife 286:1
that was the beginning of f. 24:11
Fair-spoken and persuading 262:2
Fairy: a little f. ... falls down dead 24:12
by f. hands their knell is rung 88:11
light she was and like a f. 183:9
'tis almost f. time 277:8
Faith: an event which creates f. 297:3
break f. with us who die 164:9
f. and morals ... Milton held 334:1
f. ... as the fashion of his hat 277:10
f. is ... substance of things 49:21
f. shines equal, arming me 58:12
f.'s transcendent dower 334:10
Faith (*continued*)
f. unfaithful kept him falsely true 312:4
f. without works is dead 49:25
fight the good fight of f. 49:15
I have kept the f. 49:17
I mean the F.'s Defender 68:15
just shall live by f. 47:15
more f. in honest doubt 313:1
my staff of f. to walk upon 232:12
reaffirm f. in ... human rights 319:5
reason ... soul's left hand, f. her right 100:18
remembering ... yr. work of f. 49:5
simple f. than Norman blood 313:10
'tis not the dying for a f. 315:6
we walk by f., not by sight 48:15
which constitutes poetic f. 87:19
Faithful: be thou f. unto death 50:16
ever f., ever sure 180:7
f. are the wounds of a friend 39:3
f. only he 178:18
f. to thee, Cynara! 101:11
O come, all ye f. 196:5
so f. in love ... dauntless in war 240:6
Faith-healer of Deal 12:9
Faithless: among the f., faithful only he 178:18
yr. sleeping head ... on my f. arm 20:2
Faiths: heaven smiles and f. and empires gleam 298:11
Fall: another thing to f. 273:1
A-tishoo! We all f. down 193:2
f. out, and chide, and fight 323:3
haughty spirit [goeth] before a f. 38:19
he that is down need fear no f. 63:15
held we f. to rise 60:12
higher ... the greater the f. 216:31
Humpty Dumpty had a great f. 76:8, 189:9
pride will have a f. 223:27
some by virtue f. 273:2
that strain ...! It had a dying f. 290:10
the cradle will f. 189:10
the glass will f. for ever 164:15
unless the billboards f. 186:10
upon the ground, can f. no lower 219:3
what a f. was there, my countrymen! 263:19
Fallen: awake, ... or be for ever f.! 176:7
f. out of heigh degree 80:1
f. ... that tower of strength 314:10
there has f. a splendid tear 314:4
though f. on evil days 178:20
you are f. from grace 48:21
Falling: he hath the f. sickness 262:10
what a f. off was there 249:11
Falls: between two stools one f. 207:39
like a thunderbolt he f. 312:1
nips his root, and then he f. 261:9
when f. the Coliseum, Rome shall fall 69:8
when he f., he f. like Lucifer 261:10
False: any other thing that's f. 70:14
canst not then be f. to any man 248–9:17
history must be f. 322:5
prov'd true ... prove f. again 67:17
ring out the f., ring in the true 313:4
thou shalt not bear f. witness 32:8
true to thyself, as ... not f. to others 22:17
what the f. heart doth know 270:8
Falsehood: let her and F. grapple 182:10
Falstaff sweats to death 254:9

Fame: all the family of F. 87:18
an imp of f. 259:9
Cromwell, damned to everlasting f. 203:9
f. ... is double-mouthed 181:4
f. is like a river 23:10
f. is no plant ... on mortal soil 175:2
f. is the spur 175:1
his f. soon spread around 92:9
lust of f. 58:14
nor yet a fool to f. 201:13
on F.'s eternal beadroll 305:13
physicians of the utmost f. 27:3
servants of f. 22:2
son of memory, great heir of f. 175:12
thou, whose infamy is not thy f. 297:15
Familiar: f. acts are beautiful 299:13
f. as his garter 258:7
f., but by no means vulgar 248:15
f. objects as if ... not f. 300:9
the old f. faces 156:9
too f. with disappointments 159:6
wine ... a good f. creature 279:11
Familiarity: f. breeds contempt 213:16
f. breeds contempt and children 318:14
Families: accidents ... in best-regulated f. 98:1
all happy f. resemble one another 317:13
I might ... be useful to their f. 20:6
Family: a man that left his f. 318:7
all the f. of Fame 87:18
brought up a large f. 123:19
if I heard my f. called decent 199:3
wonderful f. called Stein 13:4
Famine: die by f. die by inches 130:15
elle alla crier f. 111:6
f. grew and locusts came 315:17
she went to cry f. 111:6
Famous: awoke ... and found myself f. 71:7
but 'twas a f. victory 304:15
man can become f. without ability 295:14
Fan: she comes ... full sail ... f. spread 89:10
Fanatics have their dreams 148:1
Fancy: a f. from a flower-bell 60:13
a little of what you f. 160:5
a young man's f. lightly turns 313:15
admit those [wants] of f. 141:4
costly thy habit ... not express'd in f. 248:16
ever let the f. roam 148:3
fellow ... of most excellent f. 253:2
listen ... to the whispers of f. 141:3
sweetest Shakespeare, F.'s child 174:8
tell me where is f. bred 274:18
what I f. I feel 12:9
Fantastic: f. summer's heat 282:1
on the light f. toe 173:17
Far: a f., f. better thing that I do 99:12
beneath the good how f.! 127:2
but f. above the great! 127:2
fair and softly goes f. 213:10
f. and few, f. and few 158:5
f. as human eye cd. see 313:16
f. back through creeks and inlets 85:2
f. from de old folks 112:9
f. from eye, f. from heart 213:17
f. from the madding crowd's ... strife 126:12
from f., from eve and morning 136:7
good news from a f. country 38:29
John Peel when he's f. f. away 125:6
old Kentucky Home f. away 112:7
Far (*continued*)
one f.-off divine event 313:9
over the hills and f. away 195:3
so near and yet so f. 313:2
Thursday's child has f. to go 191:8
Farce: the farce is over 232:8
Farces: for physic and f. his equal ... scarce is 114:17
Fardels: who wd. f. bear 250–1:20
Fare: f. thee well ... for ever f. 70:16
f. thee well for I must leave thee 17:4
go farther and f. worse 214:40
Farewell: A F. to Arms 130:6
bores through his castle wall, and f., king! 283:6
can I ... bid these joys f.? 150:11
discharged his f. shot 330:3
f., a long f. to all my greatness 261:9
f., fair cruelty 290:16
f., happy fields 176:4
f., Leicester Square 329:1
f. the plumed troops ... big wars 280:2
f., the tranquil mind 280:2
hail and f. 77:17
saying 'F. blighted love' 16:12
so f. hope ... f. fear 177:14
sweets to the sweet; f. 253:4
Farmer: all ran after the f.'s wife 195:1
an old Dutch f. who remarked 159:14
this is the f. sowing his corn 194:8
Farmers: three jolly f. once bet a pound 97:2
Farthing: a f. from a thousand pounds 226:37
I will never pay a f. 94:10
two mites, which make a f. 45:15
Farthings: the Latin word for three f. 268:10
you owe me five f. 192:4
Fascination: right elbow has a f. 118:13
Fashion: art not for the f. of these times 243:19
as out of the f. 83:15
faith but as the f. of his hat 277:10
faithful ... Cynara! in my f. 101:11
nothing else holds f. 290:9
Fashioned so slenderly 134:10
Fast: a hermit's f. 149:1
f. bind, f. find 213:18
he tires ... that spurs too f. 282:4
they stumble that run f. 286:15
Faster: run far f. than the rest 27:14
Fat: f. is in the fire 213:19
f. of the land 31:13
feed f. the ancient grudge 274:7
Jack Sprat cd. eat no f. 190:7
Jeshurun waxed f. 33:7
men about me that are f. 262:9
one ... is f. and grows old 254:14
Fate: a bone to pick with f. 186:5
customary f. of new truths 138:1
f. so enviously debars 167:17
fixed f., free will 177:6
Foreknowledge, Will, and F. 177:6
hanging breathless on thy f.! 160:11
I am the master of my f. 130:10
I and my fellows are ministers of F. 288:15
limits of a vulgar f. 127:2
my dear ... my life, my f. 314:4
take a bond of f. 271:16
that one might read the book of f.! 257:4
when F. summons, Monarchs must obey 104:13

Fate (*continued*)
will in us is over-rul'd by f. 166:14
with a heart for any f. 161:2
Fates: masters of their f. 262:8
Father: as a f. pitieth his children 36:28
child whose f. goes to the devil 216:10
cry not when his f. dies 140:17
foredoom'd his f.'s soul to cross 201:11
full fathom five thy f. lies 288:1
gave her f. forty-one 14:3
hath the rain a f.? 35:13
have we not all one f.? 43:5
honour thy f. and thy mother 32:4
like f., like son 219:11
my mother groan'd, my f. wept 56:3
shall a man leave his f.? 48:25
she has deceived her f. 279:5
so were her f. and mother before 15:11
son of a dear f. murder'd 250:18
take example by your f. 98:24
wise child that knows its own f. 230:23
wise f. that knows his own child 274:12
wise son maketh a glad f. 38:8
wish is f. to the thought 230:26
Fathers: blood is fet from f. of war-proof 259:4
f. have eaten a sour grape 41:16
iniquity of the f. upon the children 32:1
Fathom: full f. five thy father lies 288:1
Fathom-line cd. never touch the ground 254:4
Fathoms: bury it certain f. in the earth 289:5
Fatigued ... tie up the knocker 201:10
Fatter: valley sheep are f. 199:6
Fault: a f. ... grows two thereby 131:9
body without f. or stain 58:6
excusing of a f. ... make f. worse 265:1
f., dear Brutus, is not in our stars 262:8
glorious f. of angels and of gods 201:7
Faultless: lifeless that is f. 219:7
Faults: be to her f. a little blind 205:5
England, with all thy f. 93:7
every man has his f. 212:32
f. are theirs that commit ... permit 213:20
f. are thick ... love is thin 213:21
friend that will tell me ... f. 215:8
his f. lie gently on him! 261:14
rich men have no f. 224:17
tell me all my f. 295:18
with all her f., ... my country 82:1
Favour: I hold with those who f. fire 113:12
king's f. is no inheritance 218:3
truths in and out of f. 113:9
Favourite: a f. has no friend 125:11
Favours: hangs on princes' f. 261:10
neither beg ... your f. 269:8
Fawning: how like a f. publican he looks! 274:7
Fear: capable not only of f. and hate 237:8
concessions of the weak are ... of f. 64:4
doth walk in f. and dread 86:16
faith ... arming me from f. 58:12
f. ... God, ... walk in ... his ways 33:1
f. no more the heat o' th' sun 247:9
f. not, said he, for mighty dread 311:4
for f. of little men 10:9
freedom from f. ... anywhere 235:4
from hope and f. set free 310:1
having little to f. ... from censure 140:4
I f. the Greeks, even when 321:2
Fear (*continued*)
I f. thee, ancient Mariner 86:9
I f. thy kisses, gentle maiden 300:7
I guess an' f. 66:13
I'll f. not what men say 63:14
irrational f. of life 90:4
many things to f. 22:14
men f. death, as children f. dark 21:9
mortality, behold and f. 25:8
needs f. no fall ... no pride 63:15
no f. in love 50:13
O word of f. 268–9:17
only thing ... to f. is f. itself 234:18
perfect love casteth out f. 50:13
quite unaccustomed to f. 16:15
who neither beg nor f. 269:8
wise f. ... forbids the robbing 82:3
with f. and trembling 48:28
with hope, farewell f. 177:14
yet do I f. thy nature 270:1
Fearful: a lovely and a f. thing 69:16
our f. innocence 333:11
our f. trip is done 325:12
snatch a f. joy 126:1
thy f. symmetry 56:5
'tis melancholy and a f. sign 69:18
Fears: bound in to saucy doubts and f. 271:6
enough for fifty hopes and f. 60:13
have f. that I may cease to be 151:7
humanity with all its f. 160:11
not without ... f. and distastes 21:14
past Regrets and future F. 110:2
so are their griefs and f. 21:17
Feast: as good as a f. 54:3
as you were going to a f. 145:9
bare imagination of a f. 282:1
chief nourisher in life's f. 270:11
company makes the f. 210:4
enough is as good as a f. 212:27
f., and yr. halls are crowded 326:10
perpetual f. of nectared sweets 172:18
Feather: birds of a f. 208:1
he stuck a f. in his cap 196:4
knocked me down with a f. 218:7
Feathers: cover thee with his f. 36:25
crow, beautified with our f. 127:6
Feats: 'twas one of my f. 70:17
February: excepting F. alone 194:6
Fed: appetite ... grown by what it f. on 248:4
bite the hand that f. them 64:16
f. with the same food 274:17
he on honey-dew hath f. 87:16
hungry sheep look up and are not f. 175:4
Federation: the F. of the world 313:17
Fee: taking a f. with a grin 117:5
Feeble: not enough to help the f. up 289:9
Feed: f. fat the ancient grudge 274:7
f. me till I want no more 329:2
f. me with food convenient 39:6
f. upon strawberries, sugar and cream 188:8
Feel: I f. it when I sorrow most 312:13
I f. no pain, dear mother 15:9
see, not f., how beautiful 87:8
to f. what wretches f. 266:14
we uncomfortable f. 120:5
what I fancy I f. 12:9
world ... a tragedy to those who f. 322:7
Feels: man is as old as he f. 220:17
Fees: as they took their f. 27:3

Feet: at the f. of Gamaliel 47:10
chase the ... Hours with flying f. 69:4
did those f. in ancient time 55:8
f. of him that bringeth good tidings 41:4
f. was I to the lame 35:10
palms before my f. 81:3
walked those blessed f. 253:14
what flowers are at my f. 150:1
Feigning: most friendship is f. 245:1
truest poetry ... most f. 245:10
Felicity: absent thee from f. awhile 253:9
our own f. we make or find 123:17
perfect bliss and sole f. 166:10
tavern chair ... throne of human f. 145:2
Felix qui potuit ... cognoscere causas 321:7
Fell: bowed himself ... and the house f. 33:22
I do not love thee, Dr. F. 59:9
it f. to earth, I know not where 160:10
Fellow: hail f., well met 309:3
you're a f. Sir ..., you're another 98:22
you threaten us, f.? 62:5
Fellow-creatures: make his f. wise 121:3
Fellow-men: one that loves his f. 137:6
Fellowship: manhood, nor good f. in thee 253:19
right hands of f. 48:20
Felony: make it a f. to drink ... beer 260:9
Felt: darkness which may be f. 31:22
Female: f. of sex it seems 180:15
f. of the species is more deadly 154:14
into the ark the male and the f. 30:20
male and f. created he them 30:3
what f. heart can gold despise? 125:10
Femina: varium et mutabile semper f. 321:3
Femme: en un mot, elle est f. 232:10
Fen: a f. of stagnant waters 333:12
Fences: good f. make good neighbours 113:13
Ferry: to row us o'er the f. 72:8
Fertile: in such a fix to be so f. 186:11
Fester: lilies that f. 294:3
Festina lente 308:3
Fettered: so f. fast we are! 60:10
Fetters: no man loveth his f. 220:16
Feu: ce qu'est au f. le vent 67:13
Fever: after life's fitful f. he sleeps well 271:4
bred a f. ... famine grew 315:17
Février: Generals Janvier and F. 187:15
Few: far and f., are the lands 158:5
let thy words be f. 39:16
miserable ... to have f. things to desire 22:14
most may err as grossly as the f. 103:8
so f. enthusiasts can be trusted 24:1
some f. [books] to be ... digested 23:7
the sound is forc'd, the notes are f. 56:14
we f., we happy f. 260:2
Fewer: the f. men, the greater ... honour 259:13
Fiat justitia, ruat coelum 213:24
Fibs: I'll tell you no f. 123:10
Fickle: woman ... f. and changing 321:3
Fiction: condemn it as an improbable f. 291:14
truth is stranger than f. 228:25
truth ... stranger than f. 70:10
Fiddle: f. while Rome is burning 213:25
fit as a f. 213:36
play first (or second) f. 223:8
the cat and the f. 189:5
Fiddler: f. statesman and buffoon 103:4
Fiddler (*continued*)
the f.'s standing by 14:15
Fiddlers: called for his f. three 192:1
Fiddlestick: my master's lost his f. 188:7
Fidele: to fair F.'s grassy tomb 88:8
Fie upon this quiet life! 254:12
Field: action in the tented f. 278:21
behold her, single in the f. 334:16
cottage small beside a f. of grain 198:4
for the f. is full of shades 316:7
happy f. or mossy cavern 149:4
in the f. after the reapers 33:27
man for the f. 314:18
never in the f. of human conflict 82:15
some corner of a foreign f. 59:5
thro' the f. the road runs by 313:11
what though the f. be lost? 175:18
Fields: 'a babbl'd of green f. 259:2
cockpit hold the vasty f. of France? 258:6
dream of battled f. no more 239:9
f. where joy for ever dwells 176:4
from the cotton f. away 112:10
pagans in those holy f. 253:14
tyrant of his f. withstood 126:11
walk through the f. in gloves 90-1:16
we shall fight in the f. 82:13
your time among green f. 324:17
Fiend: a f. hid in a cloud 56:3
a frightful f. ... behind him 86:16
ingratitude, thou marble-hearted f. 265:14
Fierce: lion is not so f. as ... painted 219:15
Fiery: Shadrach ... into the burning f. furnace 41:25
Fife: stirring drum, th'ear-piercing f. 280:2
Fifteen: at ... f., the mistress of the Earl 329:5
f. men on the dead man's chest 307:4
the maiden of bashful f. 301:17
Fifth of November: please to remember the f. 14:5
Fifty: care f. times more for a marriage 23:19
enough for f. hopes and fears 60:13
f. different sharps and flats 62:1
here's to the widow of f. 301:17
in Sodom f. righteous 31:3
one?—f. thousand! [guilders] 62:2
time-lag of f. years 324:15
Fig: they sewed f. leaves together 30:12
Fight: f. in France ... seas ... beaches 82:13
f. the good f. of faith 49:15
fought the better f. 178:19
I dare not f.; but I will wink 258:10
I have fought a good f. 49:17
man being too proud to f. 329:7
not cease from mental f. 55:8
through the perilous f. 153:6
warned them the Britain would f. on alone 83:4
we ... are baffled to f. better 60:12
we don't f. for anything 324:18
we don't want to f., but by jingo 137:4
we'll f. and we'll conquer 115:1
when the f. begins within himself 60:14
you cannot f. against the future 121:7
Fighter: fits a dull f. 255:17
Fighting: f. a liar in the quad 305:19
not conquering but f. well 91:2
were f. for the crown 190:9
Fights: he that f. and runs away 13:8
I quote the f. historical 120:4
Figs grew upon thorn 81:1

Figurative: cuts a figure—but he is not f. 152:7
Figure: fixed f. for the time of scorn 280:5
Filches from me my good name 279:15
Fill the unforgiving minute 154:20
Fille de chambre: caught hold of the f.'s 306:16
Filling: is f. his last cavity 12:7
Filths savour but themselves 266:21
Filthy lucre 49:9
Finchley: Lord F. tried to mend the ... light 27:6
Find: can't tell where to f. them 190:10
nothing seek, nothing f. 222:16
take things as you f. them 227:7
they shall f. him ware and wakin' 187:10
Finding's keeping 213:26
Finds too late that men betray 124:1
Fine arts: murder ... as one of the F. 97:6
Finer: no f. investment than ... milk in babies 83:9
Finest: men will still say, 'This was their f. hour' 82:14
this was our f. shower 197:9
Finger: have a f. in the pie 213:27
Moving F. writes; and, having writ 110:12
point his slow unmoving f. at 280:5
this is the f. of God 31:22
twist round one's little f. 228:35
Fingers: and with forced f. rude 174:12
ill cook ... cannot lick his own f. 210:9, 287:2
with f. weary and worn 135:3
Finish: tools and we will f. the job 83:2
Finished: I have f. my course 49:17
Fire: a clear f., a clean hearth 156:4
brand plucked out of ... f. 43:2
bring me my chariot of f. 55:8
element of f. is ... put out 100:16
fat is in the f. 213:19
fell in the f. ... burned to ashes 124:10
f. burn and cauldron bubble 271:11
f. is a good servant ... bad master 213:28
f. our souls to regale 56:4
foul water will quench f. 214:14
frying-pan into the f. 214:26
heap coals of f. upon his head 38:28
in the F. of Spring 109:14
like a house on f. 217:10
many irons in the f. 217:25
no f. without some smoke 221:38
no smoke without some f. 222:7
nor rain, wind, thunder, f. 266:7
now stir the f., ... close ... shutters 93:10
shd. have stood that night against my f. 267:9
spit f., spout rain 266:7
the right Promethean f. 268:14
upon a wheel of f. 267:10
warmed ... hands before the f. of life 156:11
we proceed to light the f. 116:12
what wind is to f. 67:13
who can hold a f. in his hand? 282:1
world will end in f. 113:12
Fires: keep the home f. burning 111:12
stars, hide your f. 269:12
violent f. soon burn out themselves 282:4
Firing: we shall have what to do after f. 233:6
Firmament: f. showeth his handywork 35:22
Firmament (*continued*)
the spacious f. on high 9:9
Firmness: with f. in the right 159:15
First: f. baby laughed ... f. time 24:11
f. come, f. served 213:31
f. fine careless rapture 61:3
God's f. creature ... light 23:15
last of life, for which the f. was made 62:9
the f. that ever burst into ... sea 86:4
there is no last nor f. 62:8
when f. we practise to deceive 240:8
First-born: I'll rail against all the f. 244:7
the Lord smote all the f. 31:25
Fish: he has gone to f. 158:10
I sent a message to the f. 77:1
in the belly of the f. 42:19
like a f. out of water 213:34
other f. to fry 213:35
what cat's averse to f.? 125:10
Fish-ball: no bread with one f. 156:14
Fishers of men 43:14
Fishes: if you were to make little f. talk 124:3
men that f. gnaw'd upon 285:1
the little f. of the sea 77:1
waiting for ... invasion. So are the f. 83:1
welcomes little f. in 73-4:17
when f. flew and forests walked 81:1
Fishified: flesh, flesh, how art thou f.! 286:16
Fishing: deepest water ... best f. 211:12
Fishmonger: she was a f. ... 'twas no wonder 15:11
you are a f. 249:18
Fit: all the news that's f. to print 196:9
f. for the kingdom of God 45:26
f. for treasons, stratagems 275:10
love makes one f. for any work 220:1
men ... not f. to live on land 143:21
not f. that you shd. sit ... longer 94:9
Fits: if the cap f., wear it 209:6
strange f. of passion have I known 335:2
Fittest: survival of the f. 305:3
Five: but f. upon this isle 288:11
f. reasons why we shd. drink 10:3
full fathom f. thy father lies 288:1
stand f. minutes with that man 145:4
then ye are only f. 336:6
Five-pound note: as the gen'l'm'n said to the f. 99:2
wrapped up in a f. 158:7
Fix: f. in us thy humble dwelling 325:3
in such a f. to be so fertile 186:11
Fixed the where and when 129:4
Flag: death's pale f. is not advanced 287:3
f. has braved a thousand years 72:10
keep the Red F. flying here! 90:3
spare yr. country's f. 326:7
the old f. flyin' 187:10
we shall not f. or fail 82:13
Flagons: stay me with f. 40:6
Flail: the f. of the lashing hail 298:5
Flame: adding fuel to the f. 181:6
burn always with ... gem-like f. 198:9
Chloe is my real f. 205:6
words ... full of subtle f. 25:7
Flanders: armies swore terribly in F. 306:17
in F. fields the poppies blow 164:8
Flash: he might have cut a f. 11:18
they f. upon that inward eye 331:11
Flask: a F. of Wine, a Book of Verse 109:15
Flat: your life extremely f. 120:13

Flatter: Mr. Lely, f. me not 94:10
Flattered: I have not f. its rank breath 69:5
Flatterer: scoundrel, hypocrite, and f. 55:6
Flattering: talent for f. with delicacy 21:1
Flattery: f.'s the food for fools 308:12
gained by every sort of f. 80:17
gross f. to name a coward 317:12
I can stand anything but f. 295:18
imitation ... sincerest form of f. 88:19
pernicious ... love of f. 306:6
supports with insolence ... paid with f. 140:10
what is principle against ... f. 301:18
Flavour: gives it [life] all its f. 93:8
Flaw: it is a f. in happiness 147:11
Flaws: break into a hundred thousand f. 266:4
Flax: smoking f. shall he not quench 41:2
Flea: a f. hath smaller fleas 309:4
Fleas: great f. have little f. 184:7
little f. have lesser f. 184:7
Fleckno(e) ... who like Augustus 104:13
Fled: I f. Him down the nights 316:9
whence all but he had f. 130:4
Flee from the wrath to come 43:12
Fleece was white as snow 127:11
Fleet-Street ... very animated appearance 143:14
Flesh: a pound of that same merchant's f. 275:5
a thorn in the f. 48:18
all f. is as grass 50:4
all f. is grass 40:29
all this f. keep in a little life 256:2
and f. and blood so cheap 135:4
bring me f. and bring me wine 187:2
f., f., how art thou fishified 286:16
f. is weak 45:2
f. of my f. 30:9
f. which walls about our life 283:6
from her fair and unpolluted f. 253:3
going the way of all f. 324:2
I have more f. ... more frailty 255:13
I wants to make yr. f. creep 98:19
shocks that f. is heir to 250–1:20
study a weariness of the f. 39:28
the f. to feel the chain 58:15
the soul to feel the f. 58:15
the Word was made f. 46:17
the world, the f., and the devil 52:24
this too too solid f. wd. melt 248:2
this world-wearied f. 287:4
two shall be one f. 48:25
we wrestle not against f. 48:27
what a change of f. 25:8
Fleshly School of Poetry 62:12
Fleshpots: when we sat by the f. 31:27
Flew: the white foam f. 86:4
Flies: as f. to wanton boys are we 266:20
close mouth catcheth no f. 209:33
he f. through the air 159:5
murmurous haunt of f. 150:2
Flight: beetle wheels his droning f. 126:4
swift be thy approaching f. 299:1
Flint: f. is pierced with ... shower 155:16
hard as a f. 216:11
Flirt: how can [a bishop] f.? 303:13
Floats on high o'er vales and hills 331:7
Flock: keeping watch over their f. 45:20
silent was the f. in woolly fold 147:12
Flocks: watched their f. by night 311:4
Flog a dead horse 213:39
Flogging: less f. in our great schools 143:20
Flood: bridge much broader than the f. 277:14
taken at the f., leads—God knows where 70:3
taken at the f., leads on to fortune 264:3
Flooding: comes silent f. in the main 85:2
Floods: spirit to bathe in fiery f. 273:10
Floor of heaven is thick inlaid 275:8
Florence: F., Elizabethan England 138:8
rode past fair F. 148:12
Flotte: elle f., elle hésite 232:10
Flourish: all things f. where you turn 204:4
Flourishing like a green bay-tree 36:10
Flow gently, sweet Afton 65:11
Flower: a fancy from a f.-bell 60:13
a Heaven in a wild f. 54:12
a lovelier f. ... was never sown 335:9
as a f. of the field ... he flourisheth 37:1
force that ... drives the f. 315:16
honey ... from every opening f. 323:1
London ... f. of Cities 105:4
many a f. is born to blush unseen 126:10
may prove a beauteous f. 286:11
patience is a f. 222:35
pluck this f., safety 254:10
the f. ... once has blown for ever dies 110:4
this same f. that smiles today 132:7
to me the meanest f. ... can bring 332:6
Flowers: a bunch of other men's f. 183:6
f. that bloom in the spring, Tra la 118:15
fresh showers for the thirsting f. 298:4
gather the f., but spare the buds 168:6
gave, once, her f. to love 59:6
grow f. and ... got no majesty 324:17
I cannot see what f. 150:1
late f. for the bees 147:2
on chalic'd f. that lies 246:13
say it with f. 196:10
the azure f. that blow 125:9
the blushing f. shall rise 204:4
the f. appear on the earth 40:9
with leaves and f. do cover 324:3
Flowing with milk and honey 31:18
Flown with insolence and wine 176:8
Fluffy, with no brains at all 131:5
Flügel: wo dein sanfter F. weilt 238:12
Fluttered yr. Volscians in Corioli 246:12
Fluttering and dancing in the breeze 331:7
Fly: a f. can't bird, but a bird can f. 172:6
f. away Peter ... come back Paul 195:5
I will f. to thee 149:16
man is not a f. 203:2
pigs might f. 223:5
small gilded f. does lecher 267:4
they f. forgotten, as a dream 323:6
up above the world you f. 74:9
which way I f. is Hell 177:13
Flying-fishes play 155:1
Foam: f. of perilous seas 150:4
like the f. on the river 239:10
the white f. flew 86:4
Foe: I fear no f. with thee at hand 163:7
make one worthy man my f. 201:18
overcome but half his f. 176:13
the robbing of a f. 82:3
when I ask I am a f. 218:35
who never made a f. 312:5
Foeman bares his steel, tarantara 120:5

Foes: judge a man by his f. 90:6
Fog: a London particular ... A f. 97:9
f. comes on little cat feet 238:4
hover through the f. and filthy air 269:4
yellow f. that rubs its back 106:13
Folds: tinklings lull the distant f. 126:4
Follies: the pretty f. that ... commit 274:14
Follow: f. me, and I will make you fishers 43:14
f. the Gleam 314:8
f. the river ... get to the sea 214:1
f. thy fair sun 72:12
Followed: the furrow f. free 86:4
Follows: though she draws him, yet she f. 161:6
Folly: all my joys to this are f. 67:8
brood of F. without father bred 173:5
deem it not ... presumptuous f. 129:2
fool returneth to his f. 38:31
frailty, f., also crime 69:18
learned f. is intolerable 221:22
lovely woman stoops to f. 107:5, 124:1
most loving mere f. 245:1
natural f. is bad enough 221:22
rememb'rest not the slightest f. 244:3
shunn'st the noise of f. 173:8
where ignorance ... 'tis f. to be wise 126:2
Fond: not over-f. of resisting temptation 26:3
Fonder: absence makes the heart grow f. 14:8, 25:5
Food: Continent ... good f.; ... England ... good ... manners 170:7
flattery's the f. for fools 308:12
if music be the f. of love 290:10
minds are not ever craving ... f. 93:17
no love sincerer than ... of f. 296:4
nothing to eat but f. 153:10
seeking the f. he eats 244:6
Fool: a child, nor yet a f. to fame 201:13
a f. at forty ... f. indeed 337:12
a f. his whole life long 163:2
a f. sees not the same tree 57:3
a f. the rest of his dull life 25:7
a wise man or a f. 55:7
and my poor f. is hang'd! 268:4
at thirty man suspects himself a f. 338:1
cannot play the f. on occasion 230:24
dost thou call me f., boy? 265:13
eight [hours' sleep] for a f. 225:25
even a f. ... is counted wise 38:20
f. and his money are soon parted 214:2
f. ... ask more than wisest ... answer 88:20
f. hath said in his heart 35:20
f. returneth to his folly 38:31
f. some of the people 160:1
f. that forgets himself 214:4
f. that is not melancholy 214:5
f. to the market ... f. he'll return 214:6
f. wanders ... wise man travels 214:7
how ill white hairs become a f. 258:3
I am fortune's f. 286:20
I met a f. i' th' forest 244:8
laughter of the f. 39:19
more of the f. than of the wise 22:3
no creature smarts so little as a f. 201:12
no f. like an old f. 214:3
O f., I shall go mad 266:4
rod for the f.'s back 38:30
so true a f. is love 293:20
talks to himself, speaks to a f. 227:13
the f. of love, unpractis'd 104:15
Fool (*continued*)
the wisest f. in Christendom 130:13
thou art a great f. 256:16
transform'd into a strumpet's f. 242:9
Foolish: a very f., fond old man 267:11
f. thing was but a toy 292:3
he never said a f. thing 234:11
penny wise, pound f. 223:3
Fools: a shoal of f. for tenders 89:10
all our yesterdays have lighted f. 272:10
flattery ... food for f. 308:12
f. admire, but men of sense approve 202:11
f. are in a terrible ... majority 138:3
f. are my theme 70:11
f.! for I also had my hour 81:3
f. rush in ... angels fear to tread 202:16
f., who came to scoff 122:10
fortune always favours f. 115:12
fortune favours f. 214:11
God sends fortune to f. 215:10
if f. went not to market 214:8
knaves and f. divide the world 218:6
lawyers' houses ... on the heads of f. 218:26
never-failing vice of f. 202:4
not harsh [philosophy] as ... f. suppose 172:18
Paradise of F. 177:11
poems are made by f. like me 153:9
poor f. decoyed into our condition 199:10.
suckle f. and chronicle small beer 279:8
this great stage of f. 267:8
travellers ... f. at home condemn 288:14
what f. these mortals be? 277:3
ye suffer f. gladly 48:17
you f.! I and my fellows 288:15
young men think old men f. 231:8
zeal ... is found mostly in f. 231:13
Foot: and the Forty-second F. 134:12
Feeble of f., and rheumatic 57:15
her f. was light 148:15
nay, her f. speaks 290:8
noiseless f. of Time 242:8
one f. in sea, and one on shore 277:21
one f. in the grave 222:28
put one's best f. forward 207:15
thou shalt give ... f. for f. 32:10
Thyself with shining F. shall pass 111:1
who cleft the devil's f. 101:5
ye that on the sands with printless f. 289:4
Footpath: jog on, the f. way 292:19
Footprint: looking for a man's f. 26:8
Footprints in the sands of time 161:1
Foppery: an excellent f. of the world 265:10
Forbearance ceases to be a virtue 64:10
Forbidden: wanted ... because f. 318:15
Forbids: f. the cheating of our friends 82:3
f. the robbing of a foe 82:3
Force: admit no f. but argument 60:4
f. is not a remedy 58:11
f. that through the green fuse 315:16
own no argument but f. 60:4
subtlety is better than f. 226:30
that armed f. shall not be used 319:5
use of f. alone ... *temporary* 64:5
who overcomes by f. 176:13
Ford: the time of our F. 137:8
Fordoes: either makes me or f. me 280:9
Forebode not any severing of our loves 332:5
Forecast: I cannot f. to you the action of Russia 82:10

Forefathers: rude f. of the hamlet 126:6
think of yr. f.! 9:2
Fore-finger: on the f. of an alderman 286:1
Forehead: curl ... in the middle of her f. 161:8
Foreheads: with f. villainous low 289:2
Foreign: some corner of a f. field 59:5
Foreigners always spell better 318:13
Foreknowledge absolute 177:6
Forest: a fool i' th' f. 244:8
fade away into the f. dim 149:14
Till Birnam F. come to Dunsinane 272:7
Forests: when fishes flew and f. walked 81:1
Foretell: expiring do f. of him 282:4
who can f. for what high cause? 168:5
Forever: pickets off duty f. 26:10
that is f. England 59:5
that vast f. 154:2
Forewarned, forearmed 214:9
Forget: and if thou wilt, f. 236:5
better ... you shd. f. and smile 236:2
don't f. the diver 146:14
forgive and f. 214:10
lest we f.! 155:4
look on her face and you'll f. 204:6
old men f., yet all shall be forgot 260:1
smile at us, pay us, pass us, but do not quite f. 81:9
the best sometimes f. 279:9
Forgetfulness: sleep my senses in f. 257:2
Forgets: is a fool that f. himself 214:4
Forgetting: our birth is but a sleep and a f. 332:1
world f., by the world forgot 201:9
Forgive: Father, f. them 46:13
f. and forget 214:10
noblest vengeance is to f. 229:14
to err is human, to f. divine 202:14
Forgiveness: and ask of thee f.; so we'll live 267:13
mutual f. of each vice 55:3
Forgot: shd. auld acquaintance be f.? 65:12
Forgotten: learnt nothing, f. nothing 310:12
long absent, soon f. 219:24
they fly, f., as a dream 323:6
Forlorn: f! the very word is like a bell 150:5
glimpses that wd. make me less f. 333:4
Form: ah, what the f. divine! 156:13
earth was without f. 30:1
his f. had not yet lost ... brightness 176:11
in f. and moving, how ... admirable! 250:6
the F. remains 334:9
thy f. from off my door! 200:19
Forms: by f. unseen ... dirge is sung 88:11
f. more real than living man 299:11
f. of things unknown 277:6
hope from outward f. to win 87:9
Fornication: but ... in another country 166:5
Forsake not an old friend 51:20
Fortitude: that was great f. of mind 141:14
Fortress: this f. built by Nature for herself 282:5
Fortuna: fortis f. adiuvat 315:3
Fortunate: as he was f., I rejoice 263:10
be f. without adding ... felicity 141:8
Fortune: a youth to f. and to fame unknown 126:13
children ... hostages to f. 21:19
fair face is half a f. 213:13
f. always favours fools 115:12
f. favours fools 214:11
Fortune (*continued*)
f. favours the brave 315:3
f., good night; smile once more 265:20
f. is blind 214:12
God sends f. to fools 215:10
I am f.'s fool 286:20
method of making a f. 127:3
my face is my f., sir 196:1
of f.'s sharp adversity 80:5
possession of f. ... in want of a wife 20:17
slings and arrows of outrageous f. 250:20
taken at the flood, leads on to f. 264:3
well-favoured ... the gift of f. 278:4
when f. knocks, open 214:13
when we are sick in f. 265:10
Fortune-teller: threadbare juggler and a f. 246:5
Forty: every man over f. is a scoundrel 296:16
fool at f. is a fool indeed 337:12
f. centuries look down on you 185:10
f. years on, growing older 57:15
gave her mother f. whacks 14:3
girdle round ... earth in f. minutes 276:19
he that is ... not rich at f. 216:3
his death ... at f. odd befell 134:13
I had rather than f. shillings 276:2
passing rich with f. pounds 122:9
together now for f. years 81:14
Forty-niner: dwelt a miner, f. 183:8
Forward: f. the Light Brigade! 311:10
f. tho' I canna see 66:13
look f. to with hope 113:10
those behind cried 'F.!' 163:13
Foster-child: thou f. of silence 149:6
Fought: better to have f. and lost 84:18
but what they f. each other for 304:14
f. with us upon St. Crispin's day 260:2
Foul: blood is nipp'd and ways be f. 269:1
fair is f. and f. is fair 269:4
I doubt some f. play 248:12
nothing can seem f. to those that win 255:18
so f. and fair a day 269:6
thank the gods I am f. 245:11
Foul-mouthed: the English ... a f. nation 129:9
Found: half-buried in the snow was f. 160:13
I have f. it! (Eureka!) 18:4
thou shalt not be f. out 212:20
when f., make a note of 98:3
Foundation of morals and legislation 29:1
Fountain: a woman mov'd is like a f. troubled 287:12
Fountains: and O, ye F., Meadows, Hills 332:5
passion ... life, whose f. are within 87:9
Founts: white f. falling in the Courts of the sun 81:4
Four: founded upon f. essential human freedoms 235:4
f. angels round my head 9:13
f. elements warring within our breasts 166:10
f. lagging winters and f. wanton springs 281:12
f. seasons in the mind 151:4
f. times as big as the bush 158:12
the f. pillars of government 22:8
there are f. classes of Idols 23:16
they f. had one likeness 41:21

Four (*continued*)
when angry, count f. 318:18
Four-footed: devil's walking parody on all f. things 81:2
Fourpence: took f. home to my wife 190:2
Fourscore and upward, not an hour more 267:11
Fourteen months ... idle and unprofitable 116:1
Fowl: broiled f. and mushrooms—capital! 98:17
Fox: f. from his lair in the morning 125:6
gentlemen galloping after a f. 328:10
Frabjous day! Callooh! Callay! 75:11
Fragrance: inward f. of each other's heart 148:10
Frailties: draw his f. from their dread abode 126:15
Frailty: f. folly, also crime 69:18
f., thy name is woman 248:5
love's but the f. of the mind 89:14
love's the noblest f. 104:8
more flesh ... and therefore more f. 255:13
Frame: all the human f. requires 27:4
man ... bears in his bodily f. 95:10
spangled heavens, a shining f. 9:9
France: bâton de maréchal de F. 185:13
best thing between F. and England 139:18
fair stood the wind for F. 102:9
F. is alone; and God is alone 297:4
order ... this matter better in F. 306:11
the vasty fields of F.? 258:6
we shall fight in F., we shall fight on the seas 82:13
what I gained by being in F. 144:14
Frank, haughty, rash—the Rupert 63:2
Frankfort: I went to F. and got drunk 204:13
Frankie and Johnny 15:2
Fraternity: liberty, equality, f. 17:8
Fray: latter end of a f. 255:17
Frederick: cruel F. 133:9
Free: all men everywhere cd. be f. 159:12
beauteous evening, calm and f. 333:2
flag that makes you free 336:10
her looks were f. 86:8
love Virtue, she alone is f. 173:4
man ... born f. ... is in chains 236:12
mother of the f. 28:10
o'er the land of the f. 153:7
others abide our question. Thou art f. 19:2
pure ..., majestic, f. 333:13
quite set f. ... Eurydice 174:10
so cleanly I myself can f. 102:12
so f. we seem, so fettered ... are 60:10
that Greece might still be f. 70:1
the furrow followed f. 86:4
the valiant man and f. 313:7
thought is f. 227:35
we cannot be f. men if 159:9
we must be f. or die 334:1
what a f. government is 64:17
Freed: from the thousands He hath f. 78:12
Freedom: a new birth of f. 159:13
battle for f. and truth 138:4
can do for the f. of man 153:2
every infringement of human f. 200:8
f. and Whisky 65:14
f. from fear ... anywhere 235:4
f. from want—everywhere 235:4
F. is Slavery 197:4
Freedom (*continued*)
f. of speech and expression 235:4
F. shall a-while repair 88:11
f. ... to worship God 235:4
f. with which Dr. Johnson condemns 65:6
least regard for human f. 305:6
love not f., but licence 182:11
none can love f. ... but good men 182:11
those who deny f. to others 159:9
whose service is perfect f. 52:17
yet, F.! yet thy banner 69:7
Freedoms: world ... upon four essential human f. 235:4
Freezings: what f. have I felt 294:4
French: F. are wiser than they seem 22:20
F. of Paris was to her unknowe 79:4
F., or Turk, or Proosian 120:3
F. say, there are three sexes 303:14
F. she spak ful faire 79:4
he's gone to fight the F. 146:3
how it's improved her F. 124:11
not too F. F. bean 119:5
Frenchmen: fifty million F. can't be wrong 127:10
Frenzy: demonic f., moping melancholy 179:13
poet's eye in a fine f. rolling 277:6
Fresh: bloom sae f. and fair 67:5
f. as in the month of May 79:3
I shd. feel f. and vigorous 322:14
looking as f. as paint 303:2
Freshness: glory and ... f. of a dream 331:12
Fret: nuns f. not 332:13
Frets: that struts and f. his hour 272:10
Fretted the ... body to decay 102:17
Friday: F. night is Amami night 11:3
F.'s child is loving and giving 191:8
worse on F. 193:6
Friend: a faithful f. is ... medicine 51:16
a fav'rite has no f.! 125:11
a f. ... the masterpiece of Nature 108:4
(all he wished) a f. 126:14
best mirror ... old f. 221:5
faithful are the wounds of a f. 39:3
forsake not an old f. 51:20
f. at court 214:17
f., go up higher 45:30
f. in need ... f. indeed 214:18
f. shd. bear his f.'s infirmities 264:2
f. that will tell ... my faults 215:8
f. to everybody ... f. to nobody 214:20
f. to thyself ... others will befriend 214:19
good wine—a f.—or being dry 10:3
handsome and witty, yet a f. 204:3
if I had a f. that loved her 279:2
keep thy f. under ... life's key 242:1
keep wel thy tonge ... keep thy f. 80:3
lend yr. money and lose yr. f. 218:36
loan ... loses ... itself and f. 248:17
makes no f. who never made a foe 312:5
my guide, philosopher and f. 203:11
of every friendless name the f. 140:14
only way to have a f. 108:5
open enemy than a false f. 207:19
save me from the candid f. 72:16
speak well of your f. 226:6
tolling a departed f. 256:7
trust not a new f. 228:23
up the ladder ... choosest a f. 214:39
when I lend I am a f. 218:35

Friends: a soul remembering my good f. 282:8
animals are such agreeable f. 105:16
best of f. must part 17:4, 214:23
can live without our f. 219:21
expectation of finding many f. 142:17
f. are thieves of time 214:21
f. begin to compliment him 138:10
f. in heaven and in hell 214:22
f. of the mammon of unrighteousness 46:7
f., Romans, countrymen 263:11
f. shd. be few and good 208:17
God defend me from my f. 215:3
golden f. I had 136:8
have but few f. 214:24
How to Win F. and Influence People 73:12
I love ... old f., old times 123:6
in the misfortunes of our best f. 234:9
judge ... man by his foes as well as ... f. 90:6
kiss and be f. 218:4
laughter learnt of f. 59:7
lay down his life for his f. 46:31
leaving his social f. 141:17
love, obedience, troops of f. 272:5
marriage of his f. 68:11
my f. proud of my memory 152:11
old f. ... wine are best 222:24
one of our Colonial f. 124:7
permitted to have f. in the kennel 296:15
the cheating of our f. 82:3
those f. thou hast, ... grapple them 248:15
wealth maketh many f. 38:21
wd. not enter on my list of f. 93:12
wounded in the house of ... f. 43:4
Friendship: f. hardly ever [brings money] 20:10
f. is constant ... save in ... love 277:15
f. shd. not be ... one side 214:25
higher value we ... put on ... f. 142:17
honest f. with all nations 139:9
matrimony as a sort of f. 307:7
most common ties of f. 223:36
most f. is feigning 245:1
shd. keep his f. in ... repair 142:5
that is indeed true f. 237:15
Friendships ... invalidated by marriage 68:11
Frighted: f. the reign of Chaos and old Night 176:10
sleep ... how have I f. thee 257:2
Frightened: f. a little mouse under her chair 192:7
f. Miss Muffet away. . 191:3
words that f. the birds 12:11
Frightful: a f. fiend doth ... tread 86:16
Frigid: so f. upon the fundament 186:9
Frittered away by detail 317:1
Frog: a f. he wd. a-wooing go 189:2
how public, like a f. 99:14
on a log, expiring f.! 98:21
Frogs and snails and puppy-dogs' tails 195:6
Frontier: misses the outline of the f. 319:9
Frost: comes a f., a killing f. 261:9
f. which binds so dear a head 297:9
Frosty: lusty winter, f. but kindly 243:18
Frowned: fair science f. not 126:13
Frugal: she had a f. mind 92:8
Fruit: f. of that forbidden tree 175:15
ignorance ... like delicate exotic f. 327:11
sadden after ... bitter f. 110:8
tree is known by its f. 228:20
Fruit (*continued*)
until we reach the ripest f. 166:10
Fruitful: be f. and multiply 30:4
Fruitfulness: mists and mellow f. 147:1
Fruition: sweet f. of an earthly crown 166:10
Fruitless: faint hymns to ... f. moon 276:9
Fruits: kindly f. of the earth 52:26
Frustrate their knavish tricks 73:2
Fry in one's own grease 226:17
Frying-pan: out of the f. into the fire 214:26
Fuel: report ... by adding f. to the flame 181:6
Fugitive: nature ... remembers what was so f. 332:4
Full: f. (fou) of love ... of brandy 66:4
I wasna f., but just had plenty 65:16
reading maketh a f. man 23:8
Fume: black, stinking f. thereof [smoking] 138:14
Fun: I wish I thought *What Jolly F.!* 233:1
own kin and kith more f. 186:2
to come and spoil the f. 76:1
Function: the F. never dies 334:9
Fundament: so frigid upon the f. 186:9
Funeral: f. baked meats did coldly furnish 248:8
f. marches to the grave 160:15
not a f. note 330:3
Fungus: like a f. living on ... remains 157:9
Funny: f. peculiar, or f. ha-ha? 129:5
they do taste kind of f. 13:10
Fur: Oh my f. and whiskers! 74:2
Furnace: f. for your foe so hot 261:3
into the burning fiery f. 41:25
the lover, sighing like f. 244:11
Furnish: coldly f. forth the marriage tables 248:8
f. you with arguments and intellects 123:22
Furnished: f. and burnish'd by Aldershot sun 29:12
rich men f. with ability 52:6
Furniture: no f. so charming as books 303:12
Furor arma ministrat 320:17
Furrow: the f. followed free 86:4
Fury: beware the f. of a patient man 103:9
civil f. first grew high 67:14
cunning old F. 74:1
nor hell a f. like a woman scorned 89:6
tale ... full of sound and f. 272:10
Fuse: through the green f. drives the flower 315:16
Fustian: whose f.'s so sublimely bad 201:15
Fustilarian: you f.! 256:14
Future: for I dipt into the f. 313:16
haven't any f. to think of 296:20
I never think of the f. 105:12
if you wd. divine the f. 89:3
you cannot fight ... the f. 121:7
Futurity: let f. shift for itself 304:1

Gaiety: eclipsed the g. of nations 145:1
Gain: broke the Sabbath but for g. 103:6
no painful inch to g. 85:2
Gales: cool g. shall fan the glade 204:4
Gallantly streaming 153:6
Gallantry: what men call g. 69:10
Gallery in which the reporters sit 164:4
Gallia ... in partes tres 71:11
Gallimaufry: made our English tongue a g. 305:17
Galloped: I g., Dirck g., we g. 61:6

Galloping after a fox 328:10
Gallows: his complexion is perfect g. 287:13
shall there be g. standing 253:16
Galumphing: he went g. back 75:10
Gamaliel: brought up ... at the feet of G. 47:10
Game: a rich man's g. 16:11
but how you played the g. 233:12
g. is not worth the candle 214:28
golf ... not being a g. 157:14
lookers-on see most of the g. 219:29
rigour of the g. 156:4
the g.'s afoot 259:5
win this g. ... thrash the Spaniards too 102:8
woman is his g. 314:17
Game-keeper: old poacher ... good g. 222:26
Gamesmanship or ... Winning Games Without ... Cheating 204:15
Gang: the old g. 82:4
Gaol: all ... we know who live in g. 326:15
in a g. better air, better company 143:21
Garden: a g. in her face 72:13
a g. is a lovesome thing 59:10
come into the g., Maud 314:3
dispossessed of the g. hard by Heaven 57:11
fairies at the bottom of our g. 114:11
g. ... purest of human pleasures 23:4
God Almighty first planted a g. 23:4
God the first g. made 91:12
good strawberries in yr. g. 285:3
how does your g. grow? 191:7
patience ... not in everyone's g. 222:35
put him into the g. of Eden 30:6
redbreast whistles from a g. croft 147:5
we must cultivate our g. 321:11
Garland: immortal g. is to be run for 182:4
wither'd is the g. of the war 243:6
Garment: City now doth like a g. wear 333:6
Winter G. of Repentance 109:14
Garments: g. though new-fangled ill 294:2
our purses ... proud, our g. poor 287:11
Garnish: the ... eye of heaven to g. 264:19
Garrick: here lies David G. 123:3
Garrulity: my crime, shameful g. 180:14
Garter: he will unloose, familiar as his g. 258:7
I like the G. ... no damned merit 169:9
Gas smells awful 198:3
Gash: each new day a g. is added 271:18
Gasp: at the last g. 52:10
Gate: aged man, a-sitting on a g. 77:7
at the strait g. 44:8
heavy burdens at his narrow g. 258:8
I am here at the g. alone 314:3
lark at heaven's g. sings 246:13
passion-flower at the g. 314:4
the poor man at his g. 10:5
there's knocking at the g. 272:4
willow cabin at your g. 290:15
Gatepost: you and me and the g. 207:40
Gates: such are the g. of paradise 55:3
the Gaul is at her g.! 92:1
Gath: tell it not in G. 34:10
Gather ye rosebuds while ye may 132:7
Gathering nuts in May 15:7
Gaudeamus igitur 17:13
Gaudy: express'd in fancy; rich, not g. 248:16
one other g. night 243:1
Gaul: G. is divided into three parts 71:11
hark! the G. is at her gates! 92:1
Gave: I g. you all. ... And in good time you g. it 266:1
the Lord g. and ... hath taken away 35:1
Gay: a poet cd. not but be g. 331:10
her heart was young and g. 128:1
Gaza: eyeless in G. 180:9
Gaze: show and g. o' th' time 272:13
Gazed: and still they g. ... the wonder grew 122:12
Gazes: yellow god forever g. down 129:6
Geese: all his g. are swans 214:29
six g. a-laying 194:2
where there are women and g. 230:32
Gem of purest ray serene 126:10
General: as for being a G. 320:1
caviare to the g. 250:10
of a constitution so g. 59:14
Generals: all G. ... some never grow out of it 320:1
bite some of my other g. 115:14
g. are already poring over maps 20:1
Russia has two g. 187:15
Generation: O g. of vipers, who hath warned? 43:12
one g. passeth ... another g. cometh 39:11
unto the third and fourth g. 32:1
Generations: no hungry g. tread thee down 150:4
power of books ... may endure for g. 319:6
save succeeding g. from ... war 319:5
Genius: g. (... capacity of taking trouble) 73:5
g. does what it must 170:5
g. is ... inspiration ... perspiration 105:8
good Edmund, whose g. was such [Burke] 123:1
Good God! what a g. I had 309:13
nothing to declare except my g. 328:16
since when was g. found respectable? 60:6
the G. and the mortal instruments 262:13
Gentle: a g. knight was pricking on the plain 305:10
do not go g. 315:15
his life was g. 264:7
humane and g. virtue 65:2
meek and g. with these butchers 263:7
sleep! it is a g. thing 86:13
the g. mind by g. deeds is known 305:14
this day shall g. his condition 260:2
verray parfit g. knight 79:2
Gentleman: almost a definition of a g. 187:13
always talking about being a g. 308:5
education begins a g., conversation completes 212:18
grand old name of g. 313:8
smooth-fac'd g., tickling commodity 264:13
the English country g. galloping 328:10
who was then the g.? 24:2
Gentlemanly: we must look for ... g. conduct 19:12
Gentlemen: by g. for g. 315:8
g. in England, now abed 260:2
g. of the gentle craft 96:12
G. Prefer Blondes 161:13
g. rankers out on the spree 154:15
God rest you merry, g. 15:3
not a religion for g. 78:15
we are g. of Japan 117:15

Gentleness, in hearts at peace 59:7
Gentlier: music that g. on the spirit lies 314:2
Geography is about maps 29:2
Geometry: no royal road to g. 108:27
George: any good of G. the Third 156:10
G. the First was ... reckoned vile 156:10
G. the Third ought never to have occurred 29:6
King G. upon the throne 146:3
viler G. the Second 156:10
Georgia: marching through G. 336:9,10
Georgie Porgie, pudding and pie 189:3
German: I speak ... G. to my horse 78:18
the G. dictator, instead of snatching 82:9
Germans: Don't let's be Beastly to the G. 91:9
Germany: G. G. above all 133:7
G. will be ... world power or will not be 133:1
Gert and ... Epp and ... Ein 13:4
Get: g. thee glass eyes 267:7
g. thee to a nunnery 251:2
Getting and spending, we lay waste 333:3
Ghastly: we were a g. crew 86:14
Ghost: plays to the bowling of a g. 316:7
vex not his g. 268:5
what beckoning g. ... invites my steps? 201:5
Ghosts: g. from an enchanter fleeing 299:3
haunted by the g. they have depos'd 283:6
rain is full of g. tonight 170:14
Ghoulies: from g. and ghosties and ... beasties 13:7
Giant: g.'s strength ... use it like a g. 273:6
owner whereof was G. Despair 63:11
Giants: there were g. ... in those days 30:19
Giant's-Causeway worth seeing? 144:16
Gibbon: scribble! Eh, Mr. G.? 121:13
Gibeon: sun, stand thou still upon G. 33:12
Gift: time with a g. of tears 309:15
Gifts: even when they bring g. 321:2
man's work or his own g. 181:11
rich g. wax poor 251:1
Gilded: men are but g. loam 281:8
Gilead: is there no balm in G.? 41:13
Gilpin: and G. long live he 92:13
away went G.—who but he? 92:9
John G. was a citizen 92:6
said G., so am I 92:10
Gilt off the gingerbread 227:4
Gimble: gyre and g. in the wabe 75:9
Gingerbread: gilt off the g. 227:4
Girdle: I'll put a g. round ... the earth 276:19
Girl: a g. ... cheeks are covered with paint 186:1
little g. who had a little curl 161:8
marry a country g. afterwards 295:19
naughty g. to disobey 191:9
Poor Little Rich G. 91:11
sweet g.-graduates 314:12
to the sweetest g. I know 329:1
Girlish: filled ... with g. glee 118:6
Girls: a set of wretched un-idea'd g. 141:17
all the g. ... so smart 73:3
passes at g. who wear glasses 198:2
secrets with g. ... guns with boys 94:1
servant g. in the kitchen 310:7
what are little g. made of? 195:6
where the g. are so pretty 15:10
Give: better g. a shilling 207:28
Give (*continued*)
g. all thou canst 330:11
g. me an ounce of civet 267:5
g. me back my legions 71:9
g. me my soul again 165:8
g. not thy soul unto a woman 51:19
g., oh g. me back my heart 71:1
g. one man a lecture ... another a shilling 142:10
g. us the luxuries of life 184:11
it is more blessed to g. 47:8
Mother, g. me the sun 138:5
no more g. the people straw 31:20
such as I have g. I thee 47:1
these pleasures, Melancholy, g. 173:13
when I g., I g. myself 326:3
Given: costs so much as what is g. 222:11
unto ... one that hath shall be g. 44:28
Giver: a cheerful g. 48:16
Givers: when g. prove unkind 251:1
Gives: blesseth him that g. 275:1
g. twice who g. quickly 214:35
who g. to all, denies all 214:34
Giving: g. much to the poor 214:36
not in the g. vein today 285:7
Glad: and I am g., yea g. 102:12
never g. confident morning 61:9
Glade: alone in the bee-loud g. 337:4
Gladly wolde he lerne ... teche 79:10
Gladness: sadness and g. succeed each other 224:34
teach me half the g. 300:3
Gladsome: let us with a g. mind 180:7
Gladstone's always having the ace of trumps 155:17
Glance: ten thousand saw I at a g. 331:9
whose g. was glum 121:2
Glare: maidens ... moths ... caught by g. 68:18
Glass: double g. o' the inwariable 99:4
get thee g. eyes 267:7
ghosts ... tap and sigh upon the g. 170:14
g. is falling hour by hour 164:15
g. of fashion ... mould of form 251:5
g. wherein the noble youths 256:17
grief with a g. that ran 309:15
look in thy g., and tell 293:11
made mouths in a g. 266:9
people who live in g. houses 214:37
prove an excuse for a g. 301:17
see through a g. darkly 48:7
the more women look in their g. 230:35
turn down an empty g.! 111:1
Glasses: taste, Shakespeare, and the musical g. 123:23
there were two g. and two chairs 165:2
Gleam: faiths and empires g. 298:11
follow the G. 314:8
the visionary g. 331:16
Gleamed: she g. upon my sight 334:12
Glean: thou shalt not g. thy vineyard 32:15
Gleaned ... after the reapers 33:27
Glee: filled with girlish g. 118:6
forward and frolic g. was there 239:7
piping songs of pleasant g. 56:7
Glen: down the rushy g. 10:9
Glides: still g. the Stream 334:9
Glimpses that wd. make me less forlorn 333:4

Glittering: holds him with his g. eye 85:12
long grey beard and g. eye 85:11
Globe: the great g. itself 288:16
the race dwelling all round the g. 83:14
Globule: protoplasmal ... atomic g. 118:2
Gloire: le jour de g. est arrivé 236:11
Gloom: amid the encircling g. 187:14
light to counterfeit a g. 173:9
Gloria: sic transit g. mundi 152:15
Gloriam: ad majorem Dei g. 17:11
Glories: g. like glow-worms ... shine bright 323:14
I see Heaven's g. shine 58:12
Glorious: g. the northern lights astream 302:13
Queen Bess's g. days 117:10
sons of Belial had a g. time 103:7
sunset ran, one g. blood-red 61:4
Glory: excess of g. obscured 176:11
for the greater g. of God 171:1
full meridian of my g. 261:8
g. and loveliness have pass'd 151:5
g. of Europe is extinguished 64:11
g. of the sun ... dimmed 23:23
g. of the world passes away 152:15
g. shone around 311:4
g. to Man in the highest! 310:2
g. to the new-born King 325:2
great g. in a woman 317:5
land of hope and g. 28:10
left him alone with his g. 330:4
long hair ... a g. to her 48:5
the g. of this latter house 43:1
the g. that was Greece 200:18
thine is ... power and the g. 43:24
this I count the g. of my crown 107:14
'tis to g. we steer 115:1
trailing clouds of g. do we come 332:1
triumph without g. ... without danger 90:14
uncertain g. of an April day 292:6
whose g. is their shame 48:29
Glove: hand and g. 215:40
iron hand in a velvet g. 217:24
O that I were a g. upon that hand 286:7
Gloves: walk through the fields in g. 90–1:16
Glow-worms: glories, like g., afar off shine bright 323:14
Gluttony kills more than the sword 214:38
Go: g. and catch a falling star 101:5
g. around the country—g. to ... towns ... farms 164:12
as cooks g.; and as cooks g. 237:12
better 'ole, g. to it 23:22
g. farther and fare worse 214:40
g., litel book, g. ... myn tregedie 80:6
g., put off Holiness 55:7
g. west, young man 304:9
g. West, young man 127:4
gone whar de good niggers g. 112:12
he would not let them g. 31:24
I have a g., lady, don't I? 197:7
is to g. hence unwilling 179:17
its no g. my poppet 164:15
it's no g. the merrygoround 164:14
let him g. for a scapegoat 32:13
let my people g. 31:21
the lamb was sure to g. 127:11
train ... child in the way he shd. g. 38:27
what a Rum G. everything is 324:14
whither thou goest I will g. 33:25
Go (*continued*)
with thee to g. is to stay here 179:17
year is going, let him g. 313:4
Goal: good ... the final g. of ill 312:15
grave is not its g. 160:14
Goat: with their g.-feet dance an antic hay 166:2
Goblets: my figur'd g. for a dish of wood 283:7
Goblin: spirit of health or g. damn'd 249:3
Goblins: tales ... of sprites and g. 292:13
God: a contrite heart, O G. 36:15
a lovesome thing, G. wot 59:10
a wild beast or a g. 22:21
all scripture ... inspiration of G. 49:16
all service is the same with G. 62:8
an old abusing of G.'s patience 276:3
and G. said, Let there be light 30:2
and G. said to Jonah 42:20
and G. saw everything ... he had made 30:5
and the Word was G. 46:14
are G. and Nature ... at strife? 312:16
as G. gives us to see the right 159:15
as if we were G.'s spies 267:13
being blind, the good G. prepare me 199:13
better to have no opinion of G. 22:12
Cabots talk only to G. 57:10
cannot serve G. and mammon 44:2
charged with the grandeur of G. 135:6
cry, G. for Harry, England! 259:5
destroys ... book, kills the image of G. 182:2
doorkeeper in the house of my G. 36:21
doubtless G. could have made a better berry 322:9
earthly power doth then show likest G.'s 275:1
eternal G. is thy refuge 33:9
every man ... g. or devil 103:5
fear G. and keep his commandments 40:1
fear G. Honour the king 50:5
fit for the kingdom of G. 45:26
fool hath said ..., There is no G. 35:20
for the greater glory of G. 17:11
freedom ... to worship G. 235:4
get up airly ... to take in G. 162:10
glorious the song, when G.'s the theme 302:13
glory be to G. for dappled things 135:7
glory to G. in the highest 45:22
G. Almighty first planted a garden 23:4
G. and sinners reconciled 325:2
G. appears, and G. is light 55:1
G. be praised, the Georges ended 156:10
G. be thanked ... two soul-sides 61:14
G. be with you till we meet again 233:2
G. bless ... Faith's Defender 68:15
G. bless the moon and G. bless me 190:5
G. chasteneth thee 32:24
G. comes at last 215:2
G. defend me from my friends 215:3
G. disposes 152:14
G. doth not need ... man's work 181:11
G. erects a house of prayer 96:9
G. ... esteems the growth ... of one virtuous person 182:6
G. for us all 212:31
G. fulfils himself in many ways 312:8
G. gave the increase 47:32

God (*continued*)
G. hath given liberty 95:3
G. hath given you one face 251:4
G. heals ... doctor takes the fee 215:4
G. help the poor 215:5
G. help the rich 215:5
G. helps them that help themselves 215:7
G. is alone 297:4
G. is decreeing to begin 182:7
G. is ... for the big battalions 321:17
G. is in heaven and thou upon earth 39:16
G. is love 50:12
G. is no respecter of persons 47:5
G. is not mocked 48:23
G. is our refuge and our strength 36:13
G. is thy law, thou mine 178:7
G. loveth a cheerful giver 48:16
G. made the country 93:6
G. made the wicked Grocer 81:10
G. made the woman for the man 312:2
G. made them, high or lowly 10:5
G. make me able to pay 199:9
G. moves in a mysterious way 92:15
G. must think it ... odd 155:14
g. of our idolatry, the press 93:3
G. order'd motion but ordain'd no rest 320:6
G. our help in ages past 323:4
G. ... put him into ... Eden 30:6
G. rest you merry 15:3
G. said, Let Newton be! 201:21
G. save our Gracious King 73:1
G. save the mark! 254:2
G. saw the light was good 178:21
G. send you joy 215:9
G.'s first creature ... light 23:15
G. shall add unto him 51:4
G. shall wipe away all tears 51:3
G. shed his grace on thee 25:4
G. shd. go before such villains 278:13
G.'s in his heaven 62:7
G.'s mill grinds slow 215:12
'G. tempers the wind,' said Maria 306:15
G. tempers the wind ... shorn lambs 215:11
G. the first garden made 91:12
G., who is our home 332:1
G. who made thee mighty 28:10
hath not one G. created us? 43:5
he for G. only, she for G. in him 178:3
heavens declare the glory of G. 35:22
honest G. ... noblest work of man 138:9
honest Man's the noblest work of G. 203:8
I am the Lord thy G. 31:29
I reflect that G. is just 139:13
I speak Spanish to G. 78:18
I the Lord your G. am holy 32:14
I ... thy G. am a jealous G. 32:1
if G. be for us 47:21
if G. did not exist 321:14
in apprehension, how like a g.! 250:6
in the beginning G. created 30:2
in the image of G. created He him 30:3
inclines to think there is a G. 84:14
into the hands of the living G. 49:20
isn't life ... terrible ... thank G.? 316:4
it shall please G. to call me 53:15
just are the ways of G. 180:13
justify the ways of G. to men 175:17
knowledge ... makes a G. of me 148:9
knowledge of G. ... burnt offerings 42:8

God (*continued*)
land which the Lord thy G. giveth 32:4
last and best of all G.'s works 179:10
Lord G. made them all 10:4
love, we are in G.'s hands 60:10
make a joyful noise unto G. 36:19
malt ... to justify G.'s ways to man 136:9
man proposes, G. disposes 220:21
name of the Lord thy G. in vain 32:2
nature is the art of G. 59:13
nearer, my G., to thee 9:3
new Jerusalem, coming ... from G. 51:2
not G. is greater ... than ... self 326:4
O G., O Montreal! 68:9
of such is the kingdom of G. 45:13
Oh! G.! that bread shd. be so dear 135:4
one G., one law, one element 313:9
one on G.'s side is a majority 200:3
only G. can make a tree 153:9
out of the mouth of G. 43:13
peace of G., which passeth 48:31
powers ... ordained of G. 47:28
pray G. we may make haste 282:2
prepare to meet thy G. 42:16
presume not G. to scan 203:5
pretence that G. had put it [ace] there 155:17
pure in heart ... shall see G. 43:16
remember the name of the Lord our G 35:26
resistance ... is obedience to G. 139:11
rib which ... G. had taken 30:8
rich man ... into the kingdom of G. 44:23
sabbath of the Lord thy G. 32:3
Sarah Battle, now with G. 156:4
servant of G., well done! 178:19
serv'd my G. with half the zeal 261:13
shall ... man be more just than G.? 35:2
shalt love the Lord thy G. 32:22
so G. created man 30:3
so lonely 'twas, that G. himself 87:2
souls ... in the hand of G. 51:12
stern daughter of the voice of G. 334:3
taken at the flood, leads—G. knows 70:3
thank G. we're normal 197:9
the dear G. who loveth us 87:4
the Lord our G. is one Lord 32:21
the Lord thy G. chasteneth thee 32:24
the sacrifices of G. are 36:15
there, but for the grace of G. 58:1
they [voices] come from G. 297:2
this is the finger of G. 31:22
those whom G. hath joined 53:25
thou shalt have one G. only 84:15
though G. hath raised me high 107:14
though the mills of G. grind slowly 161:3
thy G. my G. 33:25
to walk humbly with thy G. 42:24
true love's the gift which G. 239:15
turn to G. to praise 61:5
unto G. the things that are G.'s 44:25
vindicate the ways of G. to Man 202:18
voice of the people is the voice of G. 10:2
was the holy Lamb of G. 55:8
we owe G. a death 257:8
what therefore G. hath joined 45:12
when first G. dawned on Chaos 297:11
who think not G. at all 180:13
whole armour of G. 48:26
whom G. wishes to destroy 223:40

God (*continued*)
whose G. is their belly 48:29
Wonderful, Counsellor, The mighty G. 40:23
wd. G. I had died ... O Absalom 34:14
would to G. we had died 31:27
yellow g. forever gazes down 129:6
youth shows but half; trust G. 62:9
Goddess: g. and maiden and queen 310:3
g. excellently bright 145:8
Godliness: in cheerful g. 333:13
Gods: a daughter of the g. 311:15
as flies ... are we to th' g. 266:20
as g., knowing good and evil 30:11
by the Nine G. he swore 163:9
carve him as a dish fit for the g. 262:14
for the ... temples of his G. 163:10
I thank whatever g. may be 130:8
kings are earth's g. 281:4
kings it makes g. 285:12
leave the rest to G. 90:15
men call gallantry and g. adultery 69:10
no other g. before me 31:30
so many g., so many creeds 326:11
thank the g. I am foul 245:11
the darling of the G. was born 168:5
the g. are just 267:14
voice of all the g. make heaven drowsy 268:13
we thank ... whatever g. may be 310:1
wd. the g. had made thee poetical 245:9
Goest: whither thou g. I will go 33:25
Gog, the land of Magog 41:24
Going: as I was g. to St. Ives 188:3
at the g. down of the sun 54:5
Cross of Jesus g. on before 24:9
g. one knows not where 169:1
I am just g. outside 196:7
I don't feel like g. into it 237:13
men must endure their g. hence 267:12
the Lord shall preserve thy g. 37:17
where are you g. to, my pretty maid? 195:7
Gold: all is not g. that glitters 206:12
beauty provoketh ... sooner than g. 243:14
building roofs of g. 258:8
fetters, be they made of g. 220:16
floor of heaven ... with patines of bright g. 275:8
g. in phisik is a cordial 79:14
hadde he but litel g. in cofre 79:9
her locks were yellow as g. 86:8
if g. ruste, what shall iren do? 79:17
king's ... a heart of g. 259:9
led by the nose with g. 293:8
my bow of burning g. 55:8
my g.!—open the shrine 145:17
nor all, that glisters, g. 125:12
rank is good, and g. is fair 326:6
run back and fetch the age of g. 175:9
saint-seducing g. 285:19
showers ... barbaric pearl and g. 176:15
the poop was beaten g. 242:14
to gild refined g. 264:19
travell'd in the realms of g. 150:14
true love ... differs from g. 298:9
weakness to resist Philistian g. 181:1
wedges of g., great anchors 285:1
what female heart can g. despise? 125:10
when g. and silver becks me 264:16
worth his weight in g. 231:3
Golden: as they did in the g. world 243:12
from this g. rigol 257:17
girl-graduates in their g. hair 314:12
g. friends I had 136:8
g. lads and girls 247:9
g. rule ... there are no g. rules 296:11
g. slumbers kiss yr. eyes 96:11
love in a g. bowl 55:2
O polished perturbation! g. care! 257:16
silver nutmeg and a g. pear 190:1
the g. years return 298:11
waters of the Nile on every g. scale 73:17
wear a g. sorrow 261:4
Goldsmith: here lies Nolly G. ... called Noll 115:2
Golf may be played on Sunday 157:14
Golf-balls: a thousand lost g. 107:1
Gondolier: a highly respectable g. 116:8
Gone: if she's not g. ... there still 194:4
now thou art g., and never must return 174:14
thou art g., and for ever 239:10
thy thoughts, when thou art g. 300:6
what's g. ... shd. be past grief 292:14
Gongs: strong g. groaning as the guns boom far 81:5
Good: a g., unless counterbalanced by evil 144:13
all g. and no badness 302:12
all g. to me is lost 177:14
all partial evil, universal g. 203:4
all things work together for g. 47:20
and for the g. and increase 312:2
any g. of George the Third? 156:10
apprehension of the g. gives ... feeling 282:1
are you g. men and true? 278:3
as gods, knowing g. and evil 30:11
as g. as she was beautiful 199:14
as g. be out of the world 83:15
be g., sweet maid 154:2
behold, it was very g. 30:5
beneath the g. how far 127:2
best is the enemy of the g. 321:13
but what g. came of it? 304:15
care not whether man is g. or evil 55:7
chief g. and market of his time 252:17
cleave to that which is g. 47:23
Continent ... g. food ... England ... g. table manners 170:7
crown thy g. with brotherhood 25:4
curate's egg, g. in parts 210:26
enough is as g. as a feast 54:3
Evil, be thou my G. 177:14
general g. ... plea of the scoundrel 55:6
giver of all g. things 53:6
go about doing g. 94:4
gone whar de g. niggers go 112:12
g. are so harsh to the clever 330:10
g., but not religious-g. 128:9
g. enough to govern another 159:7
g. enough to shed his blood 235:9
g. fences make g. neighbours 113:13
g. for the country was g. for General Motors 329:4
g. is oft interred with their bones 263:11
g. that I wd. I do not 47:19
g. ... the final goal of ill 312:15
g., the more communicated 178:13
g. to be merry ... honest and true 16:1

Good (*continued*)
g. to be out on the road 169:1
Guinness is g. for you 11:4
he [Time] ... our g. will sever 146:1
he who wd. do g. to another 55:6
hear no g. of themselves 219:16
hold fast that which is g. 49:7
if all the g. people were clever 330:10
ill wind that blows nobody g. 217:19
it is not, nor it cannot come to g. 248:6
Joan is as g. as my lady 217:28
let him do what seemeth him g. 33:29
little of what you fancy does you g. 160:5
money ... not g. unless ... spread 22:9
never g. to bring bad news 242:16
never had it so g. 164:12
not g. that man shd. be alone 30:7
nothing ... g. or bad, but thinking makes 250:5
Oh, Sir! the g. die first 331:4
only g. Indian is a dead Indian 300:13
out of g. still to find means of evil 176:2
sermons in stones, and g. in everything 243:15
she was very, very g. 161:8
so much g. in the worst of us 133:5
some said it might do g. 63:5
the g. is the beautiful 200:13
the greatest g. 84:3
to the public g. private respects must yield 181:2
wives must be had, ... g. or bad 230:28
Good night: fortune, g. 265:20
g.? ah! no; the hour is ill 298:10
g., g.! Parting is such sweet sorrow 286:14
say g. till it be morrow 286:14
sweet ladies, g. 252:20
Goodbye to All That 125:7
Goodness: felt how awful g. is 178:10
g., what is she a-doin' of? 16:12
Goods: with all my worldly g. 53:24
Goose: g. that lays the golden eggs 217:37
sauce for the g. ... the gander 224:37
say Bo(o) to a g. 224:39
three women and a g. 227:40
Goosey, goosey gander 189:4
Gordian: the G. knot ... he will unloose 258:7
Gormed: I'm G.—I can't say no fairer 98:2
Gossip: babbling g. of the air 290:15
scandal is g. made tedious 328:3
Got: vicious place where thee he g. 267:14
Gourd: to be angry for the g. 42:20
Gout: drink, combined with g. 116:10
wine ... the g.; ... no wine ... the g. too 211:34
Gouvernement: le g. qu'elle mérite 165:3
Govern: g. another man without that other's consent 159:7
he that wd. g. others 169:2
Governed: a nation is not g. 64:5
Government: all g. ... founded on compromise 64:7
every nation has the g. it deserves 165:3
g. ... a necessary evil 197:19
g. ... framed ... in after-dinner conversations 317:2
g. of the people, by the people 159:13
g. shall be upon his shoulder 40:23
having looked to g. for bread 64:16
if any ask me what a free g. is 64:17
Government (*continued*)
one form of G. rather than another 143:7
only legitimate object of good g. 139:10
Gower: O moral G. 80:7
Gown: g. of glory, hope's true gage 232:12
like an old lady's loose g. 255:11
Gowns: robes and furr'd g. hide all 267:6
Grace: an inward and spiritual g. 53:16
divine g. was never slow 211:23
God shed his g. 25:4
g. me no g. 282:9
grow old with a good g. 306:7
he does it with a better g. 291:3
he had at least the g. 29:7
my g. is sufficient for thee 48:19
no ... beauty hath such g. 101:1
sweet attractive g. 178:3
Tuesday's child is full of g. 191:8
with one half so good a g. 273:4
ye are fallen from g. 48:21
Graced with polished manners 93:12
Gradualness: the inevitability of g. 323:8
Graduates: sweet girl-g. in their golden hair 314:12
Grain: which g. will grow ... will not 269:8
Grammar: erecting a g. school 260:11
Grammatici certant ... sub iudice lis est 135:9
Gramophone: puts a record on the g. 107:5
Granary: sitting careless on a g. floor 147:3
Grand: they said, 'it wd. be g.' 76:2
Grandchild: his little g. Wilhelmine 304:13
Grandeur: g. hear with a disdainful smile 126:7
g. that was Rome 200:18
Grandmother: teach yr. g. to suck eggs 227:17
Grandsire: proverb'd with a g. phrase 285:20
Grape: fathers have eaten a sour g. 41:16
merry with the fruitful g. 110:8
neither shalt thou gather every g. 32:15
the g. that can with Logic absolute 110:10
Grapes: our vines have tender g. 40:10
sour g. can ne'er make sweet wine 226:4
Grapeshot: a whiff of g. 73:6
Grapple them to thy soul 248:15
Grasp: a man's reach shd. exceed his g. 60:11
Grass: a snake in the g. 225:34
all flesh is as g. 50:4
all flesh is g. 40:29
cut the g. from under ... feet 210:31
g. ... as soft as ... breast of doves 90–1:16
Guests star-scattered on the G. 111:1
hare limp'd trembling through the frozen g. 147:12
his days are as g. 37:1
I am the g.; I cover all 238:5
I know the g. beyond the door 236:10
seed from the feather'd g. 148:5
two blades of g. to grow 309:1
Grate on their scrannel pipes 175:4
Gratis: he lends out money g. 274:7
Grave: a little g., an obscure g. 283:7
body lies a mould'ring in the g. 127:13
country ... a kind of healthy g. 303:18
Duncan is in his g. 271:4
eat our pot of honey on the g. 170:1
every third thought ... my g. 289:8
from g. to gay, from lively to severe 203:10
funeral marches to the g. 160:15
g. is not its goal 160:14
g. of Mike O'Day 12:8

Grave (*continued*)
g. where English oak and holly 129:2
g. where our hero we buried 330:3
g.'s a fine and private place 167:14
in the dark and silent g. 232:11
lead but to the g. 126:9
make ... turn in his g. 228:30
man ... pompous in the g. 60:3
my large kingdom for a little g. 283:7
O g., where is thy victory? 48:13
O G.! where is thy Victory? 201:4
one foot in the g. 222:28
renowned be thy g.! 247:11
see myself go into my g. 199:13
where, g., thy victory? 163:7
Graves: find ourselves dishonourable g. 262:8
talk of g., of ... epitaphs 283:5
Gravity: approach this spot with g.! 12:7
Gravy: rich wot gets the g. 16:13
Sir Humphrey Davy detested g. 29:5
Great: all things both g. and small 87:4
brilliant chief, irregularly g. 63:2
but far above the g. 127:2
even g. men have ... poor relations 97:11
g. is Diana of the Ephesians 47:7
g. is Truth, and mighty 51:6
g. men are almost always bad men 9:1
g. men ... not commonly ... g. scholars 134:6
g. ones eat up the little ones 281:5
madness in g. ones 251:6
rightly to be g. ... g. argument 252:19
rule of men entirely g. 63:3
some are born g., some achieve greatness 291:9
such g. men as these 16:14
to be g. is to be misunderstood 108:12
Great War: what did *you* do in the G.? 11:1
Greater: feel that we are g. than we know 334:10
there is no g. sorrow 95:7
thy necessity is g. than mine 302:7
Greatest: g. happiness of the g. number 29:1
g. talkers ... least doers 227:12
sooner fail than not be among the g. 152:4
Greatness: farewell, to all my g. 261:9
highest point of all my g. 261:8
some achieve g. 291:9
some have g. thrust upon them 291:9
thinks ... his g. is a-ripening 261:9
Greece: citizen not of Athens or G. 304:5
dream'd that G. ... be free 70:1
G., Italy and England did adorn 104:11
the glory that was G. 200:18
the isles of G., the isles of G.! 69:21
Greedy: not g. of filthy lucre 49:9
Greek: it is G. to me 215:33
it was G. to me 262:11
must carve in Latin or in G. 322:2
paid at the G. Kalends 71:10
small Latin and less G. 145:14
when his wife talks G. 145:3
Greeks: G. had a word for it 10:1
I fear the G. 321:2
when G. joined G. 159:1
which came first, the G. or the Romans 100:14
Green: a dyspeptic mint g. 319:9
a g. and yellow melancholy 291:7
and all the trees are g. 154:4
Green (*continued*)
drives my g. age 315:16
flourishing like a g. bay-tree 36:10
g. grow the rashes O 66:1
g. thought in a g. shade 168:1
in England's g. and pleasant land 55:8
laurel is g. for a season 310:4
making the g. one red 270:12
salad days, when I was g. 242:13
the memory be g. 247:17
their heads are g. 158:5
there is a g. hill far away 10:7
through the g. fuse drives the flower 315:16
upon England's mountains g. 55:8
voices of children are heard on the g. 56:11
when woods are getting g. 76:12
whiten the g. plains under 298:5
Greenery-yallery ... young man 119:7
Greenland: from G.'s icy mountains 130:1
Greensleeves: G. was all my joy 15:4
who but Lady G.? 15:4
Greet: how shd. I g. thee? 71:6
Grenadier: for the British G. 16:14
Grew: where only one g. before 309:1
Grey: by thy long g. beard 85:11
lend me yr. g. mare 17:5
that g. iniquity 255:1
Greyhounds: stand like g. in the slips 259:5
Grief: after long g. and pain 314:5
but for our g., as if it had not been 297:12
g. and pain for promis'd joy 66:12
g. itself be mortal 297:12
g. returns with the revolving year 297:10
g., with a glass that ran 309:15
hopeless g. is passionless 60:8
past help shd. be past g. 292:14
silent manliness of g. 122:14
smiling at g. 291:7
time and thinking tame the g. 228:1
when thou art old ... g. enough 127:5
Griefs: of all the g. that harass 140:15
secret ... are their g. and fears 21:17
Grin: g. like a dog, and run about 36:18
taking a fee with a g. 117:5
Grind: my life is one demd horrid g. 98:11
[ye] g. the faces of the poor 40:19
Grinds: with exactness g. he all 161:3
Grindstone: one's nose to the g. 222:10
Grinning: antic sits ... g. at his pomp 283:6
Grist: bring g. to the mill 215:34
Groan: bitter g. of a martyr's woe 55:5
future ages g. for this foul act 283:8
Groaned: my mother g., my father wept 56:3
Groaning: strong gongs g. 81:5
Grocer: God made the wicked G. 81:10
Groomed: nicely g., like a mushroom 157:9
Grosvenor Gallery ... young man 119:7
Grotesque: so g. a blunder 29:6
Ground: betwixt the stirrup and the g. 72:5
blood of English shall manure the g. 283:8
children of Israel ... upon the dry g. 31:26
commit his body to the g. 53:30
fathom-line cd. never touch the g. 254:4
let us sit upon the g. 283:6
massa's in de cold, cold g. 112:6
native air, in his own g. 203:20
upon the g., can fall no lower 219:3
when every rood of g. maintained 122:6
Grovel: souls that g. 72:2
Grovelled: he g. ... and my-lorded 315:10

Groves: o'er shady g. they hover 324:3
Grow: ask me where they do g. 131:13
g. up with the country 127:4
Growed: I 'spect I g. 308:1
Growled: cracked and g. and roared and howled 86:2
Growth: I cannot give it vital g. again 280:11
Grubstreet ... near Moorfields 140:6
Grudge: feed fat the ancient g. 274:7
Grumble: nothing whatever to g. at 12:13
Grumbling: the g. grew to a ... rumbling 62:3
Grundy: the end of Solomon G. 193:6
Grunt and sweat under a weary life 250–1:20
Gruntled: he was far from being g. 330:2
Gryphon: called lessons, the G. remarked 75:1
Guard: Alice is marrying one of the g. 171:6
g. the guards themselves? 146:9
Guards: up, G., and at 'em 324:9
Guerre: la g. ... industrie nationale 182:12
Guess: I g. an' fear 66:13
Guest: constant g. is never welcome 210:7
dull fighter and a keen g. 255:17
Guests: the G. star-scattered on the Grass 111:1
unbidden g. ... welcomest when ... gone 260:6
Guide: custom ... the great g. 137:2
g. me, O thou great Redeemer 329:2
my g., philosopher and friend 203:11
Guilders: 'will you give me a thousand g.?' 62:2
Guilt: other pens dwell on g. and misery 20:13
what art can wash her g.? 124:1
Guilty: better that ten g. ... escape 54:11
my soul ... g. of dust and sin 131:10
suspicion ... haunts the g. mind 261:1
we make g. of our disasters the sun 265:10
Guinea: worth a g. a box 11:10
Guinness is good for you 11:4
Gulf: a great g. fixed 46:9
Gull's way and the whale's way 168:17
Gum: Arabian trees their med'cinable g. 280–1:14
Gummidge: Mrs. G.'s words 97:13
Gunga Din 154:16
Gunner and his mate lov'd Mall 288:9
Gunpowder treason and plot 14:5
Guns: g. aren't lawful, nooses give 198:3
g. will make us powerful; butter ... fat 122:1
loaded g. with boys 94:1
strong gongs groaning as the g. boom far 81:5
Gustibus: de g. non est disputandum 210:36
Gypsies: play with the g. in the wood 191:9
Gypsy: Time, you old g. man 133:6
Gyre and gimble in the wabe 75:9

Ha, ha, ha, you and me 15:5
Habit: costly thy h. as thy purse can buy 248:16
h. is a great deadener 26:2
h. with him was all the test of truth 93:16
honour ... in the meanest h. 287:11
Habitation: local h. and a name 277:6
Habits: h. ... carry them far apart 89:2
needs reforming as other people's h. 319:1
Hackney: see to H. ('A) Marshes 25:3
Haggards ride no more 306:10
Hags: secret, black, and midnight h. 271:13
Hail: h. and farewell 77:17
h., divinest Melancholy! 173:6
h., Holy Light 177:9
h., horrors! h. 176:4
h., wedded Love 178:8
my gracious silence, h.! 246:6
the flail of the lashing h. 298:5
to be h. fellow well met 215:35
Hailed at the twilight's last gleaming 153:6
Hair: beauty draws us with a single h. 204:7
each particular h. to stand on end 249:7
graduates in their golden h. 314:12
her h. was long, her foot was light 148:15
I must sugar my h. 75:4
if a woman have long h. 48:5
Jeanie with the light brown h. 112:5
[letters] serve ... to pin up one's h. 89:11
shall I part my h. behind? 106:16
smooths her h. with automatic hand 107:5
train of thy amber-dropping h. 173:3
Hairs: given me over in my grey h. 330:6
how ill white h. become a ... jester 258:3
to split h. 226:11
Hairy: Esau, my brother, is a h. man 31:7
Hal: why, H., 'tis my vocation, H. 253:18
Half: h. a league onward 311:9
h. a trade and h. an art 138:7
h. as much as ... Mr. Toad 124:13
h.-seas over 215:38
knows not how the other h. lives 215:37
the h. that's got my keys 124:8
too civil by h. 301:12
too clever by h. 228:12
yr. servant's cut in h. 124:8
youth shows but h. 62:9
Half-a-crown: if I fling h. to a beggar 142:7
Half-a-dozen of the other 167:6, 225:26
Half-way: don't meet trouble h. 220:38
Halifax: from Hell, Hull and H. ... deliver us 216:30
Hall: bride hath paced into the h. 86:1
the Douglas in his h. 240:7
Tom bears logs into the h. 269:1
Hallelujah: h.! I'm alive 197:10
here lies my wife, h.! 12:2
Hallowed: place of justice is an h. place 23:11
Halo? ... one more thing to keep clean 114:2
Halt: how long h. ye between two opinions 34:19
Halves: never do things by h. 215:39
Hamelin town's in Brunswick 61:16
Hamlet: I saw H. Prince of Denmark played 109:2
O H., what a falling off! 249:11
rude forefathers of the h. 126:6
Hamlets brown, and dim-discover'd spires 88:9
Hammock: Drake he's in his h. 187:9
Hampden: some village H. 126:11
Hand: bite the h. that fed them 64:16
captain's h. on his shoulder smote 187:12
cold h. ... warm heart 210:2
come, give me your h. 272:4
discern between ... right h. ... left h. 42:21
earth, I do salute thee with my h. 283:1
every man's h. against him 31:1
great is the h. that holds dominion 315:17
h. and glove 215:40
h. for h., foot for foot 32:10

Hand (*continued*)
h. ... head ... heart of man go together 237:5
h. in h., on ... edge of the sand 158:9
h. open as day for ... charity 257:14
h. that signed the treaty 315:17
have still the upper h. 91:5
having put his h. to the plough 45:26
her h. on his thick skull 103:10
I fear thy skinny h. 86:9
infinity in the palm of your h. 54:12
iron h. in a velvet glove 217:24
leans her cheek upon her h. 286:7
lend thy guiding h. 180:8
let not thy left h. know 43:22
O that I were a glove upon that h. 286:7
one whose h. ... threw a pearl away 280–1:14
our times are in His h. 62:9
reason is our soul's left h. 100:18
smooths ... hair with automatic h. 107:5
the h. of war 282:5
the handle toward my h. 270:9
the larger heart, the kindlier h. 313:7
this blood clean from my h. 270:12
this my h. will rather 270:12
touch of a vanish'd h. 311:6
we are in God's h. 60:10
what immortal h. or eye 56:5
whatsoever thy h. findeth to do 39:22
when I stretched out my h. 306:16
who will stand on either h.? 163:11
will not sweeten this little h. 272:3
Handbag: an ordinary h. in fact 327:13
yes, Lady Bracknell ... a h. 327:13
Handful: just for a h. of silver he left us 61:8
Handle: and I polished up the h. 119:15
the h. toward my hand 270:9
Hands: and then take h. 287:20
by fairy h. their knell is rung 88:11
fall into the h. of the living God 49:20
he clasps the crag with crooked h. 312:1
if you believe, clap your h. 24:14
into thy h. I commend my spirit 36:3
laid violent h. upon themselves 53:27
large and sinewy h. 161:9
licence my roving h. 101:3
lift not thy h. to It 110:13
many h. make light work 216:2
mischief ... for idle h. 323:2
my h. from picking and stealing 53:14
people who have flabby h. 118:4
right h. of fellowship 48:20
swinken with his h. 79:6
the h. are the h. of Esau 31:8
the horny h. of toil 162:12
their h. are blue 158:5
took water and washed his h. 45:3
with mine own h. I give away my crown 284:2
Handsaw: a hawk from a h. 250:8
Handsome: a h., lively young fellow 301:18
h. in three hundred pounds a year 276:6
h. is that h. does 216:4
not h. at twenty ... rich at forty 216:3
Hang: a rope to h. himself 15:6
I think I will not h. myself to-day 80:20
rope enough and he'll h. himself 224:29
she wd. h. on him 248:4
we must all h. together 113:1
we will h. you, never fear 120:9
wretches h. that jury-men may dine 204:9
Hanged: as good be h. for a sheep 216:5
born, bred, and h., ... same parish 12:5
born to be h. 208:21
man knows he is to be h. 144:8
my poor fool is h.! 268:4
not h. for stealing horses 127:12
Hanging: any thing we allow ... short of h. 143:12
good h. prevents a bad marriage 290:13
h. and wiving go (goes) by destiny 216:6, 274:15
Puritane-one h. of his cat 58:2
Hangs: thereby h. a tail 279:13
thereby h. a tale 244:9, 287:9
Hanover: by famous H. city 61:16
Hans Breitmann gife a barty 159:2
Happiest: h. moments of the h. ... minds 300:10
I am h. when I am idle 322:14
Happiness: all the h. mankind can gain 104:9
boring ... somebody else's h. 137:11
divided and minute domestic h. 152:6
greatest h. of the greatest number 29:1
greatest h. of the whole 200:14
h. in marriage ... matter of chance 20:18
h. makes up in height 113:15
h. ... rare in human life 143:18
h. ... wine of the rarest vintage 303:5
in solitude, what h.? 179:3
it is a flaw in h. 147:11
life, liberty, and the pursuit of h. 139:6
lifetime of h.! ... hell on earth 296:3
look into h. ... another man's eyes 245:15
my H. ... not so fine as my Solitude 152:6
no more right to consume h. 295:11
O h.! our being's ... aim 203:7
recall ... h. when in misery 95:7
Happy: a h. bridesmaid makes a h. bride 311:7
be h. and live within our means 322:15
be h. while ... young 17:13
better be h. than wise 207:23
call no man h. until he dies 304:7
h. is England! 151:2,3
h. issue out of ... afflictions 52:30
h. the man, and h. he alone 104:16
h. the man, whose wish and care 203:20
h. ... to learn the causes 321:7
how h. ... born and taught 336:13
how h. cd. I be with either 115:7
how h. he who crowns in shades 122:7
how to be h. though married 128:6
I cd. be h. with you 329:6
little h. if I cd. say how much 277:17
methinks it were a h. life 260:13
riches of the mind ... make ... h. 224:19
the duty of being h. 307:9
this h. breed of men 282:5
Harbour: [fog] looking over the h. 238:4
Hard: h. cheese 216:13
how h. ... for women to keep counsel 263:1
nothing's so h. but search will find 132:5
Hardy: Kiss me, H. 187:7
Hare: first catch yr. h. 213:30
h. limp'd trembling through the frozen grass 147:12
mad as a March h. 220:9
rouse a lion than to start a h. 254:3
run with the h. 224:33
take yr. h. when cased 121:11

Hark: h., h. the lark 246:13
h.! the herald angels sing 325:2
Harlot: wise man that marries a h. 241:19
Harm: do so much h. ... doing good 94:4
drunken folk seldom take h. 211:40
none ... shall h. Macbeth 271:15
when loyalty no h. meant 15:12
Harmony: all discord, h. not understood 203:4
heaven drowsy with the h. 268:13
made quiet by the power of h. 335:12
such h. is in immortal souls 275:8
tie the hidden soul of h. 174:9
touches of sweet h. 275:8
Harness: die with h. on our back 272:11
Harp: David took an h. 34:6
h. not on that string 285:10
h. that once through Tara's halls 183:11
his wild h. slung behind him 184:2
praise the Lord with h. 36:4
Harps: we hanged our h. upon the willows 37:23
Harrow: lightest word wd. h. up thy soul 249:7
Harry: cry, God for H.! 259:5
not ... Amurath ... but H., H. 257:20
stain the brow of my young H. 253:15
Harsh: good are so h. to the clever 330:10
pluck yr. berries h. and crude 174:12
Harshness: not enough no h. gives offence 202:10
Harvest: like a stubble-land at h. home 254:1
seedtime and h. and cold and heat 30:23
Harwich: a steamer from H. 117:13
Haste: daffodils ... h. away so soon 132:1
h. still pays h. 273:14
h. thee, Nymph 173:16
marry in h. 220:31
men love in h. 70:7
more h. the less speed 216:15
said in my h., All men are liars 37:10
Hat: faith but ... fashion of his h. 277:10
hath no head, needs no h. 216:19
Hatch, match and despatch 216:17
Hatchet: bury the h. 208:36
I did it with my little h. 322:18
Hate: cherish those hearts that h. thee 261:12
enough religion to make us h. 309:8
generation of them that h. me 32:1
greatest h. ... from the greatest love 215:32
h. him for he is a Christian 274:7
h. the man ... you have hurt 310:9
I h. and love ... and am in torment 77:16
I h. letters 89:11
Juno's unrelenting h. 105:1
love and h. are necessary 56:15
neither beg nor fear ... favours nor ... h. 269:8
only love sprung from my only h. 286:5
politicians neither love nor h. 103:2
pomp ... of this world, I h. ye 261:10
study of revenge, immortal h. 175:18
Hated: h. wickedness that hinders loving 61:12
loved well because he h. 61:12
to be h. needs but to be seen 203:6
Hatred: h., and malice, ... uncharitableness 52:23
h. is blind 216:16
h. ... the longest pleasure 70:7
no h. or bitterness 78:1
Hatred (*continued*)
no rage like love to h. turned 89:6
stalled ox and h. therewith 38:18
Hatter: mad as a h. 220:8
Haul over the coals 216:18
Haunches: fog ... sits ... on silent h. 238:4
Haunt: murmurous h. of flies on summer eves 150:2
our life, exempt from public h. 243:15
Haunted: beneath a waning moon was h. 87:12
on summers eves by h. stream 174:7
Have: not good to want and to h. 215:20
to h. and to hold 53:22
what we h. we prize not 278:12
Havens: ports and happy h. 281:14
Haves: the *H.* and the *Have-Nots* 78:4
Havoc: Cry 'H.!' and let slip the dogs of war 263:8
Hawk: I know a h. from a handsaw 250:8
Hawks: all haggard h. will stoop 155:16
Hawthorn: gives not the h. bush a sweeter shade? 260:14
under the h. in the dale 174:3
Hay: dance an antic h. 166:2
make h. while the sun shines 220:12
Haystack: needle in a h. 221:27
He: every h. has ... a she 14:15
Head: a h. grown gray in vain 297:16
better be the h. of a dog 207:25
born about three ... with a white h. 256:9
four angels round my h. 9:13
frost which binds so dear a h. 297:9
hath no h., needs no hat 216:19
heavy weight from off my h. 284:2
here rests his h. upon the lap of earth 126:13
I ... covered up her h. 16:4
I will make you shorter by a h. 107:12
if you can keep yr. h. when all about you 154:17
in the heart or in the h. 274:18
incessantly stand on your h. 74:3
lay your sleeping h., my love 20:2
left it dead and with its h. 75:10
my h. is bending low 112:11
my h. is bloody, but unbowed 130:9
old h. on young shoulders 222:25
on the ... hands little gold h. 172:2
one small h. cd. carry all he knew 122:12
precious jewel in his h. 243:15
rise up before the hoary h. 32:17
shoot ... this old gray h. 326:7
shouting 'Off with his h.!' 74:11
talked ... after his h. was cut off 14:2
thou art a traitor. Off with his h.! 285:4
turns no more his h. 86:16
uneasy lies the h. that wears a crown 257:3
wash ... yr. h. never 229:30
weak h. with strongest bias rules 202:4
what though his h. be empty 309:7
which way the h. lies 232:13
with intention to break his h. 142:7
Headache: awake with a dismal h. 117:12
Heads: bald h. are soon shaven 206:36
h. I win, tails you lose 94:5, 216:20
houseless h. and unfed sides 266:13
mob has many h., but no brains 221:8
stars hide their diminished h. 177:12
their h. are green 158:5

Heads (*continued*)
two h. are better than one 229:1
Headstone: become the h. of the corner 37:13
Headstrong: as h. as an allegory 301:11
Head-waiter who's allowed to sit 320:2
Heal: ever h. but by degrees? 279:12
Healed: they have h. also the hurt 41:12
Healing: arise with h. in his wings 43:7
Health: a h. unto his Majesty 15:6
and h. on both! 271:7
good wife and h. ... best wealth 215:22
h.! h.! the blessing of the rich! 145:18
h. is better than wealth 216:21
h. is not valued till sickness 216:22
he that will not drink his h. 15:6
he that will this h. deny 105:7
me? In my state of h.? 146:17
the popular idea of h. 328:10
Healthy: all h. instinct for it 68:8
h. and wealthy and dead 317:6
h. citizens ... greatest asset 83:9
h., wealthy and wise 212:9
imagination of a boy is h. 147:7
nobody is h. in London 20:8
Hear: chink in the floor ... let me h. 310:7
deaf as those who won't h. 211:4
destroyer and preserver, h., oh h.! 299:4
do you h. the children weeping? 60:7
few love to h. the sins 281:3
grossly close it in, we cannot h. 275:8
h. a voice in every wind 126:1
h. dat mournful sound 112:6
h. twice before you speak 216:24
I h. thee and rejoice 336:2
never merry when I h. sweet music 275:9
the ear begins to h. 58:15
time ... when you will h. me 100:2
to h. the lark begin his flight 174:2
Heard: cuckoo is in June, h., not regarded 255:10
h. a thousand blended notes 332:7
h. melodies are sweet 149:7
I h. a maid singing in the valley 15:1
more he h. the less he spoke 231:26
not a drum was h. 330:3
voice I h. this passing night was h. 150:4
Hearing: I have heard of thee by the h. 35:15
Hears: she neither h. nor sees 334:15
Heart: a broken and a contrite h. 36:15
a h. grown cold ... in vain 297:16
a man after his own h. 34:3
absence makes h. grow fonder 14:8, 25:5
all that mighty h. is lying still 333:7
as well as want of H.! 135:1
awake, my h., to be loved 58:3
ay, in my h. of h. 252:1
because my h. is pure 314:19
blessed are the pure in h. 43:16
bring with you a h. that watches 335:8
bringing Soviet power into the h. of Western Europe 83:10
but [give] not yr. h. away 136:5
but his flaw'd h. ... too weak 268:1
cold hand ... warm h. 210:2
comes from the h., goes to the h. 88:5
enter every trembling h. 325:3
faint h. never won fair lady 213:9
fair face ... foul h. 213:12
find Calais lying in my h. 168:11
fool hath said in his h. 35:20

Heart (*continued*)
give me back my h. 71:1
Greensleeves was my h. of gold 15:4
hardened Pharaoh's h. 31:24
h. and stomach of a king 107:13
h. of oak are our ships 115:1
h. shall break into ... flaws 266:4
h.'s lightness from ... May 147:10
h. to poke poor Billy 124:10
h. upon my sleeve for daws 278:20
h. which grief hath cankered 72:1
heavy purse ... light h. 216:27
her h. was young and gay 128:1
his h. is in his mouth 216:26
his h.'s his mouth 246:10
his tiger's h. wrapped in ... hide 127:6
holiness of the h.'s affection 151:9
hope deferred maketh ... h. sick 38:13
how my h. grows weary 112:9
I feel my h. new open'd 261:10
I said to H., 'How goes it?' 27:9
I shall light a candle ... in thine h. 51:7
I sleep but my h. waketh 40:12
if thou didst ever hold me in thy h. 253:9
in the h., not in the knees 139:17
in the h. or in the head 274:18
intellect ... fooled by the h. 234:6
inward fragrance of each other's h. 148:10
it's Oh! in my h. 146:3
language of the h. 201:20
light purse ... heavy h. 219:9
like music on my h. 87:1
look in thy h. and write 302:3
love the Lord ... with all thine h. 32:22
many a h. is aching 129:1
meditation of my h. be acceptable 35:25
merry h. ... cheerful countenance 38:17
merry h. goes all the day 292:19
my h. aches and a drowsy numbness 149:13
my h. leaps up when I behold 333:8
my h. untravelled ... turns to thee 123:13
my true love hath my h. 302:2
nation ... that had the lion h. 83:14
natural language of the h. 241:18
never a crack in my h. 337:8
no longer lacerates his h. 309:11
now cracks a noble h. 253:11
open not thine h. to every man 51:18
overset the brain, or break the h. 332:12
perilous stuff which weighs upon the h. 272:6
pity ... in the h. of love 337:9
poor h. that never rejoices 223:16
pourest thy full h. 300:1
quickening life from the earth's h. 297:11
rend yr. h. and not yr. garments 42:11
rose in the deeps of my h. 337:7
serve the Lord ... with all thy h. 33:1
Shakespeare unlocked his h. 333:5
shall command my h. and me 94:3
shot through his h. on Sunday 307:1
so the h. be right 232:13
strike mine eyes but not my h. 145:10
strings, said Mr. Tappertit, in the ... h. 97:8
take thy beak from out my h. 200:19
tears fall in my h. 320:10
the h. has its reasons 198:8
the larger h., the kindlier hand 313:7
the laughter of her h. 128:1

Heart (*continued*)
the Lord looketh on the h. 34:5
the waters of the h. 315:18
them that are of a broken h. 36:7
through the sad h. of Ruth 150:4
to lose your h.'s desire ... to gain it 296:8
warm the cockles of the h. 229:28
way to an Englishman's h. 229:36
wear him in my h.'s core 252:1
wear one's h. on one's sleeve 230:1
what female h. can gold despise? 125:10
what the false h. doth know 270:8
when my h. was young and gay 112:10
where my h. lies 61:13
whose ... complexion and whose h. 293:5
wine that maketh glad the h. 37:2
with a h. for any fate 161:2
with h., and soul, and voice 186:14
with rue my h. is laden 136:8
woman with the h. 314:18
word 'Callous' engraved on her h. 241:11
Heart-ache: to say we end the h. 250–1:20
Hearts: agonies, the strife of human h. 150:11
apply our h. unto wisdom 36:24
enthroned in the h. of kings 275:1
grows old with their sick h. 146:10
h. are dry as summer dust 331:4
h. at peace, under an English heaven 59:7
kind h. are more than coronets 313:10
men with splendid h. 59:3
our h., though stout and brave 160:15
thousand creeds ... move men's h. 58:13
two h. that beat as one 162:8
wand'ring eyes and heedless h. 125:12
while yr. h. are yearning 111:12
Heat: fear no more the h. o' th' sun 247:9
have neither h. nor light 323:14
h. me these irons hot 264:18
h. not a furnace for your foe 261:3
I know not where is that Promethean h. 280:11
thinking on fantastic summer's h. 282:1
Heath: a wind on the h. 57:8
Heathen: why do the h. rage? 35:16
Heaven: a h. in a wild flower 54:12
a H. on Earth 178:2
a new h. and a new earth 51:1
all this and h. too 130:16
brightest h. of invention 258:5
builds a h. in hell's despair 56:2
created the h. and the earth 30:1
differ as H. and earth 312:6
droppeth as the gentle rain from h. 275:1
every purpose under the h. 39:14
fallen from h., O Lucifer 40:25
fantastic tricks before high h. 273:7
first h. ... passed away 51:1
floor of h. is thick inlaid 275:8
friends ... in h. and hell 214:22
gain'd from h. ... a friend 126:14
garden hard by H. 57:11
God is in h. and thou upon earth 39:16
God's in his h. 62:7
h. and earth shall pass away 240:2
h. has no rage like love to hatred turned 89:6
h. is in these lips 165:8
H. itself wd. stoop to her [Virtue] 173:4
H. lies about us in our infancy 332:1
H. tries earth if it be in tune 162:15
Heaven (*continued*)
Hell I suffer seems a H. 177:13
high H. rejects the lore 330:11
how long ... permit to H. 179:14
I see H.'s glories shine 58:12
in earth ... as it is in h. 43:24
in the nurseries of H. 316:11
joy shall be in h. 46:2
justice be done, though h. fall 213:24
keys of the kingdom of h. 44:17
kingdom of h. is at hand 43:10
leave to H. the measure ... choice 141:13
love is h. and h. is love 239:13
make h. drowsy with the harmony 268:13
marriages are made in h. 220:26
mind ... can make a H. of Hell 176:5
more things in h. and earth 249:12
new Jerusalem ... out of h. 51:2
not mad, sweet h.! 265:17
O h., were men but constant 292:11
open face of h. 151:6
or what's a h. for? 60:11
our conversation is in h. 48:30
over his living head like H. 297:13
parting is all we know of h. 99:15
places that the eye of h. visits 281:14
praise, my soul, the King of H. 163:8
progressive virtue, and approving H.! 316:13
puts all H. in a rage 54:13
reign in Hell than serve in H. 176:6
shun the h. that leads men to this hell 294:12
steep and thorny way to h. 248:14
summons thee to h. or to hell 270:10
that from H., or near it 300:1
that h.'s vault shd. crack 268:2
there was silence in h. 50:23
to be young was very H.! 334:5
to seek the ... eye of h. to garnish 264:19
top ... reached to h. 31:9
under an English h. 59:7
watered h. with their tears 56:6
when Britain first, at H.'s command 316:12
Heavens: pure as the naked h. 333:13
spangled h., a shining frame 9:9
the h. declare the glory of God 35:22
the h. themselves, the planets ... observe 290:1
till you are clothed with the h. 317:16
Heaviness foreruns the good event 257:11
Heavy: a light wife doth make a h. husband 275:12
Hebrew: called in the H. tongue Armageddon 50:27
Hector: of H. and Lysander 16:14
Hecuba: what's H. to him or he to H.? 250:15
Hedge: a voice ... from h. to h. 151:1
Heels: if yr. h. are nimble and light 189:8
to cool one's h. 210:10
Heigh! the doxy over the dale 292:17
Heigh-ho: h.! says Rowley 189:2
sing h. unto the green holly 245:1
Height: happiness makes up in h. 113:15
to the h. of this great argument 175:17
Heir: dear son of memory, great h. of fame 175:12
first h. of my invention 295:3
Heiresses: all h. are beautiful 104:10

Helen: dust hath closed H.'s eye 186:12
sweet H., make me immortal 165:8
Helena: all is dross that is not H. 165:8
Hell: a shout that tore H.'s concave 176:10
airs from heaven or blasts from h. 249:3
all H. broke loose 178:11
all we need of h. 99:15
and H. followed with him 50:22
better to reign in H. 176:6
boys, it [war] is all h. 301:20
builds a Heaven in H.'s despair 56:2
down to h.; and say I sent thee 261:2
dunnest smoke of h. 270:2
England ... h. for horses 67:10
gates of h. shall not prevail 44:16
go ... to h. in embroidery 207:29
heaven that leads men to this h. 294:12
h. and Chancery are always open 216:28
h. is a city ... like London 299:9
h. itself breathes out contagion 252:8
h. to which hate and fear ... condemn 237:8
into the mouth of H. 311:12
Italy ... h. for women 67:10
jealousy ... injured lover's h. 178:16
lifetime of happiness! ... h. on earth 296:3
make a Heaven of H., a H. of Heaven 176:5
myself am H. 177:13
no redemption from h. 224:8
nor h. a fury like a woman scorned 89:6
prompted ... by heaven and h. 250:18
road to h. is paved ... intentions 216:29
summons thee to heaven or to h. 270:10
the bells of h. go ting-a-ling 14:12
to reign ... though in H. 176:6
though h. shd. bar the way 188:2
ugly h., gape not! come not, Lucifer! 165:11
way down to H. is easy 321:4
way ... that out of H. leads 177:5
when war begins, h. opens 229:26
which way I fly is H. 177:13
women ... as Heaven and H. 312:6
Hellish dark, and smells of cheese! 308:6
Helmsman: so the h. answered 161:4
Help: a very present h. 36:13
H. of the helpless 163:5
h. yourself, heaven will h. you 111:7
hills, from whence cometh my h. 37:15
many of yr. countrymen cannot h. 142:6
not enough to h. the feeble up 289:9
O God, our h. in ages past 323:4
past h. shd. be past grief 292:14
past my h. is past my care 25:9
since there's no h. ... kiss and part 102:12
the rich can h. themselves 215:5
Helpers: when other h. fail 163:5
Helpless: Help of the h., O Abide with me 163:5
h., naked, piping loud 56:3
Hemlock: as though of h. I had drunk 149:13
Hen: two Owls and a H. 158:13
yaf nat of that text a pulled h. 79:5
Henry: the chief defect of H. King 27:2
Henry IV Part II: abdicated in favour of H. 241:10
Hens: three French h. 194:2
Heraldry: the boast of h., the pomp of power 126:8
Herbert Spencer: expression ... used by Mr. H. 95:12
Herbs: dinner of h. where love is 38:18
Hercules: and some of H. 16:14
let H. ... do what he may 253:5
Herd: lowing h. winds slowly 126:3
Here: h. he lies where he longed to be 307:6
h. is my journey's end, h. is my butt 280:13
h. lie I and ... daughters 11:17
h. lies a man who was killed 11:18
h. lies a poor woman 12:1
h. lies ... Mary Ann Lowder 12:4
h. lies my wife ... hallelujee! 12:2
h. lies my wife: h. let her lie! 104:5
h. lies ... Richard Hind 12:3
h. lies Will Smith 12:5
h. we come gathering nuts in May 15:7
I have been h. before 236:10
the ice was h., the ice was there 86:2
'tis neither h. nor there 280:7
we're h. because we're h. 17:6
Hereafter: she shd. have died h. 272:10
what is love? 'Tis not h. 291:2
what may come h. 309:18
Heresies: begin as h. ... end as superstitions 138:1
Heresy: ancient saying is no h. 274:15
there is no worse h. 9:1
Heretics: Jews, Turks, Infidels, and H. 53:4
Heritage: Americans ... proud of our ancient h. 153:1
Hermit: dwell a weeping h. there! 88:11
Hermitage: my gorgeous palace for a h. 283:7
Hermits are contented with their cells 332:13
Hero: be a h. ... must drink brandy 144:15
every h. becomes a bore 108:16
no man is a h. to his valet 91:1
see the conquering h. comes 184:6
the grave where our h. we buried 330:3
to his ... valet seem'd a h. 68:16
Herod: it out-herods H. 251:8
Heroes: fit country for h. to live in 160:9
Héros: pas de h. pour son valet 91:1
Hero-worship is strongest where 305:6
Herring: h. boxes without topses 183:9
plague o' these pickle h. 290:14
Hervey: if you call a dog H. 141:15
Hesperus: H. entreats thy light 145:8
it was the schooner H. 161:12
Hewers of wood and drawers of water 33:11
Hey: and a h. nonino 245:16
H. diddle diddle 189:5
Hickory, dickory, dock 189:6
Hid: fiend h. in a cloud 56:3
love ... cough cannot be h. 219:33
Hide: let me h. myself in thee 317:15
Hideous: ingratitude ... more h. ... in a child 265:14
Hides from himself his state 141:12
High: h. and low mate ill 326:6
means ... for contempt too h. 91:13
when civil fury first grew h. 67:14
ye'll tak' the h. road 16:10
High churchman: a zealous H. was I 15:12
Highland: my sweet H. Mary 66:3
yon solitary H. Lass! 334:16
your H. Laddie 146:3
Highlands: chieftain to the H. bound 72:8
my heart's in the H. 66:14
Hill: apart sat on a h. retired 177:6
dew of yon high eastward h. 247:16
h. will not come to Mahomet 22:4

Hill (*continued*)
laughing is heard on the h. 56:11
there is a green h. far away 10:7
to sit upon a h. as I do now 260:13
Hills: as old as the h. 222:23
floats on high o'er vales and h. 331:7
halloo yr. name to the reverberate h. 290:15
lift up mine eyes unto the h. 37:15
over the h. and far away 115:6, 195:3
the great h. of the South Country 28:2
we shall fight in the h. 82:13
Him first, h. last, h. midst 178:15
Himself: discommendeth others ... commendeth h. 59:11
man's first duty? ... To be h. 138:6
none ... liveth ... dieth to h. 47:30
shd. be the master of h. 169:2
so lonely 'twas, that God h. 87:2
Hinder end of the spear 34:13
Hindmost: devil take the h. 211:19
Hinky dinky parley-voo 236:14
Hint: upon this h. I spake 279:2
Hip: catch him once upon the h. 274:7
smote them h. and thigh 33:20
Hippo: Lord H. 27:14
Hippocrene: the blushful H. 149:14
Hireling: pay given to a state h. 140:11
Hiss: a dismal universal h. 179:12
roasted crabs h. in the bowl 269:1
Hissed all my mystery lectures 305:19
Histoire des grands événements ... h. des crimes 321:15
Histories make men wise 23:9
History: attend to the h. of Rasselas 141:3
cd. ever hear by tale or h. 276:10
ends this strange eventful h. 244–5:11
great deal of h. to produce a little literature 139:4
great dust-heap called h. 54:5
happiest women ... have no h. 105:15
happy ... country which has no h. 216:9
h. ... essence of innumerable biographies 73:10
h. is ... biography of great men 73:8
h. is bunk 111:9
h. is philosophy teaching 100:1
h. must be false 322:5
h. of England ... h. of progress 164:5
h. of the great events ... h. of crimes 321:15
h. ... register of the crimes, follies 116:3
h. repeats itself 216:32
H. ... will tell lies, as usual 295:15
no h.; only biography 108:6
Thames is liquid h. 65:7
there is a h. in all men's lives 257:5
war makes rattling good h. 128:7
we learn from h. ... nothing from h. 296:10
woman's ... h. ... h. of the affections 138:11
world h. ... world's judgment 238:13
Hit: a h., a very palpable h. 253:7
h. the nail on the head 216:33
Hitch yr. wagon to a star 108:18
Hither: come h., come h. 244:4
Hitler has missed the bus 78:11
Hive: a h. for the honey bee 337:4
Hoarded: beauty is nature's coin; must not be h. 173:2
Hobson's choice 216:34
Hodgepodge: our ... tongue a gallimaufry or h. 305:17
Hoist with his own petard 216:35
Holborn: when I was last in H. 285:3
Hold: for ever h. his peace 53:20
h. fast that which is good 49:7
to have and to h. 53:22
Hole: a better 'ole 23:22
Rooötten, Beeëastly, Silly H.! 324:12
Holes where eyes did once inhabit 285:1
Holidays: if ... year were playing h. 253:21
Holiness: go! put off H.! 55:7
h. of the Heart's affection 151:9
Hollow: we are the h. men 106:7
Holly: heigh-ho unto the green h. 245:1
the h. and the ivy 15:8
the h. bears the crown 15:8
Holy: an h. and a good thought 52:11
H. Deadlock 131:8
h., divine, good, amiable 179:10
h., fair and wise is she 292:8
h., h., h., all the Saints adore thee 130:3
hunters been nat h. men 79:5
sabbath day—to keep it h. 32:3
savage place! As h. and enchanted 87:12
the h. city, new Jerusalem 51:2
was the h. Lamb of God 55:8
ye shall be h. ... for I the Lord ... am h. 32:14
Holy Roman Empire was neither holy, nor Roman, nor an Empire 321:16
Holy writ: odd old ends ... of h. 284:14
Homage: hypocrisy ... h. paid by vice 234:7
Home: as much like h. as we can 114:5
at h. I was in a better place 244:2
blest by suns of h. 59:6
charity begins at h. 209:19
comin' for to carry me h. 17:1
don't want to go h. in the dark 131:3
dunce that has been kept at h. 93:2
east or west, h. is best 212:11
fools at h. condemn 'em 288:14
God, who is our h. 332:1
his first, best country ... h. 123:14
h. art gone, and ta'en thy wages 247:9
h. is heaven 186:3
h. is the sailor, h. from sea 307:6
h. life of our own dear Queen 13:9
h. of the bean and the cod 57:10
h. on the rolling deep 238:8
h. ... they have to take you in 113:11
hunter h. from the hill 307:6
I am far from h. 187:14
it's h. and it's h. ... fain wad I be 95:2
keep the h. fires burning 111:12
ladybird, ladybird, fly away h. 190:8
leave them alone, and they'll come h. 190:10
man goeth to his long h. 39:27
our eternal h. 323:4
pillage ... with merry march bring h. 258:8
pleasure never is at h. 148:3
returned h. the previous night 63:1
sick for h., she stood in tears 150:4
Sublimity to welcome me h. 152:6
sweet h. of ... fears and hopes and joys 149:5
that is fit h. for thee 336:4
the old Kentucky H. 112:7
there's no place like h. 199:2
they dream of h. 111:12
this little pig stayed at h. 194:7
what's the good of a h.? 127:9

Homely: home-keeping youth have ... h. wits 292:4
Homer: seven cities warred for H., being dead 132:9
shame when the worthy H. nods 135:10
with the single exception of H. 297:8
Homerus: quandoque ... dormitat H. 135:10
Homes: the stately h. of England! 91:5, 130:5
Homestead, Braddock, Birmingham 238:7
Homines: quot h. tot sententiae 315:4
Honest: armour is his h. thought 336:13
deal with none but h. men 224:13
good to be h. and true 16:1
h. God is the noblest work of man 138:9
h. man sent to lie abroad 336:11
h. man's the noblest work of God 203:8
I am not naturally h. 293:6
she was poor but she was h. 16:11
the world's grown h. 250:4
to be h. ... is to be one man pick'd out 250:1
Honesty: corruption wins not more than h. 261:12
for saving of thine h. 184:5
h. is the best policy 216:39
neither h., manhood, nor ... fellowship 253:19
no legacy is so rich as h. 242:5
Honey: and is there h. still for tea? 59:4
civil citizens kneading up the h. 258:8
eat our pot of h. on the grave 170:1
flowing with milk and h. 31:18
funny how a bear likes h.? 172:3
gather h. all the day 323:1
I always eat peas with h. 13:10
in the parlour eating bread and h. 193:5
it's no go my h. love 164:15
some h., and plenty of money 158:7
sweeter than h. and the h.-comb 35:24
Tiggers don't like h. 171:2
Honey-dew: he on h. hath fed 87:16
Honeyed middle of the night 147:13
Honi soit qui mal y pense 216:40
Honour: as h., love, obedience 272:5
brilliance ... left to the fighter's h. 130:7
can h. set to a leg? 255:21
desires h. ... not worthy of h. 211:15
drown'd my H. in a shallow Cup 110:15
fewer men, the greater share of h. 259:13
giving h. unto the wife 50:6
his h. rooted in dishonour 312:4
h. a physician with the h. due 52:3
h. all men ... h. the king 50:5
H. comes, a pilgrim grey 88:11
h. for his valour 263:10
h. hath no skill in surgery 255:21
h. is a mere scutcheon 255:21
h. is the subject of my story 262:6
h. of honourable men 319:8
h. peereth in the meanest habit 287:11
h. pricks me on 255:21
h. sinks where commerce ... prevails 123:15
h.'s thought reigns solely 258:9
h. the face of the old man 32:17
h. thy father and thy mother 32:4
I believe it is ... peace with h. 78:10
if I give thee h. due 174:1
if it be a sin to covet h. 259:14
if peace cannot be ... with h. 237:7
jealous in h. 244:11
Honour (*continued*)
loss of h. was a wrench 124:11
loved I not H. more 162:7
mine h. is my life 281:8
pledge ... our fortunes, and our sacred h. 139:7
pluck bright h. from the ... moon 254:4
pluck up drowned h. 254:4
take h. from me ... life is done 281:8
the louder he talked of his h. 108:2
there is h. among thieves 217:1
'tis for the h. of England 89:8
to h. we call you· 115:1
what is h.? A word 255:21
when h.'s at the stake 252:19
Honourable: Brutus is an h. man 263:12
Honoured: more h. in the breach than the observance 249:2
Honours: bears his blushing h. thick upon him 261:9
mindless of its just h. 333:5
Hood: can drink with him that wears a h. 307:11
Hoofs: wound ... with their horses' h. 283:1
Hook: by h. or by crook 217:2
draw out leviathan with an h. 35:14
he for subscribers baits his h. 82:3
Hook-nos'd fellow of Rome 257:13
Hooks: silken lines and silver h. 100:17
Hooting: bird of night ... h. and shrieking 262:12
Hope: abandon h. all ye who enter 95:6
because I do not h. to turn 106:1
condemned to h.'s delusive mine 140:13
from h. and fear set free 310:1
give ... h. before you blacken ... world 319:8
h. deferred maketh the heart sick 38:13
h. for the best 217:3
h. from outward forms to win 87:9
h. is a good breakfast 23:13
H. sows what Love shall never reap 236:7
h. springs eternal in the human breast 203:1
in trembling h. repose 126:15
land of h. and glory 28:10
like Lucifer, never to h. again 261:10
look forward to with h. 113:10
my gown of glory, h.'s true gage 232:12
no other medicine but only h. 273:9
nursing the unconquerable h. 19:1
our h. for years to come 323:4
pursue ... the phantoms of h. 141:3
reinforcement we may gain from h. 176:3
so farewell h. 177:14
they h. they serve God 278:13
triumph of h. over experience 143:6
true h. is swift and flies 285:12
what was dead was h. 326:13
while there is life, there is h. 219:6
worldly H. ... turns Ashes 110:1
Hopeful: hey, but I'm h. 119:6
Hopefully: to travel h. 307:10
Hopeless grief is passionless 60:8
Hopes: all the h. of future years 160:11
enough for fifty h. and fears 60:13
many the h. that have vanished 129:1
the tender leaves of h. 261:9
vanity of human h., ... public library 141:2
what are the h. of man! 145:1

Hops: Kent—apples, ... h. and women 98:18
Horatio: poor Yorick! I knew him, H. 253:2
there are more things ... H. 249:12
Horde: society is now one polished h. 70:9
Horn: Boy Blue, come blow your h. 191:1
cow with the crumpled h. 194–5:8
Triton blow his wreathèd h. 333:4
Hornby: my H. and my Barlow long ago! 316:7
Hornets: stir up a h.' nest 226:24
Horns: take the bull by the h. 227:3
Horrible: the h. *double entendre* 12:11
Horrid: sure they are all h.? 20:14
when she was bad she was h. 161:8
Horrors: I have supp'd full with h. 272:9
Horse: a dog, a h., a rat have life 268:4
behold a pale h. 50:22
cart before the h. 209:9
do not spur a free h. 226:14
fine lady upon a white h. 193:1
flog a dead h. 213:39
h. made ... wife to make 209:23
I speak ... German to my h. 78:18
king ... sent a troop of h. 60:4
know two things about the h. 13:11
lene was his h. as is a rake 79:8
looks a gift h. in the mouth 214:30
may lead a h. to the water 218:28
my kingdom for a h.! 285:16
O for a h. with wings! 247:2
on's h. back at mine hostess' door 264:11
putting money on a h. 27:14
secret ... between a rider and his h. 308:10
sell the pasture now to buy the h. 258:9
some [glory] in their h. 294:2
spit in my face, call me h. 254:15
to Oxford sent a troop of h. 318:1
where's the bloody h.? 72:6
whip for the h., a bridle for the ass 38:30
Horses: all the king's h. 76:8, 189:9
careful of the breed of their h. 199:7
England ... hell of h. 111:4, 212:24
H. and Power and War 154:9
let us take any man's h. 258:2
not hanged for stealing h. 127:12
rebels wound ... with their h.' hoofs 283:1
saddle yr. h. and call up yr. men 239:4
some trust in chariots and some in h. 35:26
swap h. in mid-stream 159:14
that h. may not be stolen 127:12
Hose: youthful h. ... a world too wide 244–5:11
Host: a h. of golden daffodils 331:7
a soundless-clapping h. 316:7
Hostages: given h. to fortune 21:19
Hostess: fairer the h., the fouler the reckoning 213:15
sits on's horse back at mine h.' door 264:11
Hot: h. as hell 310:11
H., Cold, Moist and Dry 177:8
it was h. in there 121:12
soon h., soon cold 225:41
Hotel: living in a vile h. 28:1
Hotspur: the H. of the north 254:12
Hound: a traveller, by the faithful h. 160:13
Hounds: cry of his h. 125:6
h. of spring are on winter's traces 309:14
hunt with the h. 224:33
with his h. and his horn in the morning? 125:6
Hour: but one bare h. to live 165:10
dusky h. friendliest to sleep 178:17
Eternity in an h. 54:12
fools! for I also had my h. 81:3
fourscore ... not an h. more nor less 267:11
from h. to h. we ripe ... rot 244:9
he rose in less than half an h. 28:1
how many makes the h. ... complete 260:13
I have known the lightning's h. 96:6
improve each shining h. 323:1
it chanceth in an h. 209:18
memorial ... to one dead deathless h. 236:6
one far fierce h. and sweet 81:3
that struts and frets his h. 272:10
the h. is come, but not the man 240:12
the h. is ill which severs 298:10
the wish'd, the trysted h. 66:9
this was their finest h. 82:14
wet sea-boy in an h. so rude 257:3
Hours: a heavy weight of h. has chained 299:5
golden h. on angel wings 66:3
lazy, leaden-stepping h. 181:15
lose and neglect the creeping h. 244:10
love alters not with his brief h. 294:9
six h. in sleep, in ... study six 85:9
sweetest h. that e'er I spend 66:1
three h. a day will produce 318:3
to chase the glowing H. 69:4
two h.' traffic of our stage 285:18
worst effect is banishing for h. 92:5
House: a h. where help wasn't hired 12:1
a h. wherein to tarry 207:3
a man's h. is his castle 85:8
as a moat defensive to a h. 282:5
call upon my soul within the h. 290:15
daughters of my father's h. 291:8
eaten me out of h. and home 256:15
glory of this latter h. 43:1
h. fell upon the lords, and ... people 33:22
h. is a machine for living in 90:13
h. that Jack built 194–5:8
I will build a h. with deep thatch 28:3
if a h. be divided ... h. cannot stand 45:7
in a little crooked h. 194:3
in my Father's h. are many mansions 46:30
in that H. M.P.'s divide 117:9
like a h. on fire 217:10
my h. in the high wood 28:4
my h. ... the h. of prayer 45:14
out of the h. of bondage 31:29
prop that doth sustain my h. 275:6
set thine h. in order 40:28
shalt not covet thy neighbour's h. 32:9
the h. where I was born 134:14
wounded in the h. of my friends 43:4
you take my h. when you do take the prop 275:6
yr. h. is on fire and yr. children all gone 190:8
House of Lords are never in touch 328:11
House of Peers throughout the war 117:11
Household: breathing h. laws 333:11
stables ... real centre of h. 295:17
Houses: a plague o' both your h. 286:19
h. are built to live in 23:3
h. thick and sewers annoy 179:9
if it wasn't for the h. in between 25:3
lawyers' h. ... on the heads of fools 218:26
Housewife: here's to the h. that's thrifty 301:17

Hovel: *prefer* ... a h. to ... marble halls 72:2
Hover through the fog and filthy air 269:4
How: a pretty h. town 94:13
How-de-do: here's a h.! 118:9
Howl, h., h., h., ... men of stones! 268:2
Howled: cracked and growled and roared and h. 86:2
Howling: churlish priest ... when thou liest h. 253:3
Tom went h. down the street 195:4
Hubbard: old Mother H. 192:2
Hubbub increases more they call out 'Hush!' 148:7
Hue: add another h. unto the rainbow 264:19
native h. of resolution 250–1:20
Huffy: not h. or stuffy, nor tiny 131:5
Hull: from Hell, H. and Halifax ... deliver us 216:30
Hum: busy h. of men 174:5
h. of either army stilly sounds 259:8
sad-ey'd justice, with his surly h. 258:8
Human: a fearful sign of h. frailty 69:18
Adam was but h. 318:15
all h. things are subject to decay 104:13
all that is h. must retrograde 116:4
climax of all h. ills 69:20
dignity and worth of the h. person 319:5
every h. benefit and enjoyment 64:7
full tide of h. existence ... Charing-Cross 143:14
[God] ... does a h. form display 55:1
h. on my faithless arm 20:2
h. kind cannot bear ... much reality 106:4
h. race to which ... readers belong 81:12
I may be devout, but I am h. 182:15
I wish I loved the H. Race 233:1
in h. nature ... more of the fool 22:3
purest of h. pleasures 23:4
requires the highest type of h. nature 305:2
the field of h. conflict 82:15
to err is h. 202:14, 217:11
where ... least regard for h. freedom 305:6
women—one half the h. race 23:19
Human being: remember that you are a h. 296:18
Humane: every h. and gentle virtue 65:2
Humanised: distress hath h. my soul 331:2
Humanity: h. i love you because 94:14
h. with all its fears 160:11
still, sad music of h. 335:14
Humanum est errare 217:11
Humble: neither too h. nor too great 165:4
we are so very h. 97:17
you are *not* his most h. servant 144:18
Humbly: walk h. with thy God 42:24
Humility: h. towards the Public 152:1
modest stillness and h. 259:3
Humour: deficient in a sense of h. 88:4
unyok'd h. of yr. idleness 253:20
was ever woman in this h. woo'd ... won? 284:13
Hump: a woman ... without a positive h. 315:9
camel's h. is an ugly lump 155:9
uglier yet is the h. we get 155:9
Humpty Dumpty: 76:8–10; 189:9
Hundred: about two h. pounds a year 67:17
only one religion ... a h. versions 296:17
uttered it a h. times 134:4
Hunger ... is highly indelicate 120:12
Hungry: if thine enemy be h. 38:28
Hungry (*continued*)
makes h. where most she satisfies 242:15
Hunter: h. home from the hill 307:6
Lo! the H. of the East 109:13
man is the h. 314:17
mighty h. before the Lord 30:26
Hunter Dunn: Miss J. H. 29:12
Hunters: seith ... h. been nat holy men 79:5
Hunting: h. he loved but love he laugh'd to scorn 295:4
we daren't go a-h. 10:9
wet and dirty from h. 308:8
Huntress: queen and h. chaste and fair 145:8
Hurlyburly: when the h.'s done 269:3
Hurrah! H.! we bring the Jubilee 336:10
Hurricanes: you cataracts and h., spout 266:6
Hurry: an old man in a h. 82:5
sick h., its divided aims 18:21
Hurt: cd. you h. me, sweet lips? 309:17
give delight and h. not 288:13
hate the man whom you have h. 310:9
h. with the same weapons 274:17
Hurtig: you are h. be 155:9
Husband: actors are ... h., and wife and lover 169:16
being a h. ... whole-time job 28:8
good wife makes a good h. 215:23
light wife makes a heavy h. 275:12
Husbands: flirt with their own h. 327:9
h. at chirche-dore she hadde fyve 79:15
why so many h. fail 28:8
Hush: a breathless h. in the Close tonight 187:11
they call out 'H.!' 148:7
Hush-a-bye baby 189:10
Husks that the swine did eat 46:3
Hut: love in a h. 149:1
Hymns: chanting faint h. to ... moon 276:9
Hyperion to a satyr 248:3
Hyphenated Americanism: no room ... for h. 235:10
Hypocrisy: Conservative Government ... organised h. 100:4
h. ... homage ... by vice to virtue 234:7
h. ... homage that vice pays 217:12
Hypocrite: no man is a h. in his pleasures 144:20
plea of the scoundrel, h. 55:6
Hysterica passio, down ... sorrow 265:21

I: blew hither: here am I 136:7
I am I, and you are you 61:7
I am the State 162:2
I came, I saw, I conquered 71:13
I galloped, Dirck galloped 61:6
I have a go ... don't I? 197:7
I, said the Fly 196:2
I, said the Sparrow 196:2
'I', says the Quarterly 70:17
the spot where I made one 111:1
whoso turns as I 61:5
Iacta alea est 71:12
Iago: the pity of it, I.! 280:4
Ice: as chaste as i., as pure as snow 251:3
i. in June 70:14
in skating over thin i. 108:10
like ... i. on a hot stove 113:16
pleasure-dome with caves of i. 87:15
some say the world will end in ... i. 113:12
the i. was here, the i. was there 86:2

Ice (*continued*)
thrilling region of thick-ribbed i. 273:10
to smooth the i. 264:19
Icicles: when i. hang by the wall 269:1
Ida: on I.'s shady brow 56:13
Idea: abstract I. I have of Beauty 152:6
between the i. and the reality 106:8
Ideal: the i. man ... non-attached 137:10
Ideas: nice man ... of nasty i. 309:10
ruling i. ... i. of its ruling class 168:9
Idem velle ... nolle, ... firma amicitia 237:15
Ides of March: beware the i. 262:5
Idiosyncrasy: I have no ... i. in ... humour 59:14
Idiot: it is a tale told by an i. 272:10
law is an ass—a i. 98:15
the i. who praises 118:5
Idle: as i. as a painted ship 86:5
be not solitary, be not i. 67:12
for i. hands to do 323:2
happiest when I am i. 322:14
i. that might be better employed 217:13
tears, i. tears 314:16
tongue of i. ... is never i. 228:10
Idleness: i. ... the refuge of weak minds 80:15
unyok'd humour of yr. i. 253:20
Idol: a one-eyed yellow i. 129:6
Idolatries: to its i. a patient knee 69:5
Idolatry: god of our i., the press 93:3
Idols: the i. I have loved so long 110:15
there are four classes of I. 23:16
If: i. it wasn't for the 'ouses 25:3
yr. I. is the only peace-maker 246:3
Ifs: if I. and Ans were pots and pans 217:14
talk'st thou to me of i.? 285:4
Ignorance: art has no enemy except i. 206:22
from i. our comfort flows 205:7
hold there is no sin but i. 166:3
i. is like ... exotic fruit 327:11
i. is preferable to error 139:12
i., Madam, pure i. 142:4
where i. is bliss 126:2
Ignorant: conscious that you are i. 100:11
most i. of what he's most assur'd 273:7
Ignore: aren't happy with nothing to i. 186:6
Ilium: the topless towers of I. 165:8
Ill: a fool is love ... he thinks no i. 293:20
better suffer i. than do i. 207:34
costs more to do i. 210:11
i. doers are i. thinkers 217:16
i. fares the land, to ... ills a prey 122:5
i. gotten, i. spent 217:17
i.-housed, i.-clad, i.-nourished 235:2
i. met by moonlight 276:17
love worketh no i. 47:29
marries late, marries i. 220:28
means to do i. deeds makes deeds i. done 265:2
of every i. a woman is the worst 125:3
religion an i. man is of 224:9
the final goal of i. 312:15
things bad begun make strong ... by i. 271:5
Ill-bred: nothing so ... i. as audible laughter 80:13
Illiberal: nothing so i. ... as audible laughter 80:13
Illiterate him ... from your memory 301:5
Ills: bear those i. we have 250–1:20
climax of all human i. 69:20
Ills (*continued*)
i. have no weight 163:7
to hastening i. a prey 122:5
what i. the scholar's life assail 141:10
Ill-tempered and queer 158:6
Illumine: what in me is dark i. 175:17
Image: any graven i. 31:31
are wronging your i. 337:7
best i. of myself, and dearer half 178:14
i. of war, without its guilt 304:8
in the i. of God created 30:3
Imagination: as i. bodies forth the forms 277:6
are of i. all compact 277:5
by bare i. of a feast 282:1
certain of ... the truth of I. 151:9
civet ... to sweeten my i. 267:5
i. of a boy is healthy 147:7
[indebted to] ... i. for his facts 301:19
what the I. seizes as Beauty 151:9
Imagined: exhausted worlds and ... i. new 140:19
Imitate the action of the tiger 259:3
Imitation ... sincerest form of flattery 88:19
Imlac: business of a poet, said I. 141:5
Immanuel: shall call his name I. 40:21
Immaterial: the Brighton line. The line is i. 327:14
Immortal: a thing i. as itself 249:4
grow i. as they quote 337:11
Helen, make me i. with a kiss 165:8
his biting is i. 243:8
I have left no i. work 152:11
i. longings in me 243:10
lost the i. part of myself 279:10
my scrip of joy, i. diet 232:12
such harmony is in i. souls 275:8
what i. hand or eye 56:5
Immortality: just ourselves and I. 99:17
nurslings of i. 299:11
Imparadised in one another's arms 178:5
Impatient: surprised by joy, i. as the Wind 333:1
Impediment: cause or just i. 53:18
Impediments: marriage of true minds admit i. 294:8
wife and children ... are i. 21:19
Important: little things ... the most i. 101:12
Imports be more than your exports 144:19
Importunate: rashly i., gone to her death 134:10
Importune: too proud to i. 127:3
Impossibility: begotten by Despair upon I. 167:16
Impossible: I wish it were i. 144:24
in two words, i. 124:4
pure and complete sorrow ... i. 317:14
that not i. she 94:3
when you have eliminated the i. 102:3
Impostors: treat those two i. just the same 154:19
Impotently: rolls i. on as Thou or I 110:13
Impregnable: as if this flesh ... were brass i. 283:6
Impressions: first i. are most lasting 213:32
Improbable: however i., must be the truth 102:3
Impropriety: i. is the soul of wit 169:5
use any language ... without i. 117:12
Improve: i. each shining hour 323:1

Improve (*continued*)
i. his shining tail 73:17
Impulse: i. of the moment, or ... study 21:1
one i. from a vernal wood 335:7
In: home ... you are never i. it 127:9
they have to take you i. 113:11
Incarnadine: the multitudinous seas i. 270:12
Incense: soft i. hangs upon the boughs 150:1
Inch: ay, every i. a king 267:3
give ... i. ... take an ell 214:32
no painful i. to gain 85:2
Inches: die by famine die by i. 130:15
Incident: curious i. of the dog in the night 102:1
Inclines to think there is a God 84:14
Include me out 124:5
Income: a good i. is of no avail 303:6
annual i. ... annual expenditure ... misery 97:16
innate desire ... to live beyond ... i. 68:7
Inconstant: swear not by ... th' i. moon 286:10
Incontestable: what is official is i. 114:3
Inconvenient: i. to be poor 92:3
poverty ... is confoundedly i. 303:11
Incorruptible: the seagreen I. 73:7
Increase: from fairest creatures we desire i. 293:10
God gave the i. 47:32
good and i. of the world 312:2
Ind: wealth of Ormus and of I. 176:15
Indebted to his memory for his jests 301:19
Indecency: a public i. 78:5
Independence: treacle to the wings of i. 152:9
Independent: poor and i. ... nearly an impossibility 85:4
India's coral strand 130:1
Indian: like the base I., threw a pearl away 280–1:14
only good I. is a dead I. 300:13
Indictment against an whole people 64:6
Indifferent: delayed till I am i. 142:1
Indignatio: ubi saeva i. ... lacerare nequit 309:11
Indignation: burning i. no longer lacerates 309:11
Indiscretion: a lover without i. is no lover 128:8
Individual: no i. cd. resent 308:13
not the i. but the species 141:5
Individualism: American system of rugged i. 135:5
Individuals: worth of the i. composing it 170:11
Indivisible: peace is i. 160:3
Industry: avarice, the spur of i. 137:1
i. will improve them [talents] 233:9
i. will supply their deficiency 233:9
Inebriate: cups that cheer but not i. 93:10
Inebriated with the exuberance of ... verbosity 100:8
Ineffectual: beautiful and i. angel [Shelley] 19:9
remote and i. don 27:12
Inelegance: a continual state of i. 21:4
Inert: the earth, tideless and i. 23:23
Inevitability: the i. of gradualness 323:8
Inevitable: arguing with the i. 163:1
Inexactitude: without some risk of terminological i. 82:7
Infamy: thou, whose i. is not thy fame 297:15
Infancy: Heaven lies about us in our i. 332:1
Infant: i., mewling and puking 244:11
the i. child is not aware 136:2
to a little i. ... as painful 21:10
Infection: against i. and the hand of war 282:5
Inferiority: conscious of an i. 144:6
Infidels: peace ... go sleep with Turks and i. 283:8
Turks, I., and Hereticks 53:4
Infinite: everything ... as it is, i. 57:7
how i. in faculties! 250:6
i. wrath and i. despair 177:13
Infinity in the palm of your hand 54:12
Infirmities: bear his friend's i. 264:2
bear the i. of the weak 47:31
wine for ... thine often i. 49:12
Infirmity: last i. of noble mind 175:1
Inflammation of his weekly bills 69:20
Influence: bright eyes rain i. 174:6
How to Win Friends and I. People 73:12
Influenza: call it i. if ye like 28:6
my aunt died of i. 296:22
no i. in my young days 28:6
Inform: occasions do i. against me 252:17
Information: I only ask for i. 97:18
i. vegetable, animal 120:4
know where we can find i. 143:19
Infortune: worst kinde of i. 80:5
Ingenious: neither i., sober, nor kind 12:3
Ingratitude: I hate i. more ... than lying 292:1
i., thou marble-hearted fiend 265:14
unkind as man's i. 245:1
Ingratitudes: great-siz'd monster of i. 290:6
Inhabitants: look not like th' i. o' th' earth 269:7
Inherit: all which it i. shall dissolve 288:16
i. the vasty Hall of Death 18:17
Inheritance: king's favour is no i. 218:3
Inhumanity: man's i. to man 66:8
Iniquity: that reverend vice, that grey i. 255:1
the i. of the fathers 32:1
Injury: i. ... sooner forgotten than an insult 80:10
revenge never repairs an i. 224:16
Ink: all the sea were i. 14:1
black as i. 208:3
he hath not drunk i. 268:11
whose sin ... dipt me in i.? 201:13
Inlets: far back through creeks and i. 85:2
Inn: do you remember an i., Miranda? 28:5
no room ... in the i. 45:19
warmest welcome at an i. 300:12
Innisfree: and go to I. 337:4
Innocence: our peace, our fearful i. 333:11
Innocent: better ... guilty ... escape than one i. suffer 54:11
i. of the blood of this just person 45:3
Macbeth doth murder sleep—the i. sleep 270:11
rich shall not be i. 39:4
source of i. merriment 118:11
Innocently employed than in getting money 143:13
Innovator: time is the greatest i. 22:18
Inns: shun the awful shops and go to i. 81:10
Inopem me copia fecit 197:15
Inquest: came together like the coroner's i. 89:7

Insensibility: no, Sir, stark i. 141:14
Insensible, then? Yea, to the dead 255:21
Inside: birds ... i. ... desperate to get out 183:5
returned from the ride ... lady i. 12:10
Insipid to a vulgar taste 303:5
Insisture, course, proportion, season 290:1
Insolence: flown with i. and wine 176:8
the i. of office 250–1:20
Insomnia: amor vincit i. 114:6
Inspiration: all scripture ... by i. of God 49:16
genius is one per cent i. and 105:8
Inspired: that I i. the nation 83:14
with eyes up-rais'd, as one i. 88:13
Instances: wise saws and modern i. 244:11
Instinct: all healthy i. for it 68:8
overpaying i. is a generous one 295:12
Institutions: neither for nor against i. 325:10
sought to destroy i. 325:10
Instruments: Genius and the mortal i. 262:13
make i. to plague us 267:14
Insult: add i. to injury 217:22
injury ... sooner forgotten than an i. 80:10
Insurrection: suffers ... the nature of an i. 262:13
Integer vitae scelerisque purus 135:14
Intellect: his i. is not replenished 268:11
i. is ... fooled by the heart 234:6
put on i. 55:7
Intellectual: a tear is an i. thing 55:5
being i., was amongst the noblest 72:3
I am an i. chap 117:7
the word i. suggests 20:3
thirdly, i. ability 19:12
Intelligence: pawn your i. to buy a drink 94:14
Intelligent: i. Mr. Toad 124:13
on the whole ... not i. 120:8
Intent: his first avowed i. 63:13
truth told with bad i. 54:14
Intentions: paved with good i. 216:29
Intents: be thy i. wicked or charitable 249:3
Interchange of power pressed too far 22:15
Interest: *du* [believe] in interest 162:11
Interested: whatever he is most i. in 24:15
Interesting: those ... in i. situations 20:9
Interference: no i., and freedom of movement 232:6
Interim: acting ... first motion, all the i. 262:13
Interrupt: you shdn't i. my interruptions 107:8
Interstices between the intersections 140:8
Intolerable: possession of [a thing] is i. 320:3
this i. deal of sack! 255:3
Intoxication: best of life is but i. 69:15
Introduced: when I'm i. to one 233:1
Intrudes: society where none i. 69:9
Invariable: double glass of the i. 99:4
Invasion: waiting for the long-promised i. 83:1
Invent: all the lies you can i. 54:14
more than I i. or is invented 256:8
necessary to i. Him 321:14
Invented: I have i. an ... invalid 327:8
Invention: ascend the brightest heaven of i. 258:5
first heire of my i. 295:3
necessity is the mother of i. 221:24
rhyme ... i. of a barbarous age 175:14
Inverse proportion to the sum 198:6
Investment: no finer i. ... than putting milk into babies 83:9
Invincible: none i. as they 92:2
Invisibly: silently, i., he took her 55:11
wind does move silently, i. 55:10
Involved: I am i. in mankind 101:8
Inward: flash upon that i. eye 331:11
i. and spiritual grace 53:16
Inwards: he looked i., and found her [nature] there 104:4
Iohannes fac totum: an absolute *I.* 127:6
Ireland: my love for England and I. 234:1
Irene: ill success of his tragedy [*I.*] 141:16
Irish: the I. are a fair people 143:11
the I. are not in a conspiracy 143:11
Iron: earth stood hard as i. 235:15
he shall rule them with a rod of i. 50:17
if gold ruste, what shall i. do? 79:17
i. tongue of midnight 277:8
strike while the i. is hot 226:29
the i. entered his soul 217:23
the i. entered into his soul 37:3
wink and hold out my i. 258:10
Iron curtain: i. between us and ... eastward 83:10
i. has descended across the Continent 83:11
Irons: heat me these i. hot 264:18
many i. in the fire 217:25
Irregulars: the Baker Street i. 102:4
Is: whatever i., i. right 203:4
Island: no man is an i. 101:7
our rough i.-story 314:11
we shall defend our i., whatever the cost 82:13
Zuleika, on a desert i. 26:8
Isle: but five upon this i. 288:11
I. of Beauty, fare thee well 25:5
this i. is full of noises 288:13
this sceptr'd i. 282:5
Isles: the i. of Greece 69:21
Isolation: stood alone in ... our splendid i. 124:7
Israel: as the clay ... O house of I. 41:15
children of I. ... said ... It is manna 31:28
hear, O I. 32:21
I arose a mother in I. 33:13
I., Athens, Florence 138:8
I., what doth ... God require 33:1
the children of I. ... upon the dry ground 31:26
the sweet psalmist of I. 34:15
It: Greeks had a word for i. 10:1
I. rolls impotently on 110:13
lift not thy hands to *I.* 110:13
Italian: I. to women, French to men 78:18
Turk, or Proosian, or perhaps I.! 120:3
Italy: a man who has not been in I. 144:6
I. a paradise for horses 67:10
thou Paradise of exiles, I.! 298:12
Itch: I would thou didst i. 290:4
inveterate ... i. for writing 146:10
i. of literature ... scratching of a pen 162:9
Itching: condemn'd to have an i. palm 263:22
Iteration: prone to any i. of nuptials 90:1
thou hast damnable i. 253:17
Itself: he was ... the old block i. 64:9
Iuvenes: gaudeamus ... i. dum sumus 17:13
Ivied: sat at her i. door 71:16

Ivy: i. never sere 174:12
the holly and the i. 15:8

Jabberwock: hast thou slain the J.? 75:11
Jack: all work ... makes J. a dull boy 230:40
banish plump J. 255:2
every J. has his Jill 217:26
every J. ... study the knack 121:6
house that J. built 194–5:8
J. and Jill went up the hill 190:6
J. fell down and broke his crown 190:6
J. of all trades and master of none 217:27
J. Sprat cd. eat no fat 190:6
little J. Horner 191:2
poor J., farewell! 256:2
Jack Robinson: before one can say J. 207:10
Jackdaw sat on the Cardinal's chair 24:4
Jackson standing like a stone wall 26:5
Jacky shall have a new master 193:3
Jacob: J. saw ... corn in Egypt 31:12
sold his birthright unto J. 31:6
the voice is J.'s voice 31:8
Jade: let the galled j. wince 252:5
Jades: hollow pampered j. of Asia 256:18
ye pamper'd j. of Asia! 166:12
Jail: nothing now left but a j. 97:15
taken from the county j. 118:3
want, the patron, and the j. 141:10
Jam to-morrow and j. yesterday 76:7
James, J., Morrison Morrison 171:8
Janvier: Generals J. and Février 187:15
Japan: gentlemen of J. 117:15
Jar: folk ... in front that I j. 109:1
Jardin: il faut cultiver notre j. 321:11
Javan or Gadire 180:15
Jaws: into the j. of Death 311:12
Jealous: am a j. God 32:1
j. for the cause 280:3
j. for they are j. 280:3
one not easily j. 280–1:14
Jealousy: beware, my lord, of j. 279:16
j. is cruel as the grave 40:14
nor j. ... the injured lover's hell 178:16
Jeanie: I dream of J. 112:5
Jehu: J., the son of Nimshi 34:25
like the driving of J. 34:25
Jelly: out, vile j.! 266:18
Jenny kissed me when we met 137:7
Jerusalem: black but comely .., ye daughters of J. 40:3
if I forget thee, O J. 37:26
the holy city, new J. 51:2
till we have built J. 55:8
Jeshurun waxed fat 33:7
Jessica, look how the floor of heaven 275:8
Jest: a fellow of infinite j. 253:2
a good j. for ever 254:8
his whole wit in a j. 25:7
J. and youthful Jollity 173:16
j.'s prosperity lies in the ear 268:16
life is a j. and all things show it 115:13
most bitter is a scornful j. 140:15
true word is spoken in j. 228:22
Jesting: what is truth? said j. Pilate 21:8
Jests: indebted to his memory for ... j. 301:19
j. at scars that never felt a wound 286:6
Jesu: J. by a nobler deed 78:12
J., thou art all compassion 325:3
Jesus: blood of J. whispers peace 54:4
Gentle J., meek and mild 325:1
Jesus (*continued*)
J. wept 46:28
stand up for J.! 105:2
the Cross of J. ... on before 24:9
Jesus Christ: J. her little child 10:6
J. ... the same yesterday ... for ever 49:24
the Church's one foundation is J. 307:13
Jeunesse: si j. savait 108:25
Jew: hath not a J. eyes? ... hands 274:17
Jewel: a rich j. in an Ethiop's ear 286:3
j. ... in a swine's snout 38:11
j. in a ten-times barred-up chest 281:8
the immediate j. of their souls 279:15
wears ... precious j. in his head 243:15
Jewels: dumb j. ... in their silent kind 292:7
give my j. for a set of beads 283:7
unvalued j. ... bottom of the sea 285:1
Jewish: spit upon my J. gaberdine 274:10
Jews, Turks, Infidels 53:4
Jigging veins of rhyming mother-wits 166:6
Jill: Jack and J. 190:6
make sure of his J. 121:6
Jim: they called him Sunny J. 128:3
Jingo: but by j. if we do 137:4
Joan: greasy J. doth keel the pot 269:1
J. as my Lady is as good 132:4
Job: as poor as J. 223:15
being a husband ... whole-time j. 28:8
best of a bad j. 207:16
give us the tools and we will finish the j. 83:2
heard of the patience of J. 50:3
Jobiska: to fish for his Aunt J.'s 158:10
Jocund: be gay in such a j. company 331:10
Joe: 'Poor old J.' 112:11
Jog on, j. on, the footpath way 292:19
John: Don J. of Austria is going to the war 81:5
King J. was not a good man 171:4
Matthew, Mark, Luke, and J. 9:13
O, no J., no J., no! 16:8
some said, J., print it 63:5
John Anderson my jo 66:5
John Bradford: there ... goes J. 58:1
John Brown: J.'s body ... a mould'ring 127:13
J. is filling his last cavity 12:7
J. is stowed. He watched the ads. 186:4
John of Gaunt: old J., time-honoured Lancaster 281:6
John Peel: d'ye ken J.? 125:6
Johnny: little J. Green 188–9:9
Johnny head-in-air: do not despair for J. 231:16
Little J. 133:10
Johnson: Dr. J. condemns 65:6
glad, replied J., ... that he thanks God 142:2
great Cham of literature, Samuel J. 304:3
J. said ... triumph of hope 143:6
J. scolded him [Langton] 141:17
no arguing with J. 124:2
Join: will you j. the dance? 75:3
Joined: shall be j. unto his wife 48:25
what ... God hath j. together 45:12
Joint: every j. and motive of her body 290:8
time is out of j. O cursed spite 249:14
Joking: my way of j. ... to tell the truth 295:20
Jolly: hir j. whistle wel y-wet 79:22
j. good ale 307:12
j. tars are our men 115:1
there was a j. miller once 54:1

Jonah: J., doest thou well to be angry? 42:20
J. was in the belly of the fish 42:19
lot fell upon J. 42:18
Jonathan: Saul and J. 34:11
Jones: indeed! said Mr. J. 124:8
Joneses: keep up with the J. 217:34
Jonson: O rare Ben J. 146:2
Jordan: I looked over J. 17:1
Journey: here is my j.'s end ... my butt 280:13
is yr. j. really necessary? 11:5
one of the pleasantest things ... a j. 129:11
tired and weary still j. on 157:5
will the day's j. take ... long day? 236:3
Journeys end in lovers meeting 291:1
Jours: tous les j. ... vais de mieux en mieux 91:3
Jove: daughter of J., relentless Power 126:16
J. for's power to thunder 246:10
lovelier than the love of J. 166:7
while J.'s planet rises yonder 61:5
Jowett: my name is J. 26:6
Joy: a j. for ever 147:8
and snatch a fearful j. 126:1
dreams of j. and fear 298:15
dwell in doubtful j. 271:3
fields where j. for ever dwells 176:4
glad tidings of great j. 311:4
God send you j. 215:9
grief and pain for promis'd j. 66:12
he chortled in his j. 75:11
he who bends himself a J. 55:4
impossible as pure ... complete j. 317:14
j. cometh in the morning 36:2
j. of heaven, to earth come down 325:3
j. shall be in heaven 46:2
j.'s soul lies in the doing 289:15
j. whose hand is ever at his lips 149:12
kisses the j. as it flies 55:4
let j. be unconfined 69:4
man was made for j. and woe 54:15
my scrip of j. 232:12
O j.! that in our embers 332:4
pledges of Heaven's j. 172:12
shd. allow itself a life of j. 237:8
sow in tears ... reap in j. 37:18
surprised by j., ... I turned 333:1
the deep power of j. 335:12
the oil of j. for mourning 41:11
there is ... j. for his fortune 263:10
thy j. and crown eternally 183:2
weep for j. to stand upon my kingdom 283:1
wish you the j. o' th' worm 243:9
Joyful: j. and triumphant 196:5
make a j. noise unto God 36:19
Joyous hour, we give thee greeting! 118:8
Joys: all my j. to this are folly 67:8
can I ever bid these j. farewell? 150:11
hence, vain deluding J. 173:5
j. of parents are secret 21:17
minds me o' departed j. 67:6
our youth, our j., our all we have 232:11
their homely j. and destiny obscure 126:7
unfriendly to society's chief j. 92:5
Jubilee: we bring the J. 336:10
Judas: so J. did to Christ 284:1
Judge: a j. ... no king can corrupt 261:7
a perfect j. will read 202:6
as sober as a j. 109:8
I'll be j., I'll be jury 74:1
j. none blessed before his death 51:21
Judge *(continued)*
j. not 44:5
j. of a man by his foes 90:6
J. of all the earth 31:2
marshal's truncheon nor the j.'s robe 273:4
never j. from appearances 217:30
Judg(e)ment: a Daniel come to j. 275:3
but reserve thy j. 248:16
causes ... blind man's erring j. 202:4
good j. ... relieth not ... on his own 215:18
hour of death, ... day of j. 52:25
no one complains of his j. 234:5
nor is the People's j. always true 103:8
right j. in all things 53:5
world history is the world's j. 238:13
wd. not give his j. rashly 9:8
Judges: hungry j. soon the sentence sign 204:9
Judging: want of skill appear ... in j. ill 202:
Judgments: with our j. as our watches 202:2
Jug: little brown j. 15:5
Juggler: a threadbare j. 246:5
Juice (Grease): stew (fry) in one's own j. 226:17
Julia: where my J.'s lips do smile 131:13
Juliet: it is the east and J. is the sun 286:6
Julius: many Caesars ere such another J. 247:1
July: English winter—ending in J. 70:8
Jumblies: lands where the J. live 158:5
Jump: we'd j. the life to come 270:5
Jumping from the chair 137:7
Jumps: which way the cat j. 209:14
June: cuckoo is in J., heard, not regarded 255:10
ice in J. 70:14
rose that's newly sprung in J. 66:15
she needs not J. 19:4
so rare as a day in J.? 162:15
Jungle: this is the Law of the J. 154:21
Junk: Epp's statues are j. 13:4
Juno: haughty J.'s unrelenting hate 105:1
Jury: the j., passing on the prisoner's life 273:1
trial by j. ... will be a delusion 97:4
Jury-men: wretches hang that j. may dine 204:9
Just: a beast, but a j. beast 13:6
cause or j. impediment 53:18
j. are the ways of God 180:13
j. shall live by faith 47:15
j. wore enough for modesty 62:13
memory of the j. is blessed 38:9
ninety and nine j. persons 46:2
rain it raineth on the j. 57:14
sendeth rain on the j. 43:21
the gods are j. 267:14
unjust steals the j.'s umbrella 57:14
Justice: j. be done, though heaven fall 213:24
let j. be done 109:6
much law, but little j. 221:20
place of j. is ... hallowed 23:11
religion, j., counsel 22:8
revenge is a kind of wild j. 21:12
sad-ey'd j. with his surly hum 258:8
shall temper so j. with mercy 179:11
the j. in fair round belly 244:11
though j. be thy plea 275:1
Thwackum was for doing j. 109:11
when mercy seasons j. 275:1

Justification: carry its j. in every line 90:7
Justify: j. the ways of God to men 175:17
to j. God's ways to man 136:9
use thought to j. ... wrong-doing 321:12
Justitia: fiat j., et pereat mundus 109:6
J'y suis, j'y reste 164:11

Kalendas: ad K. Graecas 71:10
Kaspar: old K.'s work was done 304:12
Kate: kiss me, K. 287:8
none of us cared for K. 288:9
Keats: who kill'd John K.? 70:17
Keen: rhy tooth is not so k. 245:1
Keener: grows k. with constant use 138:12
Keep: I k. my books at the British Museum 68:4
I love to k. it [work] by me 139:15
if you can k. yr. head 154:17
k. a thing seven years 217:32
k. up with the Joneses 217:34
Keeper: a k. is only a poacher 154:6
am I my brother's k.? 30:16
Kelly: has anybody here seen K.? 185:4
Kennel: permitted to have friends in the k. 296:15
Kensal Green: to Paradise by way of K. 81:8
Kent, sir—everybody knows K. 98:18
Kentucky: the old K. Home 112:7
Kept: that I k. my word, he said 96:15
Kettle: pot calls the k. black 223:18
Kew: go down to K. in lilac-time 188:1
His Highness' dog at K. 204:2
Key: Door to which I found no k. 110:6
with this k. Shakespeare unlocked 333:5
Keys: k. of the kingdom of heaven 44:17
send me the half that's got my k. 124:8
Khaki: one black ... one white ... two k. 13:2
Khatmandu: to the north of K. 129:6
Kick: be off or I'll k. you downstairs 74:4
hard ... to k. against the pricks 47:4
Kicked: Jeshurun waxed fat and k. 33:7
Kill: good to k. an admiral 321:10
I'll k. you if you quote it 64:2
k. a wife with kindness 287:10
k. the still-closing waters 288:15
let's k. all the lawyers 260:10
monarchize ... and k. with looks 283:6
shalt not k., but needst not strive 84:16
they k. us for their sport 266:20
thou shalt not k. 32:5
Killed: books cannot be k. by fire 235:5
I kiss'd thee ere I k. thee 281:1
k. by ... Cheltenham waters 11:17
man who was k. by lightning 11:18
who k. Cock Robin? 196:2
who k. John Keats? 70:17
Killing: k. my self, to die upon a kiss 281:1
k. of a mouse on Sunday 58:2
more ways of k. a cat 154:7
time: ... which ends in k. him 304:16
Kills: each man k. the thing he loves 326:12
gluttony k. more than the sword 214:38
k. a man k. a reasonable creature 182:2
k. me some ... dozen of Scots 254:12
k. reason itself, k. the image of God 182:2
Kin: more than k., and less than kind 247:18
one's own k. and kith 186:2
one touch of nature ... whole world k. 290:7
Kind: be to her virtues very k. 205:5

Kind (*continued*)
cruel only to be k. 252:15
dumb jewels ... in their silent k. 292:7
just the art of being k. 326:11
k. as she is fair 292:9
k. hearts are more than coronets 313:10
more than kin and less than k. 247:18
neither ingenious, sober, nor k. 12:3
what k. of people do they think we are? 83:3
Kindly: is sure of being k. spoken of 20:9
Kindness: A Woman Killed with K. 132:10
beauty lives with k. 292:9
kill a wife with k. 287:10
k. in another's trouble 124:6
save in the way of k. 317:12
tak' a cup o' k. 65:13
too full o' th' milk of human k. 270:1
unremembered acts of k., love 335:10
Kinds: soft maids and village k. 88:8
King: a little pin bores ... farewell, k.! 283:6
a new k. over Egypt 31:15
all the k.'s horses ... men 76:8, 189:9
as I have served the k. 330:6
ay, every inch a k. 267:3
catch the conscience of the K. 250:19
dainty dish, to set before the k.? 193:5
deny it [repose] to a k. 257:3
discharge my duties as K. 105:10
divinity doth hedge a k. 252:22
glory to the new-born K. 325:2
God save the K.! Will no man say amen? 284:1
have a k., and officers of sorts 258:8
he that plays the k. ... be welcome 250:7
here lies our sovereign lord the k. 234:11
I'm the k. of the castle 190:3
is the k. dead, the empire unpossess'd? 285:11
Judge that no k. can corrupt 261:7
k. is a thing men have made 241:5
k. is but a man as I am 259:10
K., observing with judicious eyes 318:1
k. of shreds and patches 252:13
K. shall do it ... shall be contented 283:7
k.'s name is a tower of strength 285:13
lad that's born to be k. 57:12
let us sing, Long live the K. 92:13
mortal temples of a k. 283:6
no bishop, no K. 139:1
Old K. Cole 192:1
old, mad, blind ... dying k. 300:5
one-eyed man is k. 208:12
our Gracious K. ... noble K. 73:1
passing brave to be a k. 166:9
so excellent a k. 248:3
sword of an angel k. 55:5
the K. asked the Queen and 171:11
the k. can do no wrong 54:10
the k. himself has followed her 122:16
the K. is strongest 51:5
the k. loved Esther 34:27
the k. never dies 54:9
the k.'s a bawcock ... heart of gold 259:9
the k. sits in Dunfermline 11:13
the K. to Oxford sent 60:4
think the K. knows all about me? 171:7
wash the balm off from an anointed k. 283:2

King (*continued*)
we will go by the k.'s high way 32:19
whatsoever K. shall reign 15:13
who Pretender is, or who is K. 68:15
with half the zeal I serv'd my k. 261:13
King Charles: in good K.'s golden days 15:12
King James ... call for his old shoes 241:1
King of the Jews: he that is born K. 43:8
Kingdom: for thine is the k. 43:24
keys of the k. of heaven 44:17
k. of heaven is at hand 43:10
my k. for a horse! 285:16
my large k. for a little grave 283:7
my mind to me a k. is 105:6
my new-found land, my k. 101:3
of such is the k. of God 45:13
stand upon my k. once again 283:1
state of man, like to a little k. 262:13
teach ... order to a peopled k. 258:8
thy k. come 43:24
thy k. is divided 42:3
Kingdoms: goodly states and k. seen 150:14
Kings: all K. is mostly rapscallions 318:9
captains and the k. depart 155:3
conquering k. their titles take 78:12
divorc'd so many English k. 257:17
dread and fear of k. 275:1
I know the k. of England 120:4
k. for such a tomb wd. ... die 175:13
k. it makes gods, and meaner creatures k. 285:12
k. that fear ... subjects' treachery 260:14
left lonely ... the k. of the sea 18:13
low ambition, and the pride of k. 202:17
mad world! mad k.! 264:12
mirror of all Christian k. 258:9
my throne, bid k. come bow 264:15
of cabbages—and k. 76:4
poor men's hovels ... K.' palaces 135:12
punctuality is the politeness of k. 162:4
sad stories of the death of k. 283:6
scorn to change my state with k. 293:17
showers on her k. barbaric pearl 176:15
such is the breath of K. 281:12
teeming womb of royal k. 282:5
the chase, the sport of k. 304:8
this royal throne of k. 282:5
King's English: an old abusing of ... the K. 276:3
Kinquering Congs their titles take 305:18
Kipling: when the Rudyards cease from k. 306:10
Kiss: ae fond k., and then we sever! 65:8
come let us k. and part 102:12
coward does it with a k. 326:12
gin a body k. a body 65:15
I dare not ask a k. ... a smile 132:2
I k. his dirty shoe 259:9
I saw you take his k. 198:11
if you can k. the mistress 218:5
k. and be friends 218:4
k. me, Hardy 187:7
k. me, Kate 287:8
k. me, sweet and twenty 291:2
k. me with the kisses of his mouth 40:2
leave a k. but in the cup 145:7
make me immortal with a k. 165:8
pale grew thy cheek ... colder thy k. 71:5
to die upon a k. 281:1
Kissed: but I k. her little sister 183:10
Kissed (*continued*)
hasn't been k. for forty years 236:14
I k. thee ere I kill'd thee 281:1
k. the girls and made them cry 189:3
k. the maiden all forlorn 194:8
Kisses: beneath the k. of Night 299:14
bread and cheese and k. 206:31
but my k. bring again 273:12
give me a thousand k. 77:15
I fear thy k., gentle maiden 300:7
I understand thy k., and thou mine 255:8
k. the joy as it flies 55:4
of many thousand k. the poor last 243:5
play'd at cards for k. 163:3
Kissing: k. don't last: cookery do! 170:4
k. yr. hand may make you feel ... good 162:1
when the k. had to stop 62:11
Kit-bag: troubles in your old k. 19:14
Kitchen: friends in the kennel, but not in the k. 296:15
taste of the k. is better 227:15
way of all flesh ... towards the k. 324:2
Kitten: rather be a k. and cry mew 255:6
Knave: a petty sneaking k. I knew 56:1
K. of Hearts, he stole those tarts 75:6, 192–3:8
Knee: not loved the world ... nor bow'd ... patient k. 69:5
silver buckles at his k. 188:5
Kneels at the foot of the bed 172:2
Knees: religion's ... not in the k. 139:17
spectacles lay on her aproned k. 71:16
Knell: by fairy hands their k. is rung 88:11
curfew tolls the k. of parting day 126:3
hear it not, Duncan, for it is a k. 270:10
Knew: fell to earth, I k. not where 160:10
I k. almost as much at eighteen 152:11
I k. him well, and every truant k. 122:11
men fell out they k. not why 67:14
new king ... which k. not Joseph 31:15
one small head cd. carry all he k. 122:12
Knife: cut it without a k. 191:4
cut off their tails ... carving k. 195:1
honey ... keeps them on the k. 13:10
smyler with the k. 79:20
Knight: a verray parfit gentle k. 79:2
gentle k. was pricking on the plain 305:10
k. of the sorrowful countenance 78:2
Knit: k. hands, and beat the ground 172:16
stuff of life to k. me 136:7
Knits up the ravell'd sleave of care 270:11
Knitting: in twisted braids of lilies k. 173:3
Knocked: k. 'em in the Old Kent Road 81:13
k. me down with a feather 218:7
Knocker: tie up the k., say ... I'm dead 201:10
Knocking: k. at Preferment's door 18:20
k. on the moonlit door 96:14
there's k. at the gate 272:4
Knocks you down with the butt end 124:2
Know: all Europe should k. we have blockheads 89:8
all ye need to k. 149:10
and when this we rightly k. 54:15
believe her, though I k. she lies 294:15
but I k. what I like 26:9
do you k. me, my lord? 249:18
does your mother k. you are out? 24:7
every wise man's son doth k. 291:1
he replied, Yes, I k. 13:1

Know (*continued*)
I don't k. anything ... really 26:9
I k. a bank ... wild thyme blows 276:20
I k. a reasonable woman 204:3
I k. the kings of England 120:4
I k. thee not, old man 258:3
I k. two things about the horse 13:11
I k. you all, and will ... uphold 253:20
I thought so once; but now I k. it 115:13
k. a subject ... k. where ... information 143:19
k. all that there is to be knowed 124:13
k. cause, or just impediment 53:18
k. then thyself 203:5
k. where the shoe pinches 225:16
little do we k. what lays afore us! 98:8
mad, bad, and dangerous to k. 156:1
no knowledge but I k. it 26:6
not to k. me ... yourselves unknown 178:9
not utter what thou dost not k. 254:11
O, that a man might k. the end 264:5
ol' man river ... must k. sumpin' 128:2
pleasant to k. Mr. Lear 158:6
she didn't k. what to do 194:5
than the devil you don't k. 207:35
they k. not what they do 46:13
this alone I k. full well 59:9
to k. that which before us lies 179:2
to k. this only, that he nothing knew 180:4
we are greater than we k. 334:10
what I don't k. isn't knowledge 26:6
what shd. they k. of England? 154:13
what the false heart doth k. 270:8
whom truly to k. is everlasting life 53:7
Knoweth: talketh what he k. 21:16
Knowing: as gods, k. good and evil 30:11
k. what shd. not be known 111:2
the misfortune of k. anything 20:15
thinking ... far from k. 227:33
Knowledge: a supercilious k. in accounts 301:9
all k. to be my province 23:14
all our k. is ourselves to know 203:12
conscious ... ignorant is a great step to k. 100:11
continual drinking of K. 152:2
darkeneth counsel by words without k. 35:12
ever-green tree of diabolical k. 301:7
fear of the Lord ... beginning of k. 38:1
having any k. of ... social order 296:9
his k. of life ... so hazy 197:11
increaseth k. increaseth sorrow 39:13
k. comes, but wisdom lingers 313:18
k. enormous makes a God 148:9
k. is of two kinds 143:19
k. is power 218:12
k. of God more than burnt offerings 42:8
night unto night showeth k. 35:23
science is organised k. 305:1
smattering of everything ... k. of nothing 99:11
still climbing after k. infinite 166:10
Thou ... art still, out-topping k. 19:2
to know no more is woman's happiest k. 178:7
Zeal without k. is fire without light 231:15
Known: best that has been k. and said 19:11
best that is k. and thought 19:8
I am k. and do not want [patronage] 142:1
Known (*continued*)
k. by the company he keeps 220:18
Knows: a woman conceals what she k. not 230:30
I never k. the children 167:6
if you k. of a better 'ole 23:22
k. nought that k. not this 289:15
no man truly k. another 59:16
nobody k. how to write letters 89:11
the more a man k. 295:19
travels far, k. much 228:18
wise father that k. his own child 274:12
Kubla: in Xanadu did K. Khan 87:11
K. heard from far ancestral voices 87:14
Kyd: Lyly outshine, or sporting K. 145:13

Labor omnia vicit ... egestas 321:6
Laborare est orare 218:16
Labour: crowns a youth of l. 122:7
ease and alternate l. 316:13
l., and do all thy work 32:3
l. and the wounds are vain 85:1
l. night and day to be a pilgrim 63:14
l. of an age in piled stones 175:11
months without ... any kind of l. 322:14
persistent l. overcame all things 321:6
six days shalt thou l. 32:3
sore l.'s bath 270:11
true success is to l. 307:10
votes L. ought to be locked up 183:7
yr. work of faith ... l. of love 49:5
Labourer: l. is worthy of his hire 45:27
now the l.'s task is o'er 107:16
Labours: children sweeten l. 21:18
Lack: sigh the l. of many a thing 293:18
Lacked: being l. and lost ... rack the value 278:12
Lacrimae: hinc illae l. 315:1
Lad: and many a lightfoot l. 136:8
cd. that l. be I? 307:3
l. that's born to be king 57:12
song of a l. that is gone 307:3
when I was a l. I served a term 119:15
Ladder: a l. set up on the earth 31:9
down the l. when thou marriest 214:39
l. of all high designs 290:2
wiv a l. and some glasses 25:3
Ladies: a lion among l. ... dreadful 276:21
eleven l. dancing 194:2
good night, sweet l. 252:20
rhyme themselves into l.' favours 260:4
sigh no more, l. 277:21
store of l., whose bright eyes 174:6
Lads: golden l. and girls ... come to dust 247:9
though yr. l. are far away 111:12
two l. that thought ... to be boy eternal 292:12
Lady: a l. of a certain age 70:4
a l. sweet and kind 17:2
and in my l.'s chamber 189:4
courting his l. in the spring 58:4
faint heart never won fair l. 213:9
fine l. upon a white horse 193:1
for secrecy, no l. closer 254:11
I met a l. in the meads 148:15
I want to talk like a l. 296:19
make a l. of my own 335:9
my l. sweet, arise 246–7:13
old l. of Threadneedle Street 227:37

Lady (*continued*)
returned ... with the l. inside 12:10
sighed for the love of a l. 121:2
swear ... like a l. as thou art 255:9
the elder unto the elect l. 50:14
the l. doth protest too much 252:4
there ain't a l. livin' 81:14
there was a young l. named Bright 63:1
they have belied a l. 278:18
went ... to tempt My L. Poltagrue 27:8
Lady Disdain! Are you yet living? 277:11
Ladybird, fly away home 190:8
Ladylike: the birch, most ... l. of trees 162:13
Lady-smocks all silver-white 268:17
Lag: in England ... a comfortable time-l. 324:15
Laid: in sad cypress ... l. 291:6
Laissez faire, laissez passer 232:6
Lake: beside the l., beneath the trees 331:7
Lamb: brought as a l. to the slaughter 41:7
did he who made the L. make thee? 56:6
go to bed with the l. 215:1
little l., who made thee? 56:9
Mary had a little l. 127:11
pipe a song about a l. 56:8
tempers the wind to the shorn l. 215:11, 306:15
was the holy L. ... on England's ... pastures seen? 55:8
wolf ... shall dwell with the l. 40:24
Lambs: death devours l. as well as sheep 211:5
little hills [skipped] like l. 37:7
while the young l. bound 331:15
Lament: have I not reason to l. 332:8
short pleasure, long l. 225:20
Lamp: I light my l. in the evening 28:2
Lamps: bright the l. shone o'er fair women 69:3
l. are going out all over Europe 127:8
who will change old l.? 18:1
Land: a traveller from an antique l. 299:7
a woman is a foreign l. 198:12
England's green and pleasant l. 55:8
gone far away into the silent l. 236:1
ill fares the l. 122:5
l. flowing with milk and honey 31:18
l. of hope and glory 28:10
l. of the free ... home of the brave 153:7
l. where the Bong-tree grows 158:8
my America, my new-found l. 101:3
my native L.—Good Night! 69:2
my own, my native l.! 239:16
o'er all the pleasant l. 130:5
ring out the darkness of the l. 313:7
stranger in a strange l. 31:16
sweet l. of liberty 303:10
they are not fit to live on l. 143:21
they came upon a l. ... always afternoon 314:1
westward, look, the l. is bright 85:3
whistles o'er the furrowed l. 174:3
Landing grounds: we shall fight on the l. 82:13
Landlord: come, l., fill the ... bowl 14:14
Lands: close to the sun in lonely l. 312:1
l. where the Jumblies live 158:5
Landscape: now fades the glimmering l. on the sight 126:4
Lane: an England while ... a country l. 198:4
Lane (*continued*)
little boy who lives down the l. 188:4
Language: if everything else in our l. shd. perish 164:3
l. in her eye, her cheek 290:8
Lord did ... confound the l. 30:27
natural l. of the heart 241:18
no l. but the l. of the heart 201:20
no tracing ... but by l. 144:23
plague rid you for learning me yr. l. 287:19
sorry when any l. is lost 144:23
stability or enlargement of the l. 140:3
sure in l. strange she said 148:17
thunder in such lovely l. 157:11
use any l. you choose 117:12
you taught me l., and my profit on't 287:19
yr. ... l. is the l. of Shakespeare 296:18
Languages: all l. living and dead 98:9
three or four l. ... without book 290:11
Languid: the l. strings do scarcely move 56:14
Lap: his head upon the l. of earth 126:13
in thy green l. was Nature's Darling 127:1
Lards the lean earth as he walks 254:9
Large as life, and twice as natural 77:5
Largest: shout with the l. [mob] 98:20
Lark: no l. more blithe than he 54:1
rise with the l. 215:1
the l.'s on the wing 62:7
to hear the l. begin his flight 174:2
Larks: hear the l. so high about us 136:6
two Owls ... four L. and a Wren 158:13
Lars Porsena of Clusium 163:9
Lashed the vice, but spared the name 308:13
Lass: I loved a l., a fair one 329:10
yon solitary Highland L. 334:16
Lasses: come, l. and lads 14:15
he dearly lov'd the l. 66:2
hours ... spent amang the l. 66:1
Last: die ... the l. thing I shall do! 198:1
filling his l. cavity. . 12:7
heard the l. of her ... I wonder! 297:5
it will not l. the night 170:13
kissing don't l.: cookery do! 170:4
l. but not least 218:18
L. of the Mohicans 90:11
l. out a night in Russia 273:3
l. taste of sweets, is sweetest l. 282:3
might be the l., my Mary! 93:13
of many thousand kisses the poor l. 243:5
rash ... blaze of riot cannot l. 282:4
the l. of life, for wh. the first was made 62:9
there is no l. nor first 62:8
well, I cannot l. ever 256:10
Late: better l. than never 207:30
good to marry l. or never 220:32
make haste, and come too l. 282:2
marries l., marries ill 220:28
never too l. to mend 221:34
too l. to save the stamp 124:9
Lately: read any good books l.? 185:3
Latin: away with him! He speaks L. 260:12
must carve in L. or in Greek 322:2
small L. and less Greek 145:14
Latter: meeter to carry off the l. 199:6
Laugh: and l. at gilded butterflies 267:13
if I l. at any mortal thing 70:2
l. and the world l. with you 326:9
l. as I pass in thunder 298:5
l. to scorn the pow'r of man 271:15

Laugh (*continued*)
l. where we must, be candid 202:18
loud l. that spoke the vacant mind 122:8
love I l. to scorn 58:14
make 'em l. ... cry ... wait 233:5
men that l. and weep 309:18
the l. broke into ... pieces 24:11
who but must l.? 201:17
Laughed: little dog l. to see such sport 189:5
no man who has ... wholly l. 73:11
when the first baby l. 24:11
Laughing is heard on the hill 56:11
Laughs: flabby hands and irritating l. 118:4
he l. best who l. last 218:21
Laughter: drinks his wine 'mid l. free 17:3
I heard the l. of her heart 128:1
invent anything that tends to l. 256:8
it wd. be ... l. for a month 254:8
L. holding both his sides 173:17
l., learnt of friends 59:7
nothing so ... ill-bred as audible l. 80:13
present mirth hath present l. 291:2
ran ... after the ... music with ... l. 62:6
sincerest l. with some pain is fraught 300:2
so is the l. of the fool 39:19
tired of tears and l. 309:18
Laundry: general idea ... in any ... l. 157:15
Laurel: burned is Apollo's l.-bough 166:1
l. is green for a season 310:4
l. outlives not May 310:4
Laurels: the l. all are cut 136:3
yet once more, O ye l. 174:12
Lavinia: she is L. ... must be loved 289:13
Law: against reason, ... of no force in l. 85:7
agree, for the l. is costly 206:9
and the l. doth give it 275:5
and this is l. that I'll maintain 15:13
dusty purlieus of the l. 312:18
every l. is a contract 241:6
glorious uncertainty of the l. 229:9
God is thy l., thou mine 178:7
good of the people ... chief l. 84:2
hard cases make bad l. 216:12
higher l. than the Constitution 241:17
I ... embody the L. 117:2
in l.'s grave study 85:9
in vice their l.'s their will 281:4
l. is a bottomless pit 218:22
l. is an ass—a idiot 98:15
l. makers shd. not be l. breakers 218:24
love ... fulfilling of the l. 47:29
love has never known a l. 326:6
may be ... good l. for all that 240:11
much l., but little justice 221:20
nature's l. that man was made to mourn 66:7
necessity hath no l. 221:23
one God, one l., one element 313:9
one l. for the rich 218:23
other sources of international l. 319:5
ought l. to weed it out 21:12
possession is nine points of the l. 223:17
pounds of l., ... not an ounce of love 227:36
rich men rule the l. 123:16
self-preservation is the first l. 225:13
take the l. into one's own hands 227:5
the l. hath not been dead 273:5
the L. is the true embodiment 117:2
the l. of the Yukon 241:15
the L. of Triviality 198:6
the l.'s delay 250–1:20
Law (*continued*)
the more l., the more offenders 218:25
these ... a l. unto themselves 47:16
this is the l. and the prophets 44:7
this is the L. of the Jungle 154:21
wedded Love, mysterious l. 178:8
windy side of the l. 291:16
wrest once the l. to yr. authority 275:2
Lawn as white as driven snow 293:3
Laws: know not whether l. be right 326:15
l. grind the poor and rich men rule the law 123:16
l. of England are at my commandment 258:2
l. of the Persians ... Medes 34:26
l. were made to be broken 187:17
let ... l. and learning die 237:10
Nature's L. lay hid in Night 201:21
religion breathing household l. 333:11
repeal of bad or obnoxious l. 125:2
sweeter manners, purer l. 313:5
Lawyers: few l. die well 213:22
let's kill all the l. 260:10
Lay on, Macduff 272:14
Lazy: liftin' the l. ones on 125:5
mentally l. ... as well be dead 324:18
Lead: do scald like molten l. 267:10
l., Kindly Light ... l. thou me on 187:14
strange ... the life he makes us l. 60:10
Leaden-eyed despairs 149:15
Leadeth me beside the still waters 35:28
Leaf: fall'n into the sear, the yellow l. 272:5
lowest boughs ... are in tiny l. 61:1
November's l. is red 240:3
take a l. out of one's book 226:38
turn over a new l. 228:31
where the dead l. fell ... did it rest 148:5
League: half a l. onward 311:9
keep a l. till death 284:4
Lean: his wife cd. eat no l. 190:7
l. and slipper'd pantaloon 244:11
Leap: a great l. in the dark 133:4
methinks it were an easy l. 254:4
Leaps: morn doth break ... l. in the sky 58:3
my heart l. up when I behold 333:8
Leapt: into the dangerous world I l. 56:3
Leap-year: twenty-nine in each l. 194:6
Lear: how pleasant to know Mr. L. 158:6
Learn: gladly wolde he l. 79:10
l. by other men's mistakes 230:25
l. to labour and to wait 161:2
live and l. 219:19
they will l. at no other 64:15
we l. nothing from history 296:10
Learned: he was naturally l. 104:4
loads of l. lumber in his head 202:15
that ... grew within this l. man 166:1
that l. body wanted loyalty 318:1
Learning: a little l. is a dangerous thing 202:5
better than a bushel of l. 216:1
l. is but an adjunct to ourself 268:12
l. makes ... better ... worse 218:30
l.'s triumph o'er her barb'rous foes 140:19
l. without thought ... thought without l. 89:4
love of money and love of l. 220:5
loyal body wanted l. 318:1
more aid than any l. 310:7
on scraps of l. dote 337:11
whence is thy l.? 115:9
Learnt nothing, and forgotten nothing 310:12

Lease: summer's l. ... too short a date 293:13
Leave: comrades, l. me here a little 313:14
fare thee well, for I must l. thee 17:4
l. me there to die 15:9
l. this barren spot to me 72:7
l. us nought but grief an' pain 66:12
Oh, never l. me! 15:1
Leaven: a little l. leaveneth ... lump 48:1
Leaves: generation of l. ... is that of men 134:8
his hoar l. in the glassy stream 253:1
l. dead are driven, like ghosts 299:3
life out of the dead l. 157:9
lisp of l. 309:14
puts forth the tender l. of hope 261:9
they sewed fig l. together 30:12
with forced fingers rude shatter your l. 174:12
with l. and flowers do cover 324:3
Leben: unnütz L. ... früher Tod 122:2
Lecher: gilded fly does l. in my sight 267:4
Lechery: an equivocator with l. 270:14
l., l.! still wars and l.! 290:9
Lectures: cannot see that l. can do so much good 143:1
I do not give l. or ... charity 326:3
Led by the nose with gold 293:8
Leer: assent with civil l. 201:16
Left: a lady richly l. 274:4
ah! he l. the thorn with me 67:7
l. for contemplation not what ... used 29:11
l. him alone with his glory 330:4
sun came up upon the l. 85:13
we that are l. grow old 54:5
Leg: can honour set to a l.? 255:21
have a bone in one's l. 208:15
here I leave my second l. 134:12
Legion: my name is L. 45:9
Legions: give me back my l. 71:9
Legislators: poets are the unacknowledged l. 300:11
Legs: a cannon-ball took off his l. 134:11
on one's last l. 218:19
vast and trunkless l. of stone 299:7
walk under his huge l. 262:8
Leicester Square: farewell, L. 329:1
Leisure: busiest men ... most l. 208:37
detest at l. 70:7
l. answers l. 273:14
Lely: Mr. L., ... paint my picture 94:10
Lend: give a shilling than l. a half-crown 207:28
I'll l. you something 291:17
men who borrow ... men who l. 156:2
when I l. I am a friend 218:35
Lender: neither a borrower nor a l. be 248:17
Lends: he l. out money gratis 274:7
three things I never l. 308:7
Length: what [happiness] lacks in l. 113:15
Leopard: can the ... l. [change] his spots? 41:14
l. shall lie down with the kid 40:24
Leprosy: her skin was as white as l. 86:8
Lesbia: let us live, my L. 77:14
vivamus, mea L., atque amemus 77:14
Less: I love not man the l. 69:9
l. than [square deal] no man shall have 235:9
one failing, had a woman ever l.? 66:6
stand ... l. betwn. me and the sun 99:19
Less (*continued*)
the little l., and what worlds away 60:15
you mean you can't take *l.* 74:10
Lessen: they l. from day to day 75:1
Lessons: reason they're called l. 75:1
Lethe: no, no, go not to L. 149:11
Letter: the l. killeth 48:14
thou unnecessary l.! 265:18
Letters: his sayings ... like women's l. 129:7
I am persecuted with l. 89:11
I pray you, in yr. l. 280:14
l. get in the wrong places 172:8
nobody knows how to write l. 89:11
Lettuces had been so soporific 204:14
Leveller: death is the grand l. 211:6
Levellers: yr. l. wish to level down 142:12
Levers to lift me up ... being down? 254:7
Leviathan: canst thou draw out l.? 35:14
Lexicographer.—a harmless drudge 140:7
Lexicography: not yet so lost in l. 140:2
Liar ... when he speaks the truth 218:39
Liars: all men are l. 37:10
great talkers are great l. 215:29
l. ought to [should] have good memories 218:40, 302:1
Libel: greater the truth, the greater the l. 215:31
Liberal: is either a little L. 117:8
Liberté: l., égalité, fraternité 17:8
O L.! que de crimes ... en ton nom! 234:16
Libertine: puff'd and reckless l. 248:14
the air, a charter'd l. 258:7
Liberty: give me l. or ... death 131:4
God hath given l. to man 95:3
L. and Union, now and for ever 323:10
l. cannot long exist 64:19
l., equality, fraternity 17:8
l. is precious ... must be rationed 159:3
l. means responsibility ... men dread it 296:12
l. ... must be limited 64:18
L. of the Press ... the *Palladium* 146:5
l.'s in every blow 67:2
l. to know, to utter 182:9
marries for wealth, sells his l. 220:27
mountain-nymph, sweet L. 173:18
O l., l., what crimes ... in yr. name! 234:16
sweet life of l. 303:10
thy chosen music, L. 333:10
Liberty Hall: this is L. 123:8
Library: a circulating l. in a town 301:7
my l. was dukedom ... enough 287:17
vanity of ... hopes ... public l. 141:2
Libre: l'homme est né l. ... est dans les fers 236:12
Licence: Government l. to print money 316:14
the rest love not freedom, but l. 182:11
Licht: mehr L.! 122:3
Lick: ill cook that cannot l. his own fingers 210:9, 287:2
to l. into shape 219:1
Licked: they l. the platter clean 190:7
Lie: a cat and a l. 318:17
a l. begets a l. 219:2
after all, what is a l.? 70:5
and they all dead did l. 86:11
Father, I cannot tell a l. 322:18
honest man sent to l. abroad 336:11
I knowed it was a l. 318:8

Lie (*continued*)
not a stone tell where I l. 204:1
nothing can need a l. 131:9
oft when on my couch I l. 331:11
painters and poets have leave to l. 222:33
seventh, the L. Direct 246:2
the L. with Circumstance 246:2
where my heart lies, let my brain l. 61:13
while you here do snoring l. 288:5
who loves to l. with me 244:4
Lied: Heart replied ... but it l. 27:9
Lies: ask no questions ... be told no l. 206:24
beats all the l. you can invent 54:14
believe her, though I know she l. 294:15
one of the social l. 138:3
one thing is certain ... Rest is L. 110:4
three kinds of l. 318:10
where my heart l. 61:13
Life: a daily beauty in his l. 280:8
a handful of good l. 216:1
a keen observer of l. 20:3
a lad of l., an imp of fame 259:9
a l. like the scriptures 152:7
a l. on the ocean wave 238:8
a space of l. between 147:7
a useless l. is an early death 122:2
after l.'s fitful fever he sleeps well 271:4
all his l. ... speaking the truth 327:18
all the blessings of this l. 53:1
all the voyage of their l. is bound 264:3
all this flesh keeps in a little l. 256:2
and l. is thorny 87:7
any practical part of l. 9:6
anything for a quiet l. 99:10, 206:18
art is long, but l. is short 132:13
as large as l. 218:17
bankrupt of l., yet prodigal of ease 103:1
before us lies in daily l. 179:2
best of l. is but intoxication 69:15
best portion of a good man's l. 335:10
brief l. is here our portion 186:13
cannot tell what you ... think of this l. 262:6
care of human l. ... not their destruction 139:10
commuter—one who spends his l. 325:8
compare human l. to ... Mansion 152:3
custom ... great guide of ... l. 137:2
dear ... as light and l. 66:3
death after l. doth greatly please 305:11
digestion is the great secret of l. 303:17
doth the wingèd l. destroy 55:4
each change of many-colour'd l. 140:19
essential thing in l. is not conquering 91:2
expect more from l. than l. will afford 143:5
fie upon this quiet l.! 254:12
giveth his l. for the sheep 46:27
he that cuts off twenty years of l. 263:3
his name out of the book of l. 50:18
I bear a charmed l. 272:12
I do not set my l. at a pin's fee 249:4
I fall upon the thorns of l. 299:5
I will give thee a crown of l. 50:16
in London all that l. can afford 144:9
in the midst of l. we are in death 53:29
is l. a boon? 120:17
isn't l. a terrible thing? 316:4
its private l. is a disgrace 14:6
I've done it all my l. 13:10
large as l. and twice as natural 77:5
Life (*continued*)
last of l. for which the first 62:9
lay hold on l. 183:2
letter killeth ... spirit giveth l. 48:14
l. for l., eye for eye 32:10
l., force and beauty must ... impart 202:3
l. ... is a continual allegory 152:7
l. is a jest 115:13
l. is as tedious as a twice-told tale 264:17
l. is but a day; a ... dew-drop 150:9
l. is but an empty dream 160:14
l. is just one damned thing after another 136:12
l. is mostly froth and bubble 124:6
l. is ... process of getting tired 68:5
L. is real! L. is earnest 160:14
l. is sweet 219:5
l. is the art of drawing ... conclusions 68:6
l. is very sweet, brother 57:8
l. isn't all beer and skittles 136:13
l., liberty, ... pursuit of happiness 139:6
l., like a dome of many-coloured glass 298:2
l. protracted is protracted woe 141:12
l. ... solitary, poor, nasty, brutish 133:3
l., time's fool 256:1
l.'s too short for chess 71:8
live a barren sister all yr. l. 276:9
love is of man's l. a thing apart 69:14
make l., death ... for-ever one ... song 154:2
makes calamity of so long l. 250–1:20
man's l. is cheap as beast's 266:2
married to a single l. 94:2
measured out my l. with coffee spoons 106:14
mine honour is my l. 281:8
modern l. ... tedious, ... and modern literature 327:7
most of the change ... in l. 113:9
no, no, no l. 268:4
nor love thy l., nor hate 179:14
not so much l. as on a summer's day 148:5
nothing in his l. became him 269:11
O for a L. of Sensations! 151:10
on human l., musing in solitude 331:3
on the Tree of L. ... sat 178:1
one good deed in all my l. 289:14
our l., exempt from public haunt 243:15
our l. is frittered away by detail 317:1
our little l. is rounded ... sleep 288:16
my l. is one demd horrid grind 98:11
my way of l. ... the yellow leaf 272:5
pass them for a nobler l. 150:11
people say that L. is the thing 303:8
preach ... doctrine of strenuous l. 235:7
promise them l. and then kill them 319:8
quickening l. from the Earth's heart 297:11
saw l. steadily and ... whole 18:14
sells us l. at a discount 114:3
she is coming, my l., my fate 314:4
short l. and a merry one 225:19
shd. ... have everlasting l. 46:21
so careless of the single l. 312:16
soldier's l. is terrible hard 171:6
spare all I have and take my l. 109:5
spend my l. in driving briskly 144:7
strange disease of modern l. 18:21
stuff of l. to knit me 136:7
sucking his l. out of the dead leaves 157:9
take away my good name ... my l. 226:39

Life (*continued*)
take honour ... and my l. is done 281:8
that a man lay down his l. 46:31
that no l. lives for ever 310:1
that state of l., unto which 53:15
the death of each day's l. 270:11
the l. he makes us lead! 60:10
the l. so short, the craft so long to lerne 80:4
the nobler modes of l. 313:5
the passion and the l. 87:9
the rest of his dull l. 25:7
there are two tragedies in l. 296:8
there is no wealth but l. 237:6
therefore choose l. 33:5
this gives l. to thee 293:15
this long disease, my L. 201:14
those with irrational fear of l. 90:4
thoughts, the slaves of l. 256:1
to the vagrant gypsy l. 168:17
travel on l.'s common way 333:13
travelled l.'s dull round 300:12
treasured up ... to a l. beyond l. 182:3
upright l., unstained by guilt 135:14
useful l., progressive virtue 316:13
variety's ... spice of l. 93:8
warmed both hands before the fire of l. 156:11
way of l. uncertain 147:7
we see into the l. of things 335:12
weariest and most loathed worldly l. 273:11
what is this l. if, full of care 96:2
what kind of l. did you give me? 324:17
while ... l. there is hope 219:6
whom ... to know is everlasting l. 53:7
yr. l. extremely flat 120:13
yr. money or yr. l.! 221:14
yr. money or yr. l.; women require 68:13
Life-in-death: the Night-mare L. was she 86:8
Lifeless: he is l. that is faultless 219:7
Lifetime: lamps ... lit again in our l. 127:8
Lift: l. not thy hands to It 110:13
l. them high ... before you drop them 319:8
oh, l. me as a wave, a leaf 299:5
Light: a certain slant of l. 99:16
apparelled in celestial l. 331:12
casting a dim religious l. 173:11
clear, unchang'd, and universal l. 202:3
come forth into the l. of things 335:6
common as l. is love 299:12
dear ... as l. and life 66:3
God appears, and God is l. 55:1
God said, Let there be l. 30:2
God saw the l. was good 178:21
God's first creature ... l. 23:15
gone into the world of l. 320:5
hail, Holy L., offspring of Heaven 177:9
Heaven's l. forever shines 298:2
Hesperus entreats thy l. 145:8
how my l. is spent 181:10
I can again thy former l. restore 280:11
in a Noose of L. 109:13
it gives a lovely l. 170:13
lead, Kindly L. 187:14
Let Newton be! and all was L. 201:21
l. breaks where no sun shines 315:18
l. that never was, on sea or land 331:1
l. the Day ... he named 178:21
Light (*continued*)
more l.! 122:3
out of Hell leads up to l. 177:5
passion for sweetness and l. 19:10
Promethean heat that can thy l. relume 280:11
pursuit of sweetness and l. 19:5
put out the l., and then put out the l. 280:11
shower of l. is poesy 150:12
teach l. to counterfeit a gloom 173:9
the dying of the l. 315:15
the l. of common day 332:2
the l. of the world 46:25
The L. that Failed 155:11
the people ... have seen a great l. 40:22
things l. and swoln ... weighty 23:10
too l. winning, make the prize l. 288:2
true l. which lighteth every man 46:15
two noblest ... sweetness and l. 308:11
what l. through yonder window? 286:6
when my l. is low 312:14
who art a l. to guide, a rod 334:3
wiser than the children of l. 46:6
with a l. behind her 120:15
Light Brigade: forward, the L. 311:10
Lighten: l. our darkness 52:20
now, the Lord l. thee! 256:16
Lighter than vanity 63:9
Lighthouse: took the sitivation at the l. 99:10
Lighting a little Hour or two 110:1
Lightly come, l. go 219:10
Lightning: I have known the l.'s hour 96:6
man who was killed by l. 11:18
the l. of the nations 299:2
thunder, l., or in rain 269:3
Lights: l. that do mislead the morn 273:12
turn up the l. ... home in the dark 131:3
Like: a God, or something very l. Him 84:14
I know what I l. 26:9
I l. two months of every year 68:17
I shall not look upon his l. again 248:9
l. and dislike the same things 237:15
l. doth quit l., and Measure still for Measure 273:14
l. to be Beside the Seaside 121:14
people who l. this sort of thing 160:2
Liked it not, and died 336:12
Liking: I have a l. old for thee 72:4
Lilac: down to Kew in l.-time 188:1
just now the l. is in bloom 59:2
Lilacs out of the dead land 107:3
Lilies: consider the l. of the field 44:3
in twisted braids of l. knitting 173:3
l. that fester smell far worse 294:3
peacocks and l. 237:3
the l. and languors of virtue 309:17
where roses and white l. grow 72:13
Lily: I am the ... l. of the valleys 40:4
to paint the l. 264:19
Limb: care I for the l., the thews ... bulk? 257:9
Limbo: into a L. large and broad 177:11
Limbs: your l. they are alive 336:6
Limericks: whose l. never wd. scan 13:1
Lime-tree Bower my prison 87:17
Limited in order to be possessed 64:18
Limits: beyond the l. of a vulgar fate 127:2
Line: l. stretch out to th' crack of doom? 271:17

Line (*continued*)
must draw the l. somewhere 211:33
the Brighton l. ... the l. is immaterial 327:14
to cancel half a l. 110:12
to l. one's pockets 219:14
we carved not a l. 330:4
Linen: choose neither ... l. by candle-light 209:25
old l. wash whitest 324:1
Lines: with silken l. and silver hooks 100:17
Lingering: something l., with boiling oil 118:14
Lingers: borrowing only l. and l. it out 256:12
Linguistics: An Essay in Sociological L. 235:14
Lining: there's a silver l. 111:12
Linnet: a l. courting his lady 58:4
come, hear the woodland l. 335:5
Lion: a l. among ladies 276:21
dar'st ... beard the l. ... The Douglas 240:7
in like a l., ... out like a lamb 220:23
l. is not so fierce as ... painted 219:15
nation ... had the l. heart 83:14
not a more fearful wildfowl than ... l. 276:21
rouse a l. than to start a hare 254:3
the devil, as a roaring l. 50:8
the l. and the unicorn 190:9
the l. looked at Alice wearily 77:6
Lions: cast him into the den of l. 42:5
Saul and Jonathan ... stronger than l. 34:11
Lip: keep a stiff upper l. 77:11, 226:20
Lips: beauty's ensign is crimson in thy l. 287:3
cd. you hurt me, sweet l.? 309:17
dear red curve of her l. 168:12
her l. suck forth my soul 165:8
her l. were red, her looks were free 86:8
take, O, take, those l. away 273:12
their l. were four red roses 285:8
through my l. to unawakened earth 299:6
truth sits upon the l. of dying men 19:3
what l. my l. have kissed 170:14
when I ope my l. let no dog bark 274:3
where my Julia's l. do smile 131:13
Liquefaction of her clothes 132:6
Liquid: Thames is l. history 65:7
Liquidation: preside over the l. of the British Empire 83:6
Liquor: l. is quicker 186:8
they sell worse kinds of l. 322:12
Lisp of leaves and ripple of rain 309:14
List: I've got a little l. 118:4
I wd. not enter on my l. of friends 93:12
l., l., O, l.! 249:7
Listen: darkling I l. 150:3
l. with credulity to ... fancy 141:3
the world shd. l. then 300:3
Listened: I l., motionless and still 335:1
Listeners hear no good of themselves 219:16
Lit again in our lifetime 127:8
Literature: he has raised the price of l. 142:3
itch of l. comes over a man 162:9
l. flourishes best when it is half a trade 138:7
that great Cham of l. 304:3
the rest is just l. 320:9
to produce a little l. 139:4
Litter: all her l. but one 256:8
Littérature: tout le reste est l. 320:9
Little: a l. of what you fancy 160:5
a l. still she strove 69:11
comrades, leave me here a l. 313:14
every l. helps 212:30
give according to that l. 51:8
goin' through so much to learn so l. 99:3
great ones eat up the l. ones 281:5
having too l. to do 155:9
I thought so l. they rewarded me 119:16
if I'm content with a l. 54:3
it was a very l. one 167:5
knows l., soon repeats it 218:14
knows l. who will tell his wife all 114:9
l. breezes dusk and shiver 313:12
l. drops ... l. grains ... l. minutes 73:13
l. things please l. minds 219:18
l. things ... the most important 101:12
l. we see in nature that is ours 333:3
love me l., love me long 220:3
man wants but l. drink below 134:2
man wants but l., nor that l. long 338:2
many a l. makes a mickle 220:22
no great ones if ... no l. ones 215:28
nor wants that l. long 122:15
obedience is ... seen in l. things 222:21
so l. done, so much to do 233:10
such a l. tail behind 27:1
the l. less, and what worlds away 60:15
the l. more, and how much 60:15
think too l. ... talk too much 103:3
through so much to learn so l. 99:3
wealth is contentment with a l. 229:39
Live: a bachelor, I l. by myself 16:3
anything but—l. for it [religion] 88:17
bear to l. or dare to die 203:7
better to l. rich 144:11
but a short time to l. 53:28
but one bare hour to l. 165:10
come l. with me and be my love 100:17, 167:1
crabbed age and youth cannot l. together 295:1
desire ... to l. beyond its income 68:7
eat to l. ... not l. to eat 212:16
I had as lief not be as l. 262:6
I marvel how the fishes l. 281:5
I with thee will choose to l. 173:13
in our embers is something that doth l. 332:4
let me l. unseen, unknown 204:1
l. a fool the rest of his dull life 25:7
l. and learn 219:19
l. and let l. 219:20
l., and move, and have our being 47:6
l. as the Romans do 10:10
l., for the truth is living 310:5
loves to l. i' th' sun 244:6
may l. to fight another day 13:8
Mirth, with thee I mean to l. 174:11
not l. by bread only 32:23
not suffer a witch to l. 32:11
other men l. to eat 304:6
rogues ... want to l. for ever? 113:5
she ... tried to l. without him 336:12
so we'll l., and pray, and sing 267:13
so wise, so young, ... never l. long 285:2
take the means whereby I l. 275:6
threatened men l. long 227:38
to l. is like love 68:8
to l. with her and l. with thee 174:1

Live (*continued*)
to l. with thee and be thy love 232:14
we that l. to please 141:1
what thou liv'st l. well 179:14
will it not l. with the living? 255:21
you might as well l. 198:3
Lived: for I have l. to-day 104:16
I have l. long enough 310:3
l. in the odium ... sodium 29:5
l. on, and so did I 86:11
who has never loved has never l. 115:8
Liver: open and notorious evil l. 53:9
Livery: in her sober l. all things clad 178:6
Lives: a history in all men's l. 257:5
all that l. must die 247:20
as a man l., so shall he die 220:19
cat has only nine l. 318:17
constancy l. in realms above 87:7
he l. ... 'tis Death is dead 297:17
he preaches well that l. well 223:25
he who l. more l. than one 326:14
l. in eternity's sunrise 55:4
l. of great men all remind us 161:1
love l. in cottages ... courts 219:40
men lead l. of quiet desperation 316:15
not how a man dies, but how he l. 143:4
one really l. nowhere 65:5
so long l. this, and this gives life 293:15
the music of men's l. 284:7
there l. more faith in ... doubt 313:1
Living: from too much love of l. 310:1
Homer ... who, l., had no roof 132:9
Lady Disdain, are you yet l.? 277:11
live, for the truth is l. 310:5
l. ... eight years with a strange man 138:2
l., shall forfeit fair renown 240:1
plain l. and high thinking 333:11
the l. need charity 18:8
the mother of all l. 30:15
the noble L. 334:6
'tis the l. up to [faith] 315:6
we have gone on l., l. and partly l. 107:9
Livingstone: Dr. L., I presume 306:4
Lizzie Borden took an axe 14:3
Load: how to l. and bless with fruit 147:1
Loaf: half a l. is better 215:36
of a cut l. to steal a shive 289:13
Loafe: I l. and invite my soul 326:1
Loan oft loses both itself and friend 248:17
Lobster: the voice of the l. 75:4
Lochinvar: never was Knight like ... L. 240:6
young L. is come out of the west 240:5
Lock: l., stock and barrel 219:22
prison with a life-long l. 118:7
Locks: her l. were yellow as gold 86:8
knotted and combined l. to part 249:7
pluck up ... honour by the l. 254:4
shaking her invincible l. 182:8
yr. l. were like the raven 66:5
Locust: years that the l. hath eaten 42:12
Lodge: where thou lodgest, I will l. 33:25
Loftiness: in l. of thought surpass'd 104:11
Lofty and sour to them that lov'd him not 262:2
Log: on a l., expiring frog 98:21
Logic: as it isn't, it ain't. That's l. 75:15
grape that can with L. absolute 110:10
l. and rhetoric [make] able to contend 23:9
un-to l. hadde longe y-go 79:7
Logs: bring me pine l. hither 187:2
Logs (*continued*)
Tom bears l. into the hall 269:1
Loitering: alone and palely l. 148:14
Lombard Street to a China orange 219:23
London: a L. particular ... A fog 97:9
as L. is to Paddington 72:17
citizen ... of famous L. town 92:6
hell is ... much like L. 299:9
it isn't far from L. 188:1
L., ... flower of Cities all 105:4
L., that great cesspool 102:5
L. ... the Clearing-house of the World 78:7
Mr. Weller's knowledge of L. 98:23
no man ... willing to leave L. 144:9
nobody is healthy in L. 20:8
our scene is L. 145:5
to L. to look at the queen 192:7
when a man is tired of L. 144:9
London Bridge is broken down 191:5
Loneliness of my country and my God 297:4
Lonely: close to the sun in l. lands 312:1
left l. for ever the kings 18:13
so l. 'twas, that God himself 87:2
wandered l. as a cloud 331:7
Lonesome: one that on a l. road 86:16
Long: a l., l. trail a-winding 153:11
a l. way to Tipperary 329:1
by thy l. grey beard 85:11
has been l. in city pent 151:6
he l. lived the pride 24:6
how l. or short permit to Heaven 179:14
I have lived l. enough 310:3
it cannot hold you l. 122:18
it shall be witty and it shan't be l. 80:18
l. after it was heard no more 335:1
l., dark, boggy, dirty ... way 123:7
l. is the way and hard 177:5
l. live the king, and Gilpin l. live he 92:13
look at them l. and l. 326:2
love me little, so you love me l. 132:3
man goeth to his l. home 39:27
nor wants that little l. 122:15
not that the story need be l. 317:4
Shenandoah, I l. to hear you 16:9
star-spangled banner! O l. may it wave 153:7
the night is l. that never finds the day 272:1
victory however l. ... the road 82:12
waiting for the l.-promised invasion 83:1
Longed: lies where he l. to be 307:6
Longest: hatred is by far the l. pleasure 70:7
Russia, when nights are l. there 273:3
Longings: I have immortal l. in me 243:10
Longitude: a l. with no platitude 114:4
Look: but westward, l., the land is bright 85:3
Cassius has a lean and hungry l. 262:9
do it with a bitter l. 326:12
has a frightened l. in its eye 302:10
houses are built ... not to l. on 23:3
I'll be a candle-holder and l. on 285:20
just to l. about us and to die 202:17
let him l. to his bond 274:16
l. at [animals] long and long 326:2
l. before you leap 219:27
l. thy last on all things lovely 96:13
mountains l. on Marathon 70:1
only a l. and a voice 161:7
shall not l. upon his like again 248:9

Look (*continued*)
to l. upon verdure ... perfect refreshment 20:12
we l. before and after 300:2
Looked: having l. to government for bread 64:16
no sooner l. but they lov'd 245:14
she l. at me as she did love 148:16
Lookers-on see most of the game 219:29
Looking-glass: not thank you for a l. 208:11
Looks: her l. were free 86:8
how like a ... publican he l. 274:7
l. the whole world in the face 161:10
love l. not with the eyes 276:12
toward school with heavy l. 286:12
woman as old as she l. 88:7
Looms: quest and passage through these l. 320:6
Loon: private buffoon is a light-hearted l. 121:5
sung ... by a love-lorn l. 121:1
Lord: a ... l., neat, and trimly dress'd 254:1
bread which the L. hath given 31:28
deputy elected by the L. 283:2
foundation is Jesus Christ her L. 307:13
from ghoulies ... good L. deliver us! 13:7
I thought ... a L. among wits 141:18
L. Finchley tried to mend ... light 27:6
L. Hippo suffered fearful loss 27:14
L. Lucky, by a curious fluke 28:1
l. of thy presence and no land 264:9
now, the L. lighten thee! 256:16
O L., thou lover of souls 51:14
one day is with the L. 50:10
praise the L. for he is kind 180:7
sing to the L. with cheerful voice 153:4
speak, L.; for thy servant heareth 33:28
the Angel of the L. came down 311:4
the day thou gavest, L. 107:17
the L. bless thee and keep thee 32:18
the L. ... chasteneth thee 32:24
the L. do so to me 33:26
the L. gave and the L. hath taken 35:1
the L. hardened Pharaoh's heart 31:24
the L. is my shepherd 35:27
the L. ... is one L. 32:21
the L. lift up his countenance 32:18
the L. make his face shine 32:18
the L. our God is good 153:5
the L. set a mark upon Cain 30:17
the L., whom ye seek 43:6
where the dear L. was crucified 10:7
whom the L. loveth he chasteneth 49:22
Lords: twelve l. a-leaping 194:2
Lose: grasp all, l. all 215:26
heads I win, tails you l. 94:5, 216:20
l. and neglect the creeping hours 244:10
l. by over-running 261:3
l. myself in other men's minds 156:6
who wd. l. ... this intellectual being 176:19
Losers: l. are ... in the wrong 219:30
l. seekers, finders keepers 219:31
Loss: buy and sell, and live by the l. 209:2
enow to do our country's l. 259:13
Lord Hippo suffered fearful l. 27:14
l. of honour was a wrench 124:11
Losses: all l. are restor'd 293:19
Lost: and she l. her maiden name 16:11
better to have fought and l. 84:18
better to have loved and l. 68:12, 312:13
Lost (*continued*)
books by which the printers have l. 114:10
field be l.? All is not l. 175:18
how art thou l.! 179:10
I have l. all the names 144:17
I have l. my reputation 279:10
I look upon every day to be l. 144:21
learning without thought is labour l. 89:4
l. causes, forsaken beliefs 19:7
never to have l. at all 68:12
praising ... l. makes the remembrance dear 242:7
sorry when any language is l. 144:23
thou art l. and gone for ever 183:8
wherever we're l. in 114:5
woman that deliberates is l. 9:5
Lot: policeman's l. is not a happy one 120:6
remember L.'s wife 46:10
the l. fell upon Jonah 42:18
Lots: so they cast l. 42:18
Lottery: marriage is a l. 220:25
Loud: I said it very l. and clear 77:3
Louder: the l. he talked of his honour 108:12
Loungers: all the l. of the Empire 102:5
Love: a little l. and good company 109:4
absence sharpens l. 205:8
ah! dearest l., sweet home of all 149:5
Alas! the l. of women 69:16
all is fair in l. and war 206:11
all l. is sweet 299:12
all mankind l. a lover 108:7
all she loves is l. 69:17
am like to l. three more 308:2
an oyster may be crossed in l. 301:3
and when l. speaks 268:13
as honour, l., obedience 272:5
be wise and l. exceeds man's might 290:5
brief ... as woman's l. 252:3
but l. is blind, and lovers cannot see 274:14
choose l. by another's eyes 276:11
comfort in the strength of l. 332:12
corner in the thing I l. 279:17
course of true l. never ... smooth 276:10
cupboard l. 210:25
dinner of herbs where l. is 38:18
dislike ... the l. of a woman ... treacle 152:9
drew them ... with bands of l. 42:10
earth's the right place for l. 113:8
familiar acts are beautiful through l. 299:13
faults are thick where l. is thin 213:21
fear the Lord ... and to l. him 33:1
few l. to hear the sins they l. to act 281:3
folly ... l. did make thee run into 244:3
for ever wilt thou l. 149:8
for I am sick of l. 40:6
for ... them that l. God 47:20
for thy sweet l. rememb'red 293:17
friendly l. perfecteth 22:1
friendship is constant ... save in ... l. 277:15
from too much l. of living 310:1
gave, once, her flowers to l. 59:6
general award of l. 148:11
God is l. 50:12
greater l. hath no man 46:31
greatest hate ... from the greatest l. 215:32
hail, wedded L. 178:8
half in l. with easeful Death 150:3
his banner over me was l. 40:5
hot l. is soon cold 217:5
how have you left the ancient l.? 56:14

Love (*continued*)
I cd. not l. thee, Dear, so much 162:7
I do not l. thee, Dr. Fell 59:9
I hate and l. ... and am in torment 77:16
I l. a lassie 157:3
I l. everything that's old 123:6
I l. not man the less 69:9
I l. sixpence 190:2
I l. thee true 148:17
I never shall l. the snow 58:5
I think my l. as rare 294:14
if music be the food of l. 290:10
is it ... a crime to l. too well? 201:6
leave to come unto my l. 305:8
lest that thy l. prove variable 286:10
let brotherly l. continue 49:23
let l. be without dissimulation 47:23
lightly turns to thoughts of l. 313:15
little brown jug ... I l. thee 15:5
live with me and be my l. 100:17, 167:1
live with thee and be thy l. 232:14
look'd at me as she did l. 148:16
l. all, trust a few 242:1
l. alters not 294:9
l. and a cough cannot be hid 219:33
l. and business teach eloquence 219:34
l. and fame to nothingness 151:8
l. and hate are necessary 56:15
l. and marriage rarely can combine 69:18
l. and meekness ... become a churchman 262:3
l. bade me welcome; yet my soul drew back 131:10
l. begets l. 219:35
l. built on beauty 100:19
l. but her and l. for ever 65:9
l. ceases to be a pleasure 26:11
l. conquers all 321:5
l. ... differs from gold and clay 298:9
l. Divine, all loves excelling 325:3
L. forgive us!—cinders, ashes 149:1
l., free as air, at sight of ... ties 201:8
l. goes toward l. ... but l. from l. 286:12
l. grows bitter with treason 310:4
l. has never known a law 326:6
l. he laughed to scorn 295:4
l. her till I die 17:2
l. I laugh to scorn 58:14
l. in a golden bowl 55:2
l. in a hut with water 149:1
l. in a palace 149:1
l. is blind 219:38
l. is enough 184:10
l. ... is exactly like war 307:1
l. is heaven and heaven is l. 239:13
l. is like the measles 139:14
l. is my religion—I cd. die 152:10
l. is not l. which alters 294:8
l. is ... sour in the ending 219:39
l. is strong as death 40:14
l. is sweet for a day 310:4
l. is the fulfilling of the law 47:29
l. itself shall slumber on 300:6
l. looks not with the eyes 276:12
l. me little, l. me long 220:3
l. me little, so you l. me long 132:3
l. me, l. my dog 220:4
l. of flattery 306:6
l. of money ... root of all evil 49:14
l. rules the court, the camp 239:13

Love (*continued*)
l.'s but the frailty of the mind 89:14
l. seeketh not itself to please 56:2
l. sought is good 291:12
l.'s the noblest frailty of the mind 104:8
l. that moves the sun 95:8
l. that never told can be 55:10
l. the brotherhood 50:5
l. the Lord ... with all thine heart 32:22
l. thy neighbour as thyself 32:16
l. thyself last 261:12
l. too much that die for l. 220:6
l., we are in God's hand 60:10
l. will find a way 220:7
l. worketh no ill 47:29
l. ye therefore the stranger 33:2
l. you because ... hard up you pawn 94:14
l. your enemies 43:20
lovers' quarrels ... renewal of l. 315:2
loyal cantons of contemned l. 290:15
man's l. ... a thing apart 69:14
many waters cannot quench l. 40:15
marry first and l. will follow 220:30
master-passion ... l. of news 93:18
me and my true l. 16:10
medicines to make me l. him 254:6
men have died ... but not for l. 245:12
men l. in haste ... detest at leisure 70:7
my dear l. sits him down 17:3
my l. and I wd. lie 136:6
my l. climbed up to me 154:1
my l. is like a red red rose 66:15
my l. is like the melodie 66:15
my L. is of a birth as rare 167:16
my l. lies underground 157:10
my only l. sprung from my only hate 286:5
my true l. hath my heart 302:2
my true l. sent to me 194:1,2
my vegetable l. shd. grow 167:12
my whole course of l. 279:1
nameless ... acts of kindness and of l. 335:10
never seek to tell thy l. 55:10
no l. sincerer than the l. of food 296:4
no rage like l. to hatred turned 89:6
none to praise ... few to l. 334:11
nor l. thy life, nor hate 179:14
not enough [religion] to make us l. 309:8
not in our power to l. or hate 166:14
nuptial l. maketh mankind 22:1
O L.! has she done this to thee? 163:4
of soup and l., the first 226:3
off with the old l. 16:1
office and affairs of l. 277:15
old l., cold l. 209:4
one does not l. a place less 20:16
one must not trifle with l. 185:6
open rebuke is better than secret l. 39:2
passing the l. of women 34:12
perfect l. casteth out fear 50:13
pity ... in the heart of l. 337:9
politicians neither l. nor hate 103:2
pounds of law, not an ounce of l. 227:36
pray you, l., remember 252:23
prosperity's the very bond of l. 293:5
prove ... the sports of l. 146:1
regain l. once possessed 181:5
rise up, my l. 40:7
said that the l. of money is the root 68:3
saying 'Farewell, blighted l.' 16:12

Love (*continued*)
seals of l., but seal'd in vain 273:12
seen ... that l. hath an end 310:3
she never told her l. 291:7
sighed for the l. of a ladye 121:2
so faithful in l. 240:6
so true a fool is l. 293:20
some are fou o' l. divine 66:4
something ... doesn't l. a wall 113:14
support of the woman I l. 105:10
that true self-l. and social are the same 203:12
that ye l. one another 46:29
the arms of my true l. 314:5
the fool of l., unpractis'd 104:15
the l. that can be reckon'd 242:10
the l. which doth us bind 167:17
the pangs of despis'd l. 250–1:20
the right true end of l. 101:2
the service of my l. 305:22
there is no fear in l. 50:13
there is tears for his l. 263:10
things that l. might 266:10
this bud of l. may prove a ... flower 286:11
this spring of l. resembleth 292:6
though I can't make her l. me 301:14
through l., through hope, and faith's 334:10
thy l. is better than wine 40:2
thy l. to me was wonderful 34:12
tired of l. ... tired of rhyme 27:10
to do justly and to l. mercy 42:24
to hold my wealth of l. 121:4
to let the warm L. in 150:7
to live is like l. 68:8
to l. and to cherish 53:22
to l. oneself ... lifelong romance 327:5
to see her was to l. her 65:9
true l.'s the gift which God has given 239:15
try thinking of l. or something 114:6
unbounded l. thou art 325:3
wanton l. corrupteth 22:1
weak man who marries for l. 144:3
what is l.? 'Tis not hereafter 291:2
what L. shall never reap 236:7
when I l. thee not, chaos is come 279:14
where both deliberate, the l. is slight 166:15
with l. in summer's wonderland 188:1
women ... have ... but two passions, vanity and l. 80:16
work of faith ... labour of l. 49:5
wroth with one we l. 87:7
you must sit down, says L. 131:11
your true l.'s coming 291:1
Loved: Alas! that all we l. of him shd. be 297:12
awake, my heart, to be l. 58:3
better l. ye canna be 185:8
better to have l. and lost 68:12
Dante who l. well 61:12
first he l. her, then he left her 16:11
God so l. the world 46:21
had we never l. so kindly 65:10
he dearly l. the lasses 66:2
he l. gold in special 79:14
I have not l. the world 69:5
I l. a lass, a fair one 329:10
I l. him not, and yet 156:12
Loved (*continued*)
I never writ, nor no man ever l. 294:9
I wish I l. the Human Race 233:1
Lavinia, therefore must be l. 289:13
l. her that she did pity them 279:2
l. I not Honour more 162:7
l. three whole days together 308:2
l. well because he hated 61:12
men l. darkness 46:22
Nature I l., and ... art 156:11
no sooner l. but they sigh'd 245:14
one that l. not wisely, but too well 280:14
she l. me for the dangers ... pass'd 279:2
sour to them that l. him not 262:2
the king l. Esther 34:27
the time and the place and the l. one 61:11
'tis better to have l. and lost 312:13
to be l. needs only to be seen 104:6
to have l. ... thought ... done 18:10
we l., sir—used to meet 60:16
where burning Sappho l. and sung 69:21
who ever l. that l. not at first sight? 166:15
who has never l. has never lived 115:8
Lovelier than the love of Jove 166:7
Loveliest: the l. things of beauty 168:12
Loveliness: enough their simple l. 151:3
glory and l. have pass'd 151:5
her l. I never knew until 85:10
l. which once he made more lovely 298:1
your L. and the hour of my death 152:8
Lovely: a billboard l. as a tree 186:10
a l. and a fearful thing 69:16
and l. is the rose 331:13
as you are l., so be various 125:8
go, l. rose 322:1
he'd make a l. corpse 98:7
I love the l. bully 259:9
look thy last on all things l. 96:13
l. and pleasant in their lives 34:11
more l. and more temperate 293:13
so l. fair and smell'st so sweet 280:6
whatsoever things are l. 49:1
Lover: a l. and his lass 245:16
a l. without indiscretion 128:8
all mankind love a l. 108:7
jealousy ... the injured l.'s hell 178:16
mother and l. of men, the sea 310:6
my fause l. stole my rose 67:7
O Lord, thou l. of souls 51:14
the l., sighing like furnace 244:11
the lunatic, the l., and the poet 277:5
thoughts will slide into a l.'s head 335:3
what is a l., that it can give? 89:13
woman loves her l. 69:17
Lovers: a pair of star-cross'd l. 285:17
all l. young, all l. must 247:10
journeys end in l. meeting 291:1
l. cannot see the pretty follies 274:14
l. fled away into the storm 147:14
l., to bed; 'tis almost fairy time 277:8
old l. are soundest 324:1
one makes l. ... as one pleases 89:13
sweet l. love the spring 245–6:16
Loves: a man l. the meat in his youth 277:22
all she l. is love 69:17
faithful l. ... moralize my song 305:9
fat white woman whom nobody l. 90–1:16
forebode not any severing of our l. 332:5
I have reigned with yr. l. 107:14

Loves (*continued*)
in her first passion woman l. 69:17
kills the thing he l. 326:12
Love Divine, all l. excelling 325:3
one that l. his fellow-men 137:6
show a woman when he l. 61:14
two l. ... of comfort and despair 294:16
who l. to lie with me 244:4
whoever l., ... do not propose 101:2
Love-sick all against our will 119:2
Lovesome: garden is a l. thing 59:10
Loveth: God l. a cheerful giver 48:16
l. him chasteneth him betimes 38:14
the dear God who l. us 87:4
whom the Lord l. he chasteneth 49:22
whom the Lord l. he correcteth 38:2
Loving: Friday's child is l. and giving 191:8
heart be still as l. 71:3
more pleasure in l. than ... loved 223:12
most l. mere folly 245:1
the night was made for l. 71:4
wickedness that hinders l. 61:12
Low: happy l., lie down! 257:3
he that is l. 63:15
her voice ... l.—an excellent thing 268:3
I'll tak' the l. road 16:10
last great Englishman is l. 314:9
sweet and l. 314:13
to cast one's eyes so l. 267:2
too l. for envy 91:13
what is l. raise and support 175:17
when my light is l. 312:14
Lowells talk to the Cabots 57:10
Lowest: matrimony at its l. 307:7
Lowly: better to be l. born 261:4
God made them, high or l. 10:5
me, made l. wise 334:4
stood a l. cattle shed 10:6
to order myself l. ... to all my betters 53:13
Loyal: that l. body wanted learning 318:1
Loyalties: home of ... impossible l. [Oxford] 19:7
Loyalty: that learned body wanted l. 318:1
when l. no harm meant 15:12
Lucifer: as proud as L. 223:32
come not, L.! 165:11
falls like L., never to hope again 261:10
how art thou fallen ... O L.! 40:25
Luck: better l. next time 207:31
I had the l. to be called upon 83:14
Lucky: better to be born l. 207:21
Lord L., by a curious fluke 28:1
Lucy: if L. shd. be dead! 335:3
Luke: L. began to slacken in his duty 332:11
Matthew, Mark, L. and John 9:13
Lukewarm: because thou art l. 50:19
Lullaby: songs and snatches, and dreamy l. 117:16
Lumber: learned l. in his head 202:15
stowed away in a Montreal l. room 68:9
Luminous: beating ... his l. wings in vain 19:9
Dong with a l. Nose 158:3
Lump: don't like it, you can l. it 219:12
Lunatic, the lover, and the poet 277:5
Luncheon: breakfast, supper, dinner, l. 62:4
Lungs: a custom ... dangerous to the l. 138:14
Lurch: leave in the l. 218:33
Lure it back to cancel half a line 110:12
Lust: for l. of knowing 111:2
l. in action; and till action, l. 294:11

Lust (*continued*)
l. of fame was but a dream 58:14
Lustre: where is thy l. now? 266:18
Lustres: unrisen l. slake the o'ertaken moon 58:3
Lute: musical as is Apollo's l. 172:18
Orpheus with his l. 261:5
Luxuries: give us the l. of life 184:11
two l. to brood over 152:8
Lying: let me have no l. 293:7
l., vainness, ... drunkenness 292:1
subject we old men are to ... l. 257:10
there is whispering, there is l. 230:13
to conclude, they are l. knaves 278:18
world is given to l.! 256:4
Lyly: didst our L. outshine 145:13
Lyme: an old party of L. 183:1
Lysander: of Hector and L. 16:14

Mab: I see Queen M. hath been with you 286:1
Macaroni: and called it m. 196:4
Macaulay: as cocksure ... as Tom M. is 169:11
Macavity: no one like M. 106:18
Machine: house is a m. for living in 90:13
maison est une m.-à-habiter 90:13
Mackerel: sprat to catch a m. 226:13
Mad: but m. north-north-west 250:8
how sad and bad and m. 60:16
I wd. not be m.! 265:17
m. as a hatter 220:8
m. as a March hare 220:9
m., bad and dangerous to know 156:1
m. world! m. kings! m. composition! 264:12
made me m. to see him shine 254:2
O, fool, I shall go m.! 266:4
O, let me not be m. 265:17
Oh, he is m., is he? 115:14
that he's m., 'tis true 249:17
to destroy, he first makes m. 223:40
we want a few m. people now 297:1
went m. and bit the man 122:19
Madding crowd's ignoble strife 126:12
Made: did he who m. the Lamb make thee? 56:6
dost thou know who m. thee? 56:9
fearfully and wonderfully m. 37:28
m. and loveth all 87:4
m. him a coat of many colours 31:10
nobody never m. me 308:1
Mademoiselle from Armenteers 236:14
Madness: devil's m.—War 241:16
great wits ... to m. near allied 102–3:17
m. in great ones ... not unwatch'd 251:6
m., yet there is method in't 250:3
melancholy and moon-struck m. 179:13
much mirth and no m. 302:12
such harmonious m. from my lips 300:3
that way m. lies 266:12
this is ... midsummer m. 291:13
work like m. in the brain 87:7
Magdalen: fourteen months at M. College 116:1
Magistrates: some like m. correct at home 258:8
Magnanimity: in all his m. of thought 338:1
in Victory: M. 83:13
you might curb yr. m. 152:12

Magnificence comes after 156:7
Magnificent: it is m., but it is not war 57:9
Magnifique: c'est m. ... pas la guerre 57:9
Magog: Gog, the land of M. 41:24
Mahomet: hill will not come to M. 22:4
Maid: a fair m. dwellin' 11:12
be good, seet m. 154:2
chariest m. is prodigal enough 248:13
I heard a m. singing 15:1
m. whom there were none to praise 334:11
Music, heavenly m., was young 88:12
O Music, sphere-descended M. 88:14
slain by a fair cruel m. 291:6
the m. was in the garden 193:5
way of a man with a m. 39:7
where are you going to, my pretty m.? 195:7
woo a fair young m. 16:3
Maiden: for many a rose-lipt m. 136:8
kissed the m. all forlorn 194:8
m. of bashful fifteen 301:17
m. ... must be slaughtered too 118:9
prithee, pretty m., will you marry me? 119:6
use a poor m. so 15:1
when a merry m. marries 116:11
Maidens: m., like moths, are ever caught 68:18
twenty lovesick m. we 119:2
Maids: eight m. a-milking 194:2
m. are May when ... m. 245:13
pretty m. all in a row 191:7
seven m. with seven mops 76:3
three little m. from school 118:6
Maimed and set at naught 68:9
Main: every man ... part of the m. 101:7
Maintaining: died m. his right of way 12:8
Majestic: his face ... m. though in ruin 177:3
Majestical: we do it wrong, being so m. 247:15
Majesty: a strange beginning—'borrowed m.'! 264:8
attribute to awe and m. 275:1
busied in his m., surveys 258:8
sight so touching in its m. 333:6
the next in M. 104:11
then our M. adorning 116:12
this earth of m., this seat of Mars 282:5
you got no-no-no m. 324:17
Major-General: model of a modern M. 120:4
Majority: m. never has right on its side 138:3
one on God's side is a m. 200:3
who makes up the m.? 138:3
Make: m. him an help meet 30:7
makes no mistakes does not m. anything 200:2
one of them said to his m. 11:15
Makes: the night that either m. me or fordoes 280:9
Male: into the ark ... m. and ... female 30:20
m. and female created he them 30:3
more deadly than the m. 154:14
Males: deeds are m. and words are females 211:11
Malice: m. never was his aim 308:13
nor set down aught in m. 280:14
with m. toward none 159:15
Malignant: a m. and a turban'd Turk 280–1:14
Malt: m. does more than Milton can 136:9
Malt (*continued*)
rat that ate the m. 194–5:8
Mammon: and M. wins his way 68:18
m. of unrighteousness 46:7
Man: a better m. than I am 154:16
a Christian faithful m. 284:15
a good old m. sir 278:9
a hairy m. ... a smooth m. 31:7
a living dead m. 246:5
a m. after his own heart 34:3
a m. can die but once 257:8
a m. can raise a thirst 155:2
a m. leave his father and mother 48:25
a m. more sinn'd against 266:11
a m. must serve his time 70:13
a m. of sorrows 41:5
a m. of such a feeble temper 262:7
a m.'s a m. for a' that 65:18
a m.'s [business] to keep unmarried 296:6
a m.'s first duty? ... To be himself 138:6
a m.'s friendships ... are invalidated 68:11
a m.'s reach should exceed his grasp 60:11
a m.'s worth something 60:14
a m. severe he was 122:11
a m. so various 103:4
a m. that is young in years 23:1
a m. that left his family 318:7
a m. under authority 44:10
a m. who cd. make so vile a pun 97:5
a m. who has not been in Italy 144:6
a m. who said 'God' 155:14
a m. who shaves and takes a train 325:8
a m. who's untrue to his wife 20:3
a m. will ne'er quite understand 198:12
a moral, sensible and well-bred m. 92:4
a nice m. ... m. of nasty ideas 309:10
a ready m. 23:8
a sadder and a wiser m. 87:5
a single m. ... a good fortune 20:17
a strong m. after sleep 182:8
a stupid m. is doing something 295:10
a very unclubbable m. 142:16
'A was a m. 248:9
a weak m. who marries for love 144:3
Adam, the goodliest m. 178:4
all my faults as m. to m. 295:18
all that was pleasant in m. 123:3
an aged aged m. 77:7
an elder m. not at all 21:21
an exact m. 23:8
an honest God ... noblest work of m. 138:9
an old m. and no honester 278:7
an old m. in a dry month 106:5
and the last m. in 187:11
Angry Young M. 199:1
any m.'s death diminishes me 101:8
apparel oft proclaims the m. 248:16
as for m., his days are as grass 37:1
ash on an old m.'s sleeve 106:10
at thirty m. suspects 338:1
away, slight m.! 264:1
beauty crieth ... no m. regardeth 68:9
became a m., I put away childish things 48:6
Benedick the married m. 277:13
better angel is a m. right fair 294:16
better spar'd a better m. 256:2
big assemblance of a m.! 257:9
both m. and bird and beast 87:3
brothers and their murder'd m. 148:1

Man (*continued*)
Brutus is an honourable m. 263:12
busiest m. who has time to spare 198:5
business of the wealthy m. 27:6
by courtesy a m. 21:5
by m. shall his blood be shed 30:24
came to the making of m. 309:15
care not whether a m. is good 55:7
caverns measureless to m. 87:11, 87:13
child is father of the m. 333:9
cloud ... like a m.'s hand 34:20
condition of m. ... condition of war 133:2
conference [maketh] a ready m. 23:8
crumbs ... from the rich m.'s table 46:8
daring young m. on the flying trapeze 159:5
Darwinian M. ... well-behaved 120:11
deep young m. 119:4
each m. kills ... thing he loves 326:12
every m. did that which was right 33:24
every m. for himself 212:31
every m. has his faults 212:32
every m. is as Heaven made him 78:3
every m. is best known to himself 212:33
every m. is wanted, no m. ... much 108:9
every m. meets his Waterloo 200:4
every m. must play a part 274:1
every m. over forty 296:16
every m.'s hand against him 31:1
every m. that cometh into ... world 46:15
every m. to his taste 212:34
every m. under his vine 42:22
every m. was ... god or devil 103:5
every woman shd. marry ... no m. 100:10
everyone has sat except a m. 94:12
expects every m. ... do his duty 187:5
face of the old m. 32:17
foolish fond old m. 267:11
foolishly-compounded clay, m. 256:8
foot-in-the-grave young m. 119:7
get a new m. 288:10
glory to M. in the highest! 310:2
God created m. in his own image 30:3
God doth not need ... m.'s work 181:11
God made the woman for the m. 312:2
God took the m. and put him 30:6
good for a m. that he bear the yoke 41:20
good name in m. and woman 279:15
greater love hath no m. 46:31
greatest m. you had ... yet seen 145:4
he thinks, good easy m. 261:9
heaven had made her such a m. 279:2
her m. ... he done her wrong 15:2
honest m. sent to lie abroad 336:11
honest m.'s the noblest work of God 203:8
how use doth breed a habit in a m. 292:10
I hate ingratitude ... in a m. 292:1
I love not m. the less 69:9
ideal m. ... non-attached m. 137:10
if a m. will begin with certainties 23:12
if any m. shall add 51:4
if I ever become a rich m. 28:3
if such a m. there be 201:17
if the m. who turnips cries 140:17
I'm truly sorry m.'s dominion 66:11
in the Parliament of m. 313:17
in the spring a young m.'s fancy 313:15
in wit a m.: simplicity a child 201:22
is m. an ape or an angel? 100:5

Man (*continued*)
it is the number of a m. 50:26
It's That M. Again 146:16
laugh to scorn the pow'r of m. 271:15
let no m. despise thy youth 49:11
let no m. put asunder 53:25
let not m. put asunder 45:12
like master, like m. 219:13
looking for a m.'s footprint 26:8
m. and wife together 53:26
m. ... bears in his bodily frame 95:10
m. being too proud to fight 329:7
m. ... born free ... is in chains 236:12
m. delights not me ... nor woman 250:6
m. for the field ... the sword 314:18
m. goeth to his long home 39:27
m. has his will,—but woman 134:3
m. in the moon 220:14
m. in the street 220:15
m. is a noble animal 60:3
m. is ... a political animal 18:5
m. is ... a religious animal 64:12
m. is a tool-making animal 113:4
m. is born unto trouble 35:3
m. is Nature's sole mistake 120:10
m. is not a fly 203:2
m. is the hunter 314:17
m. is the master of things 310:2
m. is the shuttle 320:6
m. ... killed by lightning 11:18
m. looketh on ... outward appearance 34:5
m. made the town 93:6
m. ... must get drunk 69:15
m. of upright life unstained 135:14
m. or mouse 220:20
m. proposes ... God disposes 152:14, 220:21
m., proud m. 273:7
m.'s a ribald ... a rake 120:10
m.'s inhumanity to m. 66:8
m. shall not live by bread 43:13
m. that is born of a woman 35:5, 53:28
m. that lays his hand upon a woman 317:12
m. to afflict his soul 41:10
m. wants but little 338:2
m. wants but little here below 122:15
m. was made for joy and woe 54:15
m. who knows the price 328:4
m. who sees absolutely nothing 327:1
m. who sees both sides 327:1
m. who ... sets foot upon a worm 93:12
m. with the head ... to command 314:18
manners maketh m. 328:21
met a m. who wasn't there 169:8
met a m. with seven wives 188:3
money makes the m. 221:13
Nature might ... say ... 'This was a m.!' 264:7
new m. ... raised up in him 53:10
no great m. lives in vain 73:8
no m. can serve two masters 44:1
no m. dieth to himself 47:30
no m. does [become like his mother] 328:13
no m. ever talked poetry 99:5
no m., having put ... hand to plough 45:26
no m. is an island 101:7
no m. is good enough to govern 159:7
no m. putteth new wine 45:25
no m. truly knows another 59:16
nor no m. ever loved 294:9

Man (continued)
not a dinner to ask a m. to 142:15
no-wher so bisy a m. 79:11
O good old m., how well in thee 243:19
o'er all this scene of m. 202:17
of M.'s first disobedience 175:15
old m. in a hurry 82:5
on m., on nature ... life 331:3
one m. ... appointed to buy the meat 241:5
one m. ... plays many parts 244:11
one m.'s meat is another m.'s poison 220:37
only m. is vile 130:2
open not ... heart to every m. 51:18
poor, infirm ... despis'd old m. 266:8
poor m. that hangs on princes' favours 261:10
proper study of Mankind is M. 203:5
reading maketh a full m. 23:8
rejoice, O young m., in ... youth 39:25
reminds a m. he is mortal 96:5
rich m., poor m., beggar m. 195:2
ruins of the noblest m. 263:7
sabbath was made for m. 45:6
safeliest when with one m. m.'d 101:3
same tree ... a wise m. sees 57:3
say to ... world, This was a m.! 264:7
shall mortal m. be more just than God 35:2
sleep of a labouring m. 39:17
so can I, or so can any m. 255:5
so unto the m. is woman 161:6
some new race, called M. 177:4
son of m., set thy face against Gog 41:24
stagger like a drunken m. 37:5
state of m., like to a ... kingdom 262:13
style is the m. himself 62:14
that a m. lay down his life 46:31
that m. was made to mourn 66:7
the blood of a British m. 266:17
the childhood shows the m. 180:3
the fury of a patient m. 103:9
the hour is come, but not the m. 240:12
the m. all tattered and torn 194:8
the m. hath penance done 86:15
the m. of action is called on 257:1
the m. perceives it die away 332:2
the m. that hath no music 275:10
the m., with soul so dead 239:16
the most senseless and fit m. 278:5
the proud m.'s contumely 250–1:20
the tongue can no m. tame 50:1
the whole duty of m. 40:1
the young m.'s dog with them 51:9
there came to the making of m. 309:15
There once was a m. who said 'Damn' 128:11
there was an old m. from Darjeeling 13:3
there was an Old M. who said 'Hush!' 158:12
there was an Old M. with a beard 158:13
there was a young m. of Boulogne 12:11
there was a young m. of Japan 13:1
there was a young m. of Montrose 28:9
thinking m. is bound to rebel 138:3
this is the state of m. 261:9
till one greater M. restore us 175:15
'tis strange what a m. may do 315:7
to be a well-favoured m. 278:4
to every m. a damsel or two 33:16
true love's the gift ... to m. alone 239:15

Man (continued)
valiant m. and free 313:7
vexing the dull ear of a drowsy m. 264:17
wager ... m. ... is absolutely fixed on 109:7
was there a m. dismayed 311:10
water-drops stain my m.'s cheeks 266:3
way of a m. with a maid 39:7
were m. but constant! 292:11
what a piece of work is a m.! 250:6
what bloody m. is that? 269:5
what is m., that thou art mindful 35:18
what m. has made of m. 332:8
what shall it profit a m.? 45:10
whatsoever a m. soweth 48:23
when a m. bites a dog 95:5
when a m. shd. marry 21:21
when no m. can work 46:26
when the brains were out the m. would die 271:8
whenever he met a great m. 315:10
where m. is not, nature is barren 57:6
whether ... wise m. or a fool 55:7
who kills a m. 182:2
who sheddeth m.'s blood 30:24
who's master, who's m. 309:3
who thicks m.'s blood with cold 86:8
whoso wd. be a m. 108:11
wine ... maketh glad ... heart of m. 37:2
wisest m. the warl' saw 66:2
with cords of a m. 42:10
woman is the lesser m. 313:19
wd. this m. ... ask why? 19:16
you asked this m. to die 19:16
you'll be a M., my son 154:20
Man Friday: I takes my M. with me 96:8
Mandalay: on the road to M. 155:1
Mandrake: get with child a m. root 101:5
Manger: in a m. for His bed 10:6
in the rude m. lies 175:8
the babe ... lying in a m. 45:21
Manhood: m. full and fair 58:6
neither ... m., nor good fellowship 253:19
Manhoods: and hold their m. cheap 260:2
Manifold stories ... told not to thy credit 72:4
Man-in-the-street ... a keen observer of life 20:3
Mankind: amongst the noblest of m. 72:3
example is the school of m. 64:15
gave up what was meant for m. 123:1
how beauteous m. is! 289:7
I am involved in m. 101:8
love all m., except an American 144:10
m. and posterity ... in their debt 138:8
not retreat but exclusion from m. 141:8
nuptial love maketh m. 22:1
proper study of M. is Man 203:5
seems to be all m.'s epitome 103:4
survey m. from China to Peru 141:9
to you and all m. 311:4
wd. deserve better of m. 309:1
wisest, brightest, meanest of m. 203:9
Manliness: the silent m. of grief 122:14
Manna: said one to another, It is m. 31:28
though his tongue dropped m. 176:18
Manner: cease to think about the m. 129:15
native here, and to the m. born 249:2
Manners: by nothing ... as by his m. 305:14
graced with polished m. 93:12
m. maketh man 328:21
m. of a dancing-master 141:19

Manners (*continued*)
men's evil m. live in brass 262:1
old m., old books, old wine 123:6
sweeter m., purer laws 313:5
Manservant: nor his m., nor his maidservant 32:9
Mansion: life ... M. of many Apartments 152:3
Mansions: build thee more stately m. 134:5
in my Father's house are many m. 46:30
Mantle: cast his m. upon him 34:22
cream and m. like a standing pond 274:2
morn, in russet m. clad 247:16
twitched his m. blue 175:6
Manure: blood of English shall m. the ground 283:8
Many: have the measels? ... how m.? 322:11
m. are called, but few are chosen 44:24
m. things to fear 22:14
owed by so m. to so few 82:15
the m. change and pass 298:2
the m. men, so beautiful 86:11
ye are m.—they are few 298:14
Many-splendour'd: miss the m. thing 316:10
Maps: generals are already poring over m. 20:1
Mar: oft we m. what's well 265:16
Marathon: from M. to Waterloo 120:4
M. looks on the sea 70:1
Marble: I dreamt ... I dwelt in m. halls 63:4
poets that lasting m. seek 322:2
whole as the m., founded as the rock 271:6
your dreary m. halls 72:2
March: beware the Ides of M. 262:5
droghte of M. hath perced 79:1
M. comes in like a lion 220:23
Marched breast forward 60:12
Marches: dreadful m. to delightful measures 284:9
funeral m. to the grave 160:15
Marching: as we were m. through Georgia 336:9,10
his soul is m. on! 127:13
m. as to war 24:9
Mare: lend me yr. grey m. 17:5
patience ... tired m. ... will plod 258:11
to find a m.'s nest 220:24
Maréchal: le bâton de m. de France 185:13
Margin: through a meadow of m. 301:13
Marian: Mall, Meg, and M., and Margery 288:9
M.'s nose looks red and raw 269:1
Mariner: I fear thee, ancient M. 86:9
it is an ancient M. 85:11
Mariners: ye m. of England 72:10
Marines: tell that to the M. 227:19
Mark: God save the m.! 254:2
love ... an ever-fixed m. 294:8
Matthew, M., Luke, and John 9:13
no drowning m. upon him 287:13
read, m., learn 53:2
Market: chief good and m. of his time 252:17
if fools went not to m. 214:8
school or college, kirk or m. 307:8
send a fool to the m. 214:6
women ... goose make a m. 227:40
Market-place: at noon-day, upon the m. 262:12
Idols of the M. 23:16
Marks: Signior Benedick; nobody m. you 277:11
Marlowe: M.'s mighty line 145:13
neat M. 102:11
Marmion: last words of M. 240:10
Marquis: abducted by a French m. 124:11
Marred: young man married ... man that's m. 242:4
Marriage: care ... more for a m. than a ministry 23:19
coldly furnish ... m. tables 248:8
comedies are ended by a m. 69:19
exclaim ... against second m. 109:7
eyes wide open before m. 217:35
friendships are ... invalidated by m. 68:11
hanging prevents a bad m. 290:13
happiness in m. ... matter of chance 20:18
love and m. rarely can combine 69:18
m. has many pains but celibacy has no pleasures 141:8
m. is a lottery 220:25
m. is like a cage 183:5
m. is popular because 296:14
m. is the best state for a man 144:2
m. of true minds 294:8
O curse of m. 279:17
takes two to make a m. a success 238:2
won't be a stylish m. 95:4
Married: a woman's business to get m. 296:6
as wellbred as if ... not m. 89:17
Benedick the m. man 277:13
cuckoo ... mocks m. men 268–9:17
how ... be m. without a wife? 191:4
how to be happy though m. 128:6
if ever we had been m. 115:5
live till I were m. 278:1
man who m. ... did more service 123:19
m. three wives at a time 183:1
unpleasing to a m. ear 268–9:17
wen you're a m. man, Samivel 99:3
what delight we m. people have 199:10
wd. be m. but I'd have no wife 94:2
wd. be m. to a single life 94:2
young man m. is ... marr'd 242:4
Marries: m. late, m. ill 220:28
person who either m. or dies 20:9
Marry: advise none to m. 206:7
be sure before you m. of a house 207:3
better to m. than to burn 48:3
every woman should m.—and no man 100:10
he'll come back and m. me 188:5
honest men m. soon 216:38
I can't m. you, my pretty maid 196:1
if men knew ... they'd never m. 131:2
may m. whom she likes 315:9
now that you are going to m. 143:5
to persons about to m.—Don't 231:17
when a man shd. m. 21:21
while ye may, go m. 132:8
young man shd. not m. yet 231:6
Mars: this seat of M. 282:5
Marshal: the m.'s truncheon nor the judge's robe 273:4
Martin Elginbrode: here lie I, M. 164:10
Martini: get ... into a dry M. 330:8
Martyr: bitter groan of a m.'s woe 55:5
Martyrdom ... in which ... can become famous 295:14
Martyrs: noble army of M. 52:15
Marvel: I m. how the fishes live 281:5
match me such m. 64:3
they m. more and more 27:1

Marvellous: Chatterton, the m. boy 334:8
Mary: M. had a little lamb 127:11
M., M., quite contrary 191:7
M. was that Mother mild 10:6
might be the last, my M.! 93:13
my sweet Highland M. 66:3
O M., at thy window be 66:9
Mary Ann: M. has gone to rest 12:6
nuts for M. 12:6
Mary Ann Lowder: here lies the body of M. 12:4
Mary Jane: *What* is the matter with M.? 171:10
Mary-buds: winking M. begin 246:13
Masons: singing m. building roofs of gold 258:8
Masquerade: the truth in m. 70:5
Mass: Paris is well worth a m. 130:12
Massacre: not as sudden as a m. 318:11
Masses: the m. against the classes 121:9
Mast: bends the gallant m. 95:1
Master: has a new m., get a new man 288:10
has a wife, has a m. 230:15
I am the M. of this College 26:6
in constancy follow the M. 63:13
like m., like man 219:13
man is the m. of things 310:2
M. Mistress of my passion 293:16
money is ... a bad m. 221:11
money ... will be thy m. 221:9
my m.'s lost his fiddlestick 188:7
one for the m. 188:4
that ... I wd. fain call m. 265:12
the m., the swabber, the boatswain 288:9
vice is a m. 203:6
who's m., who's man 309:3
Masterpiece: a friend ... m. of Nature 108:4
Masters: men are m. of their fates 262:8
no man can serve two m. 44:1
the people are the m. 64:8
Match: ten to make ... m. to win 187:11
Matched: thy passions, m. with mine 313:19
Mate: high and low m. ill 326:6
Mathematics: m. [make] subtile 23:9
m. possesses ... truth ... beauty 237:9
Matilda: you'll come a-waltzing, M. 198:10
Mating: come ... Only in the m. season 170:16
Matrimony: in m. ... a little aversion 301:6
take m. at its lowest 307:7
Matron: sober-suited m., all in black 286:21
Matter: a Star Chamber m. of it 276:1
all mirth and no m. 277:19
mere m. for a May morning 291:15
more m. with less art 249:16
what is M.? Never Mind 231:21
wretched m. and lame metre 175:14
Matters: where man may read strange m. 270:3
Matthew, Mark, Luke, and John 9:13
Mature in dullness 104:14
Maud: come into the garden, M. 314:3
I had written to Aunt M. 124:9
Maurice: never love the snow ... since M. died 58:5
Mawkishness: thence proceeds m. 147:7
Maxim: an old m. in the schools 308:12
it is my m. ... to enjoy it [world] 304:1
that grounded m. so rife 181:2
the m. of the British people 82:8
Maximum: marriage ... combines m. of temptation 296:14
May: fresh as is the month of M. 79:3
gathering nuts in M. 15:7
laurel outlives not M. 310:4
M. when they are maids 245:13
merriment of M. 147:10
more matter for a M. morning 291:15
ne'er a clout till M. be out 209:10
to be Queen of the M. 314:7
when M. follows ... whitethroat builds 61:2
winds do shake the darling buds of M. 293:13
Mayor: astonished M. and Corporation 62:2
Maypole: away to the m. hie 14:15
Maze: a mighty m.! but not without a plan 202:17
Mazes: in wandering m. lost 177:6
Me: blest compared with m. 66:13
but the One was M. 137:14
m. as one who loves his fellow-men 137:6
not m. for the world 304:1
terms too deep for *m.* 119:4
what shall, alas! become of m.? 163:4
ye have done it unto m. 44:30
Mead: about the new-mown m. 151:1
Meadow: a time when m., grove and stream 331:12
going through m. and village 169:1
meander through a m. of margin 301:13
the sheep's in the m. 191:1
Meadows: O, ye Fountains, M., Hills 332:5
Meads: I met a lady in the m. 148:15
Mean: I m. the Faith's Defender 68:15
in m. men we entitle patience 281:10
it all depends what you m. by 139:19
means just what I choose it to m. 76:10
tears ... I know not what they m. 314:16
try and tell you what I m. 76:12
Meanest: the m. flower that blows 332:6
Meaning: to some faint m. make pretence 104:14
word ... teems with hidden m. 120:14
Means: by honest m. ... by any m. make money 135:11
die beyond my m. 328:17
end justifies the m. 212:23
it m. ... what I choose it to mean 76:10
let us ... live within our m. 322:15
my m. ... too low for envy 91:13
Meant: more is m. that meets the ear 173:10
what those damned dots m. 82:6
Measles: have the m.: ... how many? 322:11
love is like the m. 139:14
Measure: conquests ... shrunk to this little m. 263:5
like doth quit like, and m. still for m. 273:14
m. not the work until 60:5
m. thrice before you cut 220:36
there is a m. in all things 220:35
Measureless: caverns m. to man 87:11, 87:13
Measures: dreadful marches to delightful m. 284:9
Meat: appointed to buy the m. 241:5
givest them ... m. in due season 37:30
have made worms' m. of me 286:19
I cannot eat but little m. 307:11
it snewed in his hous of m. 79:12
loves the m. in his youth 277:22

Meat (*continued*)
mock the m. it feeds on 279:16
one man's m. ... man's poison 220:37
out of the eater came forth m. 33:19
sit down, ... and taste My m. 131:11
some hae m., and canna eat 67:3
Mechanic: poor m. porters crowding in 258:8
Meddling with any practical part of life 9:6
Medes and Persians: law of the M., which altereth not 42:4
thy kingdom ... given to the M. 42:3
Medicinable: their m. gum 280–1:4
Medicine: faithful friend is the m. of life 51:16
no other m. but only hope 273:9
Medicines: given me m. to make me love him 254:6
Meditate: strictly m. the thankless Muse? 174:15
Meek: blessed are the m. 43:15
I am m. and gentle 263:7
m. shall inherit the earth 36:8
m. until they be married 220:10
taught us to be calm and m. 133:14
Meekness: love and m. ... become a churchman 262:3
Meet: extremes m. 213:6
God be with you till we m. again 233:2
if I shd. m. thee 71:6
if we do m. again ... shall smile 264:4
m. in her aspect and her eyes 71:2
never the twain shall m. 154:8
we loved, sir—used to m. 60:16
will never m. again ... on ... banks 16:10
Meeter to carry off the latter 199:6
Meeting: journeys end in lovers m. 291:1
this m. is drunk 99:6
Meetings: alarums changed to merry m. 284:9
Melancholy: bird ... most musical, most m.! 173:8
green and yellow m. 291:7
hail, divinest M.! 173:6
hence, loathed M. 173:14
m. marked him for her own 126:13
m. ... shd. be diverted 144:4
moping m. 179:13
my cue is villainous m. 265:11
naught so sweet as m. 67:8
not m. once a day 214:5
nothing ... so m. as a battle ... won 324:6
pale M. sat retired 88:13
suck m. out of a song 244:5
these pleasures, M., give 173:13
'tis m. and a fearful sign 69:18
what charm can soothe her m.? 124:1
Melodies: heard m. are sweet 149:7
Melody: from ancient m. have ceas'd 56:13
my love is like the m. 66:15
Melrose: view fair M. aright 239:12
Melted into air, into thin air 288:16
Melts: a moment white, then m. for ever 67:4
Member: ev'ry m. of the force 234:12
Members one of another 47:22
Meminisse: forsan et haec ... m. iuvabit 321:1
Memorable: finding ... he was not m. 241:10
Memorial: m. from the Soul's eternity 236:6
some ... that have no m. 52:7
Memories: creditors ... better m. than debtors 210:17
Memories (*continued*)
liars ought to have good m. 302:1
liars shd. have good m. 218:40
Memory: dear son of m., ... heir of fame 175:12
everyone complains of his m. 234:5
m. is the diary we ... carry 327:15
m. of the just is blessed 38:9
m. ... the beginning of dowdiness 328:15
mixing m. and desire 107:3
no man ... force can abolish m. 235:5
no woman shd. have a m. 328:15
peaceful hours ... how sweet their m. 92:14
pluck from the m. a rooted sorrow 272:6
shorter in wind, as in m. long 57:15
the m. be green 247:17
the M. of great Men 152:1
vibrates in the m. 300:6
Men: a sort of m. whose visages 274:2
a tide in the affairs of m. 264:3
all sorts and conditions of m. 52:27
all things to all m. 48:4
among new m., strange faces 312:7
appointed unto m. once to die 49:19
are you good m. and true? 278:3
ay, in the catalogue ye go for m. 271:1
best m. are dead 232:3
bodies of unburied m. 324:3
boon and a blessing to m. 11:8
busiest m. ... most leisure 208:37
busy hum of m. 174:5
but m. are m. ... sometimes forget 279:9
common wonder of all m. 59:15
daggers in m.'s smiles 270:16
dead m. don't bite 211:1
dead m. naked shall be one 315:14
dead m. rise up never 310:1
dead m. tell no tales 211:2
deal with none but honest m. 224:13
despised and rejected of m. 41:5
destiny with m. for pieces plays 110:11
down among the dead m. 105:7
dumb m. get no lands 212:5
England ... purgatory of m. 111:4
equal rights of m. and women 319:5
Eve upon the first of M. 135:2
even great m. have ... poor relations 97:11
evil that m. do lives after them 263:11
fair women and brave m. 69:3
fifteen m. on ... dead man's chest 307:4
finds too late that m. betray 124:1
for fear of little m. 10:9
for m. must work 154:3
give place to better m. 94:9
glory of young m. is their strength 38:25
going to dine with some m. 29:3
good will toward m. 45:22
great m. are almost always bad m. 9:1
great m. are not always wise 35:11
great m. ... not commonly ... great scholars 134:6
have m. about me that are fat 262:9
heaven ... leads m. to this hell 294:12
histories make m. wise 23:9
I said ... All m. are liars 37:10
I speak ... French to m. 78:18
I will make you fishers of m. 43:14
idols which beset m.'s minds 23:16
in mean m. we entitle patience 281:10
in most m.'s power to be agreeable 309:9

Men (*continued*)
it is the m. who make a city 220:39
jolly tars are our m. 115:1
let us now praise famous m. 52:5
lives not three good m. unhang'd 254:14
m. alone ... capable of every wickedness 90:9
m. and women merely players 244:11
m. are April when they woo 245:13
m. are but gilded loam 281:8
m. are capable ... of ... benevolence 237:8
m. are children of a larger growth 104:1
m. at some time are masters of their fates 262:8
m. below and saints above 239:13
m. ... differ as heaven and earth 312:6
m. fear death as children ... dark 21:9
m. fell out ... knew not why 67:14
m. have died from time to time 245:12
m. in great places are thrice servants 22:2
m. love in haste ... detest at leisure 70:7
m. may bleed and m. may burn 120:16
m. may come and m. may go 311:8
m. may rise on stepping-stones 312:11
m. must endure their going hence 267:12
m. of few words ... best m. 259:6
m. of good quality 322:17
m. prize the thing ungain'd 289:15
m. seldom make passes 198:2
m. that laugh and weep 309:18
m. that sow to reap 309:18
m. that were boys when I was 28:4
m. were deceivers ever 277:21
m. who borrow and m. who lend 156:2
m. will still say ... their finest hour 82:14
m. will wrangle ... write ... fight 88:17
m. with splendid hearts 59:3
m.'s natures are alike 89:2
mocks married m. 268–9:17
mother and lover of m. 310:6
my object ... to form Christian m. 19:13
new m., strange faces, other minds 312:7
nor yet favour to m. of skill 39:23
nor yet riches to m. of understanding 39:23
not as other m. are 46:11
not in the roll of common m. 255:4
old m. shall dream dreams 42:13
praise makes ... bad m. worse 223:24
praise makes good m. better 223:24
quit yourselves like m. 34:1
reputed one of the wise m. 21:21
rich m. furnished with ability 52:6
rich m. have no faults 224:17
rule of m. entirely great 63:3
schemes o' mice an' m. 66:12
sleek-headed m., and such as sleep 262:9
so are they all, all honourable m. 263:12
so long as m. can breathe 293:15
so many m., so many opinions 315:4
sons of the prophet ... brave m. 16:15
such m. are dangerous 262:9
talk of censorious old m. 77:14
that all m. are created equal 139:6
that all m. everywhere cd. be free 159:12
the breath of worldly ... m. 283:2
the clever m. at Oxford 124:13
the many m., so beautiful 86:11
the most mighty m. ... in his army 41:25
The War between M. and Women 317:9
they make their steel with m. 238.7

Men (*continued*)
thousand creeds ... move m.'s hearts 58:13
to m.'s business, and bosoms 21:7
to put confidence in m. 37:12
truth ... on the lips of dying m. 19:3
two m. look out through the same bars 156:15
we are the hollow m. ... the stuffed m. 106:7
we cannot be free m. if ... slavery 159:9
we petty m. walk under his huge legs 262:8
wealth accumulates and m. decay 122:5
what m. call gallantry 69:10
whatsoever ye wd. that m. shd. do 44:7
wisest m. have erred 180:12
wives are ... old m.'s nurses 21:20
wives are young m.'s mistresses 21:20
women are more like each other than m. 80:16
wonder m. dare trust th'selves with m. 289:10
you are m. of stones 268:2
young m. shall see visions 42:13
Mend: tried to m. the electric light 27:6
Mended: least said, soonest m. 218:32
Mene, mene, tekel, upharsin 42:1
Mens: m. cuiusque is est quisque 84:5
ut sit m. sana in corpore sano 146:11
Mentioned: and m. me to him 75:7
Merchant: m. to secure his treasure 205:6
that same m.'s flesh 275:5
Merchants: like m., venture trade abroad 258:8
Mercies: all thy faithful m. crown 325:3
His m. ay endure 180:7
Merciful as constant 125:8
Mercuries: as English M. 258:9
Mercury: words of M. are harsh 269:2
Mercy: desired m., and not sacrifice 42:8
doing justice ... leaving m. to heaven 109:11
half so good a grace as m. 273:4
have m. upon us ... sinners 52:22
his m. is for ever sure 153:4
m. I asked, m. I found 72:5
m. is above this sceptred sway 275:1
m. is nobility's true badge 289:12
'O m.!' to myself I cried 335:3
peace on earth and m. mild 325:2
quality of m. is not strain'd 275:1
render the deeds of m. 275:1
to love m., and to walk humbly 42:24
we do pray for m. 275:1
when m. seasons justice 275:1
Meridian: from that full m. of my glory 261:8
Merit: fondly we think we honour m. 202:13
I like the Garter ... no damned m. 169:9
men of m. are sought after 257:1
m. wins the soul 204:11
Satan exalted sat, by m. raised 176:15
spurns that patient m. ... takes 250–1:20
Merits: seek his m. to disclose 126:15
Mermaid: a m. on a dolphin's back 276:18
choicer than the M. Tavern 149:4
seen, done at the M. 25:7
Mermaids: I have heard the m. singing 106:16
Merrier: the more the m. 221:16
Merrily: m. hent the stile-a 292:19
m., m., shall I live now 289:6

Merrily (*continued*)
tripping and skipping ran m. 62:6
Merriment: borrow ... from the m. of May 147:10
source of innocent m. 118:11
Merry: against ill chances men are ... m. 257:11
God rest you m., gentlemen 15:3
It is good to be m. and wise 16:1
m. heart ... cheerful countenance 38:17
m. heart goes all the day 292:19
m. of soul he sailed 307:3
m. village chime 120:7
m. with the fruitful grape 110:8
m. yarn from ... fellow-rover 168:17
never m. when I hear sweet music 275:9
playing of the m. organ 15:8
short life and a m. one 225:19
so I piped into m. cheer 56:8
tonight we'll m. be 14:14
Tu-whit, Tu-who—a m. note 269:1
Merrygoround: it's no go the m. 164:14
Merryman: a m. moping mum 121:2
Message: the electric m. came 21:6
Messing: simply m. about in boats 124:12
Met: no sooner m. but they look'd 245:14
Metal: here's m. more attractive 252:2
touch of sweating m. 96:5
Meteor: shone like a m. streaming 176:9
Method: madness, yet there is m. in't 250:3
m. of making a fortune 127:3
Methods: you know my m., Watson 101:14
Methuselah: all the days of M. 30:18
Mew: rather be a kitten and cry m. 255:6
the cat will m. 253:5
Mewling: infant, m. and puking 244:11
Mexique Bay: Echo beyond the M. 167:9
Micawber, Mr. 97:15,16
Mice: best-laid schemes o' m. and men 66:12
cat is away ... m. will play 230:12
three blind m., see how they run! 195:1
Michelangelo: women come and go talking of M. 106:12
Microbe is so very small 27:13
Microscopic: has not man a m. eye? 203:2
Middle: in the m. of the woods ... Yonghy-Bonghy-Bò 158:2
wives are ... companions for m. age 21:20
Midlands: when I am living in the M. 28:2
Midnight: burn the m. oil 208:35
cease upon the m. with no pain 150:3
consum'd the m. oil 115:9
it came upon the m. clear 240:14
not to be abed after m. 290:17
of Cerberus and blackest M. born 173:14
One hour's sleep before m. 217:9
secret, black, and m. hags 271:13
see her on the bridge at m. 16:12
the iron tongue of m. 277:8
time may cease, and m. never come 165:10
we have heard the chimes at m. 257:7
Midsummer: this is very m. madness 291:13
Midwife: she is the fairies' m. 286:1
the m. laid her hand on ... Skull 103:10
Mid-winter: bleak m., long ago 235:15
Mieux: le m. est l'ennemi du bien 321:13
tout est pour le m. 321:9
Might: first in beauty shd. be first in m. 148:8
m. is right 221:3
saddest [words] ... It m. have been 326:8
Might (*continued*)
'tis m. half-slumbering 150:12
Might-have-been: my name is M. 236:8
you won't be sorry for a m. 233:3
Mightier: God ... make thee m. yet 28:10
in word m. than they in arms 178:19
Mighties: 'tis m. in the m. 275:1
Mighty: a m. man is he 161:9
death ... some have called thee m. 101:4
fear not, said he, for m. dread 311:4
God who made thee m. 28:10
how are the m. fallen! 34:9
I am weak, but thou art m. 329:2
look on my works, ye M., and despair 299:8
mean and m. rotting together 247:7
m. hunter before the Lord 30:26
this m. sum of things 331:5
Truth ... m. above all things 51:6
Mike O'Day: this is the grave of M. 12:8
Milan: retire me to my M. 289:8
Mile: he walked a crooked m. 194:3
miss is as good as a m. 221:7
yr. sad [heart] tires in a m.-a 292:19
Miles: can ye draw but twenty m. a' day? 166:12
how many m. to Babylon? 189:8
people come m. to see it 118:13
Miles gloriosus 200:15
Military: war ... too serious ... to be left to m. men 311:3
Milk: crying over spilt m. 210:24
drunk the m. of Paradise 87:16
flowing with m. and honey 31:18
m. comes frozen home in pail 269:1
no finer investment than ... m. in babies 83:9
too full o' th' m. of human kindness 270:1
Milking: going a-m., sir, she said 195:7
Milkmaid singeth blithe 174:3
Milky way: twinkle on the m. 331:8
Mill: bring grist to the m. 215:34
God's m. grinds slow but sure 215:12
in Gaza at the m. with slaves 180:9
more water glideth by the m. 289:13
Millar: I respect M., Sir 142:3
last sheet [*Johnson's Dictionary*] to M. 142:2
Miller: more water ... than wots ... m. of 289:13
there was a jolly m. once 54:1
Milliner: perfumed like a m. 254:1
Million: a m. m. spermatozoa 137:14
among so many m. of faces 59:15
the play ... pleas'd not the m. 250:10
Millionaire: I am a M. That is my religion 296:1
Millions: there are m. of us 324:18
Mills: the m. of God grind slowly 161:3
Millstone ... hanged about his neck 44:20
Milton: faith and morals ... M. held 334:1
malt does more than M. can 136:9
M.! thou shdst. be living 333:12
some mute inglorious M. 126:11
Mimsy were the borogoves 75:9
Mince: they dined on m. and ... quince 158:9
Mind: a m. not to be changed 176:5
a m. quite vacant is a m. distressed 93:4
a miserable state of m. 22:14
a prodigious quantity of m. 318:12
among all the diseases of the m. 306:6

Mind (*continued*)
better than P. of M. 231:19
blind ... judgment, and misguide the m. 202:4
born for the Universe, narrowed his m. 123:1
cheer of m. ... I was wont to have 285:14
clap yr. padlock on her m. 205:5
distressed, in m., body, or estate 52:29
dread had seized their troubled m. 311:4
education forms the common m. 203:14
fair terms and a villain's m. 274:11
farewell the tranquil m. 280:2
four seasons in the m. of man 151:4
great hills ... come back into my m. 28:2
he who does not m. his belly 142:14
I don't m. if I do 146:15
incline man's m. to atheism 22:11
it concentrates his m. wonderfully 144:8
last infirmity of noble m. 175:1
loud laugh ... spoke the vacant m. 122:8
love looks ... with the m. 276:12
love's but the frailty of the m. 89:14
love's the noblest frailty of the m. 104:8
m. ... deficient in ... humour 88:4
m. one's P's and Q's 222:32
m. that makes the body rich 287:11
m. yr. own business 221:4
minister to a m. diseased 272:6
my m. to me a kingdom is 105:6
never face so pleased my m. 17:2
no m. is thoroughly well organized 88:4
noble m. is here o'erthrown 251:5
not in my perfect m. 267:11
out of sight, out of m. 222:31
reading is to the m. 306:8
riches of the m. ... make ... rich 224:19
she had a frugal m. 92:8
sound m. in a sound body 146:11
that ... was great fortitude of m. 141:14
the gentle m. by gentle deeds 305:14
the m. is its own place 176:5
think my m. is maturing late? 186:5
'tis strange the m., that fiery particle 70:6
to the noble m., rich gifts 251:1
what is M.? No Matter 231:21
when I measure my m. against his [Shaw on Shakespeare] 297:8
when people call this beast to m. 27:1
whether 'tis nobler in the m. 250:20
with a gladsome m. 180:7
worst [tyranny] ... persecutes the m. 104:7
your m.'s cluttered up 324:17
Minds: balm of hurt m. 270:11
bringeth ... m. about to religion 22:11
great m. think alike 215:27
happiest moments of the ... best m. 300:10
lose myself in other men's m. 156:6
m. are not ever craving ... food 93:17
Nature ... doth teach ... to have aspiring m. 166:10
purest and most thoughtful m. 237:4
strange faces, other m. 312:7
the mighty m. of old 304:10
the refuge of weak m. 80:15
the religion of feeble m. 64:13
to the marriage of true m. 294:8
Mine: be m., as I yours for ever 125:8
Curly locks, wilt thou be m.? 188:8
hope's delusive m. 140:13
Mine (*continued*)
thou needest not fear m. [kisses] 300:7
'twas m., 'tis his 279:15
what's m. is my own 230:9
what's m. is yours, ... yours is m. 273:15
Miner: dwelt a m., forty-niner 183:8
Minister: canst thou not m. to a mind diseas'd? 272:6
quench thee, thou flaming m. 280:11
Ministers: angels and m. of grace defend us! 249:3
errands for the M. of State 116:13
my fellows are m. of Fate 288:15
Ministries: *Times* has made many m. 23:18
Ministry: more for a marriage than a m. 23:19
the merit of a m. 146:6
Minnehaha, Laughing Water 161:5
Minnows: Triton of the m. 246:9
Minstrel: a wandering m. I 117:16
the M. Boy to the war is gone 184:2
the M. was infirm and old 239:11
Minute: a sucker born every m. 24:10
fill the unforgiving m. 154:20
must do [good] in m. particulars 55:6
Minutes: our m. hasten to their end 294:1
round ... the earth in forty m. 276:19
see the m. how they run 260:13
Miracle: a m. ... event which creates faith 297:3
a m. of loveliness 118:13
a m. of rare device 87:15
Miranda: do you remember an inn, M.? 28:5
Mirror: best m. is an old friend 221:5
m. of all Christian kings 258:9
Mirth: all m. and no matter 277:19
bards of passion and of M. 147:6
far from all resort of m. 173:9
M., admit me of thy crew 174:1
M., with thee I mean to live 174:11
much m. and no madness 302:12
no country's m. is better than our own 145:5
old earth must borrow its m. 326:9
present m. hath present laughter 291:2
very tragical m. 277:7
Miscarriage: success and m. are empty 140:4
Mischief: no m. but a woman ... priest is at the bottom 222:1
Satan finds some m. still 323:2
to draw new m. on 279:3
to mourn a m. ... past 279:3
Miserable: a m. state of mind 22:14
me m.! 177:13
m. have no other medicine 273:9
Miseries: bound in shallows and in m. 264:3
hopes, and joys, and panting m. 149:5
Misery: dwell on guilt and m. 20:13
fallen ... into m. and endeth wrecchedly 80:1
gave to m. all he had, a tear 126:14
man ... is full of m. 53:28
m. acquaints ... with strange bedfellows 288:7
my m., the wormwood ... gall 41:18
recall ... happiness when in m. 95:7
Misfortune: the m. of knowing anything 20:15
to lose one parent ... a m. 327:12
Misfortunes: children ... make m. more bitter 21:18

Misfortunes (*continued*)
m. never come singly 221:6
m. of our best friends ... not displeasing 234:9
strength to bear the m. of others 234:4
Misgivings: I view with profound m. the retreat 83:10
Mislead: lights that do m. the morn 273:12
Miss: and mine [heart] he cannot m. 302:2
m. is as good as a mile 221:7
Missed: how I m. my Clementine! 183:10
society offenders ... who never wd. be m. 118:4
Mist: the rank m. they draw 175:4
Mistake: any m. about it in any quarter 83:6
man is Nature's sole m. 120:10
Mistakes: learn by other men's m. 230:25
the man who makes no m. 200:2
Mistress: art is a jealous m. 108:1
if you can kiss the m. 218:5
Master M. of my passion 293:16
m. of herself, though China fall 203:17
m. of the Earl of Craven 329:5
O m. mine 291:1
select ... a m. or a friend 298:8
Mistresses: wives are young men's m. 21:20
Mists: season of m. and ... fruitfulness 147:1
Misunderstood: to be great is to be m. 108:12
Misused the King's press 255:15
Mix: I m. them with my brains, sir 196:11
Moan: is not paid with m. 316:8
Moaning: no m. at the bar 311:13
Moat: as a m. defensive to a house 282:5
Mob: best ... to do what the m. do 98:20
m. has ... no brains 221:8
Mobled queen 250:11
Mobs: suppose there are two m.? 98:20
Mock: green-ey'd monster wh. doth m. 279:16
m. on, m. on, Voltaire 55:9
Mock Turtle: said the M. angrily 74:14
the M. replied 74:15
Mocked: be not deceived; God is not m. 48:23
Mockery: death itself ... a m. 299:15
Model of a modern Major-General 120:4
Moderately: love m.; long love doth so 286:18
Moderation: astonished at my own m. 84:11
m. is a fatal thing 328:14
Modes: ring in the nobler m. of life 313:5
Modesty: O m.! 'twas strictly kept 198:11
o'erstep not the m. of nature 251:9
wore enough for m. 62:13
Mohicans: The Last of the M. 90:12
Mole: wilt thou go ask the m. 55:2
Molehill: mountain out of a m. 221:19
Molly Malone 15:10
Mome raths outgrabe 75:9
Moment: all my possessions for a m. of time 107:15
happy in the m. that was present 143:18
m. foreseen may be unexpected 107:11
pleasing attentions ... impulse of the m. 21:1
snow falls ... a m. white then melts 67:4
some m. when the moon was blood 81:1
sonnet is a m.'s monument 236:6
spur of the m. 226:15
to every ... nation comes the m. 162:14
Monan's rill: the moon on M. 239:6
Monarch: becomes the ... m. better than his crown 275:1
I am m. of all I survey 93:14
Monday: hanging ... cat on M. 58:2
M.'s child is fair of face 191:8
Monde: se mêler à corriger le m. 182:14
Mondes: meilleur des m. possibles 321:9
Money: abundance of m. ruins youth 206:1
borrer the m. to do it with 322:15
business ... may bring m. 20:10
by any means make m. 135:11
dally not with m. or women 210:33
did dream of m.-bags to-night 274:13
fool ... m. are soon parted 214:2
Government licence to print m. 316:14
he lends out m. gratis 274:7
he that wants m., means 245:3
I have spent all the m. 144:17
if m. be not thy servant 221:9
innocently employed ... getting m. 143:13
lend yr. m. and lose yr. friend 218:36
love of m. ... root of all evil 49:14
marrieth for love without m. 220:29
merit will not serve ... as m. 142:10
m. begets m. 221:10
m. gives me pleasure 27:10
m. is like muck 22:9
m. makes marriage 221:12
m. talks 221:15
no man ... wrote, except for m. 144:5
no m., no swiss 222:2
pays yr. m. ... takes yr. choice 231:18
purse ... full of other men's m. 212:21
put m. in thy purse 279:6
putting m. on a horse 27:14
remember when ... m. not scarce 108:22
said that love of m. is the root 68:3
some honey, and plenty of m. 158:7
that's the way the m. goes 165:5
the want of m. is so [root of evil] 68:3
throw good m. after bad 227:41
thy m. perish with thee 47:2
your m. or your life 68:13
Mongrels: greyhounds, m., spaniels, curs 271:1
Monk: the devil a m. wd. be 185:1
Monkey: only a m. shaved 120:11
Monotony: bleats articulate m. 306:9
to chase m. 117:6
Monster: great-siz'd m. of ingratitudes 290:6
green-ey'd m. wh. doth mock 279:16
Montezuma: knows who imprisoned M. 164:2
Month: April is the cruellest m. 107:3
ark rested in the seventh m. 30:21
laughter for a m. ... jest for ever 254:8
this is the m. ... the happy morn 175:7
Months: cd. live for m. without ... labour 322:14
go right on ... for numerous more m. 322:14
Montreal: in a M. lumber room 68:9
O God! O M.! 68:9
Montrose: young man of M. 28:9
Monument: a sonnet is a moment's m. 236:6
an early but enduring m. 297:13
he replied, 'Like the M.' 141:16
if you seek my m. 337:1
Patience on a m. 291:7

Monument (*continued*)
their only m. the asphalt road 107:1
thou art a m. 145:12
Monumentum: si m. requiris, circumspice 337:1
Mood: albeit unused to the melting m. 280–1:14
in vacant or in pensive m. 331:11
sweet m. when pleasant thoughts bring sad 332:7
that blessed m. 335:11
Moon: a-roving by the light of the m. 71:4
beneath a waning m. was haunted 87:12
beneath the visiting m. 243:6
course of one revolving m. 103:4
cry for the m. 210:22
danced by the light of the m. 158:9
danced the m. on Monan's Rill 239:6
honour from the pale-fac'd m. 254:4
hymns to the cold fruitless m. 276:9
I see the m. ... m. sees me 190:5
late eclipses in the sun and m. 265:9
lustres slake the o'ertaken m. 58:3
make guilty ... the m. 265:10
man in the m. 220:14
man in the m. ... down too soon 191:6
m. in the valley of Ajalon 33:12
m. when she deserts the night 180:11
moving M. went up the sky 86:12
nor the m. [smite thee] by night 37:16
one with ... the west m. 315:14
Queen-M. is on her throne 149:16
rather be a dog and bay the m. 263:23
slowly, silently, now the m. 97:3
sung to the m. by a ... loon 121:1
swear not by the m., th' inconstant m. 286:10
the cow jumped over the m. 189:5
the m. be still as bright 71:3
the m. doth shine as bright as day 188:6
the m. lies fair 18:9
to bark at the m. 206:38
unmask her beauty to the m. 248:13
with how sad steps, O M. 302:4
Moonlight: ghost along the m. shade 201:5
go visit it by the pale m. 239:12
how sweet the m. sleeps 275:8
I'll come to thee by m. 188:2
ill met by m., proud Titania 276:17
look for me by m. 188:2
passions ... as m. unto sunlight 313:19
Moonlit: knocking on the m. door 96:14
Moons: some nine m. wasted 278:21
Moonshine: look in the almanack; find out m. 277:1
Mops: seven maids with seven m. 76:3
Moral: a m., if only you can find it 74:12
a m., sensible, and well-bred man 92:4
golf ... a form of m. effort 157:14
grandest m. attribute of a Scotsman 25:1
let us be m. ... contemplate existence 98:5
O m. Gower 80:7
point a m. or adorn a tale 141:11
Morality: give ... a lecture on m. ... a shilling 142:10
gossip made tedious by m. 328:3
m. of an action depends 142:7
periodical fits of m. 164:6
up agen middle class m. 296:21
Moralize: faithful loves shall m. 305:9
Morals: foundation of m. and legislation 29:1
Morals (*continued*)
no man's religion ... survives his m. 221:39
teach the m. of a whore 141:19
More: and penance m. will do 86:15
easy to take *m.* than nothing 74:10
enough for modesty—no m. 62:13
m. than somewhat 236:15
Oliver Twist has asked for m. 98:12
you get no m. of me 102:12
Morituri te salutant 308:4
Morn: awake, the m. will never rise 96:1
healthy breath of m. 148:4
lights that do mislead the m. 273:12
now M., her rosy steps 178:12
sang from m. till night 54:1
the m., in russet mantle clad 247:16
this the happy m. 175:7
Morning: beauty of the m.; silent, bare 333:6
day's at the morn. M.'s at seven 62:7
early one m. ... sun was rising 15:1
glad, confident m. 61:9
great m. of the world 297:11
hour in the m. is worth two 217:6
in his m. face 122:11
in the m. we will remember them 54:5
it's nice to get up in the m. 157:6
Lucifer, son of the m. 40:25
M. in the Bowl of Night 109:13
on a cold and frosty m. 15:7
peace ... dropping from the veils of the m. 337:5
sees some m., unaware 61:1
Morrow: good night till it be m. 286:14
never shall sun that m. see 270:3
trusting the m. as little as you can 135:13
Mors: pallida M. aequo ... pede 135:12
Morsel: sweetest m. of the night 256:20
Mortal: he raised a m. to the skies 103:15
her last disorder m. 122:17
reminds a man he is m. 96:5
shall m. man be more just than God? 35:2
Mortality: m., behold and fear 25:8
there's nothing serious in m. 270:15
Mortals: not in m. to command success 9:4
what fools these m. be! 277:3
Mortuis: de m. nil nisi bonum 210:37
Moses: meekness of M. ... strength of Samson 221:1
M. said, ... This is the bread 31:28
persuaded to leave M. out 29:8
Moss: a rolling stone gathers no m. 224:26
Most may err as greatly as the few 103:8
Moth: desire of the m. for the star 300:8
Mother: call me early, m. dear 314:6
dead! and ... never called me m. 330:7
disclaim her for a m. 116:1
does your m. know ... you are out? 24:7
England ... m. of parliaments 58:9
foolish son ... heaviness of his m. 38:8
gave her m. forty whacks 14:3
home to his m.'s house 180:6
I arose a m. in Israel 33:13
I feel no pain, dear m. 15:9
let ... his m. drudge ... at seventy 296:5
like m., like daughter 221:17
Mary was that M. mild 10:6
m. of the free, how shall we extol? 28:10
m., who'd give her booby for another 115:10

Mother (*continued*)
m. who talks about her own children 100:6
my m. bore me in ... wild 56:10
my m. said that I never shd. 191:9
never had any m.? 307:14
the m. of all living 30:15
the m. of months in meadow 309:14
took great care of his m. 171:8
variety ... m. of enjoyment 100:13
where a M. laid her Baby 10:6
whether his m. wd. let him or no 189:2
with the m. first begin 210:34
Mother-in-law remembers not 221:18
Mothers: all women become like their m. 328:13
people's m. always bore me 328:13
Moths ... ever caught by glare 68:18
Motion: between the m. and the act 106:8
in his m. like an angel sings 275:8
in our proper m. we ascend 176:17
no m. has she now, no force 334:15
sensible warm m. to become ... clod 273:10
Motive: morality ... depends on the m. 142:7
Motley: a m. fool 244:8
Mould: splashing the wintry m. 337:7
the m. of form 251:5
Mount: yet shall he m. [Milton] 127:2
Mountain: m. out of a molehill 221:19
robes the m. in its azure hue 72:9
tiptoe on the misty m. tops 286:22
up the airy m. 10:9
Mountains: from Greenland's icy m. 130:1
m. skipped like rams 37:7
the m. look on Marathon 70:1
two voices ... one of the m. 333:10
upon the m. of Ararat 30:21
walk upon England's m. green 55:8
Mountebank: a mere anatomy, a m. 246:5
Mourn: don't m. for me never 12:1
in summer skies to m. 147:11
makes countless thousands m. 66:8
secure, and now can never m. 297:16
that man was made to m. 66:7
to m. a mischief ... past 279:3
Mourning: with my m. very handsome 199:12
Mouse: caught a crooked m. 194:3
frightened a little m. under her chair 192:7
killing of a m. on Sunday 58:2
man or m. 220:20
the m. ran up the clock 189:6
the other caught a m. 158:11
Mouse-trap: make a better m. 108:23
Mouth: a close m. catcheth no flies 209:33
burnt his m. with ... cold plum porridge 191:6
gift horse in the m. 214:30
heart is in his m. 216:26
her m. unclosed in ... kiss 157:10
if you m. it as many ... players do 251:7
into the m. of Hell 311:12
lo, in her m. ... an olive leaf 30:22
out of thine own m. ... I judge thee 46:12
purple-stained m. 149:14
set a watch ... before my m. 37:29
spue thee out of my m. 50:19
tree whose hungry m. is pressed 153:8
wd. not melt in his m. 208:41
Mouths: blind m. that scarce ... know how 175:3
Mouths (*continued*)
have m. but ... speak not 37:8
made m. in a glass 266:9
Moutons: revenons à nos m. 17:9
Move: but it does m. 114:14
do m. a woman's mind 292:7
I will m. the earth 18:3
languid strings do scarcely m. 56:14
Moved: not m. with concord of sweet sounds 275:10
Moves: and having writ, m. on 110:12
m., and mates, and slays 110:11
m. in determinate grooves 128:11
Moving: always m. as the restless spheres 166:10
m. Moon went up the sky 86:12
Mower whets his scythe 174:3
Much: missing so m. and so m. 90:16
m. may be made of a Scotchman 143:8
m. of a muchness 320:4
m. ... said on both sides 9:8
so m., to learn so little 99:3
Muck: money is like m. 22:9
Mud: two men look out ... one sees the m. 156:15
Muddy, ill-seeming, thick, bereft 287:12
Mudie's: I keep my books at ... M. 68:4
Muffet: little Miss M. sat on a tuffet 191:3
Muffin: one caught a m. 158:11
Multiply: be fruitful, and m. 30:4
Multitudes: against revolted m. 178:19
I contain m. 326:5
m. in the valley of decision 42:14
pestilence-stricken m. 299:3
Multitudinous: the m. seas incarnadine 270:12
Munch on, crunch on 62:4
Murder: foul and most unnatural m. 249:8
I met M. on the way 298:13
m. most foul ... unnatural 249:9
m. ... one of the Fine Arts 97:6
m. shrieks out 323:15
m. will out 80:2, 221:21
then m.'s out of tune 280:12
Murdered: death of kings ... all m. 283:6
two brothers and their m. man 148:12
Murderer: Aram ... thief ... liar ... m. 72:3
Murmur: creeping m. and the poring dark 259:8
live m. of a summer's day 18:19
Muse: Fool, said my M. to me 302:3
O for a M. of fire 258:5
strictly meditate the thankless M. 174:15
the M. but served to ease 201:14
Mushroom: nicely groomed, like a m. 157:9
Mushrooms: broiled fowl and m.—capital! 98:17
Music: a reasonable good ear in m. 277:4
and let the sounds of m. creep 275:8
deep sea ... m. in its roar 69:9
fled is that m. 150:6
have m. wherever she goes 193:1
how sour sweet m. is! 284:7
if m. be the food of love 290:10
like m. on my heart 87:1
linnet, how sweet his m.! 335:5
man that hath no m. 275:10
m. and women I ... give way to 199:11
m. has charms to soothe 89:5
m. that gentlier on the spirit lies 314:2

Music (*continued*)
m., when soft voices die 300:6
never merry when I hear sweet m. 275:9
O M., sphere-descended Maid 88:14
ran ... after the wonderful m. 62:6
still, sad m. of humanity 335:14
the m. in my heart I bore 335:1
the setting sun, and m. at the close 282:3
the soul of m. shed 183:11
thou hast thy m. too 147:4
thy chosen m., Liberty! 333:10
to church ... not for the doctrine, but the m. 202:9
to hear the sea-maid's m. 276:18
uproar's your only m. 151:12
when M., heavenly maid, was young 88:12
women and m. shd. never be dated 123:11
Musical: most m., most melancholy! 173:8
we are a m. nation 316:5
Musing there an hour alone 70:1
Musty: proverb is something m. 252:6
Mutilators: borrowers of books ... m. of collections 156:3
Muttering: the m. grew to a grumbling 62:3
Mutton: Alice—M.; M.—Alice 77:10
Muzzle: shall not m. the ox 33:4
Myriad-minded: our m. Shakespeare 88:1
Myrtles: ye m. brown, with ivy never sere 174:12
Myself: awe of such a thing as I m. 262:6
best image of m. 178:14
deliver me from m. 60:2
I celebrate m., and sing m. 325:13
I like to go by m. 129:11
made m. a speculative statesman 9:6
said I to m.—said I 117:4
thought of thinking for m. 119:16
very well then I contradict m. 326:5
when I give I give m. 326:3
Mysteries: capable of being in uncertainties, m. 151:11
Mysterious: God moves in a m. way 92:15
Mystery: brave its [sea's] dangers comprehend its m. 161:4
hissed all my m. lectures 305:19
riddle ... in a m. inside an enigma 82:10
[sea's] works ... are wrapped in m. 90:8
take upon's the m. of things 267:13
the wicked grocer ... m. and a sign 81:10

Nag: forc'd gait of a shuffling n. 255:7
Nail: and Dick the shepherd blows his n. 269:1
dead as a door-n. 210:38
hit the n. on the head 216:33
Nailed: blessed feet which ... years ago were n. 253:14
Nails: nineteen hundred and forty n. 302:9
Naked: both n. ... and were not ashamed 30:10
dead men n. they shall be one 315:14
helpless, n., piping loud 56:3
left me n. to mine enemies 261:13
n. came I out of ... womb 35:1
Nakedness: and not in utter n. 332:1
Name: a deed without a n. 271:14
a good n. ... rather than great riches 38:26
a rose by any other n. 286:9
and she lost her maiden n. 16:11
conveys it in a borrowed n. 205:6
Name (*continued*)
dominion ... by a scribbled n. 315:17
gathered together in thy N. 52:19
give a dog a bad n. 214:31
good n. in man and woman 279:15
good n. is better than precious ointment 39:18
halloo yr. n. to the reverberate hills 290:15
hallowed be thy n. 43:24
he that filches from me my good n. 279:15
her n. was Barbara Allen 11:12
I remember yr. n. perfectly 305:21
I will not blot out his n. 50:18
I wd. ... my n. were not so terrible 256:11
it beareth the n. of Vanity Fair 63:9
lash'd the vice but spared the n. 308:13
let me not n. it to you, you chaste stars 280:10
local habitation and a n. 277:6
must he lose the n. of king? 283:7
my n. is Legion 45:9
my n. is Might-Have-Been 236:8
my 'oss, my wife, and my n. 308:7
n., at which the world grew pale 141:11
n. to all succeeding ages curst 102:16
nature ... a n. for an effect 93:11
not take the n. of ... God in vain 32:2
noteless blot on a remembered n. 297:15
of every friendless n. the friend 140:14
rouse him at the n. of Crispian 259:15
such weak witness of thy n. 175:12
take ... my good n. ... my life 226:39
tell your n. the livelong day 99:14
the gentleman's n. ... Worldly Wiseman 63:8
the grand old n. of gentleman 313:8
the n. of it called Babel 30:27
the n. of the slough was Despond 63:7
the very n. of [stepmother] sufficeth 226:16
the whistling of a n. 203:9
their n. liveth for evermore 52:8
to see one's n. in print 70:12
tranquillity! thou better n. 87:18
what's in a n.? 286:9
what the dickens his n. is 276:5
whose n. was writ in water 152:13
write against your n. 233:12
yet leaving here a n. 304:11
Names: call'd him soft n. 150:3
I have lost all the n. 144:17
no n., no pack drill 222:3
sick men play ... with their n. 282:7
such great n. as these 16:14
unpopular n. and impossible loyalties 19:7
Naming: to-day we have n. of parts 233:6
Naples: see N. and die 225:7
Napoleon: N.'s armies used to march 241:13
N.'s presence ... forty thousand men 324:7
the N. of crime [Moriarty] 101:16
Narr: bleibt ein N. sein Lebelang 163:2
Nasty: a nice man ... of n. ideas 309:10
something n. in the woodshed 116:5
Nation: as the clergy ... so ... rest of the n. 20:11
bind up the n.'s wounds 159:15
dedicate this n. to the policy 235:1
every n. has the govt. it deserves 165:3
hinted that we are a n. of amateurs 235:13
inspired the n. It was the n. 83:14

Nation (*continued*)
n. of shopkeepers 185:12, 303:4
n. ... perpetually to be conquered 64:5
n. shall not lift up sword agst. n. 40:18
no n. was ever ruined by trade 112:14
noble and puissant n. rousing herself 182:8
once to every man and n. 162:14
one third of a n. ill-housed 235:2
righteousness exalteth a n. 38:15
that this n. ... shall have a new birth 159:13
we are a musical n. 316:5
Nations: day of small n. ... passed away 78:8
eclipsed the gaiety of n. 145:1
equal rights ... of n., large and small 319:5
happiest n. have no history 105:15
in thy seed shall all the n. ... blessed 31:5
languages are the pedigree of n. 144:23
lasting peace ... with all n. 159:15
lightning of the n. 299:2
many n. and three continents 102:2
n. are as a drop of a bucket 41:1
n. which have put mankind ... in their debt 138:8
Privileged ... People ... Two N. 100:12
Native: content to breathe his n. air 203:20
fast by their n. shore 93:1
my n. Land—Good Night 69:2
n. hue of resolution 250–1:20
though I am n. here 249:2
Natives: the bulk of your n. ... vermin 308:16
Nativity: in n., chance, or death 276:8
Natural: as n. to die as to be born 21:10
I do it more n. 291:3
in him alone, 'twas n. to please 102:15
n., simple, affecting 123:5
Natural Philosophy [makes men] deep 23:9
Natural Selection: called this principle ... N. 95:11
Naturalists: so, n. observe, a flea 309:4
Naturally: if Poetry come not as n. as the Leaves 151:15
not n. honest 293:6
Nature: a friend ... masterpiece of N. 108:4
accuse not N.! 179:4
all n. is but art 203:4
allow not n. more than n. needs 266:2
are God and N. then at strife? 312:16
as old and new ... as N.'s self 60:13
broken N.'s social union 66:11
creatures that by a rule in n. teach 258:8
cunning'st pattern of excelling n. 280:11
disguise fair n. with ... rage 259:3
first follow N. 202:3
Force of N. cd. no farther go 104:11
fortress built by N. for herself 282:5
great n.'s second course 270:11
his n. is too noble 246:10
human n. is so well disposed 20:9
I have learned to look on n. 335:14
I love not Man the less, but N. more 69:9
in human n. ... more of the fool 22:3
in thy green lap was N.'s darling 127:1
let N. be your teacher 335:6
little we see in N. 333:3
loathed ... life that age ... can lay on n. 273:11
man is N.'s sole mistake 120:10
mute N. mourns her worshipper 239:14
N. always does contrive 117:8
Nature (*continued*)
N. and N.'s Laws lay hid 201:21
N. I loved 156:11
n. in you stands on the very verge 265:22
n. is but a name for an effect 93:11
n. is often hidden, sometimes overcome 22:26
n. is the art of God 59:13
n. lends such evil dreams 312:16
N. might stand up and say 264:7
n. ... must be obeyed 23:17
n. never did betray the heart 336:1
n. of a tragic volume 256:6
n., red in tooth and claw 312:17
n.'s law ... man was made to mourn 66:7
n.'s soft nurse 257:2
N. that framed us 166:10
o'erstep not the modesty of n. 251:9
on N., and on human life, musing 331:3
one touch of n. ... whole world kin 290:7
passing through n. to eternity 247:20
scenery is fine ... human n. is finer 151:16
spectacles of books to read n. 104:4
that N. yet remembers ... fugitive 332:4
the more man's n. runs to 21:12
the n. of an insurrection 262:13
the purpose and n. of miracles 297:3
the rest [hours] on N. fix 85:9
then N. said, 'A lovelier flower' 335:9
to write and read comes by n. 278:4
true wit is n. to advantage dress'd 202:8
unerring N., still divinely bright 202:3
where man is not, n. is barren 57:6
whose body N. is, and God the soul 203:3
woman ... one of N.'s agreeable blunders 91:14
words, like N., half reveal 312:12
yet do I fear thy n. 270:1
youth ... still is N.'s priest 332:2
Natures: men's n. are alike 89:2
Naught: it is n., it is n., saith the buyer 38:24
Naughty: a n. night to swim in 266:15
good deed in a n. world 275:11
n. girl to disobey 191:9
Navy: Ruler of the Queen's N. 119:15,16
Nazareth: can ... any good thing come out of N.? 46:18
Neaera: tangles of N.'s hair 174:16
Near: call ... while he is n. 41:8
he seems so n. and yet so far 313:2
Nearer, my God, to thee 9:3
Neat: still to be n. ... be drest 145:9
Necessary: is yr. journey really n.? 11:5
Necessities: give us the luxuries ... will dispense with ... n. 184:11
Necessity: by n. ... we all quote 108:15
make a virtue of n. 229:20
n. hath no law 221:23
n. ... is the argument of tyrants 200:8
n. is the mother of invention 221:24
no virtue like n. 281:14
sworn brother ... to grim N. 284:4
teach thy n. to reason thus 281:14
thy n. is greater than mine 302:7
Neck: a n. God made for other use 136:4
England will have her n. wrung 83:4
my n. is very short 184:5
n. or nothing 221:25
some chicken! Some n.! 83:4
Need: all we n. of hell 99:15

Need (*continued*)
friend in n. is a friend indeed 214:18
in thy most n. ... by thy side 13:5
n. to pray for fair weather 22:8
O, reason not the n. 266:2
Needle: man for the sword and for the n. she 314:18
plying her n. and thread 135:3
through the eye of a n. 44:23
Needlessly sets foot upon a worm 93:12
Needs: all this sad world n. 326:11
more than nature n. 266:2
to each according to his n. 168:7
Negative Capability 151:11
Negatives: two n. make an affirmative 229:3
Neglect: n. the creeping hours 244:10
such sweet n. more taketh me 145:10
Negligent: celerity ... admir'd than by the n. 242:19
Neiges: où sont les n. d'antan? 320:15
Neighbour: false witness against thy n. 32:8
lov'd his wicked n. as himself 103:7
love thy n. as thyself 32:16
policy of a good n. 235:1
thy n.'s wife ... manservant ... ox ... ass 32:9
worketh no ill to his n. 47:29
Neighbours: good fences make good n. 113:13
in peace ... as good n. 319:5
live without friends ... not without ... n. 219:21
Nelly: let not poor N. starve 78:16
Neptune: do choose the ebbing N. 289:4
envious siege of wat'ry N. 282:6
he wd. not flatter N. 246:10
will all great N.'s ocean wash this blood? 270:12
Nerissa, my little body is aweary 274:5
Nerves: when ... the n. prick 312:14
Nervous: Bradshaw—n. and terse but limited 102:6
Nest: to find a mare's n. 220:24
Nests: birds in their little n. agree 323:3
birds in their ... n. agree with Chinamen 27:11
built their n. in my beard 158:13
Nettle: out of this n., danger 254:10
Never: and ... n. called me mother 330:7
better late than n. 207:30
books n. die 235:5
dead men rise up n. 310:1
don't mourn for me n. 12:1
I n. shall love the snow again 58:5
limericks n. wd. scan 13:1
love that n. told can be 55:10
me and my true love will n. meet 16:10
my apple trees will n. 113:13
n. a spray of yew 18:16
n. begin than n. make an end 207:32
n. broke the Sabbath, but for gain 103:6
n. glad confident morning again 61:9
n., I ween, was a prouder 24:5
n. lov'd ... met ... parted 65:10
n., n., n., n., n. 268:4
n., n. thinks of me 17:3
n. seek to tell thy love 55:10
n. send to know for whom the bell 101:8
n. the time and the place 61:11
n. the twain shall meet 154:8
Never (*continued*)
n. to have lost at all 68:12
n. to have loved at all 312:13
n. turned his back ... n. doubted 60:12
seldom or n. the two hit it off 330:10
This England n. did nor n. shall 265:4
what, n.? No, n.! 119:11
who n. made a foe 312:5
Nevermore: quoth the Raven, N. 200:19
New: a n. broom sweeps clean 221:37
a n. commandment I give 46:29
a n. heaven and a n. earth 51:1
a n. master—get a n. man 288:10
among n. men, strange faces 312:7
as old and n. ... as Nature's self 60:13
before you are on with the n. 16:1
called the N. World into existence 72:15
[compassions] are n. every morning 41:19
conservatism? ... is ... against the n. 159:11
how strange it seems, and n.! 61:10
n. king ... knew not Joseph 31:15
n. man ... raised up in him 53:10
n. nobility ... act of power 22:7
n. philosophy calls all in doubt 100:16
n. wine into old bottles 45:25
no n. thing under the sun 39:12
old lamps for n. 18:1
old order ... yielding place to n. 312:8
piping songs for ever n. 149:9
ring in the n. 313:4
sing unto him a n. song 36:5
will not apply n. remedies 22:18
New Way to Pay Old Debts 169:3
Newcastle: coals to N. 209:8
Newcomer: O, blithe N.! 336:2
New-fangled: May's n. shows 268:9
their garments, though n. ill 294:2
News: all the n. that's fit to print 196:9
first bringer of unwelcome n. 256:7
for there is good n. yet to hear 81:8
good n. from a far country 38:29
he that tells his wife n. 227:21
ill n. comes too soon 217:18
man bites a dog, that is n. 95:5
master-passion ... love of n. 93:18
nature of bad n. infects 242:11
never good to bring bad n. 242:16
no n. is good n. 222:4
nowadays truth ... greatest n. 222:20
talk of court n. 267:13
Newspapers: n. always excite curiosity 156:8
successful n. are ceaselessly querulous 169:12
Newton: another N., a new Donne 137:14
God said, Let N. be! 201:21
Nice: a n. man ... of nasty ideas 309:10
n. to get up in the mornin' 157:6
sugar and spice and all that's n. 195:6
too n. for a statesman 123:2
Nicely: n.-calculated less or more 330:11
sick men play so n. with their names 282:7
Nickname: a n. is the heaviest stone 129:14
Nigh: the Lord is n. 36:7
Night: a braw, bricht, moonlicht n. 157:4
a casement ope at n. 150:7
a naughty n. to swim in 266:15
afraid for the terror by n. 36:26
all n. long ... on sentry-go 117:6
and darkness N. he named 178:21

Night (*continued*)
a-roving so late into the n. 71:3
as a watch in the n. 36:22
beneath the kisses of n. 299:14
calmest and most stillest n. 257:3
come, civil n. 286:21
come, thick n. 270:2
desire ... of the n. for the morrow 300:8
dog in the n.-time 102:1
done by n. appears by day 211:30
doom'd ... to walk the n. 249:6
Friday n. is Amami n. 11:3
from morn to n., my friend 236:3
gentle into that good n. 315:15
gwine to run all n. ... all day 112:4
honey'd middle of the n. 147:13
I ask of thee, beloved N. 299:1
I read much of the n. 107:4
in the Bowl of N. 109:13
in the forests of the n. 56:5
it [candle] will not last the n. 170:13
labour n. and day to be a pilgrim 63:14
let's have one other gaudy n. 243:1
like the n. of cloudless climes 71:2
moonless n. in the small town 316:2
my delight on a shining n. 16:6
ne'er saw true beauty till this n. 286:4
n. cometh, when no man can work 46:26
n. is drawing nigh 24:8
n. is long that never finds the day 272:1
n. makes no difference 132:4
n. neddying among the snuggeries 316:3
n.'s candles are burnt out 286:22
n. unto n. sheweth knowledge 35:23
odd ... it was the middle of the n. 75–6:16
out of the n. that covers me 130:8
pass'd a miserable n. 284:15
perils and dangers of this n. 52:21
poor souls who dwell in N. 55:1
reign of Chaos and old N. 176:10
remain together ... it will be good n. 298:10
returned home the previous n. 63:1
shades of n. were falling fast 160:12
she hangs upon the cheek of n. 286:3
ships that pass in the n. 161:7
silver-sweet ... lovers' tongues by n. 286:13
sing ... even in the dead of n. 290:15
singing, startle the dull n. 174:2
soft stillness and the n. 275:8
sound of revelry by n. 69:3
Spirit of N.! 298:15
stood that n. against my fire 267:9
sweetest morsel of the n. 256:20
tender is the n. 149:16
the bird of n. did sit 262:12
the black bat, n. 314:3
the n. has a thousand eyes 57:13
the n. is dark ... far from home 187:14
the n. was made for loving 71:4
the n. we went to Birmingham 81:7
the shadow of our n. 297:16
there's n. and day, brother 57:8
things that go bump in the n. 13:7
things that love n. 266:10
this is the n. that ... makes me or fordoes 280:9
this will last out a n. in Russia 273:3
to many a watchful n.! 257:16
upon a tranced summer-n. 148:6

Night (*continued*)
voice I hear this passing n. 150:4
watch that ends the n. 323:5
watchman, what of the n.? 40:26
weeping may endure for a n. 36:2
what hath n. to do with sleep? 172:15
when n. darkens the streets 176:8
wide womb of uncreated N. 176–7:19
witching time of n. 252:8
wd. not spend another such a n. 284:15
Nightingale: spoils the singing of the n. 147:11
Nightmare: the n. Life-in-Death was she 86:8
Nights: Chequer-Board of N. and Days 110:11
days of danger, n. of waking 239:9
Nile: allegory on the banks of the N. 301:11
my serpent of old N.? 242:12
pour the waters of the N. 73:17
Nimble: words that have been so n. 25:7
Nimrod: even as N. the mighty hunter 30:26
Nine: a cat has n. lives 209:13
a cat has only n. lives 318:17
how many beans make n. 218:13
n. bean rows will I have 337:4
stitch in time saves n. 226:25
Nineveh: shd. not I spare N.? 42:21
Nip: I'll n. him in the bud 234:3
No: O, n. John, n. John! 16:8
some said ... print it ... others ... N. 63:5
Noah: and N. he often said to his wife 81:11
but one poor N. 137:14
unto N. into the ark 30:20
Nobility: leave us still our old n. 237:10
mercy is n.'s true badge 289:12
new n. ... ancient n. 22:7
n. imposes its own obligations 159:4
Noble: do n. things, not dream 154:2
how n. in reason! 250:6
man is a n. animal 60:3
never enjoys h'self except for a n. purpose 131:7
n. army of Martyrs 52:15
n. Living and the n. dead 334:6
Nobleman: celebrated, cultivated ... n. 116:7
live cleanly, as a n. shd. 256:5
Nobler: n. in the mind to suffer 250:20
n. than attending for a check 247:3
Noblesse oblige 159:4
Noblest: n. Roman of them all 264:6
ruins of the n. man 263:7
the two n. of things 308:11
Nobly: both parties n. are subdu'd 257:12
n., n., Cape Saint Vincent 61:4
Nobody: don't think n. never made me 308:1
I care for n., not I 54:2
n. asked you, sir, she said 196:1
n. feels for my poor nerves 21:2
n. gets old ... godly ... crafty 337:6
n. is on my side 21:2
nothing happens, n. comes 25:11
Nod: Old N. the shepherd goes 97:1
Nodding by the fire, take down this book 337:10
Nods: N. and Becks and ... Smiles 173:16
shame when the worthy Homer n. 135:10
Nohow: looked at for nothing. N.! 75:13
Noise: a loud n. at one end 155:15
an incessant n. like ... water-mill 308:14

Noise (*continued*)
dreadful n. of waters 285:1
Fifth Symphony ... most sublime n. 112:1
never valued till they make a n. 94:1
Noises: like n. in a swound 86:2
this isle is full of n. 288:13
Noll: for shortness called N. 115:2
No-More, Too-Late, Farewell 236:8
Nonconformist: whoso wd. be a man must be a n. 108:11
None: n. of us liveth to himself 47:30
n. that ... trust in him shall be overcome 52:9
so the poor dog had n. 192:2
some believe they've n. at all 68:2
then n. was for a party 163:12
this little pig had n. 194:7
Nonsense: sounds like n., my dear 240:11
through ... realms of N. absolute 104:13
Noon: dark, amid the blaze of n. 180:10
far from the fiery n. 148:4
from morn to n. he fell 176:14
sun has not attained his n. 132:1
Noon-day, upon the market-place 262:12
Noose: in a N. of Light 109:13
naked to the hangman's n. 136:4
Normal: yes, thank God, we're n. 197:9
Norman: simple faith than N. blood 313:10
North-north-west: am but mad n. 250:8
Nor(o)way: to N., N. ... o'er the faem 11:14
Norwich: asked his way to N. 191:6
Nose: custom ... hateful to the n. 138:14
cut off one's n. to spite one's face 210:29
Dong with a luminous N. 158:3
ever and anon he gave his n. 254:1
had Cleopatra's n. been shorter 198:7
led by the n. with gold 293:8
Marian's n. looks red and raw 269:1
n. was as sharp as a pen 259:2
one's n. to the grindstone 222:10
pay through the n. 28:9, 222:38
ring at the end of his n. 158:8
snapped off her n. 193:5
to turn up one's n. 228:33
wipe a bloody n. 115:11
Noses: athwart men's n. as they lie asleep 286:1
n., ... but they smell not 37:9
nothing pay for wearing our own n. 247:1
Note: as the gen'l'm'n said to the fi' pun' n. 99:2
his merry n. unto ... bird's throat 244:4
not a funeral n. 330:3
when found, make a n. 98:3
Notes: I heard a thousand blended n. 332:7
the sound is forced, the n. are few 56:14
Nothing: book although there's n. in't 70:12
certain of n. but ... holiness 151:9
civility costs n. 209:29
days ... when ... n. goes wrong 120:13
devil, having n. else to do 27:8
did n. in particular 117:11
do n. for ever and ever 12:1
doing n. for a bribe 247:3
doings without charity are n. worth 53:3
easy to take *more* than n. 74:10
everything by starts and n. long 103:4
gives to airy n. ... habitation 277:6
he n. common did or mean 168:4
Nothing (*continued*)
he that knows n., doubts n. 218:15
I am n. if not critical 279:7
I do n. upon myself 101:6
is it n. to ... ye that pass by? 41:17
know this only, that he n. knew 180:4
learnt n., and forgotten n. 310:12
let n. you dismay 15:3
looked at for n. Nohow! 75:13
mind's cluttered up with n. 324:17
neck or n. 221:25
n. a year, paid quarterly 308:9
n—absolutely n.—half so much worth doing 124:12
n. begins and n. ends 316:8
n. beside remains. Round the decay 299:8
n. can bring you peace 108:13
n. destroyeth authority so much 22:15
n. except a battle lost 324:6
n. for n. 222:12
n. for n. 'ere 231:24
n. great ... without enthusiasm 108:3
n. happens, nobody comes 25:11
n. in excess 17:10
n. in his life became him 269:11
n. is certain but death and taxes 113:3
n. is certain but uncertainty 222:13
n. is had for n. 84:12
n. is ours but time 222:14
n. of him that doth fade 288:1
n. of itself will come 331:5
n. pay for wearing our own noses 247:1
n. seek, n. find 222:16
n. so absurd but some philosopher has said it 84:1
n. so sharply reminds 96:5
n.'s truer than them [taxes] 97:19
n. succeeds like excess 328:14
n. succeeds like success 222:17
n. to declare except my genius 328:16
n. to do but work 153:10
n. to eat but food 153:10
n. to look backward [forward] to 113:10
n. to say—say n. 88:18
n. to wear but clothes 153:10
n. venture, n. win 222:19
n. ... violent is permanent 222:18
n. went unrewarded but Desert 103:5
n. whatever to grumble at 120:13
n. will come of n. 265:6
questioneth n., n. learneth 222:15
sea ... n. but to make him sick 101:2
smattering of everything ... knowledge of n. 99:11
sound and fury signifying n. 272:10
speak ... as I am; n. extenuate 280:14
think n. done while aught remains 234:14
'tis something, n. 279:15
we brought n. into this world 49:13
yeomanry ... with whom ... n. to do 20:6
Nothingness: love and fame to n. 151:8
will never pass into n. 147:8
Notice ... you have been pleased to take 142:1
Notorious: open and n. evil liver 53:9
Nought: knows n. that knows not this 289:15
Noun: talk of a n. and a verb 260:11
Nourished: how begot, how n. 274:18
Novel: I've read in many a n. 72:2
only obligation to which ... we may hold a n. 139:3

Novel (*continued*)
when I want to read a n. 100:15
Novels: catalogue ... more entertaining than ... n. 169:6
how much wd. n. gain 70:10
November's sky ... November's leaf 240:3
Novice: young, a N. in the Trade 104:15
Now: in England—n.! 61:1
Nowhere: and n. did abide 86:12
one really lives n. 65:5
Nude: keep one from going n. 153:10
Nuisances who write for autographs 118:4
Number: count the n. of the beast 50:26
greatest happiness of the greatest n. 29:1
so teach us to n. our days 36:24
Numbers: achiever brings home full n. 277:9
divinity in odd n. 276:8
I lisp'd in n., for the n. came 201:13
perhaps the plaintive n. flow 334:17
tell me not, in mournful n. 160:14
Numbness: drowsy n. pains my sense 149:13
Nun: holy time is quiet as a n. 333:2
Nuncheon: crunch on, take your n. 62:4
Nunnery: get thee to a n. 251:2
n. of thy chaste breast 162:6
Nuns fret not at ... narrow cell 332:13
Nuptials: prone to any iteration of n. 90:1
Nurse: baby ... that sucks the n. asleep 243:11
nature's soft n. 257:2
this n., this teeming womb of ... kings 282:5
Nurseries: in the n. of Heaven 316:11
n. of all vice and immorality 109:10
Nurses: wives are ... old men's n. 21:20
Nursing the unconquerable hope 19:1
Nursling: I am ... the n. of the Sky 298:6
Nurslings of immortality 299:11
Nut: hard n. to crack 216:14
I had a little n. tree 190:1
Nutmeg: silver n. and a golden pear 190:1
Nuts: Brazil, where the n. come from 315:1
gathering n. in May 15:7
may be n. for Mary Ann 12:6
Nymph: haste thee, N. 173:16
mountain-n., sweet Liberty 173:18

O: cram within this wooden O 258:6
Oak: bend a knotted o. 89:5
grave where English o. and holly 129:2
hearts of o. are our ships 115:1
Oaks: tall o., branch-charmed 148:6
Oars: the o. were silver 242:14
with falling o. ... kept the time 167:10
Oath: a good mouth-filling o. 255:9
Oaths: full of strange o. 244:11
o. are but words 67:16
Oats: *o.* ... in England ... given to horses 140:9
sow one's wild o. 230:16
Obedience: as honour, love, o. 272:5
o. is ... seen in little things 222:21
resistance to tyrants is o. to God 139:11
Obey: safer to o. than to rule 152:16
to love, cherish, and to o. 53:23
woman to o. 314:18
Object: my o. all sublime 118:10
only legitimate o. of government 139:10
'tis for o. strange and high 167:16
Obligation: only o. to which ... we may hold a novel 139:3
Obligations: nobility imposes its own o. 159:4
respect for the o. arising from treaties 319:5
Oblivion: put alms for o. 290:6
second childishness and mere o. 244-5:11
the rest ... commend to cold o. 298:8
Oblivious: some sweet o. antidote 272:6
Obsequies: Nature ... celebrates his o. 239:14
Observance: more honour'd in the breach than the o. 249:2
with this special o. 251:9
Observation: let o. with extensive view 141:9
Observations which ourselves we make 203:13
Observed: the o. of all observers 251:5
Obstruction: to lie in cold o. and to rot 273:10
Occasion: courage mounteth with o. 264:10
Occasions: all o. do inform against me 252:17
there is o. and causes 260:3
Occupation: absence of o. is not rest 93:4
line of o. in the central sector 83:10
Occupations: worse o. in the world 306:14
Occupied: how my parents were o. and all 237:13
Ocean: a life on the o. wave 238:8
dark unfathom'd caves of o. 126:10
great Neptune's o. wash this blood 270:12
in the o.'s bosom unespied 167:8
make the mighty o. 73:13
on the o. of life we pass 161:7
painted ship upon a painted o. 86:5
pores of the o. and shores 298:6
we sail the o. blue 119:8
Odd: creators of o. volumes 156:3
divinity in o. numbers 276:8
o. because ... middle of the night 75-6:16
scarcely o. because they'd eaten every one 76:6
think it exceedingly o. 155:14
Odds: die better than facing fearful o. 163:10
the o. is gone 243:6
Odi et amo. Quare ... nescio 77:16
Odium: the o. of having discovered sodium 29:5
Odorous: comparisons are o. 278:8
Odour: in the o. of sanctity died 24:6
stealing and giving o. 290:10
Odours, when sweet violets sicken 300:6
O'erpeer: for truth to o. 246:8
Off: o. with his head! 74:11
o. with the old love 16:1
only that when ... o. [stage] he was acting 123:5
Offence: beauty ... after o. returning 181:5
dire o. from am'rous causes springs 204:5
my o. is rank 252:10
Offend: if thine eye o. thee 44:21
o. one of these little ones 44:20
Offended: for him have I o. 263:10
Offender: Clinker ... a most notorious o. 303:19
Offenders: little list of Society o. 118:4
the more laws, the more o. 218:25
Offer: never refuse a good o. 221:32
nothing to o. but blood, toil, tears 82:11
Office: hath but a losing o. 256:7
heresy ... that ... o. sanctifies 9:1
o. and affairs of love 277:15
o. and custom, in all line 290:1
the insolence of o. 250-1:20

Office boy: as o. to an Attorney's firm 119:15
Officers: a King, and o. of sorts 258:8
Official: what is o. is incontestable 114:3
Officious, innocent, sincere 140:14
Officiously to keep alive 84:16
Offspring: o. of Heaven first-born! 177:9
true source of human o. 178:8
Oft: many a time and o. 274:9
o., when on my couch I lie 331:11
Oil: lingering, with boiling o. 118:14
o'er books consumed the midnight o. 115:9
pour o. upon the waters 222:22
Ointment: good name ... better than precious o. 39:18
Old: a liking o. for thee 72:4
adherence to the o. and tried 159:11
all things worn out and o. 337:7
an o. abusing of ... patience 276:3
an o. man in a dry month 106:5
an o. man in a hurry 82:5
an o. maxim in the schools 308:12
as o. and new ... as Nature's self 60:13
call for his o. shoes 241:1
grow o. along with me 62:9
grow o. with a good grace 306:7
half as o. as time 64:3
I grow o. ... I grow o. 106:15
I love everything that's o. 123:6
if I ever grow to be o. 28:3
man ... as o. as he's feeling 88:7
never too o. to learn 221:35
new book is published, read an o. one 234:13
o. age shd. burn 315:15
o. and godly and grave 337:6
o. as he feels ... o. as she looks 220:17
o. as the hills 222:23
o. books, o. wine 123:6
o. friends and o. wine are best 222:24
o. friends are best 241:1
o. friends, o. times, o. manners 123:6
o. head on young shoulders 222:25
o. lamps for new 18:1
o. men forget 260:1
o. poacher ... good game-keeper 222:26
o. soldiers ... only fade away 16:7
o. soldiers, sweethearts ... lovers 324:1
o., unhappy, far-off things 334:17
o. wine ... o. pippins ... o. wood 324:1
one of them is fat and grows o. 254:14
ring out the o. 313:4
so o., and so profane 258:3
summits o. in story 314:14
tell me the o., o. story 128:4
the grand o. name of gentleman 313:8
the mighty minds of o. 304:10
the o. gang 82:4
the o. order changeth 312:8
the thousand wars of o. 313:6
they shall grow not o. 54:5
they think he is growing o. 138:10
when thou art o. ... grief enough 127:5
when you are o. and grey 337:10
woman as o. as she looks 88:7
young in years ... o. in hours 23:1
Old Bailey: say the bells of O. 192:4
Old Kent Road: knock'd 'em in the O. 81:13
Old Testament: prosperity is the blessing of the O. 21:13
Olive-leaf: an o. he brings, pacific sign 179:16
Olive-leaf (*continued*)
in her mouth was an o. 30:22
Oliver Twist has asked for more 98:12
Olivia: air cry out 'O.!' 290:15
Olympiades: l'important dans ces o. 91:2
Olympic Games: important thing in the O. is 91:2
Omnia vincit amor ... cedamus 321:5
On: before you are o. with the new 16:1
o., o., you noblest English 259:4
o., Stanley, o.! 240:10
Once: children ... call yet o. 18:12
One: all for o., and o. for all 105:3
animals went in o. by o. 14:9
but the O. was Me 137:14
clock struck o., the mouse ran down 189:6
dead men ... shall be o. 315:14
he replied, O.'s absurd 183:1
how to be o. up 204:16
Liberty and Union ... o. and inseparable 323:10
o. for the master ... o. for the dame 188:4
o. God, o. law, o. element 313:9
o. ... is rather coarse 13:11
o. more river to cross 14:9
o. thing ... worse than being talked about 328:6
O., two, buckle my shoe 192:3
o. to watch and o. to pray 9:13
the O. remains, the many change 298:2
to lose o. parent 327:12
true it is she had o. failing 66:6
two hearts that beat as o. 162:8
One-and-twenty: long expected, o. ... is flown 140:18
when I was o. 136:5
Oneself: to love o. ... lifelong romance 327:5
Only: not by eastern windows o. 85:3
o. thing that I ever did wrong 16:3
Onward: a little o. lend thy ... hand 180:8
O. Christian soldiers 24:9
O., the sailors cry 57:12
Open: o. and notorious evil liver 53:9
o. not thine heart 51:18
o. Sesame! 18:2
Ophir: quinquireme ... from distant O. 168:13
Opinion: error of o. may be tolerated 139:8
never in touch with public o. 328:11
no o. of God at all 22:12
of his own o. still 68:1
think the last o. right 202:12
Opinions: halt ye between two o. 34:19
proper o. for the time of year 20:4
so many men, so many o. 315:4
stiff in o., ... in the wrong 103:4
Opium: religion ... is the o. of the people 168:8
Opportunity makes the thief 222:29
Opposed: bear't that th' o. may beware 248:16
Opposing: sea of troubles and by o., end them 250–1:20
Opposition: conjunction of the mind, and o. of the stars 167:17
Oppression: lack gall to make o. bitter 250:17
Oppressor: who wd. bear ... th' o.'s wrong? 250–1:20
Oracle: I am Sir O. 274:3
Orange: ruled by an O. 241:12

Oranges and lemons 192:4
Orator: beauty ... doth ... persuade ... without an o. 295:5
Orb: monthly changes in her circled o. 286:10
smallest o. which thou behold'st 275:8
Orchard: chaffinch sings on the o. bough 61:1
Order: good o. is the foundation 64:14
in all line of o. 290:1
o. ... this matter better in France 306:11
stand not upon the o. of your going 271:9
the old o. changeth 312:8
to o. myself ... reverently 53:13
words in the (their) best 88:3
Ordered: God ... o. their estate 10:5
Ore: load ... yr. subject with o. 152:12
Organ: O. Morgan ... o. o. all the time 316:6
playing of the merry o. 15:8
Organism to live beyond its income 68:7
Organized: no mind is thoroughly well o. 88:4
Organs: hath not a Jew hands, o.? 274:17
Orgies are vile 186:3
Origin: dancing? Oh, dreadful! ... of savage o. 65:4
indelible stamp of his lowly o. 95:10
Original: a thought is often o. 134:4
their great O. proclaim 9:9
Originality: all good things ... are the fruits of o. 170:10
Originator: next to the o. of a good sentence 108:14
Orlando: run, run O. 245:2
Ormus: wealth of O. and of Ind 176:15
Ornament: rhyme being no ... true o. 175:14
Ornavit: nullum quod tetigit non o. 144:22
Orpheus with his lute 261:6
Oscar: you will, O., you will 325:7
Ostrich: America cannot be an o. 329:8
Other: after the first death ... no o. 316:1
bunch of o. men's flowers 183:6
or any o. reason why 10:3
o. times, o. manners 206:29
since then I have used no o. 232:2
Others: a corner ... for o.' uses 279:17
be not false to o. 22:17
best and distinguished above o. 134:9
England ... wont to conquer o. 282:6
fly to o. that we know not of 250–1:20
misfortunes and pains of o. 65:1
o. abide our question 19:2
pleased ourselves, we ... please o. 223:11
some ... are more equal than o. 197:1
to encourage the o. 321:10
Otherwise: some ... wise, and some ... o. 225:38, 303:20
Ounce: an o. of discretion 222:30
Ours: little we see in nature that is o. 333:3
Ourselves: fault ... not in our stars, but in o. 262:8
praise o. in other men 202:13
Out: include me o. 124:5
mordre wol o. 80:2
murder will o. 221:21
O., damned spot! o., I say! 272:2
o. of sight, o. of mind 222:31
o., o., brief candle! 272:10
o., o., hyaena! 180:16
who's in, who's o. 267:13
Outgrabe: mome raths o. 75:9
Outlive: desire shd. so ... o. performance? 256:19
Outrun: we may o. by violent swiftness 261:3
Outside: I am just going o. 196:7
Outsoared: he has o. the shadow of our night 297:16
Outward: hope from o. forms to win 87:9
o. and visible sign 53:16
Oven: in the o. for baby and me 192:5
Over: now the day is o. 24:8
'O. the hills and far away' 195:3
until it doth run o. 14:14
Over much: be not righteous o. 39:21
Over-canopied with luscious woodbine 276:20
Overcast: since first our sky was o. 93:13
Overcoat: only argument ... put on yr. o. 163:1
Overcome: nature ... sometimes o. 22:26
o. evil with good 47:27
to o. pleasure ... greatest pleasure 223:13
what is else not to be o.? 175:18
Overcomes: who o. by force 176:13
O(v)erjoyed was he to find 92:8
Overpaid: high official ... grossly o. 131:6
Overset the brain, or break the heart 332:12
Overthrow: those ... thou thinkest thou dost o. 101:4
Overwhelm myself in poesy 150:10
Overwhelmed all her litter but one 256:8
Owed: so much o. by so many to so few 82:15
Owes: he o. not any man 161:10
o. its pleasure to another's pain 93:9
Owl: moping o. does to the moon complain 126:5
nightly sings the staring o. 269:1
old o. lived in an oak 231:26
o., for all his feathers, was a-cold 147:12
the O. and the Pussy-Cat 158:7
Owls: I couch when o. do fly 289:6
two O. and a Hen 158:13
Own: came unto his o. and his o. received him not 46:16
every country but his o. 118:5
our watches ... each believes his o. 202:2
room of one's o. 330:9
we mean to hold our o. 83:6
Owner: the o. whereof was Giant Despair 63:11
the ox knoweth his o. 40:16
Ox: a stalled o. and hatred 38:18
nor his o., nor his ass 32:9
o. knoweth his owner 40:16
thou shalt not muzzle the o. 33:4
Oxenford: a Clerk ther was of O. 79:7
Oxford: ahead ... either O. or Cambridge 304:4
the clever men at O. 124:13
the king to O. sent a troop 60:4
to ... O. I acknowledge no obligation 116:1
to O. sent a troop of horse 318:1
Oxlips and the nodding violet 276:20
Oyster: an o. may be crossed in love 301:3
the world's mine o. 276:4
Oysters: 'O, O.,' said the Carpenter 76:6
poverty and o. 99:1
Ozymandias, king of kings 299:8

P's and Q's: to mind one's P. 222:32
Pace: creeps in this petty p. 272:10

Paced: bride hath p. into the hall 86:1
Pacem: qui desiderat p. 320:8
Paces about her room ... alone 107:5
Pacific: he stared at the P. 150–1:15
Pack: can p. the cards 22:16
Paddington: as London is to P. 72:17
Paddle: every man p. his own canoe 167:7
Padlock: clap yr. p. on her mind 205:5
wedlock is a p. 230:3
Pagan suckled in a creed outworn 333:4
Pagans: to chase these p. in those holy fields 253:14
Page: on a beautiful quarto p. 301:13
Pageant: this insubstantial p. faded 288:16
Paid: at cards for kisses—Cupid p. 163:3
p. at the Greek Kalends 71:10
two I am sure I have p. 254:15
well p. that is well satisfied 275:7
Pail: to fetch a p. of water 190:6
Pain: a stranger yet to p. 125:13
although p. isn't real 12:9
cease upon the midnight with no p. 150:3
hour of p. ... long as a day 217:7
I feel no p., dear mother 15:9
I love to give p. 89:12
laughter with some p. is fraught 300:2
long grief and p. 314:5
neither shall there be any more p. 51:3
not because it gave p. to the bear 164:7
not in pleasure, but in rest from p. 104:9
one who never inflicts p. 187:13
owes its pleasure to another's p. 93:9
p. clings cruelly to us 147:9
sweet is pleasure after p. 103:14
we are born in others' p. 316:8
what p. it was to drown! 285:1
when p. and anguish wring the brow 240:9
who wd. lose, though full of p., this ... being 176:19
with p. purchas'd, doth inherit p. 268:7
Painful: no p. inch to gain 85:2
one ... as p. as the other 21:10
Pains: for my p. a world of sighs 279:2
Paint: cheeks are covered with p. 186:1
good face needs no p. 215:17
looking as fresh as p. 303:2
p. my picture truly like me 94:10
p. the meadows with delight 268:17
to p. the lily 264:19
Painted: face with nature's own hand p. 293:16
idle as a p. ship upon a p. ocean 86:5
not so young as ... p. 26:7
Painters and poets ... lie 222:33
Painting a face ... not washing 114:7
Paintings: I have heard of your p. 251:4
Palace: a p. and a prison on each hand 69:6
love in a p. 149:1
my gorgeous p. for a hermitage 283:7
Palaces: cottages, princes' p. 274:6
Pale: p. cold cowardice 281:10
p. grew thy cheek and cold 71:5
Palestine: to haven in sunny P. 168:13
Pall Mall Gazette is written by gentlemen 315:8
Palladium of all the ... rights 146:5
Palm: an itching p. 263:22
bear the p. alone 262:7
Palms: before my feet 81:3
Palpable: a very p. hit 253:7
Pan: what ... doing, the great god P.? 60:9
Pancake: as flat as a p. 213:37
Pangs: more p. ... than wars or women have 261:10
p. of despis'd love 250–1:20
Panic: what a p.'s in thy breastie 66:10
Pansies, that's for thoughts 252:23
Pantaloon: lean and slipper'd p. 244:11
Paper: both sides of the p. at once 241:14
he hath not eat p. 268:11
if all the world were p. 14:1
make dust our p. 283:5
Paper-mill: thou hast built a p. 260:11
Paradise: a p. to what we fear of death 273:11
called the P. of Fools 177:11
drunk the milk of P. 87:16
England ... p. of women, the hell of horses 67:10, 212:24
P. of exiles, Italy 298:12
such are the gates of P. 55:3
this other Eden, demi-p. 282:5
to P. by way of Kensal Green 81:8
weave a p. for a sect 148:1
Wilderness is P. enow 109:15
Paragon: the p. of animals! 250:6
Parchment: inky blots and rotten p. bonds 282:6
Pard: bearded like the p. 244:11
Pardon: bret-ful of p. ... from Rome 79:19
never ask p. before ... accused 221:30
Parent: to lose one p., Mr. Worthing 327:12
Parents: joys of p. are secret 21:17
of p. good, of fist most valiant 259:9
p. we can have but once 142:17
what p. were created for 186:6
Paris: good Americans ... go to P. 328:8
P. is well worth a mass 130:12
P. vaut bien une messe 130:12
the last time I saw P. 128:1
Parish: all the world as my p. 325:4
born ... hanged ... in the same p. 12:5
Parliament: in the P. of man 313:17
Parliaments: England ... mother of p. 58:9
Parlour: 'tis the prettiest little p. 136:10
will you walk into my p.? 136:10
Parmaceti for an inward bruise 254:2
Parochial: worse than provincial—he was p. 139:5
Parody: the devil's walking p. 81:2
Parole ... donnée à l'homme pour déguiser 311:1
Paroles ... pour déguiser leurs pensées 321:12
Parson: a p. much bemused in beer 201:11
coughing drowns the p.'s saw 269:1
Part: every man must play a p. 274:1
I have forgot my p. 246:11
if ought but death p. thee and me 33:26
kiss and p. 102:12
p. of education ... p. of experience 22:13
till death us do p. 53:22
Parted: when we two p. 71:5
Partial: more p. for the observer's sake 203:13
Particle: very fiery p. ... snuff'd out 70:6
Particular: a London p.—a fog, miss 97:9
called away by p. business 301:16
Particulars: [do good] in Minute P. 55:6
Parties: both p. nobly are subdu'd 257:12
hear all p. 216:23
Parting: do not let this p. grieve thee 17:4
p. is all we know of heaven 99:15
p. is such sweet sorrow 286:14

Parting (*continued*)
stood at the p. of the way 41:22
this p. was well made 264:4
Partitions: thin p. do their bounds divide 102–3:17
Partridge in a pear tree 194:2
Parts: one man ... plays many p. 244:11
Party: ancient forms of p. strife 313:5
neither p. loser 257:12
then none was for a p. 163:12
there was an old p. of Lyme 183:1
to p. gave up what was ... for mankind 123:1
true patriotism is of no p. 304:2
Pass: his ghost. O, let him p. 268:5
I p. through the pores of the ocean 298:6
she may ... p. for forty-three 120:15
they shall not p. 199:16
Passed: he p. by on the other side 45:29
so he p. over 63:16
[time] wd. have p. in any case 26:1
Passeront: ils ne p. pas 199:16
Passes: everything p. ... perishes ... palls 228:16
p. at girls who wear glasses 198:2
Passing: did but see her p. by 17:2
P. of the Third Floor Back 139:16
p. the love of women 34:12
Passion: a master-p. is the love of news 93:18
calm of mind, all p. spent 181:8
in her first p. woman 69:17
man that is not p.'s slave 252:1
master mistress of my p. 293:16
Queen was in a furious p. 74:11
ruling p. conquers reason still 203:19
strange fits of p. 335:2
the p. and the life 87:9
Passion-flower: the p. at the gate 314:4
Passionless: hopeless grief is p. 60:8
Passions: all thy p., match'd with mine 313:19
hath not a Jew ... p.? 274:17
in truth but two p., vanity and love 80:16
Past: a mischief that is p. and gone 279:3
leave thy low-vaulted p. 134:5
p. and to come seems best 256:13
p. cure, p. care 222:34
p. help ... p. grief 292:14
p. my help ... p. my care 25:9
remembrance of things p. 293:18
study the p. ... divine the future 89:3
'Pastern' as the 'knee of a horse' 142:4
Pastoral-comical, historical-p. 250:9
Pastors: as some ungracious p. do 248:14
Pasture: sell the p. now to buy the horse 258:9
Pastures: fresh woods, and p. new 175:6
lie down in green p. 35:28
on England's pleasant p. seen 55:8
Pat-a-cake, baker's man 192:5
Path: a beaten p. to his door 108:23
p. of duty ... way to glory 314:11
Pathetic: That's what it is, P. 172:5
Pathless: pleasure in the p. woods 69:9
Paths: so many p. that wind 326:11
Patience: abusing of God's p. 276:3
how poor ... that have not p.! 279:12
in mean men we entitle p. 281:10
p. is a flower 222:35
p., money ... bring all ... to pass 222:36
Patience (*continued*)
p. under ... sufferings 52:30
sat like P. on a monument 291:7
though p. be a tired mare 258:11
though with p. He stands waiting 161:3
ye have heard of the p. of Job 50:3
Patient: a p. etherised upon a table 106:11
fury of a p. man 103:9
Patines: inlaid with p. of bright gold 275:8
Patria: dulce et decorum est pro p. mori 136:1
pro p. ... liberis ... aris 238:1
Patrie: allons, enfants de la p. 236:11
Patriot: for a p., too cool 123:2
such is the p.'s boast 123:14
Patriotic: if p. sentiment is wanted 118:1
Patriotism: I realize ... p. is not enough 78:1
p. ... last refuge of a scoundrel 143:17
true p. is of no party 304:2
Patriots: true p. we 25:2
Patron: a P., ... looks with unconcern 142:1
p. ... a wretch ... with insolence 140:10
Pattern: thou cunning'st p. of ... nature 280:11
Paul: one named Peter, the other named P. 195:5
rob Peter to pay P. 224:24
Pause: what dreams ... must give us p. 250–1:20
Pawn: p. the Bechstein Grand 91:6
you p. your intelligence 94:14
Pay: God make me able to p. 199:9
p. ... in his own coin 222:37
p. through the nose 222:38
what one can p. others to do 169:7
when will you p. me? 192:4
you ought to p., you know 75:13
Pays: he who p. the piper 222:39
p. yr. money ... takes yr. choice 231:18
Peace: a hard and bitter p. 153:1
a p. above all earthly dignities 261:11
a p. I hope with honour 100:7
all her paths are p. 38:3
better a lean p. 207:17
blood of Jesus whispers p. 54:4
calm world and a long p. 255:16
cherish a just and lasting p. 159:15
create desolation, call it p. 310:8
for ever hold his p. 53:20
for p. comes dropping slow 337:5
give p. in our time, O Lord 52:16
I am for p. ... they ... for war 37:14
I shall have some p. there 337:5
if p. cannot be ... with honour 237:7
in P., Goodwill 83:13
in what p. a Christian can die 9:12
inglorious arts of p. 168:3
live together in p. ... as good neighbours 319:5
never was ... a bad p. 113:2
no p. ... unto the wicked 41:3
nothing can bring you p. but yourself 108:13
on earth p., good will 45:22
our p., our fearful innocence 333:11
p., commerce, and honest friendship 139:9
p. for our time ... p. with honour 78:10
p. hath her victories 181:13
p. is indivisible 160:3
p. is of the nature of a conquest 257:12
p. is poor reading 128:7

Peace (*continued*)
p. makes plenty 222:40
p. of God ... passeth all understanding 48:31
p. on earth and mercy mild 325:2
p., p., when there is no p. 41:12
p., perfect p. 54:4
p. shall go sleep with Turks 283:8
the Lord ... give thee p. 32:18
the Prince of P. 40:23
the soft phrase of p. 278:21
the thousand years of p. 313:6
their bodies are buried in p. 52:8
weak piping time of p. 284:11
when ... p. he was for p. 20:4
who desires p., prepare for war 320:8
Peaceably: living p. in their habitations 52:6
Peaceful: p. hours I once enjoyed 92:14
welcome p. evening in 93:10
Peace-maker: yr. If is the only p. 246:3
Peach: do I dare to eat a p.? 106:16
p. was once a bitter almond 318:16
Peacock: as proud as a p. 223:33
Peacocks and lilies for instance 237:3
Pear: and a golden p. 190:1
Pearl: barbaric p. and gold 176:15
heaps of p., inestimable stones 285:1
hillside's dew-p.'d 62:7
like the base Indian, threw a p. away 280–1:14
one p. of great price 44:13
sowed the earth with orient p. 178:12
Pearls: he who wd. search for p. must dive 103:16
neither cast ... p. before swine 44:6
p. that were his eyes 288:1
teeth like p. 62:6
Peas: I always eat p. with honey 13:10
Peccavi [I have Sind] 185:9
Pécher en silence 182:16
Pedigree: languages ... p. of nations 144:23
Peep about to find ... graves 262:8
Peeping: came p. in at morn 134:14
Peepshow: a ticket for the p. 164:14
Peer: a rhyming p. 201:11
when daffodils begin to p. 292:17
Peg: take one down a p. 227:2
Pelican: wonderful bird is the p. 170:6
Pelting: bide the p. of this pitiless storm 266:13
Pen: before my p. has glean'd 151:7
biting my truant p. 302:3
more cruel ... p. is than ... sword 67:9
p. is mightier than the sword 63:3
poet's p. turns them to shapes 277:6
Penance: hath p. done and p. more will do 86:15
Pence: take care of the p. 227:1
Penny: back again, like a bad p. 206:32
I spent a p. ... I lent a p. 190:2
in for a p., in for a pound 217:21
not given a p. for a song 337:3
p. and p. laid up 223:1
p. for yr. thoughts 223:2
p. wise, pound foolish 223:3
shall have but a p. a day 193:3
show me first yr. p. 193:4
turn an honest p. 228:29
two a p., hot cross buns 189:7
Pens: let other p. dwell on guilt 20:13
Pensée: se servent de la p. ... pour autoriser ... injustices 321:12
Pensées: paroles ... pour déguiser ... p. 321:12
Pension: p. never enriched a young man 223:4
p. ... pay given to a state hireling 140:11
Pensive: in vacant or in p. mood 331:11
Pent: long in city p. 151:6
long in populous city p. 179:9
Penury: age, ache, p., and imprisonment 273:11
People: a glorious p. vibrated again 299:2
all p. that on earth do dwell 153:4
among a p. generally corrupt 64:19
Continental p. have sex life 170:8
decent godless p. 107:1
for God's sake look after our p. 239:2
good of the p. ... chief law 84:2
good p. all, of every sort 122:18
government of the p., by the p. 159:13
if the good p. in their wisdom 159:6
indictment against an whole p. 64:6
it is what the p. think so 64:17
let my p. go 31:21
no p. do so much harm as 94:4
no vision, the p. perish 39:5
nor is the p.'s judgment ... true 103:8
observe the condition of the p. 146:6
p. agree with me ... I must be wrong 327:3
p. are ... charming or tedious 328:1
p. have good food ... table manners 170:7
p. who like this sort of thing 160:2
p.'s mothers ... bore me 328:13
raising up a p. of customers 303:4
such trivial p. shd. muse 157:11
the Irish are a fair p. 143:11
the p. all exulting 325:12
the p. are the masters 64:8
the p. that walked in darkness 40:22
thou art a stiffnecked p. 32:12
thy p. shall be my p. 33:25
Top P. 11:9
voice of the p. 10:2
what kind of a p. do they think 83:3
wholesome ... nice English p. 295:17
win friends and influence p. 73:12
wd. all have some p. under them 142:12
you can fool some of the p. 160:1
you live with rich p. 303:7
Peopled: the world must be p. 278:1
Pepper: enjoy the p. when he pleases 74:7
peck of pickled p. 192:6
Peppered: I have p. two of them 254:15
Perceives: the Man p. it die away 332:2
Perceiving *how not to do it* 98:4
Perception: if the doors of p. were cleansed 57:7
p. that something ought to be done 324:15
Percy: I am not yet of P.'s mind 254:12
old song of P. and Douglas 302:6
Perdition catch my soul 279:14
Perfect: he was a p. cavaliero 68:16
I had else been p. 271:6
p. little body 58:6
practice makes p. 223:22
Perfection: the pursuit of p. ... is 19:5
Performance: provokes desire ... takes away ... p. 270:14
Perfume: throw a p. on the violet 264:19
Perfumed: he was p. like a milliner 254:1

Perfumes: all the p. of Arabia will not sweeten 272:3
Perhaps: in search of a great p. 232:9
Perilous: bright stars, through the p. fight 153:6
cleanse ... bosom of that p. stuff 272:6
thought without learning is p. 89:4
Perils and dangers of this night 52:21
Perish: name ... will not p. in the dust 304:11
no vision, the people p. 39:5
shall not p. from the earth 159:13
thy money p. with thee 47:2
to p. ... swallowed up and lost 176–7:19
when your time has come to p. 118:9
whosoever believeth ... shd. not p. 46:21
Periwig: new p., make a great show 199:12
Perjured, murd'rous, bloody 294:11
Perk'd up in a glist'ring grief 261:4
Perplexed: being wrought, p. in the extreme 280–1:14
p. in a world of doubts 151:12
Persecuted: I am p. with letters 89:11
Persepolis: in triumph through P.? 166:9
Persians and the Medes: among the laws of the P. 34:26
Persons: comprehended two aspicious p. 278:10
God is no respecter of p. 47:5
no respect of place, p., nor time 291:4
should certain p. die before they sing 87:10
you tossed and gored several p. 143:3
Perspiration: genius ... ninety-nine per cent p. 105:8
Persuade: beauty ... doth of itself p. 295:5
Persuadest: almost thou p. me 47:14
Persuading others we convince ourselves 146:7
Persuasive: case [against wealth] never proved widely p. 114:13
Pert as a school-girl 118:6
Perturbation: O polish'd p.! golden care! 257:16
Peru: mankind from China to P. 141:9
Pestilence: he ... breeds p. 57:2
p. that walketh in darkness 36:27
Petard: hoist with his own p. 216:35
Peter: dicky birds ... one named P. 195:5
rob P. to pay Paul 224:24
Shock-headed P. 133:11
thou art P., and upon this rock 44:16
Peter Piper picked a peck 192:6
Petty: a p. sneaking knave 56:1
Peut-être: chercher un grand p. 232:9
Phagocytes: stimulate the p. 295:16
Phantasma: like a p. or a hideous dream 262:13
Phantom: she was a P. of delight 334:12
Pharaoh: the Lord hardened P.'s heart 31:24
Philistian: resist P. gold 181:1
Philistines: Barbarians, P., Populace 19:6
Philosopher: all be that he was a p. 79:9
guide, p. and friend 203:11
nothing so absurd but some p. has said 84:1
there was never yet p. 278:17
tried ... in my time to be a p. 105:11
Philosophers: English are ... the least ... pure p. 23:20
Philosophic: gild the p. pill! 121:3
Philosophy: a little p. inclineth ... to atheism 22:11
Philosophy (*continued*)
are dreamt of in your p. 249:12
history is p. teaching by examples 100:1
how charming is divine P.! 172:18
mere touch of cold p. 149:2
new p. calls all in doubt 100:16
p. is nothing but discretion 241:3
p. will clip an angel's wings 149:3
Phoebus: and P. 'gins arise 246:13
Delos rose, and P. sprung 69–70:21
Phrase: proverb'd with a grandsire p. 285:20
the soft p. of peace 278:21
Physic: for p. and farces 114:17
take p., pomp 266:14
Physician: honour a p. 52:3
is there no p. there? 41:13
p., heal thyself 45:24
they that are whole ... no need of the p. 45:5
Physicians: few p. live well 213:22
p. of the utmost fame 27:3
Pianist: do not shoot the p. 327:19
Piccadilly: good-bye, P. 329:1
Picked a peck of pickled pepper 192:6
Picket: the p.'s off duty forever 26:10
Picking and stealing 53:14
Pickwick: Mr. P. 98:20, 22; 99:7
P., ... Owl ... Waverley pen 11:8
Pictures: book without p. and conversation 73:14
cutting all the p. out 26:14
Pie: blackbirds baked in a p. 193:5
eating a Christmas p. 191:2
finger in the p. 213:27
some of a pudding ... none of a p. 207:33
Pieces: broke into a thousand p. 24:11
Pie-crust: promises and p. ... to be broken 309:5
Pieman: Simple Simon met a p. 193:4
Pierian spring: taste not the P. 202:5
Pies: eat one of Bellamy's veal p. 200:11
Piety: nor all thy p. nor wit 110:12
renowned for larnin' and p. 125:4
Pig: a p. in a poke 209:1
stole a p. and away he run 195:4
the p. was eat 195:4
this little p. went to market 194:7
Pigeon: crooning like a bilious p. 296:18
Pigeon-livered: am p., and lack gall 250:17
Piggy-wig: a P. stood 158:8
Pigmy: darling of a p. size 332:3
fretted the p. body 102:17
Pigs: and whether p. have wings 76:4
p. might fly 223:5
Pike-staff: as plain as a p. 223:7
Pilate: P. saith ... What is truth? 46:33
what is truth? said jesting P. 21:8
Pilgrim: Honour comes, a p. grey 88:11
p. through this barren land 329:2
the P. of Eternity 297:13
to be a p. 63:13,14
Pilgrim's Progress ... interesting but tough 318:7
Pilgrimage: thus I'll take my p. 232:12
Pilgrims: we ben p. 79:21
Pill: gild the philosophic p. 121:3
Pillage ... with merry march bring home 258:8
Pillar: from p. to post 223:6
in his rising seemed a p. of state 177:3

Pillar (*continued*)
she became a p. of salt 31:4
triple p. of the world transform'd 242:9
Pillars: the four p. of government 22:8
wisdom ... hewn out her seven p. 38:6
Pillows his chin upon ... wave 175:10
Pilot: a daring p. in extremity 102–3:17
Pimples: remark these roughnesses, p. 94:10
Pin: if I sit on a p. 12:9
might have heard a p. drop 216:25
my life at a p.'s fee 249:4
serve to p. up one's hair 89:11
with a little p. bores ... castle wall 283:6
you might have heard a p. drop 234:15
Pinafore: Captain of the *P.* 119:10, 119:13
Pinch: one P., a ... lean-fac'd villain 246:5
Pine: p. for what is not 300:2
this spray of Western p. 129:2
Pined: she p. in thought 291:7
Pines: eat the cones under his p. 113:13
Pink: the very p. of courtesy 286:17
Pint: drinka p.'a milka day 11:2
Pipe: a three-p. problem 101:13
blow your p. ... till you burst 62:5
he called for his p. 192:1
in yr. p. and smoke it 223:37
p. a song about a lamb 56:8
p. to the spirit ditties 149:7
Piped: so I p. with merry cheer 56:8
Piper: Tom, he was a p.'s son 195:3
Tom, Tom, the p.'s son 195:4
who pays the p. may call the tune 222:39
Pipers: ten p. piping 194:2
Pipes: p. and whistles in his sound 244–5:11
scrannel p. of wretched straw 175:4
ye soft p., play on 149:7
Piping: helpless, naked, p. loud 56:3
p. down the valleys wild 56:7
p. songs of pleasant glee 56:7
weak p. time of peace 284:11
Pippin: right as a Ribstone p. 27:9
Pippins: old p. toothsomest 324:1
Pistol: if his p. misses fire 124:2
Pistols: young ... carry p. ... old ones grub 295:7
Pit: black as the p. from pole to pole 130:8
the bottomless p. 50:24
what is in the p. 55:2
whoso diggeth a p. 39:1
Pitch: bumping p. and a blinding light 187:11
he that toucheth p. ... defiled 51:22
Pith: arms ... had seven years' p. 278:21
enterprises of ... p. and moment 250–1:20
my rhyme ... hath in it some p. 302:11
Pitied: better be envied than p. 207:22
Pitieth: the Lord p. them that fear 36:28
Pitiful: 'twas p., 'twas wondrous p. 279:2
Pitt is to Addington 72:17
Pity: a p. beyond all telling 337:9
and never a saint took p. 86:10
and p. 'tis 'tis true 249:17
I p. the man who can travel 306:13
loved her that she did p. them 279:2
p. my simplicity 325:1
the p. of it, Iago! ... the p.! 280:4
Place: a p. called ... Armageddon 50:27
earth's the right p. for love 113:8
give me a firm p. 18:3
grave's a fine and private p. 167:14
Great God! this is an awful p.! 239:1
Place (*continued*)
love a p. the less for having suffered 20:16
never the time and the p. 61:11
p. of justice ... hallowed p. 23:11
reign in this horrible p. 93:15
savage p., as holy and enchanted 87:12
the mind is its own p. 176:5
vicious p. where thee he got 267:14
Places: all p. thou 179:17
men in great p. 22:2
praising ... exactly in the right p. 68:10
proper words in proper p. 309:2
Placid: animals ... so p. and self-contained 326:2
Plague: a p. o' both your houses! 286:19
a p. of all cowards! 254:13
a p. of sighing and grief! 254:17
make instruments to p. us 267:14
p. o' these pickle-herring! 290:14
the red p. rid you 287:19
Plagues: of all p. ... thy wrath can send 72:16.
of all the p. ... woman ... worst 125:3
p. that are written 51:4
p. with which mankind are curst 96:10
Plain: all doctrines p. and clear 67:17
did you ... see Shelley p.? 61:10
in meadow or p. 309:14
p. as a pike-staff 223:7
p. living and high thinking 333:11
pricking on the p. 305:10
virtue is ... best p. set 23:2
Plainly: honest tale ... p. told 285:9
Plaintive: the p. numbers flow 334:17
Plan: mighty maze! but not without a p. 202:17
Planet: measure every wandering p.'s course 166:10
when a new p. swims into his ken 150:15
while Jove's p. rises 61:5
Planets: the p., and this centre, observe degree 290:1
Planned: Who saith 'A whole I p.' 62:9
Plant: a Sensitive P. in a garden grew 299:14
Planted: feet firmly p. in the air 235:3
I have p., Apollos watered 47:32
Platitude: a longitude with no p. 114:4
Plato: attachment *à la* P. 119:5
P. is dear to me 18:7
Platter: they licked the p. clean 190:7
Play: all work and no p. 230:40
an hour to p. ... last man in 187:11
at Christmas p. and make good cheer 318:5
better than a p. 78:17
boys and girls come out to p. 188:6
can pack ... cards ... cannot p. well 22:16
good p. needs no epilogue 246:4
I doubt some foul p. 248:12
learnt to p. when he was young 195:3
never ... go to a p. together 89:17
p. first (second) fiddle 223:8
p. up! and p. the game 187:12
p. with the gypsies in the wood 191:9
the p. ... pleas'd not the million 250:10
the p.'s the thing wherein 250:19
they p. from ten till four 231:22
two can p. at that game 228:38
when the boys came out to p. 189:3
where every man must p. a part 274:1
Zephyrus did softly p. 305:15

Played: marks ... how you p. the game 233:12
Player: a walking shadow, a poor p. 272:10
Players: men and women merely p. 244:11
mouth it, as ... p. do 251:7
Playing of the merry organ 15:8
Playmates: I have had p. ... old familiar faces 156:9
Plays: he p. best (well) that wins 223:9
old p. begin to disgust 109:2
Plea: general good ... p. of the scoundrel 55:6
Pleasance: youth is full of p. 295:1
Pleasant: a few think him p. enough 158:6
a p. fire our souls to regale 56:4
abridgement of all ... p. in man 123:3
green and p. land 55:8
how p. to know Mr. Lear! 158:6
on England's p. pastures seen? 55:8
p. in their lives 34:11
p. thoughts bring sad 332:7
p. ... to see ... name in print 70:12
some day be p. to remember 321:1
songs of p. glee 56:7
standing on this p. lea 333:4
Pleasantest: one of the p. things ... a journey 129:11
Pleasantness: her ways are ways of p. 38:3
the p. of an employment 21:3
Please: books cannot always p. 93:17
in him alone 'twas natural to p. 102:15
live to p., must p. to live 141:1
say what they p. ... do what I p. 113:6
seeketh not itself to p. 56:2
Pleased: as p. as Punch 223:10
p. with what he gets 244:6
when ... p. ourselves, we ... please 223:11
Pleases: every prospect p. 130:2
one makes lovers ... as one p. 89:13
Pleasing: art of p. ... being pleased 129:13
Pleasure: a p. in the pathless woods 69:9
business before p. 208:39
but the privilege and p. 116:13
dissipation without p. 116:2
drinking is the soldier's p. 103:14
every p. is of itself a good 144:13
friend of P., Wisdom's aid 88:14
gave p. to the spectators 164:7
good, p., ease, content! 203:7
great source of p. is variety 144:26
happiness ... not in p. but in rest from pain 104:9
hatred ... the longest p. 70:7
love ceases to be a p. 26:11
money gives me p. 27:10
more p. in loving than ... loved 223:12
no p. without pain 222:5
no profit ... where is no p. 287:6
owes its p. to another's pain 93:9
p. ... is lost by coveting more 223:14
p. is oft a visitant 147:9
p. never is at home 148:3
p. of the fleeting year 294:4
p.'s a sin ... sin's a p. 69:13
public stock of harmless p. 145:1
refrain from the unholy p. 26:14
short p., long lament 225:20
some to business, some to p. take 203:15
sweet is p. after pain 103:14
though on p. she was bent 92:8
to overcome p. is the greatest p. 223:13
'twas for your p. you came 92:12
Pleasure (*continued*)
variety ... soul of p. 26:12
when Youth and P. meet 69:4
written without effort ... read without p. 144:25
Pleasure-dome: a stately p. 87:11
sunny p. with caves of ice 87:15
Pleasures: all the p. prove 167:1
cannot understand the p. 20:7
can sympathise ... not with their p. 137:11
in unreproved p. free 174:1
'mid p. and palaces 199:2
no man is a hypocrite in his p. 144:20
p. are like poppies spread 67:4
the purest of human p. 23:4
these p., Melancholy, give 173:13
these pretty p. might me move 232:14
we will some new p. prove 100:17
Pledge: I will p. with mine 145:7
p. to each other our lives, our fortunes 139:7
Plenty: however p. silver dollars may become 84:10
in delay there lies no p. 291:2
p. makes me 197:15
wasna fou, but just had p. 65:16
Pleure: il p. dans mon cœur 320:10
Plodders: small have continual p. ... won 268:8
Plot: the sonnet's scanty p. of ground 332:14
this blessed p., this earth 282:5
Plough: having put his hand to the p. 45:26
Ploughman: heavy steps of the p. 337:7
the p., near at hand 174:3
Plowman homeward plods 126:3
Pluck: p. from the memory a rooted sorrow 272:6
sin will p. on sin 285:6
we p. this flower, safety 254:10
Plucked: when I have p. thy rose 280:11
Plum: and pulled out a p. 191:2
supping cold p. porridge 191:6
Poacher: a p. is a keeper 154:6
old p. makes a good game-keeper 222:26
Pocket: a p. full of posies 193:2
a p. full of rye 193:5
Pocket borough: by a p. into Parliament 119:16
Pocket-handkerchief: holding his p. 76:5
Pockets: p. in none of his clothes 28:9
to line one's p. 219:14
Poem: I would rather have written that p. 330:5
ought himself to be a true p. 182:1
p. lovely as a tree 153:8
p. must ride on ... melting 113:16
p. ... worked ... not worried 113:16
Poems: dictionaries, and temporary p. 140:6
Gert's p. are bunk 13:4
p. are made by fools like me 153:9
Poesy: drainless shower of light is p. 150:12
great end of p. ... shd. be a friend 150:13
on the viewless wings of P. 149:16
overwhelm myself in p. 150:10
Poet: a p. cd. not but be gay 331:10
business of a p., said Imlac 141:5
consecration, and the p.'s dream 331:1
lunatic, the lover, and the p. 277:5
p. and the dreamer are distinct 148:2
p.'s eye, in a fine frenzy rolling 277:6

Poet (*continued*)
p.'s pen turns ... to shapes 277:6
say that when the P. dies 239:14
Swift, you will never be a p. 104:12
the p. sing it with such airs 337:3
the p.'s inward pride 96:6
Poetess: a maudlin p., a rhyming peer 201:11
Poetic: which constitutes p. faith 87:19
Poetical: gods had made thee p. 245:9
Poetry: Fleshly School of P. 62:12
homely definitions of prose and p. 88:3
if P. comes not as naturally 151:15
in p. ... in life ... ineffectual angel 19:9
mincing p. 255:7
not P., but prose run mad 201:15
p. is the record of the best 300:10
p. is the spontaneous overflow 336:7
p. lifts the veil 300:9
p. of earth is never dead 151:1
p. shd. be great and unobtrusive 151:13
p. shd. surprise by ... excess 151:14
p.'s unnat'ral; no man ever talked p. 99:5
truest p. is the most feigning 245:10
Poets: I shall be among the English P. 152:5
our clever young p. 88:3
painters and p. ... lie 222:33
p. are the unacknowledged legislators 300:11
p. [make men] witty 23:9
p. that lasting marble seek 322:2
souls of p. dead and gone 149:4
such sights as youthful p. dream 174:7
three p. in three distant Ages 104:11
translunary things ... first p. had 102:11
Point: missed the p. completely, Julia 107:7
p. his slow unmoving finger 280:5
thus I bore my p. 254:15
touch'd the highest p. of all my greatness 261:8
Poison: if you p. us, do we not die? 274:17
Poissons: nous attendons ... les p. aussi 83:1
Poke: buy a pig in a p. 209:1
p. poor Billy 124:10
Poker: stiff as a p. 226:19
Pole: beloved from p. to p. 86:13
soldier's p. is fall'n! 243:6
Police: friendship recognised by the p. 307:7
Policeman: a p.'s lot is not a happy one 120:6
want to know the time, ask a P. 234:12
Policemen: sadists ... p. or butchers 90:4
Policy: honesty is the best p. 216:39
p. of a good neighbour 235:1
turn him to any cause of p. 258:7
Polished up the silver plate 184:8
Politely: hang you ... most p. 120:9
Political: man is ... a p. animal 18:5
retired into ... p. Cave of Adullam 58:10
Politician: coffee, which makes the p. wise 204:10
like a scurvy p. seem 267:7
p. is an arse 94:12
Politicians: for P. neither love nor hate 103:2
whole race of p. put together 309:1
Politics: confound their p. 73:2
holy, mistaken zeal in p. 146:7
my p., like my religion ... accommodatin' 322:10
p. we bar ... not our bent 120:8
Poll: but talked like poor P. 115:2
Polly-wolly-doodle all the day 16:5
Poltagrue: My Lady P. 27:8
Polygamy: before p. was made a sin 102:14
Pomp: grinning at his p. 283:6
p., and circumstance, of ... war 280:2
take physic, p. 266:14
the p. of power 126:8
vain p. and glory of this world 261:10
Pompous: man is ... p. in the grave 60:3
Pomps and vanity of ... world 53:12
Poniards: she speaks p. 277:16
Pony: to town riding on a p. 196:4
Pooh: three cheers for P.! 172:11
Pooh-Bah (Lord High Everything Else) 117:14
Poor: a certain p. widow 45:15
as p. as Job 223:15
decent means p. 199:3
leave [grapes] for the p. and stranger 32:15
grind the faces of the p. 40:19
he that considereth the p. 36:12
how apt the p. are to be proud 291:11
how p. ... that have not patience! 279:12
Im one of the undeserving p. 296:21
inconvenient to be p. 92:3
it's the p. wot gets 16:13
laws grind the p. 123:16
makes me p. indeed 279:15
my friends were p. but honest 242:3
none so p. to do him reverence 263:14
plenty makes me p. 197:15
p. ... maimed ... halt ... blind 46:1
p. old Joe 112:11
poverty consists in feeling p. 108:19
simple annals of the p. 126:7
the p. man at his gate 10:5
the p. shall never cease 33:3
the riches of the p.! 145:18
to be p. and independent 85:4
too p. for a bribe 127:3
ye have the p. always 45:1
Poor relations: even great men have their p. 97:11
Pop goes the weasel 165:5
Pope: better to err with P. 70:15
Poppies: in Flanders fields the p. blow 164:8
pleasures are like p. spread 67:4
Populace: Barbarians, Philistines, P. 19:6
Population: only talked of p. 123:19
Porpentine: quills upon the fretful p. 249:7
Porpoise: there's a p. close behind us 75:2
Porridge: comfort like cold p. 288:3
supping cold plum p. 191:6
Port: any p. in a storm 206:17
p. after stormy seas 305:11
p. for men 144:15
the p. is near, the bells I hear 325:12
Porte: il faut qu'une p. soit ouverte ou fermée 185:5
Portend: late eclipses ... p. no good 265:9
Porter: Oh, mister P. 160:7
Porters: mechanic p. crowding in 258:8
Portion: any p. of the foreign world 322:16
best p. of a good man's life 335:10
he is a p. of the loveliness 298:1
Portrait of the Artist as a Young Man 146:4
Ports: all places ... are ... p. and happy havens 281:14
p. of slumber open wide 257:16
Possessed: liberty ... limited ... to be p. 64:18

Possessed (*continued*)
Webster was much p. by death 107:6
Possession: have p. of them both 152:8
p. ... is intolerable 320:3
p. is nine points of the law 223:17
prospect is ... better than p. 223:30
virtue that p. wd. not show us 278:12
Possessions: all my p. for a moment of time 107:15
Possible: O that 'twere possible after long grief 314:5
think ... p. you may be mistaken 94:7
Post: deaf as a p. 211:3
from pillar to p. 223:6
p. o'er land and ocean 181:11
Post-chaise: driving briskly in a p. 144:7
Posterity: see p. do something for us 9:11
think of yr. p.! 9:2
thy p. shall sway 92:2
what has p. done for us? 234:2
without ... hope of p. 101:9
Postscript: pith is in the p. 129:7
Postumus: alas, P., P., the fleeting years 135:15
Pot: a useful p. to put things in 172:9
crackling of thorns under a p. 39:19
death in the p. 34:24
greasy Joan doth keel the p. 269:1
p. calls the kettle black 223:18
watched p. never boils 229:32
who is the potter ... who the p.? 110:14
Potato: bashful young p. 119:5
Potomac: all quiet along the P. 26:10
Potter: as the clay is in the p.'s hand 41:15
who is the p., pray? 110:14
Pouch: spectacles on nose and p. on side 244–5:11
Poultice: silence like a p. 133:13
Pouncet-box: he held a p. 254:1
Pound: a p. of ... merchant's flesh 275:5
I'll give thee a silver p. 72:8
Pounds: about two hundred p. a year 67:17
handsome in three hundred p. a year 276:6
p. ... take care of themselves 227:1
with forty p. a year 122:9
Pour encourager les autres 321:10
Poverty: debt is the worst p. 211:8
give me neither p. nor riches 39:6
her p. was glad, her heart content 104:2
in p., hunger, and dirt 135:3
nor any crime so shameful as p. 109:3
p. and oysters ... go together 99:1
p. breeds strife 223:19
p. consists in feeling poor 108:19
p. is an anomaly to rich 23:21
p. is no disgrace ... is ... inconvenient 303:11
p. is no sin 223:20
p. is not a shame 223:21
p. will bear itself 207:4
slow rises worth by p. depressed 140:16
Power: accursed p. ... stands on privilege 27:7
beauty ... injurious ... hath strange p. 181:5
earthly p. ... likest God's 275:1
force of temporal p. 275:1
greater the p. the more dangerous the abuse 64:20
knowledge is p. 218:12
like us, though less in p. 177:4
new nobility ... act of p. 22:7
not in our p. to love or hate 166:14
Power (*continued*)
p. gradually extirpates ... virtue 65:2
p. of the press ... p. of books 319:6
p. tends to corrupt 9:1
riches, dignity and p. 28:1
the balance of p. 322:3
the certainty of p. 96:6
unequal and untimely interchange of p. 22:15
unlimited p. is apt to corrupt 200:7
Powerful: Lord, I am p., but alone 320:13
Powers: p. that be are ordained of God 47:28
we lay waste our p. 333:3
Practical: meddling with any p. part of life 9:6
Practice makes perfect 223:22
Practise what you preach 223:23
Praise: a song in thy p. 65:11
give them ... the garment of p. 41:11
let us now p. famous men 52:5
maid whom there were none to p. 334:11
p. any man that will p. me 242:17
p. at morning ... blame at night 202:12
p. is the best diet 303:15
p. makes good men better 223:24
p. the Lord, for he is kind 180:7
p. the Lord ... pass the ammunition 111:13
p. the Lord! We are ... musical 316:5
to bury Caesar, not to p. him 263:11
we but p. ourselves in other men 202:13
we ... lack tongues to p. 294:7
we scarcely can p. it, or blame 123:1
you p. the firm restraint 72:6
Praised: everybody p. the Duke 304:15
Praising: doing one's p. for oneself 68:10
Prattle: thinking his p. to be tedious 284:5
Pray: after this manner ... p. ye 43:24
came to scoff, remained to p. 122:10
I p. it be first to me 58:7
need to p. for fair weather 22:8
one to watch and one to p. 9:13
p. all the livelong day 56:4
p. without ceasing 49:6
so give alms; p. so 293:2
to God, to praise and p. 61:5
watch and p. 45:2,16
we do p. for mercy 275:1
you can't p. a lie 318:8
Prayer: four [hours] spend in p. 85:9
God erects a house of p. 96:9
more things are wrought by p. 312:9
Prayeth: p. best, who loveth best 87:4
p. well, who loveth well 87:3
Preach: practise what you p. 223:23
Preacher: vanity of vanities, saith the P. 39:9
Preaches: he p. well that lives well 223:25
Preaching: a woman's p. is like 142:13
Precept: example is better than p. 213:2
Precepts: these few p. in thy memory 248:15
Precise: too p. in every part 131:15
Precisely: thinking too p. on th' event 252:18
Prefer: folks *p.* ... a hovel to ... marble halls 72:2
Preferment: and so I got p. 15:12
tired of knocking at P.'s door 18:20
Prejudice: we all decry p., yet 305:4
Prejudices: it p. a man so [reading ... before reviewing] 303:16
Premises: sufficient conclusions from insufficient p. 68:6

Prepare to meet Thy God 42:16
Preposterous? A thorough-paced absurdity 119:3
Presbyter: new P. is but old Priest 181:12
Presence: from whose unseen p. the leaves dead 299:3
lord of thy p. and no land 264:9
p. strengthens [love] 205:8
scanter of yr. maiden p. 249:1
Present: a very p. help in trouble 36:13
both perhaps p. in time future 106:3
no time like the p. 228:4
p. mirth hath p. laughter 291:2
p. only toucheth thee 66:13
things p., worst 256:13
un-birthday p. 76:9
Presents ... endear Absents 156:5
Preservation: creation, p., and all the blessings 53:1
President: rather be right than be P. 84:9
Press: god of our idolatry, the p. 93:3
misused the King's p. damnably 255:15
written of the power of the p. 319:6
Pressed: if it were p., would run 27:14
power p. too far and relaxed too much 22:15
Pretender: who P. is, or who is King 68:15
Pretty: where the girls are so p. 15:10
Prevail: gates of hell shall not p. 44:16
passion for making them p. 19:10
Prevention is better than cure 199:5, 223:26
Prey: have they not divided the p.? 33:16
smaller fleas that on him p. 309:4
to hastening ills a p. 122:5
Price: all those men have their p. 322:4
p. of everything ... value of nothing 328:4
p. of wisdom is above rubies 35:9
virtuous woman ... p. ... above rubies 39:8
Prick: how if honour p. me off? 255:21
if you p. us, do we not bleed? 274:17
no spur to p. the sides of my intent 270:6
pat it and p. it 192:5
when ... the nerves p. 312:14
Pricking: a gentle knight was p. on the plain 305:10
Pricks: kick against the p. 47:4
Pride: he that is low, no p. 63:15
look backward to with p. 113:10
perished in his p. 334:8
p. goeth before destruction 38:19
p. of kingly sway from out my heart 284:2
p., pomp, and circumstance, of ... war 280:2
p. that licks the dust 201:19
p., the ... vice of fools 202:4
p. will have a fall 223:27
the poet's inward p. 96:6
the p. of that country side 24:6
Priest: am I both p. and clerk? 284:1
free me of this turbulent p. 130:14
I tell thee, churlish p. 253:3
p. all shaven and shorn 194:8
p. is at the bottom of it [mischief] 222:1
youth ... still is Nature's p. 332:2
Priest-craft: ere p. did begin 102:14
Priests: of p. ... a charmin' variety 125:4
Prime: having lost but once yr. p. 132:8
Primrose: p. path of dalliance treads 248:14
p. way to th' everlasting bonfire 270:13
rathe p. that forsaken dies 175:5
Prince: the P. of Peace 40:23
Princes: hangs on p.' favours 261:10
put not yr. trust in p. 37:31
that sweet aspect of p. 261:10
Principalities: against p., against powers ... rulers 48:27
Principle: a p. in life with me, sir 297:7
don't believe in p. ... *do* in interest 162:11
fundamental p. of ... constitution 54:10
what is p. against ... flattery? 301:18
Principles: first, religious and moral p. 19:12
these two p.—right and wrong 159:10
they speak of p.—look out 20:1
Print: some said, John, p. it 63:5
to see one's name in p. 70:12
Printer: almost hear the p. saying damn 319:9
Printers: books by which the p. have lost 114:10
Printing: barbarous where there is no p. 143:8
cogent reasons for not p. ... subscribers 144:17
thou hast caused p. to be used 260:11
Priority: observe degree, p., and place 290:1
Prison: come, let's away to p. 267:13
dock in a pestilential p. 118:7
Lime-tree Bower my p. 87:17
palace ... p. on each hand 69:6
stone walls do not a p. make 162:5
this p. where I live 284:6
Prisoner: the jury, passing on the p.'s life 273:1
Prison-house: secrets of my p. 249:7
shades of the p. begin to close 332:1
Prithee, pretty maiden 119:6
Private: to the public good p. respects ... yield 181:2
Privilege: accursed power which stands on p. 27:7
but the p. and pleasure ... little errands 116:13
Privileged: the p. and the people ... two nations 100:12
Prize: men p. the thing ungain'd 289:15
not all that tempts ... is lawful p. 125:12
rain influence, and judge the p. 174:6
the p. we sought is won 325:12
too light winning make the p. light 288:2
what we have we p. not 278:12
Problem: quite a three-pipe p. 101:13
Problems: the p. of victory are more agreeable 83:8
Proceedings: subsequent p. interested him no more 129:3
Process: one long p. of getting tired 68:5
Procrastination is the thief of time 337:14
Procreate: we might p. like trees 60:1
Proctors: with prudes for p. 314:12
Prodigal: chariest maid is p. enough 248:13
Shimei, though not p. of pelf 103:7
Profane: O p. one! 58:2
so old, and so p. 258:3
Profaned: province ... desolated and p. 121:8
Profess: all who p. ... themselves Christians 52:28
Professions: let in some of all p. 270:13
Profit: my p. on't is, I know how to curse 287:19
no p. ... where ... no pleasure 287:6
the winds will blow the p. 164:15

Profit (*continued*)
what p. hath a man of ... labour 39:10
what shall it p. a man? 45:10
Profits: small p. and quick returns 225:32
Progeny: a p. of learning 301:8
Prognostics do not ... prove prophecies 322:8
Progress: all p. ... desire ... to live beyond ... income 68:7
history of England ... history of p. 164:5
to promote social p. 319:5
Promethean: I know not where is that P. heat 280:11
Promise of strength and manhood 58:6
Promises: he p. himself too much 142:17
p. and pie-crust ... to be broken 309:5
p. too much ... means nothing 223:28
Promising: pretty Thomasina ... once ... so p. 113:17
Promontory: I sat upon a p. 276:18
Promotion: none will sweat but for p. 243:19
Prone to any iteration of nuptials 90:1
Pronounce: spell better than they p. 318:13
Proof of the pudding 223:29
Prop: you take my house ... take the p. 275:6
Propagate: endeavour to ... p. the best 19:8
Proper words in p. places 309:2
Properties: general p. and large appearances 141:5
Property has its duties ... rights 102:13
Prophecies: prognostics do not always prove p. 322:8
Prophecy: the trumpet of a p. 299:6
Prophesy: if you crown him, let me p. 283:8
Prophesying: ancestral voices p. war 87:14
Prophet: a p. is not without honour 44:14
methinks I am a p. new inspir'd 282:4
sons of the p. were brave 16:15
Prophetess: more than a p. ... uncommon pretty 105:13
Prophetic: O my p. soul! 249:10
to something like p. strain 173:12
Prophets: beware of false p. 44:9
is Saul ... among the p. 34:2
wisest p. ... sure of the event first 322:8
Proportion: time is broke and no p. kept! 284:7
Propose: whoever loves ... do not p. 101:2
Propriety: pleasantness ... does not ... evince ... p. 21:3
Proprium humani ingenii ... odisse 310:9
Prose: homely definitions of p. and poetry 88:3
in p. and verse was own'd ... absolute 104:13
je dis de la p. 182:13
p. run mad 201:15
talking p. for over forty years 182:13
unattempted yet in p. or rhyme 175:16
Prospect: noblest p. ... Scotchman ever sees 142:8
p. is ... better than possession 223:30
though every p. pleases 130:2
Prospects: died when his p. ... brightening 11:18
on p. drear 66:13
Prosper: treason doth never p. 128:13
Prosperity: a jest's p. lies in the ear 268:16
a man to have been in p. 80:5
him that stood in greet p. 80:1
p. doth best discover vice 21:15
Prosperity (*continued*)
p. has damned more ... than ... devils 223:31
p. is the blessing of the Old Testament 21:13
p.'s the very bond of love 293:5
you will see a state of p. 164:12
Prospers: Hope ... turns Ashes—or it p. 110:1
Protest: the lady doth p. too much 252:4
Proteus rising from the sea 333:4
Protracted: life p. is p. woe 141:12
Proud: Americans ... p. of ... ancient heritage 153:1
as p. as Lucifer 223:32
as p. as a peacock 223:33
being too p. to fight 329:7
death, be not p. 101:4
how apt the poor are to be p. 291:11
I might grow p. the while 132:2
p. me no prouds 287:1
too p. for a wit 123:2
too p. to importune 127:3
Prouder: never, I ween, was a p. seen 24:5
Prove: might p. anything by figures 73:4
prov'd true before, p. false again 67:17
Proved: likely ... to have p. most royal 253:12
p. true before, prove false again 67:17
which was to be p. 108:26
Proverb: a p. is much matter 114:8
the p. is something musty 252:6
Providence: assert Eternal P. 175:17
P. their guide 179:18
reasoned high of P., Foreknowledge 177:6
Province: all knowledge to be my p. 23:14
p. they [Turks] have desolated 121:8
Provincial: worse than p.—he was parochial 139:5
Prudes: with p. for proctors 314:12
Pruning-hooks: swords into plowshares, ... spears into p. 40:18
Prussia: war ... national industry of P. 182:12
Prussian: French, or Turk, or P. 120:3
Psalmist: the sweet p. of Israel 34:15
Psaltery: sing unto him with the p. 36:4
Public: British p. in one of its ... fits 164:6
deliberation sat, and p. care 177:3
dislike the favour of the p. 152:9
how p., like a frog 99:14
mean, stupid, dastardly, ... p. 129:12
never in touch with p. opinion 328:11
reasons for ... not speaking in p. 143:15
the sound of p. scorn 179:12
wash clean linen in p. 229:29
washing ... dirty linen in p. 327:9
Public house: vidders ... if they've kept a p. 98:24
Public meeting: speaks ... as if I was a p. 320:12
Public opinion: researchers into p. 20:4
Public schools are the nurseries of vice 109:10
Publican: how like a fawning p. 274:7
Publish: I'll p., right or wrong 70:11
p. and be damned 324:11
p. it not in the streets 34:10
Publisher: now Barabbas was a p. 72:11
Publishers: with irrational fear of life become p. 90:4

Pudding: a p. hath two [ends] 212:37
better some of a p. 207:33
proof of the p. is in the eating 223:29
Puff direct ... preliminary ... collateral 301:1
Puffing is of various sorts 301:1
Puissant et solitaire 320:13
Puking: infant, mewling and p. 244:11
Pullet-sperm: no p. in my brewage 276:7
Pulse: feeling a woman's p. 306:14
two people with one p. 165:2
when the p. begins to throb 58:15
Pumpkins: where the early p. blow 158:2
Punch: as pleased as P. 223:10
Punctuality is the politeness of kings 162:4
Punctures: pin ... p. my skin 12:9
Punishment: as I deserve, pay on my p. 180:14
the p. fit the crime 118:10
Puppets: God, whose p. ... are we 62:8
Purchased: thought ... gift of God may be p. 47:2
Pure: as p. as snow 251:3
because my heart is p. 314:19
blessed are the p. in heart 43:16
more p. than his Maker 35:2
p. as an angel 310:11
p. as the naked heavens 333:13
p. unbounded love thou art 325:3
things are p. ... lovely ... of good report 49:1
unto the p. all things are p. 49:18
Purest: garden ... p. of human pleasures 23:4
Purgatory: England ... p. of men 111:4
no other p. but a woman 25:10
Purge: I'll p., and leave sack 256:5
p. me with hyssop 36:14
Puritan: saw a P.-one hanging of his cat 58:2
the P. hated bear-baiting 164:7
Purlieus: dusty p. of the law 312:18
Purple: I never saw a P. Cow 64:1
I wrote the 'P. Cow' 64:2
p. the sails, and so perfumed 242:14
Purpose: cite Scripture for his p. 274:8
Purse: ask thy p. what thou shdst. buy 206:25
heavy p. ... light heart 216:27
light p. ... heavy heart 219:9
little and often fills the p. 219:17
p. ... full of other men's money 212:21
put money in thy p. 279:6
remedy against ... consumption of the p. 256:12
silk p. out of a sow's ear 225:24
who steals my p. steals trash 279:15
Purses: our p. shall be proud 287:11
wine and wenches empty ... p. 230:19
Purse-strings are ... common ties 223:36
Pursuing: faint, yet p. 33:17
Pursuit of perfection ... is the p. of sweetness 19:5
Pussy: Owl and the P.-cat 158:7
P. cat, where have you been? 192:7
P.'s in the well 188:9
Put: p. off holiness and p. on intellect 55:7
up with which I will not p. 83:12
Putting milk into babies 83:9
Pye: than shine with P. 70:15
Pyramides: du haut de ces p. 185:10
Pyramids: from the summit of these p. 185:10
Pyramus: Death of P. and Thisby 276:13
Pyrénées: il n'y a plus de P. 162:3
Pyrenees no longer exist 162:3

Quad: no one about in the Q. 155:14
Quadruplets, not twins 13:2
Qualified: few are q. to shine in company 309:9
Qualities: man, with all his noble q. 95:10
such q. as wd. wear well 123:20
Quality: men of good q. 322:17
q. of mercy is not strain'd 275:1
royal banner and all q. 280:2
Quantities: wept ... to see such q. of sand 76:2
Quarrel: beware of entrance to a q. 248:16
find q. in a straw 252:19
sudden and quick in q. 244:11
takes two to make a q. 229:6
Quarrelling: satisfaction in q. with her 301:14
Quarrels: bad workman q. with his tools 206:34
lovers' q. ... renewal of love 315:2
those who in q. interpose 115:11
Quarter: any mistake ... in any q. 83:6
Quarterly: 'I', says the Q. 70:17
nothing a year, paid q. 308:9
Quarto: on a beautiful q. page 301:13
Quean: the flaunting, extravagant q. 301:17
Quebec: rather have written ... poem ... than take Q. 330:5
Queen: another Sheba Q. 329:10
cruel q. died ... post-mortem ... revealed 241:11
goddess and maiden and q. 310:3
I'm to be Q. of the May 314:7
I wd. not be a q. 261:5
in good Q. Bess's glorious days 117:10
'leg of mutton,' said the Red Q. 77:10
'no!' said the Q. 'Sentence first' 75:8
q. and huntress, chaste and fair 145:8
Q. Anne is dead 223:39
Q. asked the Dairymaid 171:11
Q. of Hearts, she made some tarts 75:6, 192:8
q. was in a furious passion 74:11
q. was in the parlour 193:5
Red Q. sharply interrupted 77:8
Ruler of the Q.'s Navee 119:15,16
the mobled q. 250:11
to London to look at the q. 192:7
Queens have died young and fair 186:12
Queer: all ... q. save thee and me 197:17
drink to the q. old Dean 305:20
ill-tempered and q. 158:6
Quench: foul water will q. fire 214:14
if I q. thee, thou flaming minister 280:11
many waters cannot q. love 40:15
smoking flax ... not q. 41:2
wine in the bottle does not q. 230:20
Question: others abide our q. Thou art free 19:2
sees both sides of q. ... sees ... nothing 327:1
the q. ... wd. it bring a blush 98:16
two sides to every q. 229:4
Questions: animals ... ask no q. 105:16
answered three q. and that is enough 74:4
ask me no q. 123:10
ask no q. ... be told no lies 206:24
education ... asking q. all the time 324:18
not one of us is asking q. 324:18
Queue: an orderly q. of one 170:9

Quickly: gives twice who gives q. 214:35
good and q. seldom meet 215:14
Quiet: all q. along the Potomac 26:10
All Q. on the Western Front 233:7
anything for a q. life 206:18
holy time is q. as a nun 333:2
in q. she reposes 18:16
made q. by the power of harmony 335:12
my scallop-shell of q. 232:12
Saturn, q. as a stone 148:4
Quietness: bride of q. 149:6
king ... men ... made ... for q.' sake 241:5
Quietus: he himself might his q. make 250–1:20
Quills upon the fretful porpentine 249:7
Quince: mince and slices of q. 158:9
Quinquireme of Nineveh 168:13
Quintessence: what is this q. of dust? 250:6
Quintili Vare, legiones redde 71:9
Quintilius Varus, give me ... my legions 71:9
Quip: second, the Q. Modest 246:2
Quips and Cranks and wanton Wiles 173:16
Quires and places where they sing 52:18
Quiring to the young-ey'd cherubins 275:8
Quit: like doth q. like 273:14
q. yourselves like men 34:1
Quiver: willows whiten, aspens q. 313:12
Quod erat demonstrandum 108:26
Quotation: every q. contributes something 140:3
Quotations: a book that furnishes no q. 199:4
Quote: by necessity ... delight, we all q. 108:15
grow immortal as they q. 337:11
I'll kill you if you q. it 64:2
I q. the fights historical 120:4
Quoter: next to originator ... is the first q. 108:14

Rabbit: the r. has a charming face 14:6
Race: earth ... will no longer tolerate the r. 23:23
he rides a r. 92:9
pernicious r. ... of odious vermin 308:16
slow and steady wins the r. 160:8
some new r., called Man 177:4
the human r., to which so many ... belong 81:12
the r. dwelling all round the globe 83:14
the r. is not to the swift 39:23
whole r. of politicians 309:1
Races: human species ... two distinct r. 156:2
Rachel weeping for her children 43:9
Rack: leave not a r. behind 288:16
ship has weather'd every r. 325:12
the r. of this tough world 268:5
then we r. the value 278:12
Radical ... with both feet ... in the air 235:3
Rage: disguise ... nature with hard-favour'd r. 259:3
puts all Heaven in a r. 54:13
r., r., against the dying 315:15
Ragged: though my ryme be r., tattered 302:11
Raggedness: loop'd and window'd r. 266:13
Rags: heaven in r. than to hell in embroidery 207:29
no scandal like r. 109:3
sat in unwomanly r. 135:3
Rail: I'll r. against ... first-born 244:7
Rail (*continued*)
whiles I am a beggar, I will r. 264:14
Rain: being read to ... waiting for r. 106:5
droppeth as the gentle r. from heaven 275:1
hath the r. a father? 35:13
I dissolve it in r. 298:5
in thunder, lightning, or in r. 269:3
nor r., wind, thunder ... my daughters 266:7
r. before seven; fine before eleven 224:1
r., r., go to Spain 224:2
right as r. 224:21
ripple of r. 309:14
rudely r. beaten ... moth-eaten 302:11
sendeth r. on ... just ... unjust 43:21
still falls the r. 302:9
stirring ... roots with spring r. 107:3
the r. came heavily ... in floods 334:7
the r. is full of ghosts 170:14
the r. is over and gone 40:8
the r. it raineth every day 292:3
the r. it raineth on the just 57:14
the wind and the r. 292:3
Rainbow: a r. in the sky 333:8
add another hue unto the r. 264:19
the r. comes and goes 331:13
Rains: it never r. but it pours 224:3
Rainy: lay it up for a r. day 224:4
the weather when it is not r. 68:17
Raisons que la raison ne connaît point 198:8
Rake: every woman is at heart a r. 203:15
excuse for thus playing the r. 184:3
lean as a r. 218:29
lene was his hors as is a r. 79:8
man's a ribald ... a r. 120:10
Rampallion: you r.! 256:14
Rampart: his corse to the r. we hurried 330:3
Ramparts: o'er the r. we watched 153:6
Ran: Georgie Porgie r. away 189:3
grief with a glass that r. 309:15
the sacred river r. 87:11, 87:13
Range with humble livers in content 261:4
Rank is good, and gold is fair 326:6
Rankers: gentlemen r. 154:15
Ranks: all service r. the same with God 62:8
even the r. of Tuscany 164:1
Rap and knock and enter in our soul 60:13
Rapidity: travelling ... dull in ... proportion to its r. 237:1
Rapidly: yes, but not so r. 26:1
Rapscallions: all kings is mostly r. 318:9
Rapture: a r. on the lonely shore 69:9
first fine careless r. 61:3
Raptures: the r. and roses of vice 309:17
Rare: I think my love as r. 294:14
she was indeed a r. one 329:10
Rarely, rarely, comest thou 300:4
Rascal: a dull and muddy-mettl'd r. 250:16
get down you dirty r. 190:3
Rashes: green grow the r. 66:1
Rasselas, prince of Abyssinia 141:3
Rat: a dog, a horse, a r. have life 268:4
a r.? Dead, for a ducat 252:12
cat that killed the r. 194–5:8
Mr. Speaker, I smell a r. 234:3
to smell a r. 225:33
Rate: brings down the r. of usance 274:7

Rated: in the Rialto you have r. me 274:9
Rather: he had r. have a turnip 140:17
I live ... r. as a Spectator 9:6
Rationed: liberty ... so precious ... it must be r. 159:3
Rats: out ... the r. came tumbling 62:3
r. desert a sinking ship 224:5
r.! they fought the dogs 61:17
rid your town of r. 62:2
Rattle: spoiled his nice new r. 75:14
Rave: old age shd. burn and r. 315:15
Raven: quoth the R., Nevermore 200:19
yr. locks were like the r. 66:5
Ravens: there were three r. 11:15
Ray: gem of purest r. serene 126:10
Raze out the ... troubles of the brain 272:6
Reach: man's r. shd. exceed his grasp 60:11
Read: classic ... everybody wants to have r. 319:2
classic ... nobody wants to r. 319:2
I r. much of the night 107:4
I've r. in many a novel 72:2
r. ... as inclination leads him 142:9
r., mark, learn 53:2
sins were scarlet ... books were r. 27:5
sooner r. a time-table ... than nothing 169:6
what do you r., my lord? 250:2
without an intention to r. it 143:10
Reader: last r. reads no more 133:12
Readers: the human race, to which ... r. belong 81:12
Reading: I prefer r. 303:8
peace is poor r. 128:7
r. is to the mind 306:8
r. maketh a full man 23:8
when ... not walking, I am r. 156:6
writer's time is spent in r. 143:16
Ready: conference [maketh] a r. man 23:8
we always are r. 115:1
Real: although pain isn't r. 12:9
Realistic: when statesmen ... say ... r. 20:1
Reality: between the idea and the r. 106:8
cannot bear very much r. 106:4
Realm: this earth, this r., this England 282:5
Realms: constancy lives in r. above 87:7
who dwell in r. of day 55:1
Reap: men that sow to r. 309:18
shall r. the whirlwind 42:9
Reaped: wheat which never shd. be r. 317:17
Reason: all r. is against it 68:8
Cornish men will know the r. why 129:4
divorced old barren R. 110:9
do ... r. themselves out again 260:4
have I not r. to lament 332:8
in erring r.'s spite 203:4
no other but a woman's r. 292:5
O, r. not the need 266:2
or any other r. why 10:2
r. and energy, love and hate 56:15
r. is left free to combat it 139:8
r. is our soul's left hand 100:18
r. why I cannot tell 59:9
reasons which r. does not know 198:8
right deed for the wrong r. 107:10
ruling passion conquers r. still 203:19
teach thy necessity to r. thus 281:14
theirs not to r. why 311:11
worse appear the better r. 176:18
Reasonable: a r. good ear in music 277:4
Reasoned high of Providence 177:6
Reasons: the heart has its r. 198:8
Rebel: thinking man is bound to r. 138:3
Rebellion lay in his way 255:19
Rebels: dear earth ... though r. wound thee 283:1
Rebuke: boldly r. vice 53:8
open r. is better than secret love 39:2
Recapture: think he never could r. 61:3
Reckless what I do to spite the world 271:2
Recommendation: self-praise is no r. 225:12
Recompense: heaven did a r. ... send 126:14
Record: puts a r. on the gramophone 107:5
Recover: die of it do seldom ... r. 243:8
Recte: si possis r., si non, quocumque modo rem 135:11
Reculer: il faut r. pour mieux sauter 217:15
Red: coral is far more r. than her lips' r. 294:13
grace to get ... r. in the face 29:7
her lips were r., her looks were free 86:8
keep the R. Flag flying 90:3
like a r. r. rose 66:15
making the green one r. 270:12
nature, r. in tooth and claw 312:17
r. as a rose 224:6
r. as a rose is she 86:1
r. rag to a bull 224:7
sun ... curtained with cloudy r. 175:10
sunset ... one glorious blood-r. 61:4
the one in r. cravat 99:18
the r. plague rid you 287:19
the R. Queen 77:8,10
Red brick: not even r., but white tile 197:12
Red-breast: the r. whistles 147:5
Rede: recks not his own r. 248:14
Redeemer: I know that my r. liveth 35:8
Redemption: condemn'd into everlasting r. 278:15
no r. from hell 224:8
Redress: things past r. ... past care 282:11
Reed: a bruised r. shall he not break 41:2
r. shaken with the wind 44:11
Reeds: down in the r. by the river 60:9
Reeking into Cadiz Bay 61:4
Reeling and Writhing 74:15
References: always verify yr. r. 236:13
Reflect: when I r. that God is just 139:13
Reformation: reforming of R. itself 182:7
Reforming: nothing so needs r. as ... habits 319:1
Refrain: did ... from expensive sins r. 103:6
Refreshment: the most perfect r. 20:12
Refuge: eternal God is thy r. 33:9
God is our r. and strength 36:13
idleness ... r. of weak minds 80:15
Refugees: the guttural sorrow of the r. 165:1
Regard: where ... least r. for human freedom 305:6
Regiment: four elements warring ... for r. 166:10
led his r. from behind 116:6
Monstrous R. of Women 155:13
Region: in thrilling r. of thick-ribbed ice 273:10
Regions: double lived in r. new 147:6
r. Caesar never knew 92:2
Regret: youth is a blunder ... old age a r. 100:9
Regrets: past R. and future Fears 110:2

Reign: r. in this horrible place 93:15
whatsoever King shall r. 15:13
Reigned: I have r. with your loves 107:14
Reinforcement: what r. we may gain from hope 176:3
Rejoice: as he was fortunate, I r. 263:10
daughters of the Philistines r. 34:10
from age to age thou didst r. 333:10
good Christian men, r. 186:14
I hear thee and r. 336:2
r. with them that do r. 47:24
Rejoices: a poor heart that never r. 223:16
Rejoicing: went on his way r. 47:3
Relative: set out ... in a r. way 63:1
Relaxed: power ... r. too much 22:15
Relaxes: damn braces, bless r. 57:4
Relent: shall make him once r. 63:13
Relief: for this r. much thanks 247:13
Religion: bringeth ... minds about to r. 22:11
enough r. to make us hate 309:8
good life is the only r. 215:19
love is my r.—I cd. die for that 152:10
men will wrangle for r. 88:17
Millionaire. That is my r. 296:1
my pollertics, like my r. 322:10
no man's r. ... survives his morals 221:39
not a r. for gentlemen 78:15
one r. is as true as another 67:11
one's r. is whatever he is ... interested in 24:15
only one r., though ... a hundred versions 296:17
pure r. breathing household laws 333:11
r. but a childish toy 166:3
r. is allowed to invade 169:10
r., justice, counsel, and treasure 22:8
r. of an ill man 224:9
r. is the best armour ... worst cloak 224:10
r.'s in the heart, not ... knees 139:17
r. ... the opium of the people 168:8
superstition ... r. of feeble minds 64:13
Religious: casting a dim r. light 173:11
good, but not r. good 128:9
man is ... a r. animal 64:12
Rely upon a comfortable time-lag 324:15
Remain: as things have been, things r. 85:1
Remained: came to scoff, r. to pray 122:10
Remains: what r. is bestial 279:10
Remarkable: nothing left r. beneath the ... moon 243:6
Remedies: desperate diseases ... desperate r. 211:16
he that will not apply new r. 22:18
our r. oft in ourselves 242:2
Remedy: a r. for all ... but death 224:11
force is not a r. 58:11
knew the reason ... sought the r. 245:14
one unfailing r.—the Tankard 72:1
r. is worse than the disease 22:10
Remember: and if thou wilt, r. 236:5
bitter to endure ... sweet to r. 208:2
do you r. an inn, Miranda? 28:5
forget and smile ... r. and be sad 236:2
he'll r., with advantages 260:1
I r., I r. 134:14,15
I r. your name perfectly 305:21
I wish our ... poets wd. r. 88:3
if I do not r. thee 37:27
in the morning we will r. them 54:5
it r., whan it passed is 80:5
Remember (*continued*)
please to r. the fifth of November 14:5
r. ... best of friends must part 17:4
r. Lot's wife 46:10
r. me when I am gone away 236:1
r. now thy Creator 39:26
r. when ... money not scarce? 108:22
some day ... pleasant to r. 321:1
Remembered: r. tolling a departed friend 256:7
when we r. Zion 37:22
wd. have made myself r. 152:11
Remembering: a soul r. my good friends 282:8
r. mine affliction ... misery 41:18
Remembers: nature yet r. what was so fugitive 332:4
Remembrance: appear almost a r. 151:14
praising ... lost makes the r. dear 242:7
rosemary, that's for r. 252:23
summon up r. of things past 293:18
writ in r. more than things long past 282:3
Reminds a man he is mortal 96:5
Remorse: farewell fear, farewell r. 177:14
Remote: r. and ineffectual don 27:12
r., unfriended, melancholy, slow 123:12
Remover: bends with the r. to remove 294:8
Remuneration ... Latin word for three farthings 268:10
Rend yr. heart and not yr. garments 42:11
Render therefore unto Caesar 44:25
Rendezvous: I have a r. with Death 240:15
Renounce the devil ... his works 53:11
Renown: a citizen of credit and r. 92:6
living, shall forfeit fair r. 240:1
Renowned for larnin' and piety 125:4
Rent: what a r. the envious Casca made 263:17
Repair unto the Bell at Edmonton 92:7
Repay: I will r., saith the Lord 47:26
Repeal of bad or obnoxious laws 125:2
Repent: I do r. it from my very soul 289:14
Repentance: r. comes too late 224:12
Winter Garment of R. fling 109:14
Repented: she strove, and much r. 69:11
Repetitions: use not vain r. 43:23
Replenish: be fruitful ... r. the earth 30:4
Reply: third, the R. Churlish 246:2
Report me and my cause aright 253:8
Reporters: gallery in which the r. sit 164:4
Repose: earned a night's r. 161:11
O partial sleep, give thy r.? 257:3
r. is taboo'd by anxiety 117:12
Reposes: in quiet she r. 18:16
Reprehend: if I r. any thing in this world 301:10
Representation: no taxation without r. 222:9
Reproach: receives r. of being 294:10
sting of a r. ... truth of it 226:23
Reproof: fourth, the R. Valiant 246:2
Reprove: check the erring, and r. 334:3
Republican form of Government is the highest 305:2
Reputation: at every word a r. dies 204:8
if you esteem your own r. 322:17
purest treasure ... spotless r. 281:8
r., r., ... lost my r.! 279:10
seeking the bubble r. 244:11
sold my R. for a Song 110:15
Reputations: murdered r. of the week 89:7

Requests: thou wilt grant their r. 52:19
Require: what doth the Lord r.? 42:24
Requires: all the human frame r. 27:4
Researchers: our r. into public opinion 20:4
Resemble: when I r. her to thee 322:1
Resent: no individual cd. r. ... thousands ... meant 308:13
Resist: can r. everything except temptation 328:2
r. the devil and he will flee 50:2
Resisting: not over-fond of r. temptation 26:3
Resolute: be bloody, bold and r. 271:15
Resolution: in War: R. 83:13
native hue of r. 250–1:20
what r. from despair 176:3
Resolved to live a fool 25:7
Resolves; and re-resolves; then dies the same 338:1
Resort: far from all r. of mirth 173:9
Resource: infinite—r.—and—sagacity 155:10
Respect: is there no r. of place ... time? 291:4
the r. that makes calamity 250–1:20
Respectable: r. means rich 199:3
when was genius found r.? 60:6
Respecter of persons 47:5
Respects: he that r. not is not respected 224:14
Responsibility: liberty means r. ... men dread it 296:12
no sense of r. [baby] 155:15
Rest: absence of occupation is not r. 93:4
angels sing thee to thy r. 253:11
far better r. that I go to 99:12
God ... ordain'd no r. 320:6
run far faster than the r. 27:14
set up my everlasting r. 287:4
she's at r., and so am I 104:5
so may he r. 261:14
some ill a-brewing towards my r. 274:13
the r. is silence 253:10
the r. of his dull life 25:7
wear ourselves, and never r. 166:10
Restoration: the Church's R. in 1883 29:11
Restraint: firm r. with which they write 72:6
Resumed: democracy r. her reign 27:7
Reticulated or decussated 140:8
Retire me to my Milan 289:8
Retired into ... political Cave of Adullam 58:10
Retirement: short r. urges sweet return 179:8
Retort: first the R. Courteous 246:2
Retreat: let us make an honourable r. 245:4
Return: art gone, and never must r. 174:14
departed never to r. 67:6
short retirement urges sweet r. 179:8
unto dust shalt thou r. 30:14
Returns: and the day r. too soon 71:4
small profits and quick r. 225:32
Reveal: words ... half r. ... half conceal 312:12
Reveals: soberness conceals what drunkenness r. 225:37
Revelry: sound of r. by night 69:3
Revels: our r. now are ended 288:16
Revenge: prompted to my r. by heaven 250:18
r., at first though sweet 179:7
r. his foul ... unnatural murder 249:8
r. is a kind of wild justice 21:12
r. is sweet 224:15
r. never repairs 224:16
Revenge (*continued*)
shall we not r.? 274:17
spur my dull r. 252:17
study of r., immortal hate 175:18
sweet is r.—especially to women 69:12
sweet r. grows harsh 280:12
Revenges: time brings in his r. 292:2
Reverence: none so poor to do him r. 263:14
yet r. ... doth make distinction 247:7
Reviewing: read a book before r. it 303:16
Revolt: a r.? No, Sire, ... a revolution 234:10
inferiors r. in order that 18:6
Révolte: c'est une r.? non ... une révolution 234:10
Revolution: a revolt? No, sire, ... a r. 234:10
Révolution: une révolte? Non ... une r. 234:10
Revolutionist: not a r., is an inferior 296:9
Revolutions: state of mind which creates r. 18:6
Reward: only r. of virtue is virtue 108:5
r. of a thing well done 108:8
the Lord shall r. thee 38:28
virtue is its own r. 229:18
Rheims: Cardinal Lord Archbishop of R. 24:5
Rhetorician: a sophistical r. inebriated [Gladstone] 100:8
Rheumatic of shoulder 57:15
Rhodope: brighter than is ... R. 166:7
Rhyme: build the lofty r. 174:13
r. being no necessary adjunct 175:14
r. themselves into ladies' favours 260:4
soft names in many a mused r. 150:3
still more tired of r. 27:10
though my r. be ragged 302:11
Rialto: in the R. you have rated me 274:9
Rib: r. ... made he a woman 30:8
smote him under the fifth r. 34:13
Riband: just for a r. ... in his coat 61:8
r. in the cap of youth 252:24
Ribstone pippin: right as a R. 27:9
Rich: adversity makes ... not r. 206:5
being r., my virtue ... shall be 264:14
better to live r. than to die r. 144:11
born lucky than r. 207:21
good workmen are seldom r. 215:25
God help the r. 215:6
grew so r. that I was sent 119:16
he is r. that is satisfied 224:18
health! the blessing of the r.! 145:18
if I ever become a r. man 28:3
maketh haste to be r. 39:4
never be handsome, strong, r. 216:3
no sin but to be r. 264:14
one law for the r. 218:23
over the r. Dead 59:1
passing r. with forty pounds a year 122:9
Poor Little R. Girl 91:11
poverty is an anomaly to r. people 23:21
respectable means r. 199:3
r. can help themselves 215:5
r. man to enter ... kingdom of God 44:23
r. men have no faults 224:17
r. men rule the law 123:16
r. not gaudy 248:16
r. what gets the gravy 16:13
seems it r. to die 150:3
the r. man in his castle 10:5
victim of a r. man's game 16:11
when I grow r., say the bells 192:4

Rich (*continued*)
widows are always r. 230:14
wretchedness of being r. 303:7
Richard: body of R. Hind 12:3
we came in with R. Conqueror 287:5
Richer: for r. for poorer 53:22
r. than doing nothing for a bribe 247:3
Riches: infinite r. in a little room 166:4
of great r. ... no real use 22:25
r. are for spending 22:22
r. I hold in light esteem 58:14
r. of the mind ... make ... rich 224:19
to r., dignity and power 28:1
Richly: a lady r. left 274:4
Rickshaw: it's no go the r. 164:14
Rid: idea of getting r. of it [work] 139:15
if I can r. your town 62:2
Riddle: a r. wrapped in a mystery 82:10
Ride: a poem must r. 113:16
Haggards r. no more 306:10
r. a cock-horse 193:1
r. in triumph through Persepolis 166:9
went for a r. on a tiger 12:10
when he next doth r. abroad 92:13
Rideau: tirez le r., la farce est jouée 232:8
Rider: secret ... between a r. and his horse 308:10
Rides: and r. upon the storm 92:15
Ridicule: easier to r. than commend 224:20
Ridiculous: is not this r.? 119:3
one step above the r. 197:18
sublime to the r. 185:11
the sublime and the r. ... nearly related 197:18
Riding: r. to and from his wife 325:8
Yankee Doodle ... r. on a pony 196:4
Ridley: be of good comfort, Master R. 157:2
Rien appris ... oublié 310:12
Rifle all the breathing spring 88:8
Rift: load every r. of yr. subject 152:12
Riga: young lady of R. 12:10
Right: a r. judgement in all things 53:5
all goes r. and nothing ... wrong 120:13
all's r. with the world 62:7
an earl by r., by courtesy a man 21:5
defend to the death your r. 321:18
do the r. deed for the wrong reason 107:10
earth's the r. place for love 113:8
great r. ... a little wrong 275:2
I'll publish, r. or wrong 70:11
it must be r. I've done it from my youth 93:16
know not whether laws be r. 326:15
majority never has r. on its side 138:3
my r. there is none to dispute 93:14
never dreamed, though r. were worsted 60:12
no r. to strike against the public safety 90:10
our country, r. or wrong 96:7
rather be r. than be President 84:9
r. as a Ribstone Pippin 27:9
r. as rain 224:21
r. divine of kings to govern wrong 201:3
r. in his own eyes 33:24
shall not the Judge ... do r.? 31:2
think at yr. age, it is r.? 74:3
think the last opinion r. 202:12
too fond of the r. 123:2
two wrongs don't make a r. 229:7
with firmness in the r. 159:15
Righteous: be not r. over much 39:21
die the death of the r. 32:20
if I find ... fifty r. 31:3
judge r. judgment 46:23
souls of the r. are in the hand of God 51:12
Righteousness: r. exalteth a nation 38:15
the Sun of r. arise 43:7
Rights: endowed ... with certain unalienable r. 139:6
property has its duties ... its r. 102:13
reaffirm faith in fundamental ... r. 319:5
Rigol: from this golden r. hath divorc'd 257:17
Rigour of the game 156:4
Ring: r. at the end of his nose 158:8
spring ... the only pretty r. time 245:16
with this r. I thee wed 53:24
Ring-a-ring o' roses 193:2
Rings: my true love sent ... five gold r. 194:2
r. on her fingers 193:1
Riot: rash fierce blaze of r. cannot last 282:4
r. and dishonour stain the brow 253:15
Ripe: from hour to hour, we r. and r. 244:9
scholar ... r. and good one 262:2
Ripeness is all 267:12
Rise: r. up before the hoary head 32:17
r. up, my love, my fair one 40:7
some r. by sin ... by virtue fall 273:2
Rises: hoo-ray and up she r. 17:7
while Jove's planet r. yonder 61:5
Rising: in his r. seemed a pillar 177:3
River: Alph, the sacred r., ran 87:11
away, you rolling r. 16:9
dat ol' man r. 128:2
even the weariest r. 310:1
fame is like a r. 23:10
follow the r. ... to the sea 214:1
in the reeds by the r. 60:9
lived on the r. Dee 54:1
on either side the r. lie 313:11
one more r. to cross 14:9
r. Weser, deep and wide 61:16
snow falls in the r. 67:4
the rush of the r. 26:10
through wood and dale the sacred r. 87:13
Rivers: washed by the r., blest by suns 59:6
Rivulet: a neat r. of text shall meander 301:13
Road: does the r. wind up-hill? 236:3
good to be out on the r. 169:1
however long and hard the r. 82:12
O ye'll tak' the high r. 16:10
on a lonesome r. 86:16
on to the end of the r. 157:5
their ... monument the asphalt r. 107:1
watched the ads and not the r. 186:4
Roads: all r. lead to Rome 224:22
Roam: a dunce that has been sent to r. 93:2
ever let the fancy r. 148:3
gave, once, her ... ways to r. 59:6
Roamin' in the gloamin' 157:7
Roaming: mistress mine, where are you r.? 291:1
Roar: called upon to give the r. 83:14
r. like a bull 224:23
Roared: cracked and growled and r. and howled 86:2
Roaring: a r. in the wind all night 334:7
Rob Peter to pay Paul 224:24
Robbed: he that is r. ... not r. at all 280:1
r. that smiles steals something 279:4

Robbery: fair exchange is no r. 213:11
Robbing: forbids the r. of a foe 82:3
Robe: the marshal's truncheon nor the judge's r. 273:4
Robes: lever ... bokes ... than r. riche 79:9
r. and furr'd gowns hide all 267:6
Robin: a r. redbreast in a cage 54:13
call for the r. redbreast 324:3
Robins: alive when the r. come 99:18
Rock: R. of Ages, cleft for me 317:15
upon this r. ... my church 44:16
whole as the marble, founded as the r. 271:6
Rocks: soften r., or bend a knotted oak 89:5
with r., and stones, and trees 334:15
Rod: a r. for his own back 224:25
a r. to check the erring 334:3
can wisdom be put in a silver r.? 55:2
spareth his r. hateth his son 38:14
thy r. and thy staff they comfort me 35:29
Rode: r. madly off in all directions 157:13
r. the six hundred 311:9
she r. forth, clothed on with chastity 312:3
Roe: chasing ... deer and following the r. 66:14
Rogue: bewitch'd with the r.'s company 254:6
r. and peasant slave am I! 250:14
Rogues in buckram 254:15
Roll: not in the r. of common men 255:4
r. up that map 200:10
Rolling: just keeps r., he keeps on r. 128:2
r. English drunkard ... r. English road 81:6
Romae: si fueris R. 10:10
Romam: O fortunatam ... me consule R.! 84:8
Roman: a R.'s life, a R.'s arms 163:14
before the R. came to Rye 81:6
I am a R. citizen 84:7
neither holy, nor R. 321:16
rather be a dog ... than such a R. 263:23
Roman Conquest ... a *Good Thing* 241:8
Romance: to love oneself ... lifelong r. 327:5
Romano: si fueris Romae, R. vivito more 10:10
Romans: Friends, R., countrymen 263:11
live as the R. do 10:10
the R. counted *backwards* 241:9
Tiber, to whom the R. pray 163:14
which came first, the Greeks or ... R. 100:14
Rome: all roads lead to R. 224:22
fiddle while R. is burning 213:25
happy R., born when I was consul 84:8
I lov'd R. more 263:9
pardoun come from R. 79:19
R. shall fall; and when R. falls 69:8
R. was not built in a day 224:27
the grandeur that was R. 200:18
the hook-nos'd fellow of R. 257:13
when in R., live as the Romans do 10:10
Romeo: wherefore art thou R.? 286:8
Ronald: Lord R. said nothing ... rode ... off 157:13
Rood: when every r. ... maintained its man 122:6
Roofs: masons building r. of gold 258:8
Room: all before my little r. 59:2
although the r. grows chilly 124:10
always r. at the top 323:12
convent's narrow r. 332:13
infinite riches in a little r. 166:4
Room (*continued*)
no r. ... for hyphenated Americanism 235:10
no r. for them in the inn 45:19
not r. to swing a cat 224:28
r. of one's own 330:9
r. with a view—and you 91:7
Roosevelt: here is the answer ... to President R. 83:2
Roost (Roast): to rule the r. 224:31
Root of all evil. The want of money 68:3
Rooted: pluck from the memory a r. sorrow 272:6
Roots: stirring dull r. with spring rain 107:3
straight trees have crooked r. 226:28
Rope: a r. to hang himself 15:6
give a thief r. enough 224:29
Ropes: know the r. 218:9
Rose: a sadder ... man he r. 87:5
and lovely is the r. 331:13
as red as a r. 224:6
At Christmas I no more desire a r. 268:9
beauty's r. might never die 293:10
go, lovely r. 322:1
he's mighty lak' a r. 306:5
I am the r. of Sharon 40:4
in a twilight dim with r. 97:1
my fause lover stole my r. 67:7
my love ... like a red red r. 66:15
no r. without a thorn 222:6
not to me returns ... summer's r. 177:10
red as a r. is she 86:1
r. by any other name 286:9
r. leaves, when the r. is dead 300:6
r. of the fair state 251:5
r. or rue or laurel 309:16
the last r. of summer 184:1
the r. of youth upon him 242:20
when I have pluck'd thy r. 280:11
your image that blossoms a r. 337:7
Rosebuds: gather ye r. while ye may 132:7
r., before they be withered 51:10
Rosemary: for you there's r. and rue 293:1
r., that's for remembrance 252:23
Rose-moles all in stipple upon trout 135:7
Rose-red city half as old as time 64:3
Roses: as soon seek r. in December 70:14
ash the burnt r. leave 106:10
it was r., r., all the way 61:15
raptures and r. of vice 309:17
strew on her r., r. 18:16
their lips were four red r. 285:8
twin r. by the zephyr blown apart 148:10
where r. and white lilies grow 72:13
Rosy cheeks and flaxen curls 62:6
Rot: from hour to hour, we r. and r. 244:9
lie in cold obstruction and to r. 273:10
r. inwardly, and foul contagion spread 175:4
Rotted: do you think my mind ... r. early? 186:5
Rotten: something is r. in the state of Denmark 249:5
soon ripe, soon r. 226:1
Rotting: mean and mighty r. together 247:7
Rough: take the r. with the smooth 224:30
Rough-hew them how we will 253:6
Round: in a light fantastic r. 172:16
Rounded: our little life is r. with a sleep 288:16

Rousseau: mock on, Voltaire, R. 55:9
Roving: we'll go no more a r. 71:3,4
Rowland: Child R., to the dark tower 266:17
Rowley, powley, gammon and spinach 189:2
Royal: likely ... to have prov'd most r. 253:12
no r. road to geometry 108:27
Rub: Ay, there's the r. 250–1:20
Rubies: her price is far above r. 39:8
wisdom is better than r. 38:5
Rude: r. am I in my speech 278:21
'very r. of him,' she said 76:1
Rue: nought shall make us r. 265:5
shall I strew ... rose or r. 309:16
there's rosemary and r. 293:1
with r. my heart is laden 136:8
Rues: eye sees not, heart r. not 213:7
Ruffian: that father r. 255:1
Ruhnken: more learn'd professor R. 204:13
Ruins: I'm one of the r. 160:6
Rule: exception proves the r. 213:3
golden r. is ... no golden rules 296:11
only infallible r. we know 308:5
r., Britannia, r. the waves 316:12
r. them with a rod of iron 50:17
r. youth well for age will r. itself 224:32
Ruler of the Queen's Navee 119:15,16
Rulers: against the r. of the darkness 48:27
Ruling: the r. ideas ... ideas of its r. class 168:9
the r. passion ... conquers reason 203:19
Rum: what a R. Go everything is 324:14
Yo-ho-ho and a bottle of r. 307:4
Rumble thy bellyful. Spit, fire 266:7
Rumour: listen to popular r. 121:5
Run: gwine to r. all night 112:4
he may r. that readeth 42:26
outrun ... that which we r. at 261:3
r., r. Orlando 245:2
r. with the hare 224:33
see how they r.! 195:1
they ... r. about through the city 36:18
until it doth r. over 14:14
you r. about, my little Maid 336:6
you've had a pleasant r. 76:6
Runcible cat 158:10
Runcible spoon: ate with a r. 158:9
Running: takes all the r. *you* can do 75:12
the r. of the deer 15:8
Runs: fights and r. away 13:8
Run-stealers flicker to and fro 316:7
Rupert: frank ... rash,—the R. of Debate 63:2
Rushy: down the r. glen 10:9
Russia: I cannot forecast ... the action of R. 82:10
R. has two generals 187:15
this will last out a night in R. 273:3
Russian: he might have been a R. (Roosian) 120:3
Rust: better to wear out than to r. out 94:11
Sunday clears away the r. 9:7
Rustling in unpaid-for silk 247:3
Rusty: my ryme ... r. and mothe eaten 302:11
Ruth: sad heart of R., when, sick for home 150:4
Rye: before the Roman came to R. 81:6
comin' through the r. 65:15
fields of barley and of r. 313:11

Sabbath: child ... born on the s. day 191:8
never broke the S. but for gain 103:6
Sabbath (*continued*)
remember the s. day to keep it holy 32:3
s. ... made for man ... not man for s. 45:6
seventh day is the s. 32:3
Sabrina fair, listen 173:3
Sack: I'll purge, and leave s. 256:5
s. the lot! 109:12
this intolerable deal of s.! 255:3
Sacred: if anything is s. ... body is s. 325:11
the s. river ran 87:11, 87:13
Sacrifice: I desire mercy, and not s. 42:8
Sacrifices: the s. of God are 36:15
Sad: how s. and bad and mad 60:16
s. words of tongue or pen 326:8
when pleasant thoughts bring s. 332:7
you shd. remember and be s. 236:2
Sadder: a s. and a wiser man 87:5
Sadists: repressed s. ... to become policemen 90:4
sadness: s. and gladness succeed each other 224:34
shady s. of a vale 148:4
sickness is better than s. 225:21
Safe: better s. than sorry 207:24
I pray you ... see me s. up 184:4
I wish him s. at home 146:3
s. ... on Abraham's breast 12:6
to be s. ... never to be secure 229:37
world made s. for democracy 329:9
Safely: thro' the world we s. go 54:15
Safer: s. to obey than to rule 152:16
'tis s. to be that which we destroy 271:3
Safest: just when we are s. ... a sunset-touch 60:13
Safety: in ... multitude of counsellors ... is s. 38:10
our s. is in our speed 108:10
strike against the public s. 90:10
we pluck this flower, s. 254:10
Sagacious, bold and turbulent of wit 102:16
Sagacity: infinite—resource—and—s. 155:10
Sage: thou Goddess s. and holy 173:6
Sages: teach you more ... than all the s. 335:7
Said: best ... known and s. in the world 19:11
I hope it may be s. 'His sins' 27:5
Sail: and cried, A s.! A s.! 86:7
full s., ... fan spread ... streamers 89:10
s. near the wind 224:35
s. on, O Ship of State! 160:11
very sea-mark of my utmost s. 280:13
white and rustling s. 95:1
Sailed: they s. away ... year and a day 158:8
Sailing: three ships come s. by 14:10, 190:4
what thing ... comes this way s. 180:15
Sailor: drunken s. early in the morning 17:7
home is the s. 307:6
Sails: purple the s., and so perfumed 242:14
when we our s. advance 102:9
wind out of one's s. 227:6
Saint: and never a s. took pity on 86:10
art ... able to corrupt a s. 253:17
my late espoused s. 181:16
open the shrine, that I may see my s. 145:17
s.-seducing gold 285:19
seem a s. when ... play the devil 284:14
young s., old devil 231:9
St. Agnes Eve—Ah, bitter chill 147:12
St. Clement's: say the bells of S. 192:4
St. Crispin: fought ... upon S.'s day 260:2

Saint Empire Romain ... ni saint, ni romain, ni empire 321:16
St. George: for Harry, England, and S.! 259:5
S., that swing'd the dragon 264:11
St. Ives: as I was going to S. 188:3
St. John: awake, my S. 202:17
St. Martins: say the bells of S. 192:4
St. Paul's: 'Say I am designing S.' 29:3
Saint Vincent: nobly, nobly, Cape S. 61:4
Saints: a pair of carved s. 283:7
all the S. adore thee 130:3
Sal: down South for to see my S. 16:5
Salad: my s. days 242:13
Salisbury: Lord S. ... brought back peace 100:7
Sally: there's none like pretty S. 73:3
Salt: became a pillar of s. 31:4
coaster with a s.-caked smoke-stack 168:14
ye are the s. of the earth 43:17
Salus populi suprema est lex 84:2
Salute: s. the happy morn 68:14
s. thee with my hand 283:1
Salvation: my bottle of s. 232:12
none of us shd. see s. 275:1
visit us with thy s. 325:3
work out yr. own s. 48:28
wot prawce s.? 296:2
Samarkand: the Golden Road to S. 111:2
Same: it's the s. the whole world over 16:13
Jesus Christ the s. ... for ever 49:24
more they are the s. 146:12
no better ... much the s. 21:6
Sammy, vy worn't there a alleybi? 99:9
Samson: better than the strength of S. 221:1
Sanctity: in the odour of s. died 24:6
Sand: a world in a grain of s. 54:12
little grains of s. 73:13
on the edge of the s. 158:9
roll down their golden s. 130:1
such quantities of s. 76:2
throw the s. against the wind 55:9
Sandals were for Clementine 183:9
Sandalwood, cedarwood, ... white wine 168:13
Sandboy: jolly as a s. 217:29
Sands: come unto these yellow s. 287:20
golden s., and crystal brooks 100:17
lone and level s. stretch far away 299:8
on the s. with printless foot 289:4
wd. steer too nigh the s. 102–3:17
Sane: see where the s. ... have landed us! 297:1
Sang: he worked and s. 54:1
s. his didn't ... danced his did 94:13
Sank: but oh! the silence s. 87:1
Sans teeth, sans eyes 244–5:11
Sappho: where burning S. loved 69:21
Sarah: old S. Battle 156:4
Sashes: one of his nice new s. 124:10
Sat: as I s. on a sunny bank 14:10
we s. by the flesh pots 31:27
Satan: get thee behind me, S. 44:18
S. exalted sat, by merit raised 176:15
S. finds some mischief still 323:2
Satchel: school-boy with his s. 244:11
Satire: let s. be my song 70:11
Satisfaction: great s. in quarrelling with her 301:14
Satisfied: well paid that is well s. 275:7
Satisfies: makes hungry where she most s. 242:15
Saturday: died on S. 193:6
escaped three weeks ... o' S. 307:1
S.'s child works hard 191:8
Saturn: grey-hair'd S., quiet as a stone 148:4
Satyr: Hyperion to a s. 248:3
Satyrs: my men, like s. grazing 166:2
Sauce for the goose is s. for the gander 224:37
Saul: is S. also among the prophets? 34:2
S. and Jonathan were lovely 34:11
S. hath slain his thousands 34:7
Sautrye: fithele, or gay s. 79:9
Savage: dancing? ... of s. origin 65:4
s., extreme, rude, cruel 294:11
s. place, as holy and enchanted 87:12
so s. and Tartarly 70:17
Save: choose time ... s. time 22:19
died to s. us all 10:7
s. her from the foggy, foggy dew 16:4
s. one's bacon 224:38
Saviour: the S. of the world was born 68:14
Savour: filths s. but themselves 266:21
keep seeming and s. all the winter 293:1
salt have lost his s. 43:17
Saw: all at once I s. a crowd 331:7
coughing drowns the parson's s. 269:1
do not s. the air too much 251:7
s. the Vision of the world 313:16
ten thousand s. I at a glance 331:9
who s. him die? 196:2
Saws: wise s. and modern instances 244:11
Say: do as I s., not as I do 241:4
he may have nothing to s. 143:15
I s. it that shd. not 227:34
my people ... to s. what they please 113:6
never s. die 221:33
s. it with flowers 196:10
s. not the struggle naught availeth 85:1
s. now Shibboleth 33:18
we love best, to them ... s. least 219:36
when you have nothing to s. 88:18
Saying: ancient s. is no heresy 274:15
s. is one thing 225:1
Scald: tears do s. like molten lead 267:10
Scallop-shell of quiet 232:12
Scan: whose limericks never wd. s. 13:1
Scandal: no s. about Queen Elizabeth 301:2
public s. that gives offence 182:16
s. ... is gossip made tedious 328:3
there's no s. like rags 109:3
would the s. vanish with my life 282:6
Scandale: la s. du monde 182:16
Scanter of yr. maiden presence 249:1
Scapegoat: let him go for a s. 32:13
Scarlet: raise the s. standard high 90:3
though your sins be as s. 40:17
Scars: wars bring s. 229:27
Scatter as from ... hearth ... my words 299:6
Scattered: dead bones ... s. by 285:1
s. in the bottom of the sea 285:1
Scene: our lofty s. be acted over 263:4
s. individable, or poem unlimited 250:9
upon that memorable s. 168:4
Scenery is fine, but human nature 151:16
Scenes: busy s. of crowded life 141:9
Scepticism: a wise s. ... attribute of a good critic 162:16
Sceptre: my s. for a palmer's ... staff 283:7
s. shows the force of ... power 275:1

Sceptre (*continued*)
this unwieldy s. from my hand 284:2
Sceptred: what avails the s. race? 156:13
Schemes: best laid s. o' mice and men 66:12
Scholar: he was a s. and a ripe 262:2
what ills the s.'s life assail 141:10
Scholars: great men ... not commonly ... great s. 134:6
s. dispute ... case is still before the courts 135:9
School: every day in the life of a s. 157:12
example ... the s. of mankind 64:15
extreme busyness ... at s. or college 307:8
like snail unwillingly to s. 244:11
s. of Stratford atte Bowe 79:4
tell tales out of s. 227:8
toward s. with heavy looks 286:12
village master taught his little s. 122:11
Schoolboy: every s. knows who imprisoned Montezuma 164:2
whining s., with his satchel 244:11
Schoolboys: as s. from their books 286:12
Schooldays: in my joyful s. 156:9
Schoolgirl: pert as a s. 118:6
that s. complexion 11:6
Schoolman's subtle art 201:20
Schoolmaster: average s. ... essentially an ass 169:13
Schools: 'tis an old maxim in the s. 308:12
Schooner: the s. Hesperus 161:12
Science: fair S. frowned not on his ... birth 126:13
S. is organised knowledge 305:1
Scoff: fools, who came to s. 122:10
Scoffing: antic sits s. his state 283:6
Scorer: when the one Great S. comes 233:12
Scorn: fixed figure for the time of s. 280:5
I can s. and let her go 330:1
I s. to change my state 293:17
in s. of eyes, reflecting gems 285:1
love he laugh'd to s. 295:4
love I laugh to s. 58:14
s. not the sonnet 333:5
the sound of public s. 179:12
Scorned: nor hell a fury like a woman s. 89:6
Scorns: how Stanley s., the glance 63:2
Scorpions: they had tails like unto s. 50:25
Scotchman: a S., if he be caught young 143:9
Scot-free: to go s. 225:2
Scotland: I do indeed come from S. 142:6
I'll be in S. afore ye 16:10
oats ... in S., supports the people 140:9
stands S. where it did? 271:19
Scots: Kills me ... S. at a breakfast 254:12
S. wha hae wi' Wallace bled 67:1
S. whom Bruce has ... led 67:1
Scotsman: grandest moral attribute of a S. 25:1
Scott: not even Sir Walter S. 297:8
Scotus or Aquinas 182:5
Scoundrel: every man over forty is a s. 296:16
general good ... plea of the s. 55:6
patriotism ... last refuge of a s. 143:17
Scourge: daughter of Jove ... whose iron s. 126:16
Scratch: come up to the s. 225:3
s. my back and I'll s. yours 225:4
Scratching: cure ... but the s. of a pen 162:9
wd. ... I had the s. of thee 290:4
Scream: a s., a splash 16:12
Screw: a s. loose somewhere 225:5
s. may twist ... rack may turn 120:16
s. yr. courage to the sticking place 270:7
Scribble: always s., s., s.! ... Mr. Gibbon 121:13
Scrip and scrippage 245:4
Scripture: all s. is ... by inspiration of God 49:16
devil can cite S. for his purpose 274:8
Scriptures: life like the s.—figurative 152:7
Scruple: some craven s. 252:18
wd. not s. to pick a pocket 97:5
Scullion: away, you s.! 256:14
Sculpture: beauty cold ... like that of s. 237:9
Scum: [our army] ... s. of the earth 324:8
Scutcheon: honour is a mere s. 255:21
Scylla: between S. and Charybdis 207:38
Scythe: mower whets his s. 174:3
Scythian: snow on S. hills 166:7
Sea: all the s. were ink 14:1
alone on a wide, wide s. 86:10, 87:2
and there was no more s. 51:1
between France and England ... the s. 139:18
devil and the deep s. 211:17
down to a sunless s. 87:11
down to the s. in ships 37:4
England ... with the triumphant s. 282:6
first ... into that silent s. 86:4
from s. to shining s. 25:4
into the midst of the s. 31:26
learn the secret of the s.? 161:4
mother and lover ... the s. 310:6
my Bonnie is over the s. 16:2
never, never sick at s.! 119:11
not all the water in the rough, rude s. 283:2
on such a full s. are we now afloat 264:3
one foot in s. 277:21
one that goes to s. for nothing 101:2
out of the s. came he 85:13
over the s. to Skye 57:12, 307:3
plants His footsteps in the s. 92:15
precious stone set in the silver s. 282:5
sailed the wintry s. 161:12
scatter'd in the bottom of the s. 285:1
the kings of the s. 18:13
the rude s. grew civil 276:18
the s. is calm to-night 18:9
the s. never changes 90:8
the s.! the s.! 337:2
the wrinkled s. beneath him crawls 312:1
there is Society ... by the deep s. 69:9
till the s. ... floweth in yr. veins 317:16
to s. for nothing but to make him sick 101:2
to s. in a ... pea-green boat 158:7
two Voices ... one is of the s. 333:10
went down into the s. 85:13
went to s. in a sieve 158:4
when I put out to s. 311:13
where no s. runs 315:18
whose sound was like the s. 333:13
why the s. is boiling hot 76:4
wind of the Western S. 314:13
winds somewhere safe to s. 310:1
within a walk of the s. 28:4
worse things happen at s. 231:2
Sea-boy: wet s. in an hour so rude 257:3
Seagreen Incorruptible 73:7
Seal: all right ... you heard a s. bark 317:7

Seal (*continued*)
opened the seventh s. 50:23
Sealing-wax: ships and s. 76:4
Seals of love, but seal'd in vain 273:12
Sea-maid: to hear the s.'s music 276:18
Sea-mark: very s. of my utmost sail 280:13
Sea-monster: ingratitude ... more hideous ... than the s. 265:14
Search will find it out 132:5
Seas: foam of perilous s. 150:4
guard our native s. 72:10
I must down to the s. again 168:15–17
port after stormy s. 305:11
the multitudinous s. incarnadine 270:12
we shall fight on the s. and oceans 82:13
Seaside: I do like to be beside the s. 121:14
Season: a dry brain in a dry s. 106:6
givest ... meat in due s. 37:30
in the s. of the year 16:6
to every thing ... a s. 39:14
Seasons: as the swift s. roll 134:5
defend you from s. such as these 266:13
four s. fill the measure 151:4
four s. in the mind of man 151:4
thus with the year s. return 177:10
when mercy s. justice 275:1
Seat: regain the blissful s. 175:15
this s. of Mars 282:5
Seats: you want the best s.; we have them 11:11
Seconds: sixty s.' worth of distance run 154:20
Secrecy: for s., no lady closer 254:11
Secret: bread eaten in s. is pleasant 38:7
digestion ... great s. of life 303:17
it [love] ceases to be a s. 26:11
joys of parents are s. 21:17
learn the s. of the sea? 161:4
s., black, and midnight hags! 271:13
there is no s. so close 308:10
Secrets: s. with girls ... never valued 94:1
tell the s. of my prison-house 249:7
Sect: attached to that great s. 298:8
paradise for a s. 148:1
Sects: two-and-seventy jarring s. confute 110:10
Secure: safe ... never to be s. 229:37
s., and never now can mourn 297:16
Sedge is wither'd from the lake 148:14
See: and no man s. me more 261:8
blind as those who won't s. 208:9
come up and s. me sometime 325:5
content to s. no other verdure 151:2
did you once s. Shelley plain? 61:10
ever s. such a thing in yr. life? 195:1
forward tho' I canna s. 66:13
I did but s. her passing by 17:2
I s. the moon ... moon sees me 190:5
if thou hast eyes to s. 279:5
may I be there to s. 92:13
O! say can you s. 153:6
rather s. than be one 64:1
s. all, nor be afraid 62:9
s. her on the bridge at midnight 16:12
s., not feel, how beautiful 87:8
s. what we shall s. 225:9
shall never s. a billboard 186:10
the eye begins to s. 58:15
to s. beyond our bourn 147:11
to s. her was to love her 65:9
See (*continued*)
wait and s. 19:15, 229:22
we s. through a glass darkly 48:7
Seed: groweth s. and bloweth med 14:7
in thy s. ... all nations ... blessed 31:5
robs not one light s. 148:5
s. begging their bread 36:9
Seeds: if you can look into the s. of time 269:8
Seeing: s. is believing 225:10
worth s.? Yes; but not ... going 144:16
Seek: nothing s., nothing find 222:16
s. ye the Lord 41:8
Seeking: s. the food he eats 244:6
s. whom he may devour 50:8
we must still be s. 331:5
Seeks: he that s. trouble 225:11
whoever s. abroad may find 147:3
Seem: free we s. ... fettered ... are 60:10
s. here no painful inch to gain 85:2
s. wiser than they are 22:20
things are not what they s. 160:14
Seeming: keep s. ... all the winter 293:1
Seems: he s. so near and yet so far 313:2
how sweet and fair she s. to be 322:1
so careful of the type she s. 312:16
Seen: because thou art not s. 245:1
s. and not heard 209:21
to be hated needs but to be s. 203:6
who hath not s. thee? 147:3
See-saw, Margery Daw 193:3
Seidlitz powder: burst while drinking a s. 12:4
Seize the flow'r, its bloom is shed 67:4
Self: from thee to my sole s. 150:5
nothing ... greater to one than ... s. 326:4
to thine own s. be true 248–9:17
wretch, concentred all in s. 240:1
Self-evident: we hold these truths to be s. 139:6
Self-praise is no recommendation 225:12
Self-preservation ... first law of nature 225:13
Self-sacrifice: the spirit of s. 334:4
Self-sufficient: know how to be s. 183:3
Seldom: a woman s. asks advice 9:10
s. or never the two hit it off 330:10
Sempronius: we'll do more, S. 9:4
Senators: green-rob'd s. of mighty woods 148:6
Sensation of a short sharp shock 118:7
Sensations: Life of S. rather than of Thoughts 151:10
Sense: devoid of s. and motion 176–7:19
fools admire, but men of s. approve 202:11
live within the s. they quicken 300:6
man of s. ... trifles with [women] 80:14
Shadwell never deviates into s. 104:14
so sweet that the s. aches 280:6
sound ... an echo to the s. 202:10
take care of the s. 74:13
Sense of humour: mind ... deficient in a s. 88:4
Senseless: the most s. and fit man 278:5
Senses: steep my s. in forgetfulness 257:2
Sensibility: fine sense, yet wanting s. 93:12
Sensible: moral, s., and well-bred 92:4
Sentence: my s. is for open war 176:16
originator of a good s. 108:14
s. first—verdict afterwards 75:8
Sentimental: carry ... body around because of its s. value 114:1

Sentiments: them's my s. 315:11
Sentinels: the fix'd s. almost receive ... whispers 259:8
Sentry-go: all night long ... on s. 117:6
Separately: we shall all hang s. 113:1
Seraphs: where S. might despair 68:18
Serfs: vassals and s. at my side 63:4
Serious: nothing s. in mortality 270:15
Sermon: good example ... the best s. 215:16
preach a better s. 108:23
Sermons in stones 243:15
Serpent: my s. of old Nile 242:12
sharper than a s.'s tooth 265:15
Servant: a s. ... an impudent elf 24:3
fire is a good s. ... bad master 213:28
money ... good s. ... bad master 221:11
not his most humble s. 144:18
s. of God, well done! 178:19
speak, Lord; for thy s. heareth 33:28
yr. s.'s cut in half 124:8
Servants: England ... the purgatory of s. 212:24
his s. he with new acquist 181:8
men in great places are thrice s. 22:2
Serve: also s. who only stand and wait 181:11
let my people go ... may s. me 31:21
letters ... s. to pin up one's hair 89:11
no man can s. two masters 44:1
s. God and mammon 44:2
Served: had I but s. God as diligently 330:6
Service: all s. ranks the same with God 62:8
constant s. of the antique world 243:19
more essential s. to his country 309:1
when s. sweat for duty 243:19
whose s. is perfect freedom 52:17
Sesame: open S.! 18:2
'Sesquippledan', he wd. say 324:13
Sessions of sweet silent thought 293:18
Set: s. my bow in the cloud 30:25
virtue is ... best plain s. 23:2
Setting: I haste now to my s. 261:8
Seven: a man with s. wives 188:3
happeneth not in s. years 209:18
hewn out her s. pillars 38:6
his acts being s. ages 244:11
if s. maids with s. mops 76:3
keep a thing s. years 217:32
s. cities warred for Homer 132:9
S. Types of Ambiguity 108:24
she answered, 'S. are we' 336:5
Seventh: s. day is the sabbath 32:3
s. month, on the seventeenth day 30:21
Seventy: to be s. years young 134:7
until s. times seven 44:22
Sever: ae fond kiss, and then we s. 65:8
to s. for years 71:5
Severe: s. ... and stern to view 122:11
steer from lively to s. 203:10
Severity: summer ... with its usual s. 88:2
Severn: before the Roman ... out to S. strode 81:6
Severs: hour ... s. those it shd. unite 298:10
Sewed: and they s. fig leaves together 30:12
Sewing: no cooking, or washing, or s. 12:1
Sex: Continental people have s. life 170:8
practically conceal its s. 186:11
the s. whose presence civilises 92:5
tyrants to their s. 277:12
Sexes: there are three s. 303:14
Sexton: told the s. ... s. toll'd the bell 134:13
Shade: clutching the inviolable s. 19:1
great trees ... nothing but s. 215:30
hawthorn bush a sweeter s. 260:14
to sit in the s. on a fine day 20:12
trees ... shall crowd into a s. 204:4
under the s. of melancholy boughs 244:10
with Amaryllis in the s. 174:16
Shades: s. of night were falling fast 160:12
s. of the prison-house 332:1
Shadow: between ... falls the S. 106:8
follow ... unhappy s. 72:12
life's but a walking s. 272:10
no sunshine but has some s. 222:8
'Shadow of the Glen': writing The S. 310:7
Shadows: fills the s. and windy places 309:14
Heaven's light ... shines, Earth's s. fly 298:2
look yr. eyes once had, and ... s. deep 337:10
s. of the evening 24:8
until ... the s. flee away 40:11
Shadrach, Meshach, and Abed-nego 41:25
Shadwell: S. ... my perfect image fears 104:14
S. never deviates into sense 104:14
Shady: on Ida's s. brow 56:13
Shafto: Bobby S.'s gone to sea 188:5
Shaken: looks on tempests and is never s. 294:8
so s. as we are, so wan 253:13
when taken to be well s. 88:16
Shake-scene: is the only s. 127:6
Shakespeare: fashionable topics ... pictures ... S. 123:23
immortal S. rose 140:19
might have chanced to be S. 137:14
our myriad-minded S. 88:1
S. led a life of allegory 152:7
S. unlocked his heart 333:5
sweetest S., Fancy's child 174:8
the tongue that S. spake 334:1
what needs my S. for his ... bones 175:11
when I read S. 157:11
Shall: mark you his absolute 's.' 246:9
Shallow: Master S., I owe you 258:4
s. in himself 180:5
Shallows: bound in s. and in miseries 264:3
Shalott: the Lady of S. 313:13
Shame: ain't it all a bleedin' s.? 16:13
England ... now bound in with s. 282:6
in a waste of s. 294:11
poverty is not a s. 223:21
whose glory is their s. 48:29
Shank: too wide for his shrunk s. 244-5:11
Shape: com'st in such a questionable s. 249:3
S. of Things to Come 324:16
the other S.—if s. it might be 177:7
to lick into s. 219:1
virtue in her s. how lovely 178:10
Share: no one so true did s. it 291:6
s. and s. alike 225:15
Sharon: I am the rose of S. 40:4
Sharper: a s. played with a dupe 94:5
s. than a serpent's tooth 265:15
Sharps: fifty different s. and flats 62:1
Shatter yr. leaves before the mellowing year 174:12
Shaven: bald heads are soon s. 206:36
if I be s. ... strength will go 33:21
Shaves: a man who s. and takes a train 325:8
She: has got him a s. 14:15

She (*continued*)
that not impossible s. 94:3
the fair ... and unexpressive s. 245:2
Sheba: another S. Queen 329:10
Shed: a lowly cattle s. 10:6
by man shall his blood be s. 30:24
tears, prepare to s. them now 263:16
with ... [Edmund Burke] beneath a s. 145:4
Sheep: an old half-witted s. 306:9
baa, baa, black s. 188:4
black s. in every flock 208:6
divideth ... s. from ... goats 44:29
hanged for a s. as a lamb 216:5
hungry s. look up, and are not fed 175:4
Little Bo-peep has lost her s. 190:10
looking on their silly s. 260:14
mountain s. are sweeter 199:6
noble ensample to his s. he yaf 79:16
return to our s. 17:9
strayed from thy ways like lost s. 52:12
the s.'s in the meadow 191:1
Sheep-hook: know how to hold a s. 175:3
Sheet: a wet s. and a flowing sea 95:1
Sheets: better wear out shoes than s. 207:37
Shelley: did you once see S. plain? 61:10
Shelter: I will build a house ... to s. me 28:3
our s. from the stormy blast 323:4
Shenandoah: O, S. I long to hear you 16:9
Shepherd: as a s. divideth his sheep 44:29
Dick the s. blows his nail 269:1
every s. tells his tale 174:3
go, for they call you, S. 18:18
good s. giveth his life 46:27
homely, slighted, s.'s trade 174:15
Old Nod the s. goes 97:1
truth in every s.'s tongue 232:14
Shepherds: a sweeter shade to s. 260:14
s. abiding in the field 45:20
while s. watched their flocks 311:4
Sheridan was listened to 234:15
Shibboleth: say now S. 33:18
Shift: let me s. for myself 184:4
Shilling: better give a s. 207:28
cut off with a s. 210:30
Shillings: rather than forty s. ... Book of Songs 276:2
Shimei, though not prodigal of pelf 103:7
Shine: err with Pope ... s. with Pye 70:15
few are qualified to s. 309:9
I see Heaven's glories s. 58:12
moon doth s. as bright as day 188:6
s. so brisk, and smell so sweet 254:2
sun that warms you ... s. on me 281:11
Shines: light ... where no sun s. 315:18
Shining: from sea to s. sea 25:4
s. with all his might 75:16
Ship: a s. in a black storm 324:4
a s. is worse than a gaol 143:21
a stately s. of Tarsus 180:15
all I ask is a tall s. 168:15
as idle as a painted s. 86:5
our saucy s.'s a beauty 119:8
rats desert a sinking s. 224:5
sail on, O S. of State 160:11
the s. has weathered every rack 325:12
Ships: face that launch'd a thousand s. 165:8
I saw three s. come sailing by 190:4
our bloody s. today 25:6
seen old s. sail like swans 111:3
Ships (*continued*)
s. that pass in the night 161:7
s., towers, domes, theatres 333:6
spied three s. come sailing by 14:10
we've got the s., we've got the men 137:4
Shires and towns from Airly Beacon 154:1
Shirt: no s. or collar ... comes back twice 157:15
Shive: cut loaf to steal a s. 289:13
Shiver: little breezes dusk and s. 313:12
Shivering: grass ... s.-sweet to the touch 90–1:16
Shoal: a s. of fools for tenders 89:10
bank and s. of time 270:5
Shock: short sharp s. 118:7
Shock-headed Peter 133:11
Shocks: natural s. that flesh is heir to 250–1:20
Shoe: I kiss his dirty s. 259:9
know where the s. pinches 225:16
my dame has lost her s. 188:7
old woman ... lived in a s. 194:5
one, two, buckle my s. 192:3
Shoemakers: brave s. ... of the gentle craft 96:12
Shoe-string: a careless s. in whose tie 131:15
Shoes: better wear out s. than sheets 207:37
her s. were number nine 183:9
old s. ... easiest for his feet 241:1
s.—and ships—and sealing-wax 76:4
Shone like a meteor streaming 176:9
Shoot: do not s. the pianist 327:19
s., if you must, this old gray head 326:7
Shopkeepers: England is a nation of s. 185:12
fit only for a nation of s. 303:4
nation that is governed by s. 303:4
Shops: that men might shun the awful s. 81:10
Shore: adieu, my native s. 69:1
fast by their native s. 93:1
now upon the farther s. 107:16
rapture on the lonely s. 69:9
rocky s. beats back the envious siege 282:6
s. of the wide world 151:8
the lights around the s. 236:10
waves make towards the pebbled s. 294:1
Shoreditch: say the bells of S. 192:4
Short: if you find it wond'rous s. 122:18
s. and sweet 225:17
sweet discourse makes s. days 226:34
take a long while to make it s. 317:4
Shorter: had Cleopatra's nose been s. 198:7
make you s. by a head 107:12
Shortly: I expect a judgment. S. 97:10
Shortness: to spend that s. basely 255:22
Shot: I s. the albatross 86:3
not a soldier discharged his farewell s. 330:3
Shoulder: give the cold s. 210:3
put yr. s. to the wheel 223:38
Shoulder-blade: I have a left s. ... a miracle 118:13
Shoulders: old head on young s. 222:25
Shout: s. that tore Hell's concave 176:10
's. with the largest' [mob] 98:20
there was a s. about my ears 81:3
Shouting: after the ... music with s. and laughter 62:6
all is over bar the s. 206:13

Shovel them [bodies] under and let me work 238:5
Show: s. and gaze o' th' time 272:13
that within which passes s. 248:1
to offer it the s. of violence 247:15
Shower: drainless s. of light is poesy 150:12
this was our finest s.! 197:9
Showers: Aprille with his s. sote 79:1
fresh s. for thirsting flowers 298:4
small s. last long 282:4
Shows: May's new-fangled s. 268:9
Shreds: king of s. and patches 252:13
thing of s. and patches 117:16
Shrieking: with s. and squeaking 62:1
Shrink: all the boards did s. 86:6
Shroud: my s. ... stuck all with yew 291:6
Shrug: borne it with a patient s. 274:10
Shuffled off this mortal coil 250–1:20
Shun: s. the heaven that leads ... to ... hell 294:12
that men might s. the awful shops 81:10
Shut, shut the door, good John 201:10
Shutters: now ... close the s. fast 93:10
Shy: once bitten, twice s. 222:27
you look a little s. 77:10
Sick: can s. men play so nicely? 282:7
for I am s. of love 40:6
hope deferred maketh the heart s. 38:13
I am s. at heart 247:13
never, never s. at sea! 119:11
s. hurry ... divided aims 18:21
the devil was s. 185:1
the enterprise is s.! 290:2
tie up the knocker, say I'm s. 201:10
to sea for nothing but to make him s. 101:2
when ... the heart is s. 312:14
when we are s. in fortune 265:10
Sicklied o'er with the pale cast 250–1:20
Sickness: he hath the falling s. 262:10
in s. and in health 53:22
s. is better than sadness 225:21
Side: courtesy on one s. only 210:15
hear the other s. 206:27
look on the bright s. 219:28
nobody is on my s. 21:2
trumpets sounded ... on the other s. 63:16
which s. one's bread is buttered 218:8
Sides: buttered on both s. 208:29
laughter holding both his s. 173:17
your ... unfed s. 266:13
Siècles: quarante s. vous contemplent 185:10
Siege: rocky shore beats back the envious s. 282:6
Sieve: carry water in a s. 229:33
in a s. they went to sea 158:4
Sigh: a s. is the sword 55:5
a s. like Tom o' Bedlam 265:11
s. no more, ladies, s. no more 277:21
s. the lack of many a thing 293:18
something ... prompts th' eternal s. 203:7
Sighed: no sooner s. but they ask'd 245:14
she s., she cried 16:4
s. for ... love of a ladye 121:2
Sighing: a plague of s. and grief! 254:17
fell a-s. and a-sobbing 196:3
Sighs: for my pains a world of s. 279:2
s. are the natural language 241:18
Sight: a s. to dream of 87:6
and 'tis a shameful s. 323:3
every common s. to me did seem 331:12
Sight (*continued*)
Oh the pleasant s. to see 154:1
she gleamed upon my s. 334:12
s. for sore eyes 225:22
s. ... good for sore eyes 309:6
s. of means to do ill deeds 265:2
s. of vernal bloom 177:10
s. so touching in its majesty 333:6
to s. or thought be formed 179:10
who ever lov'd that lov'd not at first s.? 166:15
Sights: such s. as youthful poets dream 174:7
what s. of ugly death! 285:1
Sign: an olive-leaf ... pacific s. 179:16
an outward and visible s. 53:16
God made the wicked Grocer for a ... s. 81:10
Signal: only a s. shown 161:7
Silence: but oh! the s. sank 87:1
darkness again and a s. 161:7
dusky hour friendliest to ... s. 178:17
foster-child of s. 149:6
greet thee? With s. and tears 71:6
let yr. women keep s. in ... churches 48:9
mourn'd in s. and was Di-do-Dum 204:12
my gracious s., hail! 246:6
no wisdom like s. 230:22
seul le s. est grand 320:14
s. gives consent 225:23
s. is golden 226:9
s., like a poultice, comes 133:13
s. ... perfectest herald of joy 277:17
the rest is s. 253:10
there was s. in heaven 50:23
to sit in solemn s. in ... dock 118:7
Silent: burst into that s. sea 86:4
s. as the moon, when she deserts 180:11
s., flooding in, the main 85:2
s. over Africa 61:5
s. stars go by 59:8
s., upon a peak in Darien 150–1:15
s. was the flock 147:12
Silently: s., and with how wan a face! 302:4
s., invisibly he took her 55:11
wind does move s., invisibly 55:10
Silk: rustling in unpaid-for s. 247:3
Silken: s. dalliance in the wardrobe lies 258:9
s. lines and silver hooks 100:17
Silks: whenas in s. my Julia goes 132:6
Silver: can wisdom be put in a s. rod? 55:2
every cloud has a s. lining 209:34
how s.-sweet sound lovers' tongues 286:13
just for a handful of s. 61:8
polished up the s. plate 184:8
precious stone set in the s. sea 282:5
seated in thy s. chair 145:8
s. and gold have I none 47:1
s. bells and cockle shells 191:7
s. buckles at his knee 188:5
s. nutmeg and a golden pear 190:1
the oars were s. 242:14
the s. Rhodope 166:7
when gold and s. becks me 264:16
Silvia: who is S.? What is she? 292:8
Simon: Simple S. met a pieman 193:4
Simplicity: in low s. he lends out ... gratis 274:7
in ... s. a child 201:22
pity my s. 325:1
Simplify, simplify 317:1

Sin: a private s. is not so prejudicial 78:5
a s. to covet honour 259:14
as ugly as s. 229:8
before polygamy was made a s. 102:14
he that is without s. among you 46:24
hold there is no s. but ignorance 166:3
no s. but to be rich 264:14
no s. except stupidity 327:4
no s. to s. in secret 182:16
pleasure's a s. ... s.'s a pleasure 69:13
some rise by s. 273:2
some will pluck on s. 285:6
this dark world of s. 54:4
wages of s. is death 47:18
whose s. ... dipt me in ink? 201:13
Sincere: a wit shd. be no more s. 89:9
Sincerely: comes as s. from the author's soul 137:13
Sincerity: a little s. is a dangerous thing 327:2
Sind: *Peccavi* (I have S.) 185:9
Sinews: stiffen the s., summon up the blood 259:3
Sing: and I will s. of the sun 205:3
arms and the man I s. 105:1
himself to s., and build the lofty rhyme 174:13
I celebrate ... and s. myself 325:13
I do not think that they will s. to me 106:17
I'll s. ... in thy praise 65:11
I s. the sofa 93:5
lhude s. Goddamm 205:2
love, and pray, and s. 267:13
more safe I s. 178:20
now let us s., Long live the King 92:13
ord'ring yr. affairs, to s. them too 293:2
Quires and Places where they s. 52:18
s. both high and low 291:1
s., choirs of Angels, s. in exultation 196:5
s., Heavenly Muse 175:15
s. me a song ... lad that is gone 307:3
s. me a song, O! 121:1
s. no sad songs for me 236:4
s. 'polly-wolly-doodle' 16:5
s. them loud ... dead of night 290:15
s. to the Lord with cheerful voice 153:4
swans s. before they die 87:10
used to s. it—fifty thousand strong 336:9
we'd s. and pray ... livelong day 56:4
we'll s. another song 336:9
when you s., I'd have you buy 293:2
Singe: so hot ... it doth s. yourself 261:3
Singed: I have s. ... king's beard 102:7
Singing: everyone suddenly burst out s. 238:10
I'll be quit of the s. 12:1
maid s. in the valley below 15:1
s. in the Wilderness 109:15
sweet s. in the choir 15:8
Single: continued s. ... only talked of population 123:19
Sings: chaffinch s. on the orchard bough 61:1
in his motion like an angel s. 275:8
in me [summer] s. no more 170:15
lark at heaven's gate s. 246:13
s. for his supper 191:4
tell me what she s. 334:17
thrush, he s. each song twice over 61:3
Singularity: surprise by ... excess ... not by S. 151:14
Sinks: it s., and I am ready 156:11
Sinner: joy ... over one s. that repenteth 46:2
Sinners: God and s. reconciled 325:2
mercy upon us miserable s. 52:22
Sinning: more sinn'd against than s. 266:11
Sins: did ... from expensive s. refrain 103:6
few love to hear the s. they love to act 281:3
his s. were scarlet, but his books 27:5
oldest s. the newest kind of ways 257:19
other s. only speak; murder shrieks out 323:15
result of her s. was quadruplets 13:2
the multitude of s. 50:7
though yr. s. be as scarlet 40:17
Sirens: blest pair of S. 172:12
Sisera: stars ... fought against S. 33:14
Sister: a barren s. all your life 276:9
but I kissed her little s. 183:10
Sisters: his s., and his cousins, and his aunts 119:14
sphere-born harmonious s. 172:12
two s. embrace like one brother 234:1
Sit: can s. and look at it [work] for hours 139:15
here I and sorrows s. 264:15
I will s. down now, but 100:2
if I s. on a pin 12:9
not fit that you shd. s. here 94:9
shall s. and drink with me 28:4
s. every man under his vine 42:22
s. on a cushion and sew 188:8
s. upon the murdered reputations 89:7
so I did s. and eat 131:11
test my bath before I s. 186:9
there we s. in peaceful calm 137:15
to s. in ... shade ... look upon verdure 20:12
to s. upon a hill, as I do now 260:13
Sitivation at the lighthouse 99:10
Sitting: thee s. careless on ... granary floor 147:3
Situation excellent. I shall attack 111:5
Six: it's just s. of one 167:6
s. days shalt thou labour 32:3
s. hours in sleep, in ... study s. 85:9
s. of one and half a dozen ... other 225:26
Sixes and sevens: to be at s. 225:27
Sixpence: bang—went s.!!! 231:23
buy a thing that costs even s. 143:10
he found a crooked s. 194:3
I love s., jolly little s. 190:2
nothink for nothink ... little for s. 231:24
sing a song of s. 193:5
Skating over thin ice 108:10
Skies: cloudless climes and starry s. 71:2
for s. of couple-colour 135:7
his watch-tower in the s. 174:2
in summer s. to mourn 147:11
some watcher of the s. 150:15
Skill: simple truth his utmost s. 336:13
Skills: create by means of new s. 237:8
Skin: and it punctures my s. 12:9
by the s. of one's teeth 225:28
can the Ethiopian change his s.? 41:14
her s. was white as leprosy 86:8
I stuff my s. so full within 307:12
saw the skull beneath the s. 107:6
why, my s. hangs about me 255:11
Skins: all ... fancy dress ... except our ... s. 297:6
Skipped: the mountains s. like rams 37:7
Skipper: the s. had taken his little daughter 161:12

Skipping: they all went s. about 24:11
Skull: laid her hand on his thick s. 103:10
saw the s. beneath the skin 107:6
Skulls: some lay in dead men's s. 285:1
Sky: all the blue ethereal s. 9:9
clothe the wold and meet the s. 313:11
I see him ... darkening the s. 234:3
inverted bowl we call the s. 110:13
larks ... about us in the s. 136:6
lonely sea and the s. 168:15
moving Moon went up the s. 86:12
nursling of the S. 298:6
old and true as the s. 154:21
ring out ... to the wild s. 313:3
since first our s. was overcast 93:13
yon twelve-winded s. 136:7
Skye: over the sea to S. (Boulton) 57:12
over the sea to S. (Stevenson) 307:3
Slain: I am s. by a fair cruel maid 291:6
Slanders: secondarily, they are s. 278:18
Slant: there's a certain s. of light 99:16
Slaughter: as a lamb to the s. 41:7
his canon 'gainst self-s. 248:2
Slave: has been s. to thousands 279:15
here I stand, your s. 266:8
man that is not passion's s. 252:1
what a rogue and peasant s. 250:14
Slavery: choice, to be a land of s. 159:9
it cannot ... be classified as s. 82:7
Slaves: as free-men not s. 115:1
at the mill with s. 180:9
Britons never will be s. 316:12
necessity ... creed of s. 200:8
Slay: though he s. me yet will I trust 35:4
Slays: moves, and mates, and s. 110:11
Sleek: so s. and erect and eyeable 157:9
Sleep: a voice cry, S. no more 270:11
be but to s. and feed 252:17
by a s. ... end the heart-ache 250–1:20
dusky hour friendliest to s. 178:17
grey and full of s. 337:10
how s. the brave 88:10
I shall s. like a top 95:13
I s., but my heart waketh 40:12
in that s. of death 250–1:20
life is rounded with a s. 288:16
Macbeth doth murder s. 270:11
no s. till morn 69:4
nor shall my sword s. in my hand 55:8
one hour's s. before midnight 217:9
our birth ... a s. and a forgetting 332:1
peace ... s. with Turks and infidels 283:8
quiet s. and a sweet dream 168:17
rude forefathers of the hamlet s. 126:6
six hours' s. for a man 225:25
s. after toil ... greatly please 305:11
s.! it is a gentle thing 86:13
s., O gentle s., nature's soft nurse 257:2
s. of ... labouring man is sweet 39:17
s. that knits up the ravell'd sleave 270:11
s. the s. that knows not breaking 239:9
so he giveth his beloved s. 37:20
sooner it's over ... sooner to s. 154:3
such as s. o' nights 262:9
task is done, and we must s. 243:4
this s. is sound indeed 257:17
thy deep and dreamless s. 59:8
to s., perchance to dream 250–1:20
we shall not s., though poppies grow 164:9
we ... s. to wake 60:12
Sleep (*continued*)
what hath night to do with s.? 172:15
youth wd. s. out the rest 292:16
Sleeping: Capten, art tha s.? 187:9
let s. dogs lie 218:37
Sleeps: after life's fitful fever he s. well 271:4
he that s. feels not the toothache 247:12
how sweet the moonlight s. 275:8
s. as sound as Johnny underground 231:16
Sleeve: ace of trumps up his s. 155:17
ash on an old man's s. 106:10
my heart upon my s. for daws 278:20
one's heart on one's s. 230:1
Slept: I have not s. one wink 247:4
s. well ... remembers not ... s. ill 225:29
the law ... hath s. 273:5
Slew: as he was ambitious, I s. him 263:10
Slight: away, s. man! 264:1
if she s. me when I woo 330:1
Slimy: a thousand thousand s. things 86:11
Slings and arrows of outrageous fortune 250:20
Slinks out of the race 182:4
Slip 'twixt the cup and the lip 227:24
Slippery: as s. as an eel 225:30
Slips: like greyhounds in the s. 259:5
Sloth: too much time in studies ... s. 23:6
Slough: name of the s. was Despond 63:7
Slow: s. and steady 160:8
s. but sure 225:31
come he s. or come he fast 240:4
divine grace was never s. 211:23
I am s. of study 276:15
sun climbs s., how slowly 85:3
too swift ... as tardy as too s. 286:18
wisely and s. 286:15
Slowly: and s. answered Arthur 312:8
mills of God grind s. 161:3
ring out a s. dying cause 313:5
sun climbs slow, how s. 85:3
Sluggard: go to the ant, thou s. 38:4
voice of the s. 323:7
Slumber: I must s. again 323:7
love itself shall s. on 300:6
ports of s. open wide 257:16
Slumbering: poesy ... 'tis might half-s. 150:12
Slumbers: golden s. kiss your eyes 96:11
soul is dead that s. 160:14
Slung atween the round shot 187:9
Slut: I am not a s. 245:11
Small: all things both great and s. 87:4
microbe is so very s. 27:13
souls of women are so s. 68:2
when they said, 'Is it s.?' 158:12
wind ... to fire ... extinguishes the s. 67:13
yet they grind exceeding s. 161:3
Smarts so little as a fool 201:12
Smattering of everything 99:11
Smell: here's the s. of the blood still 272:3
I know ... the sweet keen s. 236:10
shine so brisk, and s. so sweet 254:2
s. far worse than weeds 294:3
taste ... better than the s. 227:15
to s. a rat 225:33
Smells: it s. to heaven 252:10
Smile: and s., s., s. 19:14
did he s. his work to see? 56:6
fortune ... s. once more 265:20
grandeur hear with a disdainful s. 126:7

Smile (*continued*)
I dare not beg a s. 132:2
if we do meet ... shall s. 264:4
my wanton, s. upon my knee 127:5
s. at us, pay us, pass us 81:9
s. on the face of the tiger 12:10
that s. we wd. aspire to 261:10
you shd. forget and s. 236:2
Smiled: s. a kind of sickly smile 129:3
until she s. on me 85:10
Smiles: daggers in men's s. 270:16
life is ... sobs, sniffles, and s. 131:1
Nods and Becks and wreathed S. 173:16
s. awake you when you rise 96:11
Smilest: Thou s. and art still 19:2
Smiling: com'st s. from the ... snare uncaught ? 243:3
like Patience ... s. at grief 291:7
Soldan of Byzantium is s. 81:4
Smilingly: flaw'd heart ... burst s. 268:1
Smite: if the rude caitiff s. the other 133:14
whosoever shall s. thee 43:19
Smith: the s., a mighty man is he 161:9
Smithy: the village s. stands 161:9
Smoke: good cigar is a s. 154:10
in yr. pipe and s. it 223:37
no fire without some s. 221:38
s. and blood is the mix of steel 238:7
Smokeless: bright and glittering in the s. air 333:6
Smooth: I am a s. man 31:7
take the rough with the s. 224:30
Smote: and s. him—thus 280–1:14
s. them hip and thigh 33:20
the Lord s. all the firstborn 31:25
Smyler with the Knyf under the Cloke 79:20
Snaffle ... curb ... but where's the bloody horse ? 72:6
Snail: a whiting to a s. 75:2
like s. unwillingly to school 244:11
the s.'s on the thorn 62:7
Snake: a s. in the grass 225:34
earth doth like a s. renew 298:11
Snapper-up of unconsidered trifles 292:18
Snare: smiling from the world's great s. 243:3
Snatch: hear a voice ... s. a fearful joy 126:1
Sneer: without sneering, teach the rest to s. 201:16
Sneezed: not to be s. at 225:35
Sneezes: beat him when he s. 74:6
Sniffles: sobs, s. and smiles ... s. predominating 131:1
Snicker-snack: blade went s. 75:10
Snob: impossible ... not to be ... a S. 315:5
Snodgrass: Mr. S. 98:20
Snoring: while you here do s. lie 288:5
Snow: birds sit brooding in the s. 269:1
bore 'mid s. and ice 160:12
half-buried in the s. 160:13
I sh. be whiter than s. 36:14
like S. upon ... Desert's ... Face 110:1
like the s. falls in ... river 67:4
naked in December s. 282:1
never ... love the s. again 58:5
[sins] shall be ... white as s. 40:17
s. had fallen, s. on s. 235:15
s. in May's new-fangled shows 268:9
when the s. lay round about 187:1
where the s. lay dinted 187:3
white as driven s. 293:3
Snow (*continued*)
whitest s. on Scythian hills 166:7
Snowing: the more it goes on s. 171:1
Snows: where are the s. of yesteryear ? 320:15
Snug: Skugg ... s. as a bug in a rug 112:16
So: if it was s. it might be 75:15
s. far, s. good 225:36
Soap: s. and education ... more deadly 318:11
used your s. two years ago 232:2
Sober: as s. as a judge 109:8
be s., be vigilant 50:8
neither ingenious, s., nor kind 12:3
tomorrow we'll be s. 14:14
Sobers: drinking largely s. us again 202:5
Sobs: with s. and tears he sorted out 76:4
Social: new stock for every s. occasion 137:12
one of the s. lies 138:3
Socialists: we are all S. now 128:5
Society: classes into which our s. is divided 19:6
no s. can surely be flourishing 303:3
one great s. alone on earth 334:6
s. is no comfort 247:6
s. is now one polished horde 70:9
s. where none intrudes 69:9
solitude ... best s. 179:8
The Affluent S. 114:12
unfriendly to s.'s chief joys 92:5
Sodden: Midlands ... s. and unkind 28:2
Sodium: odium of having discovered s. 29:5
Sodom: in S. fifty righteous 31:3
Sofa: I sing the s. 93:5
wheel the s. round 93:10
Soft: her voice was ever s., gentle 268:3
s. falls the dew 26:10
Soften rocks, or bend ... oak 89:5
Softly: fair and s. goes far 213:10
s. she was going up 86:12
sweet Thames! run s. 305:16
Zephyrus did s. play 305:15
Softness: for s. she 178:3
Soil: fame is no plant ... on mortal s. 175:2
subject is the fattest s. to weeds 257:15
Soiled: name ... s. with all ignoble use 313:8
Solace: with s. and gladness 302:12
Sold: he s. his birthright unto Jacob 31:6
s. my Reputation for a Song 110:15
Soldat: tout s. ... porte dans sa giberne 185:13
Soldier: Ben Battle was a s. bold 134:11
can always tell an old s. 295:7
drinking is the s.'s pleasure 103:14
every French s. ... in his cartridge-pouch 185:13
in the s. is flat blasphemy 273:8
s., full of strange oaths 244:11
s., rest! thy warfare o'er 239:9
s.'s pole is fall'n! 243:6
statesman, s., merchant 9:6
the boastful s. 200:15
very poor s. ... a chocolate cream s. 295:8
Soldiers: like s., armed in their stings 258:8
old s. never die 16:7
old s. ... surest 324:1
onward, Christian s. 24:9
Soliciting: this supernatural s. 269:9
Solitary: be not s., be not idle 67:12
life of a s. man 141:7
the s. child 332:9
took their s. way 179:18
Solitude: a state more gloomy than s. 141:8
as my S. is sublime 152:6

Solitude (*continued*)
in s. what happiness? 179:3
O S.! where are the charms? 93:15
race ... has ... disturbed its s. 23-4:23
s. sometimes is best society 179:8
which is the bliss of s. 331:11
whosoever is delighted in s. 22:21
Solitudinem faciunt, pacem appellant 310:8
Solomon: S. Grundy, born on a Monday 193:6
the wisdom of S. 34:17
Some: S. chicken! S. neck! 83:4
s. ... fou o' love ... s. ... o' brandy 66:4
s. glory in their birth 294:2
s. hae meat ... s. wad eat 67:3
s. talk of Alexander 16:14
Somebody: how dreary to be s. 99:14
s. bet on de bay 112:4
when every one is s. 116:15
Somer: in a s. season 157:1
Something: a man's worth s. 60:14
add s. more to this wonderful year 115:1
always doing s. for posterity 9:11
in our embers is s. that doth live 332:4
s. left to treat my friends 165:4
s. rich and strange 288:1
s. sensational to read in the train 327:16
s. ... that doesn't love a wall 113:14
s. was dead in each of us 326:13
that s. ... which prompts th' eternal sigh 203:7
time for a little s. 172:7
'tis s., nothing 279:15
what's s. rarish 12:5
Sometime: come up and see me s. 325:5
Somewhat: more than s. 236:15
Somewhere: time was away and s. else 165:2
Son: a foolish s. ... heaviness 38:8
a virgin shall ... bear a s. 40:21
a wise s. ... a glad father 38:8
as a man chasteneth his s. 32:24
he gave his only begotten S. 46:21
Jehu ... s. of Nimshi ... driveth 34:25
marry yr. s. when you will 220:34
my s., if thou come to serve 51:15
O Absalom, my s., my s.! 34:14
O Lucifer, s. of the morning 40:25
she will ... renounce me for a s. 116:1
spareth his rod hateth his s. 38:14
unto us a s. is given 40:23
Song: a s. to sing, O! 121:1
burst into a quavering s. 324:12
fierce wars ... shall moralize my s. 305:9
give ear unto my s. 122:18
glorious the s. when God's the theme 302:13
he sings each s. twice over 61:3
let satire be my s. 70:11
not given a penny for a s. 337:3
old s. of Percy and Douglas 302:6
one grand, sweet s. 154:2
pipe a s. about a lamb 56:8
run softly till I end my S. 305:16
sang a most topical s. 12:11
sea grew civil at her s. 276:18
self-same s. that found a path 150:4
sold my Reputation for a S. 110:15
s. for yr. delight 76:11
suck melancholy out of a s. 244:5
that glorious s. of old 240:14
Song (*continued*)
the Lord's s. in a strange land 37:25
this subject for heroic s. 179:6
unlike my subject ... frame my s. 80:18
we'll sing another s. 336:9
Songs: Book of S. and Sonnets here 276:2
for ever piping s. for ever new 149:9
our sweetest s. ... saddest thought 300:2
piping s. of pleasant glee 56:7
sing no sad s. for me 236:4
the s. of Apollo 269:2
their lean and flashy s. 175:4
there shall the Sussex s. be sung 28:3
where are the s. of Spring? 147:4
Sonne: when soft was the s. 157:1
Sonnet: a s. is a moment's monument 236:6
scorn not the s. 333:5
s.'s scanty plot of ground 332:14
Sonnets: onlie begetter of ... insuing s. 293:9
Sons: bears all its s. away 323:6
free as the s. of the waves 115:1
s. of Belial, flown with insolence 176:8
s. of Belial had a Glorious Time 103:7
the s. of the prophet were brave 16:15
things are the s. of heaven 140:2
Soon: belovèd Night ... come s., s. 299:1
day returns too s. 71:4
it [the future] comes s. enough 105:12
s. as she was gone ... a traveller came 55:11
s. got, s. spent 225:40
s. hot, s. cold 225:41
s. ripe, s. rotten 226:1
you have waked me too s. 323:7
Sooner it's over, the s. to sleep 154:3
Soot: black as s. 208:4
Sooth: poesy ... friend to s. the cares 150:13
Sophisters: age ... of s., economists, calculators 64:11
Sore: sight ... good for s. eyes 309:6
sleep ... s. labour's bath 270:11
trust in critics who themselves are s. 70:14
Sorrow: and not be in s. too 56:12
and wear a golden s. 261:4
any s. like unto my s. 41:17
brief s., short-lived care 186:13
down, thou climbing s. 265:21
ere the s. comes with years 60:7
from the sphere of our s. 300:8
has brought [war] untold s. to mankind 319:5
I feel it when I s. most 312:13
increaseth knowledge increaseth s. 39:13
more in s. than in anger 248:10
no more death, neither s. 51:3
O S., why dost borrow? 147:10
parting is such sweet s. 286:14
pluck from the memory a rooted s. 272:6
pure and complete s. 317:14
s. comes unsent for 226:2
s. goes, and pleasure tarries 116:11
s. will come fast enough 215:9
the guttural s. of the refugees 165:1
then to come, in spite of s. 174:2
there is no greater s. 95:7
to think is to be full of s. 149:15
truly that hour foretold s. 71:5
write s. on the bosom of the earth 283:5
Sorrows: a man of s. ... acquainted with grief 41:5
here I and s. sit 264:15

Sorrows (*continued*)
losses are restor'd and s. end 293:19
s. come ... not single spies 252:21
there are few s. ... in which 303:6
when age, disease, or s. strike him 84:14
Sorry: better ... safe than s. 207:24
dreadful s., Clementine 183:8
truly s. man's dominion 66:11
Sort: a s. of men whose visages 274:2
travel, in the younger s. 22:13
Sorts: all s. and conditions of men 52:27
Sought: that I s. to destroy institutions 325:10
the prize we s. is won 325:12
those men that s. him 262:2
Soul: a day for a man to afflict his s. 41:10
a thing which enters ... s. 151:13
all thy heart ... all thy s. 33:1
and his s. sincere 126:14
as if that s. were fled 183:11
asleep in body ... become a living s. 335:12
body Nature is, and God the s. 203:3
body presseth down the s. 51:13
breathes there the man, with s. so dead 239:16
build ... stately mansions, O my s. 134:5
call upon my s. within the house 290:15
cold waters to a thirsty s. 38:29
confession is good for the s. 210:6
distress hath humanised my s. 321:2
dull wd. he be of s. 333:6
for my s., what can it do to that? 249:4
for my unconquerable s. 130:8
foredoom'd his father's s. to cross 201:11
gain the ... world, and lose his own s. 45:10
give not thy s. unto a woman 51:19
hae mercy o' my s., Lord God 164:10
half conceal the S. within 312:12
harrow up thy s., freeze thy young blood 249:7
Helen, ... give me my s. again 165:8
her lips suck forth my s. 165:8
hidden s. of harmony 174:9
his s. is marching on! 127:13
I am black ... my s. is white 56:10
I am the captain of my s. 130:10
I ... invite my s. 326:1
iron entered [into] his s. 37:3, 217:23
it is the cause, my s. 280:10
joy's s. lies in the doing 289:15
King Cole was a merry old s. 192:1
largest and most comprehensive s. 104:3
lose his own s. 45:10
memorial from the S.'s eternity 236:6
merit wins the s. 204:11
most offending s. alive 259:14
my prophetic s.! My uncle! 249:10
my s. in agony 86:10
my s. into the boughs does glide 168:2
my s., like to a ship 324:4
my s., there is a country 320:7
no coward s. is mine 58:12
our s.'s left hand 100:18
perdition catch my s. 279:14
pouring forth thy s. abroad 150:3
praise my s., the King of Heaven 163:8
pray for my s. 312:9
prepare thy s. for temptation 51:15
rap and knock and enter in our s. 60:13
sleepless S. that perished 334:8
Soul (*continued*)
s. and ... gift of articulate speech 296:18
s. hath been alone 87:2
s. is dead that slumbers 160:14
s. is in a ferment 147:7
s. is not more than the body 326:4
s. of the Age! 145:11
s. rememb'ring my good friends 282:8
s. was sad ... glance was glum 121:2
the s. of Adonais, like a star 298:3
the s. that rises with us 332:1
the s. to feel the flesh 58:15
thou art a s. in bliss 267:10
thy rapt s. sitting in thine eyes 173:7
thy s. was like a Star 333:13
to bear my s. away 9:13
was not spoken of the s. 160:14
what a dusty answer gets the s. 170:2
what of s. was left 62:11
with all thy s. ... all thy might 32:22
yet my s. drew back 131:10
Souls: fire our s. to regale 56:4
have ye s. in heaven too? 147:6
immediate jewel of their s. 279:15
Lord, thou lover of s. 51:14
our s., whose faculties can comprehend 166:10
poor s. who dwell in Night 55:1
prosperity has damned more s. 223:31
s. of Poets dead and gone 149:4
s. of the righteous ... in the hand of God 51:12
s. of women are so small 68:2
such harmony is in immortal s. 275:8
two s. with but a single thought 162:8
unless they've s. that grovel 72:2
we that have free s. 252:5
ye have left yr. s. on earth 147:6
Sound: full of s. and fury 272:10
hear dat mournful s. 112:6
no s. save the rush of the river 26:10
sighing s., the lights around the shore 236:10
s. must seem an echo to the sense 202:10
s. of a voice that is still 311:6
s. of public scorn 179:12
s. of revelry by night 69:3
s. upon the bugle-horn 313:14
the s. is forc'd, the notes are few 56:14
the s. of his horn 125:6
to heal the blows of s. 133:13
Sounds: s. will take care of themselves 74:13
with s. that echo still 311:14
Soup: he screamed out, 'Take the s. away!' 133:8
of s. and love, the first 226:3
s. of the evening, beautiful s. 75:5
Sour: how s. sweet music is 284:7
lost his taste, sweet is s. 219:32
love is ... s. in the ending 219:39
things sweet ... prove in digestion s. 281:13
will not taste the s. 211:14
Source: true s. of human offspring 178:8
South: beaker full of the warm S. 149:14
he went by the s. 191:6
I ... go s. in the winter 107:4
Oh, I went down S. 16:5
yes, but not in the S. 205:1
South country: great hills of the S. 28:2

Southern: bore me in the s. wild 56:10
walls on the s. side 61:16
Sovereign: servants of the s. or state 22:2
Sovereignest thing on earth 254:2
Soviet power into the heart of W. Europe 83:10
Sow (noun): I do ... walk before thee like a s. 256:8
s. that was washed ... wallowing 50:9
Sow (verb): men that s. to reap 309:18
s. one's wild oats 230:16
they that s. in tears 37:18
Soweth: whatsoever ... s. ... shall he also reap 48:23
Sown the wind ... reap the whirlwind 42:9
Spade: call a s. a s. 209:5
Spain: build castles in S. 209:11
King of S.'s daughter came to visit 190:1
rain, rain, go to S. 224:2
Span: when Adam delved and Eve s. 24:2
Spaniards: S. seem wiser than they are 22:20
win this game ... thrash the S. 102:8
Spanish: I speak S. to God 78:18
Spare: I will s. all the place 31:3
s. all I have ... take my life 109:5
woodman, s. the beechen tree 72:7
Sparkling: pair of s. eyes 116:14
Sparks: born unto trouble as the s. fly 35:3
Sparrow: I, said the S. 196:2
Speak: did he stop and s. to you? 61:10
I only s. right on 263:20
I s. severely to my boy 74:7
I s. Spanish to God 78:18
never s. well of one another 143:11
now s., or ... hold his peace 53:20
one to s., ... another to hear 317:3
other sins only s.; murder shrieks 323:15
s. each other in passing 161:7
s., Lord; for thy servant heareth 33:28
s. not of my debts unless 226:5
s. of me as I am 280:14
s. roughly to your little boy 74:6
s. the speech ... as I pronounc'd 251:7
s. well of yr. friend 226:6
s. when you are spoken to 77:8, 226:7
think to-day and s. tomorrow 227:30
when I think, I must s. 245:6
when you s., ... I'd have you do it ever 293:2
Speaking: he ... [Adam] thought him still s. 179:1
Speaks: s. ill of his wife 226:8
when he s., the air ... is still 258:7
Spear: bring me my s. 55:8
Spears: stars threw down their s. 56:6
Species: especially the male of the s. 157:8
female of the s. is more deadly 154:14
not the individual, but the s. 141:5
our self-tormented s. 237:8
Spectacles: her s. ... on her aproned knees 71:16
needed not the s. of books 104:4
s. on nose and pouch on side 244–5:11
Spectator: I live ... as a S. 9:6
Spectre: grows pale and s.-thin 149:15
Speculator: I was raised by a s. 307:14
Speech: be ... never tax'd for s. 242:1
found our s. copious without order 140:1
freedom of s. and expression 235:4
let thy s. be short 52:2
rude am I in my s. 278:21
Speech (*continued*)
soul and ... gift of articulate s. 296:18
souninge in moral vertu was his s. 79:10
s. ... given to ... disguise thoughts 311:1
s. is silver 226:9
Speed: s., bonny boat, like a bird 57:12
our safety is in our s. 108:10
whose s. ... faster than light 63:1
Spell: foreigners always s. better 318:13
Spend: to s. too much time in studies 23:6
what we yet may s. 110:3
Spending: getting and s., we lay waste our powers 333:3
riches are for s. 22:22
Spends: commuter—one who s. his life 325:8
Spenser: sage and serious poet S. 182:5
Spent: all passion s. 181:8
how my light is s. 181:10
soon got, soon s. 225:40
Speranza: lasciate ogni s. 95:6
Spermatozoa: a million million s., all ... alive 137:14
Sphere: from the s. of our sorrow 300:8
their motion in one s. 255:23
world's storm-troubled s. 58:12
Spheres: as the restless s. 166:10
stand still, you ever-moving s. 165:10
stars shot madly from their s. 276:18
Spice: variety's the very s. of life 93:8
Spick and span 226:10
Spider: said a s. to a fly 136:10
there came a big s. 191:3
Spies: as if we were God's s. 267:13
sorrows ... come not single s. 252:21
Spires: City with her dreaming s. 19:4
dim-discover'd s. 88:9
Spirit: a bold s. in a loyal breast 281:8
a pardlike S. beautiful and swift 297:14
a S. still, and bright 334:14
a S., yet a Woman too 334:13
expense of s. in a waste 294:11
follow your s., and upon this charge 259:5
give me the s. 257:9
hail to thee, blithe s. 300:1
have not that alacrity of s. 285:14
history of the human s. 19:11
how oft, in s. ... sylvan Wye 335:13
I am thy father's s. 249:6
life-blood of a master s. 182:3
music ... gentlier on the s. lies 314:2
my s. is too deeply laden 300:7
pipe to the s. ditties of no tone 149:7
present in s. 47:33
rarely comest thou, S. of Delight 300:4
same s. that its author writ 202:6
s. ... is willing ... flesh is weak 45:2
s. of health or goblin damn'd 249:3
s. that will start the world along 336:9
s. to bathe in fiery floods 273:10
spur that the clear s. doth raise 175:1
the worser s. ... a woman 294:16
Wild S. ... moving everywhere 299:4
Spirits: actors ... were all s. 288:16
choice and master s. of this age 263:6
comfort and despair, which like two s. 294:16
her wanton s. look out 290:8
I can call s. from the ... deep 255:5
pluck up thy s., man 184:5
Spit: 'Please don't s. on the floor' 13:3

Spit (*continued*)
s. fire; spout rain 266:7
s. in my face, call me horse 254:15
s. upon my Jewish gaberdine 274:10
Spite: cursed s., that ... I was born 249:14
cut off ... nose to s. ... face 210:29
reckless what I do to s. the world 271:2
S. of cormorant devouring Time 268:6
s. of pride, in erring reason's s. 203:4
victory in s. of all terror 82:12
Splash: a scream, a s. 16:12
Spleen or Vapors 104:2
Splendid: and by the vision s. 332:2
in ... our s. isolation 124:7
man is ... s. in ashes 60:3
s. tear from the passion-flower 314:4
Splendour: the s. falls on castle walls 314:14
Split: part ... to make all s. 276:14
Spoil: come and s. the fun 76:1
company ... hath been the s. of me 255:12
Spoiled: had s. his nice new rattle 75:14
Spoilers of ... symmetry of shelves 156:3
Spoils: it s. the singing of the nightingale 147:11
Spoke: English as she is s. 318:14
less he s., the more he heard 231:26
put a s. in one's wheel 226:12
Spoken: sure of being kindly s. of 20:9
Spoon: dish ran away with the s. 189:5
have a long s. that sups with the devil 219:25
silver s. in his mouth 208:22
Spoons: measured out my life with coffee s. 106:14
the faster we counted our s. 108:2
Sport: detested s., that owes its pleasure 93:9
dog laughed to see such s. 189:5
S. that wrinkled Care derides 173:17
s. with Amaryllis in the shade 174:16
the chase, the s. of kings 304:8
they kill us for their s. 266:20
to s. wd. be as tedious as to work 253:21
Sported: and by him s. on the green 304:13
Sports: let us prove ... the s. of love 146:1
Spot: Out, damned s.! out, I say! 272:2
Spout: cataracts and hurricanoes s. 266:6
spit fire; s. rain 266:7
Sprang: I s. to the stirrup 61:6
Sprat: a s. to catch a mackerel (whale) 226:13
Spray: never a s. of yew 18:16
Spread: money ... like muck ... be s. 22:9
Sprightly: tossing their heads in s. dance 331:9
Spring: a linnet courting ... in the s. 58:4
absent in the s. 294:5
all the breathing s. 88:8
apparell'd like the s. 281:2
can S. be far behind? 299:6
how this s. of love resembleth 292:6
in s., when woods are getting green 76:12
in the Fire of S. 109:14
in the s. a young man's fancy 313:15
it is s., moonless night 316:2
lived light in the s. 18:10
no s. ... beauty hath such grace 101:1
sweet lovers love the s. 245–6:16
the year's at the s. 62:7
when the hounds of s. 309:14
where are the songs of S.? 147:4
Springs: four wanton s. end in a word 281:12
steeds to water at those s. 246:13
Sprites: [tale] ... of s. and goblins 292:13
Spur: do not s. a free horse 226:14
fame is the s. 175:1
no s. to prick the sides of my intent 270:6
on the s. of the moment 226:15
Spurns that patient merit ... takes 250–1:20
Spurs: let the boy win his s. 105:9
Squandering wealth was his peculiar art 103:5
Squeaking: with shrieking and s. 62:1
Squeals: if he s., let him go 189:1
Squeers, Mr. Wackford 98:9
Stable: nothing s. in the world 151:12
Stables: the s. are ... centre of the household 295:17
Stabs: with bemock'd-at s. kill ... waters 288:15
Staff: I'll break my s. 289:5
my s. of faith to walk upon 232:12
Stag at eve had drunk his fill 239:6
Stage: after a well-grac'd actor leaves the s. 284:5
all the world's a s. 244:11
frets his hour upon the s. 272:10
if ... played upon a s. now 291:14
mellow glory of the Attic s. 18:14
on the s. he was natural 123:5
s. where every man must play a part 274:1
the wonder of our S. 145:11
to this great s. of fools 267:8
two hours' traffic of our s. 285:18
your daughter on the s. 91:10
Stages: where'er his s. may have been 300:12
Stagger: they reel ... s. like a drunken man 37:5
Stain: true blue will never s. 228:21
without fault or s. on thee 58:6
Stairs: somebody stopped the moving s. 165:2
Stake: when honour's at the s. 252:19
Stamford: bullocks at S. fair? 257:6
Stamp: s. of his lowly origin 95:10
too late to save the s. 124:9
Stand: s. still, you ever-moving spheres 165:10
s. up for Jesus! 105:2
Sun, s. thou still 33:12
who will s. on either hand? 163:11
Standard: raise the scarlet s. high 90:3
Standing: Jackson s. like a stone wall 26:5
Stanley: here S. meets,—how S. scorns 63:2
on, S., on! 240:10
Stanza: pens a s. when he shd. engross 201:11
Star: and a s. or two beside 86:12
desire of the moth for the s. 300:8
dropped from the zenith, like a falling s. 176:14
eve's one s. 148:4
go and catch a falling s. 101:5
hitch yr. wagon to a s. 108:18
Soul ... rises with us, our life's S. 332:1
s. to steer her by 168:15
there was a s. danc'd 277:20
thy soul was like a S. 333:13
twinkle, twinkle, little s. 311:5
we have seen his s. 43:8
Star Chamber matter of it 276:1
Star-crossed: a pair of s. lovers 285:17

Stare: and all the world wd. s. 92:11
time to stand and s. 96:2
Starry: cloudless climes and s. skies 71:2
Stars: a country far beyond the s. 320:7
and one [sees] the s. 156:15
branch-charmed by the earnest s. 148:6
certain s. shot madly 276:18
clad in the beauty of a thousand s. 165:9
continuous as the s. 331:8
eyes, like s., start from their spheres 249:7
make guilty ... the sun ... the s. 265:10
opposition of the s. 167:17
s. above us govern our conditions 267:1
s. hide their diminished heads 177:12
s., hide your fires 269:12
s. in their courses fought 33:14
s. threw down their spears 56:6
s. through the window-pane are my children 152:6
stone that puts the S. to Flight 109:13
the silent s. go by 59:8
till you are ... crowned with the s. 317:16
true as the s. above 15:2
two s. keep not their motion 255:23
we are ... the s.' tennis balls 323:17
yoke of inauspicious s. 287:4
you chaste s., it is the cause 280:10
Star-spangled banner 153:7
Start: get the s. of the majestic world 262:7
Startle: singing, s. the dull night 174:2
s. it or amaze it with itself 151:13
Starve: let not poor Nelly s. 78:16
State: a continual s. of inelegance 21:4
all were for the s. 163:12
beat a Venetian and traduc'd the s. 280–1:14
grant me ... a middle s. 165:4
hides from himself his s. 141:12
his s. is kingly 181:11
I am the S. 162:2
I have done the s. some service 280:14
object in the construction of the s. 200:14
other two ... like us, the s. totters 288:11
the worth of a S. ... individuals 170:11
this is the s. of man 261:9
Stately: a s. pleasure-dome decree 87:11
the s. homes of England 91:5, 130:5
Statements was interesting but tough 318:7
States: many goodly s. and kingdoms 150:14
s. unborn and accents yet unknown 263:4
Statesman: a witty s. said 73:4
chymist, fiddler, s. and buffoon 103:4
speculative s., soldier, merchant 9:6
too nice for a s. 123:2
Statesmen: when s. ... say ... be realistic 20:1
Statistics: lies, damned lies, and s. 318:10
Statues: Epp's s. are junk 13:4
Status quo: restored the s. 306:2
Stay: and here I s. 164:11
without thee here to s. 179:17
wd. not s. for an answer 21:8
Stay-at-home: sweet s. 96:3
Steadily: saw life s. and ... whole 18:14
Steady, boys, steady 115:1
Steaks: smells of s. in passageways 106:19
Steal: cut loaf to s. a shive 289:13
shadows ... s. across the sky 24:8
s. from the world, and not a stone 204:1
thou shalt not s. 32:7
Stealing: not hanged for s. horses 127:12
picking and s. 53:14
s. and giving odour 290:10
wronging ... s., fighting 292:16
Steals: s. something from the thief 279:4
who s. my purse s. trash 279:15
Steed: his s. was the best 240:5
Steeds: Phoebus 'gins arise, his s. to water 246:13
Steel: clad in complete s. 172:17
foeman bares his s., tarantara 120:5
smoke and blood ... mix of s. 238:7
to thy soul with hoops of s. 248:15
Steeples: spout till you have drench'd our s. 266:6
Steer: happily to s. from grave to gay 203:10
our ... policy to s. clear 322:16
s. too nigh the sands 102–3:17
Stein: wonderful family called S. 13:4
Step: a great s. to knowledge 100:11
became ... bad in one s. 146:8
Stephen: Feast of S. 187:1
Stepmother: take heed of a s. 226:16
Stepney: say the bells of S. 192:4
Stepping-stones: on s. of their dead selves 312:11
Steps: heavy s. of the ploughman 337:7
in his master's s. he trod 187:3
invites my s. and points to yonder glade 201:5
to these dark s. 180:8
with how sad s., O Moon 302:4
with wandering s. and slow 179:18
Stew in one's own juice 226:17
Stick: a riband to s. in his coat 61:8
fling dirt ... some will s. 213:38
I am a kind of burr; I shall s. 273:13
Sticking-place: courage to the s. 270:7
Sticks and stones may break my bones 226:18
Stiff: keep a s. upper lip 77:11
s. in opinions, ... in the wrong 103:4
Stiffnecked: a s. people 32:12
Stile: merrily hent the s.-a 292:19
sixpence against a crooked s. 194:3
Still: how s. we see thee lie 59:8
mighty heart is lying s. 333:7
sound of a voice that is s. 311:6
Thou smilest and art s. 19:2
Stillness: air a solemn s. holds 126:4
modest s. and humility 259:3
soft s. and the night 275:8
Stimulate the phagocytes 295:16
Sting: death, where is thy s.? 48:13
O Death! where is thy S.? 201:4
s. is in the tail 226:22
s. of a reproach ... truth of it 226:23
where is death's s.? 163:7
Stings: armed in their s. 258:8
Stir: no s. of air was there 148:5
Stirring dull roots with spring rain 107:3
Stirrup: betwixt the s. and the ground 72:5
I sprang to the s. 61:6
Stitch: a s. in time saves nine 226:25
s.! s.! s.! 135:3
Stockings: commended thy yellow s. 291:10
Stole: fause lover s. my rose 67:7
I s. the Prince 116:8
s. a pig and away he run 195:4
Stolen sweets are best 83:16
Stomach: an army marches on its s. 185:14

Stomach (*continued*)
have the ... s. ... of a King of England 107:13
my s. is not good 307:11
Stone: heaviest s. ... the devil can throw 129:14
kill two birds with one s. 217:38
leave no s. unturned 218:34
let him first cast a s. at her 46:24
not a s. tell where I lie 204:1
precious s. set in the silver sea 282:5
rolling s. gathers no moss 224:26
s. that lieth not in yr. way 226:26
s. which the builders refused 37:13
virtue is like a rich s. 23:2
water like a s. 235:15
we raised not a s. 330:4
Stones: in glass houses ... never throw s. 214:37
inestimable s., unvalued jewels 285:1
labour of an age in piled s. 175:11
o, ye are men of s. 268:2
sermons in s. 243:15
you blocks, you s.! 262:4
Stools: between two s. one falls 207:39
Stop: Shelley ... did he s. and speak? 61:10
s.; look; listen 319:7
s. me and buy one 11:7
time ... must have a s. 256:1
when the kissing had to s. 62:11
Stopped: he [Death] kindly s. for me 99:17
it s. short—never to go again 336:8
Stoppeth: he s. one of three 85:11
Store: oft amid thy s. 147:3
s. of ladies, whose bright eyes 174:6
Storied windows richly dight 173:11
Stories: s. ... not to thy credit 72:4
tell sad s. of the death of kings 283:6
Storm: after a s. ... a calm 206:8
and rides upon the s. 92:15
any port in a s. 206:17
S. and Stress 155:12
S. in a Teacup 29:10, 226:27
lovers fled ... into the s. 147:14
the pelting of this pitiless s. 266:13
Storms: he sought the s. 102–3:17
sudden s. are short 282:4
vows made in s. are forgotten 229:21
Story: honour is the subject of my s. 262:6
in pain, to tell my s. 253:9
not that the s. need be long 317:4
our rough island-s. 314:11
place where a s. ended 106:10
shuts up the s. of our days 232:11
summits old in s. 314:14
teach him how to tell my s. 279:2
tell me the old, old s. 128:4
the s. of Sussex told 28:3
Stove: like ... ice on a hot s. 113:16
Straight trees ... crooked roots 226:28
Strain: attain to something like prophetic s. 173:12
that s. again 290:10
Strained: quality of mercy is not s. 275:1
Straining upon the start 259:5
Strains: such s. as wd. have won the ear 174:10
Straits: moon lies fair upon the S. 18:9
Strand: India's coral s. 130:1
let's all go down the S. 77:12
Strange: how s. it seems, and new! 61:10
how s. now, looks the life 60:10
misery acquaints ... with s. bedfellows 288:7
something rich and s. 288:1
s. as if ... married a great while 89:17
'tis s. but true 70:10
truth is always s. 70:10
'twas s., 'twas passing s. 279:2
very s. and wellbred 89:17
Stranger: a s. in a strange land 31:16
a s. yet to pain 125:13
love ye ... the s. 33:2
s. than fiction 70:10
the wiles of the s. 186:2
Strangers: gracious and courteous to s. 22:6
s. in the land of Egypt 33:2
we may be better s. 245:7
Strangling: other use than s. in a string 136:4
Stratford: the scole of S. atte Bowe 79:4
Straw: drowning man ... catch at a s. 211:35
find quarrel in a s. 252:19
headpiece filled with s. 106:7
last s. breaks the camel's back 218:20
scrannel pipes of wretched s. 175:4
Strawberries: feed upon s., sugar and cream 188:8
in Holborn I saw good s. 285:3
Straws: errors, like s. 103:16
Stray: if with me you'd fondly s. 115:6
nor ever ... from the Church to s. 56:4
Streaks: number the s. of the tulip 141:5
Stream: hoar leaves in the glassy s. 253:1
still glides the S. 334:9
time, like an ever-rolling s. 323:6
Streamers: sails filled and s. waving 180:15
Streams: fresh showers ... from ... the s. 298:4
thy banner ... s. ... *against* the wind 69:7
Street: have yer bought the s.? 81:13
man in the s. 220:15
Streets: through s. broad and narrow 15:10
we shall fight ... in the s. 82:13
Strength: as thy days, so shall thy s. be 33:8
better than the s. of Samson 221:1
Christ is thy s. 183:2
comfort in the s. of love 332:12
fall'n ... that tower of s. 314:10
glory of young men is their s. 38:25
if I be shaven ... s. will go 33:21
Ignorance is S. 197:4
king's name is a tower of s. 285:13
my s. is as the s. of ten 314:19
my s. is made perfect in weakness 48:19
promise of s. and manhood 58:6
s. to bear the misfortunes of others 234:4
their s. labour and sorrow 36:23
they go from s. to s. 36:20
to have a giant's s. 273:6
unity is s. 229:12
we shall fight with growing ... s. 82:13
Stretch: upon the rack ... s. him out longer 268:5
Stretched: there was things ... he s. 318:6
when I s. out my hand 306:16
Strew: shall I s. ... rose or rue or laurel? 309:16
s. on her roses, roses 18:16
Strife: agonies, the s. of human hearts 150:11
ancient forms of party s. 313:5
are God and Nature ... at s. 312:16

Strife (*continued*)
books ... dull and endless s. 335:5
ignoble s. 126:12
in the s. of Truth with Falsehood 162:14
poverty breeds s. 223:19
Strike: no right to s. against the public safety 90:10
s. while the iron is hot 226:29
take heed ... thou s. not awry 184:5
String: chewing little bits of s. 27:2
harp not on that s. 285:10
provided ... s. to tie them together 183:6
strangling in a s. 136:4
untune that s. 290:3
Strings: the languid s. do scarcely move 56:14
there are s. in the human heart 97:8
Stripes: whose broad s. and bright stars 153:6
Strive: four champions fierce, s. here 177:8
s. to set the crooked straight? 184:9
Striving to better, mar what's well 265:16
Strode: out to Severn s. 81:6
Stroke: tune of flutes kept s. 242:14
Strong: be s. and of a good courage 33:10
but wants that little s. 134:2
out of the s. ... sweetness 33:19
s.-backed and neat-bound 156:7
we know ... that the wall is s. 326–7:15
we then that are s. 47:31
what will it help ... once you were s.? 57:15
Strove: a little still she s. 69:11
I s. with none 156:11
Struggle: manhood a s. 100:9
say not the s. naught availeth 85:1
Struggling for life in the water 142:1
Strumpet: transform'd into a s.'s fool 242:9
Struts: that s. and frets his hour 272:10
Stubble: chin ... show'd like a s. land 254:1
he lies in the s. 11:18
Studies: s. serve for delight, for ornament 23:5
too much time in s. 23:6
Study: every Jack ... must s. the knack 121:6
his s. was but litel on the bible 79:13
I am slow of s. 276:15
much s. ... weariness of the flesh 39:28
proper s. of Mankind is Man 203:5
s. what you most affect 287:6
Stuff: ambition ... made of sterner s. 263:13
listen all day to such s. 74:4
'S. and nonsense!' said Alice 75:8
s. of life to knit me 136:7
such s. as dreams are made on 288–9:16
written such volumes of s.! 158:6
Stumble: they s. that run fast 286:15
Stupidity: confirm'd in full s. 104:14
no sin except s. 327:4
Sturm und Drang 155:12
Stygian: in S. cave forlorn 173:14
s. smoke of the pit 138:14
Style: le s. est l'homme 62:14
Style: s. is the man himself 62:14
true definition of a s. 309:2
Subdue: it [force] may s. for a moment 64:5
Subject: every s.'s duty ... soul 259:11
load every rift of yr. s. 152:12
poetry ... startle ... with its s. 151:13
s. to the same diseases 274:17
s. we old men are to ... lying 257:10
this s. for heroic song 179:6
Subjects: my s. for a pair of carved saints 283:7
Subjects (*continued*)
poorest s. are at this hour asleep! 257:2
Sublime: du s. au ridicule ... un pas 185:11
Sublime: from the s. to the ridiculous 185:11
my object all s. 118:10
one step above the s. 197:18
s. and the ridiculous are ... related 197:18
we can make our lives s. 161:1
Sublimity: a S. to welcome me home 152:6
Submit: King do now? Must he s.? 283:7
Subscribers: he for s. baits his hook 82:3
not printing any list of s. 144:17
Substance of things hoped for 49:21
Subtlety is better than force 226:30
Succeed: if at first you don't s. 132:11
those who ne'er s. 99:13
Succeeds: nothing s. like excess 328:14
nothing s. like success 222:17
Success: s. and miscarriage are empty sounds 140:4
s. is counted sweetest 99:13
this ecstasy, is s. in life 198:9
to command s. 9:4
to make a marriage a s. 238:2
true s. is to labour 307:10
yours [religion] is S. 24:15
Sucked: I s. the blood 86:7
Sucker: a s. born every minute 24:10
Sucks: my baby ... s. the nurse asleep 243:11
where the bee s., there suck I 289:6
Sudden storms are short 282:4
Suddenly: shall s. come to his temple 43:6
Sudetenland is the last ... claim 132:14
Sue: less used to s. than to command 239:8
we were not born to s. 281:9
Suez: somewhere East of Suez 155:2
Suffer: but doth s. a sea-change 288:1
not s. a witch to live 32:11
s. for the truth's sake 53:8
s. me to come to thee 325:1
s. the little children to come 45:13
than one innocent s. 54:11
ye s. fools gladly ... yourselves are wise 48:17
Sufferance is the badge of all our tribe 274:10
Suffered: Lord Hippo s. fearful loss 27:14
love a place the less for having s. 20:16
Suffering: been s., nothing but s. 20:16
Sufficiency: an elegant s., content 316:13
Sufficient: s. conclusions from insufficient premises 68:6
s. unto the day is the evil 44:6
Sugar: I must s. my hair 75:4
s. and spice and all that's nice 195:6
Suggests: the word Intellectual s. 20:3
Suit: silk s. ... cost me much money 199:9
Sultry: more common where the climate's s. 69:10
Summer: a wind in s. 150:8
after s., merrily, merrily 289:6
all on a s.'s day 192–3:8
bud of love by s.'s ripening breath 286:11
compare thee to a s.'s day 293:13
dry as s. dust 331:4
eternal s. gilds them 69–70:21
haunt of flies on s. eves 150:2
I only know that s. sang in me 170:15
in their s. beauty kiss'd 285:8
last rose of s. 184:1
live murmur of a s.'s day 18:19
on s. eves by haunted stream 174:7

Summer (*continued*)
one swallow does not make a s. 226:33
s. and winter ... shall not cease 30:23
s. by this sun of York 284:8
s. has o'er-brimm'd ... clammy cells 147:2
s. has set in with ... severity 88:2
s. is icumen in 14:7
s.'s lease ... too short a date 293:13
s.'s velvet buds 258:8
thinking on fantastic s.'s heat 282:1
thy eternal s. shall not fade 293:14
to ... men that sought him sweet as s. 262:2
warmed ... by the same ... s. 274:17
with love in s.'s wonderland 188:1
Summits: snowy s. old in story 314:14
Sun (*see also* Sonne): all, except their s., is set 69–70:21
and I will sing of the s. 205:3
at the going down of the s. 54:5
before the rising s. 323:5
between me and the s. 99:19
birds are faint with the hot s. 151:1
cannot make our s. stand still 167:15
close to the s. in lonely lands 312:1
dominions, on which the s. never sets 187:16
early-rising s. has not attained 132:1
eyes are nothing like the s. 294:13
far from the s. and summer-gale 127:1
follow thy fair s. 72:12
furnish'd ... by Aldershot s. 29:12
glory of the s. will be dimmed 23:23
go out in the midday s. 91:8
hath Britain all the s.? 247:5
I am too much in the s. 247:19
I gin to be aweary of the s. 272:11
just as the s. was rising 15:1
late eclipses in the s. and moon 265:9
light ... dies with the dying s. 57:13
light ... where no s. shines 315:18
love that moves the s. 95:8
loves to live i' th' s. 244:6
make guilty ... the s. 265:10
make hay while the s. shines 220:12
Mother, give me the s. 138:5
never shall s. that morrow see 270:3
no new thing under the s. 39:12
now the s. is laid to sleep 145:8
self-same s. that shines 293:4
she grew in s. and shower 335:9
so when the s. in bed 175:10
s. breaks through the darkest clouds 287:11
s. came up upon the left 85:13
s. climbs slow, how slowly 85:3
s. go down upon your wrath 48:24
s. shines upon all alike 226:31
S., stand thou still 33:12
s. that warms you ... shine on me 281:11
s. was shining on the sea 75:16
thank heavens, the s. has gone in 303:9
the chambers of the s. 56:13
the maturing s. 147:1
the rising of the s. 15:8
the s. is lost, and th' earth 100:16
the s. of righteousness arise 43:7
the s. shall not smite thee 37:16
this s. of York 284:8
to have enjoy'd the s. 18:10
white founts ... in the Courts of the s. 81:4
with the setting s. dropped from the zenith 176:14
Sunday: golf may be played on S. 157:14
here of a S. morning 136:6
killing ... mouse on S. 58:2
shot through his heart on S. 307:1
S. clears away the rust 9:7
Sunk: all s. beneath the wave 93:1
Sunless: down to a s. sea 87:11
Sunny Jim: they called him S. 128:3
Sunny pleasure-dome 87:15
Sunrise: in eternity's s. 55:4
Suns: blest by s. of home 59:6
Sunset: s. and evening star 311:13
s. ran, one glorious blood-red 61:4
Sunshine: no s. but has some shadow 222:8
the s. is a glorious birth 331:14
Sup: who sipped no s. 121:2
Supercilious: a s. knowledge in accounts 301:9
Superfluity of good things 10:8
Superfluous: in the poorest thing s. 266:2
Superior: revolt ... that they may be s. 18:6
Superiority: one shall acquire an evident s. 143:2
Superstition is the religion of feeble minds 64:13
Superstitions: new truths ... end as s. 138:1
Supper: hope is ... a bad s. 23:13
sings for his s. 191:4
to s. with a flood of tears 97:15
Support: help the feeble ... s. him after 289:9
Sure: his mercy is for ever s. 153:5
s. way to see it lost ... last ditch 65:3
Surfeit: feast ... where no crude s. reigns 172:18
Surfeit-swelled: so s., so old 258:3
Surfeiting: give me excess ... that s. 290:10
Surfeits: the s. of our own behaviour 265:10
Surgery: honour hath no skill in s. 255:21
Surmise: with a wild s. 150–1:15
Surprise: poetry shd. s. by a fine excess 151:14
Surprised by joy ... I turned 333:1
Surrender: unconditional and immediate s. 125:1
we shall never s. 82:13
Survey: monarch of all I s. 93:14
time that takes s. 256:1
Survival: s. of the fittest 95:12, 305:3
without victory there is no s. 82:12
Survive: but one ... Noah dare hope to s. 137:14
Suspects: man s. himself a fool 338:1
Suspension: willing s. of disbelief 87:19
Suspicion: Caesar's wife ... above s. 71:15
s. ... haunts the guilty mind 261:1
Suspicions amongst thoughts ... bats amongst birds 22:24
Sussex: and the story of S. told 28:3
there shall the S. songs be sung 28:3
Swagman: jolly s. camped by a billabong 198:10
Swain: no better than a homely s. 260:13
Swains: all our s. commend her 292:8
Swallow: hope ... flies with s.'s wings 285:12
one s. does not make a summer 226:33
Swallows: gathering s. twitter 147:5
whitethroat builds and all the s. 61:2
Swan: Sweet S. of Avon 145:16
Swanee Ribber: 'way down upon de S. 112:8
Swans: all his geese are s. 214:29

Swans (*continued*)
seven s. a-swimming 194:2
s. sing before they die 87:10
Swap horses in mid-stream 159:14
Swat: Akond of S. 158:1
Sway: mercy is above this sceptred s. 275:1
regions ... thy posterity shall s. 92:2
truth ... prevailed with double s. 122:10
Swear: s. me, Kate, like a lady 255:9
when very angry, s. 318:18
Sweat: blood, toil, tears and s. 82:11
in the s. of thy face 30:13
none will s. but for promotion 243:19
s. for duty not for meed 243:19
Sweating: quietly s. palm to palm 137:15
Sweats: Falstaff s. to death 254:9
Sweep on, you fat and greasy citizens 243:16
Sweet: a lady s. and kind 17:2
and s. girl-graduates 314:12
back to the great s. mother 310:6
both s. things ... all s. things 57:8
but then, how it was s.! 60:16
by any other name wd. smell as s. 286:9
deserves not the s. 211:14
each op'ning s. of earliest bloom 88:8
how sour s. music is! 284:7
how s. and fair she seems to be 322:1
how s. the moonlight sleeps 275:8
how s. their memory still 92:14
law beyond its own s. will 326:6
little s. ... kill much bitterness 148:11
love is s. for a day 310:4
love is s., given or returned 299:12
naught so s. as Melancholy 67:8
revenge is s. 224:15
sessions of s. silent thought 293:18
sleep of labouring man is s. 39:17
stolen waters are s. 38:7
s. as love 310:11
s. breathing Zephyrus did ... play 305:15
s. is pleasure after pain 103:14
s. is revenge—especially to women 69:12
s. Little Buttercup I 119:9
s. singing in the choir 15:8
s. Stay-at-Home, s. Well-content 96:3
s. Thames! run softly 305:16
s. to look into ... face of heaven 151:6
s. to taste ... indigestion sour 281:13
swing low, s. chariot 17:1
the s. o' the year 292:17
to have a s. tooth 226:35
when you speak, s. 293:2
you'll look s. upon the seat 95:4
Sweet and twenty: kiss me, s. 291:2
Sweet-briar: through the s. or the vine 174:2
Sweeten: children s. labours 21:18
civet ... to s. my imagination 267:5
perfumes of Arabia will not s. 272:3
Sweeter: anything to me is s. 133:11
s. manners, purer laws 313:5
s. than the berry 115:4
Sweetest: last taste of sweets is s. last 282:3
s. li'l feller 306:5
s. thing that ever grew 332:10
Sweethearts: old soldiers, s., are surest 324:1
Sweeting: trip no further, pretty s. 291:1
Sweetly flows that liquefaction 132:6
Sweetness: out of the strong came forth s. 33:19
passion for s. and light 19:10
Sweetness (*continued*)
pursuit of s. and light 19:5
two noblest things ... s. and light 308:11
waste its s. on the desert air 126:10
Sweets: as the last taste of s., is sweetest last 282:3
perpetual feast of nectared s. 172:18
stolen s. are best 83:16
s. and a ride in the train 171:10
s. to the sweet; farewell! 253:4
Swept: if seven maids ... s. it 76:3
Swift: Cousin S., you will never be a poet 104:12
too s. ... as tardy as too slow 286:18
Swifter than eagles, ... stronger than lions 34:11
Swim: a naughty night to s. in 266:15
but said I cd. not s. 75:7
Swine: nor yet feed the s. 188:8
pearls before s. 44:6
s., women and bees cannot be turned 226:36
Swing low, sweet chariot 17:1
Swoon: at twelve noon the natives s. 91:8
Swoons: wearied band s. to a waltz 137:15
Swop for my dear old Dutch 81:14
Sword: a Sigh is the s. of an angel king 55:5
believed he had a s. upstairs 337:3
his father's s. ... girded on 184:2
I with s. will open 276:4
is the s. unsway'd? 285:11
man for the s. 314:18
more cruel the pen ... than ... s. 67:9
nor shall my s. sleep 55:8
nor the deputed s. 273:4
pen is mightier than the s. 63:3
Swords: beat ... s. into plowshares 40:18
with paper hats and wooden s. 320:1
Swore: Frankie and Johnny ... s. to be true 15:2
Swound: like noises in a s. 86:2
Syllable: last s. of recorded time 272:10
Symmetry: frame thy fearful s. 56:5
spoilers of the s. of shelves 156:3
Sympathise: the Walrus said: 'I deeply s.' 76:5
s. with ... pains ... not ... pleasures 137:11
Sympathy: without feeling or exciting s. 141:8
System: energies of our s. will decay 23:23
Systems: our little s. have their day 312:10

Ta-ra-ra-boom-de-ay 238:11
Table: crumbs ... from the rich man's t. 46:8
Tables: to turn the t. 228:32
Tabor: as to the t.'s sound 331:15
Tail: better ... than the t. of a lion 207:25
he's treading on my t. 75:2
improve his shining t. 73:17
sting is in the t. 226:22
such a little t. behind 27:1
thereby hangs a t. 279:13
Tails: and bring their t. behind them 190:10
cut off their t. with a carving knife 195:1
frogs and snails and puppy-dogs' t. 195:6
stings in their t. 50:25
t. like unto scorpions 50:25
Take: t. a farthing away 226:37
t. any man's horses 258:2
t. away my good name 226:39
Taken: when t. to be well shaken 88:16

Takes: a man who shaves and t. a train 325:8
blesseth ... him that t. 275:1
Talcum: a bit of t. is always walcum 186:7
Tale: a round unvarnish'd t. 279:1
an honest t. speeds best 285:9
cd. ever hear by t. or history 276:10
every shepherd tells his t. 174:3
every t. condemns me 285:15
every tongue brings in a ... t. 285:15
had we lived, I shd. have had a t. 239:3
I cd. a t. unfold 249:7
it is a t. told by an idiot 272:10
point a moral, or adorn a t. 141:11
sad t.'s best for winter 292:13
t. which holdeth children from play 302:5
tedious as a twice-told t. 264:17
thereby hangs a t. 244:9, 287:9
with a t. forsooth he cometh 302:5
yr. t., sir, wd. cure deafness 287:16
Talent: one t. which is death to hide 181:10
t. does what it can 170:5
t. of flattering with delicacy 21:1
Talents: if you have great t. 233:9
Tales: and tell old t., and laugh 267:13
dead men tell no t. 211:2
natural fear ... increased with t. 21:9
tell t. out of school 227:8
Talk: Cabots t. only to God 57:10
I dont want to t. grammar 296:19
I want to t. like a lady 296:19
make little fishes t. ... t. like whales 124:3
some t. of Alexander 16:14
t. of censorious old men 77:14
t. of court news ... t. with them 267:13
t. of many things 76:4
t. of the devil 227:10
t. so like a waiting-gentlewoman 254:2
t. the hind leg off a donkey 227:9
t. what he knoweth not 21:16
think too little ... t. too much 103:3
to t. about the rest of us 133:5
Talked: being t. about ... not being t. about 328:6
he [Coleridge] t. on for ever 129:8
not to be t. of ... by men 317:5
t. like Poor Poll 115:2
Talkers: great t. are great liars 215:29
greatest t. ... least doers 227:12
Talketh what he knoweth 21:16
Talking: ears burn, someone is t. 212:7
he will be t. ... 'wit is out' 278:9
t. about being a gentleman 308:5
you go on t. and t. 324:17
you will still be t. 277:11
Talks: I wish I liked the way it t. 233:1
t. to himself, speaks to a fool 227:13
Tall: divinely t., and most divinely fair 311:15
Tally: no books but the score and the t. 260:11
Tamburlaine, the scourge of God, must die 166:13
Tameless: too like thee: t., and swift 299:5
Tamer of the human breast 126:16
Tampers with natural ignorance 327:11
Tangles: with the t. of Neaera's hair 174:16
Taper-light: with t. to seek 264:19
Tappertit: 'strings', said Mr. T. 97:8
Tara: hangs as mute on T.'s walls 183:11
Tarquin: great house of T. 163:9
Tarred with the same brush 227:14
Tarry: you may for ever t. 132:8
Tarsus: like a stately ship of T. 180:15
Tartarly: Quarterly, so savage and T. 70:17
Tarts: Queen of Hearts, she made some t. 75:6, 192:8
Task: long day's t. is done 243:4
thy worldly t. hast done 247:9
what he reads as a t. 142:9
Taste: every man to his t. 212:34
last t. of sweets, is sweetest last 282:3
let me t. yr. ware 193:4
lost his t., sweet is sour 219:32
O t. and see ... the Lord is good 36:6
they do t. kind of funny 13:10
Tasted: some books are to be t. 23:7
you have t. two whole worms 305:19
Tastes: no accounting for t. 206:3
no disputing about t. 210:36
Taught: Cristes lore ... he t. 79:18
first he wroghte ... afterward he t. 79:16
Tortoise because he t. us 74:14
Tavern: enjoy themselves ... at a capital t. 144:1
there is a t. in the town 17:3
Taxation: no t. without representation 222:9
t. without representation is tyranny 197:13
Taxes: nothing is certain but death and t. 113:3
Tea: if this is t. ... I wish for coffee 232:5
is there honey still for t.? 59:4
'take some more t.,' the March Hare said 74:10
Teach: may t. you more of man 335:7
prayer doth t. us all to render 275:1
t. the torches to burn bright 286:3
they t. the morals of a whore 141:19
Teacher: let Nature be your t. 335:6
Teaches: he who cannot, t. 296:13
Tea-cup: a storm in a t. 226:27
A Storm in a T. 29:10
Team of little atomies 286:1
Tear: a t. is an intellectual thing 55:5
all he had, a t. 126:14
and shed a bitter t. 76:3
fallen a splendid t. 314:4
he hath a t. for pity 257:14
part to t. a cat in 276:14
t. him for his bad verses 263:21
Tears: and I look through my t. 316:7
crocodile t. 210:18
drops t. as fast as ... trees ... gum 280-1:14
hence these t. 315:1
if you have t., prepare to shed 263:16
ills ... no weight, and t. no bitterness 163:7
in silence and t. 71:5
in t. amid the alien corn 150:4
nor all thy t. wash out 110:12
nothing to offer but blood, toil, t. 82:11
our t. thaw not the frost 297:9
t. fall in my heart 320:10
t., idle t. 314:16
there is t. for his love 263:10
thoughts ... too deep for t. 332:6
time with a gift of t. 309:15
tired of t. and laughter 309:18
watered heaven with ... t. 56:6
wipe away all t. 51:3
with mine own t. I wash away my balm 284:2

Teases: he knows it t. 74:6
Tedious: people are ... charming or t. 328:1
returning were as t. as go o'er 271:10
scandal is gossip made t. 328:3
t. as a twice-told tale 264:17
thinking his prattle to be t. 284:5
Teeth: bid them ... keep their t. clean 246:7
by the skin of one's t. 225:28
children's t. are set on edge 41:16
escaped with the skin of my t. 35:7
sparkling eyes, and t. like pearls 62:6
Teetotaller: I'm only a beer t. 295:13
Tell: I can t. you anyhow 64:2
I cannot t. what you ... think 262:6
never seek to t. thy love 55:10
our dead bodies must t. the tale 239:3
t. it not in Gath 34:10
t. me not, in mournful numbers 160:14
t. me not, sweet, I am unkind 162:6
t. me what she sings? 334:17
t. thee what thou art 78:6
to dream of, not to t. 87:6
when or how I cannot t. 236:10
Telling: not arguing ... I am t. you 325:6
Temper: I shall t. ... justice with mercy 179:11
keep me in t.; I wd. not be mad! 265:17
man of such a feeble t. 262:7
Temperance hotels: I prefer t. 322:12
Temperate: more lovely and more t. 293:13
Tempered by war, disciplined by ... peace 153:1
Tempers: God t. the wind 306:15
Tempests: looks on t. and is never shaken 294:8
Temple: shall suddenly come to his t. 43:6
Temples: for ... the t. of his gods 163:10
mortal t. of a king 283:6
solemn t., the great globe itself 288:16
Tempora: O t.! O mores! 84:6
t. mutantur et nos mutamur 17:14
Temporary: use of force alone is but *t.* 64:5
Tempt: t. me no more 96:6
to t. my Lady Poltagrue 27:8
Temptation: can resist everything except t. 328:2
lead us not into t. 43:24
maximum of t. ... of opportunity 296:14
not over-fond of resisting t. 26:3
prepare thy soul for t. 51:15
the last t. is the greatest treason 107:10
watch ... that ye enter not into t. 45:2
way to get rid of a t. 328:7
Tempted: My Lady, t. by a ... whim 27:8
one thing to be t., Escalus 273:1
to his ... annoyance t. him 27:8
Tempts: all that t. yr. wand'ring eyes 125:12
Tempus: fugit ... inreparabile t. 321:8
t. edax rerum 197:16
t. fugit 227:22
Ten: as the strength of t. 314:19
better that t. guilty ... escape 54:11
t. to make ... match to win 187:11
Tender is the night 149:16
Tenderly: take her up t. 134:10
Tenders: a shoal of fools for t. 89:10
Tenement: o'r informed the T. of clay 102–3:17
Tennis: we are ... the star's t. balls 323:17
Ten-sixty-six and All That 241:7
Tenterhooks: to be on t. 227:23
Tent-royal of their emperor 258:8
Terminological: some risk of t. inexactitude 82:7
Terms: fair t. and a villain's mind 274:11
Terrible as an army with banners 40:13
Territorial: last t. claim ... in Europe 132:14
Terror: so full of dismal t. was the time 284:15
victory in spite of all t. 82:12
Test: source, and end, and t. of Art 202:3
Text: of that t. a pulled hen 79:5
Thais: lovely T. by his side 103:11
Thames: every drop of the T. is liquid history 65:7
set the T. on fire 225:14
sweet T.! run softly 305:16
Thank: I t. whatever gods may be 130:8
t. me no thankings 287:1
we t. with brief thanksgiving 310:1
Thankless: to have a t. child 265:15
Thatch: build a house with a deep t. 28:3
Thaw and resolve itself into a dew 248:2
The Times: T. has made many ministries 23:18
Top People take *T.* 11:9
Theatre: as in a t. the eyes of man 284:5
Idols of the T. 23:16
Theatres: domes, t. and temples 333:6
in t. of crowded men 148:7
Their's not to reason why 311:11
Theme: fools are my t. 70:11
Themselves: are a law unto t. 47:16
Them's my sentiments 315:11
There: haven't been t. to attend to the case 117:5
is t. anybody t.? 96:14
met a man who wasn't t. 169:8
Thereby hangs a tail 279:13
Thersites' body is as good as Ajax' 247:8
Thespian: bathed in the T. springs 102:11
Thick: as t. as thieves 227:25
one can lay it on so t. 68:10
Thief: Aram ... t. ... liar ... murderer 72:3
give a t. rope enough 224:29
jury ... may ... have a t. or two 273:1
opportunity makes the t. 222:29
poor man, beggarman, t. 195:2
set a t. to catch a t. 227:26
steals something from the t. 279:4
the t. doth fear each bush 261:1
Thieves: as thick as t. 227:25
beauty provoketh t. 243:14
fell among t. 45:28
made it a den of t. 45:14
there is honour among t. 217:1
Thin end of the wedge 227:27
Thing: a lovely and a fearful t. 69:16
a most unattractive old t. 118–9:15
a tear is an intellectual t. 55:5
a terrible t., thank God 316:4
a t. of shreds and patches 117:16
a t. she had frequently done 71:16
an excellent t. in woman 268:3
any good t. come out of Nazareth? 46:18
any t. that is thy neighbour's 32:9
excuse my having such a t. 297:7
far, far better t. ... I do 99:12
first t. you'll ... want to know 237:13
foolish t. was but a toy 292:3

Thing (*continued*)
has this t. appear'd again? 247:14
if you want a t. well done 229:24
ill-favour'd t., ... but mine own 246:1
in the poorest t. superfluous 266:2
lack of many a t. I sought 293:18
laugh at any mortal t. 70:2
like this sort of t. 160:2
moderation ... a fatal t. 328:14
one damned t. after another 136:12
one t. is certain ... Life flies 110:4
only t. ... to fear is fear itself 234:18
see such a t. in yr. life? 195:1
sincerity is a dangerous t. 327:2
sleep! it is a gentle t. 86:13
spirit of youth in every t. 294:5
such a t. as I myself 262:6
swans sing ... 'twere no bad t. 87:10
sweetest t. that ever grew 332:10
the acting of a dreadful t. 262:13
the play's the t. wherein 250:19
t. immortal as itself 249:4
throw away the dearest t. 269:11
to one t. constant never 277:21
what t. of sea or land? 180:15
who Pretender ... quite another t. 68:15
Things: a thousand thousand slimy t. 86:11
a time for all t. 228:3
all good t. ... fruits of originality 170:10
all t. are artificial 59:13
all t. are lawful ... all t. not expedient 48:2
all t. both great and small 87:4
all t. bright and beautiful 10:4
all t. to all men 48:4
all t. uncomely ... broken ... worn out 337:7
all t. wise and wonderful 10:4
as t. have been, t. remain 85:1
few t. to desire ... many t. to fear 22:14
former t. are passed away 51:3
forms of t. unknown 277:6
foundation of all good t. 64:14
four t. greater than all t. 154:9
giver of all good t. 53:6
I put away childish t. 48:6
like and dislike the same t. 237:15
little t. please little minds 219:18
little t. ... the most important 101:12
look thy last on all t. lovely 96:13
Man is the master of t. 310:2
men may rise ... to higher t. 312:11
mighty sum of t. forever speaking 331:5
more t. are wrought by prayer 312:9
more t. in heaven and earth 249:12
night and day ... both sweet t. 57:8
old, unhappy, far-off t. 334:17
remembrance of t. past 293:18
right judgement in all t. 53:5
river ... drowns t. weighty 23:10
see the t. thou dost not 267:7
set yr. affection on t. above 49:4
Shape of T. to Come 324:16
sweetest t. turn sourest 294:3
sympathiseth with all t. 59:14
take upon's the mystery of t. 267:13
the day of small t. 43:3
the more t. change 146:12
the two noblest of t. 308:11
there was t. ... he stretched 318:6
t. are not what they seem 160:14
t. are the sons of heaven 140:2
Things (*continued*)
t. hoped for ... t. not seen 49:21
t. past redress ... past care 282:11
t. sweet to taste prove ... sour 281:13
t. that go bump in the night 13:7
t. that wd. astonish you 117:7
t. ... true, t. ... honest ... just ... think on these t. 49:1
t. ... we ought not to have done 52:13
t. won are done 289:15
those brave translunary t. 102:11
thou ... art all t. under Heaven 179:17
to talk of many t. 76:4
two t. about the horse 13:11
two t. stand like stone 124:6
unseen t. above 128:4
unto the pure all t. are pure 49:18
what t. ... done at the Mermaid 25:7
you worse than senseless t.! 262:4
you'll understand a good many t. 99:3
Think: books t. for me 156:6
first t., and then speak 213:33
I cannot sit and t. 156:6
I stand alone, and t. 151:8
I t. him so, because I t. him so 292:5
I t., therefore I am 97:7
if ... I t. on thee, dear friend 293:19
not so t. as you drunk 306:3
t. of yr. forefathers ... posterity! 9:2
t. to-day and speak tomorrow 227:30
t. too little ... talk too much 103:3
t. well of all men 227:31
t. with the wise 227:32
to t. is to be full of sorrow 149:15
we cannot t. alike 104:7
when I t., I must speak 245:6
world is a comedy to those who t. 322:7
Thinking: dogged as does it. It ain't t. 318:2
good or bad, ... t. makes it so 250:5
never thought of t. for myself 119:16
plain living and high t. 333:11
put on one's t. cap 223:34
talk without t. ... shoot without aiming 227:11
t. is very far from knowing 227:33
t. jest what a Rum Go 324:14
t. on fantastic summer's heat 282:1
t. on the frosty Caucasus 282:1
t. too precisely on th' event 252:18
Thinks: he t. too much. Such men are dangerous 262:9
t. what ne'er was, nor is 202:7
you do anything, he t. no ill 293:20
Third: to make a t. she joined the former two 104:11
unto the t. and fourth generation 32:1
Thirst: a man can raise a t. 155:2
Thirsty: if he be t., give him water 38:28
when you are t., to cure it 199:5
Thirteen: the clocks were striking t. 197:2
Thirty: at t. man suspects 338:1
person under ... t. ... not a revolutionist 296:9
t. days hath September 194:6
Thomasin once ... so promising 113:17
Thorn: a t. in the flesh 48:18
day as sharp to them as t. 284:3
figs grew upon t. 81:1
he left the t. wi' me 67:7
no rose without a t. 222:6

Thorn (*continued*)
snail's on the t. 62:7
Thorns: I fall upon the t. of life! 299:5
Thorny: life is t.; and youth is vain 87:7
Thou: and T. beside me singing 109:15
Thought: an holy and a good t. 52:11
best that is known and t. 19:8
every third t. ... my grave 289:8
evil is wrought by want of T. 135:1
green t. in a green shade 168:1
he t. I t. he t. I slept 198:11
I t. so little 119:16
learning without t. ... t. without learning 89:4
never t. of thinking for myself 119:16
oft was t., but ne'er so well express'd 202:8
pale cast of t. 250–1:20
sessions of sweet silent t. 293:18
sweetest songs ... tell of saddest t. 300:2
t. does not become a young woman 301:4
t. is free 227:35
to have loved ... t. ... done 18:10
two lads that t. ... no more behind 292:12
two souls with but a single t. 162:8
use t. ... to justify ... wrong-doing 321:12
use ... words ... to conceal ... t. 321:12
whose armour ... honest t. 336:13
wish was father ... to that t. 257:18
Thoughtless: the hour of t. youth 335:14
Thoughts: give thy t. no tongue 248:15
in t. more elevate 177:6
lift the t. of man 150:13
my t. are not yr. t. 41:9
my t. remain below 252:11
pansies, that's for t. 252:23
penny for yr. t. 223:2
second t. are best 225:6
Sensations rather than of T.! 151:10
speech was given ... to disguise his t. 311:1
suspicions among t. are like bats 22:24
t. of a dry brain 106:6
t. that wander through eternity 176:19
t. ... too deep for tears 332:6
thy t., when thou art gone 300:6
turns to t. of love 313:15
what fond and wayward t. 335:3
when pleasant t. bring sad t. 332:7
wording of his own highest t. 151:14
words without t. never to heaven go 252:11
Thousand: a race, 'tis for a t. pound 92:9
a t. ages in thy sight 323:5
a t. lost golf balls 107:2
a t. t. slimy things 86:11
a t. years as one day 50:10
a t. years in thy sight 36:22
after t. aves told 147:15
difference of forty t. men 324:7
face that launch'd a t. ships? 165:8
give me a t. kisses 77:15
heart-ache ... t. natural shocks 250–1:20
here's twenty t. Cornish men 129:4
I heard a t. blended notes 332:7
I, in twelve t., none 284:1
if I had five t. a year 315:12
laugh broke into a t. pieces 24:11
more than sixscore t. 42:21
my conscience hath a t. ... tongues 285:15
night has a t. eyes 57:13
O that we now had ... ten t. of those men 259:12
Thousand (*continued*)
of many t. kisses the poor last 243:5
one day ... as a t. years 50:10
one man ... out of ten t. 250:1
Shallow, I owe you a t. pound 258:4
take a farthing ... from a t. pounds 226:37
ten t. saw I at a glance 331:9
the t. creeds 58:13
the t. years of peace 313:6
t. fearful wrecks, a t. men 285:1
used to sing it—fifty t. strong 336:9
what a t. pities ... that Adam 135:2
will you give ... t. guilders? 62:2
Yesterday's Sev'n T. Years 110:2
Thousands: has been slave to t. 279:15
Jesu ... the t. He hath freed 78:12
makes countless t. mourn 66:8
slain his t. ... his ten t. 34:7
t. at his bidding speed 181:11
where t. equally were meant 308:13
Threadneedle Street: the old lady of T. 227:37
Threaten: you t. us, fellow? 62:5
Threatened men live long 227:38
Three: a t.-pipe problem 101:13
actors are ... the usual t. 169:16
all Gaul ... in t. parts 71:11
Church clock at ten to t. 59:4
going on ... for t. hundred years 328:9
handsome in t. hundred pounds a year 276:6
he stoppeth one of t. 85:11
I have answered t. questions 74:4
I spied t. ships 14:10
in married life t. is company 327:10
indicates that two and one are t. 306:9
is without t. good friends 245:3
lives not t. good men unhanged 254:14
loved t. whole days together 308:2
there are t. sexes 303:14
though he was only t. 171:8
t. acres and a cow 88:6
t. cheers and one cheer more 119:13
t. distinct terms, Barbarians 19:6
t., four, knock at the door 192:3
t. hours a day will produce 318:3
t. is company and two is none 327:10
t. jolly farmers 97:2
t. little maids from school 118:6
t. may keep counsel if two be away 227:39
t. poets in t. distant Ages 104:11
t. ravens sat on a tree 11:15
t. ships come sailing by 190:4
t. things I never lends 308:7
t. things ... too wonderful for me 39:7
t. years she grew in sun 335:9
we galloped all t. 61:6
when shall we t. meet again? 269:3
Threefold: a t. cord is not ... broken 39:15
Threescore: the days of our years are t. years and ten 36:23
Threshold: starry t. of Jove's court 172:13
Thrice: men in great places are t. servants 22:2
t. welcome darling of the Spring 336:3
weave a circle round him t. 87:16
Thrift, thrift, Horatio! 248:8
Thrifty: the housewife that's t. 301:17
Thrilling: in t. region of thick-ribbed ice 273:10

Thrive: only the strong shall t. 241:15
Throat: took by the t. the circumcised dog 280–1:14
unto the sweet bird's t. 244:4
Throne: here is my t., bid kings come 264:15
high on a t. of royal state 176:15
Queen-Moon is on her t. 149:16
Throw good money after bad 227:41
Thrush: that's the wise t. 61:3
Thumb: he put in his t. 191:2
'twixt his finger and his t. 254:1
Thunder: glorious the t.'s roar 302:13
laugh as I pass in t. 298:5
t. in such lovely language 157:11
t., lightning, or in rain? 269:3
Thunderbolt: like a t. he falls 312:1
Thunderstorm: dying duck in a t. 212:6
streams like the t. 69:7
Thursday: T.'s child has far to go 191:8
took ill on T. 193:6
Thus: why ... t? ... reason of this thusness? 322:13
Thwackum was for doing justice 109:11
Thyme: the wild t. blows 276:20
Thyself: love thy neighbour as t. 32:16
when T. with shining Foot 111:1
Tiber: Oh, T., father T. 163:14
Tickle: if you t. us, do we not laugh? 274:17
I'll t. your catastrophe. 256:14
Tickling commodity 264:13
Tide: a t. in the affairs of men 264:3
a t. in the affairs of women 70:3
call of the running t. 168:16
ev'n at the turning o' th' t. 259:1
lived in the t. of times 263:7
the t. is full, the moon lies fair 18:9
Tidings: glad t. of great joy 311:4
Tie: educational relations ... strongest t. 233:11
Ties: purse-strings ... common t. of friendship 223:36
Tiger: imitate the action of the t. 259:3
smile on the face of the t. 12:10
t., t., burning bright 56:5
t.'s heart ... in a player's hide 127:6
went for a ride on a t. 12:10
Tigers: there were no t. That was the point 107:7
Tiggers don't like honey 171:2
Time: a man must serve his t. 70:13
a t. for all things 228:3
a t. for such a word 272:10
a t. to every purpose 39:14
a t. when meadow, grove, and stream 331:12
almost fairy t. 277:8
ancient nobility ... act of t. 22:7
and in good t. you gave it 266:1
Art is long, and T. is fleeting 160:15
bank and shoal of t. 270:5
be not coy, but use yr. t. 132:8
bid t. return 283:3
busiest man who has t. to spare 198:5
but a short t. to live 53:28
conspiracy his t. doth take 288:5
cormorant devouring T. 268:6
creeping hours of t. 244:10
dark backward and abysm of t. 287:15
did those feet in ancient t. 55:8
dust on antique t. 246:8
Time (*continued*)
fixed figure for the t. of scorn 280:5
fleet the t. carelessly 243:12
fly envious T. 181:15
fool all the people all the t. 160:1
footprints in the sands of t. 161:1
friends are thieves of t. 214:21
full of dismal terror was the t. 284:15
greatest part of a writer's t. 143:16
half as old as t. 64:3
happiness takes no account of t. 216:7
he hath shook hands with t. 111:10
how long a t. lies in one ... word 281:12
I had liv'd a blessed t. 270:15
in t. all haggard hawks 155:16
in t. small wedges cleave 155:16
in t. the flint is pierced 155:16
in t. the savage bull 155:16
inaudible and noiseless foot of T. 242:8
just going outside ... may be some t. 196:7
life, t.'s fool 256:1
look into the seeds of t. 269:8
many a t. and oft 274:9
never the t. and the place 61:11
new wail my dear t.'s waste 293:18
no t. like the present 228:4
no t. to stand and stare 96:2
not of an age but for all t.! 145:15
nothing is ours but t. 222:14
old in hours if he have lost no t. 23:1
old t. is still a-flying 132:7
panting t. toiled after him 140:19
patience, money and t. 222:36
remember that t. is money 112:13
repeat how T. is slipping 110:7
seen better faces in my t. 265:19
sent before my t. into this ... world 284:10
such is T. that takes in trust 232:11
that passed the t. It wd. have passed 26:1
that t. may cease, and midnight 165:10
the Bird of T. has but a little way 109:14
the holy t. is quiet as a nun 333:2
the last syllable of recorded t. 272:10
the show and gaze o' th' t. 272:13
'the t. has come,' the Walrus said 76:4
the t. is out of joint 249:14
the t. of our Ford 137:8
the t. will come ... you will hear me 100:2
thief of t. 337:14
this bloody tyrant T. 293:12
T. ambles ... trots ... gallops 245:8
t. and chance happeneth to ... all 39:23
t. and the hour 269:10
t. and thinking tame ... grief 228:1
t. and tide wait for no man 228:2
t. enough to think of the future 296:20
t. flies 227:22
t. future contained in t. past 106:3
t. hath ... a wallet 290:6
t. is broke and no proportion kept 284:7
t. is flying 321:8
t. is on our side 121:7
t. is the greatest innovator 22:18
t., like an ever-rolling stream 323:6
t. ... man is always trying to kill 304:16
t. ... must have a stop 256:1
t. of life is short 255:22
t. of the singing of birds 40:9
t. present and t. past are both 106:3
t. spent on any item of the agenda 198:6

Time (*continued*)
T., ... subtle thief of youth 181:9
t. that takes survey of all the world 256:1
t., the devourer of things 197:16
T. travels in divers paces 245:8
t. was away and somewhere else 165:2
t. will not be ours for ever 146:1
t. will run back 175:9
t., with a gift of tears 309:15
T., you old gypsy man 133:6
T.'s winged chariot 167:13
to choose t. is to save t. 22:19
too much t. in studies is sloth 23:6
want to know the t., ask a P'liceman 234:12
whips and scorns of t. 250–1:20
whirligig of t. 292:2
with thee conversing I forget all t. 178:7
Time-honoured: old John of Gaunt, t. Lancaster 281:6
Time-table: sooner read a t. or a catalogue 169:6
Times (see also *The Times*): art not for the fashion of these t. 243:19
cowards die many t. 262:15
in pious t., ere priest-craft 102:14
lived in the tide of t. 263:7
natures of the t. deceas'd 257:5
other t., other manners 206:29
our t. are in His hand 62:9
purest treasure mortal t. afford 281:8
remember when the t. were not hard 108:22
the spacious t. of great Elizabeth 311:14
what t.! what customs! 84:6
Timor mortis conturbat me 105:5
Timotheus: let old T. yield the Prize 103:15
Tinker, tailor, soldier, sailor 195:2
Tinkers: there'd be no trade for t. 217:14
Tinklings: drowsy t. lull the distant folds 126:4
Tiny: are in t. leaf 61:1
Tiny Tim: 'God bless us ...' said T. 97:12
Tipperary: it's a long way to T. 329:1
Tippled: have ye t. drink more fine? 149:4
Tiptoe: jocund day stands t. 286:22
stand a t. when this day is named 259:15
Tired: dinner waits, and we are t. 92:10
I'm t. of love ... t. of rhyme 27:10
life ... process of getting t. 68:5
the t. waves, vainly breaking 85:2
t. eyelids upon t. eyes 314:2
t. of knocking at preferment's door 18:20
woman who was always t. 12:1
Tires: he t. betimes that spurs too fast 282:4
sad [heart] t. in a mile-a 292:19
Titania: ill met by moonlight, proud T. 276:17
Title-leaf: this man's brow, like to a t. 256:6
Titles: conquering kings their t. take 78:12
thy other t. ... given away 265:13
Titwillow, titwillow! 119:1
Toad: I had rather be a t. 279:17
intelligent Mr. T. 124:13
t., ugly and venomous 243:15
Toast: let the t. pass, drink to the lass 301:17
To-day: be wise t. 337:13
can call t. his own 104:16
hour t. is worth two to-morrow 217:8
if T. be sweet 110:7
never jam t. 76:7
To-day (*continued*)
one t. is worth two to-morrows 228:5
such a day tomorrow as t. 292:12
Toddle safely home and die—in bed 238:9
Toe: catch a nigger by his t. 189:1
on the light fantastic t. 173:17
Toes: bells on her t. 193:1
nobody knows ... how cold my t. 171:1
Together: let us never visit t. 89:17
let us remain t. still 298:10
put Humpty t. again 189:9
t. in a little crooked house 194:3
t. now for forty years 81:14
Toil: each anxious t., each eager strife 141:9
let not ambition mock ... useful t. 126:7
offer ... blood, t., tears and sweat 82:11
sleep after t. 305:11
they t. not, neither ... spin 44:3
t., envy, want, the patron 141:10
Told: t. me you had been to her 75:7
went and t. the sexton 134:13
Tolerable and not to be endured 278:6
Tolerance: practise t. ... live ... in peace 319:5
Tolerate: no longer t. the race 23:23
Toll: t. for the brave 93:1
t. me back from thee to ... self 150:5
Tolled: sexton t. the bell 134:13
Tolls: for whom the bell t. 101:8
it t. for thee 101:8
Tom: 'Come, come,' said T.'s father 184:3
poor T.'s a-cold 266:16
T. bears logs into the hall 269:1
T., he was a piper's son 195:3
T., T., the piper's son 195:4
T. went howling down the street 195:4
Tom o' Bedlam: a sigh like T. 265:11
Tom Pearse, lend me yr. grey mare 17:5
Tomb: for such a t. wd. wish to die 175:13
monument without a t. 145:12
Tommy: it's T. this, an' T. that 155:5
little T. Stout 188–9:9
little T. Tucker 191:4
Tom-tit: a little t. sang 'Willow' 119:1
To-morrow: can say, T. do thy worst 104:16
egg to-day ... hen t. 207:18
hour today is worth two t. 217:8
never put off till t. 221:31
same flower ... t. will be dying 132:7
such a day t. as to-day 292:12
think to-day and speak t. 227:30
t. and t. creeps in this petty pace 272:10
t. blossoms ... bears his blushing honours 261:9
t. is a new day 228:7
t. is our wedding day 92:7
t. never comes 228:6
t. we'll be sober 14:14
T.!—Why, T. I may be 110:2
unborn T. and dead Yesterday 110:7
To-morrows: one to-day is worth two t. 228:5
Tone: take the t. of the company 80:11
that t. and gesture bland 239:8
Tongs: the t. and the bones 277:4
touch him with a pair of t. 228:14
Tongue: an understanding, but no t. 248:11
breast forges ... t. must vent 246:10
customs, politics and t. 198:12
every t. brings in a ... tale 285:15
eye, t., sword 251:5

Tongue (*continued*)
fellows of infinite t. 260:4
give thy thoughts no t. 248:15
iron t. of midnight 277:8
keep one's t. between one's teeth 217:33
keep wel thy t. ... keep thy freend 80:3
no venom to that of the t. 229:15
one t. is enough for a woman 228:8
our English t. a gallimaufry 305:17
sad words of t. or pen 326:8
sharp t. ... edged tool ... grows keener 138:12
though his t. dropped manna 176:18
t. can no man tame 50:1
t. cleave to ... roof of my mouth 37:27
t. is not steel ... it cuts 228:9
t. of idle people 228:10
t. sounds ... as a sullen bell 256:7
t. that Shakespeare spake 334:1
use of my oracular t. 301:10
virtue dwells not in the t. 229:17
Tongues: conscience ... thousand several t. 285:15
done to death by slanderous t. 278:19
finds t. in trees 243:15
lack t. to praise 294:7
silver-sweet ... lovers' t. by night 286:13
these poor t. ... shall be silent 159:10
Tonight: along the Potomac t. 26:10
t. we'll merry be 14:14
Too: this t., t. solid flesh 248:2
t. nice ... t. proud ... cool ... fond 123:2
Tool: man is a t.-making animal 113:4
sharp tongue ... edged t. ... grows keener 138:12
Tools: bad workman quarrels with his t. 206:34
give us the t. ... finish the job 83:2
t. to work ... for those who will 162:12
Tooth: a t. for a t. 43:18
Nature, red in t. and claw 312:17
sharper than a serpent's t. 265:15
t. for t., hand for hand 32:10
to have a sweet t. 226:35
thy t. is not so keen 245:1
Toothache: endure the t. patiently 278:17
Top: always room at the t. 323:12
I shall die at the t. 309:12
sleep like a t. 95:13
t. of it reached to heaven 31:9
T. People take *The Times* 11:9
Topical: sang a most t. song 12:11
Topics: high life ... other fashionable t. 123:23
Tops: mountain t. that freeze 261:5
t. were close against the sky 134–5:15
Topses: herring boxes without t. 183:9
Topsy: persisted T., 'never had no father' 307:14
Torch: a bright t. and a casement 150:7
t. ... passed to a new generation 153:1
Torches: doth teach the t. to burn bright 286:3
Tories own no argument but force 60:4
Torment: love in a palace ... grievous t. 149:1
there shall no t. touch them 51:12
Torments: our t. ... may ... become our elements 177:2
Torn: man all tattered and t. 194:8
Tortoise: why did you call him T.? 74:14
Torture: touch him not and t. not again 297:16
Tory ... with more propriety ... the Conservative 94:6
Tossed: you t. and gored several persons 143:3
Tossing their heads in sprightly dance 331:9
Totter: charming to t. into vogue 322:6
Totters: the state t. 288:11
Touch: men t. them and change 309:17
O for the t. of a vanish'd hand 311:6
one t. of nature 290:7
that I might t. that cheek 286:7
t. him with a pair of tongs 228:14
t. not, taste not, handle not 49:3
t. wood 228:15
unkind as the t. of sweating metal 96:5
Touching: a sight so t. in its majesty 333:6
Toujours gai archy 167:3
Tous pour un, un pour tous 105:3
Tout passe, t. casse, t. lasse 228:16
Toves: the slithy t. 75:9
Tower: fall'n ... that t. of strength 314:10
King's name is a t. of strength 285:13
to the dark t. came 266:17
yonder ivy-mantled t. 126:5
Towers: burnt the topless t. of Ilium? 165:8
cloud-capp'd t., ... gorgeous palaces 288:16
Town: a tavern in the t. 17:3
in Scarlet t., where I was born 11:12
King sits in Dunfermline t. 11:13
lived in a pretty how t. 94:13
O little t. of Bethlehem 59:8
spring, moonless night ... small t. 316:2
t. ... is lighter than vanity 63:9
Town-crier: as lief the t. spoke 251:7
Toy: foolish thing was but a t. 292:3
I count religion ... childish t. 166:3
Toys: all is but t. 270:15
Trace: learned to t. the day's disasters 122:11
Traces: hounds of spring are on winter's t. 309:14
Trade: and now there isn't any t. 131:6
every t. save censure 70:13
half a t. and half an art 138:7
homely, slighted, shepherd's t. 174:15
no nation was ever ruined by t. 112:14
others ... venture t. abroad 258:8
where the old t.'s plying 187:10
Tradesmen: bow, ye t., bow, ye masses 117:1
lying ... becomes none but t. 293:7
Tradition: t. approves all forms of competition 84:17
youth of America ... oldest t. 328:9
Traduced: beat a Venetian and t. the state 280–1:14
Trafalgar Square fountains like Government Clerks 231:22
Traffic: the two hours' t. of our stage 285:18
Tragedies: all t. are finished by a death 69:19
there are two t. in life 296:8
Tragedy: go litel myn t. 80:6
t. is ... a certeyn storie 80:1
world ... a t. to those who feel 322:7
Tragical-historical, t.-comical-historical-250:9
Trail: long, long t. a-winding 153:11
Train: a man who shaves and takes a t. 325:8
something ... to read in the t. 327:16
Train-band: a t. captain eke was he 92:6

Training is everything 318:16
Traitor: thou art a t. Off with his head! 285:4
Traitors: cowards flinch, and t. jeer 90:3
translators, t. 228:17
Tram: not even a bus, but a t. 128:11
Tranquillity: dismiss it with frigid t. 140:4
emotion recollected in t. 336:7
t.! thou better name 87:18
Translated: Bottom! ... thou art t. 277:2
Translators, traitors 228:17
Transport: I turned to share the t. 333:1
Trapeze: daring young man on ... t. 159:5
Trappings and the suits of woe 248:1
Trash: who steals my purse steals t. 279:15
Travel: does not t. to see Englishmen 306:12
farther from the east must t. 332:2
I never t. without my diary 327:16
I t. light ... as a man can t. 114:1
to t. hopefully is a better thing 307:10
t. ... part of education ... of experience 22:13
Travelled: I t. among unknown men 331:6
much have I t. 150:14
Traveller: a t., by the faithful hound 160:13
a t. came by 55:11
a t. from an antique land 299:7
'anybody there?' said the T. 96:14
from whose bourne no t. returns 250–1:20
Travellers: t. must be content 244:2
t. ne'er did lie 288:14
Travelling: all t. becomes dull 237:1
Travels: fool wanders, the wise man t. 214:7
t. far, knows much 228:18
Treachery: kings that fear ... t.? 260:14
Treacle: cloying t. to the wings of independence 152:9
Tread: fiend doth close behind him t. 86:16
Treading on my tail 75:2
Treason: during his office, t. was no crime 103:7
gunpowder t. and plot 14:5
if it prosper, none dare call it t. 128:13
last temptation ... greatest t. 107:10
love grows bitter with t. 310:4
pay given to ... hireling for t. 140:11
t. doth never prosper 128:13
Treasons: fit for t., stratagems and spoils 275:10
Treasure: Bacchus' Blessings are a t. 103:14
justice, counsel, and t. 22:8
preserve it as yr. chiefest t. 26:14
privilege ... we t. beyond measure 116:13
purest t. mortal times afford 281:8
rich the t., sweet the pleasure 103:14
Treat: something left to t. my friends 165:4
Treaty: hand that signed the t. 315:17
Treble: turning again toward childish t. 244–5:11
Tree: and on the T. of Life ... sat 178:1
as the twig is bent the t.'s inclined 203:14
bark up the wrong t. 206:40
billboard lovely as a t. 186:10
ever-green t. of diabolical knowledge 301:7
fool sees not the same t. 57:3
forbidden t., whose mortal taste 175:15
I had a little nut t. 190:1
I shall be like that t. 309:12
I'll never see a t. at all 186:10
middle t. and highest there 178:1
on a t. by a river 119:1
Tree (*continued*)
only God can make a t. 153:9
poem lovely as a t. 153:8
round the elm-t. bole 61:1
this t. continues to be 155:14
t. is known by its fruit 228:20
under the greenwood t. 244:4
Trees: all the t. were bread and cheese 14:1
amid their tall ancestral t. 130:5
and all the t. are green 154:4
beside the lake, beneath the t. 331:7
birds ... hide in cooling t. 151:1
climbing t. ... they do best 171:3
finds tongues in t. 243:15
great t. ... nothing but shade 215:30
my apple t. will never ... eat 113:13
procreate like t. 60:1
see the wood for the t. 225:8
straight t. have crooked roots 226:28
the fir t. dark and high 134:15
t. ... bow themselves when he did sing 261:6
t. where you sit 204:4
with rocks, and stones, and t. 334:15
Trelawny: and shall T. die? 129:4
Tremblers: boding t. learned to trace 122:11
Tresses: fair t. man's ... race insnare 204:7
wither'd cheek and t. grey 239:11
Trial by jury ... instead of being a security 97:4
Tribe: badge of all our t. 274:10
Idols of the T. 23:16
pearl ... richer than all his t. 280–1:14
Tribes: two mighty t., the *Bores* and *Bored* 70:9
Tribute: to his feet thy t. bring 163:8
Trick: a t. worth two of that 254:5
t. of our English nation 256:10
when in doubt, win the t. 136:11
when the long t.'s over 168:17
Tricks: fantastic t. before high heaven 273:7
frustrate their knavish t. 73:2
hard to teach an old dog t. 227:16
Trident: flatter Neptune for his t. 246:10
Tried to live without him ... died 336:12
Trifle: as 'twere a careless t. 269:11
one must not t. with love 185:6
Trifles: man of sense ... t. ... humours ... flatters 80:14
snapper-up of unconsidered t. 292:18
Trip no further, pretty sweeting 291:1
Tripping hither, t. thither 116:16
Trippingly on the tongue 251:7
Triton: old T. blow his wreathèd horn 333:4
T. of the minnows 246:9
Triumph: I t. still if thou abide 163:7
meet with T. and Disaster 154:19
never dreamed ... wrong wd. t. 60:12
t. of hope over experience 143:6
Triumphs: thy ... glories, t., spoils, shrunk 263:5
Trivial: contests rise from t. things 204:5
such t. people ... such lovely language 157:11
t. and vulgar ... coition 60:1
Troop: sent a t. of horse 60:4
Troops: farewell the plumed t. 280:2
Trotting: shall we be t. home again? 76:6
Trouble: a very present help in t. 36:13
double, double toil and t. 271:11

Trouble (*continued*)
has t. enough of its own 320:9
he that seeks t. 225:11
kindness in another's t. 124:6
man is born unto t. 35:3
man ... of few days ... full of t. 35:5
never t. t. until t. troubles 221:36
where there's a will, there's t. 230:18
Troubles: arms against a sea of t. 250–1:20
don't meet t. half-way 220:38
pack up yr. t. 19:14
the written t. of the brain 272:6
Trousers: bottoms of my t. rolled 106:15
I shall wear white flannel t. 106:16
shd. never put on his best t. 138:4
Trout: rose-moles ... upon t. 135:7
Trowel: lay it on with a t. 218:27
that was laid on with a t. 243:13
Truant: a t. disposition 248:7
and every t. knew 122:11
True: a truism ... none the less t. 238:3
as t. ... as taxes is 97:19
be so t. to thyself 22:17
dare to be t. 131:9
faith unfaithful ... falsely t. 312:4
good to be honest and t. 16:1
he's mad, 'tis t.: 'tis t. 'tis pity 249:17
if all be t. that I do think 10:3
me and my t. love 16:10
nor ... people's judgment always t. 103:8
one religion is as t. as another 67:11
ring in the t. 313:4
sad reflection but a t. one 142:11
so young, my lord, and t. 265:7
to thine own self be t. 248–9:17
t. as the stars above 15:2
which was prov'd t. ... prove false 67:17
Truism: a t. is ... none the less true 238:3
Truly: whom t. to know is everlasting life 53:7
Trumpet: moved more than with a t. 302:6
the t. of a prophecy! O, Wind 299:6
to blow one's own t. 208:14
Trumpets: all the t. sounded for him 63:16
sound the t., beat the drums 103:13, 184:6
Trumps: to turn up t. 228:34
Truncheon: marshal's t. ... judge's robe 273:4
Trunk: so large a t. before 27:1
Trust: better to t. in the Lord 37:12
extreme, rude, cruel, not to t. 294:11
failing to t. everybody ... t. nobody 213:8
men dare t. themselves with men 289:10
never t. a woman who tells one her real age 328:12
none that put ... t. in him 52:9
put not your t. in princes 37:31
some t. in chariots 35:26
though he slay me yet will I t. 35:4
t. God: see all 62:9
t. not a new friend ... old enemy 228:23
under his wings shalt thou t. 36:25
Truth: a melancholy t. ... poor relations 97:11
beauty is t., t. beauty 149:10
constantly speak the t. 53:8
error ... highly heap'd for t. to o'erpeer 246:8
found t. in all but one 284:1
great is T., and mighty 51:6
greater the t., the greater the libel 215:31
habit ... all the test of t. 93:16
Truth (*continued*)
he is less remote from the t. 139:12
his t. at all times firmly stood 153:5
however improbable ... the t. 102:3
it is a t. universally acknowledged 20:17
love swears that she is made of t. 294:15
mainly he told the t. 318:6
mathematics possesses not only t. 237:9
my way of joking ... tell the t. 295:20
nowadays t. ... greatest news 222:20
one t. is clear 203:4
patiently suffer for the t.'s sake 53:8
Pilate saith ... What is t.? 46:33
Plato is dear ... dearer still is t. 18:7
simple t. his utmost skill 336:13
single hast maintained ... the cause of t. 178:19
so few enthusiasts ... speak the t. 24:1
speaking nothing but the t. 327:18
strife of T. with Falsehood 162:14
takes two to speak the t. 317:3
tell the t. and shame the devil 227:20
the t. is rarely pure 327:7
the unclouded face of t. 238:15
T. beareth away the victory 51:5
t. comes out in wine 200:17
t. fears no colours 228:24
t. from his lips prevailed 122:10
t. has such a face 104:6
t. in every shepherd's tongue 232:14
t. in masquerade 70:5
t. is always strange 70:10
t. is stranger than fiction 228:25
t. is the daughter of God 228:26
t. never grows old 228:27
t. of Imagination 151:9
t. sits upon the lips of dying men 19:3
t. ... told with bad intent 54:14
what is t.? said jesting Pilate 21:8
who ever knew T. put to the worse 182:10
whole t. and nothing but the t. 228:28
wine in, t. out 230:21
Tulip: not number the streaks of the t. 141:5
Tune: all the t. that he cd. play 195:3
Cassio kill'd! ... murder's out of t. 280:12
Heaven tries earth if it be in t. 162:15
pays the piper ... call the t. 222:39
sweetly played in t. 66:15
to the t. of flutes kept stroke 242:14
Tunes: devil shd. have all the good t. 132:12
weight of Cathedral t. 99:16
Tupman: Mr. T. 98:22
Turbulent: free me of this t. priest? 130:14
Sagacious, Bold, and T. of wit 102:16
Turk: a malignant and a turban'd T. 280–1:14
French, or T., or Proosian 120:3
Turks: peace shall go sleep with T. 283:8
Turn: fortune ... t. thy wheel 265:20
let not each gay t. ... move 202:11
one good t. deserves another 215:21
person t. in his grave 228:30
tread on a worm ... will t. 228:19
t. an honest penny 228:29
t. over a new leaf 228:31
t. the tables 228:32
t. to God to praise and pray 61:5
t. up one's nose 228:33
t. up trumps 228:34
Turned: having once t. round walks on 86:16
'in case anything t. up' 97:15

Turnips: if the man who t. cries 140:17
Turns: t. no more his head 86:16
whoso t. as I, this evening 61:5
Turpissimus: nemo repente fuit t. 146:8
Turret: Sultan's T. in a Noose of Light 109:13
Turtle: the t. lives 'twixt plated decks 186:11
voice of the t. is heard 40:9
Turtle-doves: two t. and a partridge 194:2
Tuscany: even the ranks of T. 164:1
Tutor: irreverent to my t. 141:14
Tweedledee: 'Contrariwise,' continued T. 75:15
Tweedledum and T. 75:14
Twelve: 'a parted ... between t. and one 259:1
at t. noon the natives swoon 91:8
he in t. found truth in all but one 284:1
I in t. thousand, none 284:1
in the sworn t. have a thief or two 273:1
Twenty: expenditure t. pounds ought and six 97:16
Twice: a victory is t. itself 277:9
he sings each song t. over 61:3
hear t. before you speak once 216:24
it is t. blest 275:1
Twig: as the t. is bent, the tree's inclined 203:14
Twilight: a t. dim with rose 97:1
bats ... they ever fly by t. 22:24
by the t.'s last gleaming 153:6
t. grey ... in her sober livery 178:6
Twin roses by the zephyr blown apart 148:10
Twinkle: t. on the milky way 331:8
t., t., little bat 74:8
t., t., little star 311:5
Twinkling: in the t. of a bed-staff 241:20
Twins: quadruplets, not t. 13:2
Twist: neither t. wolf's-bane 149:11
Twitched: rose, and t. his mantle blue 175:6
Two: a trick worth t. of that 254:5
bicycle made for t. 95:4
human species ... t. distinct races 156:2
I like t. months of every year 68:17
if t. are in the churchyard laid 336:6
in t. words: im-possible 124:4
only t. families in the world 78:4
only t. sorts of boys 98:14
takes t. to speak the truth 317:3
the t. noblest of things 308:11
there went in t. and t. unto Noah 30:20
t. can play at that game 228:38
t. cheers for Democracy 112:2
t. glasses ... t. chairs ... t. people 165:2
t. luxuries to brood over 152:8
t. men look out 156:15
t. mites, which make a farthing 45:15
t. things stand like stone 124:6
t. to bear my soul away 9:13
t. to make a marriage a success 238:2
when t. or three are gathered together 52:19
Type: so careful of the t. she seems 312:16
Tyrannies: of all the T. on humane kind 104:7
Tyrannous to use it like a giant 273:6
Tyranny: ecclesiastic t.'s the worst 96:10
taxation without representation is t. 197:13
Tyrant: little t. of his fields withstood 126:11
professed t. to their sex 277:12
this bloody t., Time 293:12
Tyrants: necessity ... argument of t. 200:8
resistance to t. is obedience 139:11
Tyre: village which men still call T. 111:3

U and Non-U ... Sociological Linguistics 235:14
Uglier yet is the hump 155:9
Uglification and Derision 74:15
Ugly: beauty ... that makes me u. 280:8
The U. Duckling 10:11
Umbrella: unjust steals the just's u. 57:14
Unadorned: beauty u. 26:13
Unarm, Eros ... day's task is done 243:4
Unattempted yet in prose or rhyme 175:16
Unbaptized: any that die u. 53:27
Unbelief: help thou mine u. 45:11
Unbidden guests ... welcomest when ... gone 260:6
Un-birthday: an u. present 76:9
Unborn: the children yet u. shall feel 284:3
Unburied: bodies of u. men 324:3
Uncertain: u., coy, and hard to please 240:9
u. glory of an April day 292:6
Uncharitableness: envy, hatred, ... and all u. 52:23
Uncle: my prophetic soul! My u.! 249:10
u. me no u. 282:9
Uncle Toby: our armies swore ... cried my U. 306:17
Uncle Tom Cobbleigh and all 17:5
Unclubbable: a very u. man 142:16
Uncomely: all things u. and broken 337:6
Uncomfortable: thinks he is moral ... is only u. 296:7
we u. feel 120:5
Uncommon: the thing that's most u. 204:3
Unconfined: let joy be u. 69:4
Unconscionable time dying 78:14
Uncover, dogs, and lap 289:11
Under-belly: the soft u. of the Axis 83:7
Underlings: fault ... in ourselves that we are u. 262:8
Underneath are the everlasting arms 33:9
Underpaying: better than the u. instinct 295:12
Underrate ... the duty of being happy 307:9
Understand: a man will ne'er quite u. 198:12
I u. thy kisses, and thou mine 255:8
no one can u. Ein 13:4
one half ... world cannot u. 20:7
Understanding: brute beasts that have no u. 53:19
Donne's verses ... pass all u. 138:15
give it an u., but no tongue 248:11
light a candle of u. 51:7
peace of God, which passeth all u. 48:31
Undeserver may sleep 257:1
Undeserving: Im one of the u. poor 296:21
Undo: pray you u. this button 268:4
Undone: u. those things we ought to have done 52:13
what's done cannot be u. 272:4
wish th' estate of th' world were now u. 272:11
Uneasy: this swift business I must u. make 288:2
u. lies the head that wears a crown 257:3
Uneatable: in full pursuit of the u. 328:10
Unexpected: moment foreseen may be u. 107:11

Unexpected (*continued*)
the u. ... always happens 229:11
Unfaithful: faith u. ... falsely true 312:4
Unfit: worse man ... u. for the married state 144:2
Unfold: O clouds, u.! 55:8
Unfortunate: one more U., weary of breath 134:10
Unfriendly to society's chief joys 92:5
Unhanged: not three good men u. 254:14
Unhappy: had been very u. in marriage 143:6
instinct for being u. highly developed 237:11
no one till his death ... called u. 60:5
u. family is u. in its own way 317:13
Unheard: heard melodies are sweet, but those u. 149:7
Unholy: refrain from the u. pleasure 26:14
shrieks, and sights u.! 173:14
Unicorn: lion and the u. were fighting 190:9
Unintelligible: weary weight of ... this u. world 335:11
Union: broken Nature's social u. 66:11
Liberty and U., now ... for ever ... inseparable 323:10
O U., strong and great! 160:11
Unite: workers of the world, u. 168:10
United Nations: we the peoples of the U. 319:5
Unity: brethren ... dwell together in u. 37:21
u. is strength 229:12
Universally acknowledged ... a single man 20:17
Universe: born for the U. [Burke] 123:1
wide vessel of the u. 259:8
Universities: state of both his u. 318:1
University: don't think one 'comes down' from Jimmy's u. 197:12
true U. ... is a collection of books 73:9
we are the U. 306:1
Unjust steals the just's umbrella 57:14
Unkind: Midlands ... sodden and u. 28:2
not so u. as man's ingratitude 245:1
tell me not, sweet, I am u. 162:6
when givers prove u. 251:1
Unkindest: the most u. cut of all 263:18
Unkindness: I tax not ... elements with u. 266:7
Unknown: forms of things u. 277:6
I travelled among u. men 331:6
not to know me argues yourselves u. 178:9
Paradise of Fools; to few u. 177:11
Unlamented let me die 204:1
Unlearned, he knew no schoolman's ... art 201:20
Unlucky: so u. that he runs into accidents 167:4
when you shall these u. deeds relate 280:14
Unnatural: foul, strange, and u. 249:9
let me be cruel, not u. 252:9
poetry's u. 99:5
Unobserved, home to his mother's house 180:6
Unperfect, unfinished, inartistic [of Thoreau] 139:5
Unpremeditated: my u. verse 179:5
Unprofitable: months ... most idle and u. 116:1
stale, flat, and u. 248:2
Unrespited, unpitied, unreprieved 177:1
Unrewarded: nothing went u. but desert 103:5
wit shall not go u. 289:1
Unseen: born to blush u. 126:10
leave the world u. 149:14
Unsought: Beadsman ... u. for slept 147:15
[love] given u. 291:12
Unspeakable: the u. in ... pursuit of ... uneatable 328:10
Unstable as water 31:14
Unsubstantial: an u. faery place 336:4
Untaught: better u. than ill-taught 207:36
Untimely: was from his mother's womb u. ripp'd 272:12
Untrue to his wife 20:3
Untruths: they have spoken u. ... are slanders 278:18
Untune that string 290:3
Unturned: leave no stone u. 218:34
Unvarnished: a round u. tale deliver 279:1
Unwept, unhonour'd, and unsung 240:1
Unworthy: an opinion ... u. of him 22:12
spurns that ... merit of th' u. takes 250–1:20
Up: they cannot bear levelling u. 142:12
U., Guards, and at 'em 324:9
u. so floating many bells down 94:13
U., u.! my friend ... quit your books 335:4
u. with which I will not put 83:12
Up-hill: road wind u. all the way? 236:3
Uphold: will u. the unyok'd humour 253:20
Upper classes have ... u. hand 91:5
Uproar's your only music 151:12
Upstairs and downstairs 189:4
Urn: bubbling and loud-hissing u. 93:10
Us: how different from u. 14:4
Usance: rate of u. here ... in Venice 274:7
Use: beauty too rich for u. 286:3
great riches ... no real u. 22:25
how u. doth breed a habit! 292:10
soil'd with all ignoble u. 313:8
u. a poor maiden so 15:1
u. every man after his desert 250:13
what's the u. of worrying? 19:14
Used: not what there u. to be 29:11
Useless: all art is quite u. 328:5
most beautiful things ... most u. 237:3
talent ... lodged with me u. 181:10
u. each without the other 161:6
Uses: all the u. of this world! 248:2
keep a corner ... for others' u. 279:17
sweet are the u. of adversity 243:15
Usurpation: I dare, without u. 59:12
Utter: not u. what thou dost not know 254:11

Vacant: in v. or in pensive mood 331:11
loud laugh ... spoke the v. mind 122:8
Vacations: Dotheboys Hall ... no extras, no v. 98:9
Vae victis 160:4
Vaguery: medal 'For V. in the Field' 197:11
Vain: hour when you too learn that all is v. 236:7
labour and the wounds are v. 85:1
mock on, 'tis all in v. 55:9
name of the Lord thy God in v. 32:2
no great man lives in v. 73:8
they labour in v. that build 37:19
use not v. repetitions 43:23
v. are the thousand creeds 58:13

Vain (*continued*)
v. for you to rise up early 37:20
Why, all delights are v. 268:7
youth is v. 87:7
Vaincre sans péril ... triomphe sans gloire 90:14
Vainly: tired waves, v. breaking 85:2
Valet: no man is a hero to his v. 91:1
to his very v. ... a hero 68:16
Valiant: as he was v., I honour him 263:10
he who would v. be 63:13
the v. man and free 313:7
v. ... taste of death but once 262:15
Valley: all in the v. of Death 311:9
in the v. of decision 42:14
maid singing in the v. 15:1
v. of the shadow of death 35:29
Valleys: piping down the v. wild 56:7
Valour: better part of v. is discretion 256:3
discretion ... better part of v. 211:21
for contemplation he and v. 178:3
Value: price of everything ... v. of nothing 328:4
then we rack the v. 278:12
Valued: never v. till they make a noise 94:1
Van Dycks have to go 91:6
Vanish: ah, wd. the scandal v. 282:6
Vanished: dream that v. with the morn 58:14
the touch of a v. hand 311:6
Vanity: it beareth the name of V. Fair 63:9
that v. in years 255:1
two passions, v. and love 80:16
v. of vanities, saith the Preacher 39:9
Vanquished: woe to the v. 160:4
Variable: Woman ... v. as the shade 240:9
Variation: each slight v., if useful 95:11
Variety: great source of pleasure is v. 144:26
nor custom stale her infinite v. 242:15
v. is pleasing 229:13
v. is the mother of enjoyment 100:13
v. is the soul of pleasure 26:12
v.'s the very spice of life 93:8
Various: as you are woman ... so be v. 125:8
so v., that he seem'd ... Epitome 103:4
Varium et mutabile ... femina 321:3
Vase: 'twas on a lofty v.'s side 125:9
Vassals and serfs at my side 63:4
Vasty fields of France 258:6
Vault: that heaven's v. should crack 268:2
Vaults: been in these here v. 11:17
Vegetable: my v. love shd. grow 167:12
v., animal, and mineral 120:4
Vegetate: one does but v. 65:5
Veil: this that was the v. of thee 309:16
V. past which I cd. not see 110:6
Veils: peace ... dropping from the v. of the morning 337:5
Vein: not in the giving v. today 285:7
Veins: jigging v. of rhyming mother-wits 166:6
Venetian: Turk beat a V. 280–1:14
Vengeance: noblest v. is to forgive 229:14
rarer action ... virtue than in v. 289:3
v. is mine ... saith the Lord 47:26
Veni, vidi, vici 71:13
Venice: here with us in V. 274:7
in V., on the Bridge of Sighs 69:6
Venom: no v. to that of the tongue 229:15
Vent: ce qu'est au feu le v. 67:13
Vent: what his breast forges, that his tongue must v. 246:10
Venture: nothing v., nothing win 222:19
Ventures: take the current ... or lose our v. 264:3
'Verboojuice': 'Sesquippledan v.' 324:13
Verbum sapienti sat est 229:16
Verdict: Sentence first—v. afterwards 75:8
Verdure: content to see no other v. 151:2
different shades in the v. 141:5
Verge: on the very v. of her confine 265:22
Verified: they have v. unjust things 278:18
Verify: always v. yr. references 236:13
Veritas: in vino v. 200:17
Vermin: yr. natives ... race of little odious v. 308:16
Verse: bumbast out a blank v. 127:6
curst be the v. 201:18
Flask of Wine, a Book of V. 109:15
my unpremeditated v. 179:5
ornament of poem or good v. 175:14
the v. you grave for me 307:6
Verses: Donne's v. ... pass all understanding 138:15
tear him for his bad v.! 263:21
Vessel: wide v. of the universe 259:8
Vessels: empty v. make the most noise 212:22
Vest: casting the body's v. aside 168:2
Vestal: happy is the blameless v.'s lot 201:9
Vestry: see you in the v. after the service 303:13
Vesture: this muddy v. of decay 275:8
Veterans: how the world its v. rewards 203:16
Vex not his ghost. O, let him pass! 268:5
Vexes: the other v. it 148:2
Vexing the dull ear of a drowsy man 264:17
Vibrated: strings ... better not ... v. 97:8
Vibrates: music ... v. in the memory 300:6
Vicar: I'll be the V. of Bray, Sir 15:13
Vice: any taint of v., whose ... corruption 292:1
boldly rebuke v. 53:8
homage paid by v. to virtue 234:7
hypocrisy ... homage that v. pays 217:12
in v. their [king's] law's their will 281:4
lash'd the v., but spared the name 308:13
mutual forgiveness of each v. 55:3
no v. but beggary 264:14
prosperity doth best discover v. 21:15
public schools ... nurseries of all v. 109:10
subject ... to this v. of lying! 257:10
that reverend v., that grey iniquity 255:1
the raptures and roses of v. 309:17
v. is a master of so frightful mien 203:6
Vice versa: good for General Motors and v. 329:4
Vices: of our pleasant v. make instruments 267:14
through tatter'd clothes small v. 267:6
Vicious: restraint of ten v. 182:6
Victim: some day ... a v. must be found 118:4
v. of a rich man's game 16:11
Victoria Station: the cloak-room at V.? 327:14
Victorious, happy and glorious 73:1
Victory: a v. is twice itself 277:9
and shouted V.! 240:10
better a lean peace than a fat v. 207:17
but 'twas a famous v. 304:15
grave, where is thy v.? 48:13
however long ... for without v. ... no survival 82:12

Victory (*continued*)
in V., Magnanimity 83:13
O Grave! where is thy V.? 201:4
peace hath her v. 181:13
problems of v. are more agreeable 83:8
v. in spite of all terror 82:12
welcome to yr. gory bed, or to v. 67:1
Westminster Abbey or v. 187:4
where, grave, thy v.? 163:7
Victuals: picks it up and buys v. 142:7
the German dictator, instead of snatching the v. 82:9
Vieillesse: si v. pouvait 108:25
View: observation with extensive v. 141:9
View halloo: Peel's v. wd. a-waken the dead 125:6
Vigilance: condition ... liberty ... eternal v. 95:3
Vigorous: shd. feel fresh and v. enough 322:14
Vile: better to be v. than v. esteemed 294:10
cd. make so v. a pun 97:5
from living in a v. hotel 28:1
out, v. jelly! 266:18
v., but viler George the Second 156:10
wisdom and goodness to the v. seem v. 266:21
Village: loveliest v. of the plain 122:4
through an Alpine v. passed 160:12
v. ... men still call Tyre 111:3
Villages: dollar ... no ... devotees in these ... v. 138:13
Villain: condemns me for a v. 285:15
determined to prove a v. 284:12
fair terms and a v.'s mind 274:11
hungry, lean-fac'd v. 246:5
O v. ... condemned into ... redemption 278:15
Villainous: foreheads v. low 289:2
Villains: God shd. go before such v. 278:13
Villainy: thus I clothe my naked v. 284:14
Vinci: they spell it V. 318:13
Vindicate the ways of God to Man 202:18
Vine: Daughter of the V. 110:9
every man under his v. 42:22
Vines: bless with fruit the v. 147:1
our v. have tender grapes 40:10
Vineyard: thou shalt not glean thy v. 32:15
Violence: to offer it the show of v. 247:15
Violent: laid v. hands upon themselves 53:27
nothing ... v. is permanent 222:18
so over v. or over civil 103:5
Violet: the nodding v. grows 276:20
the v. smells to him as ... to me 259:10
throw a perfume on the v. 264:19
Violets: breathes upon a bank of v. 290:10
daisies pied and v. blue 268:17
from her ... flesh may v. spring 253:3
odours, when sweet v. sicken 300:6
Vipers: generation of v. 43:12
Virgin: a v. shall conceive, and bear 40:21
Virtue: a fugitive and cloistered v. 182:4
admire v. ... follow not her lore 180:1
assume a v. if you have it not 252:14
enterprises ... of v. or mischief 21:19
every v. ... founded on compromise 64:7
forbearance ceases to be a v. 64:10
if V. feeble were 173:4
lilies and languors of v. 309:17
love V., she alone is free 173:4
Virtue (*continued*)
much v. in If 246:3
O infinite v., com'st thou smiling? 243:3
only reward of v. is v. 108:4
power ... extirpates ... gentle v. 65:2
rarer ... in v. than in vengeance 289:3
saw v. in her shape how lovely 178:10
some rise by sin, and some by v. fall 273:2
there is no v. like necessity 281:14
useful life, progressive v. 316:13
v. dwells not in the tongue 229:17
v. is ... best plain set 23:2
v. is its own reward 229:18
v. never grows old 229:19
v. of necessity 229:20
v. only makes our bliss below 203:12
v. that possession wd. not show 278:12
wars that makes ambition v. 280:2
Virtues: be to her v. very kind 205:5
lady ... of wondrous v. 274:4
their v. we write in water 262:1
world to hide v. in? 290:12
Virtuous: be in general v., and ... happy 112:15
think, because thou art v. 291:5
Visages: whose v. do cream and mantle 274:2
Vision: a v. or a waking dream? 150:6
baseless fabric of this v. 288:16
by the v. splendid ... attended 332:2
not disobedient unto ... heavenly v. 47:13
saw the V. of the world 313:16
where ... no v., the people perish 39:5
write the v., ... make it plain 42:26
Visionary: whither is fled the v. gleam? 331:16
Visions: young men shall see v. 42:13
Visit: let us never v. together 89:17
v. us with thy salvation 325:3
Visiting the iniquity of the fathers 32:1
Vital: I cannot give it v. growth again 280:11
Vitality: extreme busyness ... deficient v. 307:8
Vive: Napoleon's armies ... shouting 'V. l'intérieur' 241:13
Vocabulary: the v. of Bradshaw is nervous 102:6
Vocation: no sin ... to labour in his v. 253:18
'tis my v., Hal 253:18
Vogue: charming to totter into v. 322:6
Voice: a certain what-is-it in his v. 330:2
a distant v. in the darkness 161:7
a still small v. 34:21
a v. cry, Sleep no more 270:11
bird, or but a wandering v.? 336:2
every man thy ear, but few thy v. 248:16
harmonious sisters, V. and Verse 172:12
hear a v. in every wind 126:1
heart and soul and v. 186:14
her v., and her hair, and eyes 168:12
her v. was ever soft 268:3
his big manly v. 244–5:11
I sing with mortal v. 178:20
its familiar v. wearies not ever 299:12
lost my v. most irrecoverably 324:5
my v. ... lost it with hallooing 256:9
no v.; but oh! the silence sank 87:1
no v. but the v. of complaining 184:10
no v. I'll be quit of the singing 12:1
sing to the Lord with cheerful v. 153:4
so charming left his v. 179:1

Voice (*continued*)
sound of a v. that is still 311:6
still raise ... the supplicating v. 141:13
the v. is Jacob's v. 31:8
the v. of all the gods 268:13
the watchdog's v. that bayed 122:8
'tis the v. of the Lobster 75:4
'tis the v. of the sluggard 323:7
v. ... crying in the wilderness 43:11
v. I hear this passing night 150:4
v. of the people ... of God 10:2
v. of the turtle is heard 40:9
v. ... run from hedge to hedge 151:1
v. whose sound was like the sea 333:13
warm, thrilling v. cry out 197:10
Voices: ancestral v. prophesying war 87:14
I hear the gentle v. calling 112:11
music, when soft v. die 300:6
two v. are there 333:10
two v. are there ... of ... deep ... of sheep 306:9
v. of children ... on the green 56:11
v. telling me what to do 297:2
Void: have left an aching v. 92:14
without form, and v. 30:1
Volscians: flutter'd yr. V. in Corioli 246:12
Voltaire: mock on, V., Rousseau 55:9
Volume: desideratum of a v. 156:7
foretells ... a tragic v. 256:6
Volumes: borrowers ... creators of odd v. 156:3
written such v. of stuff! 158:6
Vomit: dog is turned to his ... v. 50:9
dog returneth to ... v., ... fool ... to ... folly 38:31
Vorpal blade went snicker-snack 75:10
Vote: v. ... as ... leaders tell 'em to 117:9
Voted at my party's call 119:16
Votes: anyone who v. Labour 183:7
Vow: I v. to thee, my country 305:22
Vows made in storms are forgotten 229:21
Vox populi, vox dei 10:2
Voyage: about to take my last v. 133:4
Voyager: lands the v. at last 107:16
Vulgar: familiar, but by no means v. 248:15
think with the wise, but talk with the v. 227:32

Wabe: gimble in the w. 75:9
Wacht am Rhein 238:14
Wade: shd. I w. no more 271:10
Wages: be content with your w. 45:23
home art gone, and ta'en thy w. 247:9
w. of sin is death 47:18
Wagon: hitch yr. w. to a star 108:18
Wail: with old woes new w. ... time's waste 293:18
Wailing for her demon lover 87:12
Wait: learn to labour and to w. 161:2
make 'em laugh ... cry ... w. 233:5
time and tide w. for no man 228:2
w. and see 19:15, 229:22
who only stand and w. 181:11
Waiter roars it through the hall 156:14
Waiting for the long-promised invasion 83:1
Waiting-gentlewoman: talk so like a w. 254:2
Waits: everything comes to him who w. 212:36
the dinner w., and we are tired 92:10
Wake: do I w. or sleep? 150:6
Wake (*continued*)
held we ... sleep to w. 60:12
w. up, America 114:16
w. up, England 115:15
you must w. and call me early 314:6
Waked: you have w. me too soon 323:7
Wakes: and whoever w. in England 61:1
Walcum: a little talcum is always w. 186:7
Walk: can two w. together? 42:15
doth w. in fear and dread 86:16
w. humbly with thy God 42:24
w. upon England's mountains green 55:8
we w. by faith, not by sight 48:15
where'er you w., cool gales 204:4
will you w. a little faster? 75:2
will you w. into my parlour? 136:10
within a w. of the sea 28:4
Walked: as I w. through the wilderness 63:6
when she has w. before 122:16
Walking: I nauseate w. 89:16
life's but a w. shadow 272:10
Walks: having once turned round w. on 86:16
I wish I liked the way it w. 233:1
she w. in beauty, like the night 71:2
w. the night in her silver shoon 97:3
Wall: green hill ... without a city w. 10:7
Jackson standing like a stone w. 26:5
know ... the w. is strong 326–7:15
little pin bores through his castle w. 283:6
serves it in the office of a w. 282:5
something ... that doesn't love a w. 113:14
washes its w. on the southern side 61:16
weakest goes to the w. 229:38
Wallet: his w. lay ... in his lappe 79:19
time hath ... a w. at his back 290:6
Wallow naked in December snow 282:1
Wallowing: sow ... to her w. in the mire 50:9
Walls: banners on the outward w. 272:8
stone w. do not a prison make 162:5
w. have ears 229:23
watches from his mountain w. 312:1
Walrus and the Carpenter 76:2–6
Waltzing: you'll come a-w., Matilda 198:10
Wander: whither shall I w.? 189:4
you shall w. hand in hand 188:1
Wandered: I w. lonely as a cloud 331:7
when we have w. all our ways 232:11
Wandering: a w. minstrel I 117:16
w. between two worlds 18:15
w. Dong through the forest goes! 158:3
Want: Adam ... did not w. the apple 318:15
all we w. is a limousine 164:14
freedom from w. ... everywhere 235:4
I shall not w. 35:27
if you w. to get somewhere else 75:12
not good to w. and to have 215:20
the w. of money is so [the root of all evil] 68:3
w. it [advice] most ... like it least 80:12
w. of a thing is perplexing 320:3
w. of Thought ... w. of Heart 135:1
waste not, w. not 229:31
worth ... best known by w. 231:4
you w. the best seats 11:11
Wanted: every man is w., ... no man is w. much 108:9
map ... not be w. these ten years 200:10
Wanting: robb'd, not w. what is stol'n 280:1
weighed ... and art found w. 42:2
Wanton: w. love corrupteth 22:1

Wanton (*continued*)
weep not, my w. 127:5
Wantonness: kindles in clothes a w. 131:14
Wants: but w. that little strong 134:2
man w. but little here below 122:15
w. money, means, and content 245:3
War: advise none to ... go to w. 206:7
all is fair in love and w. 206:11
Americans ... tempered by w. 153:1
ancestral voices prophesying w. 87:14
desires peace, prepare for w. 320:8
Don John of Austria is going to the w. 81:5
ease after w., death after life 305:11
he that first invented w. 166:8
I know the disciplines of w. 259:7
image of w. without its guilt 304:8
in w. ... no winners, ... all are losers 78:9
in W.: Resolution. In Defeat: Defiance 83:13
infection and the hand of w. 282:5
let slip the dogs of w. 263:8
looks on w. as all glory 301:20
love ... is exactly like w. 307:1
magnificent, but ... not w. 57:9
marching as to w. 24:9
my sentence is for open w. 176:16
neither shall they learn w. 40:18
never was a good w. 113:2
pride, pomp, and circumstance of ... w. 280:2
so dauntless in w. 240:6
some ... depos'd, some slain in w. 283:6
stupid crime ... devil's madness—W. 241:16
succeeding generations from ... scourge of w. 319:5
the arts of w. and peace 69–70:21
The W. between Men and Women 317:9
to w. and arms I fly 162:6
w. ... endless w. still breed? 181:14
w. is done and youth stone dead 238:9
w. is ... national industry of Prussia 182:12
W. is Peace, Freedom is Slavery 197:4
w. makes rattling good history 128:7
w. ... too serious ... to be left to military 311:3
w. upon this bloody tyrant, Time 293:12
when I speak, they are for w. 37:14
when the blast of w. blows 259:3
when there was w., he went 20:4
when w. begins, hell opens 229:26
wither'd is the garland of the w. 243:6
Women ... and Power and W. 154:9
Warble his native wood-notes wild 174:8
Ward: thou knowest my old w. 254:15
Ware: I shd. dine at W. 92:11
Warm: let the w. Love in 150:7
this sensible w. motion to become 273:10
Warmed: w. and cooled ... winter and summer 274:17
w. both hands ... fire of life 156:11
Warn: to w., to comfort, and command 334:14
Warned: be w. by me that breakfast 27:4
Warring within our breasts 166:10
Wars: end to the beginnings of all w. 235:6
fierce w. and faithful loves 305:9
let w. give way to peace 84:4
more ... fears than w. or women 261:10
still w. and lechery! 290:9
Wars (*continued*)
the thousand w. of old 313:6
w. and rumours of w. 44:27
w. bring scars 229:27
w. that makes ambition virtue 280:2
Wars of the Roses: leave Moses out of the W. 29:8
Warts: roughnesses, pimples, and w. 94:10
Wash: bid them w. their faces 246:7
I w. away my balm 284:2
tears ... w. out a word of it 110:12
w. dirty linen in public 229:29
w. me ... whiter than snow 36:14
w. the balm ... from ... anointed king 283:2
w. ... yr. feet seldom ... head never 229:30
will all great Neptune's ocean w. this blood 270:12
Washed the dishes with his wife 184:8
Washes: river Weser ... w. its wall 61:16
Washing: no cooking, or w., or sewing 12:1
painting a face ... not w. it 114:7
w. ... clean linen in public 327:9
Waste: barrel of meal shall not w. 34:18
in a w. of shame 294:11
wail my dear time's w. 293:18
w. not, want not 229:31
Wasted: some nine moons w. 278:21
Wasteful and ridiculous excess 264:19
Wastes: tell her that w. her time and me 322:1
Watch: has a w. and chain, of course 234:12
keeping w. over ... flock by night 45:20
one to w., and one to pray 9:13
our w. ... have indeed comprehended 278:10
secret whispers of each other's w. 259:8
take ye heed, w. and pray 45:16
w. and pray, that ye enter not 45:2
W. on the Rhine 238:14
w. that ends the night 323:5
w. to babble and to talk 278:6
Watchdog: the w.'s voice that bayed 122:8
Watched: he w. the ads and not the road 186:4
o'er the ramparts we w. 153:6
w. pot never boils 229:32
Watcher of the skies 150:15
Watches: a heart that w. and receives 335:8
he w. from his mountain walls 312:1
with our judgments as our w. 202:2
Watching: Big Brother is w. you 197:3
Watchman, what of the night? 40:26
Watch-tower: from his w. in the skies 174:2
Water: as w. unto wine 313:19
blood is thicker than w. 208:13
by w. and the Word 307:13
carry w. in a sieve 229:33
deepest w. ... best fishing 211:12
Eeyore ... looked at himself in the w. 172:5
give him w. to drink 38:28
I came like W. 110:5
I don't care where the w. goes 81:11
like w. off a duck's back 229:34
may lead a horse to the w. 218:28
more w. glideth by the mill 289:13
name was writ in w. 152:13
never know the worth of w. 218:10
not all the w. in the rough rude sea 283:2
smooth ... w. where the brook is deep 260:8
unstable as w. ... shalt not excel 31:14

Water (*continued*)
virtues we write in w. 262:1
w. is best 200:5
w. out of a stone 229:35
w., w. every where 86:6
Watered heaven with ... tears 56:6
Waterfall: from the w. he named her 161:5
(A)-Watering the last year's crop 105:14
Waterloo: battle of W. was won ... Eton 324:10
bodies high at Austerlitz and W. 238:5
every man meets his W. at last 200:4
Marathon to W. 120:4
Water-mill: noise like that of a w. 308:14
Water-rugs: shoughs, w., and demi-wolves 271:1
Waters: a fen of stagnant w. 333:12
beside the still w. 35:28
cast thy bread upon the w. 39:24
cold w. to a thirsty soul 38:29
dreadful noise of w. in my ears 285:1
fades o'er the w. blue 69:1
kill the still-closing w. 288:15
many w. cannot quench love 40:15
still w. run deep 226:21
stolen w. are sweet 38:7
w. of the heart push in their tides 315:18
Watson: you know my methods, W. 101:14
Wave: all sunk beneath the w. 93:1
chin upon an orient w. 175:10
glassy, cool, translucent w. 173:3
lift me as a w., a leaf 299:5
walk o'er the western w. 298:15
Waved: long has it w. on high 134:1
Waves: sons of the w. 115:1
the tired w., vainly breaking 85:2
w. make towards the pebbled shore 294:1
when ... w. went high ... sought ... storms 102–3:17
Wax-works: if you think we're w. 75:13
Way: a damned long, dark ... w. 123:7
all taking the easiest w. out 324:18
catch the nearest w. 270:1
every day, in every w. ... better 91:3
go by the king's high w. 32:19
gull's w. and the whale's w. 168:17
keep his distant w. [Milton] 127:2
long is the w. and hard 177:5
love will find a w. 220:7
perilous w. from a tree's summit 150:9
plods his weary w. 126:3
primrose w. to the ... bonfire 270:13
roses, roses all the w. 61:15
set out ... in a relative w. 63:1
steep and thorny w. to heaven 248:14
the w. of all flesh 324:2
the w. to dusty death 272:10
travel on life's common w. 333:13
w. of an eagle ... serpent 39:7
w. was long, the wind was cold 239:11
where there's a will ... a w. 230:17
which w. shall I fly? 177:13
Ways: among the untrodden w. 334:11
gave once ... her w. to roam 59:6
he had his little w. 171:4
her w. are w. of pleasantness 38:3
let all her w. be unconfined 205:5
Mr. Facing-both-w. 63:10
neither are yr. w. my w. 41:9
oldest sins the newest ... w. 257:19
Ways (*continued*)
when ... w. be foul 269:1
We: put it down a w., my lord 99:8
Weak: bear the infirmities of the w. 47:31
concessions of the w. 64:4
idleness ... refuge of w. minds 80:15
surely the w. shall perish 241:15
to be w. is miserable 176:1
w. and therefore pacifistic 20:1
Weakest goes to the wall 229:38
Weakness: show no more w. than is natural 317:5
silence ... all else is w. 320:14
w. is thy excuse 181:1
Wealth: as their w. increaseth, so inclose 166:4
bear w. 207:4
consume w. without producing it 295:11
he that marries for w. 220:27
health is better than w. 216:21
let w. and commerce ... die 237:10
love rememb'red such w. brings 293:17
neither wit nor w. 15:6
squandering w. ... his ... art 103:5
there is no w. but life 237:6
w. accumulates and men decay 122:5
w. is contentment with a little 229:39
w. is not without its advantages 114:13
w. maketh many friends 38:21
where w. and freedom reign 123:15
Weapons: hurt with the same w. 274:17
in this war ... books are w. 235:5
women's w., water-drops 266:3
Wear: better to w. out than ... rust out 94:11
better w. out shoes than sheets 207:37
if the cap fits, w. it 209:6
our souls ... will us to w. ourselves 166:10
to w. the breeches 230:2
w. him in my heart's core 252:1
Wearied: wherein have I w. thee? 42:23
Weariest: even the w. river ... safe to sea 310:1
Weariness: much study ... a w. of the flesh 39:28
Wearing: everything is the worse for w. 212:38
Weary: age shall not w. them 54:5
how my heart grows w. 112:9
how w., stale ... uses of this world 248:2
long w. day have end 305:8
sae w., fu' o' care 67:5
Unfortunate, w. of breath 134:10
Weasel: as a w. sucks eggs 244:5
pop goes the w.! 165:5
Weather: I like the w. 68:17
if it prove fair w. 308:2
need to pray for fair w. 22:8
no enemy but winter and rough w. 244:4
the w. the cuckoo likes 128:10
two Englishmen ... talk is of the w. 140:12
what dreadful hot w.! 21:4
who's there, besides foul w.? 266:5
you won't hold up the w. 164:15
Weave: tangled web we w. 240:8
w. a circle round him thrice 87:16
Weaving: I work at the w. trade 16:3
Web: w. of our life ... mingled yarn 242:6
what a tangled w. we weave 240:8
Webster was ... possessed by death 107:6
Wed: with this ring I thee w. 53:24

Wedding: has bought her w. clothes 9:10
Wedding-day: brightly dawns our w. 118:8
said John, 'It is my w.' 92:11
tomorrow is our w. 92:7
wager ... w. ... is ... fixed on 109:7
Wedding-gown: I chose my wife, as she ... her w. 123:20
Wedding-guest: O W.! this soul hath been 87:2
Wedge: thin end of the w. 227:27
Wedges: in time small w. cleave 155:16
w. of gold, great anchors 285:1
Wedlock is a padlock 230:3
Wednesday: he that died o' W. 255:21
married on W. 193:6
W.'s child is full of woe 191:8
Wee, sleekit, cow'rin' ... beastie 66:10
Wee-wee-wee: little pig cried w. 194:7
Weed: O thou w. who art so lovely 280:6
pernicious w. whose scent ... annoys 92:5
Weeds: her winter w. outworn 298:11
lilies ... smell far worse than w. 294:3
subject is the fattest soil to w. 257:15
worthless as wither'd w. 58:13
Week: in his beak enough food for a w. 170:6
murdered reputations of the w. 89:7
no admittance till the w. after next 77:9
rust of the whole w. 9:7
takes me as much as a w. 318:12
Weeks: love alters not with ... w. 294:9
Weep: I w. for Adonais—he is dead! 297:9
I w. for joy to stand 283:1
'I w. for you,' the Walrus said 76:5
men that laugh and w. 309:18
no, I'll not w. 266:4
or ere I'll w. ... I shall go mad 266:4
such ... tricks ... the angels w. 273:7
that he shd. w. for her? 250:15
'tis that I may not w. 70:2
w., and you w. alone 326:9
w. no more, my lady 112:7
w. not for little Leonie 124:11
w. not, my wanton, smile 127:5
w. with them that w. 47:24
who wd. not w., if Atticus were he? 201:17
Weeping: all de darkies am a w. 112:6
dwell a w. hermit there 88:11
I have full cause of w. 266:4
Rachel w. for her children 43:9
the children w., O my brothers 60:7
w. may endure for a night 36:2
Weeps: our country sinks .. it w., it bleeds 271:18
Weighed: thou art w. in the balances 42:2
Weight: able and willing to pull his w. 235:8
he carries w.! he rides a race 92:9
heavy ... weary w. ... of ... world 335:11
heavy w. from off my head 284:2
w. of Cathedral tunes 99:16
Wein, Weib und Gesang: wer nicht liebt W. 163:2
Welcome: advice is seldom w. 80:12
constant guest is never w. 210:7
eat and w., fast, and heartily w. 212:14
he that plays the king shall be w. 250:7
so let us w. peaceful evening 93:10
thrice w., darling of the Spring 336:3
warmest w. at an inn 300:12
w. is the best cheer 230:4
w. to yr. gory bed 67:1
Welcomes: and w. little fishes in 73-4:17
Well: all is not w. 248:12
all is w. that ends w. 206:14
Chaucer, w. of English undefiled 305:13
deep w. of unconscious cerebration 139:2
did nothing ... did it very w. 117:11
he preaches w. that lives w. 223:25
lov'd not wisely, but too w. 280:14
not feeling very w. myself! 232:3
prayeth w. who loveth w. 87:3
Pussy's in the w. 188:9
worth doing is worth doing w. 230:8
Well-a-way: made every youth cry *W.*! 11:12
Wellbred: as w. as if ... not married 89:17
moral, sensible, and w. man 92:4
very strange and w. 89:17
w. Captain of the *Pinafore* 119:13
Well-content: sweet W. 96:3
Weller: Mr. W.'s knowledge of London 98:23
Well-favoured: to be a w. man is the gift of fortune 278:4
Weltgeschichte: die W. ... Weltgericht 238:13
Wen: fate of the great w. [London] 85:5
Wenceslas: good King W. 187:1
Wench: beside the w. is dead 166:5
Wenches: getting w. with child 292:16
Went: and she w., and came, and gleaned 33:27
when there was war, he w. 20:4
Wept: my mother groan'd, my father w. 56:3
they w. like anything to see 76:2
West: East is East, and W. is W. 154:8
go W., young man 127:4, 304:9
Lochinvar is come out of the w. 240:5
West port: open the W., and let me gang free 239:4
Westen: im W. nichts Neues 233:7
Western: All Quiet on the W. Front 233:7
wind of the W. Sea 314:13
Westminster Abbey or victory 187:4
Westward: but w., look, the land is bright 85:3
Wet: out of ... w. clothes and into a dry Martini 330:8
to w. one's whistle 230:6
w. and dirty from hunting 308:8
Wetting: saved his friend from a w. 172:11
Whale: gull's way ... w.'s way 168:17
sprat to catch a w. 226:13
very like a w. 252:7
Whales: they wd. talk like w. 124:3
What-is-it: a certain w. in his voice 330:2
Wheat: orient and immortal w. 317:17
Wheel: a w. ... in the midst of a w. 41:21
fortune ... turn thy w. 265:20
put a spoke in one's w. 226:12
put yr. shoulder to the w. 223:38
upon a w. of fire 267:10
w. is come full circle 267:15
Wheelbarrow: as she wheeled her w. 15:10
Wheels: all the w. of Being slow 312:14
w. within w. 230:10
Where: leads—God knows w. 70:3
w. are the snows of yesteryear? 320:15
w. ish dat barty now? 159:2
Wherefore: for every why he had a w. 67:15
never mind the why and w. 120:1
w. stopp'st thou me? 85:11
Whiff: a w. of grapeshot 73:6

Whig: first W. was the Devil 144:12
Whigs: caught the W. bathing 100:3
W. ... no force but argument 60:4
Whim: tempted by a private w. 27:8
the strangest w. has seized me 80:20
Whimper: not with a bang but a w. 106:9
'twixt a smile and a w. 299:10
Whipped: she w. them all soundly 194:5
Whipping: who shall 'scape w.? 250:13
Whips and scorns of time 250–1:20
Whirligig of time brings ... revenges 292:2
Whiskers: runcible cat with crimson w. 158:10
Whisky: freedom and W. ... thegither 65:14
Whisper: hush! hush! w. who dares! 172:2
Whispering: where there is w. ... lying 230:13
Whispers: blood of Jesus w. peace 54:4
secret w. of each other's watch 259:8
Whist: loved a good game of w. 156:4
Whistle: as clean as a w. 209:30
hir joly w. wel y-wet 79:22
to wet one's w. 230:6
Whistles o'er the furrowed land 174:3
White: a moment w., then melts 67:4
as w. as leprosy 86:8
fleece was w. as snow 127:11
I shall wear w. flannel trousers 106:16
in winter, when the fields are w. 76:11
my soul is w. 56:10
one w., and two khaki 13:2
[sins] shall be ... w. as snow 40:17
some gave them w. bread 190:9
the w. foam flew 86:4
the W. Man's Burden 155:6
two blacks do not make a w. 228:37
w. radiance of Eternity 298:2
yr. hair has become very w. 74:3
Whiten: w. the green plains under 298:5
willows w., aspens quiver 313:12
Whiter: I shall be w. than snow 36:14
Whites: don't fire ... see the w. of their eyes 205:4
Whitethroat builds, and all the swallows 61:2
Whither: one knows not w. nor why 169:1
soul ... driven ... I know not w. 324:4
w. goest thou? 46:32
w. is fled the visionary gleam? 331:16
Whiting: said a w. to a snail 75:2
Who: w. killed Cock Robin? 196:2
w. kill'd John Keats? 70:17
w., or why, or which 158:1
w. was then the gentleman? 24:2
Whole: all ... parts of one stupendous w. 203:3
saw life steadily, and saw it w. 18:14
they that are w. 45:5
Who saith 'A w. I planned' 62:9
Whooping: wonderful ... out of all w. 245:5
Whore: like a w., unpack my heart 250:18
'Tis Pity She's a W. 111:11
Wicked: God made the w. Grocer 81:10
lov'd his w. neighbour as himself 103:7
no peace ... unto the w. 41:3
pomps ... of this w. world 53:12
Wickedness: men alone ... capable of every w. 90:9
spiritual w. in high places 48:27
w. of a woman 52:1
Wicklow: chink in the floor of the old W. house 310:7
Widdicombe Fair: for to go to W. 17:5
Wide: alone on a w. w. sea 86:10, 87:2
Wider still and wider shall thy bounds be set 28:10
Widow: a certain poor w. ... threw in two mites 45:15
care for ... his w. and his orphan 159:15
here's to the w. of fifty 301:17
Widows: be very careful o' w. (vidders) 98:24
when w. exclaim ... against second marriage 109:7
w. are always rich 230:14
Wife: a light w., a heavy husband 275:12
all the world and his w. 231:1
and Noah he often said to his w. 81:11
by degrees dwindle into a w. 89:18
Caesar's w. ... above suspicion 71:15
choose a w. ... by yr. ear 209:24
chose my w. ... nct for ... glossy surface 123:20
good w. and health ... best wealth 215:22
good w. makes a good husband 215:23
has a w., has a master 230:15
he that hath w. and children 21:19
he that speaks ill of his w. 226:8
he that tells his w. news 227:21
here lies my w.—hallelujah! 12:2
his w. cd. eat no lean 190:7
his w. looked back 31:4
honour unto ... w. as ... weaker vessel 50:6
horse made ... w. to make 209:23
how ... be married without a w.? 191:4
if w. shd. dine at Edmonton 92:11
Intellectual suggests ... untrue to his w. 20:3
kill a w. with kindness 287:10
married, but I'd have no w. 94:2
must be in want of a w. 20:17
naked, the man and his w. 30:10
need makes the old w. trot 221:26
never lend—'oss, ... w., ... name 308:7
not covet thy neighbour's w. 32:9
remember Lot's w. 46:10
riding to and from his w. 325:8
roaring of the wind is my w. 152:6
tell his w. all he knows 114:9
this is my w.—look well at her 306:1
took fourpence home to my w. 190:2
when his w. talks Greek 145:3
whose w. shall I take? 184:3
Wights: descriptions of the fairest w. 294:6
Wild: and her eyes were w. 148:15
bore me in the southern w. 56:10
kind of w. justice 21:12
piping down the valleys w. 56:7
Wilderness: one crying in the w. 43:11
scapegoat into the w. 32:13
the w. of this world 63:6
W. is Paradise enow 109:15
Wiles: of w., more unexpert, I boast not 176:16
Quips and Cranks and wanton W. 173:16
Will: a man's ... w. ... invalidated by marriage 68:11
complies against his w. 68:1
law beyond its own sweet w. 326:6
man has his w. ... woman has her way 134:3
puzzles the w. 250–1:20
serveth not another's w. 336:13
the w.! the w.! ... Caesar's w.! 263:15

Will (*continued*)
the w. to do, the soul to dare 239:7
their law's their w. 281:4
thy w. be done 43:24
unconquerable w., and study of revenge 175:18
where there's a w. there's a way 230:17
where there's a w., there's trouble 230:18
w. in us is over-rul'd by fate 166:14
William: you are old, Father W. 74:3
Williamanmary ... ruled by an Orange 241:12
Willow: a w. cabin at yr. gate 290:15
a w. grows aslant the brook 253:1
w., titwillow 119:1
w. w. waly 119:6
Willows: our harps upon the w. 37:23
w. whiten, aspens quiver 313:12
Wills: choose executors and talk of w. 283:5
the w. above be done 287:14
women must have their w. 230:36
Win: heads I w., tails you lose 94:5, 216:20
hope from outward forms to w. 87:9
nothing ... foul to those that w. 255:18
Wind: a roaring in the w. all night 334:7
absence is to love what w. is to fire 67:13
all aloud the w. doth blow 269:1
and the w. shall say 107:1
bayed the whispering w. 122:8
blow, blow, thou winter w. 245:1
blow w., come wrack 272:11
fair stood the w. for France 102:9
frosty w. made moan 235:15
gentle w. doth move 55:10
God tempers the w. ... shorn lamb 215:11
hey, ho, the w. and the rain 292:3
hope constancy in w. 70:14
how the w. doth ramm! 205:2
ill w. that blows nobody good 217:19
impatient as the W. 333:1
know which way the w. blows 218:11
like W. I go 110:5
likewise a w. on the heath 57:8
man in the w. 315:14
more gentle than a w. in summer 150:8
O Wild West W. 299:3
only argument ... with an east w. 163:1
readers ... sway in the w. 106:2
reed shaken with the w. 44:11
roaring of the w. is my wife 152:6
sail near the w. 224:35
shorter in w., as in memory long 57:15
streams ... *against* the w. 69:7
swoln with w. and the rank mist 175:4
tempers the w. ... to the shorn lamb 306:15
the w. of. change is blowing 164:13
they have sown the w. 42:9
when the w. is southerly 250:8
where the w. comes from ... goes 171:5
w. bloweth where it listeth 46:20
w. blows it back again 55:9
w. blows, the cradle will rock 189:10
w. of the Western Sea 314:13
w. out of one's sails 227:6
w. that follows fast 95:1
w.'s like a whetted knife 168:17
words but w. 67:16
Window: at my w. bid good morrow 174:2
love comes in at the w. 219:37
the little w. where the sun 134:14
what light through yonder w.? 286:6
Windowed: loop'd and w. raggedness 266:13
Window-panes: fog ... rubs its back upon the w. 106:13
Windows: cleaned the w., ... swept the floor 119:15
not by eastern w. only 85:3
storied w. richly dight 173:11
Winds: blow, w., and crack yr. cheeks 266:6
courted by all the w. 180:15
four-square to all the w. 314:10
rough w. do shake the darling buds 293:13
so perfumed that the w. were love-sick 242:14
the w. will blow the profit 164:15
w. somewhere safe to sea 310:1
wound the loud w. 288:15
young w. fed it with ... dew 299:14
Windy: keep o' th' w. side of the law 291:16
Wine: a little w. for thy stomach's sake 49:12
as water unto w. 313:19
bring me flesh ... wine 187:2
cedarwood, and sweet white w. 168:13
conversations over the w. 317:2
good w.—a friend—or being dry 10:3
good w. needs no bush 215:24
happiness ... w. of the rarest vintage 303:5
I love ... old books, old w. 123:6
I'll not look for w. 145:7
if it doesn't get into the w. 81:11
mine host's Canary w. 149:4
new w. into old bottles 45:25
old friends and old w. are best 222:24
old w. wholesomest 324:1
Sans W., sans Song 110:3
sour grapes can ne'er make sweet w. 226:4
the blude-red w. 11:13
thy love is better than w. 40:2
truth comes out in w. 200:17
w. and wenches empty men's purses 230:19
w. gives great pleasure 144:13
w. in the bottle does not quench 230:20
w. in, truth out 230:21
w. is a good familiar creature 279:11
w. is a mocker 38:22
w. is in ... wit is out 26:4
w. is the strongest 51:5
w. that maketh glad the heart 37:2
w. ... the gout; ... no w. ... the gout 211:34
wolf's-bane, ... for its poisonous w. 149:11
Wine, woman and song: who loves not w. 163:2
Wing: got to take under my w., tra la 118:15
Lo! the Bird is on the W. 109:14
the lark's on the w. 62:7
Winged Cupid painted blind 276:12
Wings: and whether pigs have w. 76:4
beating ... his luminous w. in vain 19:9
beating of his [Death's] w. 58:8
cloying treacle to the w. 152:9
golden hours on angel w. 66:3
ill news hath w. 102:10
in the shade of your soft w. 238:12
love ... spreads his light w. 201:8
O for a horse with w.! 247:2
Oh that I had w. 36:16
under his w. shalt thou trust 36:25
under the shadow of thy w. 35:21
viewless w. of Poesy 149:16
with healing in his w. 43:7
Wink: I have not slept one w. 247:4

Wink (*continued*)
w. and hold out mine iron 258:10
Winners: in war ... no w., ... all are losers 78:9
Winning: not w., but taking part 91:2
too light w. make the prize light 288:2
Wins: and Mammon w. his way 68:18
plays best (well) that w. 223:9
who loses and who w. 267:13
Winter: a sad tale's best for w. 292:13
cold ... heat ... summer ... w. 30:23
cooled by the same w. 274:17
English w.—ending in July 70:8
for, lo, the w. is past 40:8
her w. weeds outworn 298:11
hounds of spring are on w.'s traces 309:14
I ... go south in the w. 107:4
if W. comes, can Spring be far behind? 299:6
in w., when the fields are white 76:11
it was the w. wild 175:8
like a w. hath my absence been 294:4
my age is as a lusty w. 243:18
nor the furious w.'s rages 247:9
red blood ... in the w.'s pale 292:17
savour all the w. long 293:1
the w. evening settles down 106:19
w. and rough weather 244:4
w. is come and gone 297:10
w. is icummen in 205:2
w. of our discontent 284:8
Winters: four lagging w. ... wanton springs 281:12
Wisdom: apply our hearts unto w. 36:24
can w. be put in a silver rod? 55:2
excess leads to ... palace of w. 57:1
fear of the Lord ... beginning of w. 37:6
for w. is better than rubies 38:5
friend of Pleasure, W.'s aid 88:14
how can he get w.? 52:4
in much w. is much grief 39:13
knowledge comes ... w. lingers 313:18
more of w. in it 335:5
no w. like silence 230:22
the price of w. ... above rubies 35:9
to hear the w. of Solomon 34:17
unsearchable dispose of Highest W. 181:7
w. and goodness to the vile 266:21
w. hath builded her house 38:6
Wise: a word is enough to the w. 229:16
all things w. and wonderful 10:4
be not w. in yr. own conceits 47:25
be w. today ... madness to defer 337:13
be w. with speed 337:12
better ... happy than w. 207:23
exceeding w., fair-spoken 262:2
fool ... holdeth his peace is counted w. 38:20
give unto me made lowly w. 334:4
good to be merry and w. 16:1
great men are not always w. 35:11
he that is not ... w. at fifty 216:3
histories make men w. 23:9
holy, fair and w. is she 292:8
I care whether ... w. man or a fool 55:7
I heard a w. man say 136:5
more of the fool than of the w. 22:3
nor ever did a w. one 234:11
reputed one of the w. men 21:21
same tree ... a w. man sees 57:3
so w., so young ... never live long 285:2
Wise (*continued*)
some are w., ... some are otherwise 225:38
some folk are w. ... some are otherwise 303:20
that's the w. thrush 61:3
the least foolish is w. 218:31
the only wretched are the w. 205:7
'tis folly to be w. 126:2
to a w. man ports ... havens 281:14
to be w. and love 290:5
w. after the event 212:13
w. father ... knows his own child 274:12
w. man that marries a harlot 241:19
w. ones [marry] not at all 216:38
Wisely: one that lov'd not w., but too well 280:14
thou dost not inquire w. 39:20
Wiser: be w. ... but do not tell 80:8
French are w. than they seem 22:20
sadder and a w. man 87:5
Spaniards seem w. than they are 22:20
world would be w. than ever 330:10
Wisest: fool ... ask more than ... w. ... can answer 88:20
in the mouths of w. men 181:2
Wish: I w. I had said that. You will 325:7
I w. our clever young poets 88:3
my oft-expressed personal w. 159:12
who wd. w. to die? 57:8
w. is father to the thought 230:26
w. was father ... to that thought 257:18
Wished she had not heard it, yet she wished 279:2
Wishes: everything ... exact to my w. 12:1
Wit: a w. shd. be no more sincere 89:9
age is in, the w. is out 278:9
bold and turbulent of w. 102:16
brevity is the soul of w. 249:15
he is only a w. among Lords 141:18
his whole w. in a jest 25:7
I wish him neither w. nor wealth 15:6
impropriety ... soul of w. 169:5
in w. a man: simplicity a child 201:22
neither w., nor words, nor worth 263:20
no man's w. can well direct 100:16
nor all thy piety nor w. 110:12
prize of w. or arms 174:6
too proud for a w. 123:2
true w. is nature to advantage 202:8
want of w. is worse 229:25
wine is in ... w. is out 26:4
w., if not first, in ... first line 123:4
w. shall not go unrewarded 289:1
w. that can creep 201:19
w. with dunces ... dunce with wits 201:2
your men of w. will condescend 308:12
Witch: not suffer a w. to live 32:11
Witchcraft: only ... w. I have used 279:2
Witching: very w. time of night 252:8
With: not w. me is against me 44:12
Withal: Time ambles w., ... trots w. 245:8
Withered: rosebuds, before they be w. 51:10
so w., ... wild in their attire 269:7
Withers: our w. are unwrung 252:5
Within: life whose fountains are w. 87:9
Witness: shalt not bear false w. 32:8
such weak w. of thy name 175:12
Wits: great w. ... to madness near allied 102–3:17
home-keeping youth ... homely w. 292:4
Witty: a w. statesman ... prove anything 73:4

Witty (*continued*)
it shall be w. and it shan't be long 80:18
not only w. in myself 256:8
Wive: hard to w. and thrive ... in a year 230:27
Wives: a man with seven w. 188:3
married three w. at one time 183:1
profane and old w.' fables 49:10
sky changes when they are w. 245:13
some poison'd by their w. 283:6
w. are young men's mistresses 21:20
w. must be had ... good or bad 230:28
Wiving: hanging and w. goes by destiny 274:15
Wobbly: my spelling is w. 172:8
Woe: a thurghfare ful of w. 79:21
all our w., with loss of Eden 175:15
bitter groan of a martyr's w. 55:5
can I see another's w.? 56:12
cry w., destruction, ruin 283:4
life protracted is protracted w. 141:12
man was made for joy and w. 54:15
the w.'s to come 284:3
trappings and the suits of w. 248:1
Wednesday's child is full of w. 191:8
w. to the vanquished 160:4.
w. to them ... at ease in Zion 42:17
w. unto them that call ... good evil 40:20
Woes: with all w. new wail 293:18
Wold: fields ... that clothe the w. 313:11
Wolf: keep the w. from the door 230:29
to cry 'W.' 210:23
w. ... shall dwell with the lamb 40:24
Wolf's-bane, tight-rooted 149:11
Wolves: inwardly ... ravening w. 44:9
Woman: a fair w. ... without discretion 38:11
a perfect W., nobly planned 334:14
a Spirit, yet a W. too 334:13
a virtuous w. is a crown 38:12
a w. is a foreign land 198:12
a w. is only a w. 154:10
A W. Killed with Kindness 132:10
a w. mov'd ... a fountain troubled 287:12
a w. sat, in unwomanly rags 135:3
a w. seldom asks advice 9:10
a w.'s face ... hast thou 293:16
a w.'s preaching is like 142:13
a w.'s whole history 138:11
a w., therefore to be won 260:7
a w. who tells her ... age 328:12
a w. with fair opportunities 315:9
a w. yet think him an angel 315:7
a worthy w. al hir lyve 79:15
a young w. called Starkie 13:2
an uncommon pretty young w. 105:13
as you are w., so be lovely 125:8
believe a w. or an epitaph 70:14
but what is w.? 91:14
but w. has her way 134:3
constant ... but yet a w. 254:11
die because a w.'s fair 329:11
do you not know I am a w.? 245:6
dumb jewels ... move a w.'s mind 292:7
every w. false like thee 180:16
every w. is at heart a rake 203:15
every w. is ... to be gained by ... flattery 80:17
every w. shd. marry—and no man 100:10
fat white w. whom nobody loves 90–1:16
frailty, thy name is w. 248:5
Woman (*continued*)
give not thy soul unto a w. 51:19
God made the w. for the man 312:2
great glory in a w. 317:5
had a w. ever less? 66:6
her voice ... soft—an excellent thing in w. 268:3
I could be a good w. if 315:12
I know a reasonable w. 204:3
if a w. have long hair 48:5
in a post-chaise with a pretty w. 144:7
in argument with men a w. 181:3
in her first passion w. 69:17
lays his hand upon a w. 317:12
love and good company improves a w. 109:4
man that is born of a w. 35:5, 53:28
never yet fair w. but 266:9
no other but a w.'s reason 292:5
no other purgatory but a w. 25:10
no w. shd. ... be quite accurate 327:17
no w. shd. have a memory 328:15
none of w. born shall harm Macbeth 271:15
nor hell a fury like a w. scorned 89:6
O W.! in our hours of ease 240:9
of every ill, a w. is the worst 125:3
old w. lived under a hill 194:4
old w. who lived in a shoe 194:5
one tongue is enough for a w. 228:8
poor w. who was always tired 12:1
seven [hours' sleep] for a w. 225:25
she is a w., ... may be woo'd ... won 289:13
teaches such beauty as a w.'s eye 268:12
the rib ... made he a w. 30:8
the worser spirit a w. colour'd ill 294:16
there's a broken-hearted w. 129:6
this w. to thy wedded wife 53:21
thought does not become a young w. 301:4
'tis w.'s whole existence 69:14
to show a w. when he loves 61:14
wavers ... in a word, she is a w. 232:10
when lovely w. stoops to folly 107:5, 124:1
who can find a virtuous w.? 39:8
wickedness of a w. 52:1
wit no more ... sincere than a w. constant 89:9
without the ... w. I love 105:10
w. as old as she looks 88:7
w. ... at the bottom of [mischief] 222:1
w. conceals what she knows not 230:30
w. ... fickle and changing 321:3
w. for the hearth 314:18
w. ... if she have the misfortune 20:15
w. in this humour woo'd ... won? 284:13
w. is his game 314:17
w. is the lesser man 313:19
w.'s at best a contradiction 203:18
w.'s happiest knowledge 178:7
w. that deliberates is lost 9:5
w. to obey 314:18
w. wailing for her demon-lover 87:12
w. will be the last thing civilized 170:3
w. with the heart 314:18
worse occupations ... than feeling a w.'s pulse 306:14
yield to one of w. born 272:12
Womb: from his mother's w. untimely ripp'd 272:12
this teeming w. of royal kings 282:5

Womb (*continued*)
through the foul w. of night 259:8
Women: a bevy of fair w. 179:15
alas! the love of w. 69:16
an experience of w. which extends 102:2
Bah! I have sung w. 205:3
by bad w. been deceived 180:12
dally not with money or w. 210:33
discreet w. ... neither eyes nor ears 211:20
England ... a paradise for w. 67:10
England is the paradise of w. 111:4, 212:24
fair w. and brave men 69:3
for w. to keep counsel 263:1
from w.'s eyes this doctrine I derive 268:14
goes with w., and champagne 27:7
happiest w. ... have no history 105:15
how w. pass the time when ... alone 131:2
I speak ... Italian to w. 78:18
Italy ... hell for w. 67:10
let your w. keep silence in ... churches 48:9
loved Esther above all the w. 34:27
Monstrous Regiment of W. 155:13
most w. are not so young as ... painted 26:7
music and w. I ... give way to 199:11
other w. cloy the appetites 242:15
passing the love of w. 34:12
souls of w. are so small 68:2
sweet is revenge—especially to w. 69:12
the more w. look in ... glass 230:35
the third wrote, W. are strongest 51:5
three w. ... goose make a market 227:40
tide in the affairs of w. 70:3
where there are w. and geese 230:32
W. and Horses and Power 154:9
w. and music shd. never be dated 123:11
w. are always in extremes 230:33
w. are angels, wooing 289:15
w. are glad to have been asked 197:14
w. are necessary evils 230:34
w. become like their mothers 328:13
w. ... care ... more for a marriage 23:19
w. in London who flirt 327:9
w. ... more like each other than men 80:16
w. must have the last word 230:37
w. must have their wills 230:36
w. must weep 154:3
w. never look so well as when 308:8
w. require both 68:13
w. sit or move to and fro 325:9
w.'s letters ... pith is in the postscript 129:7
w.'s weapons, water-drops 266:3
w. ... talking of Michelangelo 106:12
w., worst and best 312:6
Won: a woman, therefore to be w. 260:7
marks—not that you w. or lost 233:12
melancholy as a battle w. 324:6
prize we sought is w. 325:12
things w. are done 289:15
woman, therefore may be w. 289:13
w. on the playing fields of Eton 324:10
Wonder: all the w. that wd. be 313:16
and still the w. grew 122:12
how I w. what you are! 311:5
how I w. what you're at 74:8
the common w. of all men 59:15
we ... have eyes to w. 294:7
Wonderful: all things wise and w. 10:4
how w. is Death! 298:7
O w., w. ... out of all whooping 245:5
Wonderful (*continued*)
W., Counsellor, The Mighty God 40:23
Wonderment: I'm always moved to w. 186:9
Wonders: His w. to perform 92:15
w. will never cease 230:38
Won't: will you, w. you, will you, w. you? 75:3
Woo: was to w. a fair young maid 16:3
Wood: my house in the high w. 28:4
old w. burn brightest 324:1
one impulse from a vernal w. 335:7
see the w. for the trees 225:8
springeth the w. new 14:7
through w. and dale the sacred river 87:13
Woodbine: over-canopied with luscious w. 276:20
Woodman, spare the beechen tree 72:7
Wood-notes: his native w. wild 174:8
Woods: a pleasure in the pathless w. 69:9
and the w. have no voice 184:10
in spring, when w. are getting green 76:12
senators of mighty w. 148:6
the w. shall to me answer 305:7
though he build his house in the w. 108:23
tomorrow to fresh w. 175:6
we'll to the w. no more 136:3
w. or steepy mountain yields 167:1
Woodshed: something nasty in the w. 116:5
Wooed: beautiful, and therefore to be w. 260:7
woman in this humour w. 284:13
woman, therefore may be w. 289:13
Wooing: a frog he wd. a-w. go 189:2
women are angels, w. 289:15
Wool: have you any w.? 188:4
pull the w. over a person's eyes 230:39
Word: a character dead at every w. 301:15
a tale unfold whose lightest w. 249:7
at every w. a reputation dies 204:8
by water and the W. 307:13
every w. stabs 277:16
every w. that proceedeth 32:23
fairer than that w. 274:4
four ... winters ... springs end in a w. 281:12
Greeks had a w. for it 10:1
his w. was still 'Fie, foh, and fum' 266:17
in the captain's but a choleric w. 273:8
in w. mightier 178:19
Latin w. for three farthings 268:10
let the w. go forth 153:1
many a true w. ... in jest 228:22
Mum's the w. 88:15
nor all thy tears wash out a w. of it 110:12
some with a flattering w. 326:12
suit ... the w. to the action 251:9
that I kept my w., he said 96:15
the W., and the W. was with God 46:14
the W. was made flesh 46:17
there wd. have been a time for such a w. 272:10
what is honour? A w. 255:21
'when I use a w.,' Humpty Dumpty said 76:10
whose w. no man relies on 234:11
women must have the last w. 230:37
w. for w. without book 290:11
w. is as good as his bond 216:37
w. ... teems with hidden meaning 120:14
yawning at every other w. 77:6

Word (*continued*)
yesterday the w. of Caesar 263:14
Words: actions speak louder than w. 206:4
all sad w. of tongue or pen 326:8
as many w. into the last line 13:1
best w. in the best order 88:3
comprehending much in few w. 52:2
dumb jewels ... more than quick w. do move 292:7
eat one's w. 212:15
few w. are best 213:23
her last w. on earth 12:1
in two w.: im-possible 124:4
let the w. of my mouth ... be acceptable 35:25
let thy w. be few 39:16
like a whore, unpack my heart with w. 250:18
long w. Bother me 172:4
men of few w. ... best men 259:6
much matter decorated into few w. 114:8
my w. fly up, my thoughts remain 252:11
neither wit, nor w., nor worth 263:20
noun ... verb ... abominable w. 260:11
oaths are but w. ..., w. but wind 67:16
on the pedestal these w. appear 299:8
proper w. in proper places 309:2
report thy w. by adding fuel 181:6
scatter ... my w. among mankind 299:6
the w. of Mercury are harsh 269:2
use ... w. only to conceal ... thoughts 321:12
what do you read ... ? W., w., w. 250:2
when you let proud w. go 238:6
w. are the daughters of earth 140:2
w., like Nature, half reveal 312:12
w. may be false 241:18
w. ... so nimble ... full of ... flame 25:7
w. that frightened the birds 12:11
w. will never hurt me 226:18
w. without thoughts never to heaven go 252:11
Wore enough for modesty 62:13
Work: a w. that aspires to ... art 90:7
all in the day's w. 206:10
all things w. together for good 47:20
all w. and no play 230:40
because he can't w. any faster 193:3
day is short ... w. is long 210:35
doing more w. than I shd. do 139:15
I have left no immortal w. 152:11
I have protracted my w. 140:4
I like w.; it fascinates me 139:15
I w. at the weaving trade 16:3
if any wd. not w., neither shd. he eat 49:8
men must w. and women must weep 154:3
my w. is left behind 28:2
night ... when no man can w. 46:26
no more hard w. for poor old Ned 112:12
nothing to do but w. 153:10
old Kaspar's w. was done 304:12
smile his w. to see 56:6
so w. the honey bees 258:8
sport wd. be as tedious as to w. 253:21
strive on to finish the w. 159:15
the way to spread a w. 143:10
there is always w. and tools to w. 162:12
to w. is to pray 218:16
whose w. is not born with him 162:12
woman's w. is never done 230:31
w. ... curse of the drinking classes 328:18
Work (*continued*)
w. expands so as to fill the time 198:5
w. like madness in the brain 87:7
w. yr. hands from day to day 164:15
Workers of the world, unite 168:10
Workhouse: Christmas Day in the W. 302:8
Working: another for w.-days 277:18
fiery Soul, which w. out its way 102:17
Workman: a bad w. quarrels ... tools 206:34
Workmen: good w. are seldom rich 215:25
Works: devil and all his w. 53:11
faith without w. is dead 49:25
its [sea's] w. ... are wrapped in mystery 90:8
Saturday's child w. hard for his living 191:8
World: a balm upon the w. 148:2
a citizen ... of the w. 304:5
a man if he shall gain the whole w. 45:10
a w. in a grain of sand 54:12
a w. of happy days 284:15
a w. too wide for his shrunk shank 244-5:11
a w. where nothing is had for nothing 84:12
aching void the w. can never fill 92:14
all de w. am sad 112:9
all sorts to make a w. 206:16
all's right with the w. 62:7
all the uses of this w.! 248:2
all the w. and his wife 231:1
all the w. as my parish 325:4
all the w. is queer 197:17
all the w.'s a stage 244:11
all this sad w. needs 326:11
all this the w. well knows 294:12
an excellent foppery of the w. 265:10
and all the w. would stare 92:11
another W., the happy seat 177:4
any author in the w. 268:12
any portion of the foreign w. 322:16
any way to perpetuate the w. 60:1
as good be out of the w. 83:15
as they did in the golden w. 243:12
banish ... Jack and banish all the w. 255:2
before my time into this breathing w. 284:10
body is aweary of this great w. 274:5
brave new w. ... such people in't 289:7
Britain is a w. by itself 247:1
called from the w. 12:4
cankers of a calm w. 255:16
Clearing-house of the w. 78:7
commodity, the bias of the w. 264:13
compare this prison ... unto the w. 284:6
consider the w. as made for me 304:1
constant service of the antique w. 243:19
contain and nourish all the w. 268:14
deceits of the w., the flesh, and the devil 52:24
enthusiasm moves the w. 24:1
ever shall be: w. without end 52:14
fast, and the w. goes by 326:10
flash in this w. of trouble 11:18
funniest joke in the w. 295:20
gave me ... a w. of sighs 279:2
get the start of the majestic w. 262:7
gone into the w. of light 320:5
greatest thing in the w. 183:3
had we but w. enough, and time 167:11
he doth bestride the narrow w. 262:8

World (*continued*)
he is a citizen of the w. 22:6
hold the w. but as the w. 274:1
hope before you blacken their w. 319:8
how the w. its veterans rewards 203:16
how this w. is given to lying! 256:4
I called the New W. into existence 72:14
if all the w. were paper 14:1
in this harsh w. draw thy breath in pain 253:9
into the dangerous w. I leapt 56:3
justice ... though the w. perish 109:6
knaves and fools divide the w. 218:6
laugh, and the w. laughs with you 326:9
leaves the w. to darkness and to me 126:3
light of the bright w. dies 57:13
love is enough though the w. 184:10
love makes the w. go round 220:2
mad w.! mad kings! 264:12
more ... wrought by prayer than this w. dreams 312:9
nature is too noble for the w. 246:10
never enjoy the w. aright 317:16
no enjoying the w. without [health] 145:18
not loved the w., nor the w. me 69:5
nothing stable in the w. 151:12
official ... undercuts the problematical w. 114:3
on ... shore of the wide w. 151:8
one half ... w. cannot understand 20:7
reckless what I do to spite the w. 271:2
ring'd with the azure w. he stands 312:1
same the whole w. over 16:13
Saviour of the w. 68:14
saw the Vision of the w. 313:16
so shines a good deed in a naughty w. 275:11
some say the w. will end in fire 113:12
the correction of the w. 182:14
the Federation of the W. 313:17
the ... increase of the w. 312:2
the light of the w. 46:25
the rack of this tough w. 268:5
the workers ... have a w. to gain 168:10
the wilderness of this w. 63:6
the w. forgetting, by the w. forgot 201:9
the w. is too much with us 333:3
the w. must be peopled 278:1
the w. shd. listen then 300:3
the w.'s great age begins anew 298:11
the w.'s grown honest 250:4
the w.'s mine oyster 276:4
the w. was all before them 179:18
this dark w. and wide 181:10
this dark w. of sin 54:4
this happy breed ... this little w. 282:5
this is the way the w. ends 106:9
this w. ... a thurghfare ful of wo 79:21
thro' the w. we safely go 54:15
to save your w. you asked 19:16
two soul-sides, one to face the w. 61:14
up above the w. so high 311:5
vanity of this wicked w. 53:12
vile blows and buffets of the w. 271:2
weight of ... unintelligible w. 335:11
when all the w. is young 154:4
when Rome falls—the W. 69:8
where in all this small-talking w. 114:4
whole w.'s in a state o' chassis 196:8
wondrous architecture of the w. 166:10

World (*continued*)
word of Caesar ... against the w. 263:14
w. grew pale 141:11
w. history is the w.'s judgment 238:13
w. is a comedy ... a tragedy 322:7
w. is charged with the grandeur 135:6
w. must be made safe for democracy 329:9
w. of doubts and fancies 151:12
w. of vile, ill-favour'd thoughts 276:6
w.'s great snare uncaught 243:3
w.'s storm-troubled sphere 58:12
w. to hide virtues in 290:12
w. wd. be wiser than ever 330:10
w. wd. go round ... faster 74:5
you shut out the w. 324:17
Worldly: name ... was Mr. W. Wiseman 63:8
with all my w. goods 53:24
Worlds: best of possible w. 321:9
exhausted w., and then imagin'd new 140:19
the little less, ... what w. away 60:15
wandering between two w. 18:15
Worm: concealment, like a w. i' th' bud 291:7
early bird catches the w. 212:8
tread on a w. and it will turn 228:19
who ... sets foot upon a w. 93:12
wish you joy o' th' w. 243:9
Worms: have made w.' meat of me 286:19
I was one of the w. 90:5
talk of graves, of w. and epitaphs 283:5
w. have eaten them 245:12
you have tasted two whole w. 305:19
Wormwood and the gall 41:18
Worried: poem ... not ... w. into being 113:16
w. the cat that killed the rat 194–5:8
Worry: no one to w. ... to hurry us 91:7
Worse: as Heaven made him, and ... w. 78:3
goes by the w., whatever be her cause 181:3
make the w. appear the better 176:18
really w. than interrupting 107:8
remedy is w. than the disease 22:10
sell w. kinds of liquor 322:12
there is no w. heresy 9:1
w. than being talked about 328:6
Worship: are come to w. him 43:8
with my body I thee w. 53:24
Worshipper: Nature mourns her w. 239:14
Worst: do your w., blow your pipe 62:5
hope ... best and prepare for the w. 217:3
so long as we can say 'This is the w.' 266:19
so much good in the w. of us 133:5
things at the w. will mend 227:29
things present, w. 256:13
whose puppets, best and w. 62:8
women, w. and best 312:6
Worth: doings without charity are nothing w. 53:3
none was w. my strife 156:11
slow rises w., by poverty depressed 140:16
w. a guinea a box 11:10
w. ... best known by the want 231:4
w. doing ... w. doing well 80:9, 230:8
w. of a State ... w. of ... individuals 170:11
w. reading ... w. buying 237:2
w. seeing ... not w. going to see 144:16
Worthington: daughter on the stage, Mrs. W 91:10
Worthless as wither'd weeds 58:13

Worthy: labourer is w. of his hire 45:27
Worts: went to W. 204:13
Wound: did help to w. itself 265:4
jests at scars that never felt a w. 286:6
take away the grief of a w. 255:21
what w. did ever heal? 279:12
w. the loud winds 288:15
Wounds: bind up the nation's w. 159:15
faithful ... the w. of a friend 39:3
gash is added to her w. 271:18
labour and the w. are vain 85:1
talk ... of guns ... and w. 254:2
these w. in thine hands 43:4
Wrangle: men will w. for religion 88:17
Wrapped up in a five-pound note 158:7
Wrath: day of w., that dreadful day 240:2
infinite w. and infinite despair 177:13
sun go down upon your w. 48:24
the w. to come 43:12
Wreck: decay of that colossal w. 299:8
Wrecks: like w. of a dissolving dream 298:11
Wren: four Larks and a W. 158:13
robin redbreast and the w. 324:3
Sir Christopher W. said 29:3
the w. goes to't 267:4
Wrestle: we w. not against flesh 48:27
Wretch: excellent w.! 279:14
needy, hollow-ey'd ... w. 246:5
patron.—commonly a w. 140:10
w., concentred all in self 240:1
Wretched: scrannel pipes of w. straw 175:4
the only w. are the wise 205:7
the w. child expires 27:4
w. matter and lame metre 175:14
Wretchedness: the w. of being rich 303:7
Wretches: poor naked w., wheresoe'er you are 266:13
to feel what w. feel 266:14
Wrinkled: the w. sea beneath him 312:1
w. with age ... Old Nod 97:1
Writ: if this be error ... I never w. 294:9
over that same door was ... w. 305:12
Write: as much as a man ought to w. 318:3
contrive to w. so even 20:19
firm restraint with which they w. 72:6
hope to w. well hereafter 182:1
I never read books—I *w.* them 232:1
look in thy heart and w. 302:3
to w. and read comes by nature 278:4
when I want ... novel I w. one 100:15
why did I w.? 201:13
w. God first 278:13
w. me down an ass 278:16
Writers of small histories, dictionaries 140:6
Writes: the moving finger w. 110:12
Writing: in w. or in judging ill 202:1
true ease in w. comes from art 202:10
w. [maketh] an exact man 23:8
Written: what I have w. I have w. 46:34
w. such volumes of stuff 158:6
Wrong: and if you w. us, shall we not revenge? 274:17
but he done her w. 15:2
fifty million Frenchmen can't be w. 127:10
for telling a man he was w. 85:6
house of Tarquin ... suffer w. no more 163:9
I always feel I must be w. 327:3
King can do no w. 54:10, 218:1
losers are always in the w. 219:30
Wrong (*continued*)
never dreamed ... w. wd. triumph 60:2
only thing that I ever did w. 16:3
or whether laws be w. 326:15
our country, right or w. 96:7
physical effect is good ... action ... w. 142:7
right divine of kings to govern w. 201:3
something ... w., however slightly 204:16
something w. with ... ships 25:6
stiff in opinions, always in the w. 103:4
to do a great right do a little w. 275:2
we do it w., being so majestical 247:15
w. never comes right 231:5
Wrong number: if I called the w., why ... answer? 317:8
Wrote: no man ... ever w. except for money 144:5
who w. like an angel 115:2
Wroth: to be w. with one we love 87:7
Wrought: being w., perplexed in the extreme 280–1:14
first he w., ... afterwards he taughte 79:16
more things are w. by prayer 312:9
Wye: turned to thee, O sylvan W. 335:13

Xanadu: in X. did Kubla Khan 87:11

Yankee Doodle came to town 196:4
Yarn: all I ask is a merry y. 168:17
web of our life ... a mingled y. 242:6
Year: about two hundred pounds a y. 67:17
add ... to this wonderful y. 115:1
any book ... not a y. old 108:17
before the mellowing y. 174:12
each day is like a y. 326–7:15
grief returns with the revolving y. 297:10
how many days will finish ... y. 260:13
I like two months of ... y. 68:17
if ... y. were playing holidays 253:21
in the season of the y. 16:6
measure of the y. 151:4
pleasure of the fleeting y. 294:4
proper opinions for ... time of y. 20:4
say no ill of the y. 224:40
stolen ... my three-and-twentieth y. 181:9
sweet o' the y. 292:17
the y. is going, let him go 313:4
the y.'s at the spring 62:7
twentieth y. is well-nigh past 93:13
wive and thrive both in a y. 230:27
Yearning: man of y. ... aspiration 236:9
Yearnings for equal division 107:18
Years: a thousand y. as one day 50:10
age ... not weary ... nor the y. condemn 54:5
alas, Postumus, the fleeting y. 135:15
all the hopes of future y. 160:11
before the beginning of y. 309:15
come to the y. of discretion 53:17
cuts off twenty y. of life 263:3
eight y. with a strange man 138:2
evil days come not ... y. draw nigh 39:26
forty y. on 57:15
fourteen hundred y. ago were nail'd 253:14
hasn't been kissed for forty y. 236:14
if the British Empire ... last for a thousand y. 82:14
Myself with Yesterday's Sev'n Thousand Y. 110:2
O for ten y. 150:10

Years (*continued*)
our hope for y. to come 323:4
parted ... to sever for y. 71:5
sorrow comes with y. 60:7
tell me where all past y. are 101:5
the thousand y. of peace 313:6
three y. she grew in sun and shower 335:9
time-lag of fifty y. 324:15
together now for forty y. 81:14
y. a mortal man may live 260:13
y. that the locust hath eaten 42:12
young in y. ... old in hours 23:1
Yellow: come unto these y. sands 287:20
commended thy y. stockings 291:10
green and y. melancholy 291:7
her locks were y. as gold 86:8
the sear, the y. leaf 272:5
y., and black ... and hectic red 299:3
y. god forever gazes down 129:6
Yeomanry ... people with whom 20:6
Yeovil: our H.Q. at Station Road, Y. 204:17
Yes, and back again 189:8
Yesterday: children dear, was it y.? 18:12
dead Y., why fret? 110:7
not born y. 208:24
O, call back y., bid time return 283:3
Yesterdays: all our y. have lighted fools 272:10
Yet: young man shd. not marry y. 231:6
Yew: my shroud ... stuck all with y. 291:6
never a spray of y. 18:16
Yield: courage never to submit or y. 175:18
to get rid of temptation ... y. 328:7
Yo-ho-ho and a bottle of rum 307:4
Yoke: our country sinks beneath the y. 271:18
savage bull sustains the y. 155:16
shake the y. of inauspicious stars 287:4
that he bear the y. in his youth 41:20
who best bear his mild y. 181:11
Yonghy-Bonghy-Bo: lived the Y. 158:2
Yorick: a Cock and a Bull, said Y. 307:2
alas, poor Y.! 253:2
York: glorious summer by this sun of Y. 284:8
You: Daddy, what did y. do? 11:1
for y. but not for me 14:12
I am I, and y. are y. 61:7
room with a view—and y. 91:7
sight of y. is good for sore eyes 309:6
y. too, Brutus? 71:14
Young: America ... country of y. men 108:21
compliment him about looking y. 138:10
crime of being a y. man 200:6
happy while we are y. 17:13
I have been y., and now am old 36:9
if ... world and love were y. 232:14
my heart was y. and gay 112:10
no y. man believes he shall ... die 129:10
not so y. as they are painted 26:7
old are more beautiful than the y. 325:9
our clever y. poets 88:3
so y. and so untender? So y. ... and true 265:7
the embarrassing y. 115:3
to be seventy years y. 134:7
to be y. was very Heaven! 334:5
when all the world is y. 154:4
y., and so fair! 134:10
y. blood must have its course 154:5
y. ones ... pistols: ... old ones grub 295:7
Yours: as I y. for ever 125:8
what's mine is y., ... y. is mine 273:15
what's y. is mine 230:9
y. [religion] is Success 24:15
y. is the Earth 154:20
Yourself: *do it y.* 24:3
Youth: a y. of frolics, an old age of cards 203:16
a y. to fortune and to fame unknown 126:13
age ... perform the promises of y. 141:3
crabbed age and y. 295:1
good ... that he bear the yoke in ... y. 41:20
home-keeping y. have ... homely wits 292:4
I wd. ... that y. would sleep 292:16
if only y. knew 108:25
let age approve of y. 62:10
let no man despise thy y. 49:11
loves the meat in his y. 277:22
made every y. cry *Well-a-way!* 11:12
mewing her mighty y. 182:8
must be right ... done it from my y. 93:16
noble y. did dress themselves 256:17
our y., our joys, our all 232:11
rejoice ... in thy y. 39:25
remember ... thy Creator in ... y. 39:26
riband in the cap of y. 252:24
rule y. well 224:32
spirit of y. in every thing 294:5
the hour of thoughtless y. 335:14
the rose of y. upon him 242:20
the y. ... still is Nature's priest 332:2
Time, the subtle thief of y. 181:9
war is done and y. stone dead 238:9
when Y. and Pleasure meet 69:4
y. and age will never agree 231:10
y. grows pale and spectre-thin 149:15
y., I do adore thee 295:2
y. is a blunder 100:9
y. is full of pleasance 295:1
y. like summer morn 295:1
y. of America ... oldest tradition 328:9
y. of England are on fire 258:9
y. of labour ... age of ease 122:7
y. shows but half 62:9
y. who bore 'mid snow and ice 160:12
y. will be served 231:11
y. will have its course (fling) 231:12
y.'s a stuff will not endure 291:2
Yukon: this is the law of the Y. 241:15

Zeal: holy, mistaken z. in politics 146:7
not too much z. 311:2
serv'd my God with half the z. 261:13
z. is ... found mostly in fools 231:13
z., when ... a virtue 231:14
z. without knowledge 231:15
Zeal-of-the-Land Busy 145:6
Zed: whoreson z.! ... unnecessary letter! 265:18
Zenith: dropped from the z., like a ... star 176:14
Zenocrate: fair Z.!—divine Z.! 166:11
Z., lovelier than the love of Jove 166:7
Zephyr: roses by the z. blown apart 148:10
Zion: at ease in Z. 42:17
one of the songs of Z. 37:24
wept, when we remembered Z. 37:22
Zuleika on a desert island 26:8